Dedication

Dedicated at the feet of my mother Mdm.Santhanamary Sinnappen and
to the memory of my dearly missed father,
Santiago Arokiam Esq.(1929-2004).

MULTIHUED MULTITUDE

OR UNITED WE STAND
OR MALAYSIA TRULY ASIA
OR 1 MALAYSIA

PANNIR SANTIAGO

ISBN 979-8-89322-619-5

Contents

Preface

Can a book write itself? This one pretty much did. Having just returned to Malaysia for good in March 2008 (and boy, does it feel good!) after fourteen years vagabondage in the United States, I began scribbling notes on scrap sheets, my contemplation of Malaysia and Malaysians. It seemed almost like a reverse culture shock, I taking the role of an outsider looking in. No, it didn't take long for me to get into an all Malaysian mode of mind. Soon enough, what seemed like a plot and structure became apparent. The general theme evokes isomorphism, the Marriage and Family Therapy concept that individuals across family generations exhibit many similarities of behavior and personality – what we commonly call, "running in the family". As a nation, we are a family whose members have similarities and disparities.

It is as if we live in twilight zone-like parallel universes. Except for the 9 to 5 interim when these universes briefly brush by each other in the school, business, or work-place setting, we are virtually aliens to each other. Come twilight, we retire into our own little conformal, communal, connubial, conventional, convivial, customary cultural cocoons, like cuckoos in roost, cooing in chorus crescendoing confoundingly.

These parallel universes existing side by side, is what makes Malaysia unique in the larger cosmos. Despite each race enjoying its own creole, culture, customs, cuisine, couture, quirks, and confounding curiosities, we are still Malaysians first, doing justice to Aesop's phrase, *United We Stand, Divided We Fall*. Our own national motto, *Bersekutu Bertambah Mutu* – "Unity is strength" agrees. Different, but one. Indeed, the Indonesian national motto *Bhinneka Tunggal Ika* ("It is different, [yet] it is one") speaks to that. Despite the obvious differences in the details, we are structurally similar. Different in form but alike in substance. Alike in the unalike ways we do things. The reader will be forgiven if s/he, reading through these topics feels like being in a time-loop movie, popping in and out into the same subject but in a different culture context.

Somewhat a **curry** (Tamil [1681]: *"a food, dish, or sauce in Indian cuisine seasoned with a mixture of pungent spices"* – Merriam-Webster), we are more like the **agar-agar** (Malay [1820]: *"a gelatinous colloidal extractive of a red alga"* – Merriam-Webster). Curry, you see, is a stew of many spices, some vegetables and a meat, all melting into each other and becoming a monochromatic mush. We are that. We are also **chop suey** (Chinese –Cantonese [1888]: *"a dish prepared chiefly from bean sprouts, bamboo shoots, water chestnuts, onions, mushrooms, and meat or fish and served with rice and soy sauce"* – Merriam-Webster). The ingredients still retain their crip individualities.The *agar – agar cermin* (glass jelly), is little solid cubes of different colored jellies (jello, in American), suspended in a clear gelatinous base. We are, most of all, like the agar-agar. Separate, but hanging together. Different in colour, flavour and figure but alike in taste and texture. This alikeness, averts any danger of stereotyping, for unalikeness is when a single group is likely to be noticed and picked out for negative commentary.

Malaysian political leaders have always (when it suited them) highlighted this unique "condition" of ours, and Malaysians in general like to boast about it to our visitors. The established fact is, nowhere else in the world is this the norm. Each race has its own national vernacular school system, its own public radio and TV station etc, something unheard of in America. Is this Malaysian mélange an artificial situation? A social experiment by the British, who introduced the Chinese and Indians (representing ⅔ of humankind) into the local mix? Not necessarily. Check out the article on origins. We've all been on this same boat for quite a while, since before Britain herself was a faraway, forlorn, forsaken, foreign colony of Rome, and English was the lingo of a tiny band of primitive Atlantic islanders. Or, read the article on Malaccans. All of us wuz here before the European arrived hither. Before we were Malaysia, Malaya, Malacca, Golden Chersonese, Suvarnabhumi (golden land), Terra Incognito, we were all here – refer to the article on human origins.

By no means is this a text book, much less an encyclopedia, on Malaysian matters. Rather, it is a summative commentary, or a compendium of simple info, delivered in bite-sized morsels for easy digestion. It could be taken by

Malaysians as a pocket reference, to better understand our neighbours and their behaviors. Perhaps textbook won't be a bad idea afterall, if used in a class on national unity. I remember those primary school days in the late sixties, when we had civics class that included learning about others' cultures. Not a travelogue or travel guide, this can be a Malaysia bound traveller's companion, to help decipher its diverse people and their peculiarities and idiosyncracies. A travel guide is big on places and spaces, but stinges on the heart, mind, and soul behind the faces. This book might fix that.

Being an attempt at a light-hearted look at our collective selves, hopefully this will provide an easy reading experience. No willful putdowns of any group or individual is intended. Being one individual's rampant, rambunctious ramblings, the opinionated offerings herein presented are unapologetically, the writer's only. Direct quotes or reports are excepted (not accepted) as reasons for brickbats, of course. Hey, I am only reporting. However, your keen observations, conscientious objections, and constructive opinions will be embraced with much gratitude. My E-mail is pathungum_puli@yahoo.com.

There is no deliberate omission or minimization of any sub-group of Malaysians. In the interest of simplicity, Malays and their culture are treated as representative of the Bumiputras ("sons of the soil"); Taoist Chinese as par for all Chinese, including Babas; and Tamils are taken as token of Indians in toto. To say that every single strand and shade of Malaysian ethnic, cultural, and religious fabric contributes to the overall matrix, is an understatement. We are perhaps the most mixed (not mixed-up) people on the planet. The Americans may claim the most nationalities and ethnicities under their spacious sky represented within their long borders, but they are culturally, linguistically, philosophically, politically, and virtually homogenously Anglo-Saxon Protestant in outlook. They are mixed up to the point of sameness. We are a "mix".

Finally, a friendly nod to our neighbours to the south. Our differences, if there are any, are merely a matter of politics, rather than of history. As a matter of fact, Singapore and Peninsular Malaysia are way closer culturally, ethnically, linguistically, historically, and not to mention geographically, than the Malaysian states of Sabah and Sarawak are to the mainland.

Surely, we are Siamese twins, separated only by the slim straits of Johore, yet attached by the kinship cord of causeway.

(AD 2008)

NB: Most of the ensuing material was already written down around this time, with some recent edits and updates.

Acknowledgement

My *Sittrannai/Chinnamma* ("Little Mother", or mother's younger sister, or paternal uncle's wife), Mdm.Nalini Matilda, certainly tops every list of acknowledgements for every positive thing that I have achieved or will ever. Since my childhood (and hence), she continues to be my cheerleader-in-chief. To her goes my *Muthal Mariyaathai* (pre-eminent first respects).

Much gratitude is due the bloggers– for some of the insights gleaned from them. The blogosphere is the garden which produced the raw material, for me to assemble and dish up this book. Immeasurable gratitude also goes to Wikipedia and the World Wide Web (WWW). They have provided the condiments which went into this confection.

I have been too lazy to seek out cultural consultants. Sorry. But thanks to Malaysians, who by their words and behavior, as reported in the media, have allowed me to form some idea of who, why, and where and how we are.

Finally yet infinitely, I am indebted indeed to Saroja and Salome, the two women in my life. The former, I took. The latter, I gave away. The one taken for better, for worse. The other, given away for good – to a good man, David Shroder.

Music

Drums: Gong, Gendang, Ghatam

During the intermission of a *Bharathanatyam* (Indian classical dance) performance in Malaysia many years back, the compere did a vocal rendition of his own. He gave an explanation of how a South Indian percussion piece, the *mrdangam* drum, was made. Hollowed out Jackfruit tree trunk for body, leather membrane for drumhead, black rice paste at the centre of the smaller face and so on. In the course of the discourse, he also gave an interesting thesis on the origin of the names of drums, beginning with "drum".

Drum, according to him, is an onamapatoeia, i.e., something named after the way it sounds. The Greeks created the word "barbarian" to describe their Teutonic northerners, based on their unintelligible language, which to them sounded like, "bar, bar bar." Likewise the verb "murmur" apparently results from the sound "mur..mur..mur..mur", emitted when the murmuring is done. Interestingly, the Tamil verb for mumbling, independently derived, is to *"murumuru"*. The word drum, imitates the sound it makes. "Drrrrummm" as in "drrrrummm rrrollll !" The announcer extended his argument to the name of the *mrdangam* like this – "Mrr… Danggam! Mrr…Danggam! Dangg gamm! Mrr..Danggam!"

If we apply this test to Malaysian drums, would it look like this?

Kompang (Malay tambourine) – "Kom..Pangg! Kom..Pangg! KomPangg! KomPangg!"

Gendang (Malay Barrel Drum) – "Dangg! Dangg! Gen..Dangg!"

Dholak (Bangra drum) – "Dhol Dhol Dholak Dholak Dhol Dhol!

Tabla (Hindustani twin drum) – "Tabak tabak tabla tabak tabak!"

Gong (Chinese cymbal) – "Gonggggggggggg!

Just as the different languages sound different, the various drums make strange noise to different hearers. All music is beautiful and meaningful, in context. All drums can evoke varying responses in different hearers. It is as if they speak the language of the particular culture to which they belong. A Malay buddy once shared a joke he heard on RTM (in the 70's). The TV comedian (Badul? Hamid Gurkha? Jamali Shadat?) had paired the sounds made by the ethnic drums, to the business experience of the culture it represented, as follows:-

Chinese:	Un tonggg! Un Tongg!	(gibing the gong)	*"Profit! Profit!*
Malay:	Tak Un tong! Tak Un tongg!	(copying the kompang)	*"No profit ! No profit!"*
Indian:	Kadang Kadang Untongg!	(mimicking the mrdangam)	*"Occasional profit!*

The humour nothwithstanding, Malaysian ethnic drums are heard within their cultural locales and seldom blend their beats. Chinese gongs and cymbals are heard at lion dances, chingay processions and Chinese wayang or opera performances. Live Malay Gamelan these days, is heard exclusively at dinners shows fabricated for foreign tourists, Wayang kulit performamances, and at royal functions. Indian Carnatic sounds are heard at temple functions, at Baratha Natyam *arangetrams* (debutante performances), or other cultural fetes. Will we ever hear the sounds fuse? The only fusion that happens is during the one minute sound bite in a promo ad about national unity, national day, 1 Malaysia and what not. Yet these Asian sounds have on their own, successfully created fusion albums with western music. Shouldn't it be about time Malaysian classical musicians of all stripes thought about sitting in a circle and collaborating? The buoyant, bouncy baby of that mixed marriage is bound to be a blast. A true Malaysian indeed, if ever there is to be one.

Now, if you thought that the earlier poke about the different ethnic drums "talking" about their business fortunes was plausible, it may be because drums actually have their own dialects. And we are not talking about the African talking drums (tom-toms) here. We identify the sound of each with its ethnic culture. More importantly, they actually mimic the sound of the respective language. For instance the crackling notes of Indian, especially Carnatic music, echo the rapid tongue rolling of Tamil, Telugu, or Malayalam. The different instruments in a Carnatic *Kacheri* (concert) do seem to be having a spirited debate among themselves. If it can be measured on a musical heart monitor, it would probably have clumps of uneven peaks and valleys, like a heart arrhythmia (tachycardia) patient's. The Chinese drum, flute, or cymbal have the tonal quality of the Chinese dialects. That is to say, the musical phrases are sonorous somnolent single syllable notes strung together like beads of equal size, volume and pitch. The booming big drums would look like the spiky waves on the heart monitor attached to a marathoner. Listen carefully to a Gamelan ensemble, and you might recognize the native sounds of the Nusantara (Malay archipelago) languages. The tinkling of the kettles would look like the shallow, even waves on the heart monitor on a beachcomber.

Now, a little bit about the different representative percussion instruments in the title of this article. The gong is a Chinese instrument that has been adopted into the classical music of South-East Asia. It has a prominent place in the Gamelan orchestra and in Filipino music. In fact, the different metal kettles of Gamelan are gongs resting on the floor (bonang), or suspended (gong). The image that comes to mind is the suspended bassy voiced brass vessel that the Chinese emperor strikes, when he wants to summon court attendants. A variation of this is the tam-tam, a mainstay of western classical orchestra.

The Gendang is a medium sized barrel drum with leather beat surfaces on both ends. It adds to the assortment of percussion pieces in a Gamelan emsemble, providing another steady layer of beat.

In the South-Indian Carnatic tradition, the Ghatam is actually a large round red clay pot, shaped like the spherical pots they used to cook western missionaries in, per cartoon caricatures. This one is strictly not for cooking, but great sounds are concocted on it when flying fingers furiously fandangle on its shiny smooth surface. The metalic sound resembles the clinking of eversilver tumblers somersaulting in a concrete drain. No doubt, it also has versitile shades of sound such as bass, treble, depending on how or where it is tapped. Slapping the mouth of the pot gives a hollow, bassy burp.

So, what we have are three representative drums, the gong, gendang and ghatam. All are different in make up, i.e,, metal, leather, and clay, respectively. All make different sounds, like the languages of the cultures they represent. But all can converse together. In Gamelan, the gong and gendang are co-actors. The gendang has a genetic kinship with the Indian mrdangam, in size, shape, sound as well as source material. The body of both drums is from the jackfruit tree. How is that for unity in diversity?

Reeds: *Nada*Swaram, Sheng, Serunai

Reed, or wind instruments are natural accompaniments to the percussion instruments. Drums can be considered the first musical instruments, the hand clap qualifiable as percussive music. A mirthful babe in arms spontaneously scoops and sandwiches its soft spongy palms together to make soundless symphony. Or, when the toddler thumps its feet in happiness, evoking the African American, *stomp*. As the child matures, he learns to purse his lips and make a whistle – the first wind music. Priorly, he had probably espied sweet music escaping from a bug drilled bamboo infiltrated by a blustery breeze. This, quite possibly, after he had made a percussion piece out of broader bamboo – antedating the *angklung*.

The flute is the instrument to imitate the sound of birds of all feathers. It is an indispensable member of any Malaysian ethnic music ensemble.

The *naadaswaram* (*naayanam*) is a double reed woodwind instrument which is the precursor of the North Indian *shehnai*. Its bold, vibrant, almost metallic sound is akin to the saxophone's, and considered auspicious music (*mangala isai*) by Tamils. This instrument is "among the world's loudest non-brass acoustic instruments", according to those who should know it. It is accompanied by the loquacious *thavil*, a double sided drum equivalent to a marching band drum.The naadam is the requisite music during Hindu weddings and temple functions. At the moment of the tying of the thaali, the up tempo flourish of thavil and naadaswaram sounds like the applause of a thousand hands. It may be the Indian equivalent of the Western recessional, as the newlyweds march out of the chapel. A typical quartet consisting of twin naadaswarams and twin thavils, doesn't need any amplifier, thank you. The sound can even fill an open space, as in a temple chariot street procession.

The Hindustani *shehnai*, is slightly smaller, slimmer, and shorter than the *naadam*. If the western equivalent to the naadaswaram is the trumpet, the shehnai's is the oboe. Although known for its upbeat sound at auspicious events such as weddings, the shehnai is the opposite to the Naadaswaram in terms of emotive content. If the Naadaswaram is a happy, joyful music, the shehnai can be the weeping cousin. The shehnai sound is what tugs at your heartstrings during a melodramatic moment in Bollywood movies, heightening the pathos.

The *sheng* is one of the ancient Chinese instruments, going back 3500 years. It is one of the main pieces in Chinese opera. In today's large Chinese orchestras it provides melody as well as accompaniment.

It is a mouth-blown free reed instrument consisting of a bunch of vertical pipes. Imagine a frozen stiff Scottish bag-pipe. A spherical air chamber with a dozen reed pipes of various heights, rising rigidly from it. The extended mouthpiece attached to the sphere is both blown and sucked, ensuring continuous wind movement. The effect is akin to playing a harmonica or an accordion. With all those tubes, holes and buttons, it is a non-homophonous one instrument orchestra, producing sounds ranging from trills, whistles, chirps, horns, drones, to what else have you. Its close cousin is the hulusi, also from China, which is slightly smaller.

The *serunai* is a traditional wind instrument, famously, from the Minang community in Indonesia. It is heard at their weddings, silat events and padi plantings. With Minangkabau migration to other parts of Nusantara from their home in West Sumatra, the serunai has naturalized into a key instrument in Gamelan, Wayang Kulit and regional folk music.

Having a name and look similar to the *shehnai*, the serunai is said to have come from North India. It probably came with the cargo of Gujarati Muslim traders. The two sounds are similar, with even musical tones, unlike the naadaswaram which has a more "vocal" quality.

Suppose, we have all the reeds playing together (in concert)? It won't be a lot of hot air, for sure. Perhaps, plenty hot arias.

Strings: Gambus, Veenai, Guqin

The music of stringed instruments cannot be duplicated by human body parts (hands, lips). So stringed music, whether plucked, struck, or caressed with horsehair bow was a later addition to the ensemble. It probably had its genesis in the constant quest and creative curiosity of man, as he fiddled (!) with anything he could get his hands on. What if he had pulled on a vegetable fibre, and it let out a sound? The three modes of music making namely, percussion, wind, and string, can be considerd the holy trinity of the art. And all ethnic traditions have incorporated them, including Malaysia's own regional varieties.

The string of the Malays, is the *gambus,* which originated in the Middle East. The *banjo* of American Country Music, is from West Africa, by way of the African slaves who were shanghaied there in the 18th century. We don't know if both (gambus and banjo) are connected by a common ancestor, but their sounds are quite alike. We know that the Spanish guitar is gambus inspired, since Spain was ruled by the Arab Moors for a while. The lute and harp however, predate the gambus (Arabic – qanbus). The body of the gambus reminds you of a pear cut in half.

The gambus immediately evokes the form of Malay music called the *ghazal*, which is arabesque. Naturally. Its deep bass, nasal sound lends itself well to the Malay vocals, which the singer renders in an Arab "voice", or intonation. The word ghazal itself means different things to different regions or the world. In the Middle-East and North Indian/ Pakistani tradition it is sung to couples in love, and in bereavement. Often, it is religion oriented as in the Sufi tradition.The Malay ghazal tradition and with it, the gambus, seems to have retreated back to the Riau region of Indonesia from whence it made a footfall in Johor in the 19th century.

Hence, If we want to cite a true Malaysian bumiputra, it would be the *sape/sapit*. This boat shaped instrument originating in the Orang Ulu (upriver people) of Sarawak/Central Borneo, namely the Kenyah, Kayan and Kelabit tribes. Ibans and Dayaks also perform this. Unlike the guitar or gambus with the hollow opening upwards to the playing surface, the sape is hollowed out at the back. The sound is less bassy than the gambus, but with base and melodic notes that soothe and evoke the surrounding forest. Originally employed in longhouse spirituals and inducing trance in the last century, it has come to be widely used in social settings such as marriages, births, harvests as well as accompaniment to dances such as the *ngajat* (kind of a war dance) and *datun julud* (women imitating a hornbill in flight). The ngajat is Iban and the datun julud is Kenyah.

The *veenai*, with its bassy nasality is the sound that tugs the heartstrings (!) of South Indians. It is the ancestor of the *sitar*, which evolved as the North Indian version, in the courts of the Moghul emperors (Arab/ Persian influences). The difference twixt the two, the sitar is held diagonally upright to the opposite shoulder, while the veenai rests horizontally across both laps of the player. Soundwise, the veenai's is a vibrant deep drone, while the sitar makes scintillating shimmer, like a thousand tiny silver bells. Both these strings are lively, though the veenai can also be plucked to produce melodramatic tones. It's the music played on national radio (Minnal FM) during the wake for a head of state/government.

Veenai music is part of the carnatic genre of Indian classical music. It is music that is often incorporated into Hindu devotionals, or bhajans. Besides being an accompaninent to carnatic vocal concerts, it is often a lead piece in instrumentals. With its unique human-like sound, the veenai gives "voice" to Tamil movie songs and instrumentals.

Guqin is a seven-stringed zither. Zither (German) from Cithara (Latin), also Guitar (Spanish). A zither is many strings stretched across a flat board.The guqin is among the most classical of Chinese instruments, with over 3000 years of history. Its name says so. *Gu* means "ancient" and *qin* is a general term for any string instrument. Therefore, Guqin = ancient string. It has enjoyed a high status among the ancient intellectuals and sages such as Confucius, who was a keen practioner. As such, it is very well documented and its repertoire of compositions well preserved.

Yangqin, is a struck string instrument, originally from Persia. The piano is actually a stringed instrument. It's keys, when struck activate arms that in turn, strike tuned strings. That it can be used for Asian classical works, speaks to the versatility of both instrument and musical genre.

Classical Music: Carnatic, Yayue, Gamelan

Classical music in Malaysia as a whole (Indian Carnatic, Chinese operatic, and Malay Gamelan), antedates the western by double digit centuries. Western classical music was codified in the 16th century AD. The Sanskrit *Sama Veda* ("Knowledge of melody") written circa 1000 BCE has detailed instructions on musical composition. The Tamil epic, *Silappadhikaram* ("The Ankle Bracelet" – circa 100 AD) has numerous references to music and styles of it. In China, the Imperial Music Bureau was first established during the Qin Dynasty (221-07 BCE), to develop Chinese music. Music in the European classical tradition can be said to have begun from after the fall of the Roman Empire, in 476 CE.

For classical Malay music one has to turn elsewhere in the Nusantara. A drum and gong ensemble known as the gamelan is one of Indonesia's best known classical music forms, mixing it up with Sundanese, Javanese and Balinese strains. In Javanese mythology, the gamelan was created by Sang Hyang Guru, a god who ruled from mount Maendra in Java (c. AD 230),. Hindus would quickly pick up the scent of Shiva here. *Guru* is another appellation for Shiva, who abides in his mountainous abode of Kailasam aka Mahendragiri (mount Mahendra). Shiva is considered the progenitor of Indian arts, including music. The famous dancing Shiva statue *Nataraja*, in Chidambaram, Tamil Nadu, is the universal symbol of Indian culture. This bronze Shiva is synonymous with music and dance. Hence, the connection of Shiva to Gamelan music is not unusual, or unlikely.

Carnatic (ancient Tamil name, Pannisai), the classical music form of South India is also ascribed divine origins, like the other arts, such as Barathanatyam, astrology, etc. The ancient manuscripts, such the *Silappadhikaram*, the Tamil epic poem of the first century AD, and Bharata's *Natya Shastra* (Sanskrit codex) describe its musical aspects, such as *swaram*, *raagam*, and *taalam*. These are terms that are familiar to speakers of Malay, too. The oldest Tamil book, the Tholkaapiyam (approx. 1000 BCE) mentions musical phrases and practices that pre-date and antecede the present carnatic tradition (orig.12th century AD).

Etymologically speaking, Carnatic derives eponymously from the region including north-western Tamil Nadu, namely the Deccan ('south').

Eventhough currently enjoying high status, its origins may be not that glorious. *Karu Nadu*, from which carnatic derives, means "dark country". Like "Dark Continent", it probably refers to an unmapped or underdeveloped region. Anyhow, carnatic couldn't have just appeared on the scene. Its origins must lie in the Tamil folk music that has survived to the present. When a Tamil wants to label you as *pucca* (typical) old school, he'll say you are *karnadakam* – "primitive"

The above treatises ascribe the origin of the swarams (notes) to the sounds of animals and birds. Carnatic music has 7 Swarams, which are building blocks of music making, Sa Ri Ga Ma Pa Tha Ni Sa, which is similar to the western Do Re Mi Fa So La Ti Do. Raagam, refers to a set of rules for building a melody or rhythm – much like the Western concept of mode. Taalam refers to the beat of a composition (a measure of time). They have cycles of a defined number of beats and rarely change within a song.

Carnatic concerts, being largely vocal based, are solo rather than choral and sung mostly in undertones. The droning effect is most akin to a Quran recital. Hence its soothing cadence has a meditative property. No wonder that, unlike in other music, carnatic events witness a sea of swaying heads and slo-mo hand movements keeping time as if, conducting the thing. Contrast this with the wild bouncings and "head bangings" at a rock cocert.

Easily, the number of terminologies and sub-categories of these terms is dizzying for a non-musical person. While carnatic *katcheris* (concerts) are carnivals and mega events in Tamil Nadu, Malaysian Indians do not have a tradition of carnatic music appreciation, except for the occasional musical accompaniments in temples and weddings, or the vocalist on radio. Na. Mariappan is one Malaysian who has had intensive training in India. His fellow Penang pal, the late Re. Shanmugam was another accomplished composer/singer who had done quality work in Radio Malaysia and Singapore Broadasting Corp. One excellent musical happening in Malaysia is the annual *India Beat* series, the latest being the 6[th,] in 2011. However, it is only a sampler plate with small servings of assorted instruments, vocal and dance. With renewed interest in their mother culture, Indian parents are sending their children to traditional arts houses such as Barathanatyam and music studios. The Temple of Fine Arts has been the drum major in this march towards traditional arts.

Singing is king in Carnatic music, with instrumental accompaniment exactly that, accompaniment or fillers.Vocals can stand on its own needing only the *Oththu* (drone), for timing. While the singing is always based on lyrics, the Carnatic tradition has a unique non-verbal form called *konokkol*, very similar to the African American *scat-singing,* nonsense sounds in the jazz genre popularized by the likes of Louis Armstrong and Ella Fitzgerald. Scat – *"shaba didoo doo da dah, lidi didoo rab bab haa."* Konokol – *"ta ka di mi thom, ta di ki na thom, taki ta ta ka dhim mi, ta ka dhim mi ta ka ta ki ta"*. As in music generally, the Indian system of beats is a very mathematical affair. More to rhythm. konokkol sometimes even replaces the drum.The instrumental ensemble is minimal – Mridangam (drum), flute, and violin, a later import. In the absence of the vocalist, instruments can also provide a great Carnatic experience. In this case, flute, violin, mandolin etc will take centre stage, while Mridangam is everyones' companion. In the case of temple and wedding music, it's the *Nadaswaram, Tavil* and the *Oththu,* a nadaswaram-like drone accompaniment that means "agree".

Chinese classical music harks back to Ling Lun, who in mythical times, made bamboo pipes which mimicked bird sounds. Later in historical times (Qin dynasty 221-07 BCE), the Imperial Music Bureau was established and expanded by Emperor Han Wu Di (140-87 BCE). Outside influences, like Central Asia, greatly influenced the music in the succeeding dynastic periods.

Like his imprint on many aspects of the culture, Confucius is surmised to have written the oldest known music, the *Youlan* or *Solitary Orchid.* We remember that Confucius was also a qualified practionioner of the *guqin* string instrument. Realizing that all music originated as folk music, Chinese emperors went all out to collect the common people's music. The *Shi Jing* (The Classic of Poetry), a Confucianism inspired work, included folk songs from 800 BCE to 400 BCE.

Yayue. That is the name for Chinese classical music. Meaning 'elegant music', it was associated with Confucian ritual, and hence was the state music of the time.

"The word ya (雅) was used during the Zhou Dynasty to refer to a form of song-texts used in court collected in Shijing. The term yayue itself first appeared in the Analects, where yayue was considered by Confucius to be the kind of music that is good and beneficial, in contrast to the popular music originated from the state of Zheng which he judged to be decadent and corrupting. Yayue is therefore regarded in the Confucian system as the proper form of music that is refined, improving, and essential for self-cultivation, and one that can symbolize good and stable governance. It means the kind of solemn ceremonial music used in court, as well as ritual music used in temples including those used for Confucian rites. In a broader sense, yayue can mean a form of music that is distinguishable from the popular form of music termed suyue (俗樂) or "uncultivated music", and can therefore also include music of the literati such as qin music." – Wikipedia. Malaysians often hear "suey!" being used for "damn!"

The most recognizable Chinese classical music in most Malaysian minds, is the all so familiar lion or dragon dance music. In fact, it is an international icon of Chinese culture, heard around the world on Chinese New Year.

Chinese classical music is pentatonic in scale (black keys in a piano) – five notes per octave. In layman language, it is catchy music such as found in military marches, childrens's songs, hymns ("Amazing grace"), Gamelan, Jazz etc.

It is melodic rather than harmonic, which means that songs are sung by individuals (solo) rather than groups (choral).

The qin is perhaps the most revered instrument in China, even though very few people know what it is or seen and heard one being played. The zheng, a form of zither, is most popular in Henan, Chaozhou, Hakka and Shandong. The pipa, a kind of lute, believed to have been introduced from the Arabian Peninsula area during the 6th century and adopted to suit Chinese tastes, is most popular in Shanghai and surrounding areas.

Chinese opera has been hugely popular for centuries, especially Beijing opera. The music is often guttural with high-pitched vocals, usually accompanied by suona, jinghu, other kinds of string instruments, and percussion. Other types of opera include clapper opera, Pingju, Cantonese opera, puppet opera, Kunqu, Sichuan opera, Qinqiang, ritual masked opera and Huangmei xi.

Han folk music thrives at weddings and funerals and usually includes a form of oboe called a suona and percussive ensembles called chuigushou. The music is diverse, sometimes jolly, sometimes sad and often based on Western pop music and TV theme songs.

Guangdong Music or Cantonese Music is instrumental music from Guangzhou and surrounding areas. It is based on Yueju (Cantonese Opera) music, together with new compositions from the 1920s onwards. Many pieces have influences from jazz and Western music, using syncopation and triple time.

The Malay Gamelan is distinct from the Javanese or Balinese Gamelan, not so much in the instruments used but rather in the music played. The gamelan was brought over to Pahang in Malaysia in 1811 from Riau-Lingga (Zakaria Ariffin 1990) and spread to Terengganu shortly afterwards through a royal marriage. From the over 60 songs initially brought over, about half died with the original players and of the 30 remaining only about 12 are regularly performed today. Malay gamelan music is very simplistic in that nearly all instruments play the melody, unlike the intricately locked parts of the Javanese gamelan. There is currently a revival of interest in Malay gamelan music, led by Ariff Ahmad of Universiti Malaya, with many new pieces being written out for the ensemble. Cipher notation, common to Javanese gamelan and Chinese music, is used. Instruments used include: *saron* (a metallophone), *gambang* (a xylophone), *keromong* or *bonang* (sets of small kettle gongs), *kenong* (larger kettle gongs), *gong* and *gendang* or drums. As is customary in gamelan performance, players move around between instruments from piece to piece. Malay gamelan music is usually played during royal and formal occassions and performers are specially trained in royal palaces. Ariff Ahmad would like to see gamelan music being performed more frequently for all occassions and has expended much effort in promoting and writing music for the Universiti Malaya gamelan troupe which performs regularly for various occassions. Besides Universiti Malaya, various other local insitutions of higher learning have set up their own gamelan troupes, the most prominent of these being the Universiti Sains Malaysia group in Penang which in 1995 performed the Concerto for Piano and Gamelan by Lou Harrison.

The term refers more to the set of instruments than to the players of those instruments. "Gamelan" comes from the Javanese word "gamel", meaning to strike or hammer, and the suffix "an", which makes the root a collective noun. Real hammers are not used to play these instruments as heavy iron hammers would break the delicate instruments.

Angklung – bamboo based wind-chime like instrument produces a tingling sound like a mountain brook. Another type of this sound is that made by marbles or beans as they cascade down inside an inverted length of bamboo – a rainstick, from South America. So it makes the sound of a flowing creek.

Other forms of classical Malay music are – keroncong (Portuguese influenced), ghazal (Persian), zapin (Arab), that have been relegated to the backstage of the cultural scene.

We have observed that Chinese music, like its speech is tonal, so its layers are less. Carnatic, on the other hand, is very voluble and garrulous. The lead instrument in an instrumental performance takes the role of a vocalist, with the percussion [(mrdangam, kanjira (midget kompang lookalike), or ghatam (earthen pot), or tabla] playing back-up, or *pakkavaathyam* (litt: "side music"). All the instruments appear to be having a lively conversation. In the middle of a performance, the main instrument (wind, string, or vocal) takes a break, and the percussions have the dais to themselves, a brief moment in the limelight, for a heated debate in a call and response session of short and elongated notes. The challenger makes notes that progress from basic to very complex, and the responder is supposed to duplicate that at every stage. It makes for an interlude of comic relief, like the joker in an Elizabethan play. Such interludes are called *Thani Aavarthanam* ("solo percussion") in Tamil.

Folk Music: Shan'ge, Dondang Sayang, Themmaangu

Music of the folk variety, in any language, seems to touch an emotional chord, and pluck at heart strings. That is probably because the singer sings it from deep within his soul. Soul music? Now, if a non-native, listening can feel that, how much more the enjoyment to a person who can understand the words. The lyrics of a folk song, being a reflection of the soil and its smells, do indeed strike deeper than most other genres. I don't know if

I can speak for the youth of today, who favour the wordy, rap (hip-hop). That too, can be can be considered folk, unlike the angry snarls of hard rock, drowned out by the growl and scream of electric guitar. Even in the West, country music, which approximates folk, is much easier on the ears and mind than the jarring heavy metal rock. Country and Western, even to an alien non-dixie like me, is more soul stirring than any other of the English language music except perhaps, opera.

Chinese folk music was adapted very early in the day, to royal command performances. In fact the emperors, swooning to folk songs, dispatched cultural agents to round up and record the peasants' songs so as to access their general thoughts and desires. Goes back to the question of soul music.

Chinese music, as most other things, is conveniently split into Northern and Southern schools. Southern music, which is the music of Malaysian Chinese, is softer and melodious. This is explained by the fact that the South is well endowed with good weather and good life. Northern folk music, due to the harsh cold and dry clime, is rather "hard-rock" and jarring. This dichotomy is seen in the Peking (Baiguan – "northern") opera and the Cantonese (Nanguan – '

"southern") opera.You would guess that as the soil is, so goes the soul and its expression. Soul music. Soil music.

Mo Li Hua which means 'Jasmine Flowers', is a popular Chinese folk song. It was created during the Qianlong Emperor period of the Qing Dynasty. The melody is familiar to the West, as part of Giacomo Puccini's opera Turandot. It was sung by a Chinese lass at the closing ceremony of the 2004 Summer Olympics in Athens, Greece, to introduce the next Olympic Games venue and played at the awards ceremonies of the 2008 Beijing Olympic Games.

Interestingly, the Tamil word for *Mòlìhuā*, is *Malligai* or Jasmine. The Malay equivalent is M*elor,* which could be from the Tamil *Malligai* or *Malar* (flower).

Mo Li Hua

What a beautiful jasmine flower
What a beautiful jasmine flower

Sweet-smelling, beautiful, stems full of buds
Fragrant and white, everyone praises
Let me pluck you down
Give to someone
Jasmine flower, oh jasmine flower

Malay folk music of the *Dondang Sayang* variety are kinda love ballads, using pantuns (quartrains) for lyrics. *Dendang* means "to sing". *Sayang* is "love". Got it? It is believed to originate from the 15th century Malacca Sultanate era. It is always a duet between a man and a woman, in a call and answer format. With the lyrics being all poetic (pantun), and a wooing, starry-eyed tone, the whole effect is indeed romantic. The music, consisting of the violin, 2 rebana (drums) and a tetawak (gong) adds to the mood. The violin is the main instrument, accompanying the vocals. Nothing can beat a romantic fine dining with a dondang sayang music lifting the mood higher.

The music itself is said to be influenced by Portuguese folk music. Afterall, they were the ones who replaced the Sultanate. Interestingly, *Keroncong* the Indonesian folk tradition *(Bengawan Solo* etc) is also Portuguese influenced. It is observed that Keroncong has shades of *Mariachi* the Mexican strolling band — carousing. Dondang Sayang lives today mainly in exhibition concerts and dinner shows, not in mainstream venues. The older generation can only reminisce fondly, the many clubs devoted to the genre. The Baba Nonya community had a great investment in it up to the early sixties.

These days, the art form has been basically grandfathered, meaning Dondang Sayang (2018), along with Mak Yong (2005) will at least live on in the UNESCO's list of intangible cultural heritage of humanity. Exist on paper, not in popular consciousness?

Tamil folk music, like its ancient literature, has a long history. It is the beat of the common agricultural classes, and sung while working the fields, during festivals, in love, in war (marches), at funerals and lullabies and every other aspect of life. Most often, the music is robust and stirring, similar to the Punjabi bhangra, another Indian folk style.

Themmangu from *Thein Paangu* ("honey like"). Sung while working, riding bullock carts the songs can be solos or duets in a question and answer (prompt – response) format. The more robust versions are: *Oppaari* (laments at funerals), *Kummi* (joy at harvest time), *Thaalaattu* (lullaby), speaking of which, it has even entered the international scene. *Pi's Lullaby* from the Hollywood film *Life of Pi*, sung by Bombay Jayashree, is a *thaalaattu*, with Tamil lyrics. It was a frontrunner for best original song at the Academy Awards 2013.

Unlike Tamil popular (film) music, the folk music genre has not germinated well in Malaysia. Neither has the listening of India origin ballads. It is absent from the repertoire of Minnal FM, the Tamil department of Radio Malaysia, Except, perhaps a few filmy foksy songs on Ponggal, the harvest festival. A very few local born folk songs that come mind from the past and recent past are *"Chow Kit Roadu Santhaiyilae – 'Evening at the Chow Kit Road Market …..'"* and *"Ponnu parka ponen……"* By RK Prakash – *"I went bride hunting and …."* It's a kind of comic blues ballad with chorus in Minangkabau dialect – *"apo kono enko termeno, pompuan mano enko semanjo?"*

Music: Pop Yeh Yeh, Mellisai, C-Pop

Like the respective classical music of the Malaysian ethnicities, their pop songs are also strange to each others' ears. The Malay thinks Tamil pop and cinema songs are just so much noisy chatter. The Indian thinks Chinese ballads are such sonorous, somnolent same-tone drawls. The Chinese thinks Malay pop all sound the same, through the ages. To one's ears, those other tunes are a monotony. The various listeners quickly turn the dial to their language stations. To each, his own. But in many ways there are similarities.

No matter the language, the chief form of the songs are ballads.

Then there are those enduring tunes that, despite their ethnic colouration have "crossed over." The older Malay, even today will remember a few lines from the early 60's Tamil song, *"Allo Miss, Allo Mi..iss, Enge Poreenga,"* – "Hello Miss, Hello Miss, where are you going?" Every Malaysian teen in the 70's could mouth at least a few lines of the Chinese (Teresa Teng), "Woh Ai Te Ni Ah, Woh Ai Te Ni…" – "I love you, oh I love you." The Malay songs of the 60's and 70's were eminently mouthable ballads. "Hitam manis, hitam manis. Yang hitam manis." "Oh sweet dark one, oh sweet dark one.." The P.Ramlee – Saloma marital and musical pair from the 60's have their own category in the playlists of radio stations.

Current songs somehow do not cross over so easily, probably due to the lack of attributes stated above. However, the often incomprehensible, sometimes reprehensible rap and Hip-Hop of the West finds such welcome among all Malaysian youth, as elsewhere around the world. Rap and Hip-Hop has become a distinct genre in local the Malay, Chinese and Tamil music scene. Its catchy acapella (strictly vocal) sound keeps youth in rhythm, just as disco kept their parents in the groove, and rock and roll kept their grandparents in the jive. Homegrown Rap and Hip-Hop groups abound in the Malaysian music charts. Local Tamil musicians have appeared in Tamil movies made in India. While local Tamil compositions have existed since the fifties, it is only in the last decade that they have proliferated. The earlier ones were rhythmic ballads, the current ones are mostly raps, remixes of movie hits, and love songs. Homegrown Tamil music has finally come of age.

Malay:

A major part of this section on Malay music is quoted en bloc from the WWW.

"Malay pop music is descended from traditional *asli* ("pure" or "original") music popularized in the 1920s and 1930s by Bangsawan troupes. These are a type of Malaysian opera influenced by Indian opera, at first known as Wayang Parsi (Persia) which was started by the rich *Parsees* of *India*. They portrayed stories from diverse groups such as Indian, Western, Islamic, Chinese, Indonesian and Malay. Music, dance, acting with costumes are used in performance depending on the stories told. The musicians were mostly local Malays, Filipinos and Goans (from Goa, India). They ruled the stage, in the days before the wireless. Does that make it, days of the wireless-less.

One of the earliest modern Malay pop songs was *"Tudung Periok"*, sung by Momo Latif, who recorded it in 1930. In the 1950s, P.Ramlee became the most popular Malay singer and composer with a range of slow ballads such as *"Azizah"*, *"Dendang Perantau"* and the evergreen *"Di Mana Kan Ku Cari Ganti"*.

Pop Yeh-Yeh was a popular genre in the 1960s, influenced by western sounds. It ruled the airwaves of Malaysia, Singapore, and Brunei from 1965 to 1971. The music and fashion of The Beatles and other British rock and roll bands during the 1960s were a strong influence of the pop yeh-yeh bands and also generally influenced the Malay music industry of that period. As a matter of fact, *"pop yeh-yeh"* came from a line from the popular Beatles song, "She Loves You" ("she loves you, *yeah-yeah-yeah*".) While the term itself was never used in the 1960s until its revival in the 1980s by M. Shariff & The Zurah.The first song in the Pop Yeh-Yeh mode was, *"Suzanna"*, sung by M Osman in 1964.

Western, fast tempoed and using electric guitars and drums, the bands began to be called *kugiran*, by the first Malay DJ, M.I.A (Mohd. Ismail Abdullah), on Radio Singapore. Ku-gi-ran is an acronym for *kumpulan gitar rancak*. Say, "rock group". Another story goes, that P. Ramlee coined the word to differentiate it from the earlier, combo style bands, like Frank Sinatra and his gang.

"Some of the singers who made their name during that period include M Osman, A Ramlie, Jeffrydin, **Roziah Latiff** & The Jayhawkers, Adnan Othman, Halim "Jandaku" Yatim, Afidah Es, J Kamisah, Siti Zaiton, **J. Sham**, A Rahman Onn, Hasnah Haron, J Kamisah, Fatimah M Amin, Asmah Atan, Orkid Abdullah, A. Remie, Zamzam, Salim I, Kassim Selamat, M Rahmat, A Karim Jais, M Ishak, Hussien Ismail, Jaafor O, A Halim, Azizah Mohamed, S Jibeng and **L.Ramlee**. The names in bold are those from Malaysia. You can count on one hand! The Singaporean majority in the list explains why Singapore was the hub of music production in the earlier days.

Other popular rock and pop bands of the period include The Rhythm Boys, The Siglap Five, The Hooks which featured A Romzi as their lead vocalist (they scored a hit with the song *"Dendang Remaja"*), Siglap Boys, Les Kafilas, Cliffters featuring Rikieno Bajuri, Impian Bateks featuring Rudyn Al-Haj with his popular number "Naik Kereta Ku" and a acappella like "Oh Posmen", "Gadis Sekolah" etc. The Swallows featuring "La Aube", "Angkut-angkut Bilis" etc whose vocalist was Kassim Selamat and the EP was featured in a radio station in Germany. There, "La Aube" was in the German pop chart. Orkes Nirvana, The Sangam Boys and Les Flingers were Malaysian bands. The music and lyrics were usually composed by the bands themselves. The band leaders were also the producers of the albums of the period."

The golden age of pop yeh-yeh started to dwindle in 1971. With the slump in pop-yeh-yeh's popularity, the gravitational center of the Malay music industry shifted up north from Singapore to Kuala Lumpur, Malaysia. Loads of composers, songwriters, lyricists, singers, and producers started to establish themselves in Kuala Lumpur, Johor Bahru and Ipoh to stake out opportunities in the swiftly transforming face of the Malay music industry.

DJ Dave, Hail Amir and Uji Rashid introduced Hindustani-flavoured (*Dangdut*, in Indonesia) music in the 1970s. Between the late 1970s and mid 1980s, the market for local recordings and artistes was in great demand, bands and musicians performing in clubs and pubs were contracted to record. This was the time when non Malay artistes, bands and businessman ventured into the Malay music industry. Bands like Alley Cats, Discovery, Carefree and my own cousins, Cenderawasih took pop music further. Soloists like Sudirman, and Sharifah Aini expanded the borders".

Sisters' act Cenderawasih, by the by, have done very well, thank you. I am proud to claim them as my first cousins. Since exiting the Malaysian music scene, both have graduated from the prestigious Juilliard School of Music in Boston, USA. Helen and her husband organize an annual Jazz festival in Switzerland, among other things. Her international orchestra has performed at the Kuala Lumpur Symphony hall in 2009. Her younger sister and fellow Cenderawasih Irene, founded and captains the ICOM (International College of Music) in KL.

"Before the mid 1980's another genre of music appeared. This time it was slow rock, heavy metal, hard rock and the blues. Popular bands from the west like Scorpions, Led Zeppelin, Deep Purple, Def Leppard were some of the major influences for these Malaysian bands. Former Singaporean M. Nasir, played a leading role in shaping rock music in Malaysia as a song writer and producer for a period of almost ten years. He produced local rock bands like Search and Wings and took them to their highest level of Malaysian rock music.

Between the mid 80's and early 90's, R&B and Pop music became the focus of the urban youngsters. This music was cosmopolitan and catered to a professional and educated crowd. In 1985 Sheila Majid a singer groomed by engineer/producer Roslan Aziz made a debut album called dimensi baru which was financed and produced by Roslan Aziz himself. With a lovely mellow voice together with a bunch of creative musicians like Mac Chew and Jenny Chin both influenced by R&B, fusion and jazz achieved their dreams and set a new direction for many Malaysian R&B artistes to come. This was evidently clear when her second album EMOSI was released in Indonesia and earned the BEST R&B ALBUM in the prestigious BASF awards in 1986.This historical release has changed the facet of the music industry. In the mid 1990s, the rap group 4U2C with 7 young boys was introduced by Zman Production and a producer mansenoi & mam rap and they had made a big hit in the market and received few gold and platinum and <u>KRU</u> a vocal group composed of three brothers among others developed Malay rap and hip-hop."

"In 1991, an environmental album recorded by Zainal Abidin, songs written by Mukhlis Nor and produced by Roslan Aziz was released. This was received very positively by the public and the international music scene especially in Asia. Around this time nasyid pop music which was a form of Islamic religious which utilized a vocal group and accompaniment of only percussions music entered the market. Developed by vocal groups like Raihan, Rabbani and Brothers, this music got a lot of support from the countryside and religious fans.

In 1996 a school girl by the name of Siti Nurhaliza from a rural town Temerloh in the state of Pahang released an album produced by a talented pop music producer named Adnan Abu Hassan. This album of Malay Pop genre was a huge success. She included different genres such as Malay pop, R&B and Malay Traditional music in her later albums with much success." She is the current diva."

Tamil music in Malaysia has had some developmental disabilities. It is only recently, that a robust homegrown industry has begun to emerge, despite a miniscule market. The recent, second local music awards presentation, bespeaks this fact. Weekly *Top Ten* of Malaysian Tamil songs, aired on the local private Tamil station THR Raaga, is another proof. Minnal FM, the Tamil section of Radio Television Malaysia RTM) also runs a weekly hour long program featuring local artists and releases.

This is indeed a healthy development, in terms of showcasing local talent and content. Astro Vaanavil channel, in 2012 showcased a hugely successful singing talent contest called *Vaanavil Superstar.* It included international contestants from India, Sri Lanka, Australia and Canada.

There has always been an abundance of local singing talent on TV, Radio and the concert stage, but they have had to parrot songs originally composed and sung in India. These days, some of the Malaysian Tamil rappers have even been invited to sing for Tamil movies in India. Two decades before, a Malaysian singer did break through the Tamil film Industry and make a successful career out of it. Malaysia Vasudevan, a popular playback singer, was feted and celebrated in Malaysia for his lifetime of music. Vasudevan was pigeonholed as a *dappanguthu* (folksy) singer, eventhough he could carry classical tunes well. A Singaporean Tamil, Mohamed Rafee Yakob, has scored music for both Indian (*Jaggubhai*) and Malaysian Tamil films, which is supposed to be big achievements indeed. Malaysians have always scored music and composed songs for the healthy local Tamil movie industry.

These movements in the local Tamil music, are just a drop in the bucket against the huge music industry in India – Folk, Carnatic, Religious, Patriotic, Pop and Movie included. Tamil music, especially the movie songs are vibrant and current with the latest technologies. Once localized, regional, and playing second fiddle to Hindustani melodies, Tamil movie music has now surpassed Hindi compositions, which now copy from Tamil tunes. Ilayaraja, started the trend by infusing folk and country (village) elements to the popular light music genre. A.R. Rahman, son of a Tamil music director himself, debuted in Tamil movies and is now in high demand worldwide. Having composed for the British stage and collected two Oscars for *Slumdog Millionaire,* he was nominated again for 2010. His tune, *Chinna Chinna Aasai* ("A teeny weeny wish"), in his first movie, the Tamil film *Roja,* has been dubbed in many languages and cited in Time Magazine as one of the top 100 tunes of the 21st century.

In November 2011, a laidback *Tanglish* tune (English words, Tamil grammar/accent/melody) composed, written and sung on spot (in a jam session) became viral on youtube, securing 30 million views in a month). *Why this Kolaveri, Kolaveri, Kolaveri, Kolaveri di,* showed how cross-bred material can cross-broaders. Kolaveri (Tamil: *kola(i) –murder; veri – rage, mania)*, enjoyed a brief moment of its *veri* own rage. At the end of the year, it had won a gold medal from youtube, and citations in Time Magazine and CNN, as the top song of 2011. A.R.Rahman, called this phenonom a "clutter buster", meaning, an unpretentious, hummable tune and threadbare lyrics, which even the non-singer could easily perform. Compare it to the *Ayy Macarena* craze of the mid 90s which Malaysian kids mechanically mouthed on every corner.

"C-pop is an abbreviation for Chinese popular music, a loosely defined musical genre by artists originating from mainland China, Hong Kong, and Taiwan. Others come from countries where the Chinese language is used by much of the population, such as Singapore and Malaysia. C-pop is sometimes used as an umbrella term covering not only Chinese pop but also R&B, ballads, Chinese rock, Chinese hip hop and Chinese ambient music, although Chinese rock diverged during the early 1990s.

There are currently three main subgenres within C-pop: Cantopop, Mandopop and Hokkien pop. The gap between Cantopop and Mandopop has been narrowing in the new millennium. Hokkien pop, initially strongly influenced by Japanese enka, has been re-integrating into C-pop.

Chinese popular music was initially a vehicle for the Cultural Revolution and Maoist ideologies; however, during the country's extensive political and cultural changes of the past 50 years, it has lost much political significance; and now closely resembles the styles of K-pop and J-pop, from South Korea and Japan, respectively.

There has been a local Malaysian Chinese recording industries since the 1960s with generations of Chinese singers involved in Mandopop music. In the 1960s singers such as Poon Sow Keng achieved notable success in the region, and in the 1970s and 80s, Malaysian Chinese pop singers such as Wong Shiau Chuen, Lan Yin, Donny Yap, and Lee Yee were popular. In more recent times, popular singers include Eric Moo, Lee Sin Je, Fish Leong, Z Chen, Penny Tai and Daniel Lee."

For some reason, most of the scores of singers/lyricists have based themselves in Hong Kong, Taiwan, or mainland China. The one guy who consistently (controversially) presents himself in the Malaysian space is *Namewee* (Wee Meng Chee), with his hip-hop singing, composing, filmmaking, and acting and resulting occasional public stirs.

Classical Dance: Makyong, Yangko, Barathanatyam

The dance, like talking and singing, is a sibling that is born with us (inborn). It begins with the joyful jumping and whooping of a happy child. Observe, a child welcoming its parent back home from work, or as it receives a present. Who taught it how to dance?

Western, and African, or most other dances are mostly focused on the movement of the feet, with some minor role for the arms. Consider ballet or tango. The legs travel all over the dance space. If you are a competitor on, "So you think you can dance?", you are expected to cover or "work" the stage – no points for taking centre stage. Pun indeed intended.

Asian classical dance doesn't need legs, thank you. That is a joke, but not entirely. What I mean is, Asian dances like the Barathanatyam from Tamil Nadu, the Legong from Bali etc. are generally less spatial and more "facial". Case in point, The Barathanatyam exponent dances on spot and moves a deliberate step at a time, in a square, forward, backward, sideways etc movement. Facial expressions and neck movements are paramount. The Malay Asli and Inang styles of dancing are, hands and hip rather than foot based. The Mak Yong, out of Kelantan, is danced mostly seated on the floor.The ballet dancer on the other hand, swirls, swooshes, prances and pirouettes in a circular ambit, making it a whole body experience.

Makyong is a traditional form of dance-theatre from northern peninsular Malaysia, especially the east coast state of Kelantan. It is probably the most descriptive of Malay performing arts, largely devoid of external flavours. Although most traditional Malay dances were influenced by India, Java and other parts of Southeast Asia, Mak Yong has its own musical and movement style. Most of its themes stem from Kelantan-Pattani mythology.

The prelude incudes paying of respect and offerings to the spirits (*semah kumpung*). Dancing, acting and impromptu dialogues ensue. Three hour performances extend over several nights. The pak yong, dressed as a king, is the main character. Then, there is the queen, palace maids, and the jester, who is the only male performer. The *Jong Dongdang*, a chorous group, provides song and dance between acts. The tiny mak yong musical ensemble include the three-stringed spiked lute, drum (gendang) and a pair of gong. Additionally, the flute (serunai), keduk drums and small cymbals (kesi).

Today there are less than ten veteran mak yong performers. Although there have been a few attempts to revive the art form, the urbanized, monetized mak yong of today is a far cry from of rural performances of yore. Young people are wary of the rigorous apprenticeship so the art is now on the wane towards total eclipse.

Mak Yong was originally a form of folk theatre involving rituals connected with propitiation as well as healing. It is believed to have begun in the Pattani kingdom currently a province of Thailand. It could be almost a millennium old. Legend generally credits the dance to a rice spirit called Mak Hiang but a later belief tells that it was created by the clown-like divinity Semar. Mak Yong was patronized by all layers of society to pay respect to spirits, give thanks for the harvest or to cure illnesses.

The traditional Mak Yong survived into the 1960s and 70s but was banned by the Islamist PAS when it took control of Kelantan in 1991. They cited the immodest costume and such. Although many old performers defied the ban, Mak Yong could no longer be shown in public. Until UNESCO declared it a masterpiece of mankind's heritage in 2005, Mak Yong was an atrophying art. Eventhough there has been some effort to preserve Mak Yong outside Kelantan, lack of interest among the younger generation is another stumbling block.

These days, Mak Yong rarely gets staged at cultural shows, losing out to modern Malay ethnic group dances like Joget. It is sometimes still staged at weddings, to celebrate a state's independence or to pray for the king's long life. But these modern, shortened performances are stripped of the old animist rituals and their music is simplified because the songs are played so infrequently. There are only a few troupes left who perform traditional Mak Yong in the villages of Kelantan and Terengganu. With the current ongoing "arabization" of Malay society, many cultural arts with non-islamic origins, are slowly shriveling off. It can be somewhat similar to the cultural cleansing of ancient artifacts, as happened during the raging rape by the Taliban (Bamian Buddhas) and ISIS (Iraqi museum).

The Yangko dance, also called twisting Yangko dance, is a traditional Chinese folk dance commonly performed in the Northern provinces of China. The dance is smooth and compact in rhythm, featuring its jolly scene, abundant dance language, exuberant gestures, and vivid performing style. Therefore, people often take the Yangko dance during the spring festival or some other special celebrations.

The Yangko dance was created by the farmers when they worked in the rice field in the Song Dynasty, and is used to worship the god of farming to pray for harvest in ancient times. Year after year, the Yangko dance constantly absorbed techniques and forms from farming songs, folk songs, folk Kungfu, acrobatics and dramas. Until the Qing Dynasty, "the Yangko dance" had been popular around the whole country.

Because of the differences of regions and customs, some variations exist in the Yangko dances. To identify different kinds of Yangko dances, the name of the region or the feature of the dance is often added ahead. For example, the "Drum Yangko dance" in Shandong Province, the "Shanbei Yangko dance" in Shanbei Area, the "Field Yangko dance" in Hebei, Beijing and Liaoning Provinces, and the "Manchu Yangko dance" in the Northeast China.

There are three types of performance in Chinese Yangko dance: the song-and-dance duets, Yangko performed on the ground and Yangko preformed on the stilts. The major accompanied instruments of Yangko dance include suona (trumpet-like wind instrument), small cymbals, drum, flute, erhu (alto fiddle) and zhuban (bamboo clappers). Yangko dancers usually wear bright and colorful costumes, and their movements are vigorous and quick, with distinguished local flavor.

Yangko dance is more than a kind of performing art in China, because many Chinese people take it as an important method of relaxing. They would like to organize Yangko dance matches or performances during grand ceremonies and also in their daily life.

It is basically a public parade, with men and women marching and swaying holding fans, kerchiefs, and twirling umbrellas. A free-for all conga line, with no touching.

The Barathanatyam, originally called, "Sathiraattam", hails from the Tamil country of India. It has three divisions, namely the *Nritta* (pure dance), *Nritya* (Facial expressions) and *Natya* (the dramatic, or story telling part). All three combine to provide the Bharathanatyam full experience, although they can on their own, provide a huge stand alone entertainment/edutainment.

Nritta – movements are angular. Arms fold and extend laterally like those of an earth excavator, and similarly, the main movement is the bend at the hips. The upper body of the dancer is stiff like that of a gymnast on a balance beam. The legs are worked but they do short moves like heavy thumps on the floor,. The taps, unlike the tap-dancer's or river dancer's, is flat footed, to the basic beat of *tat-tit, tat – taa* etc. These movements, called *adavu*, are the basic vocabulary in the language of dance. The sequences of these adavus, or *korvai* (string), form the pure dance i.e no story is conveyed. The body and limbs move according to the beat and tempo – the foot thumping, voice (konnokkol), and or percussion.

Nritya – the expressive, emotive aspect. It includes *Mudra* – hand gestures: *Bheda* – head, neck, eye movements; *Bhava* (facial expressions by the dancer which convey mood. There are eight altogether – love, joy, sorrow, anger, energy, fear, disgust and astonishment. *Rasa* refers to emotion created in the spectator, corresponding to the eight *Bhavas*).

In fact, the foot taps and jingle of the *salangai* (ankle bells) can suffice for musical accompaniment. In a certain sense, Barathanatyam is akin to a robot dance or a break dance, especially the rubber neck side to side jerks, and arm extensions. Those jerky movements sometimes remind you of the Chinese Lion dance movements. Those Lions can be frisky kitties indeed, incessantly twisting their heads this way and that, while pretending to taunt and leap.

On another level, the multidirectional arm/leg bends and body twists especially by a "twin" pair of dancers is very co-ordinated and mirror imagish. Imagine a pair of synchronized swimmers doing their thing on stage. While the synchronous swimmers do the *nritta,* the barathanatyam exponent does the *natya.*

Except for short leaps, the dancer does not need much space. And for such a space and movement limited dance, it gives the impression of a full bodied, stage-wide performance. The portions where the dancer draws a circle while doing fine footworks and bending at the hip as if strewing flowers, and short "leaps" like a deer, are the extent of larger movements. If at all there is a swirl, it more like a single 360° slow turn. The focus is on facial expressions and hand movements – much like a mime artist. It is also like sign language – the dancer miming the story that the singer sings.

The Bharathanatyam and Balinese dances are also identical in their usage of the neck. The difference is, Bharathanatyam's lateral neck jerks, giving the effect of the head dislocating/or relocating sideways. Whereas, the Balinese chin appears to be oscillating pendulum-like. Bharatham shares the demi-plié stance (knees half-bent sideways and feet squarely on the floor) of ballet. That's the gist of it, which has a confounding list of sub categories to the above aspects.

As for the costume, it is colourful, to say the least. Being of silk, the reds, greens and yellows look metallic. It is somewhat a restyled silk saree, adapted for free movement.

Street Theatre: Theru Koothu, Ziqu, Wayang Kulit

Theru Koothu (Litt: "street bash") is a traditional Tamil folk dance drama characterised by story telling through a combination of dialogues, songs, and dance. It is usually performed in rural areas of Tamilnadu in the Tamil months of *Panguni* (March – April) and *Aadi* (July-August). Theru Koothu can be classified into Valli Koothu, Kuravai Koothu, Samaya Koothu, Pei Koothu, Thunangai Koothu, and Porkala Koothu that depict the life styles of ancient Tamil people.

Theru Koothu was the only form of entertainment for the people when movies and television or modern drama had not made an entry into the world. The play usually starts in late evening with artistes and music troops performing on a wooden bench in open air and goes on upto the small hours of the morning. The performance of artistes is so captivating that people sacrifice their sleep and enjoy the performance throughout the whole night.

To perform Theru Koothu, one must have a thorough knowledge of make-up and costumes. Theru Koothu is usually dominated by male artistes who also perform female roles. They took stories from the great epics of India – Ramayana and Mahabharata, or ancient Tamil legends. Sometimes, current news stories also prevail in their performance. Theru Koothu is conducted during temple festivals mainly in the months of Panguni and Aadi.

As with many folk cultural traditions, Malaysian Indians have become detached from their folk dance traditions, having been distracted by concerns of work and survival in the colonial dispensation. However, that does not prevent them from vicariously identifying with and experiencing the ethos and pathos of these forms as they watch those in concerts and in movies.The freestyle *Dappangutthu,* or *Kutthu* dances that modern youth have taken to, don't count. They are more social or, party, or festival dance.

"The Painted Face role, or *jing,* is a feature unique to Chinese opera, and is a crucial element in identifying the character's specific role (there are four jing roles, as will be discussed below). The Painted Face involves not only facial makeup, but also headdress as well as a specific costume to fit the specific role of the character. The Painted Face no doubt originated as a device to disguise a male actor as a female, but from there it was expanded to the jing role, and as such imparting important symbolism to the audience.

Red in Chinese opera, like in Feng Shui, carries a traditional well-loved radiance. The color red in an opera is understood to symbolize positive traits such as intelligence, heroism, integrity and loyalty.

And when the art or costume director tires of red on stage, he or she can bring in the slightly less utilized color purple. Purple conveys the same positive perception as red, but with the added attributes of respect, sophistication, nobleness and a sense of justice.

When black is used as the foundation of a mask on stage it is seen as a neutral. A black face represents characteristics like impartiality with a hint of altruism.

Add in traditional bravery and a bit of stubbornness and you have a character depicted by the color blue, which in the opera may represent a certain level of vigour coupled with audaciousness. The person wearing this mask might be a spirited young person who remains in love despite the consequences.

On the other hand, the color yellow without dispute portrays characteristics like treachery, ferociousness, and the character's overall performance will be marked by slyness. The audience can rest assured that masks of this nature represent the adversary to the red or blue-faced protagonist.

So, if you find yourself in a Peking opera don't worry if you don't understand Mandarin, allow color to be your translator and guide you through the performance." – Wikipedia

Alas, as in many things cultural, Malaysia has lost its right to claim the Wayang Kulit (Shadow Puppet Play) as its own. All this is of its own doing, with the PAS (islamist party) ruled Kelantan state, its last bastion, banning it from the social space and popular concience. As it is (or, was) performed in the open, we shall consider the art is as street theatre.

"Wayang kulit (Javanese: ꦮꦪꦁꦏꦸꦭꦶꦠ꧀) is a traditional form of puppet-shadow play originally found in the cultures of Java and Bali in Indonesia. In a wayang kulit performance, the puppet figures are rear-projected on a taut linen screen with a coconut-oil (or electric) light. The dalang (shadow artist) manipulates carved leather figures between the lamp and the screen to bring the shadows to life. The narratives of wayang kulit often have to do with the major theme of good vs. evil. Wayang kulit is one of the many different forms of wayang theatre found in Indonesia; the others include wayang beber, wayang klitik, wayang golek, wayang topeng, and wayang wong. Wayang kulit is among the best known, offering a unique combination of ritual, lesson and entertainment. On November 7, 2003, UNESCO designated Wayang the flat leather shadow puppet (wayang kulit), the flat wooden puppet (wayang klitik), and the three-dimensional wooden puppet (wayang golek) theatre, as a Masterpiece of the Oral and Intangible Heritage of Humanity. In return for the acknowledgment, UNESCO required Indonesians to preserve the tradition." – Wikipedia

In the days prior to movies, TV, or stage dramas, the Wayang used to be the "Screen"entertainment of the day. *Wayang* means "show" as in wayang gambar "picture show." It is related to *tayang* or "display" and in the case of the wayang kulit, to *bayang* or "shadow" or, "imagine". Even if it hadn't been banned, arts like Wayang Kulit, Mak Yong, and Wau kite would have no chance against their technologically superior modern avatars like movies, pop concerts and drones.

Stage Drama: Bangsawan, Medai Naadagam, Chinese Opera

Bangsawan is a type of traditional Malay opera. It was known to have developed from a sort of Indian theatre performance during the 19th century by visiting Indian travellers.

Bangsawan is similar to western opera, the stories drawn from diverse sources, such as Indian, Western, Islamic, Chinese, Indonesian and Malay. Music, dance and costumes are used depending on the story told. As the name suggests, Bangsawan storylines revolve around royalty and aristocracy, bangsawan being 'nobililty', in Malay

Nowadays, it is difficult, if not impossible to find any bangsawan troupes in Malaysia.

"It was originally an Islamic religious sacrificial dance drama introduced from Persia. The subject matter was limited to the story of Islamic prophets and heroes, and later it gradually described history and real life. Around 1870, a Persian Wayang troupe arrived in Penang and gained a reputation.

The early Bangsawan plays had a strong primitive religious color, and the content of the plays mostly came from domestic and foreign myths, fables, and historical stories. For example, "Alibaba and the Forty Thieves" and "Aladdin and the Magic Lamp" are popular plays. In the 1930s, Bangsawan dramas began to reflect real life. The themes focused on punishing evil and promoting good and admonishing the world. It became a popular drama in Malay-speaking regions (including Indonesia) before the 1940s.

"Between Two Coffins" premiered in 1935, Johor, depicting the story of pagans being indicted after their marriage and death.

"Who's Blame" was first performed in 1938, Singapore, describing an unfilial son being struck to death by lightning and exposing the evil consequences of enslaving education.

"The Rebellious Son" was first performed in Johor in 1932, depicting a young man who abandoned his wife and continued to marry others, swallowing his family wealth, and finally ended in prison. – Wikipedia

In the 1950s, the drama entered its heyday. The work echoes the awakening of the Malay nation, and the representative work are "Water Ghost", "Johor Tiger", and "Tun Sri Lalang". Garam Hamidi's "Children of Magnificence" is considered an excellent drama with originality.

Usman Awang (1928~)'s representative play "Uda and Dara" is a tragedy depicting the innocent love of young men and women, and condemned the feudal system. The one-act play "Guest on Kenny Hill" describes the situation of a senior official who is plagued by various contradictions, exposing various contradictions in real life. His plays "From Stars to Stars" (1965), "Under the Sun" (1969), "Curtain of the Times" (1969), "Red Morning" (1971), etc. concentratedly reflect the achievements of Malay drama creation in the depth and breadth of realism." – Wikipedia

"Malaysian Tamils adopted street drama in the rural Malaysia and stage drama in the urban areas. In the early days of the Twentieth Century so many stage artists with their theatre have visited Malaysia. These theatre artists have also trained the local artists in Malaysia. The Theatre artists in Tamil Nadu who later became Cine Artists also have contributed their part in the development of stagecraft in Malaysia. Therefore, there is a similarity in the stagecraft of Tamil Nadu and Malaysia. Though after the Second World War, Malaysian Tamil stage tried to establish its own base, it has the resemblance of Tamil Nadu stage. Before the Second World War, the themes were Puranas and later social themes after thirties. The plays of many are dramatists like Sankaradas Swamigal, Pammal Sambanda Mudaliar have been staged here and through them Malaysian stage was developed." – Prof.Dr V. Sabapathy, Universiti Malaya

"Two different types of plays make up the Cantonese Opera repertoire—Mo, meaning "martial arts," and Mun, or "intellectual"—wherein the melodies are entirely secondary to the lyrics. Mo performances are fast-paced, involving stories of warfare, bravery and betrayal. The actors often carry weapons as props, and the elaborate costumes may be as heavy as actual armor. Mun, on the other hand, tends to be a slower, more polite art form. The actors use their vocal tones, facial expressions, and long flowing "water sleeves" to express complex emotions. Most of the Mun stories are romances, morality tales, ghost stories, or famous Chinese classic tales or myths.

One notable feature of Cantonese Opera is the makeup. It is among the most elaborate makeup systems in all of Chinese Opera, with different shades of color and shapes, particularly on the forehead, indicating the mental state, trustworthiness, and physical health of the characters. For example, sickly characters have a thin red line drawn between the eyebrows, while comic or clownish characters have a large white spot on the bridge of the nose. Some Cantonese Operas also involve actors in "open face" makeup, which is so intricate and complicated that it resembles a painted more than a living face". – Kallie Szczepanski, 06. 02. 2019

"Award-winning filmmaker Chong Keat Aun's *Snow in Midsummer* movie depicts the rise and fall of a Cantonese opera troupe in Kuala Lumpur during the '80s. His tired expression speaks volumes about the state of Malaysian Chinese opera. 'The sad reality is that in my 17 years of documenting traditional arts of the local Chinese community, we may be looking at Chinese opera's extinction in the next decade,' he states solemnly. 'And it's not just because we don't have the financial support or the lack of awareness. It's more how [Malaysian Chinese opera] cannot keep up with the times, especially since people these days prefer instantaneous entertainment'." – Koyyi Chin, 22.09.22

Small Screen Series: Inspector Segar (1966-69), Empat Sekawan (1966-88), Gerak Khas (1999-2021)

The Inspector Segar cop serial was telecast in RTM. Written and directed by Major V.I.Joseph and produced by RTM. It was Malaysia's 1st Tamil Mega series (1964-1969) and filmed on 16mm film camera. Before the days of Astro multichannels, this once a week entertainment was eagerly awaited. I remember 12 year-old me sneaking off to the neighbour's to watch the black and white flick. It was contemporary to *Run Buddy Run and Daktari*. Remember those? The protoganist inspector, was played by V.I. Joseph himself. His brother V.I.Stanley was an accomplished showman himself, famously known for his stage comedy skits (*Ayyaa Koyaa*) with Ayyappan.

He was the straight man (*Dean Martin, Bud Abbot*) to Ayyappan's comic character (*Jerry lewis, Lou Costello*).

RTM telemovies were the much anticipated Deepavali entertainment in the 60's and 70's, in addition to the one movie feature from India. Today. You have the nauseating non choice (Hobson's/Sophie's?) of non-stop Tamil movies on Astro and the weekly once on RTM. But then the latter are all imported films. Local TV dramas are regular weekly fare on RTM.

Gerak Khas (Special Force) is a Malay police television drama series, first aired on 5 April 1999 on Radio Televisyen Malaysia's TV1 and later TV2. It is the longest-running action drama series on Malaysian television.

Datuk Yusof Haslam directed both the series and its film adaptations and produced by his company, Skop Productions. The series received recognition from The Malaysia Book of Records as the country's longest running television drama series (20 seasons and 1054 episodes) from 5 April 1999 and ended on 27 March 2021

Pi Mai Pi Mai Tang Tu ("Going around, Coming around") – (1985-2004) is a popular sitcom TV show rose to fame in the '80s and was aired on TV3. The sitcom talks about the life of the multi-ethnics staying in Flat Seri Wangi. You have the likes of the character of Pak Busu, Lucy, Budin, Ravi, Pak Uda, Mak Ngah and many more.

It ran from 1985 to 2004. Once the show was over, its legacy still lived on when it was picked as a musical and also was featured weekly as a newspaper comic strip.

On top of these and the few dramas by the likes of Rahim Razali, RTM churns out tons of somnolent, indolent melodramas.

Empat Sekawan (The Four Friends) or, *Sei Hei Lam Mun* in Cantonese, starred four actors – Lai Meng, Hon Ying, Hoi Yong and Wong Hor. It was a hitcom sitcom that ran from 1966 to 1988. Holy smoke! that is equal to *Gunsmoke* (1955-1975). Empat Sekawan actually began during pre-Merdeka days as a radio show, where it was recorded in a makeshift studio in Kuala Lumpur, and broadcast to the New Villages. (New Villages were set up by the British as a way to contain the communist insurgency by corralling the rural Chinese populace).

The radio show was so well-received that it evolved into an even more popular television show. Malaysian sitcom Empat Sekawan actress Datuk Lai Meng passed away recently at 90 years of age. She and her co-stars had acted on the same set for 20 years. It is clearly the longest running show in Malaysia.

All said, the good news about Malaysian television today, is the availability and multiple choice of local entertainment. The flip side however, is not everyone seems to be watching the local shows because Hollywood, even Korean progamming in a horde of channels is kidnapping viewers. Whereas, in the old days, people waited with bated breath for that once a month or once a week showtime on RTM. Nowadays, RTM begs for viewership. Kinda brings to mind the Tamil saying, *Kenjinaa Minjurey, Minjinaa Kenjurey* – "When I plead you're sombong (cocky), When I'm sombong you plead."

Cinema: Hang Tuah (1956), Raththa Pei (1969), The Journey (2014)

Art appreciation, being a very subjective matter, this essay is just a brief, basic browse, and not a comprehensive capture of the subject.

The *Bujang Lapok* Trilogy, *MaduTiga*, *Hang Tuah* (1956) are some of the memorable movies of yore, all featuring the multitalented P.Ramlee.

Hang Tuah (Director: Phani Majumdar) is another retelling of Malaysia's historic icon, Hang Tuah. The film depicts the rise and fall of the legendary warrior, similar to Ivanhoe or Sir Lancelot. It was the first Malay film to be shot in colour! It was even nominated for the highly-coveted Golden Bear at the Berlin Film Festival, receiving international acclaim.

From the first Malay film *Laila Majnun* (1933) directed by B.S.Rajhan, the directing was monopolized by Indians (Majumdar, and Malaysian L.Krishnan). Tan Sri Krishnan is widely considered to be the father of Malay movies. The production/distribution side was controlled by the Chinese (Shaw Brothers, and Cathay-Keris). Even today much of the international award winners have been directed by Malaysian Chinese. Currently, Malays are in all aspects of filmmaking.

1972's, *Satu Titik di-Garisan* was the last of the (Cathay-Keris) big studio movies from Singapore. Thereafter, like the music industry, movies began coming out of Kuala Lumpur. For a time, in the 70-80's Malay audiences depended on Indonesian imports to satisfy r their movie appetite and to supplement the small number of local productions.Today the local Malay moviedom is self-sufficient and thriving. The golden age of malay cinema, that coincided with characters like P.Ramlee and his contemporaries is still appreciated by the current generation as witnessed by their recurrent reruns on RTM.

Malaysia's first Tamil film is *Raththa Pei* (Blood thirsty ghoul) starring Kalaikkumar Chinnasamy, Susheela Devi, Sivaji Raja, M. Baharudeen, Mukesh, Vijaya Gowri and Malaysia Vasudevan. It was shot in Golden Studio, Chennai and directed by Mooban. Music and background score of the film was composed by G. K. Venkatesh. Shooting of the film began in year 1968 and was released on 14 January 1969. Although it was shot in Tamilnadu, it is most certainly a Malaysian movie. The production and acting crew were from Malaysia.

Jagat – (from the Malay word jahat, "naughty") is a 2015 Malaysian crime drama film. directed by Shanjhey Kumar Perumal. Set in the early 1990s, a critical period in Malaysian Indian history, the coming-of-age story subtly underlines the plight of the Indian Malaysians who were forsaken by the estate owners and forced to move to the cities, surviving under harsh circumstances. The story follows a mischievous 12-year-old boy named Appoy and his relationships with his father, Maniam, and his uncles, former drug-addict Bala and local gangster Dorai. Perumal has described the film as semi-autobiographical, having lived for two years in squatter areas with his family.

The film had won the Best Malaysian Film award in the 28th Malaysia Film Festival in 2016, whereas its director Shanjhey Kumar won the award for Best Director. The film also represented Malaysia at Asean Film Fest 2017.

'*Chemman Chaalai*' (The Laterite Road, 2005) is a lesser-known Malaysian film, but it has made waves internationally.

This Tamil language film tells the story of a young Malaysian girl named Shantha, and her family, who live in a remote estate. Shantha dreams of pursuing an education in spite of the many challenges she and her family face from living in poverty.

Chemman Chaalai received international acclaim and was screened at a number of film festivals, including the Rotterdam, San Francisco, Pusan, Barcelona, Fukuoka, Bangkok, and Nantes International Film Festivals.

The Journey (2014) is Malaysia's second highest-grossing film. This Malaysian-Chinese film is about a conservative father who embarks on a journey throughout Malaysia to hand-deliver wedding invitations alongside his daughter's British fiancé.

The Journey won a number of awards at the Malaysia Film Festival on the year of its release.

This heartwarming film also shows how people from two different worlds understand each other's cultures, and is definitely something every Malaysian can be proud of.

2014 Malaysian comedy-drama film directed by Chiu Keng Guan and written by Ryon Lee. The film stars Ben Andrew Pfeiffer, Lee Sai Peng and Joanne Yew Hong Im. The story follows a father that finally allows her daughter to wed an English lad with a condition that he shall follow him on a journey around the nation to deliver their wedding invitation

In its final theatrical run, the film raked in a total of RM16.87 million. That achievement would later be surpassed by 2015's Polis EVO with its collective gross of RM17.74 million.

Even if not a Malaysian production, nor a Malaysian story, *Everything, Everywhere, All At Once*, deserves a place here due to it's Malaysian thespian Michelle Yeoh bagging the 2022 Oscar for Best Actress. The first for an Asian.

Social Dance: Joget, Dappangguthu, Ballroom

Modern Malaysians don't practice a traditional form of social dance. The social dancing that happens in nightclubs are imports. Malaysians of all races up to the 50's were active party goers, dancing the joget and western ballroom dances. Turn the black and white photo albums of your grandparents, and notice their slick ballroom moves. Later, your parents were grooving to the music of rock and roll, the twist, disco and what not.

Malay social dancing scene was active in the 50's with the *joget* form, practiced during weddings and social gatherings. It is identified with the likes of 60's icons, the P.Ramlee, Saloma pair.

With joget practically extinct as a social dance (as opposed to performed dance), we'll have to look to East Malaysia for it. The Kadazan-Dusun *Sumazau*, can be assumed to represent the bumiputras. It can qualify as a social dance, where males and females can hit the floor, with its simple steps. It can also double as a staged performance.

Malaysian Indians have not had a social dancing tradition unti recently. Modern Indian youth have taken to the *kutthu* dance at weddings and birthdays. *Kutthu* or, *Dappanggutthu* is a virile shake-a-leg to vibrant native vibes. Take the disco drums of the 90's and amplify it two knotches up. It is still part of the impromptu moves of youngsters in Tamil Nadu, at temple festivals and funerals. Malaysian Indian youth, thanks to Tamil cinema, have now adopted it as part of their social outlook.

Chinese social dancing was nonexistent until the introduction of the western ballroom dancing. Western ballroom dancing became popular in the 20th century. Previously, it would not have been permissible for men and women from respectable families to dance together. It was popular in the 1940s Shanghai nightclubs, and early Communists leaders such as Mao Zedong and Zhou Enlai were also avid Soviet-style ballroom dancers. Ballroom dancing however later disappeared after the Cultural Revolution to be replaced by massive group dances such as yangge dance. Ballroom dances however reappeared after the liberalisation of China later in the century, and it is now commonly found performed by many people in public parks in the morning as exercise.

These days, youth and the youthful of every community might be found dancing away at nightclubs, weddings and new year bashes.

Animated dance: Wǔshī, Poikaal Kuthirai, Kuda Kepang

Lion dance (*wǔshī*) is a traditional Chinese dance form that has athletic young persons doing lion-like movements. You will have to ask a lion if indeed, the movements are accurate. The sharp, angularly jerky movements remind you more of a frisky kitten than a majestic lion. Perhaps a lion cub might do that movement.

The lion dance is often mistaken as dragon dance. An easy way to tell the difference is that a lion is operated by two people, while a dragon needs many people. Also, in a lion dance, the performers' faces are covered, since they are inside the lion. In a dragon dance, the performers can be seen since the dragon is held high upon poles. Basic lion dance fundamental movements can be found in Chinese martial arts.

During the Chinese New Year, lion dancer troupes from the Chinese martial art schools or Chinese guild and associations will visit the houses and shops of the Chinese community to perform the traditional custom of "cai ching", literally meaning "plucking the greens". The lion has to pluck the auspicious green usually a vegetable like lettuce, 'cái', that sounds like "fortune" and auspicious fruit like oranges tied to a red *Ang Pao* envelope containing a stash of cash. It is either hung up or placed on a table at the entrance in front of the premises. The "lion" will dance and approach the veg and red evelope like a prowling cat, to "eat the green" (dollar) and "spit" out the "leaves". The lion dance is believed to bring good luck and fortune to the business and the troupe is rewarded with the "red envelope".

The lion dance and the dragon dance are also usually performed at many other important grand occasions, including Chinese traditional, cultural and religious festivals, business opening events, birthday celebrations, honour guests, welcoming and wedding ceremonies by the Chinese communities.

The *Poikaal Kuthirai* ("False leg horse") is a popular traditional dance unique to Tamil Nadu, India. "Popular", not in the sense of being well patronized, but in the sense of being the common people's dance. The artistes dress and dance in such a way that it looks like an old time royal riding a real horse. The difference between the lion and horse dance is that while the lion dancers are hidden inside the lion apparatus, the horse dancer is visible from above the hip, as if seated on the horse. The papiere mache horse shell is slung over the shoulders, and the "rider's" legs are free to move any which way. The thing which facilitates the horses' trotting, rearing, whirling around, and yeah bucking bronco, is the foot high stilt on which the riders's feet rest.

Poikkal kuthirai dance is also called *Puravai Attam* (Horse Dance). Or, dummy horse, if you please.The horse sans legs, is made up of a variety of materials such as jute, paper, cardboard, and glass. A male – female pair perform together, with the richly decorated cardboard horses making them look like real raja and rani on horseback ride, swordfights, and generally challenging each other. The music, like tamil folk music will make you jump off your seat and make you want to do some galloping yourself. Needless to say, the successful performance of this dance needs years of practice and experience. There's no horsing around, here. And no horseshit, either!

While the Poi kaal Kuthirai, like the lion dance, is 3-dimensional, the Malay *Kuda Kepang* ("Flat Horse") is a 2-dimensional horse. Kuda Kepang is a traditional dance much enjoyed by the Malay community, especially those of Javanese descent. Kuda Kepang is a woven frame that looks like a legless horse. It is typically a mat made from woven strands of bamboo or animal hide that is coloured and patterned to make it more attractive.

"Usually, a group of Kuda Kepang performers are made up of 10 to 15 dancers. One of the dancers, called a 'dayang' will lead the dance. In the early part, all of the dancers' movements are controlled by the dayang, using a thin strand of rope. This performance is typically displayed at communal ceremonies to celebrate auspicious occasions such as welcoming honoured guests, weddings and festivities. There are several schools of thought on how the dance originated.

There is a theory that links the origin of the dance to Wali Songo, who lived in Java during the 15th Century. In his efforts to expand the teachings of Islam in the depths of the Javanese rural communities, Wali Songo was facing difficulties to get connected to the people there. He had an idea to dance whilst on horseback. Over time, the woven frame made of bamboo or animal hide replaced the real horses initially used. Another school of thought related the origins of the dance to Saidina Ali. The dance was to emulate the movement of Saidina Ali's armies during battle, and that was how Kuda Kepang came to be.

Others believe the origins had a link to the mystic realm. A celestial horse by the name of Kuda Sembrani was slated to have come down from the heavens to Java to look for a lost friend. When reunited, both danced in joyous union.

Kuda Kepang has elements of mystery, spiritism etc and performers can sometimes be overwhelmed by mystical forces. Special ceremonies must be performed before the dance, to avoid unwanted accidents. The special ceremony entails rituals of spirit worship. The bomoh also prepares a feast for the spiritual guardian, consisting of coconut, rice, ripe banana, incense, white cloth, needle, thread, white feathered chicken, eggs and a special mix of fresh flowers and herbs. The minimum number of dancers is 9, to a maximum of 15.

There are only male dancers. Choreography includes Sola dance, Selendang Pak Tani, Pucuk Rebung, Perjuangan, Mempertahankan Diri and so forth. The dance movement is called Lenggang Kiprah.

Quite often dancers succumb to a trance like states at the end of the performance. They dancers would begin sequences of humanly impossible movements like jumping to heights of six to seven feet. During their trance, the musical accompaniment continues, to calm them.

The typical musical instruments that perform the accompanying music are anklong (main instrument), gendang, gong (a bronze disc instrument), kinong (a smaller version of the gong), jidor (similar to a rebana besar), soron kecil (a copper instrument shaped like a bamboo) and bonang made of copper, with a nipple in the middle)."

Other animal-like dances among Malaysians, are the Indian Peacock dance (*mayilaatam*), where the dancer dressed in a green suit and peacock feathers imitates the big bird. The snake dance (*paambattam*) is another female performed dances that is suited to the stage. A dance rarely found in Malaysia but common in Tamilnadu, is the tiger dance, (*puli attam)*. The dancer paints his bare body in bright yellow with black stripes. Standing upright, he prances, strides zig-zag fashion, making striking motions.This is usually peformed at the head of funeral or temple processions.

Self Defence: Silat, Shaolin, Silambam

Eventhough Malaysians have always dabbled in their respective arts of self-defence, the Kung Fu (Wushu, Qigong) films out of Hong Kong in the 60's spurred a renewed interest. Self-defence has its origins in national defence. The original proponents were frontline soldiers who had to also train in hand to hand combat tactics. The formal armed combat invariably degraded into a free for all and good 'arm' tricks determined victory on the field.

Vestiges of armed combat still survive in modern self-defence. The Kung-Fu employs the use of chain whips (recall the nunchaku). *Silambam* refers to the bamboo staff used in the fighting, and also uses arm and fist moves. Silat uses the *keris* (*kris*), the wavy edged dagger and hand tricks.

The native form of the art is Silat, or its full form Pencak Silat. The name evokes its origins in Indonesia. *Pencak* was the term used in central and east Java, while *silat* was current in Sumatra. In modern terminology, pencak and silat are used to refer to different facets of the art, pencak being the performance aspect and silat, the fighting and defence aspect. The etymology of *pencak* and *silat* has not been determined. Some believe that pencak comes from the Sanskrit word *pancha,* meaning five, or from the Chinese *pencha* meaning avert or deflect. Silat might derive from the Minangkabau word *siliek* (meaning – *"clay",* or slickness thereof). In fact, they practiced on clay or muddy paddies. Another theory is it comes from "sekilat", "as swift as lightning". Or, could it be related to *silambam,* the Tamil art of self-defence? As a matter of fact, there is a branch of silambam in India called *sillaathu silambam,* that has no link to silat.

A writer on the matter says, "India and China were the first civilisations from outside Southeast Asia with whom Indonesia made contact. Both countries influenced the local culture, religion and martial arts. Bas-reliefs in Srivijaya depict warriors wielding such weapons as the jian or Chinese straight sword, which is still used in some styles today. Additionally, Javanese blades are of Indian derivation. It was during this period that pencak silat was first formulised (sic)." History has recorded for us that Tamils traded and culturally influenced Sumatra and Java (see the section on language/scripts). We have to thank Chinese Buddhist travellers Fa-Hisen, I-Ching and others, for the copious travelogues of their stay in Srivijaya (Sumatra) en route to India. Sumatra especially, has had ample contact with Chinese culture and arts. Over a thousand Buddhist monks from around South-East Asia were living and studying at the Buddhist centre of Srivijaya, at its apogee (zenith).

In a further manifestation of how interlocked our cultures are, Shaolin Kung Fu is said to be introduced by a South Indian prince. Chinese records point to a Tamil prince of the Pallava dynasty, Bodhidarma, as the originator of the Shaolin school of self-defence. He is regarded as a *Bodhisattva* in Buddhist records, the 27th incarnation of Buddha and the first Buddha in the *Chan* (Zen) tradition. Chan = Dhyana (Skt – "Meditation").

An account was written by Tánlín (曇林; 506-574), a disciple of a disciple of Bodhidharma. Tánlín's brief biography of the "Dharma Master" is found in his preface to the *Two Entrances and Four Acts*, a text traditionally attributed to Bodhidharma, and the first text to identify Bodhidharma as South Indian:

"The Dharma Master was a South Indian of the Western Region. He was the third son of a great Indian king of the Pallava Dynasty. His ambition lay in the Mahayana path, and so he put aside his white layman's robe for the black robe of a monk [...] Lamenting the decline of the true teaching in the outlands, he subsequently crossed distant mountains and seas, traveling about propagating the teaching in Han and Wei". (citation: Wikipedia)

Bodhidharma, noticing the weak physical state of the Shaolin temple monks, instituted some physical strengthening exercise regimes, drawing from his martial background in India. Not that he started them on a martial track. That would have been antithetical to Buddhism. Anyway, Shaolin tradition credits him with founding the Kung Fu martial arts.

"According to Southeast Asian folklore, Bodhidharma travelled from south India by sea to Sumatra, Indonesia for the purpose of spreading the Mahayana doctrine. From Palembang, he went north into what are now Malaysia and Thailand. He travelled the region transmitting his knowledge of Buddhism and martial arts before eventually entering China through Vietnam. Malay legend holds that Bodhidharma introduced preset forms to silat." (Wikipedia)

This sea route would be the more digestible itinenary, compared to some accounts that say Bodhidarma entered China by land route through North India. The Pallava Tamils had by this time already found the sea-route to China. The islands and mainlands of South-East Asia had already been Indiannized by them. The Angkor Wat's (Cambodia) layout is a carbon copy of the Perumal (Vishnu) temple in Sirangam, Tamil Nadu. The royal names ending in Varman such as Purnavarman (Tarumanagara kingdom, Java); Jayavarman I and II (Khmer kingdom); and Mulavarman (Kutai kingdom in East Borneo), are reflections of the names of Pallava kings such as, Narasimhavarman son of Mahendravarman. Hence it would be no surprise for a Pallava prince to reach China through Viet Nam.

That would point to a *silambam – shaolin* connection, wouldn't it? With this, the art of self-defence in Malaysia has come to a full and convoluted circle. Silambam stimulates *silat*. Shaolin Kung-Fu borrows from silambam. Shaolin in turn, enriches silat. It is possible even, that *silat* has contributed to *silambam* and *shaolin*, in a reverse osmosis of the art. There is a type of *silambam* in India, called *sillaathu silambam,* or *silat silambam.*

Silambam (silambu = staff), is the armed form of self defence/offence. *Adimurai* ("strike method"), *Kuththu varisai* ("pummel series"), and *Varma kalai* ("art of vital points") are the unarmed aspects. All four are different aspects of the same game. Varma kalai, as it name implies, refers to disabling and reviving the nerves of the opponent, hence encompasses medical knowledge.

There is a localized version of Chinese martial arts, that has taken on shades of silat. This is the *kuntao* style, which in Hokkien translates as, "way of the fist." First brought to South East-Asia by various classes of Chinese migrants, it incorporates many of the moves in silat. Sometimes, it is called *Kuntao-Silat.* Kuntao angin or silat angin (meaning "wind kuntao/silat") was founded in 1977 by Yap Mat from Kedah, Malaysia by combining silat seni gayong with the knee and elbow strikes of *tomoi* (Malaysian version of *muay thai*), the hand techniques of Wing Chun and the energy drills of yiquan. It is known for its deceiving circular attacks and nerve point manipulations.

The earliest evidence of pencak silat being taught and fought comes from the empire of Srivijaya on Sumatra island, where folklore tells that pencak silat was created by a woman who witnessed a fight between a tiger and a large bird. There are several variations of this story depending on the region where it is told. On Bawean island, the woman is believed to have watched monkeys fighting each other while the Sundanese of West Java believe that she witnessed a monkey battling a tiger. Notwithstanding the details of it, the fact that it is a woman who created the art, says much about women's role in those societies.

Compared to the "stand up and fight" style of western boxing and wrestling, Asian self defence incorporates a lot of deviousness. And silat is the most underhanded and deflective, with the practioner squatting, bending low and trying to knock off opponents with circular kicks. Kind of brings to mind the 1976 clash of Muhammad Ali (boxer) and Antonio Inoki (wrestler) at the Nippon Budokan Arena in Tokyo. While Ali bounced around, Inoki was on his back most of the time, trying to kick Ali. That was a failed experiment, and called a draw.

After the Tamil Cholas sacked Srivijaya in the 12th century, it declined. Shortly thereafter, so did the Mataram and Sailendra kingdoms of Java. The newly ascendant Majapahit empire in Eastern Java brought the big islands of Indonesia together, and pencak silat was the beneficiary of its renaissance. Pencak silat became refined, and Majapahit weapons were in great demand elsewhere, including Malacca. Hang Tuah's magical kris, the *Taming Sari* was minted there. Pencak silat is not going away anytime soon, as it is a popular mainstay in Indonesian movies, especially historical, "period" pieces. In Malaysia, it enjoys popularity as Silat Seni Gayong.

Fine Art: Chinese Brush, Indian Bronze, Malay Wood

Before there was Picasso, there was the Chinese brush painter. Methinks Chinese painting may be considered the original abstract art. The stylistic strokes that suggest rather shout out loud, makes you stay awhile and surmise/survey/suppose the picture before you.

Starting around 4000 B.C. traditional Chinese painting has developed continuously over a period of more than six thousand years. Its growth has inevitably reflected the changes of time and social conditions. In its early stage of development, Chinese painting was closely related to the other crafts, from pottery to the decorations used on the bronzes, carved jade and lacqerware.

Following the introduction of Buddhism into China from India during the 1st century A.D. and the consequent carving of grottoes and building of temples, the art of painting religious murals gradually gained in prominence.

"The range of subject matters depicted in the paintings was extended far beyond religious themes during the Song dynasty(960-1127). Paintings of historical characters and stories of everyday life became extremely popular. Techniques were also further refined.

Landscape painting had already established itself as an independent form of expression by the 4th century. Then it gradually developed into the two separate styles of "blue-and-green landscapes" and "ink-and-wash landscape". The blue-and-green landscape used bright blue, green and red pigments derived from minerals to create a richly decorative style. The ink-and wash landscape relied on vivid brushwork and varying degrees of intensity of ink to express the artist's conception of nature, and his own emotions and individuality.

Flower-and-bird painting was separated from decorative art to form an independent genre around the 9th century. A great many artists painted in this genre during the Song dynasty and their subject matter included a rich variety of flowers, fruits, insects and fish. Many of the scholar painters working with ink and brush used a great economy of line. They produced paintings of such things as plum blossoms, orchids, bamboo, chrysanthemums, pines and cypresses, using their subject matter to reflect their own ideals and character.

Fifthly, there is composition and space. Since the creative requirements of Chinese painting do not demand strict adherence to reality or to a particular angle of view or source of light, the painter has complete freedom in terms of artistic conception, structural composition and method of expression. To give prominence to the main subject, it is quite permissible to omit the background entirely and simply leave it blank. At the same time, since the sizes and shapes of the spaces in the painting are different, the very absence of content can itself create rhythm and variety. Sometimes the variety and balance created in this way is further enriched by the addition of inscriptions in the empty space.

Chinese landscape painters' aim is to depict the familiar mountains and rivers of China from the perspective of nature as a whole and on the basis of their understanding of the laws of nature. Most landscape paintings create the impression that the scene is viewed from high in the air, as if seen through the eyes of a bird.

With flower-and-bird paintings, sometimes a single flower hangs as if suspended in space, or the flowers and plants of different seasons appear together. Explained by one of the Ming painters, Wang Fu(1362-1416), as "likeness through unlikeness" and Qi Baishi (1863-1957) as "subtlety of a good painting lies in its being alike and yet unlike the subject" Chinese painters attach great importance to reality, science, space and time and yet manage to disregard them at the same time. The laws of these things must come second to the requirements of artistic creation and should not become shackles that bind artistic expression.

One of the distinctive characteristics of Chinese painting is the use of inscriptions in poetry of calligraphy and of special seals as part of the painting itself. In ink-and-wash paintings, the bright red seal add a final touch of beauty. Calligraphy, to be sure, is a distinct, developed, art by itself.

The simplest inscription consists of the artist's name and the date. Sometimes the inscription could include the occasion for the painting and the name of the person for whom the painting was done. It could be about the subject and style of the painting. Quite often the artist might include a piece of poetry or a literary allusion. These are all followed by the artist's own seal. When using red seal on a monochrome painting, it is said to be 'adding the eye to the dragon'."

Paleolithic cave paintings of up to 30 millenia ago exist in Tamil Nadu. The 1,011 year old Big Temple in Tanjavur, hides "technicolour" life size murals of the same period, in the dark depths of its inner rooms. However, that art form has not extended to the present day. Rather, Tamils opted to achieve their greatest artistry in Bronze (Copper – Tin alloy) work. The hollow statues are achieved by the "lost wax" method. The world famous *Nataraja* (King of Dance) is a shiva statue at the temple in Chidambaram. His Tamil title is *Sabesan* (Sabaiyil Aadum Eesan), or the "Lord who dances in the assembly". It is an international icon of india. Naturally, there have been tons of statues of all dieties since the beginning of the 1000 year-old Chola bronze history. Even today, such statues keep being produced in Thanjavur. Coincidendally, the equally famous Thanjavur genre of painting is entirely colourful canvas cn depictions of deities.

Thanjavur is also famed for its silk weaving and the thalayaatti bommai ("jiggling head doll"). But those come under the crafts category.

"The Malays have a long tradition of woodcarving stemming from the availability of timbers for constructing buildings (palaces, mosques and private houses), boats and boat heads (*bangau*), weapons, tools and decorative items; the wealth of the natural environment as well as the influence of the Islamic religion for inspiring forms and motifs; the innate creativity and skill of the craftsman and continuous royal patronage.

Traditional Malay woodcarving employs two main techniques: *ukiran timbul*, in which floral and geometric designs are carved in relief, usually on panels, walls, pillars and doors of traditional Malay palaces and houses; and *ukiran tebuk*, which involves piercing or cutting out patterns in the wood, used for parts of a building where ventilation is required, such as windows, fanlights, partitions and railings. These carvings may sometimes be enhanced with gold paint. Outstanding examples of woodcarving are especially manifested in old palaces, such as Istana Kenangan in Kuala Kangsar, Perak, on roof ridges and eaves, fanlights and friezes.

The type of wood used depends on the purpose of the carving but two hardwoods, cengal (*Neobalanocarpus heimii*) and jati (teak, *Tectona grandis*), are widely used because of their durability. Standard tools include saws, planes, files, borers, shavers and knives.

The motifs on woodcarving, some of them ancient, reflect a combination of indigenous Malay, Indian and Middle Eastern elements, the latter through Islam. Motifs from nature, in stylised or abstract form, are based on flowers, such as the frangipani (*cempaka*), lotus (*teratai*) and jasmine (*melur*), and betel leaves (*daun sirih*).

Islamic influence is best reflected in designs on pulpits (*mimbar*) as well as in the form of calligraphy (*khat*) in Arabic or Jawi script. Short passages or verses (*ayat*) from the Holy Qur'an serve to decorate the interiors of mosques. Framed calligraphy done on wooden panels also finds a place in almost every Muslim house, as do carved Qur'an stands (*rehal*).

Ukiran also appears on items of daily use, such as furniture, walking sticks, coconut scrapers (*kukur kelapa*)—the older examples of which are carved in the shape of animals, particularly a horse—as well as in traditional weapons such as the keris hilt, often based on dragon (*naga*) or bird motifs.

Traditional Malay woodcarving continues to this day as a vibrant form of art and craft" – Ghulam – Sarwar Yousof.

Word Art: Khat, Chinese Calligraphy, Tamil Epigraphy

Calligraphy, from the Greek kallos ("beautiful") is the artistic form of day to day writing, text or script. *Khat* art, i.e, painted, pencilled, digital etc, is an art form advanced from its beginngs in the Umayyad period (661-750 AD).

It is a truism that necessity is the mother of invention, or innovation as the case may be. Islam's injunction against the use of animal forms in art necessitated the use of inanimate shapes such as geometric and floral motifs. The stylistic use of the Arabic script was another area of such ingenuity that was expressed on the walls of marble mosques and mausoleums. *Khat*, as it is called, is the art of choice that adorns the homes of Malays/Muslims in Malaysia.

Although it is cultural rather than religious, modern khat presents itself as mosty quranic verses in a stylized form. The most common words are *Allah*, *Bismillah*, and *Halal*. We are dealing with khat as art, rather than as script. So, taking leave of conventions and conformity, the normally straight "lines" (*Khatt* in Arabic) weave and heave and twist and turn hither and tither like Chinese noodles. It is often like abstract art, stopping you in your tracks until you are able to decipher it. Modern khat takes all kinds of shapes. There are circles, as in *Bismillah,* water droplet as in the *Al Jazeera* logo, and squares as in the one replicating a QR code. Or, the one that really amazes, like a maze, really. Interestingly, the QR code and khat lookalike, are encoded with secret messages! Figure it out, if you can. Animal shapes abound. There is peacock, tiger (Saidina Ali), lion, horse, man praying etc. Apparently animal shapes are OK as long as it is abstract, not actual depiction.

The material is varied. There is the master who carves on wood, the painter who swirls his brush, the sculptor who chisels marble, and the digital artisan who commands his computer. Batik style for fabrics, metals, glass etc. are all proof of the adaptability and versatility of the art.

Chinese calligraphy, like the ink painting, is very abstract. Both do not pretend to depict reality but suggest it. Besides, both are partners in crime. Doesn't every Chinese ink painting have a brush stroke signature identical to the art itself?

Chinese calligraphy, along with with brush painting, playing stringed instruments, and the board game called "Go", is considered the favourite pastime of the ancient elites. Today, it is the domain of specialist artisans.

With its swirls, twirls and flourishes of brush, the art renders a feel of ballerina in motion just as we get when watching the calligrapher's hands perform it.

Rules of modern calligraphy: The characters must be written correctly (duh!). Calligraphers often use variant Chinese characters, which are deemed correct or incorrect case-by-case, but in general, more popular variants are more likely to be correct.

The characters must be legible. As calligraphy is the method of writing well, a calligraphic work must be recognizable as script.

The characters must be concise. Good Chinese calligraphy **must be unadorned script**. It **must also be in black ink** unless there is a reason to write in other ink.

The characters must be **aesthetically pleasing**.

Surprisingly, Tamils do have a tradition of word art. Not in moderm times, but in ancient times. As in the section on language (scripts), they were fond of chiseling anything from royal decrees, land deeds and war reports, to business transactions, on stone. Besides stone, the royals also wrote on copper plates, while the ordinary householder scratched names on earthern pots.That is why over 50% of all archeological finds (rock inscriptions etc) in India are in Tamil Nadu, or in Tamil. The recent (2020-21) discovery of potsherds with Tamil scribblings in Keezhadi have been dated back to 580 BC.

Even China must have had experts who carved Tamil inscriptions onto stone. In 1911, S.H.Thomlin, a British Public Works engineer discovered a 4' 9'' x 2'6'' x 5" slab of rock In Galle, Sri Lanka while doing ditchwork. It had been mis(used) as a bridge over the ditch! What was it and how is it related to the Chinese Admiral Zheng He? From the contents of the inscriptions on it, it was a gift from China that paid obeisance to Buddha, the Hindu God Tenavarai Nayanar, and to Allah, written in Chinese, Tamil and Persian (Arabic script) respectively. The stele contains a date, 15 February 1409 when Zheng He installed it. It corresponds to his 2nd visit to the Indian Ocean area. He had visited Ceylon all of the 7 times he visited the region. Anyway, one must conclude that there must have been some Chinese or Tamil craftsman present at Nanjing or Galle, 1409 when the inscriptions were made.

Fabric Art: Kanjeevaram, Songket, Kesi

Weaving silk is itself an art, be it by the worm or the human. Fabricating it into eye-catching, soft caressing material is high art indeed. One origin story from the writings of Confucius credits silk manufacture to Empress Leizu, wife of the Yellow Emperor (Shih Huang Di). In about 3000 BC, a silk worm's cocoon fell into her teacup. Extracting it from the drink, long fibers unravelled from the cocoon.

India is famous for its silk from places as far flung as Kashmir, Kanjeevaram (Kanchipuram), and Mysore to Benares (Varanasi).

"Kanchipuram is located very close to Chennai, the capital of Tamil Nadu. From the past, Kanchipuram Silk sarees stand out from others due to its intricate weaving patterns and the quality of the silk itself. Kanchipuram silk sarees are large and heavy owing to the zari (gold thread) work on the saree. Kanchipuram attracts large number of people, both from India and abroad, who come specifically to buy the silk sarees. Most of the sarees are still hand woven by workers in the weaving unit. More than 5000 families still indulge in silk weaving." – Wikipedia

Kanchipuran is the go to silk saree for Tamil weddings, both in India and in Malaysia. Malay ladies are nowadays prone to buy these sarees at Little Indias to turn into baju kurung. Priorly, the sole material for high class Malay fabrics was the kain songket, out of the east peninsular states of Kelantan and Trengganu.

"*Songket* is a *Tenun* (woven) fabric that belongs to the brocade family of textiles of Brunei, Indonesia, Malaysia and Singapore. It is hand-woven in silk or cotton, and intricately patterned with gold or silver threads. The metallic threads stand out against the background cloth to create a shimmering effect. In the weaving process the metallic threads are inserted in between the silk or cotton weft (latitudinal) threads in a technique called supplementary weft weaving technique.

The term *songket* derived from the Malay word of *sungkit*, which means "to hook". It is referred to the method of songket making; to hook and pick a group of threads, and then slip the gold and silver threads in it. Another theory suggested that it was constructed from the combination of two terms; *tusuk* (prick) and *cukit* (pick) that combined as *sukit*, modified further as *sukit* and finally *songket*. Some says that the word *songket* was derived from *songka*, a Palembang cap in which gold threads was first woven." – Wikipedia

"Kesi is the essence of traditional silk art in China. Since the Song and Yuan Dynasties, the royal family has monopolized its production. Kesi was used to weave the emperors' and empresses' apparels, imperial images and famous paintings. Because of the extremely meticulous weaving process and its rich and elegant character, Kesi is known as 'an inch of Kesi and an inch of gold' and 'the Holy of Weaving'

Kesi adopts a weaving method that passes through the warp and breaks the weft, which makes the work look like being carved and engraved, and has a rich double-sided three-dimensional effect. The Kesi craftsmanship was already extremely superb in the Tang Dynasty, when craftsmen were able to use a variety of valuable materials such as pure gold and silver threads, peacock feathers to weave Kesi. Moreover, the strength of Kesi is much higher than that of any silk handicrafts, therefore Kesi is the best preserved work among all the silk art that has survived to this day.

The nobility of Kesi comes from its need of huge man-hours and meticulous techniques with thousands of threads. As an ancient craftsmanship, Kesi has its own special loom that cannot be replaced by modern machines. Craftsmen must not only master the weaving skills, but also understand painting knowledge in order to combine rich colors with sophisticated techniques. Even a small handtowel-sized work of the highest quality contains thousands of gradient colors, often requires the exchange of tens of thousands of shuttles, and several months for a senior craftsman to complete.

In 2006, Kesi was selected into the first National Intangible Cultural Heritage List. In 2009, Kesi as Chinese silk tapestry weaving" – Wikipedia

Speaking of fabrics and art, batik is an art form that jumps to mind. "Batik is an Indonesian technique of wax-resist dyeing applied to the whole cloth. This technique originated from the island of Java, Indonesia. Batik is made either by drawing dots and lines of the resist with a spouted tool called a *canting*, or by printing the resist with a copper stamp called a *cap*. The applied wax resists dyes and therefore allows the artisan to colour selectively by soaking the cloth in one colour, removing the wax with boiling water, and repeating if multiple colours are desired." – Wikipedia

It appears that all (Indian, Chinese, and Malay) arts, crafts, and culture in Malaysia have origins outside of the Malay peninsula, going by google. The silliest aspect of this is the Malay culture, claiming a nativist narrative, being shown in google as emanating from Indonesia. Why blame google when we ourselves are iconoclastically annihilating the culture. Look at the situation of Makyong, Bangsawan, and Wayang Kulit, where attempts at whitewashing under the pretext of exterminating non-islamic content looks very much like throwing the baby out along with the bathwater. Which leaves no option but to scramble replace with/replicate another culture, or attempt to create a fake national culture. The ongoing arabization of Malay culture, is a case in point.

House of God: Kaaba, Kovil, Kong, Kirk

Bulbous onion domes of mosques (and the twisted garlic domes of Russian Orthodoxy), highrise pyramidal temple gopurams, buffalo horn-like Taoist roofs, meaning a mosque is not mosque without the signature dome and minaret, a kovil is not one without the gopuram and the tokong is not a tong without the dragon roof. This is what one observes, as one gets around the country – neighbourhood after neighbourhood of mind numbing sameness, come prayer time.

The question then arises, if God is the creator par excellance and all creativity is of Him, why then are buildings dedicated to his worship so preset and predictable? The initial buildings or prototypes, were indeed awesome wonders. However, Malaysian religious architects seem to have fixed on to a formula and stuck with it. If imitation is a form of flattery, then kudos to the copyrighter. Zeros to the copycatter.

Prof Dr Mohamad Tajudin Bin Mohamad Rasdi who writes the "Architecture Inside Out", column in *The Star,* opines that a religious building should be subservient to the nature around it. He was commenting in the context of the current craze of erecting increasingly bigger domes and taller minarets in modern mosque construction. His view is that the creation of man (i.e. buildings) should not supercede the creation of God (i.e. the natural environment). That is to say, human handiwork should blend into God's handiwork, and not stick out like a sore thumb. *Au Contraire*, the cathedral builder would say that you should feel very small inside the grand edifice.

Ain't it a paradox of paramount proportions, profoundly puzzling? Skyward reaching cathedral spires, mosque minarets, and temple gopurams are considered outward expressions of human devotion to God, while at the same time allowing room for human ego massage. The builder usurps God's glory while trying to glorify HIM! The original mosque was the Prophet Muhammad's simple house. He also appropriated the millennium old *Kaaba*, an unassuming structure in Mecca dedicated to pre-islamic Arab dieties, as a focal point (*kiblah*) of all muslim worship. Eventhough it (the Kaaba) is not a place of worship, all mosques and praying spots are aligned to it. Like the original masjid, the original churches were "house churches", meaning, they met in individual homes. The home being where the heart is, the church was anywhere the believers met, be it open space, under the tree, or in a grand cathedral.

On a recent religious program on Minnal FM radio (Tamil channel), the Ustad (religious teacher) while appreciative of the impressive mosque designs of recent times, lamented the fact that in a building to house a thousand, there were often only fifty worshippers during non Friday *solat* (prayer times). That can be said of Christian cathedrals too. Awe inspiring on the outside on any day, but awfully empty on the inside on Sundays. The Hindu, and the Chinese prayer, of course is almost always an individual act and not congregational. So forget full houses at worship time, except for the occasional temple festival, Thaipusam etc. Even Batu Caves Thaipusan, despite the million crowd, is strictly not congregational, but individual devotion, gawking, hawking, and touring.

While on the subject, a Muslim architect friend concurs that the cental dome is not Islamic in origin as seems the fervent belief of some. Rather, it was the Romans who built the first techonologically advanced domes (the Pantheon – rebuilt by Emperor Hadrian in about 126 AD), and continued with the Byzantines. The Byzantine domes were in turn, influenced by the Sassanids (a pre-Islamic Iranian kingdom). When Muslim armies conquered the Sassanids and Byzantium, they made the dome their own, adding their distinctive four minarets, geometric designs etc. The minaret was used as a vantage point from which the muezzin or bilal recited the *azan*, or call to prayer. Today, with loudspeaker technology, minarets are still a fixture, albeit decorative.

The *Hagia Sophia*: Greek – "Holy Wisdom (of God)" is the mother of all domed mosques and churches. Completed in 537 AD, the Byzantine edifice was the premier cathedral for 1500 years until its 1453 conversion into a mosque. It stayed a mosque until 1993, when it morphed into a museum. It is the model for all domed mosques that have followed, including the

Blue Mosque (Turkey) and the Dome of the Rock (Palestine), and for the Russian Orthodox domed cathedrals.

Speaking of domes, South Indian Hindu temples have always incuded a dome (*Vimaanam*), above where the *Karuvarai* (Garbha Graham, Holies of Holies, or Sanctum Sanctorum) where the main deity abodes. This dome outdates, or is at least contemporary with the Byzantine dome. The Sikh temples have always had a dome, e.g the Golden Temple of Amritsar. Since Sikhism is a relatively new kid on the believers' block, it is uncertain as to whether it downloaded the dome from Muslim or Hindu architecture. Why not say both, since Sikhism includes aspects of Hindu and Muslim codes in its theology.

Buddhist Viharas are commonly domes or more like bells, with their rims resting right on the ground, instead of on raised towers. The Burmese have plain white stupa(s) that remind you of the hand bell of your neighbourhood icecream man. They take after the stupas of India and Sri Lanka, where they are called dagoba(s). The Thai peaked roofed temples are generally more similar to the Taoist temple, although there are ample stupas in Thailand. The difference is, Thai stupas are bright and golden, with rich encrustatuions and ornamentations, while the Burmese and Sri Lankan ones are plain and whitewashed in chalk.

The religious fervor (*bhakti*) that drove the Tamils to build tiered temple towers (*Raja Gopuram)* was that they could derive the benefit of the lord's *darisanam* (visitation/epiphany) at the gateway itself. Or by merely contemplating the gopuram from a distance. The gopuram is reckoned to be the feet of the lord (or lady) that resides inside. Hence, you might notice a Hindu tapping her cheeks as the bus she rides in, passes a temple. That is, by way of acknowledging the god/dess. Similarly, her Muslim fellow passenger might do a silent prayer of her own, cupping her palms when the *Azan* comes on the bus radio. The Catholic guy up front might do the sign of the cross as the Cathedral comes into view.

The Hindu temple layout represents a human body lying on its back, the head facing the South. If the *Gopuram* (entrance tower) is the lord's feet, the *Karuvarai* (Garbha Graham, in Sanskrit) meaning "womb chamber", is the head. It is where the temple's principal deity is installed in the main sanctum, at the back. Its location is indicated by the domed *Vimaanam* (above the sanctum) that acts like a pin drop on a google map.

Chinese temples are an exception to the skyscraper craze. They are unpretentious, flat and low by design (!), i.e, following Confucian dictates. While colourful and eye-catching enough, they are generally horizontal, and low roofed. They however, build temples of a different kind that are grand structures. Their devotion to education shows through, again thanks to Confucius' concern for knowledge. Chinese private schools are temples par excellence compared to government school buildings, which are bland, unimaginative, box-like structures created out of dusty, decades old blueprints.

Many concerned Malaysian Indians bemoan the fact that their community does not give a fraction of the importance to schools that they do to erecting elaborate temples. Their leaky longsuffering schools are dependent on government handouts. It is all a matter of priorities. The community has begun to introspect its educational and cultural needs. Indeed much acitivity of the educational kind is happening in temple community halls, ranging from book exhibitions, to educational and religious seminars. The Chinese bring a religious fervor to the god of education, while the Hindu favours devotion to his agamic gods. While the Bumiputra enjoy the comforts of their special political status; and the Chinese cherish their businesses and schools; the Indians' most conspicuous area of growth, seems to be their temples. Everywhere, you see new constructions, renovations, and *kumbabishekam* (reconsecration) in progress. Old temples are torn down and rebuilt in a bigger way, and roadside shrines become grand sanctuaries. This Hindu resurgence might be a reaction to the *koyil idippu* (temple demolition) incidences in KL and Selangor. It might also be a kind of collective statement about their much publicized marginalization in other sectors. "Hey look! We are everywhere, and we (Hindus) are not going away anywhere, anytime soon." The Chinese, with their strong focus on vernacular education, are making a similar statement. "You bet! Our language and culture are here to stay". There is nothing like a community's perceived threat to its valued ideals, to rally the troops.

To be fair, all places of worship are also places of instruction. Religious, that is. Buddhist viharas are especially diligent in this matter. And churches have special classes called Bible studies, or Sunday schools (for the young) and Gospel meeting or seminars. *Cheramah* (lectures) and *Khutbah* (sermons) happen regularly in mosques. Hindu temples conduct *Thevaram* (devotional recitation) classes.

Taoist temples, while devoid of sky seeking spires, have their own grammar and formalized formulations of form and function. Usually, four main structures are seen, beginning with the tall, square, red entranceway that leads into a spacious courtyard. There may be a small adjunct building housing smaller shrines, incense urns, an incinerator for burning "heavenly notes", or a carp or tortoise pond. The main temple building rises in three separate units as if on terraces. The effect of big, bigger, biggest from front to back, is quite dramatic. Stairway to Heaven?

You also get the sense of mountain ranges that rise step-wise from the darker foothills to the gradually hoary and misty peaks, similar to those depicted in Chinese water colour paintings. It is a great technique, to effect an emotional response such as this. A tribute to the artistry and creativity of the original architect, who overcame the Confucian limitations of flat, shallow building, and created a place of awe inspiration.

Like the South Indian Hindu temple with its ornate encrustation of idols, brass pots etc. on its gopuram, the Taoist temple is ornamentally studded with colourful embellishments of snarling dragons, gargoyles, bamboo motif tiles etc. These intricate constructions of immaculate conception, nevertheless fully conform to confucian constrictions against religious ostentation. The basic form and structure remains true to Confucius' edicts, but human creativity finds expression in the details! Necessity being the mother of invention, the Taoist, given a lemon maketh sweet lemonade indeed.

The pointy pagoda, while associated with Chinese Buddhist architure, is an elongated version of the of the steeple or spire. Or, a vertically stretched version of the dragon roof. The pagoda's name itself is Sanskrit. Penang's Kek Lok Si pagoda has different tiers in Thai, Burmese and Indian styles.

Just when you were beginning to think that Malaysian religious buildings are as different and distant from each other as the adherents of the various faiths, there comes a surprise. We have not been always this apart and aloof. There was a time in our our collective past (about half a millennium = 500 years) ago, when the lines were less demarcated. In Malacca's jalan Tukang Emas (Goldsmiths's street), stand the oldest functioning places of worship in Malaysia. They are the Sri Poyyatha Vinayagar ("the never lying Ganesha") temple built in the 18th century. Three shophouses away, is the Kapitan Kling Mosque (18th century). Nearby, is the Cheng Hoon Teng Taoist temple – 17th century). "Kapitan Kling" suggests that it was built and patronised by the Tamil Muslim merchants of those days. The Hindu temple, the Indian Muslim mosque, and church in close proximity, is typical of towns in Tamil Nadu, India. There, religious strife is non-existent, unlike in North india, with its recent Babri Masjid debacle and Hindutva (hinduistic) agenda.

The roof of the Kapitan Kling Mosque is three tiered like a Taoist temple. The only difference being, the mosque roof is a four faced pyramid, while the typical Taoist roof is a two faced folddown, an expansive 'A' – frame. The minaret is a pagoda look-alike, with tiers and all. The mosque is ornamented with typical Chinese adornments depicting nature, horn-like eaves, Chinese looking characters. The educated guess of the experts, of the "why?" of this is, Chinese temple artisans were readily available and were hired to build the mosque. The Cheng Hoon Teng, down the street, is as old a Chinese temple as you can find in South-East Asia.

Another such "street of harmony", is in Georgetown, Penang. On Pitt Street, there is St. George's Church on one end and the Kapitan Keling Mosque (again?) at the other. In between, there is the Sri Maha Mariamman temple and the Goddess of Mercy Taoist temple. Is there any doubt that it might be for exactly such a living cultural wonder, that Penang and Malacca have been declared joint UNESCO heritage sites? Hey, wouldn't it be grand if Malaysia is declared the world's first UNESCO heritage nation? It certainly won't happen anytime soon. The 1 Malaysia, Abah ("dad") Muhyiddin, and Keluarga Malaysia (Malaysian family) are slogans of 3 different governments within a period of 2 years. They remain just slogans.

In an interesting study of adaptatation in building design, the Malaysian Hindu temple, while replicating everything of a Tamil Nadu temple, lacks the *Teppakulam*. It is a huge (basketball court sized) rectangular pond ("tank") with steps on four sides leading down to it. Ritual cleansing (*snaanam*) and other ceremonies are done in it and beside it. The glaring absence of it in Malaysia, may be explained by the fact that the huge ponds need extra land. Besides, why have an algae pond, when there is running water? One notices that quite a few temple plots in new housing schemes are allocated near sewerage treatment ponds, by monsoon drain reserves, or water tanks. Is this by design, according to temple vasthu shastra dictates requiring a water body?

Talking of water, it seems to be an important part of all houses of worship. Beside the temple pond mentioned above, mosques, churches and Taoist temples have a water element somewhere in the blueprint. The Mosque has a public tank or washing area for *wuduk* (ablutions) before prayers. Returnees from the hajj to Mecca often come back with bottles of water from Zam Zam, the biblical site where God provided a well for Hagar. The Taoist temple usually has a carp pond in its compound, with an arched bridge across and landscaping. Supposedly the water body is a feng shui enhancer. Catholic church entrances have a font which holds the holy water for signing the cross. All churches of Christ have a water tank called baptistry, in which they perform the adult "believer's baptism" – immersion in water to signify a rebirth, or, a "resurrection" to a new life.

The Gurdwara (Sikh temple), has its own distinctive architecture. While Sikhism is not a particularly evangelistic (or missionary) religion, it does reach out to the public in a different way. An important part of its temple design is the community kitchen, called *Guru Ka Langar*. Interestingly, Muslims of the Sufi persuasion also conduct such kitchens, also called Langar. It is an all year round "open house". The kitchen prepares enough vegetarian food for members of the public to come and dine. Many a tourist on a shoe string budget, can thank the Gurdwara for 'saving' them during a critical time.

Hindu individuals often do what is called *Annathanam*, or "food donation." As fulfillment of wows or expression of thanks, vegetarian food is usually prepared and served for the poor in the temples' community halls, or care homes. Churches often have what is called "agape (love) feasts", where sharing of meals in a potluck style is done. Muslims hold special *kenduri* in mosques. During Hari Raya Haji (the feast of sacrifice), beef is slaughtered in the compound and distributed to the poor. The Hindu devotees of the village gods, like Madurai Veeran and Muneeswaran, slaugher goats and cook mutton curry. In Malaysia, these are usually the little shrines that have sprung up everywhere there were estates. Buddhist temples have communal vegetarian feasts. Hence, worship houses are homes in every sense, not merely the spiritual.

Whereas the building of grander houses of worship is all well and good, we humans (not Malaysians only) tend to be minimalists when it comes to observing religious precepts. That is to say, we resist going the extra mile, even if not all the way. For instance, the Muslim will not consume alcohol but will smoke stacks of cigarettes. Conversely, you won't catch a Sikh puffing, but he will certainly drink mugsful of ale. When the Quran or Hadith made the injunction against drinking, smoking tobacco was non-existent, except in native America. What the Islamic injunction likely meant was, avoid all things harmful to one's body. Now, the Sikh situation is a puzzle. Does the *Shri Guru Granth Sahib* (Sikh holy scripture) allow that which existed then (alcohol) and forbid that which didn't yet (i.e. smoking)?

The Mormons (considered a deviant cult by most Christians) avoid drinking coffee, because apparently their 'Prophet" Joseph Smith had a revelation about its evil effects. They can and will drink cocoa and tea simply because it is not mentioned in their teachings. Despite the practices of some individuals, most believers, by and large follow their internal spiritual compass to avoid harmful and injurious habits. Their bodies afterall, are a 'Temple of God' as the Bible puts it. You don't want to desecrate it with harmful things.

The nomenclature of houses of worhip speaks of their purpose. *Masjid,* or Mosque derives from "Sajed" or "sujud" to prostrate. Hence it is a place of prostration before the Almighty.

Church is a Germanic term (Kirche, Kirk etc) from the Greek *ecclesia,* which means, to call out (or summon). When the called out gather together, it becomes an assembly or community. Hence, church ultimately means community, or *koinonia* in Greek. Of believers, that is. It does not refer to the physical place of the gathering. By the way, what is the connection between ecclessia and the Malay Gereja? *Ecclessia* is rendered *igreja* in Portuguese (*iglesia* in Spanish), and there you have it.

Vihara is the Pali term for a Buddhist monastery. It originally meant "a secluded place in which to walk", and referred to "dwellings" or "refuges" used by wandering monks to shelter during the rainy season. *Biara,* (Malay version of Vihara) means monastery of any sort..

A Chinese Taoist temple, generally called *Gong (Kong),* Guan or Miao in Chinese, is the holy hall where Taoists perform their religious ceremonies. "Gong" means "palace" referring to a complex of buldings in a religious compound. You notice cognates in connection with temples, such as *Gong-Fu* (martial arts practiced in Shaolin temples), and Falung Gong (a controversial Chinese religious sect). Perhaps it has something to do with happines, as in *Gong Si Fa Cai* – Litt. "Congratulations on increasing your prosperity" Now Kongsi among Malaysian Chinese, refers to clan associations/houses. By extension, can Gong mean a communal place of worship? *Kongsi,* has entered the Malay language, with meaning, "to share."

Gurdwara means "Doorway, or gateway, to the Guru." The Guru in this case, possibly refers to the Guru Granth Sahib, the holy book that rests on a canopied dais. Interestingly, Guru is also the designation for Shiva, or Hari. But *Gurdwar* doesn't refer to Shiva's gateway. *Hardwar,* does. It is a popular Hindu pilgrimage destination in the Himalayas meaning, "Gateway to God." It is a Shaivite site, since Shiva's abode is *Kailasam,* always depicted as a snow shrouded Shangri-la surrounded by silvery mountain peaks.

The Hindu holy space is the *kovil* or *koyil,* (*kuil,* in Malay). The literal meaning is, "abode of the king". "Ko" is king or the supreme one, in Tamil. "Il" (illam) is home. So, Kovil will be the king's abode, or palace. Interestingly, the Chinese temple, Gong (Kong) also means a palace. The

Malay "Agong", *supreme ruler,* derives from the Tamil *Kon*. Any relation to King, Koenig, Khan?

House of Man: Minangkabau, Estate lines, Shophouse_

Malaysians live in houses whose design is based on European blueprints. Brick and mortar houses are not indigenous but are a European colonial influence. Single and semi-detached bungalows (fr. Bengali, *bangla*) are based on English or European cottages. The most popular, or rather, the most affordable houses are the so called terraced houses, either single or double storied.

"Terraced house" refers to rows or blocks of living units, linked together in neat lines.Their prototypes are are found in the tenements or townhouses of Europe. Rows and rows of these modular homes now stand where infantry formations of rubber and oil palm trees stood at attention not too long ago, stiff and stalwart. The green jungle has been overrun by the white-washed concrete one. Rubber and oil palm estates have turned into housing estates. Have you wondered why these housing schemes are called estates, when you don't see manors or mansions in them? No matter how much the developers come up with new designs, you cannot escape the sense that the terraced house is a case-study in anonymity, iniquity and ubiquity, although not necessarily inequity. A mindless maze of the mass produced mundane monotony. These are only a notch better than our flats, apartments, and condomiums in their borabilty. They are basically rows of trerraced houses stacked on top of each other. What my Kiwi bro-in-law calls "pigeon holes".

Our "shophouses" of course, take their shape from the business buildings and guild halls of cities like Amsterdam and Hamburg. The shophouse, as the name suggests, consists of business at the ground floor (Shop) and living quarters upstairs (House). It is a rarity these days, as businessmen would certainly like to live in gated communities, just like their customers. Most daily trading activities these days, are conducted in terraced multi storied blocks, similar to the shophouse. The corporate businesses, have the own named buildings or rent their premises thereat.

The only residences that can claim authentic Malaysian pedigree are the quaint Malay kampong houses and Iban longhouses. Those too, are a fast disappearing act, as Malays keep moving into the towns and cities. The grand old houses of Kampung Abdullah Hukum in Bangsar Road have been swallowed alive by developments in adjacent Bangsar and the Mid-Valley scheme. The graceful has turned garish in Kampung Baru in mid KL, as old homes there are being replaced by concrete cargo containers. Is it any surprise then, that Malay houses are on display at the National Museum or at the Mini Malaysia Park in Air Keroh, Malacca? Isn't that a scary sign of the times? A museum is no place for a living, lived – in abode.

Mirroring the pedestrian nature of mass produced Malaysian homes, is the vexious naming of the vicinities. Roads in the housing estates are routinely named after trees, or flowers etc or worse, unknown local council officers. To name all the roads in a sitting, use the prime name followed by a letter and or number. E.g. Jalan Kubah U8/50 in Bukit Jelutong, Shah Alam. It is just like serializing the auto registration number plates. The bigger joke is the naming of the sections or subdivisions as the Yankees call them. You affix a prefix or suffix to a designated name, and voila!, problem solved. Take Damansara for instance, youll get: Seri Damansara, Saujana Damansara, Sungai Damansara, Alam Damansara, Ara Damansara, Aman Damansara, Bukit Damansara, Bayu Damansara, Desa Damansara, Kota Damansara, Kiara Damansara, Mutiara Damansara, Bandar Damansara, Danau Damansara, Denai Damansara, Prima Damansara, Putra Damansara, Putri Damansara, Pantai Damansara, Tasik Damansara etc. Affix the suffix, and you get you get Damansara Utama, Damasara Jaya, Damansara Baru, Damansara Lama. Damansara Heights, Damansara Damai, Damansara Ehsan, Damansara Indah, Damansara Idaman, Damansara Impian, Damansara Perdana, Damansara Permai, etc. In reality, half of these names already exist! The cross-breeding of this shortlist of words only breeds a nauseating brood of inbred clones. It is a smart, albeit banal way to mass produce place names. You have 32 base words here including Damansara and if you multiply into it by itself (32), you get $32^2 = 1024$ configurations. Wow! How's that for a super efficient way for the powers that be, to name a thousand subdivisions in a few seconds on the calculator! Just pick a main name like Klang, Petaling, Puchong, Selayang, Ampang etc, and compute your toponymic permutation for the entire district. Your heart goes out to the clueless residents, and the baffled visitors to these abstruses, er, addresses. It reminds you of a line from the old Glen Campbell song, "Show a little kindness." Adjusted for this situation, it might go like this:

If you show a little kindness, you'll pardon the mundane madness

Of the humdrum little streets, of the hamsap housing schemes*

*"Perverse" in Cantonese.

While the Malay house is the indigenous form of the bungalow, the Iban/Penan longhouse of deep Sarawak is the native counterpart of the terraced house. Like the kampung house, the longhouse not only stands on stilts, it is also very rural, natural, cultural, agricultural, and pastoral. More about these in a minute, but the Malaysian Chinese and Indians do not have their own native home. For one, the British planter who inducted the indentured Indian worker provided wooden housing quarters called *coolie lines* or *Layams (Tamilized),* which immediately evokes "terrace" houses. Similarly, the British colonial administration provided the Indian railway worker and civil servant with terraced concrete houses called *government quarters.* Growing up in Sentul in the 60's, I remember the *artisan quarters* of the railway workers, the *waterworks ("wotroks") quarters, and the "*kosu layam*" (mosquito quarters,* in Tamil*)* of the KL municipality workers, among other quarters in the neighbourhood. The name of the latter derives from the mosquito collecting work of the municipal health department staff. At night, these workers would climb into mini huts on stilts at strategic locations, and trap the vermin that try to suck their blood.

As for the Chinese, the businessmen built rowed shophouses, and the tin mine tycoons were lords of concrete mansions in Ipoh and Jalan Ampang in KL. Another form of stately homes were the Baba-Nonya house in Malacca and Penang. Now, mostly museums or boutique hotels. As for Indian mansions, the Chettiar's Hall, located between the Sri Thandayuthapani national school and the Sri Subramaniyar temple in Jalan Ipoh, is an accurate facsimile of a chettiar foyer. Spacious, colonnaded, high ceilinged, and black/white tiled chequerboard floor, imitate the teak wood internal structures of the once prosperous nagaraththaar (naatukottai chettiar) community. They had once ruled financing (money lending) from Burma to Singapore. True to form, the place even has a *thinnai,* on both sides of the doorway. It is a raised cement platform, 2½ feet high, where family and neighbours gathered to socialise. It also served as a open verandah where stangers and travellers are free to spend the night, before continuing the journey the following morning.

The Chinese mine coolies were provided common quarters, called *kongsi*. Paralleling the Indian coolie lines of the rubber estates. The word has come to mean, "to share" (verb) and "partner" (noun) in the national language. Indeed, the kongsi system was a business partnership. It also referred to social clubs (especially Cantonese) that helped new immigrants get settled in South-East Asia and the US. Then of course, there is the Kongsi system, based on clan memberships. The Khoo Kongsi in Penang, is an outstanding Hokkien clan house that is both historic and a tourist magnet.

With their living space thus provided for, the Indians and Chinese had little scope for distinctive house design. The only unique building form brought by them is their temple design, which is discussed in the preceding chapter, on houses of worship. They may have lost their dwelling designs, but their temples, they will always have.

Back to indigenous home design, both the Malay house and the Iban longhouse are functionally, fundamentally and philosophically cogent and environmentally sustainable.

The Orang Asli house can be the foreunner of the modern Malay house. They are much smaller models raised above ground by short, thin stilts. Attap and bamboo are common materials. Many are very basic shelters, almost like lean-tos suitable for the nomadic lifestyle of some groups like the Bateq negroid race of Taman Negara.

The Malay house and the Iban longhouse have what is called the *Rumah Ibu*, or "Mother House." It is somewhat like the "Mother Ship" in a space craft. It is the main house, that sits above ground and on pillars or stilts. It consists of the living area or *ruang tamu*, which is as open and spacious as the heart of the owner. Given a half chance, he would persuade you inside to sit on the mat with him, serve you tea and *kuih-muih* (sweet and savoury snacks), and ask you about your health, family and more. He would also regale you with stories galore, both tall and true. As Sir Frank Swettenham wrote a hundred years ago in, *The Real Malay (1900).*

"He is a good talker, speaks in parables, quotes proverbs and wise saws., has a strong sense of humour and is very fond of a good joke. He takes an interest in the affairs of his neighbours and is consequently a gossip".

Part of the entire house, but slightly detached on ground level, is the kitchen (*dapur*). The entrance to the kitchen is through a ladder/stairs at the back of the main structure, or doors on the ground level. The logic for this concept is that, the *dapur* could be easily kicked away from the *rumah ibu,* in case of a kitchen combustion.

The Malay traditional house follows a linear flow from entrance to kitchen. The front staircase leads onto the *Anjung or Serambi* (verandah/porch), where initial niceties or entire entertainment may be held. Stepping inside gets you into the main living space, the *Ruang Tamu ("Guest Space"),* which is basically an open square area with sitting, dining and TV sections just like in any other modern Malaysian living room. Bedrooms are set off to the sides. Moving further in gets you to the stairs leading down to the kitchen on ground level.

The roof can range from zinc to clay tile, while the older houses used to be covered with attap. Attap, or palm thatch, as well as the raised wooden super-structure is optimal natural air-conditioning. There is continual air-flow in and out of the house. As for the shape of these roofs, it ranges from the normal double pitched inverted V, to the steep A-frame of Malacca houses, to the Minagkabau, which are similar to a butterfly roof but smoother, curvier and more pronounced. While the butterfly is like an opened book, the minang is like the alphabet C turned turtle, almost a U. The ends of the U curve skyward like aerobatics planes doing the vertical ascent. It is named after the horns of a water buffalo (kerbau/carabao).

While most kampong houses nowadays have the latest designer furniture, the living space is still broad and inviting. Why build on stilts? For one, Malays and other native Malaysians usually built their settlements on or close to river banks. Those were the days when the only form of travel was up and downriver. The stilts assured the inhabitants protection from flooding. With stilts, the *tapak* (footprint) of the house was very small, leaving more ground exposed. Less ground under concrete means that rain water seeps underground faster, unlike in cities where graveled roads, building floors and even cemented courtyards leave no room for rainwater seepage, resulting in flash floods.

Another functional reason for stilts was protection from wildlife. Building on stilts affords domestic animals the space to move around at night. Wild animals could freely loiter under the floor and through the yard, assuring environmental balance. You wonder how the domestic animals, that were tied to pillars, were protected from the wild? Perhaps they may have fenced up the entire outer pillars with thatch. Prior to the days of mosquito coils, sprays or electric tablets, they would light a bonfire under the house to keep mosquitos away from the sleeping tenants above ground, and the domestic animals warm.

House of Government: Moorish, Minangkabau, Mosque-form

Public buildings in Malaysia have gone through spurts of style changes, reflecting its ongoing identity crisis.

The earliest brick and stone buildings in Malaya were a style known in British times, as Moorish. This style is represented In the complex of government offices around the *Selangor Padang* in KL, what is now known as the *Dataran Merdeka,* or Independence Square. The mother ship in that fabulous fleet is the Sultan Abdul Samad building, initially the Selangor government secretariat, and now in its umpteenth avatar. These buildings are currently in an "empty nest" mode, since the federal administrative offices moved to Putrajaya. Other examples of the Moorish that have survived are the Railway (KTM) Headquarters building, the Railway stations of KI, Ipoh and other towns. Many of the old mission schools like St. Johns Institution of KI and government schools like Victoria institute and Penang Free school sport a variety of classical looks, including 'Grecian Spanish'. The Kuala Kangsar Malay College sports Greek columns and gables.

Moorish is a British misnomer for the North Indian style of building. Moorish is another name for Islamic or Muslim. Though it was influenced somewhat by Persian forms, it is a native Indian. Think, the Moghul Taj Mahal and the palaces of Delhi, and the Hindu Rajahdoms of Rajasthan.

Art Deco style is represented in the Central Market building rebuilt in 1937. Art deco style is a mix of the classical richness with the modern, especially cubic and square looks. The British era buildings have that exuberant spirit that makes you stop and do a double-take, unlike the easily passed over glass towers of today.

In the 60's and 70's, government started thinking of a fashion change. Something embodying a national style. The power players of the time decided on the Minagkabau architechture as representative of Malaysia. So for a while, everything from the National Museum to the police pondok (beat hut), to the outdoor noticeboard sported the Minangkabau roof. The Malay roof of Perak/Selangor was incorporated into the National Museum in Kuala Lumpur. Designed by Ho Kok Hoe, and rebuilt on the site of the former Selangor Museum, it was opened on Independence Day 1963. The Putra World Trade Centre (1985) also evokes the Malay roof, exterior and interiors.

The current rage in buildings and building styles, is the so-called Islamic style, which are basically buildings capped with a dome. While the dome itself is not Islamic in origin, geometric shapes are. In the truer sense of Islamic, it is the geometric designs on building such as the Tabung Haji headquarters, the octagonal girth of the twin towers, etc., that make them definitive structures.

Putrajaya, as the fairly recent administrative centre of Malaysia, is the place to start on current government office styles. However the style is varied. The Islamic or Moorish influence is seen in the domes of the the Palace of Justice, Perdana Putra building, Seri Perdana (Prime Minister's residence), as well as in the arches of the Finance Ministry building and Putrajaya Corporation building. And then there is a mix of the archaic and the ultra modern. The building housing the legal affairs department is designed based on the Neo – Raj palace with architectural expression of colonnades, porticos, archways and screens. The hilltop Putrajaya International Convention Centre (PICC) is a ultra modern futuristic form (reminds me of a just landed UFO). It falls in the same category as the Sydney Opera House. The National Registration Department Building, the Domestic Trade Ministry Building, and the Plantation Industry and Commodities Ministry building, Putrajaya, all have a similar look – Art

Deco. The jade green, glass clad buildings like the Attorney General's Chambers, Ministry of Transport, the Boulevard Building, and the Energy Commission (diamond shaped) Building are cooling to the eye. The Malaysian Islamic Development (JAKIM) Building, is a surprise – a modern, non-islamic façade. In short, Putrajaya has all the styles and designs for the student of architechture.

Chilling Out: Lepak, Arattai, Xiánguàng

The *lepak* syndrome is not an exclusively Malay, or even Malaysian trait. It is international. Its short explanation is to chill, as in chilling out at the Mall or relaxing in the living room. Just take take break, take it easy, and watch the world go by, as they say. Children everywhere do, and are expected to chill at certains times of the day. The Spanish *siesta* takes it to a whole new level. Businesses close and everybody goes home to take a after lunch snooze. They start up again at 4.00 pm. It derives from Latin *Sexta Hora* – "sixth hour" or Noon.

The Malays have mastered the art of lepak, which is more complex than merely taking a break. It includes fine conversation of the robust variety, such as gossip and ghost stories; jokes and joviality; politics and ponzi schemes; sports and sordid things; tattles and tall tales. A lepak session is not a mid-afternoon siesta and can be rather rowdy, with friendly shoving and cacophonous laughter. Or, it can just be sitting around and watching the world go by. Somebody could say, "give the Malay a public space, and he will sit down in small groups engaging in small talk". In New Zealand, they actually say, "Give the Indian a corner (football phrase), and he will build a grocery shop there." The space in front of the Sogo department store in KL, seems to be a magnetic place for such (lepak) activity. Or it could be any Mall or Medan, or tourist attraction or Taman Tasik (Lake Gardens). Malays dominate the public park, as they stroll in family groups. The men (not necessarily acquainted in any way) naturally form groups on the grass, as their wives congregate nearby. The children, naturally don't need nudging, to initiate their raucous rowdy running around.

A distinct behavioral characteristic of Malays, is their earnest presence and participation in public gatherings of the civic kind. Government sponsored do's like the independence day celebrations, public concerts, etc will witness this phenomenon. A kind of mass lepak, if you will.

Hospital visiting times are social gatherings, where whole family systems of 3 generations gather around the bed of the patient. While the children run around squawking under the bed, the adults are not to be outcone. If it happens to be mealtime, why the food from home becomes part of the menu. The children and adults join in the feast. It is a virtual picnic.

The Tamil version is to make *arattai*, conveying the sense of chatterboxes chit-chatting nonchalantly and nonsensically. To *arattai*, is to yak about anything and everything, but nothing in particular, if you get the drift. This is a lepak lookalike, because the action is done by those who have nothing better to do. It is commonly said of preteens, who are loud and chatty at that stage.

It seems that gathering in public parks is not a big draw for Indian adults, though they are not averse to small talk with their neighbours. Their big draw is religious gatherings like the Thaipusam celebrations, or a free Indian concert in open fields. The crowds at the MIC, PKR organized grand do's is an example.

While adults elsewhere may congregate at the local bar to relax, most Malaysians generally prefer the mamak stall or corner curry house. The former, are the first successful 24 hour eateries anywhere. While everyone has gone to sleep, the mamak stall will be just starting its graveyard shift. What did we do in days before electricity and street lights? The night hawker (not the bird of prey) in those days, would come around the neighbourhood with his pushcart before closing shop at 8.00 pm. We didn't have the luxury of late nights, as teenagers do these days. You simply did not risk being subjected to parental interest, or worse inquiry, or worser, interrogation, or worst, inquisition.

The young Malaysians, in the range of 20 to 30 years have turned night hawks. It is a lifestyle that appeals to them. They would probably hate to live in small town, USA or any town, NZ, as shops and restaurants there close by about 9 pm. In the winter, it gets dark and dreary by 4 pm in those temperate places. Kuala Lumpur's golden triangle district has a nightlife that appeals to our foreign guests, who would like to lepak all night long too.

The Chinese idea of lepak, at least in the 50's, was to sit at the white marble topped table in the neighbourhood coffeeshop (koptiam) and hang out with friends over a porceline cup of black coffee, with condensed milk at the bottom of the cup. The old Chinaman would sit on the stool, one foot on it and one on the floor. With arms hugging his thigh and bent leg, he seemed most comfortable. Imagine a crane (migrating bird).To make himself even more comfortable, the gent would roll up his white cotton, crocodile brand singlet/T-shirt up to his chest. Air-conditioning, see? He stirred the black coffee and milk to his required sweetness and poured the coffee into the saucer before sipping from it! The bigger surface area and shallowness of the saucer, cooled the coffee faster. Since this was usually a morning ritual, the fried bread, Char Koay, dipped in the black coffee, was a standard accompaniment. Or it might be "conjugal bread", *roti kahwin,* a conjoined sandwich of butter and kaya on toasted white bread. While the methods of coffee drinking may have changed, the gatherings have not. Even today, elderly Chinese can be seen congregating in coffee shops or local parks, chilling or chigong-ing together, as the case may be.

Like the Indians and unlike the Malays, Chinese seem to have better things to do than to hang out in large groups in public. If they are in the park, you would see them doing their own thing, exercising or jogging. The older set are habituated to gather at their clan houses to practice *Tai Chi Chuan* or *Chigong*. In earlier times, the oldies would be engaged in the game of *Mahjong*, the fat porcelain bricks rattling loudly as they were shuffled about on the marble table. The kopitiam is a popular destination for the youth of every ethnicity.

The younger set of Chinese prefer hanging out at the local kopitiam or mamak corner. So, chill, as you will as you gulp that swill.

Headlines: The Tamil wobble, Chinese nod, Malay salam

All creatures and their cultures have their signals for indicating approval and disapproval. The Romans started us off with the, now universal, thumbs up and thumbs down. Suppose you rode a time machine to an ancient Roman arena and found yourself the loser in a gladiatorial combat. All it took was a thumb sign from Caesar and your fate was sealed, depending on how it pointed. Up, you lived to fight another day. Down, the victor's sword travels through your heart.

When frustrated with a teammate's miscue or a wrong pass, you might throw your arms up in the air. Or, you may throw up your arms while throwing back your head. Or, you might hang your head down while slightly slumping your shoulder, accompanied by a deep sigh. Some soccer players have been known to sink to the ground on their knees, in frustration and in elation.

We learn from infancy – its an inbuilt automatic response – to turn our heads left and right to indicate "no" or a refusal. It probably originates with the child averting its head this way and that, from that spoonful of unexciting food coming at it. But how about the "yes" response, the up and down bobbing of the head? That too, seems inborn, as if to say, "come" or, "bring it (the food) to me". The baby, at this time, still has not got complete motor function of its hands and fingers. You know that when the child is a little older, it will be able push away food with its arms, or extend it to reach the food. Even elephants and horses sometimes do this head bobbing or swiveling, for perhaps the same reasons.

Then, there is the curious and peculiar case of the Tamil, who has developed a third head movement, that has puzzled and fascinated many. This is the famous Tamil head wobble which looks like a "no" but means a loud "yes!" It is an automatic, unconscious response and takes a non-Tamil (even fellow Indians) to notice this peculiarity. While the universal, "no" head shake is straightforward and turns through a single plane, the Tamil wobble is all over the place. The head, if you pretend that it is the felt tip of a marker pen, basically traces the infinity sign ∞ in the air. It's the same shape the sun makes if you snapshot it from the same spot, same time for a whole year – an Analemma.

This head movement expresses agreement, affirmation, appreciation, enjoyment, and encouragement. Attend a Carnatic music *katcheri* (South Indian classical music concert), and witness the phenomenon in all its glory. The music afficionados, mostly older gentlemen, will be doing synchronized slow motion head wobbles, eyes closed in deep concentration or total immersion, and restless fingers keeping time with the beats. This is a picture of joyful bliss, and spurs the musicians on.

Meanwhile on stage, the musicians are wobbling too, with little head jiggles in between, while playing their instruments. During the short interludes, the main musician encourages and cheers his accompanists by moving heads and fingers. Everyone else (the rest of the world) exhibits their enrapt enjoyment by stiff and still immersion in the experience. The hopping, screaming delirium combined with headbanging, of youth at a rock concert is another. Different form but same substance.

All this is puzzling to the non-Tamil and sends somewhat of a double-bind message. A double-bind is a psychological anomaly in which the verbal message is incongruent with the body language. Case in point: A mother saying, "I love you" to her infant child, while wearing a scowl on her face. So how does this head wobble, which looks like a negative head-shake, mean the affirmative? Any wonder it turns the heads of others? Psst: Doesn't a double negative mean a positive? "You ain't no fool" means "you are a fool". My enemy's enemy is my friend, isn't s/he?

The Chinese have a tendency to make rapid head bows when addressing important people, or when thanking a gift or good deed. *Toh cheh,* or *Mm koi,* Cantonese for *"thank you"*. These mini bows may be the smallest movements on the range from *Mm Koi* to *Kow Tow* (Cantonese – *"knocking head on floor"*).

Malays are wont to shake their head slowly, three middle fingers on forehead, while humming, "mmh, mmh, mmh, m...mh!", when puzzled or perturbed by something.

Sometimes, people make head movements while in prayer. The Muslims, in congregational prayer, do the slight side-to-side rhythmic motions that is possibly for balance or circulation, or other practical reason. May be it is a religious requirement. Likewise, the orthodox Jew does the back-and-forth rocking motion while praying at the wailing wall in Jerusalem. These are certainly not trances, even if thy might look like it. At the end of a prayer, (congregational or otherwise) the Muslim turns his head to the right and to the left. He is acknowledging the two angels on his right shoulder who record his good deeds and the angel on his left who records his bad deeds. Another version is: to pass the blessings of Allah to all the people of the world by the act of turning to the right and to the left and giving the salaam.

The Tamil wobble comes close to a trance (musical ecstasy?) during classical concerts. Certain persons with autism do rock back and forth, and it seems to give them a sense of soothing and stability similar to that experienced by an infant rocked by its mother.

This might seem exotic to westerners, but Asians and Malaysians in particular, are fond of using their heads to communicate non-verbally. When someone is at a distance and trying to sign language something to you, you make a quick backward jerk of the head with a slight squint in your eyes, to indicate,"what is it?" or, "what's the matter?"

Someone asks where the key to the cabinet is, and you point your nose in the direction of it, holding the stance for a few seconds. No mouth, no hands. A short, quick jerk to the side with a frown may mean a simple, "go away!" The same, done almost imperceptibly, can be a cue for someone to perform a pre-arranged task.

A talking head beside you has the floor, saying things that do not impress you. How do you convey your thoughts to the one across you? Well, the side of your mouth forms a crooked pout, like you are having a stroke, your eyebrows rise knowingly, and your head traces a slight arc in the direction of the speaker. You have just made a comment that can mean anything from, "Did you hear that?" to, "He's at it again!" Take away the pout and raised brows, replace it with smiling eyes, and a grin, and message becomes, "Impressive, huh?" or, "Look, he is speaking our language" (saying we want to hear).

While still on the subject, a relative of mine quotes a TV (Astro) motivational speaker as saying that people do actions with the head that are significant. For instance, she gives the example of the *pottu* or mark that Hindus wear on their foreheads. The married woman has a round black one and the unmarried woman wears a red one. Sure saves a lot of awkward moments for the young buck on the lookout for a prospective doe, doesn't it? Then, there are those who smear, or dab holy ash on the forehead when they attend Friday temple prayers. Thaipusam devotees, go further, and daub their entire bodies with ash. Hindu ash represents humility and nothingness before the deity. Meanwhile Jews of the Old Testament spread ash on themselves as a sign of grieving or repentence.

Anyway, she cautions against laughing at ash smearing as bordering on clown make-up or the pottu as forehead tattoo. Doesn't almost everybody do a form of action or other with their foreheads? The Muslim bows low and touches his forehead to the ground in obeisance to his Almighty. In fact some Muslims wear a dark patch on their forehead (from years of forehead – ground contact) as a badge of honour.The Catholic dips his finger tip in holy water and makes the sign of the cross on his, guess what, as he enters the sanctuary. The citizen raises the fingers of his right hand to his right temple, as he salutes the flag. The Indian, Thai, Burmese, Cambodian, Sri Lankan brings his clasped hands to the forehead in greeting. The Malaysian does the same when approaching royalty. All this, is by of way acknowledging a higher power or authority, or acknowledging other humans. Of course, the head being the summit of our body, is the part reserved for doing such solemn functions.

Salutations: Gong Si, Assalamu Alaikkum, Vanakkam

And of course, you notice variety in the way we "wish", i.e, greet each other. When a mother wants to show off her baby's budding social skills, she is likely to encourage it by saying, "sweetie, go and wish auntie." And sweetie goes and says, "Good morning Auntie." How sweet!

The Malay child learns to say, *Assalaamu Alaikkum*, which in Arabic means, "Peace to you." This is acknowledged with, *Alaikkum Salaam*. It sounds and reads very similar to the Hebrew, *Shalom Aleichem* or *Aleichem Shalom*. When context is mundane, or when greeting a non-Muslim, the Malay would say *Selamat Pagi* or "A safe morning to you"; or *Selamat Jalan* meaning, "Have a safe trip", "Bon Voyage", Good Bye." After the handshake, which is usually a light brush with the tips of the fingers, he brings the hand to his chest. It is an indication that the greeting was heartfelt. Often, the junior will brush the senior's extended palm with both hands and bring them up to his/her chest.

A more down to earth and casual way of saying it is, *Apa Khabar?*, or "what's the news?" Asking for the news suggests an invitation to stay awhile and chat over coffee, as opposed to Selamat Pagi, which sounds like something said in passing. There is not much body language accompanying the greeting, except for a big smile or a miniscule head nod. When you are greeting *apa khabar* from afar, you would shout out the greeting while raising your right hand, in the style of His Excellancy, the late great Tunku Abdul Rahman. The independence declaration by the first Prime Minister, as he punched his hands three times into the air, is an iconic moment indeed in Malaysian history. Even more laconic then apa khabar is, *Amacam?*, basically a, *Whazzup?* distilled from *Apa macam?*, it means, "How's it?" or, "How's it going?" A non-committal, humourous answer to Amacam? might be, "Macam, macam" – "Every which way." I would just as casually answer Whazzup? with, "somethings up, somethings down."

The English goodbye is a contraction of "God be with ye" from the late 14th Century. It has its echo in the Spanish, *Vaia con Dios*, "Go with God". The Tamil sendoff is, *Poi Vaa*, "Go and come back." An interesting homophone Is the Spanish Vaa, meaning "Go" and the Tamil Vaa, meaning "Come." Brings to mind the cultural faux pas by Volkswagen when they introduced a model named NOVA ("New") – "No Go" in Mexico! WV quickly learned its lesson when there was "no sale".The English of Poi Vaa will be, "go and come back" or See you soon". Of course, the German *Auf wieder sehen*, means the same,"Till we see each other again".

The Chinese courtesy, on occasion, is accompanied by a curt curtsy, especially when saying *Gong Ci Fa Cai*, which is basically a new year greeting. Otherwise the normal greeting is "Ni how?" or "Ni how ma?" meaning, "how are you?" "Nee" also means, "You" in Tamil. So, you can see the possibilities. "Nee How Ma?". "You how, mom" ?

In the New Year (CNY) greeting, before you make the slight bow from the waist, you clench your right fist and lightly punch it into the other palm, as you bring both up to chest level. The gesture evokes the customary bow of combatants in martial arts tournaments of old Kung Fu movies.

The Kung Fu bow is a flowing movement that includes many phases. With erect posture and feet together, the arms rise from the sides of the body to mid-chest level, travelling in a smooth arc towards the centerline at chest level.The right hand closes into a fist and meets the open, vertical left palm at the centerline.The fingers of the left hand are kept vertical and close together, with the thumb tucked in.The right horizontal fist is centred into the open left palm.The right fist remains placed in the open left palm as the body bends slightly forward from the waist and the arms push slightly outward.The bowed position is held for a second or two, then the body returns to an upright position and the arms return to the sides of the body.

An interpretation of the entire process is as follows:-

1. The shape of the open left palm represents the moon, and Yin aspects pertaining to the theory of Yin and Yang, such as passiveness, yielding, rest and reflection, intellect, ethics.
2. Four fingers close together represent equality and mutual respect of everyone in the martial arena.
3. The thumb represents yourself. It is bent to signify your humility; you don't regard yourself as being superior to others.
4. The shape of the right fist represents the sun, and Yang, aspects such as strength and determination, movement and action.
5. Hands Travelling: The right fist and open left palm travelling towards each other symbolize the efforts towards the merging of the ideals of Wen and Wu, or total physical and intellectual balance and harmony. In this way, the martial skills are never employed without the balance of martial virtue.
6. Hands Meeting: The true martial artist cultivates both their intellectual and physical abilities, combining both towards self-understanding and refinement. The meeting of both hands represents the combination of the two principles.
7. Left Hand Covering the right fist reflects that the principles of martial arts are rooted in theory, philosophy and virtue. The theory (left hand) covers, and governs the fighting aspect (right fist). The techniques of combat are thus dictated by the principles of civility, peace and etiquette.
8. Hands Merged, Moving Forward represent sincerity, good intentions and the ongoing quest for self-improvement. The martial artist goes forward with forthright honesty and righteousness, never driven by ego or desire. One stands for truth and justice, adhering to their beliefs. Zheng Yi or true righteousness, doesn't sway. (*Condensed from Chung Wah Kung Fu International System website*)

The Indian greeting, accompanied by the palm sandwich, is *Vanakkam, Namaskaaram,* or *Namaste,* depending on which part of India the speaker is from. *Vanakkam* simply means, "my obeisance to you", and is usually said without the clasped palms, except on formal occasions. This gesture that accompanies the greeting, is found in many South-East Asian cultures, the legacy of Tamil traders and missionaries who visited these shores in the 3rd century AD onwards. In Thailand, it accompanies the *Sawadee kaap,* In Cambodia the *Susadei*, in Myanmar, *Nei kaurn thala*, in Bali *Om Suastiastu*. In Malaysia, the vestiges of the clasped palm survive in the royal court ceremonies, where the Prime Minister, or Menteris Besar do obeseisance before the Agung or Sultans respectively, to the accompaniment of *Ampun Tuanku,* or "I beg your indulgence my leige." The palms clasped symmetrically, the heels are raised to the top of the forehead, that is slightly bent forward.

The Indian, perhaps because he is the one who invented and propagated this palm clasp, has developed many variations of it. I faintly remember some Indian expert explain the various positions of this salutation, for the different occasions. At the beginning and ending bow, the Barathanatyam dancer brings the palms down against her sternum, which squares her shoulders. Don't ask me why she does that, but it just seems to make her more graceful and "proportionate", like Hollywood's Oscar. You bring the thumb nails to nose tip level, when greeting an equal or your constituents, if you happen to be a politician. Bring the base or heels against the forehead if greeting a revered personality, or the Agung as in the Malay court practice. Devotees of Hindu deities raise the clasp above their head and rest it on the crown. The devotee who is in a state of enthrallment will fully stretch his sandwich up vertically, especially in crowed situations like the Thaipusam chariot procession. He wants to make sure that the deity sees his obeisance. Sometimes, he might stand on his toes, or do little hop, just to be certain.

The Indian palm sandwich, the *Anjali Mudra* (Sanskrit: "Salutational Gesture"), is a non-contact, non-verbal communication, distance no bar. Like the military salute, it can be performed between individuals at any distance, even through Skype or Zoom. During the recent Covid-19 worldwide pandemic, it came into some use with international figures, like US President Trump trying it some.

The most common, universal non-verbal greeting is the hand wave.This all-place, all-purpose, all-time standby has no particular gammar to it, except for styles such the royal, papal, nazi, and nasty (mid-finger) etc.

The Tiff: Merajuk, Oodal, Sā jiāo

To get into a pouty, petulant, sulky pique is quite common in relationships with loved ones. When you have this, you emotionally withdraw from the significant other. Or rather, you simply change from being tender towards the significant other, to a self-absorbed dither.

The Malays have a word for this attitude of mind. *Merajuk.* The Malay/ English author Adibah Amin writes, that there is no accurate equivalent in the English lexicon. *Merajuk,* from the base word, *rajuk* is a verb meaning, "to sulk". This feeling or attitude can be described of adults as well as children. Most children, and some adults, throw tantrums when they don't get their way. Others retreat to their rooms or into themselves, shutting out communication in a show of merajuk. It is a way of getting back at the perpetrators for perceived wrongs done to them.

Merajuk can happen in all kinds of situations. The aspiring politician can merajuk if not given a 'seat'. In the general elections/cabinet, that is. The Hon. Minister will feel slighted if not given the protocol due him. Thats it! How about: Feel slighted = merajuk? The wife will suffer an attack of *merajukitis majorii* if hubby does not remember their wedding anniversary. Forget the fact that its hubby's anniversary too, and she could have "remembered". It is usually a female, rather than a male malaise.

The Tamil equivalent to this is more specific in it's application. *Oodal,* a noun prounounced as in "oodles of noodles", is used solely for lovers and young married couples. The closest English descripton is the mutual aloofness following a lovers' tiff. Tamil poets like to pen volumes on this emotion, which is said to be a delicious feeling indeed. This temporary separation affords the couple a forced period of privacy and space. It need not be a physical separation, as in the case of newlyweds. The couple might communicate, but may be reserved in their love language, focusing instead, on more mundane matters.

"Have you eaten?".

"Ya".

"Any letters today?"

"nope".

And this is not too bad. At least, they are talking now. At the earlier stage, the chill is suffocating and the silence deafening. It seems *oodal*, like grief and loss, is a process. First, there is simmering resentment, followed by silent treatment, like ignoring and withdrawal. The other person is no more a person, but *persona non grata*. Quite often, you speak to each other through a third person, like a child or a friend. Conversation is in bits and mini-bytes (not megabytes), followed by longer responses, and attempts at small talk and humour making which does not quite get the laugh. And then is the catharsis, like grey clouds lifting and the sun making a grand entrance, which leads to the feeling of falling in love again. It is as if you are falling for the other for the first time.The lovers had missed each other, yearned for the other's company. It is now time to "make up" for lost opportunities, passion crescondoing to the levels of ther initial love. When they reunite, the 'high' of love is supposedly accentuated, like aged wine. If this sounds even the slightest bit poetic, it is no wonder Tamil poets have sung so strenuously about this emotion through the 3 millenia, or so, of Tamil secular literature.

The emotive range of the *oodal*, is apty captured in an old Tamil movie that culminates in a song sequence. The movie starred Gemini Ganesan and Savithri, a real life couple too, for good measure. In the scene, the couple behaves as if singing to their little son, but you get it that they are actually speaking to each other. The husband is trying to reconnect with his wife by appreciating her art, which was the cause of the war, in in the first place. It goes something like this.

Gemini: Ask her why she has she ignored her art, my dear.
Look at the painting she has created, my son. (painting of him she'd thrown down)

Savithri: Housekeeping art is enough, my son
Why the need for this art, my dear ?

Gemini: Where is the girl who loved me, my son?
Why has she changed after marriage, my son?

Savithri: Tell him the girlfriend is now wife, my dear.
Why was he quiet about it then, my dear?

The back and forth goes on for a while, with the subject matter closing in on the denouement. All the while, the child is pulling them closer together. In the end, the husband and wife are joined. That's all it takes. That's all that matters.

Here again, one is hard put to find a suitable word in English, despite it having the world's largest vocabulary. This is not for want of similar feelings among English speakers. This may have more to do with the fact that Asians put more weightage to matters of personal relationships (?). For instance, take the noun "Love". (Affection, Adoration, Agape, Amore, Passion etc, are discounted because they are not English originals)

English   : Love, infatuation.

Malay   : Cinta, Kasih, Sayang, Minat, Memuja.

Tamil   : Anbu, Aasai, Bakthi, Kaathal, Maiyal, Moham, Nesam, Neyam, Paasam, Premai, Priyam, Poosaitthal, Sneham, Viruppam, Yaasam.

Mandarin : Ai, Ai qing,

This may, or may not, apply in Malaysia, but it is based on a westerner's observation of the pout in China, *sā jiāo*. Michael Hurwitz, datelined October 24,2013, writes that it may be connected to Chinese concepts of feminism or feminity.

sā (撒) literally means "to give expression to" or "to cast out and let loose,"

jiāo (娇) means "lovely," "charming," "delicate" or "to pamper or spoil."

Unlike the western, or even malaysian scene, where gender equality prevails, females in China, even if they are successful and otherwise independent, expect their boyfriends or husbands to "spend"/indulge their needs. The men are expected to buy things for them. 照顾 (zhào gu), which literally means "to attend to" or "take care of". Hurvitz has witnessed scenes of, "Grown women (and occasionally men) will stop in the street or sidewalk and cross their arms, stomp their feet and refuse to utilize their senses of reason until the demand at hand is met." – a typical childish tantrum. "If a woman doesn't *sā jiāo* from time to time, her peers might not regard her as feminine enough." Opposed to the western concept of female individuality, this is about "asserting (Chinese) feminine identity." And the payoff for Chinese men? Most of them seem to enjoy it! – it gives them a sense of being "needed".

Concurrent to this, is the case of 剩女 (shèng nǔ) or "leftover women". "Often high-earning, they are Chinese women who are considered either too old or too successful to get married. Men are often intimidated by them, and it's becoming increasingly difficult for these women to find quality partners."

Sulking in all its various forms. Just another flavour of life. Just, so long as it is not carried to extremes. Many are the cases of slight that result in suicide, when the victim decides to "get even", wanting to "guilt trip" the offending family member. A case of no winners.

Silly Street: Road Hogs, Hell Drivers and Handicapped Spot Stealers

Eventhough Malaysians of different ethnicities exhibit divergent behavior patterns, they also show unity of bizarre behavior on streets and roads. The road hogs, hell drivers, middle finger maestros, and auto boombox boors are found in all communities, though it is not widespread.

One thing that western visitors quickly observe, is our impatience on the road even in the micro level. Say, for instance you have already turned your nose onto a side road at a T-junction – you are turning from the main road. A lady veers past you, onto the main road. This happened to me today. There is a German MM2H (Malaysia, My Second Home) expat, who in his youtube channel says he'd had a few chilling close calls with cars dashing at high speed while traversing a zebra crossing. Of course, it doesn't happen in his culture, where cars slow down and come to a complete stop. Here, you will be the be the barricade that stops said car.

Another street behavior is the usage of overhead bridges. It is my unfortunate conclusion that the overwhelming majority of us will jaywalk across the road rather than use the government built overhead bridges. What adds to the amazement scale is that we would cross the road right under the bridge, in its shade! From the perspective of the bridge, talk about rubbing chilli powder on an insult. The bookie is better off not betting his filthy lucre on the probability, that a loafer (jaywalker) might opt to walk on the bridge.

Still on roads, how proud I am about the Malaysian government's concern for the cyclists and motorcylists! In KL and KV (Klang Valley), it has built motorcycle lanes off and parallel to highways. We may be the only nation to do so. But look at the supposed beneficiaries. Most of the time, these lanes are abandoned and the two wheeler jockeys and desperados would druther weave and meander between four wheelers on the autoway. They will proffer the excuse of avoiding highway muggers hiding in the tunnels and underpasses. So, what is anyone, including the authorities, doing about it?

Highways have extra lanes on the left-most side, reserved as emergency lanes. The emergency may be an overheated engine or a stalled car which can be pushed on to the lane. Most importantly, it is for emergency vehicles such as ambulances, police, and fire engines. Usually, in a free flowing traffic, they are kept free. However, let the congestion thicken into a jam and everyone wants to spread it into the reserved space. Many have been the instances where an ambulance has been late to the ER by an hour, because of selfish ones trying "beat" the jam. Does it help? It only gets the jam in one's face. Enjoy the sandwich ya, bugger?

Bad behavior on roads seems almost inbuilt or inborn in humans. One impatient solipsist weaves in and out of lanes and causes another one of his kind to react by chasing the former down. He wants to get infront of him and shake his booty in a dance called "brake checking", i.e the the act of constantly slamming the brakes for no good reason, except to inconvenience the driver on your rear. PM Anwar Ibrahim's daughter, Nurul Ilham was such a victim. The opposte also happens when the car behind does the dance called "tailgating". Same thing, but different positions. Those are non-verbal abuses, as is giving the mid-finger, clenched fists etc. And then, there are honking, shouting etc. Public roads seem to bring the worst in us.

One profoundly puzzling highway phenomenon, if you haven't experienced it, is the jam spread on it! It is AOK if an accident has slowed it down. But why on earth, should the opposite direction also be jammed? Sneaking a

Peek? Poking Nose? Cat's curiosity? Trying to help? Sometimes, it happens for no reason at all, clearing up suddenly. Perhaps it is no fault of a hog or a hare, but a tortoise that holds up the traffic.

Coming to city streets, we have another kind of hog. There is one that double parks in engaged gear and runs into the shop for a "quick" trip. Meanwhile the legally parked car is hemmed in, prevented from getting out. At least he could leave it in neutral so that the car could be moved aside. Another double parker likes to sit across two bays spots. An even wilder boar (boor) likes to make itself at home in handicapped parking spaces. The two-wheeled baby pig, insists on parking in the middle of the car spot. Ya, you also pay road tax, but shouldn't you find your motorbike spot? Even if you park on the line, it might be OK. How boarish can one get? There is something about a road that turns normal people into hogs, which turns others to rage. Then there are the circus acrobats ("Mad" Rempits) treated in another section – Medicine: Psychology

We are not talking here about H.O.Gs, namely the worldwide Harley Owners Group, who roam in droves and are genteel enough. There is an order and system to their mass migration and road navigation.

Behavior: The way we do business

The Malaysian way of doing business can sometimes be confounding to the outside observer. From cabinet level meetings to kitchen counter encounters, preambles can be quite prolonged. Beginning with acknowledging the chairman, down the hierarchy to the ordinary members can sometimes seem like an eternity. Say you are the MC at a wedding reception, you would give a nod to every VVIP, VIP, IP, and P present, before you come to the subject matter. Starting with the *YAB* (Rt. Hon.), the *YB* (Hon.), to your regular *Yang Dihormati* (Respected). There may may others like, *Yang Mulia* (Esteemed), *Yang Arif* (Learned). And so on. Looking at the equivalents in English, do you suppose that we got this from the British? The Americans address their supreme leader simply as, "Mr.President". Here, it is "The Right Honorable, Tengku, Tun, Tan Sri, Dato Seri, Dato, Dr. Soh And Soh." Similarly, a mention of his name in the government gazette would be followed by a goods train of his awards. Dr.Soh And Soh, (MBSB, PHD, PSMN, PMN, PJN, AMN, KMN, PJN, PJK) yada yada yada.

A friend has an interesting theory about why Malays tend to do things the way they do. He has observed that they tend to do business by committee or consensus, taken to extremes. Whether it be a government department, or village leadership committee (JKKK), things are laid back and relaxed. Every precaution is taken to not rock the boat, the issue of "face" being of paramount importance. No one pushes the boss for a quick implementation or resolution, or offers a contrary view. You definitely don't want to, *"menjatuhkan"* someone's *"air muka"*, (Litt: "drop his water face" or "make him lose face"). *Air muka*, refers to countenance, or a person's honour.The term "Saving face", is an oriental concept for maintaining mutual dignity, honour, respect, and diplomacy. Committee members, being careful not to step on each other's toes, action gets delayed. It gets done, nevertheless. He notes that even decisions such as organizing a dinner, can get bogged down. A rather interesting thing, is the emphasis on big catered lunches during such meetings. Lesser meetings will at least, get a comprehensive breakfast menu or at least tea and tit bits.

Many foreign businessmen with proposals to set up business in Malaysia, have expressed puzzlement at delays and lethargy at government decision making levels. But things do get done ultimately, as can be seen in the vast amount of businesses being approved every year.

The "face" factor can been noted in the way UMNO (United Malays National Organization), leadership is run. It is the main political party in the country (or was). There has never been, and perhaps never will be, a challenger who wins the party's presidency. It has always been a handover, or smooth transition, even if the incumbent reluctantly gives up the reins. In leadership crisis situations, someone invariably steps up to the plate to facilitate a compromise. The one time there was a direct challenge, the party briefly split into UMNO Baru and Semangat 46. And then it reconstituted, as homeostasis (steady state) returned.

The leadership style is very similar to the way things are done in the Malay family. Face, unity, and respect for the elders are of ultimate importance. In Family Theory (a Marriage and Family Therapy concept), the self-appointed intermediary or facilitator, is equivalent to the 'Joker'. The joker is the one who distracts the quarreling parents or family members by troublesome behavior or comic action, thereby taking the focus off the main issue. During a bullriding session, clowns enter the ring to divert the bull from goring a fallen rider.

But when forced against a corner, the Malays have shed their gentle demeanor and become ferocious fighters. Mat Salleh of Sabah and Mat Kilau of Pahang are examples. Likewise, there was a time when the Malay was pushed too far, he would run amuck (mengamok) seeking vengeance, In that state of mind, he would slash the nearest human, even his family or neighbour. Going postal, killing spree, running amuck, rampaging, mass murder.

The Chinese way of doing things is still largely based on face (mianzi). However the difference is, things get done faster. Hospitality is paramount. Deals are made over sumptuous lunches or dinners in upscale hotels. Thanks to Confucius, nobody is as cool as the Chinese. C for cool confucian Chinese. But this a generalization. When situations call for it they are capable of public hairpulling. Every once in a while, the world gets to witness the Taiwanese parliament, where chairs fly as fluently as words. The only all-Chinese Party in Malaysia, MCA (Malaysian Chinese Association), has seen its fair share of public dogfights and leadership tussles. Nevertheless, the losers do not go start splinter parties, as the Indians do.

The Malayan Communist Party aka MPAJA (Malayan Peoples' Anti-Japanese Army) led by Chin Peng had a lengthy agitation against the British, post WW11. It was mostly Chinese, even if some Malays and Indians participated.

Indians are prone to speak their minds. Whether they realize it or not, they have largely tended to be vociferous and boisterous in agitating for their rights. A survey of the movers and shakers in the Malaysian trades union sector, shows an improportionate preponderance of Indians. Face is observed, as a matter of course, up to a certain point. And then, the fangs and claws come out. The illegal rally of Hindraf (Hindu Rights Action Front) outside the British Embassy in 2007, is considered by political analysts to be one of the catalysts for the then ruling coalitions's, especially MIC's, election setbacks in that year.

Is this quarrelsome garrulousness the reason why, when the British left India with a democracy, Indians formed a million political parties? They have run away with democracy, to the extremes of it. But notice also, that the British evacuation was preceded by that most face-saving of agitations – the Non-Violent Movement (Ahimsa) by Mahatma Gandhi. During WW11, Indians in Malaya were equally involved in Gandhi's Ahimsa as well as (Subash Chandra) Bose's militaristic Indian National Army. Malaysians Indians have the indubitable, as opposed to dubious, honour of having the most number of registered political parties in proportion to population.

Speaking of agitation, it is at first glance, rather difficult to assign this as an indian trait. The South Indians, especially Tamils, were seen as docile and hardworking coolie material. Hence, they were brought here, and to South Africa, Mauritius, Reunion, the Caribbean, as well as Fiji and Sri Lanka, as indentured labourers. Fortunately for them, this was after the abolition of slavery by Britain. Janakiraman Manickam, son of estate workers, in his book *Malaysian Indian Dilemma: The Struggles and Tribulations of the Malaysian Indian Community*, writes that the British had earlier experimented with Chinese labour. They had soon enough proved to be difficult to manipulate, therefore the British turned to the Indians. After a period of peaceful appeals for fair treatment, general strikes became the norm in estates beginning 1939. The first demand out of 12, was equal pay with their Chinese co-workers. Things built up to a crescendo on May 12, 1941, with the indian workers and MMIS facing off the estate managements and the colonial government. A crowd of workers from the surrounding estates had gathered at the Klang police station. The Punjab regiment and other army outfits were called in, resulting in 5 deaths. To the victor goes the spoils, and so Mr.Raman concludes that this incident doesn't even get a footnote in the history books. If anything came of it, the British realized that when push came to shove, even the docile will fight back.

An English writer Ainsworth, in his *The Confessions of a Planter in Malaya: A Chronicle of Life and Adventure in the Jungle* (1911) quotes an English estate owner. The planter describes his Tamil labourers as, *"weak and timid, in both body and spirit, pitiable and and without life force. Due to a famished state, all the Tamils were without any grip on life and dissatisfied with their own race. What was surprising was the blind faith they had, on their white employers.*" The dissatisfaction was due to the treatment they had received from the so-called higher castes among their countrymen. In other words they were conditioned to a slave-like state of mind by the Hindu caste system. One infamous line by the British colonial adminsistrator of the time, Sir Thomas Hislop, regarding the importation of Indian labour, was, "*We need only Indian indentured coolies. Independent persons are not needed*". The British only continued the policy of the Hindu caste system. It is a testament to the multicultural democratic system of Malaysia, that the descendents of these Indians have found their voice. They have further voice training to do, though.

Malaysian Indians have subscribed to both forms of agitation – violent and non-violent. They have been supporters of Subhas Chandra Bose's militaristic INA (Indian National Army) as well as Gandhi's Satyagraha movement. Just as the above influences came from India, perhaps the same is the case, of the Malayan Chinese led communist insurrection. They had direct influence from 'Red China', or communist mainland China. I remember, as a primary school student, hearing a Chinese woman lambasting the Tunku Abdul Rahman cabinet, in flawless classical Tamil (!), on shortwave radio. It was the accent that gave her away. I do remember my father saying that it was illegal to listen to that.

Unlike the Malays and UMNO, Indians and MIC (Malaysian Indian Congress) have no real sense of "us". They are divided into castes, and caste politics is said to be rife there. Recent leadership positions have tended to be determined by caste sentiments. One leader was notoriously branded as using ruffians of his caste to rough up his opponents. That was not always the case, though. The earlier leaderships were focused on common interests and social upliftment.

The alternate mainstream political party, the Peoples' Justice Party (PKR), seems to be the harbinger of a new style. Here is an untried experiment in multi-racial political machinery. But thus far, leadership therein seems cronyistic too. There are family politics in PKR and DAP too, as in UMNO, where children are enlisted into the leadership. The Democratic Action

Party (DAP) and Gerakan, while claiming to be multiracial, have not had much Malay focus or support, and have been dominated by the Chinese. PKR has representation in all three ethnicities. The success of the PKR experiment is yet to be established. It will have to weather many more years of political monsoon before that will be proven.

This section is not about religious faith and tradition`. That is treated under the section on Religion. The beliefs considered here, are non religious and purely cultural. In fact, most are anti-religious or extra-religious, being somewhat of an accessory to bona fide religion. These are assumptions and practices not based on scientific evidence, or are pseudo-scientific, at best. There are lots of hearsay (heresy?) and personal testimonials that are given by the so-called masters of these crafts, to convince you of their efficacies.

This is Malaysia, representing the largest ethnic groups in the world — Chinese, Indian, and Austronesian. Interestingly, they are from the Asian landmass, which we all know, is the birthing ground of all the significant religions in the world — Christianity, Islam, Judaism, Buddhism, Hinduism, Taoism, Jainism, Zoroastrianism, Bahai'ism, Shintoism, etc. Paradoxically, Asia is also home to the biggest array of non-religious nonsense — Fung Shway (*Fool's Way*), Vasthu Shastra (*Voodoo Shitz-ter*), Astrology (*Assinine Logic*), Numerology (*No more logic*), sex-fiendish gurus etc.

Should you happen to think that I am being unfair on that last category (extra-religious beliefs), none of that has any basis in religion. The practitioners cannot quote any religious scripture that supports such beliefs or practices. While written religious scripture is generally logical and scientific, these are loco and sceptic. While there are copious old shastras (literature) and ithikasas (traditions) that have codified these ideas, these are later writings that have parasited (attached) themselves to the bona fide vedas (scriptures) to gain a semblance of reliogiosity.

Beliefs originate from what we hear — and keep on hearing from others, ever since we were children (and even before that!). The sources of beliefs include environment, events, knowledge, past experiences, visualization etc. One of the biggest misconceptions people often harbor is that belief is a static, intellectual concept. Nothing can be farther from truth! Beliefs are a choice. We have the power to choose our beliefs. Our beliefs become our reality.

"Beliefs are not just cold mental premises, but are 'hot stuff' intertwined with emotions (conscious or unconscious). Perhaps, that is why we feel threatened or react with sometimes uncalled for aggression, when we believe our beliefs are being challenged! Research findings have repeatedly pointed out that the emotional brain is no longer confined to the classical locales of the hippocampus, amygdala and hypothalamus. The sensory inputs we receive from the environment undergo a filtering process as they travel across one or more synapses, ultimately reaching the area of higher processing, like the frontal lobes. There, the sensory information enters our conscious awareness. What portion of this sensory information enters is determined by our beliefs. Fortunately for us, receptors on the cell membranes are flexible, which can alter in sensitivity and conformation. In other words, even when we feel stuck 'emotionally', there is always a biochemical potential for change and possible growth. When we choose to change our thoughts (bursts of neurochemicals!), we become open and receptive to other pieces of sensory information hitherto blocked by our beliefs! When we change our thinking, we change our beliefs. When we change our beliefs, we change our behavior."

"A mention of the 'Placebo' is most appropriate at this juncture. Medical history is replete with numerous reported cases where placebos were found to have a profound effect on a variety of disorders. One such astounding case was that of a woman suffering from severe nausea and vomiting. Objective measurements of her gastric contractions indicated a disrupted pattern matching the condition she complained of. Then a 'new, magical, extremely potent' drug was offered to her, which would, the doctors proclaimed, undoubtedly cure her nausea. Within a few minutes, her nausea vanished! The very same gastric tests now revealed normal pattern, when, in actuality, she had been given syrup of ipecac, a substance usually used to induce nausea! When the syrup was presented to her, paired with the strong suggestion of relief of nausea by an authority figure, it acted as a (command) message to the brain that triggered a cascade of self-regulatory biochemical responses within the body. This instance dramatically demonstrates that the influence of placebo could be more potent than expected drug effect." – wikipedia

NOWHERE to 'NOW HERE'. Just by splitting the word, you change your perception, that changes your belief, that changes your biochemistry in an instant! It goes to indoctrination – how Nazis, Fascists, ISIS, Al-Qaeda, RSS and cults like Heaven's Gate brainwash their neophytes.

Astronomy

Astrology: Vaana Sasthiram, zhàn xīng xué, Ilmu Nujum

Now, astronomy is an exact science that has developed lately, in terms of the timeline of human thought development. Preceding that was what is known as astrology, a wannabe science at best, or wanton nonsciense. Astrology is primitive man watching the movement of stars with the naked eye. Astronomy is modern man studying the stars with high powered telescopes. Astronomy is an eternal baby, always seeking and searching. Astrology is an inscrutable old man, fixated on former findings and hung up on hoary hypotheses.

The brute human mind, unused as yet to critical reasoning, witnessed grand natural phenomena and quickly formed its conclusions. The stars became manifestations of gods and thus you have *Zeus*, god of the sky and lightning; *Poseidon* god of the sea, *Ra* and *Surya*, sun gods etc. Sun and moon, became divinities, and so did the planets because they had power over you. They were god's born of fear and thus you had to perform obeisance and the natural progression is rituals to appease them. Today's astrologers are the current high priests of these gods, who prescribe such *pradosham* (propitiations). They'll ask you to change the colour of your dress, the type of stone on your ring, your personal number etc. They base your star on your number and vice versa. It's interliked.

Even today, it recurringly affects our daily lives. The days of the week are named after planets and gods. Sunday (Sun's day); Monday (Moon's day);Tuesday (Tiu's day); Wednesday (Woden's day); Thursday (Thor's day); Friday (Freya's day); Saturday (Saturn's day). "Hindu" astrology goes even further and creates nonexistant 'shadow' planets called *Raagu* and *Kethu* and call certain times of the day called *raaghu kaalam* (auspicious time) and *kethu* (inauspicious time). Why would you imagine a non-existent planet to scare people? Would you call this the science of objective observation or the nonsensical non-science of subjective subversion? The purveyors of astrology (*jyotidam*), usually temple priests, cannot quote original Hindu scripture (*vedas*) that teaches such things. What they do quote are *sastras* (treatises) and *ithikasa* (traditions) and *vedangas* (vedic interpretations) written by humans. Human writings cannot be imputed to divine revelation. Do it, and it opens the gate to all kinds of interpretations, interpolations and interesting insinuations. Islam accepts the Hadith and human traditions, apart from the Koran. Whereas, the Bible claiming itself to be complete and self-contained, does not accept extra-biblical texts as binding. Catholics, Lutherans and Methodist add extra-biblical teachings such as catechisms and papal fiats, encyclicals. Hence, the variant human interpretations and insinuations have given rise to a thousand sects and denominations.

Editor's Note: Suzanne White a so-called, "High Priestess of Chinese and Western Astrologies" explains the Chinese calendar, thusly: –

"Like our own western astrology, Chinese astrology uses twelve different signs or symbols to define twelve basic categories of human beings. Similarly to western astrology, the Chinese system uses a person's birth date as the basis for his sign, so in some ways the two systems are alike. Now, let's have a look at how they differ.

Our own astrological signs are monthly. Each of our signs has a different heaven-inspired mythological name and corresponds to a period equivalent to a single Sun cycle. If you were born in the Sun cycle period labeled Aquarius, then in western astrological terms you are an Aquarian. Chinese zodiacal signs are yearly. Each Chinese sign has a different animal name and corresponds to a period equivalent to an entire Chinese calendar year. If you were born in a yearlong period which the Chinese label the Dragon Year, then in Chinese astrological terms you are a Dragon. Simple? Yes.

Chinese astrology is so simple that you need only know the year of your birth to find out which of the twelve signs is yours. But there is one tricky aspect to consider. The Chinese New Year falls on a different date every year. This holiday can occur as early as mid-January or not until late February. If you were born in either January or February, that is, if you are either Capricorn or Aquarius in western astrology, you need to know whether you were born before or after the Chinese New Year. This interpretation has calculated that information for you.

The Chinese animal symbols are: Rat, Ox, Tiger, Cat, Dragon, Snake, Horse, Goat, Monkey, Rooster, Dog and Pig. These animals always appear in the same order. Since the beginning of recorded Chinese time, 2637 B.C., the animal sequence has recurred faithfully every twelve years. It always begins with the Rat and ends with the Pig. And to make things even more convenient for us Twentieth-Century Westerners, 1900 was a Rat year. That means that the next Rat year was 1912 and 1924, 1936, 1948, 1960, 1972, 1984 were all Rat years. Anybody born in any of these years is a Rat.

Chinese astrology, in one form or another, was widely used all over the Orient from the fourtieth century B.C. It became especially popular between 2953 and 2838 B.C. under the Emperor Fu Hsi and again under Shen Nung, who was born in the twenty-eighth century B.C. The zodiacal system and its philosophies as we know them today were codified by Ta Nao, an able minister of Emperor Huang Ti, born about 2704 B.C. It was made official in 2637 B.C. and was formally inaugurated, as were other historical events, at the sixtieth anniversary of the same popular Emperor Huang Ti's accession to the throne. For forty-six centuries thereafter, this system was used as the national standard and touched on all state affairs in China."

Suzanne goes on to explain the characteristics of the different beasts. I had, even in those days, wondered if people of the same age everywhere, displayed the same type of beast behavior. Horrors! What a boring world the classrooms would be!. If this sounds absurd, it is only a simplified extension of western astrology which determines one's character on the month of birth. The "hindu" system at least covers its bases, by taking into account other factors at the instance of birth, such as the correlations of the constellations in connection to the orientation and location of the occasion of parturition (birth).

"The medieval Muslims took a keen interest in the study of the heavens: partly because they considered the celestial bodies to be divine, partly because the dwellers of desert-regions often travelled at night, and relied upon a knowledge of the constellations for guidance in their journeys.

After the advent of Islam, the Muslims needed to determine the time of the prayers, the direction of the Kaaba, and the correct orientation of the mosque, all of which helped give a religious impetus to the study of astronomy and contributed towards the belief that the heavenly bodies were influential upon terrestrial affairs as well as the human condition. The science dealing with such influences was termed astrology (Arabic: علم النجوم Ilm an-Nujūm), a discipline contained within the field of astronomy (more broadly known as علم الفلك Ilm al-Falak the science of formation [of the heavens]'). The principles of these studies were rooted in Arabian, Persian, Babylonian, Hellenistic and Indian traditions and both were developed by the Arabs following their establishment of a magnificent observatory and library of astronomical and astrological texts at Baghdad in the 8th century." – Wikipedia. In Malay culture, this well depicted in the P.Ramlee starred (!) *"Nujum Pak Belalang"*, a comedy of errors.

Numerology

Numerology: Jílì ≠ bùjí, En Kanitham, Al-dalalat

Now, the KL Sentral complex in Brickfields is a multinational, multi-talented, cyberrific, intellectually and intelligently happening place. The Plaza Sentral building there, is a 25 story office edifice that has its lifts numbered arithmetically correctly, except for 3A in place of 4, 13A instead of 14, and 23 A in lieu of 24.

I don't know what to make of it, but my artless arithmetic informs me of a pattern. There appears to be a gap of 10 between these numbers. That does not tell me much, but I know for a fact that 3A should actually be 4 and I know from my Chinese buddy, that 4 sounds like the word "sei", meaning "die" in his language. Perhaps the KLS management wants to respect Chinese sensibilities (oops!, sensitivities), about that number. But what about 14 and 24? 14 (1+4 = 5) and 24 (2+4=6), evil numbers too? If that be the case, floors 5 and 6 should have it tagged differently, too.

I think that the common denominator in all these is the number 4. That certainly is it. Even the western phobia of 13 is not taken into account, and there are a whole lot of them westerners working there. The Malays seem to like the number 4 (empat), which if you apply the "sound principle", gets you *cepat* (quick) and *dapat* (get). However, that is most unlikely. They would reckon that is mostly to do with the low value of motor registration numbers like 4, 44, 444 4444, having been shunned by the Chinese. Indeed, an inordinate number of Malay owned vehicles with configurations of 4 seems to bear this out.

The double helping of 4 (4+4=8) is actually good! How can? Beg pardon, how so? The number 8, in Chinese sounds like the word for prosperity, "Phat". There is a big "phat" chance of happiness if you surround yourself with no. 8s – no slim pickins, but phat portions. So, auto registration numbers especially the 8, 88, 888, 8888 are booked ahead and fetch premium prices.

8, according to Hindu numerology, ain't so good, or so-so at best. You take big risks with it because 8 is either very good or extremely bad. No middle ground, see?. My Hindu friend explains it as a double trouble, double zeros one piled on top of the other. Others may interpret it as an inconvenient infinity, double zeros placed side by side ∞ and hence, endless trouble. The Chinese might see it (prone position 8) as infinitissimal joy. What does it matter whether the 8 is standing or sleeping, as long as it is "phat". The number 9 (*Nava*) for Hindus, is good all round. *Navagraham* (nine planets), *Navarasam* (the nine emotions or affects), *Navamani* (nine precious stones), *Navarathiri* (nine holy nights) etc, attest to that. Why 9? It is the number of Brahma, completion, fulfilment, wisdom and leadership. In the Christian context the number 9 is related to finality as the last and biggest digit in the series from 1 to 9. It occurs as the 9 fruits and the 9 gifts of the Holy Spirit, the ninth hour which is the hour of prayer etc. In Islam 9 is associated with the nine openings in the human body, and 9 months of gestation of a human foetus. These are merely observations, with no supernatural potency asssigned to the number. Chinese naturally love 9 (Jiu) as it means everlasting.(Eternity!)

While the Chinese react with paranoia to sound and appearances (colors, shapes etc), the Hindus claim scientific basis for their beliefs, namely astrology – the study of the firmaments and their effects on things. The Chinese style is more reading tea leaves or shells. If the leaves gather in a certain way, or looks like something, then that is it. While the Chinese system is simplistic and almost endearingly childlike, the Indian system looks insidious in trying to frame a superstition, or a supposition, as natural law. This is due to the Hindu propensity to look at every aspect of culture as having divine origins. Music, dance, medicine, and what have you, are all deemed to derive from the devas and the vedas. No modern scientific research that I know of, has been done, that supports astrological efficacy or numerological accuracy. The only "logic" in these, seems to be in the '… logy' itself.

The habit of 'seeing things' and perceiving certain attributes based on the shape and sound of things continues into other aspects of everyday life. If they see that that the sound of the number four is akin to that of "death" in Chinese, then that is that is to be avoided. Noodles (面条; miàntiáo) uncut – long life, food items shaped like certain organs of the body positively affect those. For instance, Mandarin orange (瓯柑; ōugān) – gold, wealth, Pomegranate (石榴; shíliu) – many offsprings.

Just as playing Lotto or Magnum 4-digits is a game of pure chance, numerology appears to be a manipulating of numbers masquerading as science. An inexact science, a quasi science, a pseudo science, and a science wannabe or pretender, seems more like it. Science is about crunching numbers with logic while numerology crunches numbers with what looks like white magic. Logic and Magic. The difference between the two is like day-light and mid-night. If numerology is a discrete science, it should be taught in the science labs of all schools, colleges, and universities.

The astrologist, numerologist, geomantist, feng shui shifu, vasthu shastra vendor, bomoh, pawang, voodoo shaman, exorcist, palm reader, tea-leaf reader, glass orb gazer, soothsayer, peerer into the future, seer (of the unseeable), ahli sihir, hearer (of voices), false prophet, swindling swamy, scary sorcerer, occultic oracle, and others of their ilk exist because man has refused to dialog direct with God. If you need an intermediary, an intercessor, interpreter, interloper, spokesman, "consultant", you might get skinned by cheats and charlatans. To meet one's maker face to face, one doesn't have to be in the hereafter. You can do it in the here and now. Deal or No Deal? Deal direct with the divine, and you might put the charlatans out of business. Many realize, usually after the fact, that these so-called experts are not there to do service out of the goodness of their hearts. Their fear-mongering usually has a monetary motif to it.

"Early mathematicians like the great Pythagoras are said to have deeply indulged in numerology, as we understand it here. However, modern scientists consider it a pseudomathematics. The early Christian Church disapproved of the practice of numerology. In 325 A.D., following the First Council of Nicaea, departures from the beliefs of the state Church were classified as civil violations within the Roman Empire. Numerology had not found favor with the Christian authority of the day and was assigned to the field of unapproved beliefs along with astrology and other forms of divination and "magic". Despite this religious purging, the spiritual significance assigned to the here-to-fore "sacred" numbers had not disappeared; several numbers, such as the "Jesus number ["The name "Ιησους" (Iesous = Jesus) has the numerical value 888]', have been commented and analyzed by Dorotheus of Gaza and numerology still is used at least in conservative Greek Orthodox circles."

There is another class of numerologists today, who spend their lives seeing mathematical patterns in practically everything, They are the movies. Case in point, movies like the matrix, π, da vinci code and the TV series NUMBRS. etc.

The problem with numerology as a whole, is that there is no codified, unified, systematic set of principles governing it, like bona fide science does. Chinese, Indian, Middle Eastern, and European numerologies greatly differ from each other. Even in European numerology, there is no standard meaning or value attached to the numbers. One common example is:

0. Everything or absoluteness. All
1. Individual. Aggressor. Yang.
2. Balance. Union. Receptive. Yin.
3. Communication/interaction. Neutrality.
4. Creation.
5. Action. Restlessness.
6. Reaction/flux. Responsibility.
7. Thought/consciousness.
8. Power/sacrifice.
9. Highest level of change.
10. Rebirth.

The Chinese determine the efficacy or negativity of numbers by the way their sounds are homonymic to other words. As we saw earlier the number 4 in Cantonese is homonymic (similar sounding) to *sei* or die. By that token, numerology in the other Chinese dialects mean different things. The following number meanings in Cantonese:-

1. (yat) — sure
2. (yi) — easy (易/yi)
3. (saam) — live (生/saang) Does 23 – yi saang equal "easy life"? That's a toast during CNY
4. (sei) — considered unlucky since the pronunciation of 4 is a homonymous with the word for death or suffering (死/sei).
5. (ng) — the self, me, myself (吾/ng), nothing, never (唔/ng, m)
6. (luk) — easy and smooth, all the way
7. (chat) — a slang/vulgar word in Cantonese.
8. (baat) — sudden fortune, prosperity(gau) — long in time (久/gau), a slang/vulgar word in Cantonese

Some lucky number combinations include:

- 99 — doubly long in time, hence eternal; used in the name of a popular Chinese-American supermarket chain, 99 Ranch Market.
- 168 — road of prosperity or to be prosperous together literal translation is "continuing to be wealthy"— many premium-pay telephone numbers in China begin with this number. It is also name of a motel chain in China (Motel 168).
- 518 — I will prosper, other variations include: 5189 (I will prosper for a long time), 516289 (I will get on a long, smooth prosperous road) and 5918 (I will soon prosper)
- 814 — Similar to 168, this means "be wealthy, entire life". 148 also implies the same meaning "entire life be wealthy".
- 888 — Three times the prosperity, means "wealthy wealthy wealthy".
- 1314 — whole lifetime, existence.

Many young Chinese are seemingly not buying into the dark age superstitions of their elders. In times past, no normal Chinese person would be caught dead in a black car. Certainly, he would, but only if it was a black funeral hearse. These days, it is a favourite color of the young uns. The deathly number 4 is now the number of choice on their registration plates. Whereas the sound "sei" used to determine their choice, nowadays, it is the sight or appearance of it that tips it. You see, the number 4 resembles someone sitting cross-legged, which indicates a life of ease and luxury! Imagine a retired young millionaire lounging on a beach chair, somewhere. From the number 4 as a feared symbol of death to a symbol of wealth and health. Tell me if that is not a peerless paradigm shift of unparalleled proportions!

Based as it is, on sights, sounds, and sensations, Chinese phobias and paranoia are easily dispelled by reframing the feared object. That is, to give an alternate, new meaning to it. The Hindu fears are not so easily dispersed, since they are couched in spiritual and supernatural terms. To do so, would need an intellectual sea change of tsunami proportions. To give up numerology and astrology, would be a below belt blow to the very core of Hinduism, as purveyed by the priests and purohits. They won't tell you that fundamental Hinduism doesn't teach such stuff.

Everything from naming ceremonies, picking names, to engagements and weddings is centered on a balance of numbers. As each number is associated with a particular sign of the zodiac, which in turn is related to a planet.The dates and names should correspond to the best alignment of these forces in the constellation. Most times astrologer/numerologist's explanation of one's current life situation and his birth numbers seem very plausible. He would suggest that you use this knowledge proactively to overcome these negative situations.

That doesn't explain the millions of non Hindus or non Taoist who do very well, thank you, without the aid of number manipulation. The numerologist would have to say that their (other's) numbers are already well aligned. Wouldn't it be fair to protest, why only Hindus are so cursed that they need to read their numbers? Horoscopes, in the wrong hands, become "horror-scopes", with charlatans preying on the fears of the gullible.

While the numerology subscribers are of the proactive, fate overcoming camp, the rest of us are in the fatalist camp. These are the one's who sing, "Que sera, sera. Whatever will be, will be." They leave every aspect of their destiny to God and proclaim, "Let God be God, and man be man." Of course, if God the creator is the decider of our future, one has no need to lose sleep. He cares enough to provide our needs.

God provides our every need. It is only when we have "wants" that you find people scurrying to numerologists, and four digit sellers. Wants, you can do without. Needs, you must have. The fatalist camp does very well without numerological intervention, because they work for their needs. That work produces enough to supply their wants too.The numerology camp must be trying to avoid work and get freebies and goodies that don't cost blood, sweat and tears. It seems akin to gambling, embezzling, bribing and cheating. It also smacks of wishful thinking and fantasizing. In the end, perhaps the only one gaining anything from numerology is the numerologist! Couldn't he numerically configure his own bright future so he doesn't have to sit behind a stack of almanacs and charts? Oh yes, he sits on a goldmine. Mining your fears, anxieties, and insecurities, naturally.

Malays used to be generally fatalistic in their outlook. Insha Allah, which means, "If God wills it", is a common phrase. When something beyond one's control happens, it is Takdir or fate. That, does not prevent them from getting up at dawn to pray, to plow the paddy, go to the office, or run the business, and plan for the future. Que Sera, Sera.Whatever will be will be, but whatever happens will be for the best. That is the Hindu deity Krishna, coaching Arjuna, in that portion of the Mahabaratha called the Bhagavad Gita. "Whatever has happened has happened for the best. Whatever is happening is happening for the best. Whatever will happen will happen for the best." Notwithstanding this soothing scripture, the temple priest/astrologer/numerologist, vasthu expert will mine your fears and insecurities, saying that things are not going too well in your life. You need to do something monetary about it.

Seriously, if numbers and positions of objects in certain cardinal directions, have the power to make or break us, then doesn't that take personal responsibility and accountability away? Whine and blame the stars for all our inadequacies. Blame the time you were born, blame your parents, blame your name. Isn't that the game? Take the easy way. Move some objects around, or change the numbers. Everything will be hunky dory. No need to do deep thinking, to find solutions to problems. Leave that to the number expert or feng shui master.

Though Malays do not consult numerologists or astrologers for important endeavours of life, they have been known to lean on bomohs or witchcraft practioners. The hope is, this is a declining practice.

The Chinese, risk takers as they are in business, do consult numerologists and soothsayers, to set up auspicious dates and times. Their actions are based on a beliefs in the efficacy of numbers, as stated at the beginning of this article. House and vehicle numbers are meticulously chosen to avoid bad Qi (Chi) or vibes. Numerology consultancies do a thriving business amongst the business houses.

Physiognomy: Mian Xiang, Svetasvatara Upanishad, 'ilm al-firasah, Cephalic index

Wittingly or unwittingly, willingly or unwillingly, wantonly or unwontonly, everyone practices physiognomy, which is the tendency to assign unwanted characterictics to persons or populations on the basis of their physical appearances. That is to say, prejudice, prejudgement, preconception, predisposition, preference, prepossession, predilection, preclusion, predetermination, presumption, presupposition, propensity, proclivity, proneness. Don't we all?

On a very general level, skin colour determines nobility or nobody in a society. Lets be honest about it. You "friend" and fete a caucasian tourist in your country. You trip over yourself, bend over backwards, and go the extra mile to please him. At the same time you disdain and disregard the dark dude who came over on the same flight, same visa, spending the same amount of money. Then we have the scientific classification of the human race into the Caucasoid, Mongoloid and Negroid. Some outside observers have said that the Caucasus (kavkas) region, especially Georgia has the most beautiful women on earth. In a way, the above classification could be considered scientific, as it is based on observable physical traits. Way down in the dumps of human categorization is the attribution of negative traits to certain tribes, castes or "other".

And then there are beliefs about things and natural occurrences. Those come from deep conditioning, strong convictions based on continuous listening to elders, compounding it in our minds. In short, beliefs are not inborn or inherent. They are acquired post birth. What shapes our beliefs is the shape of that (mindset) which shapes our beliefs and behavior.

A curious case of physiognomy is (or was, since its not current anymore) is that of Cesare Lambroso. He was an Italian criminologist of the mid eighteenth century who developed the idea that criminals are born, not created. He would predict the criminality of a person based on the dimensions of his or her cranium (skull), ears etc. In a way he took away the onus of responsibility from the criminal – to the accident of birth. Doesn't that somehow bring to mind the artificially concocted villainy of such freaky old characters as the Hunchback of Notre Dame and Fankenstein? Or the Incredible Hulk.

In Chinese face reading, the face shapes are vividly described with ten Chinese characters, namely '甶', '田', '目', '同', '用', '由', '甲', '申', '𠘨', and '王', which have the following features respectively:

'甶' Shaped

It belongs to the round face.

This kind of people is easy-going, compassionate, helpful, generous, considerate, honest and tolerant and they are good at handling interpersonal relationships. Also, they are softhearted and never want to harm others or look out others' harming. Being careless, they are the adaptable optimists and most of Buddhists have this kind of face.

'田' Shaped – The outline of face roughly resembles a square.

People with '田' shaped face are rich, smart, energetic, motivated, unflappable in the face of anything and skilled in diplomacy. Also, they are humorous, noble-hearted and popular with others, especially the opposite sex. However, they are impatient, stubborn and quite self-esteemed.

'目' Shaped – It belongs to the long face.

Those with '目' shaped face are resolute, stubborn, decisive, highly subjective, bad-tempered, suspicious and inflexible. It's hard to get along with them. They are hard-working and well-planned but often focus on one thing and ignore the trivial matters. Women with the '目' shaped face are unrestrained, frank, competitive and career-oriented rather than family-oriented.

'同' Shaped – It also belongs to the long face but is wider and more masculine, featuring straight nose, low forehead and well-developed cheeks which look like the two vertical strokes in '同'.

This kind of people is quite subjective and emulative. With good physical strength, they are tough and can always overcome the difficulties. Also, they are frank, honest, serious and responsible, demanding the payment matching the work they do. Though they are impulsive, they can restrain at the most impulsive moment. The biggest shortcoming lies in that they are overly emotional and softhearted.

'由' Shaped – Evolving from the '田' shape, it features the small forehead and wide chin.

The '由' shaped faces are prudent, practical, persevering, frank and ready to promise others. They have poor luck in early years and good kinship because they are family-oriented. At the same time, they are stubborn and impatient and cannot get along with others. Though women with '由' shaped face are not gentle, they can assist their husbands to build up a family and embark upon a career.

'甲' Shaped – Also evolving from the '田' shape, this kind of face features broad forehead and small chin and belongs to the currently popular 'V' face in China.

Full of ideas, people with '甲' shaped faces have good perception, memory and imagination. They are the ambitious entrepreneurial talents yet not good at interpersonal relationships. With good luck in early years, they enjoy success when young but tend to be lonely in old age.

'申' Shaped – Small in both upper and lower part, this type of face features narrow forehead, big and protruding cheeks, and pointed chin.

The '申' shaped faces tend to be in the complicated dual disposition. They are smart, rational, emotional, highly adaptable and long-sighted. Meanwhile, they are indecisive, think a lot messily, lack of confidence, and hardly carry out a plan. Also, they are self-interested, lack of self-control, often tell a lie, have many schemes and always need praise from others.

'爪' Shaped – Just like the Chinese character '爪', this kind of face is flat and defined with the broad forehead, flat cheeks, broad and plump chin.

People with '风' shaped faces are easy-going, resigned to the situation and not aggressive. They move about all their life, leave the hometown in early years, move here and there at the age of about 20 and will succeed if they get help from the benefactor. After the age of 40, they have better luck and lead the good life in old age. The shortcoming lies in their greed.

'王' Shaped – This kind of face is big, bony and defined with the protruding cheeks and forehead, and straight nose.

Those with '王ir' shaped faces are intelligent, vigorous, capable and of distinctive character. They have a clear-cut stand on what to love and what to hate, and the courage to take the blame for what they do, and try their best to help those in trouble. At the same time, they are capricious and moods change according to environment. Also, they are highly vengeful, greedy and selfish, have no sense of responsibility the family and will harm others to benefit themselves by fair means or foul. They tend to live a hard life with bad luck.

'用' Shaped – Resembling the Chinese character '用', it belongs to the square face yet features more protruding chin and cheeks.

People of this face shape are generally irritable, tenacious, loyal to friends and of strong self-consciousness.

Svetasvatara Upanishad (500 BC), an Indian text on physiognomy mentions the following traits in humans.

Round (moon Face) – lazy, jovial, imaginative, domestic

Square (Earth Face) – tough, offensive, sociable – good for physical work

Rectangular faces – diplomatic, honest, leadership, – professional, executive

Triangular (upright) – narrow forehead – anger, low talent, boastful

Triangular (inverted) – pointy chin, broad forehead. – cheerful, bright, sensitive, hyperactive – disturbed marriage.

On side profile, it has this: –

Straight – balanced

Concave – dark side of life

Convex – happy disposition

It also has ideas on the shape of the eyes, lips, nose, ears etc

In Muslim culture, *al-Firasah* (face reading) has died out as a valid science, since Islam warns people to "beware of the firasa of the believer". – i.e the special ability to see/know the unseen. The Koran also denounces the practice accusing that the divinators get their info from Jinns who get it by spying on the angels' conversations.

The Doctrine of Signatures

The shape of a particular vegetable may be of special benefit to its correspondingly shaped body organ. It reminds you of the saying, "You are what you eat, so eat well." The following is a verbatim quote from an on-line article.

"A stupendous insight of civilizations past has now been confirmed by today's investigative, nutritional sciences. They have shown that what was once called 'The Doctrine of Signatures' was astoundingly correct. It now contends that every whole food has a pattern that resembles a body organ or physiological function and that this pattern acts as a signal or sign as to the benefit the food provides the eater.

Here is just a short list of examples of Whole Food Signatures.

A sliced Carrot looks like the human eye. The pupil, iris and radiating lines look just like the human eye...and YES science now shows that carrots greatly enhance blood flow to and function of the eyes.

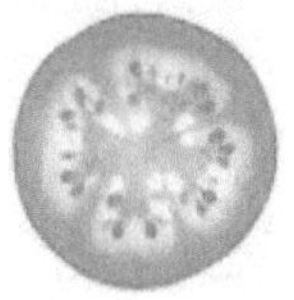

A Tomato has four chambers and is red. The heart is red and has four Chambers. All of the research shows tomatoes are indeed pure heart and blood food.

Grapes hang in a cluster that has the shape of the heart. Each grape looks like a blood cell and all of the research today shows that grapes are also profound heart and blood vitalizing food.

 A Walnut looks like a little brain, a left and right Hemisphere, upper Cerebrums and lower cerebellums. Even the wrinkles or folds are on the nut just like the neo-cortex.We now know that walnuts help develop over 3 dozen neuro-transmitters for brain function.

 Kidney beans actually heal and help maintain kidney function and yes, they look exactly like the human kidneys.

 Celery, Bok Choy, Rhubarb and more look just like bones. These foods specifically target bone strength. Bones are 23% sodium and these foods are 23% sodium. If you don't have enough sodium in your diet the body pulls it from the bones, making them weak. These foods replenish the skeletal needs of the body.

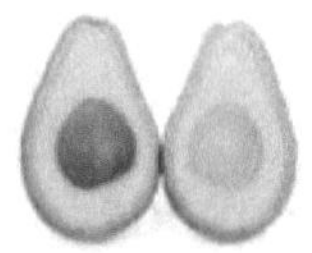 Eggplant, Avocados and Pears target the health and function of The womb and cervix of the female – they look just like these organs. Today's research shows that when a woman eats 1 avocado a week, it balances hormones, sheds unwanted birth weight and prevents cervical cancers. And how profound is this?. it takes exactly 9 months to grow an avocado from blossom to ripened fruit. There are over 14,000 phytolytic chemical constituents of nutrition in each one of these foods (modern science has only studied and named about 141 of them).

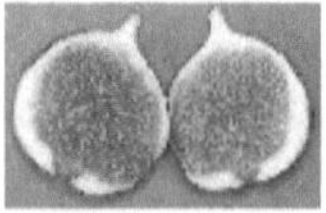 Figs are full of seeds and hang in twos when they grow. Figs increase the motility of male sperm and increase the numbers of sperm as well to overcome male sterility.

 Sweet Potatoes look like the pancreas and actually balance the glycemic index of diabetics.

Olives assist the health and function of the ovaries

Grapefruits, Oranges, and other Citrus fruits look just like the mammary glands of the female and actually assist the health of the breasts and the movement of lymph in and out of the breasts.

Onions look like body cells.Todays research shows that onions help clear waste materials from all of the body cells. They even produce tears which wash the epithelial layers of the eyes.

Bananas, Cucumber, Zucchini and more target the size and Strength of the male sexual organ. It's true!

Peanuts have a profound effect on the testicles and sexual libido. Peanuts were banned as a food for males by the church during the middle ages. Most people don't realize that arginine, the main component of Viagra, comes from peanuts.

For a Chinese and Indian take on a similar belief about food, see "The shape of food" in the food section.

Geomancy: Feng Shui, Vasthu Sastra, Tiang Seri

Geomancy, from Greek *geōmanteía* translates literally to "foresight by earth"; it is a direct translation of the Arabic *'ilm al-raml,* or the "science of the sand". Other Arabic names for geomancy include *khatt al-raml* and *darb al-raml.* Our Malay word ramal (predict) looks like a cognate.

Geomancy as an art is supposed to have its origins in the Middle East. The reference in Hermetic texts, to the mythical Ṭumṭum al-Hindi potentially points to an Indian origin. Having an Islamic or Arabic origin is most likely, since the expansive trade routes of Arabian merchants would facilitate the exchange of culture and knowledge. It is theorized that related systems of divination in sub-Saharan Africa, such as Ifá and sikidy, either were based on or co-developed with Arabic divination systems.

European scholars and universities began to translate Arabic texts and treatises in the early Middle Ages, including those on geomancy. They produced oft-cited and well-studied treatises on geomancy, along with other philosophers, occultists, and theologians until the 17th century, when interest in occultism and divination began to dwindle due to the rise of the Scientific Revolution and the Age of Reason.

The Arabic tradition consists of sketching sixteen random lines of dots in sand.

In Africa, one traditional form of geomancy consists of throwing handfuls of dirt in the air and observing how the dirt falls. Ifá, one of the oldest forms of geomancy, originated in West Africa, and uses the same sixteen geomantic figures as in Arabic and Western geomancy, with different meanings and names. In China, the diviner may enter a trance and make markings on the ground that are interpreted by an associate.

Feng shui, *fung-shway* in Mandarin or *fung-shooy*, is an ancient Chinese system of aesthetics believed to use the laws of both Heaven (astronomy) and Earth (geography) to help one improve life by receiving positive qi. The original designation for the discipline is *Kan Yu* literally: (*Tao of heaven and earth*).

The term *feng shui* literally translates as "earth-water" in English. This is a cultural shorthand taken from the following passage of the *Zhangshu* (Book of Burial) by Guo Pu of the Jin Dynasty:

"Qi rides the wind and scatters, but is retained when encountering water".

Traditional feng shui practice always requires an extremely accurate Chinese compass, or *luo pan*, in order to determine the directions in finding any auspicious sector in a desired location.

The history of feng shui covers 3,500+ years, before the invention of the magnetic compass (China, 206 BC). It originated in Chinese astronomy. The goal of feng shui as practiced today is to situate the human built environment on spots with good qi. The "perfect spot" is a location and an axis in time.

"Qi (roughly pronounced as the sound 'chi' in English) is either a movable positive or negative life force which plays an essential role in feng shui. In Chinese martial arts, it refers to 'energy', in the sense of 'life force' or élan vital. A traditional explanation of qi as it relates to feng shui would include the orientation of a structure, its age, and its interaction with the surrounding environment including the local microclimates, the slope of the land, vegetation, and soil quality.

Polarity is expressed in feng shui as Yin and Yang Theory. Polarity expressed through yin and yang is similar to a bipolar magnetic field. That is, it is of two parts: one creating an exertion and one receiving the exertion. Yang acting and yin receiving could be considered an early understanding of chirality. The development of Yin Yang Theory and its corollary, Five Phase Theory (Five Element Theory), have also been linked with astronomical observations of sunspots.

The five elements of feng shui (water, wood, fire, earth/soil, metal) are made of yin and yang in precise amounts (Greater wood has less yin than lesser wood, but not as much yin as water, and so forth). Earth is a buffer, or an equilibrium achieved when the polarities cancel each other. While the goal of Chinese medicine is to balance yin and yang in the body, the goal of feng shui has been described as aligning a city, site, building, or object with yin-yang force fields.

Even today feng shui is so important to some people that they use it for healing purposes, separate from western medical practice, in addition to using it to guide their businesses and create a peaceful atmosphere in their homes. In 2005, even Disney acknowledged feng shui as an important part of Chinese culture by shifting the main gate to Hong Kong Disneyland by twelve degrees in their building plans, among many other actions suggested by the master planner of architecture and design at Walt Disney Imagineering, Wing Chao."

Modern criticism differentiates between feng shui as a traditional proto-religion and the modern practice: *"A naturalistic belief, it was originally used to find an auspicious dwelling place for a shrine or a tomb. However, over the centuries it, has become distorted and degraded into a gross superstition."* There has been little systematic scientific research into feng shui, since the general scientific consensus is that it is superstition.

Many of the superstitions are actually commonsense. <u>Cemetaries</u> – *"Living next to a burial ground, the people in your home will feel general uneasiness, discomfort or paranoia"*. True, you don't want to be reminded of death everday. <u>Railway tracks</u> – *"The fast-moving train will contribute unnecessary stress to your home's occupants, resulting in needless quarrels and disagreements"*. Noise pollution is major cause of stress. <u>T-Junctions</u> – *"In classic Feng Shui, T-junctions are referred to as "Tiger Eyes" as oncoming cars with headlights shining into the house. It is also called the "Poison Arrow" as cars are approaching with relatively high speed. This creates Sha Qi towards the house, resulting in negative energy"*. – naturally.

Vastu Shastra ("science of construction", "architecture") is a traditional "Hindu" system of design based on directional alignments. It is primarily applied in Hindu architecture, especially for Hindu temples, although it covers other applications, including poetry, dance, sculpture, etc. The foundation of Vastu is traditionally ascribed to the mythical sage Mamuni Mayan. Some have found Indian motifs in the mayan ruins of the central America.

While Vastu had long been essentially restricted to temple architecture, there has been a revival in India in recent decades, notably under the influence of V. Ganapati Sthapati of Chennai, Tamil Nadu (b. 1927), who has been campaigning for a restoration of the tradition in modern Indian society since the 1960s.

Basically, forgetting the complicated rules and regulations, vaasthu is presented on paper as a Mandala, a four cornered diagram similar to the Indian astrological chart called the Kattam. Prana is equivalent to the Chinese Chi. *"Vastu shastra prescribes desirable characteristics for sites and buildings based on flow of energy (prana in Sanskrit). Many of the rules are attributed to cosmological considerations – the sun's path, the rotation of the earth, magnetic field, etc. The morning sun is considered especially beneficial and purifying and hence the east is a treasured direction. The body is considered a magnet with the head, the heaviest and most important part, being considered the North Pole and the feet the South pole. Hence sleeping with one's head in the north is believed to cause a repulsive force with the earth's magnetic north and thus considered harmful. Bedrooms are therefore designed keeping this in mind. This is a wide spread practice in India even today."*

"Energy is primarily considered as emanating from the northeast corner and many site and building characteristics are derived from this. Sites sloping down towards north or east from higher levels of south and west are considered good. Open spaces in site and openings in the building are to be more in the north and east than in the south and the west. No obstacles are to be present in the north and the east. Levels and height of buildings are to be higher in the south and west when compared to the north and east. The southwest corner is to be the highest, followed by southeast, then by northwest and finally by northeast. The triangle formed by joining the southwest, southeast and the northwest corner of the site is attributed to the moon and the triangle formed by joining the northeast, northwest and southeast corner of the site is attributed to the sun. The former are prescribed to be heavier and higher and the latter light and lower. Sites having a longer east-west axis are considered better. The diagonal connecting southwest and northeast is to be longer than the diagonal connecting southeast and northwest. An extended northeast corner is considered beneficial".

Tiang seri means "shining pillar" and is the Malay pseudo-science of metaphysical and geomantic principles considered when siting or designing buildings to improve well-being. It was traditionally practiced by shamans (dukun or bomoh) and architects from Malaysia and Indonesia.

The word tiang seri refers to the main pillar of traditional Malay houses. The system is also called *tajul muluk* after a famous book on the subject.

Some of the terminology used are: –

- tiang ibu ("mother pillar"): Alternative term for the main pillar
- depa (armspan): The matriarch's armspan, used as a unit of measurement
- rumah ibu ("mother house"): The main part of a house
- baris Laksmana: A symbol drawn onto a beam to protect the house from evil. Named after the magic line drawn by Lakshmana to protect his sister-in-law, Seetha

"Malay geomancy has always been passed down orally so not much is known about its early history. Although its age may be unknown, tiang seri contains cultural symbolism of Indian origin, indicating that it has existed as far back as the Hindu period of Southeast Asian history.

Originally tiang seri had no name and its principles were referred to more specifically as adat mendirikan rumah (house-building customs), petua tinggi rumah (house height rules), etc. These concepts were later written about in a book for Achehnese royalty. The book was called Taj-al-Mulk (meaning "Crown Of Kings" in Arabic) and covered a number of other subjects including herbal medicine, astrology and dream interpretation. The title was pronounced Tajul Muluk in Malay so people often referred to tiang seri as ilmu tajul (knowledge of tajul) before it eventually became known as tajul muluk.

Tiang seri was a common practice on the east coast of Malaysia, an area often called the "cradle of Malay culture" because many traditions originated there. This continued in rural areas through European colonisation and some of the rites were recorded by British authors such as William Skeats' book Malay Magic published in 1900. After the Islamic revival of the 1980s, animistic and Hindu-Buddhist aspects of Malay culture were discouraged. Today tiang seri is considered a superstitious relic of the past and books written on the subject are sometimes banned in Malaysia out of fear that they could mislead Muslims. Nevertheless, there are those who believe geomancy is worth researching, particularly the common ground between the Malay, Chinese and Indian systems, all of which have traditionally been practiced in the Malay Peninsula."

Ancient Malay society was matrilineal and this is reflected in old building principles. The main part of traditional Malay houses is called the *rumah ibu* (mother house) and the house's main pillar is often called the *tiang ibu* (mother pillar), thereby acknowledging the mother's role as homemaker. Their construction is based on the length of the matriarch's outstretched arms, called one *depa*. Tiang seri uses this unit of measurement in everything from the siting to the construction of the home's main area.

"This ritual is carried out by a dukun or bomoh to select a house site. The shaman begins by smoking the area with incense. He then measures one

depa of bamboo and sticks it in the ground together with a container of water. Incense is burnt again as the dukun recites incantations. At dawn the next morning, the stick and water are checked. If the pail of water has spilled or the bamboo has shortened, the plot is bad luck. If the water has overflowed or the stick has lengthened, it is very auspicious. Once the site has been chosen, a hole is dug in the ground for the house's main pillar. The shaman places seven grains of rice into the hole and recites mantera before inserting the pillar. If any of the rice grains are missing the next day, the site has negative energy. It is important to note however that an area which is bad for one family may be good for another since the ritual is based on the matriarch's armspan.

Another method involves a mother's dreams. After clearing the area, the dukun places four sticks in its centre. He then takes a handful of soil and chants to the local spirits. The chant as recorded by William Skeats goes as follows:-

Ho, children of Menteri Guru; Who dwell in the Four Corners of the World; I crave this plot as a boon; If it is good show me a good omen; If it is bad show me a bad omen.

The soil is then wrapped in white cloth, fumigated with incense and placed under the mother's pillow at night. The house can be built there if she has a good dream but if she has a nightmare, the area would be unlucky for her. This method is rarely practiced today."

Astrology and numerology, and geomancy which includes Feng Shui, Vasthu Shastra, and Tiang Seri, seems to have degraded into superstition and mindless mumbo-jumbo. It may have started as perfectly logical common sense. For instance, the Chinese dread (Feng Shui) of buying a house located at a T-junction may have been prompted by a concern that a lorry hurtling down the street might crash into the house. The Indian concern about bulding a house facing the direction of the setting sun, may be because the residents, when sitting in the verandah in the evening, would get the sun in their faces. In time, these and similar concerns probably became entrenched, and codified as laws. The headscratching begins when these so called codes become generalized to all situations.

As usual, the Indian practitioners, have imputed religious overtones into it, as in astrology, numerology and what have you. These practioners being usually the temple priests, have always had a motive – monetary – in scaring people into subscribing to these falsities. The poor ignoramuses buy these wholesale, and pay purohits (priests) for services ranging from house warmings to fortune telling. The Hindu religion itself does not say anything on the matter. Hinduism does not have a uniform code. The various sects have their own traditions or *ithikasa*s. Numerology and vashthu shastra are human creations that have been co-opted or integrated into the religion. In fact, all religions disawow such fearmongering and superstitions. The wonder of it is, these practices have only increased in popularity in this age of nuclear science and information technology. Many only turn to science after shamanism fails to get results. Consult the bomoh first, before going to the hospital. That seems to be the prevailing thought.

A simple test to prove the ridiculousness of this fung shui (*fool's way*)/vasthu sastra (*voodoo rasta*) mumbo-jumbo, is to ask oneself this question: If you believe in a God or gods, as the case may be, why do you need all this sweat and expense of trying to find human "solutions"? Why do you need amulets; reconfiguring of birth numbers and names; shifting of furniture; and observing of auspicious times, in order to protect yourself? Wouldn't a loving God do it in the first place? Isn't that His job description? Would the practioners of geomancy, numerology etc., practice what they practice if it is a clear indication of their lack of faith in their God, to supply all needs? God says, "*If you need an amulet, what am I for?*" Man says, "*No offense God, but I need to cover all the bases.*"

The Torah says, "*If you follow my decrees and are careful to obey my commands, I will send you rain in its season and the ground will yield its crops and the trees of the field their fruit.*" – Leivticus 26: 3

The New Testament says, "*God shall supply all your needs*" – (Phillippians 4: 19)

The Quran says, "*Allah is sufficient for us and He is the best guardian*". (Surah Al-Imraan v. 173)

The Tamil god Murugan says, "Yaam irukka bayam ein?" Or, "*Why fear, when We are here?*" (the "we" is the royal "we").

And we humans proceed to do our own thing, anyway. We would rather listen to the fortune-teller or Feng Shui master, than the God who created them. Although my difficulty with these quasi (crazy?) sciences arises out of their unbelievable and unproved claims, I have had my share of close encounters with them, that have reinforced my doubts. One memorable one, is a radio interview given by a certain "Dr.....", in a series of weekly infomercials. It is the day after the disastrous earthquake and tsunami in Japan (March 11, 2011). Veteran radio personality, V. Arumugam is conducting the interview on Minnal FM (RTM's Tamil station). The script goes such (Get the transcript if you can):

Arumugam : Dr...., the day before the tsunami, it was reported that a large number of fish had died and were found floating in the sea, just off Los Angeles, USA. What are your thoughts on this?

Dr. What's-his-name : (*Without skipping a heartbeat*). It's all related. Before the earthquake happened, gases were released into the ocean, that sucked out the oxygen. The fishes died of suffocation. Everything is related."

Arumugam : (*Matter-of-factly*). "So, an action in one part of the world has direct consequences in another?"

Dr. Know-it-all : (*Emphatically*) "Yesss! Blah-blah-blah......blah.......... It is all related"

Arumugam didn't need to ask why the fishes around ground zero (Japan) didn't die. We get it. Now, this guy holds a doctorate in gemology (not geology), but I would have taken my hat off to him and worshipped his feet had he said, "Sorry, that is not my field of expertise. Ask me about gemstones and ways to improve your life." But this one, like most funky shooists (*feng shui*) and wasted sods (*vastu sastra*), must have his two cents worth in. You see, he'll tell you anything to sell gemstones, and especially enjoys pushing a holy nut called *utthraksha*. What is it that compels these types to presume to know the answers and solutions to all the problems of the world? Reputation! Image! Even if they don't have an answer, they must "seem" to have one. That is their bread and butter. The slightest hint of hesitation, or doubt, and their aura of infallibility dissipates.

Perhaps, his die-hard customers should convert his shop in Klang's Little India into a temple, since he is all-knowing. Why seek God, when this one can solve all your issues, eh?

Having said so much about the pseudo sciences such as palmistry and astrology, what about the solid sciences, such as physics and astronomy? Modern scientists like Stephen Hawkings have an equally surprising take on the realm of religion and God. While the pseudoscientists think that inanimate objects (charms, amulets) and rituals can replicate the functions of the divine, the hard scientists believe solely in the efficacies of human knowledge (science and technology). While both (pseudo and exact sciences) place their faith on something other than God for the salvation of the human race, the middle way (a working relationship with a personal God) has the majority of takers.

Seers: Kili Jothidam, Tukang Tilik, Suan Ming

Then, there was Paul, the omniscient octopus which became famous for predicting the winner of the July 2010 world cup in South Africa. It died 3 months later, probably unaware of its doomsday. Before that, there was the Indian parrot jothidam. The parrot fortune teller, with his couple of parrots in a little green lunchbox of a cage, was a ubiquitous street curiosity in the those days. He has now disappeared except in little India in Klang and five foot ways elsewhere. His green backed, red beaked fortune telling fowl was a fixture in the local scene.

The modus operandi was simple enough. He had trained his parrots well, to "randomly" pick from a stack of envelopes that each contained a tarot card sized picture of a Hindu god or goddess. At the back of the picture was a write-up that foretold the future. Sometimes, it also "post-told" the past and "now told" new info. Everything was positive in tone, of course, and the customer carried on with his life, a spring in his gait. Even though the little birdie appeared to move only three or four cards each session, it somehow seemed a random pick. A fine actor indeed, with his deliberate, "thoughtful" moves. It might seem a tad childish to the curious observer. But to many, parrot tarot, is not for the birds. Serious business indeed.

Parrot fortune telling is the first cousin of tea leaf reading, palm reading, crystal ball peering, zodiac gazing and the rest. However, using wild animals is in a class of its own. Malaysians have been consulting these animal mediums forever, it seems like. The latest craze in Malaysia is the would be world famous, wildboar windfall Woodstock. A rendevouz of wild beast and wild-eyed gambler, acting in concert for mutual benefit. A séance of bipartisan back scratching. This is how it must have happened. A herd of four-digit fanatics had somehow persuaded a band of boars to a tryst at the edge of the Ampang forest reserve, just outside Kuala Lumpur. It has since, become a daily circus. Food is used to grease the deal. The punters meditate on their favourite four digit combination whilst stroking the backs of these jungle hogs, hoping for big payouts from the 4-D bookies. Alternately, they would rub a piece of paper inscribed with four digits, on the backs of the willing beasts. The swine get to swallow their favourite fare. Or, perhaps they enjoy the backrub, as a bonus?

This mania is not the first in Malaysia. It has a precedent near a Taiping forest reserve, where the swine get to pig out on nasi lemak parcels. And as you can expect in any gold rush, there will always be the sure winners — the suppliers and outfitters. In this case, it is the small time entrepreuner who hits it big time. The nasi lemak seller strikes the jackpot. What a lucky guy, snagging so many losers in one place! The wild beast are luckier still. Does anybody know how or where the whole shebang started? Should we consult a fortune teller? This particular practice is predominantly a Chinese phenomenon, although when it comes to gambling, no ethnicity is aloof from it. Where there is a remote probability, the faintest whiff of easy money, you'll find them all clamouring and clambering over each other.

I recall about 20 years back, a Malay colleague had witnessed a pig laden lorry tip over on its side. The pigs were squealing, still enclosed in their individual rattan baskets. His decision to punt 4-D with the lorry's licence plate number, resulted in a big payoff for him. He swore that pig related accidents never fail to produce winning numbers. In my un-enlightened days, yours truly, was "blessed" by a bird. Let's say it was a close encounter of the fowl (foul) kind. As I walked through a cloud of airborne pigeons outside Vaithy clinic in Brickfields, I experienced an illegal mid-flight dumping of avian poop. What a fowl deed, it was. The chalky goo landed and nestled in a corner of my moustache. Lo and behold, there was a 4D shop right at the scene of the crime (still exists). Perhaps, I had remembered someone say that its was good luck to be stink-bombed by birds, which made me want to test the theory. The number I booked there (my motorbike's registration) won me a hundred ringgit. It was the first and last gambling "win" of my life, thankfully. If I had to spend $10,000.00 to win a $100.00, what kind of win would that be? Phyrrhic? For every "winner", there are 10,000 losers. So, how do they prove those animal tales? Coincidence?

While the Indian predator, er, predictor uses the parrot to parry his trade, other Malaysians use birds of other feathers. Singing birds (*merbok, murai, mynah, shama* = magpie robin) are a predominantly Chinese and Malay preoccupation. Bird owners gather regularly in open fields, hoisting their cages on tall poles in a forest of other poles. The ideas is to appreciate the sweet songs, but you can bet (!) that illegal gambling also happens, as can be expected in any competition. Cockfighting. Of course the race horse is the universal provider of betting opportunities. Winner or loser, all hang their hopes on a horse, eventhough neither rider nor horse predicts a race winner. Only the gambler does. And then, there are the dogs, cocks, and even frogs and cockroaches and ants that people use as betting tools. Ultimately, the biggest bets are probably on soccer, cricket teams and other athletes.

In other animal tales, after the winter in North America, the possum is looked to for prediction of Spring. Apparently, they have been predicting precisely since the founding of European settlement there. However, that doesn't involve gambling.

Superstitions: Petanda, Suei, Sagunam

A superstition is simply an overgrown fear. So, you happened to walk under a ladder one day. It so happened that the painter standing on the ladder dropped his paint on you. It was so awful that everytime you saw a leaning ladder, you gave it a wide berth. That is not so bad, is it? What is bad is the belief (a conviction) that every time you walked under a ladder, some bad luck will definitely befall you.

Superstitions do have elements of psychological phenomena like Paranoia, Phobia, Post-Traumatic Stress Disorder (PTSD), Perfectionism, Anxiety and

Obsessive – Compulsive Disorder (OCD). A paranoia is a mistrust, distrust, suspicion of things. A phobia is an irrational fear of something. PTSD is a recurring flashback of a traumatic experience. Perfectionism is a fear of failing, or being second best. Obsessive-Compulsive Disorder (OCD) is related to anxiety and the sufferer's compulsive actions to overcome it.

As we have seen, superstitions start their life as a logical apprehension of certain phenomena. Walking along at night, our ancestor might have tripped and fallen on a black cat. He would have told his family members not to cross paths with black cats. In time, it became a part of the culture and mindset. A Tamil proverb says," "*arandavan kannukku irundathellaam pei*" "to a startled person, everything dark is the devil."

Since superstition has cultural origins, lets look at some of them in their natural habitat.

Indian – *Sagunam*. If you see a black cat as you head out the door, it is *ava sagunam* (bad omen). You need to go back into the house, and come out again when the coast is clear. Even If doing that causes you to miss an important job interview it is OK, because you would not have got the job anyway.

Crow crap is good luck, as is coming across an elephant (representing Ganesha, the remover of obstacles). In gift giving, round figure means completion, while adding a dollar (incomplete) ensures continuous prosperity. House cleaning after dark stops Lakshmi (goddess of wealth) from entering the home. A mirror falling and breaking on its own is a sign of death. A black *pottu* on a baby's cheek will avert bad things, like a distraction. Try figuring out the reasons.

Chinese – *Suei* – Gifting clocks (sounds like zhōng, meaning "the end". Countdown to the underground? The colour red is great because, blood represents life. House facing the north, is bad chi. While a pet turtle is a symbol of longevity, it also said to slow down a business. Number 4 is bad and number 8 is good, based on their sounds. Why not change the word?

Malay – *Petanda* – a sign – Sitting or stepping on a book makes one stupid. Opening an umbrella inside the house brings bad luck. Drinking water that has ants in it, makes you forgetful. Clipping fingernails at night shortens your life. Peeping in girl's showers makes you blind (duh!).

Peeping through a keyhole has resulted in many an eye poked with a twig by the person on the other side. While the above observations may seem silly, they started out as good advice. Only in the course of time their actual purpose and meaning may have changed entirely. Don't we know of words that have changed meaning? Take *awful* and *awesome*, which both meant the same thing, a reverential fear of God. Now, they mean opposite things.

Talismans/Amulets: Thayithu, Tangkal, Hùshēnfú, Kara, Crucifix

This topic should come under the section on religion, as talismans are closely identified with the respective religions. However, it is placed here because not every believer of a certain religion wears it or subscribes to its efficacy. It is A-OK if a religion endorses the wearing of a talisman. But it is completely another matter if people, due to personal paranoia or bomoh induced phobia, resort to ornamenting themselves like Christmas trees.

A talisman is an object having magical and luck bringing properties. An amulet is supposed to protect against evil, danger or disease. A Good-Luck Charm is both. These are equivalent to your childhood security blanket to hide from the bogeyman.

An overwhelming number of Hindus in this country have resorted to tying the *Thaayithu, or kayiru. A* few strands of coloured string tied around the wrists. It is supposedly blessed by a priest and believed to ward of evil or grant protection. This is not to be confused with the *Raakhi*, a North Indian custom where unmarried girls tie a similar string around the wrists of their 'brothers' during the *Holi* festival. As in most aspects of the recent Hindu "awakening" in Malaysia, they have begun wholesale importation of some forgotten practices, along with the coming of temple priests from India. While the practice of tying the *Thayithu* is not new in Malaysia, you hardly saw anyone tie it on the wrist about fifteen years ago, when I left for the US. Back then, the Thayithu was believed procured from a *manthravathi* (Shaman) and tied around the biceps and conveniently hidden under the shirt sleeves. Very few wore it, anyway. The old Tamil movies usually depicted villains sporting that. So, it was quite a culture shock for me to witness this widespread, new fangled fashion of kayiru (rope), especially by the young Hindus.

Tamils used to wear the *Puli Naham* (Tiger Claw) around the neck. It is rare these days but still strong in Thai and other communities, as a dispeller of evil. The Hindu god Murugan is said to have said, *"Yaamirukka Bayamaen"*, meaning, "why fear, when we

am here?" Why fear anything at all, or need anything at all, if the self is assured?

In Chinese folk tales, tigers kill evil men and protect good men. Tiger charms are used to keep away disease and evil, and babies are given colourfully embroidered tiger shoes for protection. The "Tiger Claw" (*hu chao*) amulet is believed to ward off sudden fright and give the wearer the courage of the tiger. Because the tiger wards off disasters, it is popular as one of the nine gods worshipped at the New Year Festival.

Aside from amulets (protection), Chinese are prone to the talisman (good luck) aspect of it. More so, is their fixation on health especially sexual health. In that regard, you see the usage of rhino horns and other animal parts. China is the biggest black market for Jaguar parts out of South America. Gangs harvest jaguars for their fangs, skins, claws and even their testicles, Sarah Stoner, senior investigations manager at the Wildlife Justice Commission, a Netherlands-based foundation, told EFE news agency.

There is across the board belief among Malaysians, that inanimate objects prayed over or "blessed" can somehow be endued or infused with powers only the Divine and the human psyche can have. The Roman Catholic believes in the efficacy of so called "holy water" blessed by padres. Muslims invest their hopes in the supposed power of blessed water from the well of Zam-Zam. Hindus wear the holy red thread on their wrists. Buddhists also wear a similar yellow string. The rationalist would argue that when objects are assigned power, they become idols. When idols can innoculate you from evil, then the immortal becomes the immaterial. True believers don't subscribe to outward forms to assure them of security. The belief in an almighty, rules out dependence on all things made by human hands. Doesn't such practice send the message that the almighty is actually "all-most" or, "all, but"?

An Indian Muslim neighbour had a bottle with zam-zam water tied to a corner of the ceiling. Another had a rolled up piece of paper with koranic writing inside the bottle. Such practices are rare in the urban areas.

Some sport tattoos blessed by Thai Buddhist monks. Supposedly elephants, won't approach you and wild animals will be kept at bay. Those are smarter than that – they will keep their distance from the true (human) predator. Don't these people watch the National Geographic Channel?

A cousin wears a tattoo (from India) depicting a *swastika* with a star at its centre. It was a bad job – lousy colour and an open infection. He keeps tapping the star with his middle finger, in the belief that it recharges his luck. It had become his idol.

Similarly, verses of scripture are written and are supposed to have a curative effect on the believer. But the danger is in using these without understanding. Meaninglessly mouthing it or mounting it on a wall, makes it a magic pill, whereas scripture wants the adherent to understand its meaning. Religion is psychological in the sense that it changes the mind (psyche). Karl Marx was right when he said that religion is the opium of the masses – when they use it as a crutch. He was wrong on the other hand, when he said that religion itself was an opium. Rather, it is an agent of positive change.

The Kara is a steel bracelet that our Sikh brother wears. It is one the five "K" identying marks of the Khalsa (brotherhood). It also reminds the wearer of restraint in their actions and remembrance of God at all times. So, in this case the kara cannot be considered a talisman. So is the wearing of the crucifix. About the wearing of amulets, the Bible says thus:

"I am against your magic charms with which you ensnare people like birds and I will tear them from your arms; I will set free the people that you ensnare like birds. I will tear off your veils and save my people from your hands, and they will no longer fall prey to your power" (Ezekiel 13: 18, 20,21,).

The Muslim/Malay equivalent to the Talisman/Amulet is the *Tangkal/ Azimat*. Another name would be the *Taweez*, which people seek out for becoming attractive and to make others fall in love with them. They contain spells as requested by the wearer. Clearly, it against the Muslim faith. One Hadith says, *"Rasoolullah sallahu alayhi wasallam said:*

"Whoever ties on an amulet has committed Shirk"

(al-Silsilah as-Sahihah, # 492)

While one's choices are unquestionable, isn't it very questionable if that one chooses two diametrically opposing choices? For instance, a fervent believer in God (the source of all knowledge), consulting a medium to solve his problems). It is equivalent to a two-timing husband (*main kayu tiga*, in Malay).

Ghosts and Spirits: Langsuir, Ba Ji Gui, Aaavi

Everyone loves/fears a campfire ghost story session. Perhaps that explains its prevalence in all cultures, and its prominence as a popular movie genre.

All three of the above ghosts have an affinity for trees. The *Pontianak* (Malay Vampire) and the *Ba Ji Gui* (Chinese one) tend to live in banana trees, while the Indian *Veythaalam* (a haunted undead) hangs like a bat on a drumstick (murungai) tree. In Tamil usage, when someone says the "veythaalam has climbed the murungai tree again", he means that an episode is repeating or that someone is back to his old tricks. It comes from an old tale about King Vikramaditya who was manipulated into bringing a spirit undead by a sorcerer, for purposes of gaining powers. The veythaalam would tell a story everytime Vikrama carried him on his back, and would jump back into the tree everytime the king couldn't answer a question based on the stories. Apparently the spirit was well intentioned, as it was trying to provide clues to Vikrama to defeat the sorcerer. It is somewhat remiscent of Shaherzad's *Alf Laylah wa-Laylah* (One Thousand and One Nights). Or, to the "Time Loop" style of movies like "Groundhog Day".

The *Pontianak, Kuntilanak, Matianak or "Boentianak"* (as known in Indonesia, sometimes shortened to just kunti) is a type of vampire in Malay and Indonesian folklore, similar to the *Langsuir* ("eagle"). Pontianak and langsuir are women who died during childbirth and became undead, seeking revenge and terrorizing villages. The name "pontianak" seems a corruption of the Bahasa Indonesia *"perempuan mati beranak"*, or "woman who died in childbirth".

While Pontianak and Langsuir are blood sucking female vampires, the former are said to be beautiful and dressed in white, while the latter are ugly and scary. Both are spirits of women who died in childbirth, and nightstalk their victims by the wayside. Paul Theroux, in his writings, notes that the myth was created by Malay women, to dissuade their husbands from engaging in carnal night prowling of their own! Pontianak are associated with the strong smell of the *cempaka* (Magnolia Champaca) flower.

Behold the list of Malay hantu as follows:-

- *Bajang*: the spirit of a stillborn child in the form of a <u>civet</u> cat (*musang*).
- *Bota*: a type of evil spirit, usually a giant
- *Hantu belian:* an evil <u>tiger</u> spirit that enters the body of a human and <u>runs amok</u>[2]
- *Hantu galah*: a ghost with legs and arms as long and slender as bamboo poles.
- *Hantu kopek*: a female ghost with large bosoms who lures men who cheat on their wives
- *Hantu kum-kum*: the ghost of an old woman who sucks the blood of virgin girls to regain her youth.
- *Hantu lilin*: a wandering spirit that carries a torch or a lit candle at night
- *Hantu Pemburu*: the Spectral Huntsman whose head is always looking upwards with a shoot growing from his neck
- *Hantu punjut*: a ghost that takes children who wander into the forest late at night
- *Hantu tinggi*: lit. "tall ghost", a type of giant that will flee at the sight of a naked body
- *Jembalang*: a demon or evil spirit that usually brings disease
- *Lang suir*: the mother of a <u>pontianak</u>. Able to take the form of an owl with long talons, and attacks pregnant women out of jealousy
- *Mambang*: animistic spirits of various natural phenomena
- <u>Orang minyak</u>: a cursed man covered in oil, who rapes women at night
- <u>Pelesit</u>: a type of grasshopper that precedes the polong's arrival.
- <u>Penanggal</u>: a flying head with its disembodied stomach sac dangling below. Sucks the blood of infants.
- *Penunggu*: tutelary spirits of particular places such as caves, forests and mountains.

- <u>Pocong</u>: a ghost wrapped in white burial shroud
- <u>Polong</u>: a spirit resembling a thumb-sized woman.
- *Puaka*: nature spirit of a place which are typically said to reside in abandoned buildings
- <u>Raksaksa</u>: humanoid man-eating demons. Often able to change their appearance at will.
- *Toyol*: the spirit of a stillborn child, appears as a naked baby or toddler

– Wikipedia

In Tamil culture, *Kolli vai pisasu* (Flame mouthed spirits) are strange, smoky semblances seen at zero hour. As this usually occurs in paddy fields, it is said to be a manifestation of methane gas igniting.

Raththa Kaateri (Blood Vampire) roam at midnight. A form called *Kaateri Amman* (Mother Vampire) is worshipped by some Indian and diaspora Tamils, as a healing goddess. Malaysia's first Tamil movie venture, the 1968 production *Raththa Pei* (Blood fiend) deals with this stuff.

Muni appear at high noon or midnight and children and women are prohibited from the open fields or trees at that hour. Generally not vindictive, they are said to slap anyone who crosses their path at that hour. One of my grand uncles got seriously slapped to the ground as he carried wildboar meat in the Glenmarie Estate of over a hundred years ago. Another form of Muni, is the deified type worshipped as *kaaval deivam* (guardian deity) in many-festations such as *Muniandy, Muneeswaran, Muniappan, Munisamy* etc. They are said to be the spirits of those who fell in battle. A colleague, who happened to be outside his DID quarters in Brickfields at an ungodly hour, witnessed – or sensed – a coconut tree height Muniswaran towering over his roof. *Mohini*, are ghosts that haunt old wells, coconut trees and forests and attack couples. They are supposed to be the spirits of women who killed themselves without ever knowing romantic love. They have a strong, deadly fragrance (Jasmine) and legs of fire.

Chinese folklore has categorized many kinds of ghosts. In the Śūraṅgama Sūtra, ghosts are depicted as the souls of wicked humans who, after undergoing punishment for their offenses in the afterlife, are eventually reborn as demons. Like the immortal xian, the text describes ten types of ghosts, characterizing each type with their principal offense and their unique ability:

Weird ghosts (怪鬼; 妖鬼; yāoguǐ or guàiguǐ) were consumed by materialism in life and can transform into any physical object.

Drought ghosts (魃鬼; báguǐ) were consumed by carnal lust in life and can create hot, dry winds.

Trickster ghosts (魅鬼; mèiguǐ) caused confusion in life and can transform into animals.

Venomous ghosts (蠱毒鬼; gǔdú-guǐ) were hateful to others in life and can transform into insects.

Pestilence ghosts (疠鬼; lìguǐ) harbored grudges in life and can cause disease and decay.

Hungry ghosts (饿鬼; èguǐ) were arrogant in life and can take on gaseous forms.

Nightmare ghosts (魇鬼; yǎnguǐ) were frauds in life and can transform into pure darkness.

Goblin ghosts (魍魉鬼; wǎngliǎng-guǐ) were corrupted by their desire for insight in life and are formed from the essential energy within rocks and trees.

Servant ghosts (役使鬼; yìshǐ-guǐ) were corrupted by their desire for accomplishment in life and can transform into blinding light.

Messenger ghosts (传送鬼; chuánsòng-guǐ) were litigious in life and can transform into any person.

The most famous or common ghosts in the Malaysian context, are the hungry ones. In Taoist tradition hungry ghosts arise from people whose deaths have been violent or unhappy. Both Buddhism and Taoism share the idea that hungry ghosts can emerge from neglect or desertion of ancestors.

A non-ghost or human form of the *Gui*, or, *Kui* in Malaysian Chinese circles, is the *guailo* or, "Foreign Devil". In Hong Hong, it refers specifically to Caucasians. However in Malaysia, it is used for all non-chinese. *Maalai Kui* (Malay devil), *Keeling Kui* (Indian devil) are some. It seems rather harmless, and not derogatory. Just a way of referring to an "other".

She-wear Formal: Sarong kebaya, Sari, Cheongsam

The sarong, or "sheath" in Malay is the archetypal attire of the Malay masses. Men and women have wrapped these tubes around the waist for ever. While the the baggy *Baju Kurung* is the customary couture in both formal and informal situations, we shall categorize it under informal wear. The *Sarong Kebaya,* rather, qualifies as more elegant, formal, sexy with its tight body fit. Perhaps due to this, the cultural gestapo of Malaysia has sent it to the gas chambers, along with the bangsawan, and the makyong. Recall those days in the sixties or earlier when the likes of Saloma dazzled us as she danced the joget on screen? Elsewhere, we hear of efforts to recover cultural arts/artifacts that have been gradually lost over centuries, but here we have a deliberate, Taliban/ISIS type of cultural extermination. If the baju kurung (Litt: "lock-up dress") is your ideal formal wear, why then do you send miss universe contestants in weird costumes? Today, the sarong kebaya survives in the Baba-Nyonya culture and as the national dress of Indonesia. It is also the uniform of Malaysia, and Singapore Airlines flight attendents.

The kebaya refers to the top jacket in the *sarong-kebaya* combo. It opens at the front and is traditionally made from lightweight fabrics such as brocade, cotton, gauze, lace, or voile, sometimes adorned with embroidery. The front is secured with either buttons, pins, or brooches. The lower garment for the outfit is known as sarong, kemben or kain, a long piece of cloth wrapped and tucked around the waist and made of batik, ikat, songket or tenun (types of weaves or prints).

Interestingly, kebaya is not local etymology. It draws from *qaba*, or "vesture" in Arabic. More interestingly, it was the Portuguese who introduced the term caba, cabaya, cabaia, to describe the half robes worn by the muslim rulers in India. The "short kebaya" is said to have been copied by the Malaccan Malay women from the waistcoats (breastplate, cuirass) of the Portuguese administrators and soldados.

The *sari* is simply a drape. Its waist high and 6 yards length of material is perhaps the only national dress without a single stitch. Being a drape, it fits all sizes. The modern sari has three components – the *ravukkai* (blouse), the *ul paavadai* (inskirt) and the *seelai* (drape). Even so, the seelai alone will suffice for a full dress. Even today, older women in the villages of Tamil Nadu, are apt to be fully and modestly attired in a single sheet.

There are as many versions of the sari as there states in India. And there are styles of the different South Asian countries. There are as many materials such as silk, cotton, woolly georgette, nylon etc. There as many weaves such as the Banares, Mysore and Kanchipuram silks, and the *sungudi* and *kandaangi* cottons of Madurai and Karaikudi respectively. Considering the rich colours and designs of silk saris from India, Malay women have begun shopping at saree centres. They cut it to stitch their baju kurung.

The *Paavaadai-Thaavani* is a "stick-on" version of a saree. Call it a "training sari", worn by pubescent Tamil girls. It consists of the *paavaadai* (long skirt) and *thaavani* (blouse), as in the regular saree. However instead of being part of a one-piece saree, the *mundhanai* or pallu is a 2 meters long separate sheet. One corner is stuffed into the front left side of the waist and the rest gathered around the buttocks and thrown over and across the left shoulder making it a very saree (not, "very sorry") lookalike.

The *cheongsam* is a body-hugging outfit of Manchu origin. It is a one-piece dress for women; the male version is the changshan, also known in English as a mandarin gown. The stylish and often tight-fitting cheongsam or qipao (chipao) that is most often associated with today was created in the 1920s in Shanghai and was made fashionable by socialites and upperclass women. The name itself is Cantonese, while its Shanghainese name is zansae.

The modernized version is noted for accentuating the figures of women, and as such was popular as a dress for high society. As Western fashions changed, the basic cheongsam design changed too, introducing high-necked sleeveless dresses, bell-like sleeves, and the black lace frothing at the hem of a ball gown. They are depicted in some Chinese movies such as in the 1960s film *The World of Suzie Wong*, where actress Nancy Kwan made the cheongsam briefly fashionable in Western culture.

The 1949 Communist Revolution ended the cheongsam and other fashions in Shanghai, but the Shanghainese emigrants and refugees brought the fashion to Hong Kong where it has remained popular. Recently there has been a revival of the Shanghainese cheongsam in Shanghai and elsewhere in Mainland China. The Shanghainese style functions now mostly as a stylish party dress. They are also uniforms of flight stewardesses of China and Hainan airlines.

She Wear Informal: Baju Kurung, Maxi, Samfoo

The Malay *makcik* wears her loose baju kurung at home and on formal occasions. The Indian *Aachi* wears sarees only on special occasions and dons the two-piece "maxi" on social visits. Both will wear the sarong pelekat and blouse at home. Whereas, the Chinese *Ah Soh* has largely stopped wearing the Cheongsam except for certain occasions. For outings, she wears a pair of loose pants and blouse that falls just below her hips, the Sam Foo. By the by, *Makcik, Aachi, Ah Soh* all refer to "Auntie" in Malay, Tamil and Chinese respectively.

The *baju kurung* has become the national dress of Malay women, overtaking the *sarong kebaya* that used to reign up until the 60s. Remember the Diva Saloma and company? Then, the baju kurung was the dress of the homebodies and servants, while the aristocracy and upper class wore the kebaya. Today, the baju is worn by everybody from children and teenage schoolchildren, working adults, suri rumahtangga (homemakers), grandmothers, and Her Highness Raja Permaisuri Agung herself.

The baju, these days, is a three piece suit comprising the loose sarong, that falls to the ground almost, and the equally billowy long sleeved blouse of the same material, that hangs just below the knees. *Kurung* literally means, to "enclose" or "confine". Is it a surprise then, that the entire body below the neck is comfortably corralled inside the kurung. The *tudung* (scarf) completes the confinement, save the face. Saving face, in the sense that it is the only exposed part of the body. Saving face, in the sense that modesty is immaculately maintained. At home, the Makcik might wear kain pelekat (batik sarong) and kurung blouse.

The younger women and some of their working kakak have turned to the comfortable huggy pants/jeans, and long sleeved blouse that dips to just above their knees. Again, fancy tudung completes the attire. Very rarely do you see Malay women wear skirts, midi or maxi, much less a mini. Hotel and office receptionists may be an exeption.

The Malaysian Indian *Aachi* seems to have abandoned the saree as outdoor or in home wear. Weddings and temple functions are the last repository of the saree. *Maami*(s) (Brahmin matriarchs) and some older women still hang on to it as daily wear. The rest have comfortably co-opted the *Maxi*, for its comfort and ease of wearing. It is a long, loose skirt that falls to the ankles and topped by a short sleeved slack blouse of the same fabric. It is the Indian version of the baju kurung. Alternatively, you might see the aunties in one piece gowns that hang to just above the ankles. It is similar to the kaftan, but without the flowing "wings" or the heel touching length.

The young Indian female, generally prefers the Punjabi suit. It consists of the *shalwar* or loose pants, the *kameez* (long sleeved, flowy blouse that hangs below the knees, and the shawl (*dupatta*). Actually the rage is the *churidar*, or slimmer blouse with tights for the shalwar. Otherwise, she may also, like her Malay sisters, don the pants and a blouse that reaches her waist. She might also, wear a midi and blouse.

With Indian women, both young and old, abandoning the saree as a normal wear, you wonder where those ubiquitous saree houses in Little India get their business. What do they do, who throng those places, looking for bargains in silk and chiffon sarees. Stock up for occasions? I am given to understand that Malay women also buy the richly embroidered silk sarees to fashion their their baju kurung.

The Chinese *Ah Soh* wears a light pants and blouse at home, for shopping or for social gatherings – the Sam Foo (Cantonese: "Coat-trousers"). Like the other races, this is an evolution in apparel. I remember the vegetable gardener Ah Soh and the Nyonya Kuih seller Ah Soh of my primary school days, who bartered a kuih for dried ikan bilis (anchovie) heads. She wore a loose pajama-like pants of flowered print. Her body hugging blouse, of the same material, had no sleeves and reached to her waist. The neck was raised, like that of a *cheongsam*. The cut of her dress, from her right collar, diagonally across her left breast, formed a flap, like a pocket into which she tucked her handkerchief. To protect her bare arms from the sun, she pulled on a pair of white arm sleeves, which was anchored to her neck like a sling, by thin string-like "handles". To top it (!), she wore the familiar broad brimmed bamboo hat, with a Mount Fuji peak.

The young Chinese miss is wont to wear anything from jeans and T-shirt, to skirt and blouse, to shorts and tank tops as a matter of casual wear. For formal wear, she would wear a midi skirt and blouse, or the knee length cheongsam, or the regular business suit – long pants and untucked long sleeved shirt.

Knits, Prints, Weaves: Gongbi, Batik, Kanchipuram

Silk has been known to us for ages as fabulous fabric, and silk weaving or printing is an old art among the Malaysian races.

Chinese, as the discoverors of silk, have a long tradition of weaving and printing it.

"Most art historians believe that the Chinese silk painting was incepted during the Warring States period in 476 BC. But for concluding that the artistic style gained prevalence in the time of the Western Han Dynasty in 206 BC."

"There are two ways of creating a silk painting and these are the Gongbi technique and the Shuimo technique. Gongbi roughly translates to meticulousness, which is aptly termed for how effortful the work is in nature. An artist will require a detailed brushwork to create a Gongbi-style silk painting while Shuimo simply follows a monochromatic palette to create impressionistic artwork." – ChinaArtLover.

The shuimo technique appears to be your regular watercolor or graded wash technique, whereas, gonjin ("tidy") is "meticulous". Gongjin – realist. Shuimo – abstract. Both styles are similar to the Malaysian batik, in the sense that gongjin starts with fine outlines and then paint fill, while shuimo is paint wash.

"The word *batik* is Javanese in origin. It comes from the Javanese *ambatik* that consists of *amba* means "wide" or "large", and *tik* or *nitik* means "dot" or "make a dot". The word *bathikan* also means "drawing" or "writing" in Javanese". – Wikipedia

Batik fabric are of two styles – stamp (cap) and paint (lukis), but the main base in both is wax. In the stamping method, a square copper cap ("chop") with designs, is dipped in wax and stamped on the fabric. When the cloth is dipped into a basin of dye, the wax "resists" it leaving the design untouched. The process can be repeated to add different overlays of design and colour. This process makes for mass production. The batik sarong is thus made in this style.

As for the painting type, outlines are drawn by using the canting, a pen-like tool with a little container and tiny spout (cucuk). The artists dips into molten wax and draws the picture with the spout end. Then he fills the spaces in between the wax, with vibrant colours and washes. In both processes, the crumpling of the cloth to dip in another dye creates fine lines like a network of neurons. The material made in process is entirely used for men's long sleeved shirts or ladies' baju kurung, scarfs, handkerchiefs etc.

As for silk prints, tenun (weaving) and songket (weaving with gold and silver threads added) has been inscribed (2021) on the Representative List of the Intangible Cultural Heritage of Humanity.

Indian silks are primarily focused on wedding sarees and named after their centres of production, namely Benares, Mysore and Kanchipuram etc. These handloom handiworks end up as heirlooms in family trophy rooms, or as hundred year old hand-me-downs across generations.

In the Tamil country of South India, cotton is a convenient conduit for comfortable couture. Chettinadu and Koorainadu are two regions in Tamil Nadu that adopt the traditional *Kandangi* style. However, many new types of Kandangi were introduced by the Tamil Nadu government. Kandangi saree received a geographical Indicator tag on 30 August 2019. A Chettinadu style saree is usually 48 inches wide and 216 inches long, and usually made with maroon, mustard, and black colours. *Sungudi* sarees are traditional cotton sarees from the Madurai area. This is a tie-and-dye technique. It gives the wearer a sexy rural feel.

The Scarf: Selendang, Mukkadu, wéijīn

The usual tudung is actually a selendang (scarf) that is folded in half and the base of the triangle placed slightly overhanging the forehead, the tip of the triangle hangs out down the back (out, down, back!). One of the points of the base is then gathered around the front of the neck, brought up near the ear to below the other ear and pinned with a brooch. The result is a headcovering that traces the contour of the head and has subtle peak at the forehead, like that of a GI (US army) helmet.

Necessity being innovation's mother, and invention's intention, the Malay scarf has latterly evolved into an artform. That is, in the sense of colourful prints, styles of tying and variety of shapes. There are dozens of styles including the wedding, shawl, turban and bawal (pomfret) adorning tudung boutiques.

Indian muslim women do the veil with their sarees (*seelai/pudavai*) at all times, while Hindu women, and some Catholic ones veil themselves at worship time and in the outdoors. The *mundhanai* (the free hanging portion of the saree) may cover the entire head from the forhead, or it may cover half the head as it anchors on the hair knot (*Kondai*). The veil that reveals itself (!) as the saree is draped around the head is the *mukkaadu*, and is rare as modern women prefer to show off their coiffure. The closest that the *mundhanai/pallu* gets to being a scarf, is as a drape over the shoulder, (shawl?) giving the wearer a quality of noble gentility, or gentle nobility.

Time was, when Catholic women and girls were seen in white lace scarfs at Sunday masses. Not only that, Western women and Hollywood actresses found it fashionable in the sixties. Add a pair of sunglasses, and you feigned a Jacqueline Kenndey.

The Chinese don't wear the headscarf as a habit, nowadays. The Chinese vegetable gardener and the woman who hawked door to door on a bicycle in the 60's was distinguishable by her bandana underneath the broad bandolero-like bamboo hat. Sometimes, she would wrap it over the hat and knotted under her chin, as if to it secure from the blustery wind. Not only that, she covered her arms with a special white arm-glove. Her two piece suit (samfoo) consisted of a loose pajama-like pants and a short-sleeved shirt that hangs out to the hips (a Shkirt ?) cut out of the same material.

And then, Chinese lasses were depicted in their samfoos and scarves on red Chinese posters of the sixties. Chinese made silk scarves are internationally prized and collected.

He wear Formal: Baju Melayu, Kung Fu Jacket, Vesti Sattai.

The ethnic dresses of Malaysian men also have pedigrees dating back centuries. As with the women, all races reserve the use of these clothing for special occasions such as religious, cultural or community functions. Often these are used as the uniforms of front office staff in culture specific organizations such as museums, heritage houses etc..

The Malay male wear is the *Baju Melayu*, meaning, "Malay dress". It seems like a name cooked up impromptu, in response to a curious tourist's question. The original name of this attention getting gear with its ancient Malay Royal court and martial background, is lost in history. These days, it is a three piece suit with a loose trouser, a loose untucked shirt and a mini sarong *(samping)* between the two. The samping, also meaning "besides," is generally of *songket* material, or hand embroidery. Those days (think Hang Tuah and company), the additional headgear *(tengkolok)* of the same material would be used instead of today's songkok. A kris tucked in at the waist, somewhat like a gunslinger's, made it picture perfect.

As in many things Malaysian, one runs into oxymoronic surprises with the *baju*. It may be called Malay dress, but its components proclaim a different story. For one, the light and airy pants and the loose fitting, long sleeved shirt are very much Chinese in origin and appearance. Pictures of old Malacca Babas as well as Chinese mainlanders bear this out. The Chinese "Nehru collar" (actually, the Mandarin collar), is the prototype of the stiff Baju Melayu collar called *cekak musang* ("civet's noose").

The samping, tightly wrapped around the waist, is a curious quirk. From a certain angle, it could almost pass for a manly mini skirt or a quaint kilt. Yet, it may not be that difficult to trace its genesis. Hindus priests, as they approach the deity, and Indian servants as they approach their employer, have always tied their cotton shawls (*Angavastiram/Thundu*) around the waist in similar fashion. Tamil kings and the Hindu god-king Rama during his forest exile, is depicted in similar fashion, a yellow waist cloth over his white trouser-like dhoti. This samping tying thing could well have its origins in Malacca's Hindu past, especially as a sign of respect and humility befor the ruler. Like the Indian mid-section piece, the samping might have functioned as a belt to hold the pants up (and the private part under wraps). We are assuming there were no belts in those days. In Europe of the 17th or 18th centuries, it was fashionable for army officers to sport a cummerbund at the waist.

The tengkolok could well derive from the non-urban tamil turban, a haphazardly informal wrap, unlike the elaborately symmetrical Sikh turban. The modern Malay wears the songkok, which definitively has it origins in the middle-east. Clearly, even in this piece of national dress, you find the unity of cultures. A kind of wearable 'One Malaysia', shouldn't you think?

The Malay baju is the most conspicuous part of the royal regalia. The material is usually silk or satin. The most common colors seem to be yellow for the Sultans of the states. In the requiste framed photos in public and private establishments, the Agong always appears in a black baju Melayu, and a black jacket with gold trimmings. The royalty wear white bajus for funerals. Malay males in multicoloured Baju Melayu assemble at Friday prayers at mosques. Malay ministers wear them at official functions, dutas (ambassadors) don them at diplomatic dos, and Muslim men do it too, at Aidil Fitri (Ramadan) and Aidil Adha (Haj) celebrations. It is the requisite suit of a different kind of royalty too. You can wager that the Malay groom, *raja sehari* ("king for a day") as he is, will invariably be in it.

The Chinese celebratory wear is a Baju Melayu forebear. Dragon Shirt, Kung Fu Shirt & Mandarin Shirt – they all seem to refer to the same item. The general appellation is *Tang Zhuang*, and the style is of Manchu origin. The only spottable difference between Malay and Chinese, is the buttons. Whereas the Malay shirt has conventional buttons, plain, clip on or screw on, the Chinese shirt buttons are usually the frogged fastening (Chinese: pankou) type, similar to what Napoleon Bonaparte would have had on his chest. Made of silk and elaborately patterned, or plain, young and old wear it at home during Chinese New Year. Bright or maroon red, turquoise blue, or beige, would be the colors of choice.

On other days, it can be found in Baba-Nonya museums or other heritage houses. Or, you can catch Jackie Chan modeling it on a Kung Fu flick.

Indians wear their own Mandarin/baju Melayu style shirts and collars, to temples and social gatherings. The *jibba* (from the Arabic *Jubah?*) is a loose, long sleeved shirt that hangs to the knees, almost. There is a collarless version, the *motta kalutthu* ("bald neck"). Remember the cheese cloth jippas of hippie times? The *Kurta* is a similar suit made of thicker material, fashioned after the Moghul royal style. Here again, the collar is akin to the mandarin and baju melayu.

The standard traditional attire of Indian men for auspicious, and suspicious, occasions is the *vesti* (dhoti) and *sattai* (shirt). The vesti is a seamless length of white cotton cloth that is wrapped tightly around the waist, unlike the ubiquitous *sarong*, which is a tube. It is the male equivalent of the saree. The shirt that goes with it is also white, long-sleeved, low hemmed, and has the traditional collar (i.e. neck tie collar). A folded shawl hung over the left shoulder (*Angavasthiram)*, makes it a three piece white suit. Watch MIC delegates at their annual convention paint the assembly hall white. Indian women don't usually wear white sarees, as it indicates mourning widows, Hindu nuns, or Mother Theresa types. The exception may be Malayalee women, who favour the white-beige (with gold border) kasavu saree for weddings, onam etc.

He wear casual: Sarong, Shorts, Singlet, Sandals

The Sarong used to be common household gear for most Malaysian men, but obviously no more the case. When I was in the US for close to 15 years, I wore the sarong exclusively, at home. On more than one occasion I have refuelled my car in the middle of winter (Midwest US) in the sarong and sandals. Crazy? And the air conditioning was …….

American foreign missionaries or soldiers on foreign "missions" generally experience something called "reverse culture shock" when they return home. That, is a feeling of alienation from the culture of your homeland. When I re-entered Malaysian space, I did not experience that. The closest to that would be my amazement at the near extinction of the saronged man at home. Everywhere I turned, the multi pocket, knee length shorts appeared to be the domestic fashion of choice for young and old men. What happened to the good old sarong? Sayang! (what a pity).

The sarong – singlet synergy is something like a love marriage. Look at the convenience of it. Before you can get into a pants and shirt, I could get into four changes of the sarong and singlet. Just hop into the tube and pull on the singlet. The thin cotton fabric is ideally suited to our climate, which explains why it is so widespread across South, South-East, Middle-East Asia, Horn of Africa and Oceania. Ironically, the sarong is worn formally on occasions like the muslim friday prayers, in these places.

Latter day alternate casualwear is the shorts and round necked T-shirt with flip-flops. That is convenient for getting around, and for chilling out. While shying away from the sarong, there are men who are not shy about hanging out bare bodied. And not necessarily at the beach or the swimming hole. But you rarely see workers labour bare bodied, digging holes or chopping trees. So whats the need for baring your body when your'e not sweating in the sun?

"On hot summer days in Beijing and other places, it is a common sight to see men running around without shirts or with their shirts rolled up under their armpits exposing their bellies. They hang around, play cards, drink tea, stroll on the sidewalks without their shirts, exposing their less than ideal bodies. Flabby tummies and spares tires are the norm, not rippling abs. They also like to pull up their trousers past their belly button, with the legs rolled up. One Chinese academic told the Los Angeles Times, "Foreigners who visit always ask why are there so many half-naked men in Beijing."

Even though men from a wide range of ages engage in the custom, those that do it are smirkingly known as *bang ye* ('exposing grandfathers'). One man spotted with his flabby tummy exposed told the Los Angeles Times, 'I don't know, it just feels cooler. Look, you just shake your shirt to create breeze.' [Source: John Glionna, Los Angeles Times]

One is reminded of our own yesteryear's Ah Pek (Chinese uncle), sitting at a round marble table, sipping his cuppa, with crocodile T-shirt rolled up to his chest. It was a common spectacle at kopitiams. Likewise, the Indian uncle (ayyah) no longer wears veshti at home, as his father used to. Even if he wears it to the temple or wedding is questionable. He usually wears trousers with a floral short sleeved shirt, hanging out. At home, he'll wear shorts and singlet.

As for the yet young, jeans and t-shirt is the common mode of wear for office, outdoors, occasions or otherwise. Shorts also come into play in casual situations.

Teen Wear: Jeans n' Top, Shorts, Churidar

Teenage leisure wear. The after school, off-day, weekend clothing that they wear to the park or the neighbourhood mall, is the topic of discussion here. The mall, favourite chill space of teens, may be best place to observe them and their fashion sense, as they rove in droves in the corridors. Actually, sightings of cliques of chicks and gangs of guys, like everything else about people watching, the following observations have to be approximations, not generalizations. Besides, these observations may not hold true in time, due to the creeping changes in fashion

The teenage Malay lass wears the *tudung*, most times. However, take it off, and you could still make a correct ethnic identification by the jeans and T-shirts she favours. Malay teens are Levi-Strauss' biggest Malaysian clients, it seems. Almost every *Cik Adik* (Sis) can be seen wearing a pair light blue or navy blue denim. The Chinese Ah Moi (Miss) is quickly identifiable by her invariably black (or dark) shorts and black body glove type T-Shirt. Does the dark hued hottie panty ostensibly accentuate the lassie's silky smoothy cheddar cheesy chicken thighsy splendour, you wonder? She is the most up to date in western teen fashion.The Indian *Thangachchi* (Lil Sis) is prone to sport a long pants of light material and loose T-shirt or mid-thigh skirt. Occassionally, she may opt for short pants, and loose T-shirt. No particular colour requirements. It goes without saying, that the varieties of handbag is a universal accessory.

Aside from the obvious western (or modern) focus of these casual wear, the teens do also wear native gear. For instance, The Cik Adik can often be seen in Baju Kurung, even in casual settings. In keeping with the requirements of religion, and the need for convenience, they often opt for the long pants and long-sleeved loose shirt with the tudung. The Ah Moi can be observed in miniskirt and blouse. The Thangachchi sports the churidar, or Punjabi suit. Long ago, the Ah Moi's *Po Po* (grandmother) was wearing the *Sam Foo,* and double high pigtails and bangs as a teenager. You don't see it today except in period dramas on TV. Or little girls dressed up in red velvet samfoos for Chinese New Year. Likewise, the Thangachchi's *Paati* (granny) wore the *Paavaadai Thaavani,* which has joined the dinosaur, except in rura Tamil Nadu. The *Paavadai* (heel length skirt), *Thaavani* (short-sleeved blouse), plus the *Mundhanai* (length of soft shawl) make for a good imitation of the saree worn by the older women. The pavadai is worn by the young, tween and teen. Hence, a training saree. She may often be seen in a Churidar or its lookalike, the Salwar Kameez. The churidar skirt hangs down to the ankles, while the kameez drops till the knees.

All male teens sport the shorts, especially Indians and Chinese. Malays can be spotted in their jeans and Ts. Many Indian youth seem to favour the black T-shirt for some reason. Perhaps it affords a leaner look, like dusk masks daylight. Compared to adult fashion, youth trends continue to evolve faster and the locals catch on just as fast.

Birthday Suit: Tattoo, Pottu, Wen Shen, Tutang

There is a kind of fabric free "attire" that can pass for a dress. The ancient body art of tattooing is the rave among today's youth, with syndicated TV shows showcasing the latest designs. Some so completely "cover" themselves, that they might walk the streets naked and hardly get a second look. While I personally consider the current tattooing craze to be an environmental pollution on God's gift of body, I do respect native sentiments and traditions. The tribes of *the* Amazon forest, Ibans of Sarawak, tribes of China, consider it a decorative, even religious, act. The ancestors of the Native Americans (Red Indians), used to war-paint themselves, as do the Australian Aborigines.

Tamil men used to sport a tiny green dot tattoo on their foreheads, of 4 mm diameter. Forehead mark is *pottu.* Indian women wear a round curcuma (from KumKum) dot on the forehead as sign of their marital status. A red pottu indicates an unmarried woman. A black one denotes a married woman. That, and the *thaali,* the blessed marital string and pendant. No confusion about a person's marital status. The men used to wear a ring on their right, second toe. The eligible woman, who usually who was not supposed to look a man square in the face, looked down at a man's toe to see if he was eligible.

Tattooing was popular among many ethnic minorities in China since ancient time. However, among the Han Chinese (the major ethnic group) tattoo has been associated with barbaric, criminals, gangsters and bandits since at least Zhou Dynasty (1045 BC to 256 BC). Tattooing Chinese character "Prisoner" (囚) or other characters on convict's or slave's face was a practice until the last dynasty Qing Dynasty (1644 to 1912).

The traditional Han Chinese view especially Confucianism believes that the body is a gift of parents and continuation of the bloodline of the ancestors. Damaging the body is a grave offense. Tattooing and piercing (except women's ear piercing) are generally not accepted by the community. This view can be reflected by the fact that many Han Chinese were killed at the beginning of Qing Dynasty when they refuse to obey the Manchu government's order that all Han Chinese men to shave their forehead (the Manchu hair style). Certain tribes such as the Dai wear tattoo traditionally.

While Chinese tattooing, i.e Chineses designs. Are enjoying universal popularity the danger of being lost in transition land Is everpesent. 'There is the story of a young man in England who thought he was having the Mandarin characters for "Love, honor and obey" tattooed on his arm. He later found out from a Chinese woman that what he actually had tattooed on his arm said "At the end of the day, this is an ugly boy."

Chinese tattoos can be beautiful and powerful tattoos, but you should do thorough research before getting any Chinese tattoo put on your body. It is, after all, going to be with you the rest of your life.' – A History of Chinese Tattoos and Chinese Tattooing Traditions, October 1, 2018

People of Dayak, Kenyah, Bahau, Iban, Kayan have tattoos, as a mark of respectability and nobility. They are broad strokes and use black ink. Like the Chinese patterns like writing characters and dragons, Dayak designs have gained international following.

Hirsute: Meesai, Janggut, húzi

Facial hair has had many uses from badge of maleness, to mark of male beauty, to mask of abnormality (i.e. receding chin), to face warmer, to hider of true identity. Along with the haircut, beard and moutache have their catalogue of styles.

While most cultures would consider a definitive beard as a mark of masculinity – a mark of manliness, the Tamil is most fond of his moustache.

If he were to throw a challenge, "I dare you to….", he would usually prefix it with, "if you are truly a mustachioed man …..".

Meesai murukku (the twirled moustache) refers to a person's comportment/deportment. The upturned spike of hair suggesting a sword. The Chinese moustache – downturned and saggy, along with a wisp of silvery beard indicates wisdom and learnedness. Think Confucius or LaoTze. Eventhough north Indians generally have the beard – moustache combo (Sikhs, Sadhus etc) South Indians go for all sorts upper lip hair – the full moustache of the Tom Selleck/Sam Elliot variety or other style.

You find depictions of big shot characters in Tamil cinema twirling their moustaches to highlight their commanding presence.

Malays wear the Muslim beard and moustache, imitating Prophet Muhammad. Many muslims of the Indian sub continent like the plain beard without moustache – the "chin strap". Or, the plain goatee.

When human groups settled in warmer climates, such as much of eastern and south-eastern Asia, facial and body hair became less necessary, so their bodies did not evolve to express those genetic features as much. Another supposed reason is low testorone levels, which is debatable, since the Far East and South East of Asia is the most populous ! More accurately East Asians have lower androgen receptors – which prevents testosterone from reaching hair follicles.

A reason for the lack of beards in China or on Chinese people is their generally thin follicles, leading to uneven distribution, leading to an unkempt appearance, especially if it happens to be a white beard like LaoTze's. That would be a good enough reason if they don't fall back on the time management excuse. Cleanshaven-ness also needs time. So does dressing up.

Exercise: Yoga, Sema, Chiqong

Malaysians have a good repertoire of mind-body meditative exercises. Yoga, Chigong are the main forms, thanks to Indian and Chinese cultures. The Bumiputra society does not seem to posess a specific exercise with a physical – mental nexus. The *Ruku* during prayertime can pass as exercise. While focussing their minds on the creator, they also do physical flexes and folds of their arms and legs in the Ruku – note section on religion ("the shape of religion"). So, we will go further afield to a form of Islamic discipline called Sufism for that, especially the trance-like swirling (*Sema*) that they do. The swirls demand balance, concentration, and more as the passive observer feels giddy just watching.

There are certain elements of meditative exercise preceding malay dances such as the Javanese Kuda Kepang.

All three place emphasis on breathing and slow movements, which equals meditation and mindfulness.

Yoga *asanas* ("seat" or postures), involve contorting and twisting the body "out of shape", that is supposed to get you physically pliable and in shape. Some of the asanas remind you of those young Chinese acrobats, who are always touring some part of the world at any one time. Chigong movements are like a slow motion of someone fighting off a swarm of mosquitos. While silat itself, is remiscent of the above exercises, the warm-ups are akin to yoga and qigong. All these exerscises can be considered as under the category of stretching and breathing. The others being aerobic and weight exercises.

The practice of yoga is thought to date back to pre-vedic Indian traditions; possibly in the Indus valley civilization around 3000 BCE – as a seal depicting a yogi-like figure is one of the the Harappan finds. Yoga is mentioned in the Rigveda, and also referenced in the Upanishads, though it most likely developed as a systematic study around the 5th and

6th centuries BCE, in ancient India's ascetic and Śramaṇa movements. The Yoga Sutras of Patanjali date from the 2nd century BCE, and gained prominence in the west in the 20th century after being first introduced by Swami Vivekananda.

The Sanskrit noun योग yoga is derived from the sanskrit root *yuj* (युज्) "to attach, join, harness, yoke". It is cognate with the English, "yoke". There is a Tamil word *"Oham"* that equates with yoga, found in the classical era writings of the Siddhars (early Tamil savants). Now, if one were to consider that the inhabitants of The Indus Valley civilization were indeed Dravidians, as most scientists believe, and who also believe that yoga was present in that civilization, then might it not be reasonable to expect that yoga existed in Dravidian literature much before the Sanskrit? A simple syllogistic logic.

Yoga consists of *asana* or posture, *pranayama* or breathing, *Pratyahara* ("Abstraction"), *Dharana* ("Concentration"), *Dhyana* ("Meditation"), *Samadhi* ("Liberation").

"In the early 11th century, the Persian scholar Al Biruni visited India and translated Patanjali's Yogasutra. Al Biruni's translation preserved many of the core themes of Patañjali 's Yoga philosophy, but certain sutras and analytical commentaries were restated making it more consistent with Islamic monotheistic theology. Al Biruni's version of Yoga Sutras reached Persia and the Arabian peninsula by about 1050 AD. Yoga was, however, not accepted by mainstream Sunni and Shia Islam. Minority Islamic sects such as the mystic Sufi movement, particularly in South Asia, adopted Indian yoga practises, including postures and breath control. Muhammad Ghawth, a Shattari Sufi and one of the translators of yoga text in the 16th century, drew controversy for his interest in yoga and was persecuted for his Sufi beliefs."

Malaysia's National Fatwa Council in 2008 passed a decree, prohibiting Muslims from practicing yoga, saying it had elements of Hinduism and that its practice was blasphemy, therefore haraam. Some Muslims in Malaysia who had been practicing yoga for years, criticized the decision as "insulting." Sisters in Islam, a women's rights group in Malaysia, also demurred, saying yoga was just a form of exercise. This fatwa is legally enforceable. However, Malaysia's prime minister clarified that yoga as physical exercise is permissible, but the chanting of religious mantras is prohibited.

Sema or whirling dervishes are a part of the practices of the Mevlavi Sufi order of Turkey. The physical-spiritual act of whirling is supposed to facilitate closeness to God. If Sufism is an attempt to get up close to God through austerity, why wouldn't it be pro – Islam? If that is against islam, wonder what is fasting during Ramadan or the Shiite practice of *Ashura* (self-flagellation)? Perhaps, with the growing incidence of materialism and corruption everywhere, the Sema might just be the medicine this world needs.

Qigong is another mind-matter discipline that has received international acceptance.

"The origin of qigong is commonly attributed to the legendary *Yellow Emperor* and the classic *Book of Internal Medicine*. Archaeological evidence such as the *Mawangdui Silk Texts* (168 BC) shows a series of *Tao Yin* (導引) exercises that bears physical resemblance to some of the health exercises being practiced today." The Taoist writings of *Laozi* (~400 BC) and *Zhuangzi* (~300 BC) both describe meditative and physical exercises to extend one's lifespan and as means of accessing higher realms."

Buddha himself is seen "enlightened" in the padmasana, or lotus posture. "On reaching China, Buddhist practices mixed in with the Chinese forms, birthing the Chinese Buddhist qigong tradition. Chinese Buddhist practice apexes with *Chán* (禪) Buddhism in the 7th century AD. Meditative practice was emphasized and a series of qigong exercises known as the *Yijin Jing* ("Muscle/Tendon Change Classic") was attributed to Bodhidharma, the Tamil prince turned missionary to China. The Chinese martial arts community eventually identify this Yijing Jing as one of the secret training methods in *Shaolin martial arts*."

Tai chi chuan is often described as being Taoist in origin, while *Shaolin* martial arts is named after the famous Buddhist Shaolin temple. Qigong is not just a set of breathing exercises as it encompasses a large variety of both physical and mental training methods designed to help the body and the mind based on Chinese philosophy.

Court Games: Sepak Raga, Sadu Gudu, Wushu

Sepak takraw, or kick volleyball, is the indigenous pastime of Southeast Asia, being the national sport of many SEA countries. While its exact origin is uncertain, sepak takraw is thought to have been introduced by the Chinese by way of the traditional games, *cuju*, an ancient chinese military exercise, where soldiers would try to keep a feathered shuttlecock airborne by kicking it back and forth between two people. As the sport developed, the animal hide and chicken feathers were eventually replaced by balls made of woven strips of rattan.

Sepak takraw differs from the similar sport of footvolley in its use of a rattan ball and only allowing players to use their feet, knee, and head to touch the ball. In Brunei, Indonesia, Malaysia, and Singapore it is commonly called sepak takraw. It can be known as sepak raga as well in Indonesia and Malaysia. In the Philippines, the sport is also called "sepak takraw", resembling the related native sport known as sipà. Sepak, or "to kick", is Malay, while Takraw is Thai for "rattan ball".

The earliest historical records in Malaysia occur in the *Sejarah Melayu* ("Malay Annals") as played in the 15th century Malacca Sultanate. It details the incident of Raja Muhammad, a son of Sultan Mansur Shah who was accidentally hit with a rattan ball by Tun Besar, a son of Tun Perak (the Prime Minister), in a Sepak raga game. The ball hit Raja Muhammad's headgear and knocked it down to the ground. In anger, Raja Muhammad immediately stabbed and killed Tun Besar, whereupon some of Tun Besar's kinsmen retaliated and wanted to kill Raja Muhammad. However, Tun Perak managed to restrain them from such an act of treason by saying that he would no longer accept Raja Muhammad as the Sultan's heir. As a result of this incident, Sultan Mansur Shah ordered his son out of Malacca and had him installed as the ruler of outlying Pahang.

International play is now governed by ISTAF, the International Sepak Takraw Federation. Major competitions for the sport such as the ISTAF SuperSeries, the ISTAF World Cup and the King's Cup World Championships are held every year.Sepak takraw is now a regular sport event in the Asian Games and the Southeast Asian Games, in which Thailand has won the most medals.

Sepak takraw sport is played on a court similar to a badminton doubles court. Area of 13.4 by 6.1 metres (44 ft × 20 ft) free from all obstacles. Sand and grass court not advisable. The width of the lines bounding the court should not be more than 4 centimetres (1.6 in) measured and drawn inwards from the edge of the court measurements. All the boundary lines should be drawn at least 3.0 metres (9.8 ft) away from all obstacles. The centre line of 2 cm (0.79 in) should be drawn equally dividing the right and left court. The net is similar to badminton's.

A match is played by two teams called 'regu', each consisting of three players. On some occasions, it can be played by only two players (doubles) or four players (quadrant) per team.

One of the players shall be at the back; he/she is called a "Tekong" or also known as the "Server". The other two players shall be at the net, one on the left and the other on the right. The player on the right is called a "feeder/setter/tosser" and the player on the left is called a "attacker/striker/killer". The feeder tosses the ball in a low arc to the tekong's foot, who lifts the ball towards the net, whereupon the killer executes a kind of bicycle kick (aka scissor kick, overhead kick). It is supposed to stun the opposition with its force and sneaky stealth. The opposition is on to your schemes and its killer waits at the net with his own back flip. And so the back and forth goes on till the ball hits the court, or goes off it, like in volleyball. A far cry from solo footbag.

Sadu Gudu, as we played in childhood, is now officially Kabaddi. There is even a thought that kabaddi itself may have a Tamil origin, namely *kai pidi* or Kai (hand) + pidi (hold). It is a contact team sport, a mix of tag and wrestling. Played between two teams of seven players on opposite courts, the objective of the game is for a single player on offence, referred to as a "raider", to run into the opposing team's half of a court, tag out as many of their defenders as possible, and return "home" to his own half of the court, all without being tackled by the defenders. Like a deep sea diver seeking pearls, the raider has to finish his mission in a single breath. Lose your breath, lose your play and sit it out. To satisfy the referee that you are on the single breath, you are required to chant "kabaddi, kabaddi", "sadu gudu, sadu gudu", or some other phrase. It is obviously difficult to steal a second breath. Reminds me of a caregiver administering pills to a delinquent resident. She makes conversation during the process. You just can't hide the pill under your tongue while having to talk, hee heeee!

The team being "raided" hold hands to form a chain to encircle and ambush the intruder. You attack the fringes and if tackled, struggle home even if you barely touch your boundary. Points are scored for each player tagged by the raider, while the opposing team earns a point for capturing the raider. Players are taken out of the game if they are tagged or tackled, but are brought back in for each point scored by their team from a tag or tackle.

If Sepak Takraw has South East Asian nativity, Kabaddi has a South Asian habitat. It is played in India, Pakistan, Sri Lanka, Bangladesh, Nepal and Maldives.

In the international team version of kabaddi, two teams of seven members each occupy opposite halves of a court of 10 by 13 metres (33 ft × 43 ft) for men, and 8 by 12 metres (26 ft × 39 ft) for women. Each has five substitutes. The game is played with 20-minute halves with a 5-minute half break in which the teams exchange sides.

Wushu, or Chinese Kungfu, is a hard and soft and complete martial art, as well as a full-contact sport. It has a long history in Chinese martial arts. It was developed in 1949 in an effort to standardize the practice of traditional Chinese martial arts, yet attempts to structure the various decentralized martial arts traditions date back earlier, when the Central Guoshu Institute was established at Nanking in 1928.

"Wushu" is the Chinese term for "martial arts" (武 "Wu" = military or martial, 術 "Shu" = art). In contemporary times, Wushu has become an international sport under the International Wushu Federation (IWUF), which holds the World Wushu Championships every two years. Wushu has become an official event at the Asian Games, Southeast Asian Games, and the World Combat Games among other multi-sport events.

Competitive Wushu is composed of two disciplines: *taolu*, which is a kind of individual, exhibition style and *sanda* sparring and actually resembles Thai kickboxing. But it has other disciplines, like self defense, breaking hard objects with fist, and other related practices, that are not performed in competitions. Aside from barehand combat, including the long fist, Tai

Chi Chuan, weapons are also used like swords (broad and straight) as well as cudgels and spears.

Board Games: Mahjong, Thaayam, Congkak

Mahjong is a Qing era table game that has internationalized. Though not exactly a board game, it is a tile game similar to dominoes, which in turn, is traceable to the Song dynasty of China. It is commonly played by four players and is akin to rummy, the western card game, requiring strategy and serendipity.

"The game is played with a set of 144 tiles based on Chinese characters and symbols, and each player begins with 13 tiles. In turns, players draw and discard tiles until they complete a legal hand using the 14th drawn tile to form four melds (or sets) and a pair (eye). A player can also win with a small class of special hands. There are fairly standard rules about how a piece is drawn, how a piece is robbed from another player, the use of suits (numbered tiles) and Honors (winds and dragons), the kinds of melds allowed, how to deal the tiles and the order of play. Despite these similarities, there are many regional variations to the rules including rather different scoring systems, criteria for legal winning hands, and even private table rules which distinguish some variations as notably different styles of mahjong."

In Chinese, the game was originally called 麻雀 (pinyin: máquè)—meaning sparrow—which is still used in some languages in southern China. It is said that the clacking of tiles during shuffling resembles the chattering of sparrows. Suffice to say that that it can take whole book to explain the intricacies.

Chinese checkers is a board game that is not even Chinese! It belongs to Germany, where it is called *Sternhalma*. *Stern* ("star") refers to the star shaped board.

Thaayam or dhaayam, is a Tamil game that is comparable to the North Indian pachisi. It is a lesser known board game compared to its more famous India export, chess or sathurangam. The thaayakattam or board can be standard chessboard size, or drawn on the floor with chalk or charcoal. The thaayakattam is of 3 concentric squares (7x7, 5x5, and 3x3) for a total of 83 squares (Chess has 64). The central square is called *manai*, or home. Interspersed around the perimeter, certain squares are marked with an X called *malai*, or "hill" which are safe zones where you cannot be kicked out by a pursuing opponent. The clear squares are the risk areas where collisions happen and chips get run over.

Thaayakattai, or a pair of elongated 4-sided metal dice. The sides have from zero to 3 indentations, making a maximum number of 6 advances per throw.

4 players can play at one time, and each will enter from the middle peripheral square on their side. The basic rule of this game of chance is to get a zero on the dice throw to get a chance to begin. Proceed to complete the outer perimeter before attempting to move in to the inner perimeters and on to home. Each player, with his own coloured set of 6 chips or *kaai* ("unripe fruit") must herd it all to the manai where it becomes *palam* ("ripe fruit"). The first to complete the process is the winner. One who loses all his kaai will have start over again. Naturally, there are further rules and complexities that enhance the thrill factor.

"Congkak is a popular game of logic played throughout Asia, Africa and the Americas, with many adaptations. Known elsewhere as mancala, the version commonly played in the Malay Archipelago requires two players to share a wooden board with one row of seven holes along each side, and one bigger hole at either end. The two rows of seven holes are designated as "houses" in the "village" (kampong) while the last two larger holes serve as "storehouses", although there are variations. Seeds are placed in each hole, and then redistributed according to the rules of the game. The objective is to gain as many seeds in one's storehouse as possible. A popular game in the past, the attractiveness of congkak began declining in the 1980s as Singapore became more urbanised." – extract

"The game is believed to have originated from the Middle East, where it was known as mancala (Arabic for "move") in Arabia. The earliest discovery of the board game was made in Jordan, dating between 7,000 BC and 5,000 BC. The game was probably brought by Arab or African traders travelling to China and beyond on their trade travels. The game is believed to have spread throughout Southeast Asia, similarly through merchants via the trading post of Malacca. The game became popular among the wider population, particularly among Malays and Peranakans

or Straits-born Chinese. There are thus unique Malay terms for the rules of the game." – quote. The game is known as *pallaangkuzhi* or (pathinaalaam kuzhi – "fourteeth pit") in Tamil. It is a game from Chola times, whose merchants were here some milleniums ago.

Ethnic Games: Kavanda Kavandi, pīng pāng qiú, Gasing

How many scores of childrens' games have become extinct due to modernization and shrinking public spaces! With children confined to rooms and friendless, electronic games are their sole entertainment. Pastimes like kite flying, marbles, hopscotch and 'police and thief' needed open space. And the equipment were simple, or none, without need for electrical plug-ins.

Kavanda-kavandi (kaunda kaundi) was a childrens' game till the sixties, of unkown etymology. It was played with a foot long stick with which to hit a shorter, 4 inch stick, like a cricket ball. Accompanied by a meaningless sing-song phrase, *"kavanda – kavandi kavandikku lavandi"*, its exact rules are lost. I remember that a little hole was scratched in the ground and the shorter piece placed across it. It was flipped as far as possible, with the longer stick. Like in cricket, the opposing team had to catch the airborne little stick and throw it back at the hole. Failing to catch meant that the other team would continue hit it further afield. When it finally manages to catch it, the opposing team would then have to return the stick to the starting point while singing the above tune, "kavanda kavandi kavandikkku lavandi." In the absence of any specific ethnic origin to the sport, the "Tamil-ness" of the phrase, as we played it, would probably make it Indian.

Chinese folk games are not to be found in Malaysia, at least not in these modern times. Hence it would be fun to describe a game or two that the Chinese love and dominate in, but cannot claim as theirs. *"Although the game (yǔ máo qiú) may have originally developed among expatriate officers in British India, where it was very popular by the 1870s, yet China regularly takes home the gold in badminton during the Olympic Games. It is often played casually in the park or in local or national competitions. Casual badminton players have no problem playing outside, but more serious players prefer to play inside to avoid possible disruptions by the wind."*

"In the 1930s, Edgar Snow commented in Red Star Over China that the Communist forces in the Chinese Civil War had a "passion for the English game of table tennis" which he found "bizarre". Probably, this sport doesn't need much introduction. Not only is pīng pang a national sport of China, but it is also fairly cheap in terms of setup and supplies. You don't need to construct or pave a court. The tables used in ping pong are portable, and they can fold up to save space. Ping pong is the most played recreational sport in China, with over 300 million players."

Boy, talk about not claiming it, but owning it!

While kite flying and top spinning are simple and universal enough pastimes, the Malays have turned it into an art form. The *Wau Bulan* ("moon kite") is an elaborately built big bird in the sky, complete with sound effects made by a built-in vibrating bamboo sliver.

Likewise, top spinning, has graduated from a kid to an adult game. "Giant top spinning is no child's game! Each gasing or top weighs approximately 5kg and the wooden tops are as big as the size of a dinner plate. It calls for strength, coordination, and skill. The gasing, if expertly hurled, can spin for as long as 2 hours. Top spinning competitions are an annual feature in the east coast of Peninsular Malaysia especially Kelantan and Terengganu."

The winner is determined by the length of time it takes till the top's tilt, wobble, and final topple. Whereas adult top spinning has survived as a cultural and tourist exhibit, regular tops have bitten the dust of modernity. Requiem.

Word Games: Berpantun, Paatukku Paatu, ...

Call – response games are usually of a verbal nature, including exchanges of poetry, song lyrics, drums, etc

Main pantun (poetry play) is a type of call and response in traditional Malay society, probably from the time of the Malacca Sultanate – which explains why Baba-Nyonya are/were also great practioners of it. Pantun is a poetic quartrain, with the top two lines being *pembayang* (precursor) and the bottom two, *maksud* (crux). An example follows: Excuse the amateur translate!

Jual ("Sell")

Panas-panas makan semangka
Makin segar jika ditambahkan gula
Apabila engkau tahu jawabnya
Binatang apa yang ekornya ada dikepala?

Beli ("Buy")

Daun jambu tertiup melambai
Jatuh tertimbun bagai sampah
Ekor itu saperti belalai
Belalai milik si hewan gajah

Translation:

Call

Watermelon eaten in hot weather
Fresher yet with sugar added
When you do know the answer
What animal has tail on its head?

Response

Guava leaves in wind billows
like a thrash heap a'fallen
The tail a trunk mirrors
Belongeth to the elephant

When professional bards go at each other with this style of entertainment, you definitely feel the artistry, romance, humour and class. It was in the realm of the upper class, and has now been relegated to the performing stage. In a romantic type of call-response, it is between a male and female in a sing-song courting format, praising the partner's beauty, and virtue.

In the 60's and 70's radio and live performances and S.M Salim and

Paatukku-paatu ("song for a song"), is a latter day tamil brain game similar to the hindi *antakshari* ("last letter"). It is a parlour game, or road trip entertainment, where two teams or two people try to come up with popular song phrases. When the first person stops a line of song at any point, the next person will have to come up with another song beginning with the first letter of the last word. Lets try one.

A: "By the the rivers of Babylon, where we sat down ...."   (Boney M)
B: Daddy doesn't pray anymore
     I guess he's finished talking to the Lord
     He used to fold his hands and bow his head down to the floor
     But daddy doesn't pray anymore   (Chris Stapleton)

The other team should sing a song beginning with "A", and so on. Hours could be spent in such activity.

Although an ecquivalent activity is yet to be found in Chinese culture, the Baba-Nonya (A Chinese people) have a history of excelling in the Malay tradition of berpantun. Shaped by Chinese folktales and unique legendary characters, they gave rise to a unique Sino-Malay literature.

There exists a database of 11,204 pantun, syair and dondang sayang written by babas over 100

Years. However, the practice of spontaneous, extemporaneous, impromptu delivery of the pantun and dondang saying has slowed, except for literary programs organized by Baba associations in Penang, Malacca and Singapore.

Open House: Hari Raya Puasa, Chinese New Year, Deepavali, Wesak Day

The festivals celebrated in Malaysia are generally religious, with the exception of Chinese New Year (CNY), Gawai/Keamatan, and Ponggal, which are cultural or agricultural related. Hari Raya Puasa, "The high feast of the fast" – celebrates the end of the month long fast during Ramadhan. Deepavali – "The way of light" – commorates the defeat of the demon Narakasura by the lord Krishna.

These festivals are observed exclusively by the respective ethnic or religious groups. However all races come together to enjoy the holiday in a queer arrangement called the "Open House". While the main celebrant plays host, their "non" friends are expected to drop in on the party in a, "come and go" basis. There is usually a time-frame such as, "day one, from 12.00 noon to 5.00 PM". Very often, no invitation is extended, as invitations are insinuated by the term, Open House. Foreign tourists walking into such a home, are appreciated and warmly feted. No questions asked. This must be the only place anywhere one can do it without feeling like a gate crasher. The above scenario is largely history now. The only "open house" happens when friends and office mates are invited – you don't crash anymore – and during staged shindigs set by political parties.

Festivals such as Hari Raya, CNY, Christmas, Deepavali, Vesak etc, are the high points in the

celebratory calendar of the respective groups. As such, they are accorded public holiday status. That, is reason enough for celebration all round. And what better way to frolic in the fiesta, than to flock to your friends' homes for free food, fine fellowship, and fabulous fun. The fantastic fun is usually the domain of the children, who receive bright red *Ang Pow* packets (little envelopes with money) from the elders. What began as a Chinese custom, is now practiced by everybody else. Muslims are giving out green packets on Hari Raya Puasa. Hindus may get saffron packets. Christians, of course, exchange gifts under the Christmas tree.

Ang Pow ("Red Packet"), are a sign of good luck. The notes inside are usually the red 10 ringgit ones. Mandarin oranges, symbolizing gold are also handed out. The focus is so much on financial prosperity, that the celebrants don't sweep the house for a week. The adults don't really believe it (the thing about good luck, etc.). Everyone just goes along with the pretense, just for fun, and for the sake of it. It is similar to Santa Claus at Christmas time, when adults put on santa suits, and a show, for the benefit of children.

With the exception of perhaps Hari Wesak, most of our major festivals seem to have become highly commercialized. The days leading to Hari Raya see retailers jostling for customers with new banners and sales events. Small time vendors selling sweetmeats and savories for buka puasa (opening of fast) do their best sales of the year. Deepavali too, has become detracted from its spiritual focus, to the physical. Big city Little Indias drown in colour and clamour. Car parks (KL Sentral) and road pavements sprout stalls of all kinds. Chinese New Year is the time you see red. Red banners, buntings, and beach balls hang from walls and in malls. All this deviation from the spiritual focus to the physical owes, perhaps, to Christmas celebrations – the mother of festive flatulence. It is all about satisfying physical wants. "All I want for Christmas is my ...." Somewhere in the clamour, a hoarse voice croaks, "Christ is the reason for the season." Or, not the debauchery of overindulgence.

Since visitors will be expected, the homes are spring cleaned and spruced up with new coats of paint and colourful buntings, drapings, hangings and floorings. Also part of the logistics is a whole lot of baking, cooking and storing for the big day. Ironically, they don't sweep the house from the first day of CNY until Chap Goh May, 2 weeks later! Neither do they take out the garbage, cut hair, use knives, break things, wash clothes. In extreme cases, they don't shower. The operating principle is, you don't want to sweep out, or throw out lady luck along with the bath water. Or is it, throw out the baby along with the thrash? Lady luck along with the trash.

In House: Moon cake, Kartikai Theebam, Gawai Dayak

You need some strictly all in the family celebration too. So, there are festivals that you celebrate behind closed doors, in the privacy of your home. These are the festivals that are low key and don't get national holiday status. You don't even take out an annual leave for it. Do it in the evening, after coming back from work.

The Chinese moon cake (Mid Autumn) festival is one such family affair. Well, not quite. You do get a moon cake from the celebrant friend. A month before the festival, shopping outlets put out those sweet delights in various flavours. The filling is almost always bean or pumpkin seed paste. What is a moon cake and what is the festival about, anyway?

"The festival is held on the 15th day of the 8th month of the Chinese lunisolar calendar with a full moon at night, corresponding to mid-September to early October of the Gregorian calendar. On this day, the Chinese believe that the Moon is at its brightest and fullest size, coinciding with harvest time in the middle of Autumn. (Harvest Moon?).

The festival was a time to enjoy the successful reaping of rice and wheat with food offerings made in honor of the moon. Today, it is still an occasion for outdoor reunions among friends and relatives to eat mooncakes and watch the Moon, a symbol of harmony and unity. During a year of a solar eclipse, it is typical for governmental offices, banks, and schools to close extra days in order to enjoy the extended celestial celebration an eclipse brings. The festival is celebrated with many cultural or regional customs, among them." Wiki

"The Kartikai month starts on the day of Deepavali. From that day till the end of the month, oil lamps are lit every day. On *Karthikai Pournami* (full moon of Karthikai month) oil lamp with 365 wicks, prepared at home, are lit in Lord Shiva temples. Apart from that, on Kartikai Pournami fasting is observed till sunset, every day for the whole month.

Rows of *agal vilakku* (clay oil lamps) are lit in every house. Karthigai is essentially a festival of lamps. The lighted lamp is considered an auspicious symbol. It is believed to ward off evil forces and usher in prosperity and joy. While the lighted lamp is important for all Hindu rituals and festivals, it is indispensable for Karthigai. This festival is also celebrated to commemorate the bonding between brothers and sisters in south India (analogous to the North Indian Bhaiya-Dhuj and Raakhi). Sisters pray for the prosperity and success of their brothers and light lamps to mark the occasion." – Wiki

In the Islamic the calender, festivals are generally of the public kind, i.e. mosque, mecca, or mass gathering based. The Gawai festival of the Dayaks (Ibans, Bidayuh et al.) of Sarawak can be a good candidate for this section. Eventhough, it involves the whole longhouse (virtually a village of 30 to 130 families), it is nevertheless, a "house" satisfying the title of this piece.

"According to Agas, this is when each family in the longhouse will reveal their own "family *tuak*", brewed to be as strong as possible.

The whole village will line up at one end of the longhouse and make their way down, visiting each home (apartment). At each home, there will be a representative from the family to pour out their family's *tuak* recipe for everyone who stops by.

Since a longhouse can house anywhere from 30 to 150 families (virtually a village) depending on its size, if you join the line you'd be drinking that many sips of *tuak* all through the night– and straight on 'til morning! Of course, there has to be a free flow of food to match the free flow of drinks too. In fact, according to Agas, the food will be hosted by the community in a pot-luck fashion, so party-goers can eat whenever they want to." – Anne Dorall, May 29, 2021. TRP

Gawai and Keamatan, the Sabah version of the same, is a harvest festival, both falling on the dead centre of the year. Gawai is enlivened by traditional music and dance, the Ngajat.

Processions: Thaipusam, Chingay, Awal Muharram,

There are open house celebrations and there "closed house" ones. If the open house festivals discussed above are cause célèbre for everyone, and closed ones are family affairs. A third category is a mix of both. You may not be an active participant in it, but can witness and ogle at the public dispay of religion. The above festivals consist of processions long and short, from the half kilometer march from a park to mosque, to the 11 km parade from the Sri Maha Mariamman temple in downtown Kl to the Batu Caves shrine.

While Muslim, Christian, and even the Sikh faith have a tradition of corporate (communal) worship, Hindu and Taoist worship is almost entirely individual. That is to say, the devotee comes to the temple and has personal contact with the deity. Very little social element is present. However, when it comes to the festival procession kind of worship they do it with a bang, literally. Clanging of cymbals and banging of drums, add to the crush of thousands and even millions as in the case of the Batu Caves Thaipusam. The Chinese Hungry Ghosts festival is a spectacle of opera, decorated stalls with food for the ghosts, etc. even so, it is still a personal and individual walk of faith, rather than congregation. There is not co-ordinated schedule of activity. You go and come at your own pace. Someone has observed that it is the loneliest feeling to be in a crowd, especially when you are not socializing with the others.

Awal Muharram, or Maal Hijrah marks the first day of the Muslim calendar when Prophet Muhammad migrated from Mecca to Medina to escape persecution. In other words, it is the Muslim new year. Processions are organized on a national scale in the capital to recall that great hijrah, or exodus. In Muslim minds, that depicts a paradigm shift from bondage to freedom. Also from sinfulness to worthiness.

While the Maal Hijrah procession is quiet and straightforward enough, accept for perhaps some nasyid chorusing, both Thaipusam and Chingay recall *Mardigras* elsewhere in terms of colourful fabrications, cantankerous music, and ….. theatrics.

Thaipusam commemorates Lord Murugan's destruction of the evil demon, Soorapadman. Every year, thousands of visitors and devotees throng to witness this spectacle of epic proportions. In a show of faith and devotion, Hindus (including quite a few Chinese and foreigner caucasians) in a trance carry magnificent kavadis that are anchored into their bodies with hooks or balance pots of milk carried on heads as offerings to Lord Murugan.

The kavadi represents the weight of sin.. types ans designs

The three-day event includes a silver chariot procession where the statue of Lord Murugan makes its way from a temple in the George Town heritage enclave of Penang to a hilltop temple in Waterfall Road. As the chariot passes the streets, devotees smash coconuts as offerings and to give thanks to the deity. The KL – Batu Cave procession is the longest (11 km) and biggest convergence of devotees (1 million at last count).

The festival falls on the full moon in the Tamil month of *Thai* (January/February), usually coinciding with the *Poosam* star. The day after Murugan arrives at the destination temple, like Batu Caves, devotees carrying Kavadis ascend the 272 steps to get his darshan (blessings).

Chingay began in Penang in the late 18th century as a Chinese street procession with floats and street performers to honour the deities and welcome in Spring. Today, Chingay is largely associated with a procession of giant flags on bamboo poles measuring up to 20 feet tall, skillfully balanced and transferred on the foreheads, chests and shoulders of Chingay exponents – a veritable circus act. Picture a pro footballer executing an exhibition of soccer foot and headwork. Johore Bahru is the other centre of Chingay display.

It is a Taoist thing, celebrating their gods. Chingay, from Mandarin *zhenyi*, meaning "true art" is awash in red in banners, lanterns and t-shirts. Floats carrying deities, people dressed as Chinese deities, and dragon acts form part of the parade.

The Lantern (*Tangling*) festival is something that was prominent in the sixties. With young folk carrying animal shaped lanterns hanging from bamboo poles, it very much reminds one of the Trick or Treating during Halloween in the US. Both events are chiefly childrens' processions in the neighbourhood, both are conducted at night, and both are supervised by adults. It happens in the time of Chap Goh May? Lanterns in the shape of fish, duck, rabbit etc are formed of bamboo frames and wrapped in colourful ..... paper. A candle placed inside the lantern brightens it against the night, reminding you very much of the candle-lit Hallowen pumpkin face.

As for the Catholic church, they do have solemn night processions around the cathedral on Palm Sunday (Easter week) – recalling Jesus' symbolic entry into Jerusalem as the Messiah. The devotees carry and wave palm fonds or makeshift crosses made of coconut frond. A completely opposite, anti-spiritual procession occurs just before Easter season in catholic majority places like Baton Rouge, Lousiana, Haiti and Brazil, that has raucous music, colourful apparel and suggestively dressed women romping on the streets. Why would anyone engage in such undecorous acts, just before a holy season? Someone has ventured to say that, they let loose because *Lent* (40 days of Easter) was a period of utmost chastity, non meat fasting and prayer). In neighbouring Phillipines, you sometimes hear of someone being raised on a cross. Again, Mardigras (French for "Fat Tuesday") only happens in certain parts of the world.

Sleepless in Spiritual: Lailatul Qadar, Vaikunda Ekadasi, Midnight Mass

Lailatul Qadar or "malam seribu bulan", or "night equivalent to a thousand months". It is staying up late reciting certain verses and in prayer, based on the following verse of the Quran.

"We have sent it [the Quran] down in the Night of Qadr. And what may let you know what the Night of Qadr is? The Night of Qadr is much better than one thousand months. The angels and the Spirit descend in it, with the leave of your Lord, along with every command. Peace it is till the debut of dawn" (Q. 97).

"Laylatul Qadr, often translated as the Night of Power, or Night of Decree, or Night of Glory falls in one of the last ten nights of the month of Ramadan. This is the night in which God began the revelation of the Quran. Worship done in this single night is equivalent to 84 years—basically, a lifetime—of worship outside this night. It has the potential, when approached with sincerity, to gain a person grand forgiveness and mercy from God. One narration says, "Whoever prays on Laylatul Qadr out of faith and sincerity, shall have all their past sins forgiven"[Bukhari and Muslim].

Today, many Muslims spend these nights in the mosque where there are programs dedicated to foster an extra spiritual environment. Some take off days from work to ensure they can stay up all night without having to worry about their jobs. After the Taraweeh prayers, the imams will give a talk encouraging Muslims to tie their belts and hit the ground running in these final days. It is very possible a lot of people feel burnt out toward the end of the month, but this is the time that matters most! The boost is needed from the scholars of the community to ensure people exit the month on a high note." – Wiki

Ekadashi is the 11 th day after the full moon and the 11th day after the new moon.

Vaikunta Ekadashi is a special Ekādaśī, observed on the 11th lunar day of the waxing lunar fortnight of the solar month of Marghazhi. This falls between 16 December and 13 January in the English calendar.

"The Vaishnava (Vishnu devotees) sect believes that 'Vaikunta Dwaram' or 'the gate to the Lord's Inner Sanctum' is opened on this day. Special prayers from Vedas, Divya Prabhandham, Sri Vaikuntha Gadhyam (sometimes additional Gadhyams by Ramanuja are also chanted).

Vaikuntha is the *Supreme Abode* of God Vishnu and called, *the place of non-hindrance*. Mortals find it in the feet of God Vishnu as *Vishnupada*, or *Parama Padam*, as it is a place for God Vishnu and his devotees to reside in the *suddha-sattva*, or the supreme state of purity and goodness.

According to the Vishnu Purana, fasting on Vaikuntha Ekadashi is equivalent to fasting on the remaining 23 Ekadashis of the (Hindu) year. However, according to Vaishnava tradition fasting is mandatory on all Ekadashis of both Shukla paksha and Krishna paksha. Fasting on Ekadashi is considered holier than any other religious observation. Complete Fasting has to be observed on Ekadashi, the 11th day of the Paksha. 1 Paksha = 15 days, One month (maasa) has 2 pakshas in Hindu Lunar Calendar.) That is why the meal on Dwadashi (12th Day) is designed to be wholesome, nutritious, and filling." – wiki

My only understanding of Ekadasi was sitting in a cinema hall, watching 2 back to back matinees with my hindu friends. How's that for keeping awake on that night?

Staying up late also happens in the catholic church. They follow the big Christmas Eve mass is traditionally live telecast from the Vatican and Bethlehem, the actual venue. Locally, catholics around Sentul would walk in the cool night breeze to worship at the St. Joseph's church. The parishioners spilled over into the compound, and the nons who came to gawk would walk around and ogle at the girls. Both the Ekadashi and midnight mass episodes were my personal experiences in the mid sixties of the last century. I am unsure if the same thing happens now, in the 20s of the current century.

Late night worship (Watchnight Service) also happens among the so-called "high churches" like the Catholic, Lutheran and Methodists on New year's eve. The other Christians, and non-celebrants wake up for other reasons, like the year end midnight countdown and the ball drop in New York.

While African Americans (Aframericans?) do observe watchnight services, theirs has gained extra significance, as they had gathered in churches for the expected emancipation proclamation by President Abraham Lincoln at zero hour on the 1st of January 1862. On top of welcoming the new year, they also got to welcome the new freedom. Yayy!

Sacrifice: Muneeswaran, Jingxiang, Hari Raya Korban

According to the Chinese custom, the first day of the tenth lunar month is the Ancestors' Sacrifice Festival.

In order to show their loyalty and respect, since ancient times people have been holding ceremonies to offer sacrifices, usually grains, to their ancestors after harvest. Sacrificial ceremonies may be held at home or in front of tombs. Such a custom is widely accepted both in the north and in the south. Up to now, it is still practiced in many parts south of the Yangtze River.

As the first day of the tenth lunar month is the very beginning of winter when the weather begins to become cold, paper clothes are among the most important necessities together with food, paper money and candles on sacrifical ceremonies. They are afraid that their ancestors do not have enough clothes. On the ceremony, they burn paper clothes to send them to their beloved ones. In this case, the Ancestors' Sacrifice Festival is also known as the "Clothes-burning Festival".

Note: Taoism forbids food and animal sacrifices to god's, and incence, images and bank notes are considered as a form of sacrifice.

Hari Raya Korban or Aidil Adha marks the end of the Haj pilgrimage period made every year by millions of Muslims to the Holy Land of Mecca. Performing the haj is one of the five tenets of the religion which every Muslim should attempt to perform at least once, as long as they have the means to do so, and are in good health.

The day honours the commitment made by Abraham who was ready to sacrifice his only son when commanded to do so by God. At the crucial moment God spared Abraham's son and revealed to him that he was testing his faith (a ram was sacrificed in little Ishmael's place.

Animal sacrifices, especially cattle, are done at mosques and suraus and the meat distributed to the poor. The Tamil muslims sacrifice camels (?) in Tami Nadu. They are specially brought down from Rajasthan state.

The agamic sects of Hinduism (Shaivism, Vaisnavism, Kaumaram etc) do not have the practice of sacrifice, be it animal or otherwise. The folk denominations, such as Muneeswaran, Ayyanar worship etc do have animal sacrifices. Male goats are sacrificed (*Kadaa Bali)* to muneeswraran as well as chicken, and community cooked for common meals. Muneesaran presents as a stern, brawny deity who acts as the village guardian. He is depicted holding an aruvaal (machete) and smoking a cheroot. A more popular deity (just as stern and protective) is the mother goddess, Mariamman. She too gets goats and chicken, though they are no more being sacrificedin her temples.

Temple Festivals: Kovil Thiruvila, Feasts of Patron Saints.

Kovil Tiruvila, or "Holy festival of the temple", is the festival dedicated to the presiding deity of the temple. They are restricted to the particular temple of the area. Although, certain festivals are of a national holiday type. The Thaipusam celebrations at Batu Caves, is an approximation, on a bigger scale, of a village temple festival. In the old country of Tamil Nadu, the village temple festival is the highlight of the calendar year, with the deity taken around in processions. But, it is not so much worship, as it is fun fairs and games, open air concerts and fireworks. It is the excuse to *"balik kampong",* or visit the village, and draws visitors from other villages too. It attracts a lot of hawkers and gawkers (tourists i.e) as well. *Avul* and *Vellam* (puffed rice and unrefined cane/palm sugar) are special snacks associated with these festivals.

In Malaysia, there doesn't seem to be much of such. There used to be grand festivals when there used to be estates. That is, before the migration of estate Indians to the towns. I vividly remember, as a very young 'un, the *Pangguni Utthiram* festival in my estate, Bukit Badong

Estate, care of Golden Hope Plantations Ltd. I didn't understand then, what it was all about, and who the the deity was. I still don't. My father, the estate school headmaster's house was situated away from the labour lines, near the manager's bungalow. But, I could discern the sound of throbbing drums and the preparations from afar. I could feel a tangible sense of gaiety and gala, camaraderie and carefree. On the day of the procession, we children would lurk behind bushes near the school, both anxious and curious, as the procession of the deity finally began afar off. There was a whole lot of drumming and shouting. As the troupe neared, led by men in a hopping frenzy with spokes through their cheeks and *aruval* (parang/machete) in hand, we would scurry (scamper off in a hurry) to hide behind our parents. That evening, we would we would be treated to an open air, black and white MGR or Sivaji Ganesan Movie. The historical, *raja – rani* films are especially memorable. I preferred to sit on the grass outside with my friends, while my parents had first class seats (stools) inside Mr. Matthew's sundry shop. My favourite experiment was to inspect the movie images on both sides of the screen, to see if they were exactly alike. It was, except that it was like a mirror. On the other side of the screen, the hero held the sword with the other hand. Some years, there would also be concerts, with skits and, song and dance, by local talent.

St Anne's feast, Bukit Mertajam and St.Anne's in Port Klang are examples of area code specific celebrations for the catholics. Each parish church named after a "patron" saint, will have a parade and mass on that particular saint's "day". Like the Hindu presiding deity (moolavar) festival, this is a one day, annual event.

Although there are mosques named after the prophet, his companions, and caliph's etc there is no festival dedicated to them, other than the regular universal schedule of events.

Likewise, Taoist temples conduct special festivals on a grand scale but not specific to that temple. It may be a festival that is generally or generically celebrated everywhere. The Nine angels festival – 9 days of festivities – stictly vegetarian – bazaar like stalls etc. Nine days? Recalls the Hindu Navarathri ("nine nights") in honour of goddess Durga. Falling twice a year, the latter date in the month of Ashwini (September-October) and coincides with the Nine Emperor Gods Festival of Taoism. The above mentioned temple is in Teluk Pulai, Klang, opposite the Komuter station of that name.

Without saying, all Buddhist viharas celebrate Buddha and his teaching, nothing temple specific – duhh!

Festivals of Fire and Water: Songkran, Nanneeratu, Mandi Safar, Lianhou

Water seems to be an integral part of the culture of Malaysians. Aside from the pre-worship washing rituals of Wuduk, Snaanam etc, there is a cultural component to it. The Malays have Mandi Safar

It is a thing, like the mak yong, Wayang kulit, joget, becoming a distant memory for Malaysians. *Temasya mandir safar* used to a beach party in some sections of the Malay community, especially in Melaka (Tg.Keling/ Tg. Beruas) and in Penang. It had an Islamic face to it although there is no koranic edict to practice it. Apparently the Arabs considered the Safar to be a month of bad karma, and that Allah would send quite a few misfortunes to earth during the month especially on the last Wednesday. Hence they (the Arabs) would vacate their homes on that day. Safar means "empty". The Malaysian fiesta however, is said to be pre-islamic, and obviously Hindu in origin. The Malays, especially those living by the river or sea, would group in knee deep water and splash water on top of each other and exchanging pantuns (quartrains). Mandi Safar continues comfortably on the cultural calendar of communities in the island of Borneo (including Tg.Aru in our own, Sabah), and other parts of Indonesia, where they are tourist atteactions.

"Mandi Safar is a Muslim bathing festival unique to Malaysia. This holiday, which is observed during the month of Safar, was originally believed to commemorate (Muhammad's cure from disease).. the last time Muhammad was able to bathe before his death. Muslims wearing bright colors visited beaches for a religious cleansing of the body and soul with water. There is no mention of the rite in the Qur'an (the Muslim holy book), and orthodox Muslims consider it nothing more than a picnic. It continues as a merry holiday. The best-known gathering places are the beaches of Tanjong Kling, near Malacca, and of Penang."
– www.tourismmalaysiausa.com

The Thais have a water festival where they splash H2O on each other, called Songkran. The Malaysian Thais in Kedah and Perlis, would subscribe to that.

The Hindus have a water festival called Nanneeratu (not in Malaysia) in Tamil nadu and Sri Lanka. Purpose – religious. The Hindu tamils of the islands of Mauritious and Reunion (French territory) have a twist on Thaipusam, where they gather on the beaches to celebrate. Matter of Fact, Mrs Reginald Sanders …. (18…) says that, "the Tamils would go the seaside at Thaipusam for seabath.

On a personal level, I witnessed several marriages as a kid in the 1960's where the day after, a *thombu* (tong) is filled with cool water mixed with turmeric paste. Every body and anybody would dip cupped hands and splash each other staining whites into yellows. Me included. Don't ask me why they did it. Someone says that turmeric is the ancient Dettol, a bacteria batterer. But what does that have to do with the day after the wedding? Before the splashing good time, the crowd gathered around the newlyweds, who stood on opposite sides of a narrow necked *sombu/ kudam* or brass pot. A ring would have been dropped into it. At the signal, the couple was supposed to "dive" into it and retrieve the ring. The winner was supposed to the "boss" in the family. The idea of was to provide fun for the onlookers, as the forearms of the young couple get stuck in the pot opening and the struggle that ensues. It was a kind of ice breaker for the newlyweds, before the first night that would follow. The groom usually "loses" not wanting to hurt his wife, or wanting to be the gentleman.

The annual Water Splashing Festival of the <u>Dai ethnic minority</u> falls during the New Year celebrations of the Dai Calendar. It is the most important festival observed by the Dai ethnic people of Xishuangbanna Prefecture, and, similar to neighboring Thailand's Songkran Festival, it involves three days of celebrations that include sincere, yet light-hearted religious rituals that invariably end in merrymaking, where everyone ends up getting splashed, sprayed or doused with water.

As for the fire element in worship, Hindus observe walking on hot coals during Amman festivals. Called *theemithi thiruvila* (firewalking festival) is observed by Tamils in India, Sri Lanka, Malaysia, Medan, Singapore,

South Africa and outposts like Fiji, Mauritius, Reunion and Guadalupe/St. Martinique. It also known by *poomithi* (walking on flowers). Youtube has a video of such a festival in Singapore, dated 1913. The motive for this is remembrance of Draupadi (Amman)'s proving her purity by fire in the Mahabaratha story.

A 16 foot long shallow/narrow trench is filled with glowing embers from a priorly burned bonfire. A goat might have been sacrificed at the pit. Under the gaze of idols brought in procession, devotees take turns to walk across, some carrying children and others bunches of neem leaves or swords. Drums beat constantly to the crowd's ceaseless chant of *Om Sakti, Om sakti, Om Sakti Om*. At the end of the trip the devotees step into a pit filled with milk.

Fire also burns constantly in the temple in the form of sweet smelling camphor.

Chinese temple worship includes burning of joss stick and joss paper, as well as oil lamps. Firewalking is a folk festival called *lianhou* in Xhejiang province in Eastern China. Like the others, this too, is to ward off evil. There is a video footage of men prancing across a fire trench in the Nine Emperor temple in Kuala Lumpur on October 25,1963. It is a rarity these days, but Chinese are said to participate in the Hindu fire walks.

Self – "torture": Self-flagellation, Azhagu Kavadi, Self-Crucifixion,

Is this a human reasoning about buying one's redemption, the thinking error that some self inflicted pain can cancel one's self committed stain. Or, could it be a stretching of the "no pain no gain" truism to the realm of religion. So you have committed a big boo-boo, lets clean the slate by some self-punishment. This just seems another version of penance or pradosham prescribed by priests. Worse, one could even buy one's forgiveness. From God's perspective, does that constitute true repentence? In psychology, the habit of "cutting" or gashing one's wrists apparently relieves the person's emotional pain. It is replacing one pain with another.

Maybe I am way off the mark here. Perhaps the self-inflicted pain, though religious in nature, is more a tradition and culture phenomenon? That would make it fine. Look at the lengths people go seemingly torturing themselves throwing and tossing rotten tomatoes towards each other leading to bloody looking torsos. No harm done.

Ashura, the Shiite festival commemorating Muhammad's grandson Hussain's martyrdom involves self-flagellation, as form of mourning. Since it happens on such large scales, perhaps mob psychology is also invoved. When everybody is doing it, it is somehow less painful and less self-conscious? Such mass self pain is also observed by certain Indian groups during Thaipusam or Amman festivals. Devotees carry kavadis – piercing their cheeks and backs wth skewers and hooks with no sign of pain. Trance and spiritual frenzy may be attributable. The Amman devotees also engage in firewalking on bare feet. Taoists also walk on embers, dipping hands in boiling oil, walking on a ladder of blades etc. The occasional Filipino also hoists himself up in self crucifixon during Lent.

Strong emotional bouts have seen the mind taking a leave of absence often leading to self – murders. Among the Tamil community of India, many a neophyte/follower had self-immolated at the death of his leader. The Sri Lankan Tamil Tigers were the pioneer suicide bom squad during the height of the civil war there. Al-Qaeda also appropriated it shortly therafter.

Well, you might run as far as you could, but once stopped by a wall, you will face the foe and fight back. Now, the fear is gone and the fight is on. Somehow you have that overwhelming will to wallop the enemy. What is the psychology? In one instance the person gives in and dies. In another, he turns around and fights. In another instance, he invites pain in the name of devotion to a deity or a cause.

Unlike the Shiites, the Malay, who is a Sunni muslim, has no such displays of despair. He just leaves everything in the hand of God as takdir, or will of God. At the end of the day, no amount of anguish or angst is going to change things. Que Sera Sera, whatever will be, will be. Krishna says in the Bhagavat Gita, "whatever has happened has happened for good. Whatever is happening is happening for good. Whatever will happen will happen for the good". That takes the onus away fro us.

Harvest Festival: Zhong Qui Jie, Thai Ponggal, Hari Gawai/Keamatan

In the days of yore, before vegetables sprouted in supermarket shelves and dairy milk came in cans and bottles, there was such a thing as communal farms. Harvests marked the end of the planting and growing season and were naturally celebrated with thanksgiving and gaiety. They were festive seasons then, and continue as such, to this day. Every one of Malaysia's ethnicities has an equivalent harvest event.

The August Moon Festival or the Mid-Autumn Festival or more commonly, the Moon Cake Festival is one of the most celebrated Chinese festivals. Mid Autumn Festival occurs on the 15th day of the 8th lunar month which is in September or early October in the Gregorian calendar, close to the autumnal equinox. Chinese have Moon Cakes during the festival. Friends and relatives send Moon cakes to each other as a way of giving and receiving. At this time, the moon is at its fullest and brightest which becomes an ideal time to celebrate the abundance of the summer's harvest. The Round moon cakes are baked and enjoyed, ornate lanterns are made and hung, and lovers are encouraged to come out of their homes and relax in the glow of the full moon. The moon is said to be brightest and most spherical on this day. Harvest Moon?

The August Moon festival (*Zhong Qui Jie*) is often recognized as the Women's festival. The moon symbolizes beauty and elegance and is also referred as a female principle and is a trusted friend.

Many ancient August Moon folktales are about a Moon Maiden. On the 15th night of the 8th lunar moon, little children on earth can see a lady on the Moon. And those who make wishes to the Lady on the Moon will find their dreams come true.

Mid-Autumn is a time for family, friends and loved ones to gather and enjoy the full moon that is a symbol of abundance, harmony and luck. Families enjoy picnics or special dinners. Along with the delicious moon cakes, children enjoy puppet shows and lantern processions.

Ponggal, is the archetypal or typical festival of the Tamil culture rather than religious. Each religionist might celebrate it in his own way, though. The Catholic celebrate 'The Three Wise Men' ponggal, after the characters in the Bible. The Muslims may celebrate their own version of ponggal in their privacy. Generally, there are three days of celebration, each dedicated to a significant matter to the farmer. The first day is *bhogi* – old household stuff are gathered outside and burnt. The second is, *veetu ponggal*, or house ponggal, where the actual ponggal boiling happens. The last one is the *maattu ponggal*, or cow ponggal where the cow is pampered. Cow ponggal happens in India and includes the spectacle of bull runs (*manju virattu*) and bull taming (*jallikattu*). Currency coins (*salli*) are tied (*kattu*) to the bulls' horns and youths are challenged to retrieve the money for themselves, by literally trying to take the bull by its horns. Unlike the Spanish spectacle, no bull is maimed or killed in this sport. Perhaps, the other way – participants might get killed by the bull. There is no such tradition among Malaysian Indians, as there are no village structures here for them. The closest thing to a village was the rubber estate, which is fast becoming a distant memory for most Indians. Besides, the estate was an artificial set-up, not a treasure trove of tradition. There is even a fourth ponggal called *kaanum ponggal* ("sightseeing ponggal") which is when families gather outside, like the beach or park.

Ponggal means, "boiling over" or the end product, "that which is boiled." In the old country, the entire village gathers, each family with its earthern pot, and boils freshly harvested rice in fresh milk, and freshly squeezed sugar cane juice. Nuts, lentils, raisins, and scraped coconut are added. A portion of the harvest (first fruits) would have been set aside for this purpose, before the continuing with the rest of the harvest. *Ponggal* signifies joy and hearts overflowing with thankgiving to the Almighty, at a good year's yield.

As the pots are laid out in a row on open fires, everybody watches in anticipation. There is a kind of tension, as an unspoken, unintended competition brews. Whose pot will be the first to boil over? As the pot or pots start to foam over the top, shouts of "Ponggolo Ponggal!" pierce the air. It could mean something like, "Oh Boy! What a Boil!" There are no prizes for the first pot to erupt, but everybody rejoices. Everybody shares their family pot's porridge with their neighbours.

The Bornean states of Sabah and Sarawak are the torch bearers for native bumiputra culture in Malaysia. *Kaamatan* Harvest Festival in Sabah (30th and 31st May) and *Gawai* Harvest Festival of Sarawak (1st and 2nd June) are like mirror images, including the dates.

Kaamatan is a Kadazan-Dusun term for "harvest" and is celebrated during the entire month of May. It is normally celebrated by the ethnic *Kadazan-Dusuns*, as well as by *Muruts* and *Rungus.* Whereas, the Gawai is celebrated by many different Sarawakian ethnic groups such as *Iban, Bidayuh, Kenyah, and Kelabit* (collectively known as *Dayak*).

The Raison D'etre for keamatan rests on *Kinoingan*, a god, who took pity on the people who were suffering from a great famine. In order to save them, he sacrificed his daughter, *Huminodun*, and sowed her over the land. The resulting padi crop was harvested and the people were saved. The spirit of Huminodun is embodied in the rice and is therefore known as *Bambarayon* or *Bambazon*.

The *Bobohizan* (high priestess) plays an important role in the festival, which consist of several ceremonies. These ceremonies include tying 7 stalks of rice together and placing them in a tadang or basket, and moving them into a rice hut. Each ceremony is important and ensures the farmers will be able to harvest again in the next planting season.The *Humabot* Ceremony is the closing ceremony, which happens on the last day of Kaamatan. It includes a variety of activities, entertainment, dances, food, and delicacies throughout the day.

From home-brewed rice wine called *tapai* and *lihing*, to local delicacies like *hinava* (raw fish marinated in lime and citrus), *bambangan* (a seasonal wild mango fruit) and *butod* (sago grub), it is a real feast. The Dayak version of the brew is called *tuak*, and is made by fermenting glutinous rice and homemade yeast. On Gawai eve, glutinous rice is roasted in bamboo known as *ngelulun pulut*, along with a multitude of traditional dishes such as *pansoh* manok, chicken and lemongrass cooked in a bamboo log over an open fire. Traditional treats are prepared from glutinous rice flour mixed with sugar, such as *sarang semut* (ant nest cake), *cuwan* (molded cake), *kui sepit* (twisted cake), and *penganan iri* (a discus-shaped cake).

Sumazau is the traditional folk dance of the Kadazan Dusun. The dance is inspired by an eagle in flight as observed by farmers in the field during harvest time. Similarly for the Dayaks, the main dance is the Ngajat, with its own eye-catching costumes.

New Year: Awal Muharram, Puththaandu, Chūnjié

As a year completes its course and the New Year reaches out to accept the baton, everyone is suddenly excited about the possibilities. As if every month, week, and day does not have possibilities. The DJ on the Radio asks you what the last year brought you and what you expect in the new one. You hear callers inevitably talk about how lucky it was or wasn't in the year that was, and how the new year promises so much. This is the time of year when we seem ripe for the picking by Feng Shui fraudsters and Vastu Shastra charlatans and their shenanigans, who will sell you on rearranging the furniture or reorienting this or that.

Spring Festival or the Lunar New Year (Chūnjié), is the festival that celebrates the beginning of a new year on the traditional lunisolar Chinese calendar. In Chinese culture and East Asian countries, the festival is commonly referred to as Spring Festival as the spring season in the lunisolar calendar traditionally starts with lichun, the first of the twenty-four solar terms which the festival celebrates around the time of the Lunar New Year. Marking the end of winter and the beginning of the spring season, observances traditionally take place from New Year's Eve, the evening preceding the first day of the year to the Lantern Festival, held on the 15th day of the year. The first day of Chinese New Year begins on the new moon that appears between 21 January and 20 February

After the English new year, CNY is is most widely known and widespread around the world. The eve of the New Year's Day is frequently regarded as an occasion for Chinese families to gather for the annual reunion dinner. It is also traditional for every family to thoroughly clean their house, in order to sweep away any ill-fortune and to make way for incoming good luck. The reverse happens after that, when floors are not to be swept until after the 15 days of celebration are over. You don't want to sweep away the luck. Another custom is the decoration of windows and doors with red paper-cuts and couplets. Popular themes among these paper-cuts and couplets include good fortune or happiness, wealth, and longevity. In Mandarin, "Happy Chinese New Year" is **"xin nian kuai le"**. In this part of the world, we are more familiar with the poetic, *Gong Xi Fa Cai* ("Wish you enlarge your wealth").

Other activities include lighting firecrackers and giving money in red paper envelopes. The obligatory Lion/Dragon dance performances during the festivities, is treated in the section on animated dance.

The habit of naming the years at CNY after animals is unique. The zodiac consists of 12 animals from the runty rat to the husky horsey. The habit of assigning the personalities of the creatures to humans born in that year is probably in jest, as is attributing the year's outlook to the animals characteristics. New Year 2021 was the year of the bull. There was a cock and bull tale of how the year was going to be financially bullish, but as it turned out it was more bullsh**, or as the American is wont to say, "baloney!" Continuing the rat year's Covid19 contagion, the bull year was a blooming disaster overall.

Awal Muharram or Maal Hijrah is an important day for Muslims, as it marks an important event that occurred in Islamic history, which is commemorating the migration of Prophet Muhammad from Makkah to Medina in 622 AD. It is a public holiday in Malaysia.

The Hijri Calendar did not officially begin during the Prophet's lifetime. This calendar only dates from the time of the second Caliph Arrasyidin, Saidina Umar al-Faruq. Muhammad's followers made several suggestions for the *Taarrikh* (date/chronology) for Medina at that time. Some suggested that the year of Islam begin from Prophet Muhammad's birth, some advocated his prophethood call, but the majority opinion was for the *Hijrah* (Flight to Medina).

Awal Muharram (also called Maal Hijrah) celebrates the beginning of the Islamic New Year. Muharram, deriving from the word haram, which means forbidden, is a month considered most sacred of all besides the month of Ramadan. During this time, Muslims are forbidden to fight; hence, a time of meditating and peace.

The importance of hijrah comes from the paradigm shift that it created in Islamic history. From a motley group of neophytes shunned by the Meccans, the Hijrah to Medina evolved into a strong government and a worldwide movement.

Following the month of Maarghazhi, Puthaandu or New Year in Tamil, is the first day of the month of Chithirai of the lunisolar Hindu calendar. It falls on or about 14 April every year on the Gregorian calendar. The same day is observed elsewhere in South and South East Asia as the traditional new year, but is known by other names such as Vishu in Kerala, and Vaisakhi or Baisakhi in central and northern India.

"There are several references in early Tamil literature, to the April new year. Nakkirar, the Sangam era author of the *Neṭunalvāṭai*, wrote that the sun travels from Mesha/Chitthirai through 11 successive signs of the zodiac. Kūdalūr Kizhaar refers to Mesha Raasi/Chitthirai as the commencement of the year in the *Puṟanāṉūṟu*. The *Tolkaapiyam* is the oldest surviving grammar book (Late BCE to Early CE) that divides the year into six seasons where Chitthirai marks the start of the Ilavenil season or summer. The *Silappadikaaram* mentions the 12 Raasis or zodiac signs starting with Mesha/Chitthirai. The *Manimekalai* alludes to the Hindu solar calendar as we know it today. Adiyarkunallaar, an early medieval commentator or Urai-asiriyar mentions the twelve months of the Tamil calendar with particular reference to Chitthirai. There were subsequent inscriptional references in Pagan, Burma dated to the 11th century CE and in Sukhothai, Thailand dated to the 14th century CE to South Indian, often Vaishnavite, courtiers who were tasked with defining the traditional calendar that began in mid-April.

The day is spent quietly, with a visit to the temple and a simple family lunch.

Are bedtime stories still fashionable? I remember us children gathering around our father's easy chair for that after dinner, before bedtime, nightly ritual. TV was unheard of then, and radio was dearly beloved, in that estate environment. It did not matter if some of father's stories were reruns – it always felt like a new story. There were stories about kings, peasants, animals and what not. Baby boomers of all sections of society can recall those days and times. Alas, babies of today are bummed out by technology and cartoons for their portion of bedtime stories.

Cunning Critters: Sang Kancil dan Sang buaya, hǎi guī and qīng wā, and Kurangum Muthalaiyum

The fairy tales we grew up with are fairly universal. Aesop's famous fables are said to have originated from India's Jataka tales, by way of Roman and Greek retellings. Malay folk tales like Pa' Kadok, Pa' Pandir, Lebai Malang, Pa' Belalang, and Si-Lunchai. Animal tails..oops tales, like Sang Kancil are also local to the Nusantara (litt: "in-between region" or Austronesia). The stories are possibly a redaction from the Jataka tales. Chinese tales are awash with dragons and tortoises, and Tamil tales also abound with cunning foxes, being a part of the Jataka tales milieu. The American equivalent of these fables, such as Br'er Rabbit, originates from the Akan people of West Africa. Now, we know how West Africans were spirited away to America by slave traders. The common thread of these appealing apologues are the morals they impart and presence of mind of potential victims in the face of the cunningness of the trickster characters.

The title above translates as: *Sang Kancil dan Sang Buaya* (Mr.Mousedeer and Mr. Crocodile), *hǎi guī and qīng wā* (The tortoise and the frog), and *Kurangum Muthalaiyum* (The monkey and the crocodile). They are actual titles of fables in the three languages. The *Sang* in the Malay story is the honorific "Mr". Interestingly it carries the same sense in Japanese (*-San*), and the Cantonese (*Saang*) which also means "mister".

Mr. Mousedeer and Mr.Crocodile (*Sang Kancil dan Sang Buaya*), is a Malay minor/junior story that is told at kindergarten or pre-school. It goes,

"Once upon a time, there was the most intelligent animal on earth, the mousedeer. The other animals came to it for help with problems. Even so, it was not haughty. One day, as Mr. Mousedeer was foraging in the forest beyond his neighbourhood for food, thirst drove him to seek a river. Finally, finding a river with clear water, Mr. Mousedeer immediately drank his fill.

He continued walking along the river, until fatigue made him lie down under a shady beringin tree. He continued his hunting trip along the river until he spied an open area on the opposite bank, that was an orchard in full fruit. He wanted very much, to be there. While wondering how to get there, he noticed a croc sunning himself nearby. Immediatedly approaching Mr. Crocodile, and exchanging pleasantries, Mr. Mousedeer said that he had some good news. It got the crocs's attention.

Upon hearing that mousedeer had been asked by King Solomon to do a census of the crocodiles in the river, the crocodile immediate left to call his friends. "Hai all, King Solomon wishes to take a census of you, and has a present for you today, so please line up from this bank to the other." As they got in formation, Mr.Mousedeer hopped all the way counting and knocking the head of each crocodile. Once on the other side he shouted with joy, "Hey crocodiles, do you know that you have been had and there is no gift from King Solomon?" Hearing this, the crocodiles vowed to get him. The mousedeer hopped off into the orchard to enjoy the ripening fruits.

The Frog and The Turtle (*hǎi guī + qīng wā*), is a Chinese childrens' story. It goes thus:-

There was a frog that lived in a shallow well.

"Look how well off I am here !" he told a big turtle from the Eastern Ocean. "I can hop along the coping of the well when I go out, and rest by a crevice in the bricks on my return. I can wallow to my heart's content with only my head above water, or stroll ankle deep through soft mud. No crabs or tadpoles can compare with me. I am master of the water and lord of this shallow well, What more can a fellow ask ? Why don't you come here more often to have a good time ?"

Before the turtle from the Eastern Ocean could get his left foot into the well, however, he caught his right claw on something. So he halted and stepped back then began to describe the ocean to the frog.

"It's more than a thousand miles across and more than ten thousand feet deep. In ancient times there were floods nine years out of ten, yet the water in the ocean never increased.

And later there were droughts seven years out of eight yet the water in the ocean never grew less. It has remained quite constant throughtout the ages. That is why I like to live in the Eastern Ocean."

Then the frog in the shallow well was silent and felt a little abashed.

The Tamil tale is so similar to the Malay one, that it could also have come from the Jataka tales. In The Monkey and the Crococodile (*Kurangum Mudhalaiyum*), the character of the mousedeer changed to the monkey. Only minor details have changed.

The location is the same – an orchard beside a river. The monkey is enjoying ripe mangoes, and the crocodile initiates the conversation, appreciating the mangoes – initial small talk. One day, appreciating the monkey's generosity providing mangoes daily, the croc invites the monkey to a lunch he would prepare on the other side of the river. The unwitting monkey accepts the invite and rides the croc's back.

Well, wouldn't you know? Halfway across, the crocodile begins to dip, to which the monkey asks what was happening. The Croc replies that his wife wanted so much, to taste monkey heart. "Alas!", Mr.Monkey tells Mr. Crocodile. "I have left my heart in the trees". Crackbrained croc quickly u-turns. As they reach the bank, the story ends like the Malay version, with the primate regretting their permanently fractured friendship owing to the reptile's hypocrisy.

Fairy Tales: Bawang Putih, Bawang Merah; Ye Xian, Nalla Tangaal

Fairy tales, naturally must be about fairies and how they intervene in human dramas. Sometimes, handsome princes are involved.

Bawang Putih *(Garlic)* **Bawang Merah** *(Onion)* is one of the more famous of the old Malay fairy tales (*dongeng*), passed down orally through the generations. Like most, the story is laden with lessons regarding familial values, patience in the face of adversity, and that ultimately good will be rewarded and the evil will be punished. If the names of the main characters grow a frown in your brow, consider the western characters like *Snow White* and *Red Riding Hood*.

The story takes place in a simple village household. The head of this family has two wives, and each wife has their own daughter. Bawang Merah and her mother are jealous of the attention the father gives Bawang Putih and her mother. When the father dies, Bawang Merah and her mother take charge of the household and bully Bawang Putih into servitude. Bawang Putih's mother stands up for her daughter but she soon dies prematurely, in some versions due to sickness and in some versions due to the intentional malice of Bawang Merah's mother.

With her biological mother and father dead, the gentle and obedient Bawang Putih is left alone to be tortured by her cruel stepmother and half-sister. Though Bawang Putih suffers, she is patient. One day, when she is out in the woods, she sees a pond containing a live fish. The fish is able to speak, and tells her that it is her mother who has came back to comfort her. Bawang Putih is overjoyed to be able to speak with her mother again, and secretly visits the pond whenever she can.

One day Bawang Merah notices Bawang Putih sneaking off and secretly follows her to the pond, where she witnesses Bawang Putih talking to the fish. After Bawang Putih leaves, Bawang Merah lures the fish to the surface of the pond and catches it. Bawang Merah and her mother kill the fish, cook it and feed it to Bawang Putih without telling her where it came from. Once Bawang Putih finishes eating, her stepmother and stepsister reveal where they obtained the fish. Bawang Putih is repulsed and filled with remorse over this revelation.

Bawang Putih gathers the fish bones and buries them in a small grave underneath a tree. When she visits the grave the next day, she is surprised to see that a beautiful swing has appeared from one of the tree's branches. When Bawang Putih sits in the swing and sings an old lullaby, it magically swings back and forth.

Bawang Putih continues to visit the magic swing whenever she can. One day, while she is on the magic swing, a Prince who is hunting nearby hears her song. He follows the sound of her voice, but before he approaches her, Bawang Putih realizes that she is not alone, she quickly runs back home.

The Prince and his advisors eventually find the home of Bawang Putih and Bawang Merah. (In some versions this happens immediately after the Prince's first sighting of Bawang Putih, but in other versions it happens after a long search made by the Prince's advisors). Bawang Merah's mother, seeing the opportunity, orders Bawang Putih to stay hidden in the kitchen. The Prince asks about the swing and the girl who sat in it. Bawang Merah's mother says that the girl he heard is her beautiful and talented daughter Bawang Merah. Though the Prince agrees that Bawang Merah is beautiful, he requests that she show him how she sang in the magical swing.

Bawang Merah and mother reluctantly follow the Prince and his advisors back to the magic swing. Bawang Merah sits in the swing and attempts to sing so that it will move, but she fails. The Prince, now angry, ordered Bawang Merah's mother to tell the truth. Bawang Merah's mother is forced to confess that she has another daughter hidden in her house.

The Prince brings Bawang Putih back to the swing, and as she had done many times before, the magic swing starts moving as soon as she begins singing. The Prince is overjoyed and asks Bawang Putih to marry him. She agrees and they live happily ever after

Ye Xian/Yeh Hsien/Yeh Shen

First published in the Tang dynasty compilation *Miscellaneous Morsels from Youyang* written around 850 CE by Duan Chengshi. The Ye Xian, a story similar to the fairy tale Cinderella, appears in Chapter 21. The story was allegedly told by Duan's servant Li Shiyuan, a native from what is now Nanning. It is set during the late 3rd century BCE. The exact location is unknown, but the most likely candidate is Guangxi, where the shoe eventually found its way to a king from an island.

A scholar named Wu, who is chieftain of a community of cave-dwellers, had two wives and a daughter by each of them. Yeh-Shen is Wu's beautiful daughter of one wife, and she is intelligent, artistic and gifted in many skills. In contrast her half-sister, Jun-li, is spoiled, self-absorbed and lazy.

When her mother and then her father die from a local plague, Yeh-Shen is forced to become a lowly servant and work for her father's other wife, named Jin (Yeh's evil stepmother) and her daughter, Jun-li. Despite living a life burdened with chores and housework, and endless suffering at her stepmother's hands, she finds solace when she ends up befriending a beautiful, 10-foot-long (3.0 m) fish in the lake. With golden eyes and scales, the fish is the reincarnation of her mother, who now watches out for her.

Angry that Yeh-Shen has found happiness, Jin kills the fish and serves it for dinner for herself and her daughter. Yeh-Shen is devastated until a spirit appears and tells her to bury the bones of the fish in pots at each corner of her bed. The spirit also tells her that whatever she needs will be granted if she talks to the bones. Déjà vu? You bet. It's the Bawang Putih, Cinderella story.

The local Chinese New Year takes place, where many young women will have the opportunity to meet potential suitors. Not wishing to spoil her own daughter's chances, Jin forces her stepdaughter to remain home and clean their cave-house. After her stepfamily has left, Yeh-Shen is visited by her mother's spirit again. Her mother tells her to dig up the pots containing the fish bones and Yeh-Shen finds fine clothes, including a cloak of feathers, jewellery, and a pair of golden slippers to wear to the festival.

Yeh-Shen dons the clothes and goes to the festival by foot. She stays and enjoys herself until she realizes her stepmother may have recognized her and leaves, accidentally leaving behind a golden slipper. When she arrives home, she hides the clothes in the pots beneath her bed again. When her stepfamily returns, they discuss Jun-li's marriage prospects and also mention a mysterious maiden who appeared. They are unaware that it is Yeh-Shen they are speaking of.

The golden slipper is found and traded by various people until it reaches the hands of a nearby king. He orders a search to find the maiden whose foot will fit the shoe and proclaims he will marry that girl. The shoe eventually reaches the cave-house of Yeh-Shen, Jun-li and her mother try to put on the shoe and fail. The shoe ends up fitting Yeh-Shen's foot perfectly.

In an attempt to dissuade the King from marrying Yeh-Shen, Jin declares that it was impossible for Yeh-Shen to have been at the festival. She saw the maiden who owns the golden slipper at the festival, the fine clothes she wore, and also mentions that Yeh-Shen was at home the entire time. Yeh-Shen proves her wrong by bringing out and putting the clothes she wore at the festival and the other golden slipper and the King, awed by Yeh-Shen's beauty, affirms that he will marry her, and she will become his chief wife in his palace. Jin makes a final attempt to dissuade the King from marrying her stepdaughter by accusing Yeh-Shen of stealing the maiden's golden shoe. The King catches on and her evil plan are exposed. To punish Yeh-Shen's stepfamily for their cruelty and dishonesty, he forbids Yeh-Shen from bringing them to live with her. Jin and Jun-li were banished to a cave, where they would spend the rest of their lives until a shower of falling stones kill them.

Nalla Thangaal

There is a serious lack of a Cindarella in Tamil folklore, although other Indian sub-cultures do have more identical cinderalla stories. Not that there is no concept of the wicked stepmother or step-siblings in Tamil either. Or, a lack of fairy godmother. Most Cinderella stories contain magical elements and happy endings. The Tamil story Nalla Tangaal (Cinderalla type) is more legend than fairy tale, without magic or happy endings. It is etched in popular culture.

The selfish father of Nalla Tangaal fails to provide dowry for her marriage, because of objections by his second wife, whose sexual favours he craved. So, Nalla had to return to her father's house as a *valaavetti* ("failure in life"). The plot thickens with Nalla Tangaal's baby thriving on her ample milk, and her stepmother's child being a sickly one due to her lack of milk. In the nights, the stepmother switches the the positions of the two babies, so her own child will have milk. Nalla Tangaal, already tired by being overworked (you know it had to happen), notices her child getting sicklier by the day, so one night she picks the child next to her and jumps into a well. Not sure whose child it was – but shouldn't there be a poetic justice?. Nalla Tangaal's father, learning of the matter, chases away the stepmother, and raises his surviving grandson. C'mon, this is no fairy-tale ending! But, the similarities to Cinderalla are present in this story. The father character is actually the stepmother, and his second wife is more of a step-sister.

Court Jesters: Tenali Raman, Pak Belalang, Dongfang Shuo

He could be a juggler, confidant, scapegoat, prophet, and counselor all in one. If we follow his family tree along its many branches we encounter musicians and actors, acrobats and poets, dwarfs, hunchbacks, personal confidants, tricksters, madmen, and mountebanks. There is one court official whom the king keeps close to his heart and close by. He is is the one who ultimately solves his doubts. He is serious and straight thinking, but his actions appear comical. This not deliberate, but his fellow court personnel resent him and try to undermine him. No matter what they do, to sabotage him, his advice or solution always turns out right. Therein is the comedy of it, much like a Shakespearian scene where the audience is privy to what is going happen next to the bad guy.

Tenali Raman is the south Indian version of Birbal, the Moghul emperor Akbar's confidant. Or, the mulla Naziruddin tales. Tenali was an accomplished Telugu poet with good acumen and, what a wit. He had, by his insightfulness gotten into Vijayanagara king, Krishnadevarayar's inner circle, always consulted on important matters. Of the dozens of episodes, this is one:

One day, when king Sri Krishnadevarayar was sitting in court, he heard a commotion outside the palace gates. He commanded the guards to find out what it was. A guard came with a man who identified himself as the village head. The king asked him what the matter was. The man replied, "Your majesty, our village is infested by rats. The rats are destroying our food grains and creating chaos in the village. Please save us."

The king assured the village head by saying, "Fear not, my good man. I will consult with my courtiers and find a solution to your problem."

King Sri Krishnadevarayar ordered his ministers to arrive at a solution. One of the ministers stood up and said, "Your majesty, since cats eat rats, we can solve this rat menace by giving one cat to each household in the village." "But how would the poor villagers feed the cats?" asked another minister. The minister suggested that they could give a cow along with a cat so that the cats can feed on milk.

The king agreed to this solution. All the villagers began feeding the cats with milk. And as days passed by, the cats became healthy and lazy. Tenali Raman observed this and thought, "There is something wrong with this solution."

The next day, Raman placed a hot bowl of milk in front of one of the cats. As soon as the cat spotted the milk, it rushed to drink it and burned its tongue. The cat ran away and never touched milk again.That cat began to hunt, and the owner's house was clean of rats.

One day, the king wanted to review the situation and ordered the villagers to get the cats to the court. The villages complained that their cats haven't been hunting rats, except the one owner whose cat stopped drinking milk thanks to Raman. The king asked the cat's owner, "Why is only your cat hunting rats? Haven't you been feeding it with milk?" Raman stepped up and said, "Your majesty, it is not the owner's fault this cat refuses to drink milk."

"A cat that doesn't drink milk? How is that possible, Raman?" asked the king. "Let me show it to you, your majesty," said Raman and asked the guards to get a bowl of milk. As soon as the cat saw the bowl of milk, it ran away.The surprised king asked for the reason behind it. Then, Raman said, "Your majesty, I had given the cat a bowl of hot milk which burnt its tongue. From that day onwards, this cat never drank milk."

"But, why did you do so?" inquired the king. Raman replied, "Your majesty, cats would hunt the rats only when they are hungry. By drinking milk every day, the cats have become healthy and lazy and do not hunt for the rats. To show you this, I gave hot milk to one of the cats."

The king understood the flaw in the solution. He asked the ministers to find another solution to help solve the problem. He also rewarded Raman handsomely.

Pak Belalang, is a Malay folk character, who started off as a lazy layabout who somehow got appointed the Sultan's astrologer and problem solver-in-chief. Thanks to his little son Belalang (grasshopper), Pak Belalang (Daddy Grasshopper) was serendipitously saved from many a "situation". One of the episode is as follows:

They saw that Sultan of Masai's delegation was peaceful and without troop accompaniment. This was because they knew they did not have the military strength to oppose Beringin Rendang kingdom, so they came there on intelligence scouting. At the palace, the two sultans met.

Sultan of Masai made a wager on the wisdom of the astrologers of the two countries, and risked losing his country. Sultan Shahrul Nizam thought for a moment before putting his full confidence in Pak Belalang who did not actually have any intellect. After signing an agreement between the two countries, Masai's astrologers popped the question (s):

"There is a beautiful piece of wood. Which is the top and which one is the base?"

"There are two ducks that have just hatched. How do I know which one is male and which one is the female?"

"There is a problem. One, a lot. Two, a little bit. Three, rarely. Four, sometimes. What is it?"

"Where is the strength of Datuk Laksamana Hang Tuah? On the dagger? Or is it in his power?"

After listening and assessing situation in the palace, Pak Belalang was horrified that the sultan was willing to risk the country by putting his full trust in him, who really knew nothing. He went home and told Grasshopper to find a boat to escape while he packed up essentials. At the port, Belalang tried to take Sultan Masai's boat but when he wanted to push the boat, Sultan Masai's entourage arrived. The grasshopper entered the boat and snuck under a seat as the ship sailed to Masai.

On the way, Sultan Masai persuaded his astrologers to tell him the puzzle's answer and eventhough he forbade all the crew who heard him from coming ashore, all the answers were heard by Grasshopper. The grasshopper swam home and told his father all the answers he heard.

On the appointed day, Pak Belalang was ready with the answer given by Belalang. This is how it went:

"There is a beautiful piece of wood. Which top and which one is the base?"

Pak Belalang took a beautifully snatched wooden stick and put it in the water and saw the wood there was an end that arose and the other sank. Dad grasshopper said that the tip arose and that the base was sunk due to "every tip being lighter than the base".

There are two ducks that just hatched. How do you know which one is male and which one is the female?

Pak Belalang carried a male and female duckling that had just hatched and let then float. One duck swam in front and another followed. Pak Belalang said that in duck front was female the laggard was male. The reason was, "the norm of the world" because the male will always chase the female.

There's a problem. One, a lot. Two, a little bit. Three, rarely. Four, sometimes. What is it?

Pak Belalang replied, "marriage" because "One married person means many in this world. Two, somewhat, means, a person who marries two (twice) is less than a once married person. Three, rarely, means, thrice married people are rarely heard of. Four, sometimes, meaning, we sometimes have four times married people.

Where is the strength of Datuk Laksamana Hang Tuah? On the dagger? Or in his power?

Pak Belalang replied "The strength of Datuk Laksamana Hang Tuah lies not in the keris or in his energy but lies in the alphabet Ta which strengthens the name Tuah ("Lucky"), Ta – Wau – Alif – Ha: Tuah, If the Ta is converted to Ba, it will sound 'Fruit'. Lucky Pak Belalang

With Beringin Rendang winning, Sultan of Masai suspected that his astrologer had colluded with Beringin Rendang. He then asked another question. Pak Belalang disagreed but Sultan Shahrul Nizam persuaded him to take up his challenge. Sultan Masai took something out of his grasp and told Pak Belalang to guess what it was. Pak Belalang realizing that he could not answer groaned and murmured while calling the name "Belalang" blaming his stubborn son for the situation. Sultan Masai who heard it, hunched down. Sultan Shahrul Nizam asked why and he replied that Pak Belalang's answer was correct because what he was holding was a grasshopper. Thus, Beringin Rendang had an absolute victory and Masai fell to Beringin Rendang. This is the version portrayed in the 1959 film Nujum Pak Belalang (Grasshopper's dad, the Astrologer), directed and starred by the inimitable P.Ramlee. The film won the best comedy film award at the 7th Asian Film Festival in Tokyo, Japan.

Dongfang Shuo, is a character similar to the other two. This time, as advsor to emperor Han Wu Di. While entertaining himself in Shanglin Garden, Emperor Wu Di of the Han Dynasty pointed at a tree and asked Dongfang Shuo, "What is that called?"

"It's called Goodness." replied Dongfang Shuo nonchalantly. Wu Di had it written down.

Several years later, playing in the garden again, Wu Di saw the tree and turned to Dongfang Shuo to ask its name. "it's named Jusuo (Overlooking all)." said Dongfang Shuo again casually.

Wu Di's expression changed, "You have been cheating me over the years. How can the same tree have different names?"

Dongfang Shuo defended himself with fervor and assurance. "A horse is called a horse only when it grows up; it is a foal when young; chicken is the name for a chick when it becomes older; and a cow is called a calf when born. So it is with human beings: They are called infants when born and old men when aged. The tree was Goodness several years ago and is now Overlooking-All. All the objects in the universe change. Don't you think that is the truth?"

Satisfied with Dongfang Shuo's reply, Wu Di laughed heartily. "

Fables: Aesop's, Badang, Panchatantra

Fables are lasting stories of the people, spread across borders through word of mouth. Indeed India has many fables that are attributed as the source of many of aesop's stories. They consist almost entirely of animal, plant and other non-human characters that deliver moral solutions. Jataka tales.

The Panchatantra – "five principles" is a collection of fables, designed for teaching group daft royal siblings. "The introduction to the Panchatantra tells of how Vishnu Sharma created the collection of fables. There was a ruler of a kingdom who had three sons. The king, named Sudarshan, was apparently quite intelligent and powerful, yet his sons were not a source of pride to him. The sons had no inclination or ability to learn anything. In fact, they were quite unimaginative, slow, and rather stupid. In desperation, the king turned to his counselors for advice.

Only one of the ministers, Sumati, seemed to make sense to Sudarshan. Sumati told the king that the things the princes needed to learn—namely politics, diplomacy, and the sciences—were difficult and would take a lifetime of hard study and dedication. Now, you see, both Sudarshan and Sumati knew that the princes were incapable of such strict discipline.

Sumati gave the suggestion that rather than having the princes learn scriptures and texts, it would be better to directly teach them the essential attributes conveyed by those scriptures and texts.

Sumati said the most likely man to take on that task was Vishnu Sharma, an aged scholar. The king wasted no time in inviting Vishnu to court and offered him a hundred land grants if he could turn the princes into learned scholars. Vishnu refused the gift, saying he did not sell knowledge and that he would take on the task and within six months make the princes wise so they would be able to rule as wisely as their father.

Now, the method Vishnu devised was to gather and adapt ancient stories that had been told in India. He then created an interesting, entertaining work of five parts which he called the Five Principles and that became the Panchatantra. *Pancha* means "five," and *tantra* means "treatises."
– Wikipedia

Interestingly, Munshi Abdullah (1796-1854) had translated a Tamil edition of panchatantra into Malay, as Hikayat Panca Tanderan.

Chinese Fables and Folk Stories, a compilation of 37 tales, was billed as the first book of Chinese fables ever printed in English when it was published by American Book Company in 1908. The co-authors were Mary Hayes Davis and Chow Leung. Widely reprinted today and also translated into French, *Chinese Fables and Folk Stories* has been noted as one of the most "reliable" works by Western scholars on Chinese folktales published before 1937. Each tale in the book is accompanied by an illustration, attributed to unnamed "native" Chinese artists.

The professor and the melon is one such story. "Wu-Kiao was a professor in a large Chinese university, and a very proud and learned man. Hundreds of students were under his teaching, and many thousands honored him. When he went out of his house, five people followed, singing and playing the drum all the way down the street, and eight men carried his chair. At home he had six servants about him. During each meal, thirty dishes were served at his table.

The professor was a great man. Through his wisdom and out of his deep knowledge, he explained all questions to the people.

One day Wu-Kiao sat in the shade of a tree in his garden. He turned his head and saw a watermelon lying on the ground, nearly covered with its green leaves. Then, seeing the fig tree with many figs on it, he said, "*I think the Creator should have made the melon grow on this tree.*"

He touched the tree and said, "*How strong you are; you could bear larger fruit like the watermelon.*" And he said to the vine, "*You, so thin and small, should bear small fruit like the fig. Things are not well ordered. Mistakes are made in creation.*" Just then a fig dropped from the tree on his nose, and he was a little bruised.

Then he said, "*I was wrong. If the fig tree bore fruit as large as the watermelon and dropped it on my nose, I think I should be killed. It would be a dangerous tree to all people. I must study more carefully. I know many things and many people; and if I study and think more deeply, it may be I shall come to know that the Creator's works are perfect.*" – Wikipedia

"Animal fables are often used to explain certain natural phenomena. Other times, they are simple moral tales. In almost all instances, the animals in these stories possess the ability to speak, reason and think like humans, similar to Aesop's Fables.

The *kancil* or mouse-deer serves as the main character in a number of the stories. The Malays regard this humble animal in the highest esteem due to its ability to overcome obstacles and defeat adversaries despite of its rather small and benign appearance. The mouse-deer appears in the state herald of Melaka and even plays a part in the legend of Malacca›s founding.

Below are listed some of the common fables as well as their approximate title translations. (Note that the word *sang*, an Old Malay honorific meaning "revered", appears in all instances preceding the name *kancil* to indicate respect)

Kisah Sang Kancil dengan Buaya – The tale of the mouse-deer and the crocodile

Kisah Sang Kancil dengan Monyet – The tale of the mouse-deer and the monkey

Kisah Sang Kancil dengan Harimau – The tale of the mouse-deer and the tiger

'*Kisah Sang Kancil dengan Gajah* – *The tale of the mouse-deer and the elephant*

Kisah Sang Kancil dengan Sang Sempoh – The tale of the mouse-deer and the bison

Kisah Anjing dengan Bayang-bayang – The dog and the shadow

Kisah Burung Gagak dan Merak – The crow and the peacock

Kisah Burung Gagak yang Haus – The thirsty crow

Kisah Labah-labah Emas – The golden spider

Kisah Labah-labah dengan Burung Merpati – The spider and the pigeon

Kisah Kerengga dengan Pemburu – The fire-ant and the hunter

Kisah Burung Murai – The mockingbird

Kisah Burung Kakak Tua – The cockatoo

– Wikipedia

General Peace: Hang Tuah, Sun Zi, Madurai Veeran

Not only kings and presidents preponderantly populate the popular consciousness. So do their knights and generals. Sir Lancelot of King Arthur, General Malik Kafur of Moghul Emperor Allaudin Khilji, General Grant of President Lincoln etc.

Hang Tuah is the chief of the *Hangs* of Malacca during the sultanate of Mansur Shah. He is the Sir Lancelot equivalent of Baginda Sultan, a knight in kris. Probably of the rank of *Panglima*, his fellow braves are Hang Jebat, Hang Kasturi, Hang Lekiu, and Hang Lekir. The fantastic 5. Is that why a general is called Pang-lima (five), you think? You also wonder if the *Hang* that precedes the names is a title like Sir, or a name. Could it be similar to the *Sang* of Sang Kancil and Sang Buaya?

Hang Tuah and his band of brothers have earned an enduring place in folk memory. Their exploits are read in school history books. It tells of his impeccable loyalty. One story tells of how he even withstood and fought his comrade, in defence of his liege.

Generals in Tamil culture are not only many but many of them have joined the host of Hindu pantheon of gods. The custom of ancient Tamils was to erect rock pillars to soldiers in the place where they fell in battle. They are called hero stone or nadukal (Litt: "planted stone"). These became shrines and pilgrimage sites. Some of the popular gods not associated with the trinity (Brahma, Siva, Vishnu) and their various manifestations and consorts, were such generals. Case in point, Madurai Veeran, Muneesvaran, Karuppasaamy, Sandi Kavalan etc. These are the ones that get goat sacrifices, unlike the vedic gods who only get flowers and vegetarian offerings. These appear to be the attendents of Ayyanar, a popular village guardian deity, or *kaaval deivam*. So, a general who not only defends his land till death, but also thereafter? Must have been some hero.

Chinese – General Sun Zi, or Sun Tzu, ("Master Sun") was a prominent military general during the Spring and Autumn Period (770-476 BC) who is always regarded as one of the greatest military strategists in China and even the World. Sun Zi wrote the famous war strategy book "The Art of War", which highlights his military philosophy in only 13 chapters with

5,000 words. Today, many political leaders and entrepreneurs in the world use "The Art of War" as a guide for strategy and leadership.

One of the better-known stories about Sun Tzu, taken from Sima Qian, illustrates Sun Tzu's temperament as follows: Before hiring Sun Tzu, the King of Wu tested Sun Tzu's skills by commanding him to train a harem of 180 concubines into soldiers. Sun Tzu divided them into two companies, appointing the two concubines most favored by the king as the company commanders. When Sun Tzu first ordered the concubines to face right, they giggled. In response, Sun Tzu said that the general, in this case himself, was responsible for ensuring that soldiers understood the commands given to them. Then, he reiterated the command, and again the concubines giggled. Sun Tzu then ordered the execution of the king's two favored concubines, to the king's protests. He explained that if the general's soldiers understood their commands but did not obey, it was the fault of the officers. Sun Tzu also said that, once a general was appointed, it was his duty to carry out his mission, even if the king protested. After both concubines were killed, new officers were chosen to replace them. Therafter, both companies, now well aware of the costs of further frivolity, performed their maneuvers flawlessly.

Sima Qian claimed that Sun Tzu later proved on the battlefield that his theories were effective (for example, at the Battle of Boju), that he had a successful military career, and that he wrote The Art of War based on his tested expertise. However, the Zuozhuan, a historical text written centuries earlier than the Shiji, provides a much more detailed account of the Battle of Boju, but does not mention Sun Tzu at all.

America's Asian conflicts against Japan, North Korea, and North Vietnam brought Sun Tzu to the attention of American military leaders. The Department of the Army in the United States, through its Command and General Staff College, has directed all units to maintain libraries within their respective headquarters for the continuing education of personnel in The Art of War. The video game Age of Empires II: Definitive Edition contains challenge missions based on Sun Tzu's The Art of War, which explains the military tactics and strategies.

Myths: Monkey King, Puteri Gunung Ledang, Thirumal

A myth is an improbable story that formed in the fertile minds of our forefathers, way back in the blurry brume of the bygone. The word itself conjures up confounding plots and superhuman beings.The gigantic gods of Greek, Roman, Norse, Hindu and Chinese mythologies doing phantasmagoric battles with mean demons come to mind.Thunderbolts and lightning rods zip past, and planets collide, reminding you of *Star Wars* or *The War of the Worlds,* or *Ultraman*. The movies, that is.

While no degree of archeology has been able to uncover evidence of mythological creatures, and places, some of the fantastic objects like spaceships and missiles have inspired modern man to actually invent these. Examples of these abound in Hindu, Chinese, or Greek and Roman mythologies. If you were to watch an old black and white Tamil mythological flick, you would notice gods and asuras firing flaming arrowheads and maces at each other and airborne space chariots! The resemblance to modern surface to air, or air to surface missiles is uncanny.

While fables seem to be chiefly moral education devices for children, myths appear to serve the same purpose for adults. Was it a ploy by the priestly classes to keep the common man subdued? It does seem like it. The Brahmin priest of today is an expert at explaining these mythical stories, or *Puraanau*. He will explain these divine politics and powerplays of the gods (*thiru vilayadal*) as evidence of the deities' power and compassion on the *bhaktas*, or devotees. Just trust the gods, do the required appeasements, and you will be fine. No scientific *whys* and *wherefores* of their existence is asked for, or given. In the Hindu mind, the mythical events are very real indeed. So is it in Taoist thinking.

In a sense, every adult is prone to be possessed of myths. If very young children can actually believe in fables, fairy tales, Santa Clauses and Sasquatches, so do we tend to buy in to racial, caste, and national superiority myths. Apartheid, Nazism, Segregationism (US casteism), "Manifest Destiny" (the US idea that native American lands were theirs to annex) were myths that were once bought and sold wholesale. Untouchability, the idea that some people are born dirtier than dirt, still exists due to being embedded in the Hindu religion. Dirt, they can handle. The Jewish idea of a "chosen people of God", finds its echoes in the

American sense of God given supremacy (manifest destiny), that exceeds ordinary patriotism. There is a myth hiding in all of us. It goes by different names: phobia, paranoia, distorted thinking, xenophobia, hatred, nazism, or fascism etc. Do you think that yours is a superior race, or have a "siege mentality" that you'll be subsumed by a minority race group. Well, you have a blockade myth, an ethnic mind block.

Ok, let's get back to the old myths.

Sun Wukong – the monkey king. Excerpt: "He is the most famous monkey in China. He is one of the main characters in a Chinese classic, *The Journey to the West*. At first Sun Wukong is a very naughty monkey, eager to take over the world, and it costs Buddha a lot of effort to tame him. He later becomes a loyal companion to the monk Xuanzang on his adventurous journey from China to India and back again." Ed's Note: Wonder if he ever met Hanuman, the Indian Monkey King ?

Excerpt: "In Malay History, Puteri Gunung Ledang (*The Princess of Mount Ophir*) is said to be very beautiful to the point desired by Sultan Mahmud Shah of the Sultanate of Malacca. The emissaries that were sent were Admiral Hang Tuah, Tun Mamat and several others. As a child, Hang Tuah had crossed over Gunung Ledang and was familiar with the road to the top. By this time, however, he was too old to get to the top of Mount Ledang.

With that, Tun Mamat was assigned to the top and met an elderly grandmother or better known as Grandma Kebayan who was actually a alter ego to Puteri Gunung Ledang. Puteri Gunung Ledang is said to have rejected Sultan Mahmud's proposal by imposing seven conditions that could not be fulfilled, namely:

1 gold bridge from Gunung Ledang to Malacca.
1 silver bridge from Malacca to Gunung Ledang.
7 trays of mosquito liver.
7 trays of mite liver.
7 jars of virgin tears.
7 jars of young betel juice. (Note: Betel nut has no Juice)

Sulalatus al-Salatin (*The Malay Annals*) masterpiece by Tun Sri Lanang tells of Sultan Mahmud's willingness to fulfill all these conditions by wishing to marry Puteri Gunung Ledang after his wife's death: (... He did not want to marry an ordinary princess because it meant the same as other kings. He wants to look different from the others. He said, "... *Which we desire that which no other kings do, that is what we want to be found. Now, we want to ask the Princess of Gunung Ledang;.......*")."

Well, long story short: Princess interested in Hang Tuah. Hang Tuah indebted to Sultan. You decide the denouement, because there are many versions.

Excerpt: "Tamil literature, in tandem with Sanskrit literature, forms a major source of information regarding ancient Hindu culture. The ancient epics of Tamilakam detail the origin of various historical figures in Hindu scripture, like Agathiyar, Iravan, and Patanjali. Ancient Tamil literature contains mentions of indigenous deities like Perumal, Murugan, and Kotravai. Tolkappiyam hails Shiva as Brahman, Murugan as *Seyyon* (the red one), and Kotravai as the goddess worshipped in the dry lands. This literature serves as a springwell of history, as referenced by inscriptions upon major temples like the Pundarikakshan Perumal Temple, Nataraja Temple, Chidambaram, Ranganathaswamy Temple, Srirangam, Tirupati, Meenakshi Temple, Madurai Koodal Azhagar temple."

Since hindu mythology is vast and multibranched, one can take one's pick of a mythical character. Each one has its convoluted story based on where one is, in India. Each will have a many-festation in many a milieu.

Legend: Kumari Kandam, Mahsuri Langkawi, Sun Goddess

A legend, unlike a myth, has a tinge of truth in it. It sounds very plausible but does not have enough historical proof (yet) in order to make a firm determination. A legend may have started as a real person or event that has, over aeons become blurred and fuzzy. It is somewhat like a fallen tree that, in the swift current of time, lost its original shape and become driftwood. Indeed, many legends have actually been realized by archeologists who have followed their instincts and leads. The Indus valley civilization of India and the Terracotta army of China were probably excavated due to leads taken from local folklore. King Solomon's mines or El Dorado or Shangri-la may be next.

The lost continent mentioned in ancient Tamil records, is a supposed massive land that was swallowed by a series of huge tsunamies in hoary times. Tamils claim their origins from there, which they call *Kumari Kandam*, or "Virgin Continent." Sangam Literature, the 3,000 year old classical Tamil literary corpora, speak of a thriving civilization with its capital Madurai, shifted inland three times, after each *Kadal Kol* ("captured by the sea"). Kadal kol, is the ancient Tamil name for continental submergence by tsunami (*Aazhi Peralai* – "Gigantic Seawave")*. The present metropolis of Madurai (number 3), in Taml Nadu, has been in continuous existence for over 2,000 years. Gives you an inkling of the age of the legend.

Lost continents are not a new thing. The Atlantic, Indian and Pacific oceans each have a lost city or continent called Atlantis, Kumari Kandam (Lemuria), and Te Rea respectively. Lemuria was coined by a German zoologist Phillip Sclater (1864) from *lemur*, the primate that lives exclusively on Madagascar in the, you guessed it, Indian Ocean.

When the Indian Ocean tsunami of Boxing Day 2004 slammed 15 countries, on three sides of it, the probability of Kumari Kandam became quite real. It came even closer home to Tamils spread out in India, Myanmar, Medan, Malaysia, Mauritious, Singapore, Sri Lanka, South Africa, Seychelles, Thailand, and Reunion island, where the tsunami lapped. On hindsight, it seems probable that a colossal wave many times the size of the 2004 edition could have washed away a continental landmass over a few increments.

"The Langkawi myth happens around the reign of Kedah Sultan Ahmad Tajuddin Halim Shah (1803-1843). A Thai couple from Phuket, Pandak Mayah (Indonesian) and Endak Alang (Chinese decended) along with their daughter Mahsuri are settled on Langkawi. Suffice to say that Mahsuri was born in magical circumstances (there are too many versions). She is very beautiful.

As Mahsuri blossomed into a young lady, she became a magnet for suitors, including the Penghulu (Sultan's representive on the island) Wan Yahya. Naturally, his wife, Wan Mahora. becomes jealous and angry. She succeeds in instigating the folk of Kg.Mawat and all Langkawi about Mahsuri's alleged adultery. While tied at the stake, she tells them her blood would flow white rather than red, as a sign of her innocence. Their spear wouldn't penetrate her. She tells them her body would only receive her family heirloom spear/or kris in a another version. They find it and use it. As a result of Mahsuri's curse, Langkawi would be doomed for 7 generations." Now, it is a tourism draw. While every geographical locale has its own legend, it works well as a selling point – tourism wise. For sure, a place wouldn't be hip without the hype.

Chinese culture has no shortage of myths and make belief, but none that qualifies as a legend – i.e has a touch of reality.

Excerpt: "The Sun Goddess had 10 sons with the Supreme God, who all acted in turn as 10 suns. Every morning, the Goddess would send one of her sons to be on duty in the sky, sending light to the earth.

One day, the 10 sons decided to travel to earth together for a visit. Unfortunately, as these 10 fiery beings got close, their intense heat began scorching the world and everything that lived in it. The people's desperate pleas to be saved were heard by the Supreme God, who didn't want to see the earth destroyed, and sent for Hou Yi (后羿), a legendary archer with a magical bow.

Angered by the suffering of the people, Hou Yi began shooting down the suns one by one. As he was aiming for the last one, the people stepped in and told him they need the sun for light and warmth. Hou Yi was revered for this courageous act, and this is why we have one sun in the sky."

All good: Dum good briyani, Bak good teh, and Tom yumm!

This section is the fattest in this volume, almost a cookbook in its own right. Skip it if you are not a fan of food. Proceed with it, and you may be in danger of drooling, or dripping digestive juices already. Before perusing the separate menu items, it would do well to do a brief survey of the core philosophies of the separate cuisines.

You get an idea of what food means to Malaysians by our standard greeting. "Have you eaten, yet?" "Dah makan?" "Saaptiyaa?" "nǐ chīfàn le ma?" All these, in place of "How do you do?"

When it comes to Malaysian fare, the different cuisines are as varied as sugar and salt and pepper. For one, the Chinese add sugar generously to their dishes, while the Indians prefer their entrees savoury, using salt generously. Their food philosophies are equally different, but similar. The Malay food philosophy is a class of its own, having a lot in common with the regional tastes like Thai, Indonesian, and Filipino, but also heavily ingested with Indian infusions. The Malay cuisine is currently co-opting more Chinese styles to its repertoire. *Pao* (steamed rice flour buns with meat or bean paste stuffing), Hainanese Chicken Rice, *Char Koay Tiao* (fried savoury pasta) etc, are part of the daily offerings in Malay eateries. Halal Chinese Muslim restorans are also increasingly making their appearance. Names like Mohammad Chan and Rahmat Tan beckon Malay clients to try conscionable Chinese cuisine.

Malay cooking is fundamentally a herb-based rather than spice based style. Eventhough the Malay area, or Nusantara (spice islands) is a where some of the most exotic spices originated, the Indians have made the most of it in their dishes (before the Europeans caught on). As I see it, Malay food most readily brings to mind the smell and taste of kaffir lime leaves, lime juice, ginger, galangal, turmeric roots which are herbs and roots, as well as ample usage of coconut milk. The base of the cooking is a paste made by pounding any combo of the above items, together with garlic, onions and chillies. All that, makes for a tantalising nose taunting smell and tangy tongue triggering taste. It is no wonder that its northern cousin and everyones' darling, Thai Tom Yam, is now such a part of Malay restaurant fare.

Variety is the spice in Malay food. The traditional culinary style has been greatly influenced by the long-ago traders from neighboring countries, such as Indonesia, India, the Middle East, and China.

Malay cooking incorporates ingredients such as lemon grass, pandan (screwpine) leaves, and kaffir lime leaves, ginger and lengkuas (galangal). Fresh herbs, such as daun kemangi (a type of basil), daun kesum (polygonum or laksa leaf), nutmeg, kunyit (turmeric) and bunga kantan (wild ginger buds) are often used. Traditional spices such as cumin and coriander are used in conjunction with Indian and Chinese spices such as pepper, cardamom, star anise and fenugreek. Seasonings play an important role in Malay cooking as they often enhance the food taste and flavors. Many of the seasonings are not dried spices but are fresh ingredients such as fresh turmeric, galangal, fresh chili paste, onions, and garlic. A combination of these seasonings and dried spices are normally pounded together to make a fine paste and tempered in oil. Fresh coconut milk is often added.

But what is the definitive philosophy of Malay cuisine? Not easy to pin point – due to its thorough marination and integration with other cuisines. With its emphasis on the abpve named herbs and roots it is definitely earlier in the progression of cooking. Er, vintage?

Basic Chinese cooking, except for the spicy Szechuan style, is mostly bland and comfort foodish. Lots of hot hearty soups, stir fries using soy and oyster sauce, or an abundance of garlic and ginger are what you need on a cold night or for a stuffy sinus. The one thousand and one different recipes and tastes, using few spice and lots of local indredients, attest to the creativity of the Chinese chef. The Chinese five spice powder consisting of cinnamon, cloves, star anise, fennel seeds and Sichuan pepper, is the open secret behind the popular Bak Kut Teh stew. The fragrance of it, has a way of making you sit up and take notice, like *Chicken Soup for the Soul.*

Chinese cooking has less to do with taste (now, now, hold your horses!) but more to do with texture. While the individual Indian entrees each have their own distinct taste (sweet, sour, salty, bitter, pungent etc.), Chinese entrees incorporate a blend of tastes (sweet n' sour; pungent n' salty; sour n' pungent with a hint of bitterness etc). What you see in Chinese food, is an emphasis on how food feels in the mouth. Is it crunchy, crispy, creamy, chewy, chunky, cheezy or custardy etc.? Confucius is credited with codifying this circa 500 BCE. It also emphasises how the food looks – eye appeal and colour. A stir-fried vegetable dish has orange (carrot), green (beans), black (shiitake mushroom). And there is white (bean sprouts), bamboo shoots (yellow), Chilly (red). Care is taken, to ensure that food is not overcooked to discolouration.

Take a Chinese 12-course dinner for example. First, comes the four season platter – a collection of four types of Hors d'oeuvre or appetizers. They represent the four seasons, no doubt.

Would you take up a challenge to find an Indian, especially Tamil, dish that has no spice? Even the mildest dish will have a spice – like turmeric for instance. Unlike Chinese cooking, which often adjusts for seasonal availabilty, the Indian recipes are pretty static. This is because the basic ingredients are *available* year round and many are dry ingredients. Even in this age of refrigeration, Tamil cooking includes sun dried mutton and vegetables called *Vatthal* (litt: "reduction"). Naturally, the Chinese have Peking duck and every Malaysian knows dried salted fish and ikan bilis.

The food philosophy of Indian cooking is based more on taste than texture, as I sees it. The Tamil Siddha system of medicine has the algorithm that food ought to be medicine and medicine food (*Unavey marunthu, Marunthey unavu*). It lists lists six types of types of taste (*Arusuvai – six flavours or tastes*) that must be present in every Tamil meal, for it to be complete. They are: – salty (*uvarppu*), sweet (*inippu*), bitter (*kaippu*), pungent (*kaarppu*), astringent (*tuvarppu*) and, sour (*pulippu*). The sugar in Indian food comes last, in the form of desserts, like payasam, kesari etc. The entrées have salt added, astringency, or tanginess as in rasam, thairu; bitterness of bitter gourd asofoetida; sourness of pickles and chutneys. If we are what we eat, then it makes sense that the different tastes or properties will work on the different conditions in the body, namely acidic, alkaline, bile etc. Traditional Indian food is more vegetarian, believing that plant sources contain all the elements needed. The meat is an occasional occurrence, and if it is more common nowadays, it is only due to affluence and availability.

As for presentation, colour is not paramount. In fact, Indian food is often a mash (mush?) of fully cooked ingredients. It is more to tongue appeal as opposed to the Chinese need for eye appeal.

Chinese entrees stand apart from Indian and Malay food in their made to order freshness. The food is actually individually prepared and served steaming hot to the table. Malay and Indian food are usually prepared in advance in large pots, and kept on warmers. That is not a bad thing, considering that fish curry, like old wine, actually tastes better when *sund*(ed) ("reduced") the next day! But pre-cooked veggies? – Hmmn! The made to order food in Indian restaurants are usually the snack type (dosai, roti canai, and chapatti, and of course mamak mee.

Malay ccoking methods include '*Tumis*' (pan fry with small amount of oil), '*Salai*' (to smoke, grill or roast), '*Sangai*' (slow fry with dried spices), '*Layur*' (dry cooking with low heat), '*Tanak*' (pot-cooking, especially for rice), '*Jerang*' (to boil, mostly for soups), '*Celur*' (to blanch in hot water) and '*Reneh*' (to simmer). Wiki – Malaysian Cuisine: Kaleidoscope of Flavours

Food, being the epitome of hospitality, it commonly occurs in the local idiom. Tamil has a folk saying that, hospitality/feasting (*Virunthu*) and medicine (*Marunthu*) are only for 3 days. It is understood by this, that just as cold medicine is prescribed for 3 days, you don't overstay your welcome by more than three days. Is that why the average hotel booking is three days and two nights? Go figure.

Yin and Yang

In Chinese culture (and elsewhere) it's believed that the universe is held together by the balancing of positive (yang) and negative (yin) energy. This philosophy of balancing positive and negative forces in order to create a harmonious state is found throughout all aspects of Chinese life from politics to cookery.

Some foods are yin or 'cold' food e.g. bean sprout, bananas, coconut, water chestnut, while others are yang or 'hot' food e.g. garlic, aubergine, pineapple, turkey, pizza. Deficiencies in or excess of these positive or negative foods can lead to illness and it's a cook's responsibility to create a balanced meal.

Yi xing Bu xing

Skip this paragraph if you have a weak stomach! The Chinese rarely waste potential food, meaning there is no part of the animal that they won't eat. In addition, they believe in Yi xing bu xing'. In other words, by using a particular part of an animal's body, the human equivalent will be strengthened. So eat monkey brains for wisdom and tiger testicle for male stamina. However, these are considered delicacies and only served at banquets and special occasions.

The eight major traditions of Chinese cuisine

"Shandong cuisine, Lu cuisine – North eastern.The masterly cooking techniques include bao (爆; quick frying), liu (溜; quick frying with corn flour), pa (扒; stewing), kao (烤; roasting), zhu (煮; boiling), and using sugar to make fruit and crystallising with honey.

Sichuan cuisine – It has bold flavours, particularly the pungency and spiciness resulting from liberal use of garlic and chili peppers, as well as the unique flavour of Sichuan pepper. Kung Pao chicken, Sichuan hot pot

Cantonese cuisine – Yue Cuisine – The Teochew cuisine and Hakka cuisine of Guangdong are considered their own styles, as is neighboring Guangxi's cuisine [zh] despite also being considered culturally Cantonese. Its prominence outside China is due to the large number of Cantonese emigrants. Many cooking methods are used, with steaming and stir frying being the most favoured due to their convenience and rapidity. Other techniques include shallow frying, double steaming, braising and deep frying. Black bean, hoisin, oyster sauces. Sweet and sour sauce. Century egg, Char siew, sweet sour pork, stir-fried kangkong. Cantonese Kong Foo Cha, Hor Fun (Singapore mee hoon), Yee mee, Wonton Mee, Chee Cheong Fun, Siu Mai, red bean/mung bean pao. Soups – sharksfin, bird's nest, sea cucumber. Congee – rice porridge, ABC. Dim Sum or,"little heart" is usually a breakfast meal.

Fujian cuisine – Min/Hokkien – Unique seasonings from Fujian include fish sauce, shrimp paste, sugar, shacha sauce and preserved apricot. Fujian is also well known for its "drunken" (wine marinated) dishes and is famous for the quality of the soup stocks and bases used to flavour their dishes, soups and stews. Bak Kut The (meat bone tea), Popiah, mee sua. Hokkien Mee

Jiangsu cuisine – Su. In general, Jiangsu cuisine's texture is characterised as soft, but not to the point of mushy or falling apart. In addition, Jiangsu cuisine also focuses on heating temperature. Braised spare ribs

Zhejiang cuisine – Zhe. Stewed pork belly, beggar's chicken

Hunan cuisine – Xiang. Both Hunan and Sichuan cuisine are perhaps significantly oilier than the other cuisines in China, but Sichuan dishes are generally oilier than Hunan dishes. Another characteristic distinguishing Hunan cuisine from Sichuan cuisine is that, in general, Hunan cuisine uses smoked and cured goods in its dishes much more frequently.

Anhui cuisine – Hui. similar to Jiangsu cuisine." – Wikipedia

Outside the eight traditions of Chinese cuisine above, other regional styles are very familiar to Malaysians. Teochew food from the area around Swatow in China is another style noted for it's delicacy and natural favorite. It is known for it's seafood and Char Kway Teow (stir-fried flat rice noodles) with cockles, beansprout and prawns. It has to have chilly paste stirred in. Also Teochew (Chaoshan) Food – Teochew Porridge (Congee), Egg Fooyong (omelette)

Hakka food is another Malaysian mainstay. It is known for the use of preserved meats and tofu as well as stewed and braised dishes. You have to thank them for Yong Tau Foo. It consists primarily of tofu that has been stuffed with either a ground meat mixture or fish paste (surimi). Slit lady's finger, bitter gourd, and egg-plant can also be used as containers for the fish paste, which are then steamed and eaten with chillie and hoisin sauce.

Hainanese Food – Chicken Rice, Chicken Chop (modified from British chop) – The Hainanese were, afterall, the favourited personal cooks ("cookies") of the British administrators and entrepreuner alike.

Tamil cuisine has its regional variations, like Chettinadu, Kongunadu, Madurai and Thanjavur styles, although Madurai is the more standard in Malaysia. Likewise Malay rice dishes (pilafs) reflect various regions as nasi ulam, nasi kerabu (Kelantan), nasi minyak, nasi dagang (Trengganu), nasi ambeng, nasi tumpeng (Javanese), nasi padang (Minangkabau), nasi kandar (Indian Muslim) not forgetting the universal nasi lemak. A national icon. And then, there is any number of nasi like nasi beriani, nasi minyak (Indian inspired), nasi ayam (hainanese), nasi campur (chinese), nasi tomato, nasi arab (?).

Now, let us look at the different items on the plate. They are listed in groups, not necessarily in any particular order, either of full course meal, or alphabetical. All good: Dum good briyani, Bak good teh, and ....

Preliminaries: Bismillah, Grace, Kaakkaa Soru, Ancestral Offering

Naturally, food is something that everyone is thankful for whether one verbalizes it or not. Indeed, physiological need (food inclusive) is the most basic of Abraham Maslow's five tier hierarchy of needs. Every religion has its own form of what is known as *saying grace*, or thanksgiving.

Muslims worldwide, mouth the Arabic: *"Bismillahi wa barakatillah".* English: "In the name of Allah and with the blessings of Allah". This is before the meal. Unique to them, they also say a post meal thanksgiving in Arabic: *"Alhamdulillah".* English: "Praise be to Allah". The language doesn't seem specific to food. So, perhaps it could apply to any legal activity.

The Bismillah and Alhamdulillah are generally said individually, each person saying it softly or silently even while dining in a group. Grace, in the Christian setting is often said by an appointed person or head of the table. While the Islamic grace is fixed, the Christian grace is usually free form.

Grace is from the Latin *gratia*, or thanks (gratitude, gratefulness). In Christian theology, it also denotes the unmerited (freely given) favour of God, from the Greek *charis* (graciousness, gratis). Hence Christians say *grace* (gratia/thanks) for the *grace* (charis/favour) from God. It commonly follows this formula: *"Bless us, oh Lord, and these thy gifts which we are about to receive from thy bounty through Christ our Lord. Amen".*

One Tamil meal prayer goes: *"Oh supreme one of South Madurai, Sokkanaatha (Siva) who creates all worlds, give me the heart to serve you and to think of you everyday".* Again, this is not meal specific and could apply to any valid activity.

Not current in Malaysia, but Hindu Tamils of the old country practice the habit of *Kaakkaa Soru* ("Crow Rice") – the feeding of some of the rice to crows first, before sitting down for their meals. It is understood that the crows represent their *Pithru,* or ancestors.

A Hindu prayer in Sanskrit, called the *Bhojana Mantra,* litt. "Meal Prayer", is:

"Aum, beloved Shakti of Siva, fullness everlasting and fully manifest as this food; O, Mother of the universe, nourish us with this gift of food so that we may attain knowledge, dispassion and spiritual perfection. Goddess Parvati is my mother. God Maheshvara is my father. All devotees of Siva are my family. All three worlds are my home. Aum, that is Fullness. Creation is fullness. From Divine Fullness flows this world's fullness. This fullness issues from that Fullness, yet that Fullness remains full. Aum, peace, peace, peace. Aum, this I offer unto Siva".

Like most things Buddhist, the pre meal prayer is a chant. This a Theravada chant. When the Five Reflections are chanted before a meal, these four lines are added after the Fifth Reflection:

"The first morsel is to cut all delusions.
The second morsel is to maintain our clear mind.
The third morsel is to save all sentient beings.
May we awaken together with all beings".

Like the Hindu offering to the the ancestors, Buddhist's feed their bhikkus (monks) food as alms. While no record exists for Taoist grace, they do offer their ancestors sweetmeats and savouries at Chinese New Year. Another occasion of feeding is the Hungry Ghost festival where the spirits of ancestors come to roam the earth in search of food. And there always some fresh fruit or food on the family altar.

Taoism teaches that food on the altar will be consumed by "someone, namely, higher powers or "masters". They in turn give back when requested. It is a two way barter, like the sky giving up its excess (Rain) and the earth giving up its excess (heat and humidity). A constant recycling that happens in the earthly cycle of life. Ultimately, it is a form of thanksgiving to nature.

One man's <u>meat</u>: Beef, Mutton, Pork

One won't touch it because of its holiness. One won't be caught dead with it because of its uncleanness. And another considers both game (!). When it comes to eating habits or preferences, Malaysians are as diverse as beef, mutton and pork.

In fact, one might even address the three major racial groups of Malaysia as cows (Malays), goats (Indians) and pigs (Chinese). Afterall, we are mammals too. According to a book written on the infamous May 13th 1969 racial riots in Kuala Lumpur, some Malays in Kampung Baru were heard saying, "we're done with the pigs, now lets finish off the goats."

Now, that dark day was an unfortunate and forgettable stain on our collective history, but in current day-to-day Malaysia, these distinctions are another colourful strand in our multihued social fabric. We have become so identified with these meats that it is not a slur, but a badge of instant identification.

Malays are enjoined by their Islamic code, to stay away from hogs (or swine). It is an extension of the Mosaic law against anything to do with animals with cloven hoofs, of which pigs are a part. Part of this Semitic culinary proscription has to do with proper, prescribed methods of slaughtering the approved "halal" animals. The Muslim butcher, would need to say a certain prayer ("With the name of Allah .....") and draw blood in a way that would cause the least amount of pain to the food source. Anything contrary to this procedure is "haram" or unclean. By this definition, I suppose fresh road kill, even if is still alive at the time, is unacceptable.

How interesting! Muslims and Jews united in at least this matter. When living in the States for 14 years, I noticed Muslims could buy meat slaughtered by Jews, without question. Indeed, my Muslim American friends say that buying from a Jewish butcher is more than acceptable because the Jewish ("Kosher" = "Halal") code is even more stringent than the Muslim one.

What a place, then, to start the journey of peace in the Middle East. *Shalom* and *Salaam* at the dining table! Today in Israel, Jewish food is indistinguishable from the Palestinian. Both love falafel, the common snack of the Middle-East.

Back in Malaysia, even though we have mutually exclusive meat habits, there is peace in the land. Aside from the meat untouchables, we love digging into each other's plates, both figuratively and literally. Festival days are times to look forward to, and open houses awaited with much anticipation of bounteous buffets of the host's ethnic cuisine.

It can be assuredly assumed that the nexus of greatest unity is food. Not only do we frequent the other ethnic restaurants (except for Muslims who avoid pork based Chinese restaurants) our specific cuisines and spices overflow into each other's pots. Case in point: Curry Mee = **Curry** (Tamil) + **Mee** (Chinese); Roti Canai = **Roti** (Hindi) + **Canai** (Malay); Apam Balik = **Apam** (Tamil) + **Balik** (Malay); Tek Tarik = **Teh** (Chinese) + **Tarik** (Malay). And so on.

In this connection, Indian eateries appear to be savouring the best of all worlds in terms of the varieties of customers. Malay ethnic restaurants draw mainly Malay customers. Chinese restaurants are frequented by Chinese and Indian diners. The Indian (including Mamak) establishments get diners of all races. Often you'll find all of them represented at a table. Even the European back-packer tourist knows how to ask for the roti canai. Apparently that fulfils their need for bread as well as local content in their food. Perhaps the draw for Indian cuisine is because the meats served are acceptable to all. Or, perchance it has to do with the recent published studies of the anti-cancer properties of curry spices such as turmeric etc? It is more likely, the former.

While on the topic of Malay meat preferences, the other indigenous people (Bumiputra) such as the Kadazan-Dusun of Sabah and the Iban of Sarawak, as well as the aboriginals (Pribumi) have their own preferences. They, like the Chinese, are likely free to eat as they fancy. Coming of age, the Iban youth goes out on his own to hunt his food. Likely, it would be monkeys, with their blowpipes.

The Indians, who are themselves a hodge podge, potpourri, include Muslims and some Christians who eat beef. The Hindu's and Sikh's religious sentiments steer them away from beef, although a section of Hindus do eat beef. The Hindu reasoning for beef avoidance is, the cow is a sacred icon in Hinduism, equivalent to milk giving mother. And you don't eat your mother. However, I cannot figure out why you can't eat the bull which is not a holy figure (except as Shiva's vehicle, Nandi). Or, what about the water buffalo, a different species? Doesn't the female goat give milk too? Or, the whale? Why wouldn't they count as mother.

To be fair, many Hindus together with most Buddhists, eschew (don't chew?!) meat entirely and opt for vegetarianism altogether or veganism. Chinese Buddhists have found a superbly creative way of producing meat flavoured food from vegetable sources, particularly soy. There are special restaurants dedicated to this kind of cuisine. They originated in Buddhist monasteries. But then, if you truly want to be vegetarian why hanker after the animal flavours? That sounds suspiciously like wanting to keep your cake and eat it too. Wouldn't true abstinence mean abstaining from any hint of meat at all?

Tamil Muslim (Mamak) restaurants, perhaps in deference to their Hindu brethren, are not known to serve beef in their menu, whereas all Malay restaurants serve beef exclusively as their preferred red-meat. Fact is, Indian Muslims, at least the Tamil Muslims in South India, do not consume beef. This may be due to the abundance of mutton there. It may also be said of the Arabs, where sheep and camels are the readily available meats. Muslims in Tamil Nadu go to great lengths to slaughter camels imported from Rajasthan in North India, during the Korban festival of Eid-il – Adha corresponding to the end of the Hajj season. Recently, at a Sri Melor (Indian Muslim restaurant chain) outlet in Klang, the waiter asked if I preferred my *rava thosai* with vegetarian dips. If only everyone could exhibit such cultural competence. No, I wanted fish curry, thank you.

The curiosity of how Indian Muslims came to be "Mamak" deserves some explanation. There is no Malay word "Mamak". "Maama", is a Tamil term of address for your maternal uncle, father-in-law, or, your older sister's husband. Often, a wife calls her husband, "Maama", just for kicks, and having had no previous family ties to him. This harks back to a time it was fashionable, for girls to be married off to the mother's younger brother (maama).The Indian Muslim stall owners, being commonly brothers and uncles and nephews, and Malay customers hearing the frequent use of "maama" in the hawkers' conversation, started calling them all "mamak". That is the most certifiable theory of mamak name origin, that I have heard. Another theory, albeit a little distant in time, alludes to the influence of Tamils in the royal court of Malacca. Some were even Sultans, Prime Ministers and advisors and commingled and intermarried with the Malay royalty. Hence, the *Maamas* – maternal uncles and fathers – in – law in the court, and out.

The Chinese, generally have no qualms about meat consumption. He is wont to boast about eating, "anything that moves." This must have something to do with those great famines of old in China, where their forebears had to eat most anything to survive. It must be mentioned here, that the Chinese Hailam (from Hainan island) cooking is pork free, to the extent that Malays and other Muslims are comfortable dining there.

The overall top choice in Chinese chow, is pork, the "other white meat", as the American Pork Board advertisement goes. It is deep-fried, stir-fried, steamed, baked, boiled, broiled, or roasted in various sauces and marinades. Roast pork of two kinds, Char Siew and Siu Yuk, are favourites to go along with Chicken rice. Suckling pigs (2 to 6 month old piglets) are also a delicacy. The boiled, soup dish Bak-Kut-Teh is a popular menu, especially in Klang, the Bak-Kut-Teh capital of Malaysia.

Nowadays, the Chinese restaurateur or stall-holder is careful to ask his non-Chinese patrons if they would like pork (Ba) in their noodle or fried rice. He may even ask his Chinese customer the same question, especially since the outbreak of the swine epidemic (Japanese Encephalitis) of 1999. So you might opt for Chick-Kut-Teh (Chicken).

Speaking of chicken, it is the great common denominator of food. Everyone is able to enjoy it. You only have to visit the local KFC outlet and see the full house, of all races. They may be a cow, goat or pig, but each will prepare a chicken dish on their special festive days so that their open-house guests will have a sure thing on their plates.

The Chinese, as we have seen, are like the "Fear Factor" sportsmen – prone to try anything. The back lanes in Chinatown are bound to yield soups or entrée of almost any critter of your choice. Turtle soup?, monkey brain, dog dish anybody? Try Madras lane, off Petaling Street in KL's Chinatown.

The Indians are particularly identified with the "udumbu", or Iguana/ monitor lizard. Even in the old days a very few deliberately hunted and cooked them. These days there are almost none, but the identification of Indians as Iguana eaters has stuck. As a young boy, I have heard said that when you eat udumbu, make sure you don't vomit it out. Bad things will happen to your stomach, like being knotted up in excruciating pain.

From what I heard from connoisseurs in those days, iguana tastes like chicken, which reminds me of foolhardy foodies who say the same thing about snakes and alligators. I once went to a Spanish restaurant, the Don Quixote, in Valparaiso, Indiana our hometown of 2½ years in the US of A. He serves bison, ostrich, alligator and other exotic meat on a particular day in a year, at a great discount. But alas, we went on the wrong day, and so missed the experience. But we did have alligator stew at a black restaurant in town, and it tasted like chicken alright.

About 4 four years earlier, when we were domiciled in Abilene, Texas, we seldom missed the annual Rattlesnake Roundup in the small town of Sweetwater down the highway to the west. That was a take on the "rodeo", that every town in the west holds annually. Rodeos have to do with cattle roundups, bucking broncos and bulls, piglet catching (for the future cowboys), and food and fair rides. The rattlesnale roundoup is all these, without the catttles and horses.

A few days before the event, locals scour the arid countryside for snakes (rattlesnale only). They are poured into a pit in the arena, for view. They are taken out by an expert handler for demonstration on poison milking, skinning, and butchering and cooking demos. Kentucky fried rattlers tasted like the real thing, eventhough the bones were bushy like the seed of the *buah kedondong* (ambarella, amra).

While cooking technology may have changed, cooking techniques have not. My grandmother, who was a young maiden at the beginning of the last century, often marvelled how a simple chicken gravy with minimal spices and water (cooking oil unavailable then!), *"would give a smell that wafted 7 houses away."* In fact, the smells and flavours of those times are somehow difficult to duplicate in the present time.

Table Manners: Banana leaf, Chopstick, Clean Plate

Is there anywhere, etiquette is more full flavored than at the dining table? Hence, table manners, along with the unspoken signals and gestures that inform the waiter of one's needs.

Etiquette involves rules of social conduct, such as awaiting one's turn at the table as the turn table (Lazy Susan) turns bringing food in turns, your way, which attitude in turn returns a good turn for you by establishing you as a respectable member of society. It is polite conversation, which means listening actively before responding. It means not being a "Greedy Pig", a 'euphemism' for gluttony. While etiquette generally refers to interaction between guests co-equally seated at a table, there is a parallel interaction that goes on between table guest and table waiter – an unspoken communication, with its own rules of grammar and vocabulary. At a Chinese restaurant, you politely top up the teeny weeny tea cups of the others before you fill up your own. When the teapot gets empty, you dangle its little lid diametrically across the mouth of the pot. It signals to the waiter, "refill please." As he does does it, your surreptitiously tap your index and middle fingers on the table edge, as a way of thanking him.

The seating arrangement in a typical Chinese dinner is predictable. The Confucian banquet etiquette requires guests to sit according to their rank, presumably in a sliding scale. So, does junior get the bones (?!). What rank? At a round table (full circle), don't the most senior and most junior end up sitting side by side? Even if ranking may not be the practice in these latter days, most often than not, Chinese eat at a round table of 10 or more people. It is considered a symbol of perfection. The elder usually gets to sit at the head of the table (wherever he sits), and even serves the juniors. It is similar to the American table at Thanksgiving, where the family head has the honor of carving up the Turkey.

Chopticks are an extension of your fingers. You don't hold them carelessly, in a way that the tips point at the person across the table. Its rude, like pointing or accusing. Hold it such that they point downwards, toward the food, or lay it on the chopstick rest. Neither should you touch the chopstick of the others, as would likely happen if louts lewdly lunge for that luscious last morsel. Back off! And don't stick the chopsticks (!) into the little bowl of rice. You'll be committing a big boo boo and break a major taboo. That "sticky" situation resembles incence sticks stuck into the little red bowls in front of the ancestral altar. Hints of death and human impermanence have no place in the dining room, see?

Someone may stand up and reach to serve the others, especially from the soup basin. As in the Western scene, it is also common to pass the platters. It is most unwelcome and unsightly to pass them over your neighbours head! Decorum, please!

In an Indian home or restaurant after a satiating *saadham* (rice) on banana leaf, the guest folds the leaf towards himself or herself. It sends the universal message of a satisfied customer, "compliments to the chef." Folding the leaf towards you indicates appreciation and means in effect, "I shall return". Folding the leaf away from yourself says, "the food and service was not that great" or, "I won't be returning here anytime soon." The action resembles an infant pushing away food it doesn't fancy.

This is quite similar to the old Jewish custom. If the guest or master of the house wishes to go the restroom and plans to return and continue the meal, all he has to do is neatly fold the napkin and lay it on the table. It basically says, "I'll be back!" If he doesn't intend to return or is done eating, he will simply crumple the napkin and chuck it on the table.

Christians see a significant connection between this Hebrew habit and the biblical account of Christ's resurrection. When the Roman guards entered his empty tomb, they found Jesus' funereal sheet neatly folded up. The parting words of Christ before his ascension, "I will return", makes the message more sublime in context.This Jewish gastronomic morse code of the folded napkin gels well with Christian eschatology, i.e the study of end times and the Judgement Day.

At the end of a meal, Indians and Malays, especially of the earlier generation, often sprinkle a little water onto the plate. As most often happens, you will probably get a thousand explanations if you asked around. You have the feeling that it might be a kind of metaphor for eating, the act of wetting the plate mirroring the quenching of the dry, hungry stomach. Or, it may be the conscious act of a conscientious consumer concerned that the cutlery cleaner not have to contend with a parched curry crusted plate.

Malays and Indians typically eat with their hand. And, the right hand please, even if you are a lefty. The right hand is the "good" hand, that greets, writes, salutes etc. The left is the one that does the 'dirty work', suffice it to say. It frequently happens, when eating with your hands, that your left elbow wants to rest on the table. It might be OK if you do it at home, but it is supposedly rude in front of company. I have had that pointed out many a time by my elders. Reason? It indicates a slouch, shall we say? And that is not the optimum position for food intake. For that matter, you don't slouch anywhere – in classroom, in the presence of company, in prayer to your creator. Except, perhaps, in your private cloister.

Corporate dinners come with their own innuendo encoded cues. At a Chinese boardroom banquet, if a steamed fish platter is placed with the head facing you, Quick! Duck! Fish head pointing at a person means that he is being fired. Hopefully, thats just ancient legend.

In Malay custom, by way of Islamic tradition, waste is frowned upon. Therefore, guests are expected to scoop just enough food onto the plate so as to "clean it". You can always add another instalment if able to finish it. It is a polite gesture to show the host your satisfaction in the meal. How? It is OK to show overt delight or gusto when accepting a serving of food. The Spanish *Mi Gusto Mucho* means, "I like it very much!". It is even better if you can burp, or fake it in the Arab way!

The Shape of Food:

The habit of 'seeing things' and perceiving certain attributes based on the shape and sound of things continues into other aspects of everyday life. If they sense that the sound of the number four is akin to that of "death" in Chinese, then that number is to be avoided.

For instance,

Mandarin (瓯柑; ōugān) – gold, wealth,

Pomegranate (石榴; shíliu) – many offsprings,

Noodles (面条; miàntiáo) uncut – long life,

Besides ascribing positive qualities to food that look like organs, the Chinese nowadays, or at least some of them, even go to the extent of eating animals organs to impute their qualities to their own organs. For example, eating pig testicles or vagina is good for the reproductive processes of the male or female respectively, and so on.

The western take on this has already been dealt with in the section on beliefs. J. Crow, suggests that the shape of food foreshadows its use, as per the saying, "you are what you eat". He believes that this concept, the archaic "Doctrine of Signatures", has been confirmed by nutrition science. Every natural food that has certain anatomical shape, directly benefits the corresponding human organ. This is quite relatable to the Chinese foot reflexology (acupressure) mapping of the foot corresponding to the human anatomy. For example, if you apply pressure to the "neck" of second and third toes, you are accessing the eyes."

In indian culture/cuisine, shapes and colours also played a role in their choice as food. *"The key to human use of plants was hidden in the forms of the plant itself (signature); so close observation helps to recognize the utility of the plants, the hidden treasures of the Almighty, for the benefit of life."* – Dr. Arpita Mondal.

My mother told me to finish up my beetroot – it was good for the blood. She also said murungai leaves were good for the eyesight. Don't ask me what medical text she got that from.

To make it simpler, lets just eat what God has provided for us, and let nature take care of the benefits. The doctrine of signatures has been, like other pseudo-sciences, been disowned by precise science.

Breakfast: Nasi Lemak, Idli – Thosai, Youtiao

Breakfast is the only meal that is specific and unchanging. Say, an American breakfast of sausage and biscuit plus coffee, or a continental one of bread with butter and jam, plus scrambled egg and tea. Would you have those for lunch or dinner? Yet, you will have any number of things for lunch or dinner, right?

Likewise it is with Malaysian breakfast. Yes, you might have a few variations once in a while but what immediately comes to mind at breakfast time – Nasi Lemak, Idli – Thosai and Youtiou/Dim-Sum. These three are the representative ethnic fast breakers of Malaysia.

Nasi lemak has earned its position as the national breakfast, nay, national dish of Malaysia. In 2018, Time magazine even included it in the top 10 healthiest breakfasts of the world. Cooked in coconut milk, you woud think, "healthy?" Some say that the distinction came as a result of comparing a small packet of NL to the heavier american breakfast.

That argument aside, there is no denying the observable fact that Nasi Lemak is the undisputed favourite at breakfast. Eventhough the roti canai (RC)/roti prata is a strong rival, RC is an any time food, unlike NL. Other items in the Malay breakfast menu can include soto, a range of kuih, rice with rendang etc.

The Indian home, or restaurant evokes Idli or thosai plus saambhar. The World Health Organisation (WHO) had designated Idli as the healthiest food. Why not? With ¾ portion special rice and ¼ portion black gram (ulundhu) soaked overnight and ground you get the right proportion of carbohydrate and protein. The batter fermented overnight provides the probiotics. The steaming adds to the positive factors. The saambhar (lentil stew) that goes with the idli adds another layer of spice, protein and vegetable.

Besides, idli the other items can be the thosai, a crepe made with a similar batter to the idli's. Then there is the idiyappam (stringhoppers), paal appam, vadai varieties and roti canai/chappati to choose from.

The trademark Chinese breakfast is the youtiao (char koay tiao) and black coffee, followed by Dim Sum. A morning Dim Sum session can be likened to a layman's multicourse dinner. You wave down the waiters drifting by with their trays of tapas and choose your morsels, much like you would from a sushi train.

Other runners up can be a range of noodles like wan tan, Singapore mee, curry laksa, and steamed items like yam cake and chee cheong fun.

Breakfast, being the first meal of the day, seems to enjoy its own mood and grammar. It has to be specific, wholesome and inviting as if to a vacation, after a long period of bed bound boredom.

The Banquet: Kenduri, Virunthu, yàn huì

The Chinese wedding binge makes for a deliberate, delectable, delicious, delightful by design dining experience, with each course a mélange of small morsels. Reminds you somewhat, of the Spanish pub crawl or bar hop experience, where the *tapas* they serve are bite sized canapes, hors d'ouevres, that you down with drinks. Similarly, the Chinese banquet is generous with the ale and alcohol, as the guests crawl leisurely from one course to another. No, aa-ii-yaa, the courses are brought to the their table lah!

Humankind's love affair with flavourful food is nicely summed up by this Chinese aphorism: *"Born to the earth are three kinds of creatures. Some are winged and fly. Some are furred and run. Still, others stretch their mouths and talk. All must eat and drink to survive."* – (Lu Yu, Ancient Chinese Philosopher)

A typical Chinese 10 course dinner may look like this:

Fried chicken, (butter chicken, sweet sour etc); Fish (crispy sweet sour, steamed etc); mushroom platter (shiitake, abalone); a Pork item (baked, braised, or barbequed); Shrimp (butter prawn, salted egg, kung pau); Four seasons vegetable; Julienned abalone, sea cucumber etc combo (chewy cruncy texture). Fried Rice. Sweet sea coconut for dessert. The soup usually appears in the middle of the dinner. It is usually a bird's nest, sharksfin or chicken with veggies soup, the last being the least ostentatious. It is always a fine dining experience.

What is the significance of these arranging of foods? Chinese focus on texture. Indians focus on pungency and spiciness. Malay focus on gingery, lemony, tanginess.

In the Indian indulgence, whether it be a buffet or banana leaf table service or dome style, all the various dishes are slapped together on a dish or leaf. Unlike the Chinese experience, what you plop onto your plate as dictated by your palate, makes for a palatable palette on your eversilver platter. You mix the items with rice or straight, dispatching it down the gullet.

At the buffet line, it is a mad dash to the hash. Afterall, the Tamil truism, *Panthikku Munthu, Padaikku Pinthu* means, "hurtle to the feast, hang back on the battlefield." In the battle between heroism and hedonism, gutsy and gluttony, valour and victual, courage and cuisine, the latter usually wins. Another similar Tamil saying, "*It's the crying baby that gets the milk*", describes our attitude to food. "First come, first served" is what everyone is familiar with. That doesn't mean we shouldn't serve our neighbour first. Only means, "makanlah, don't be shy."

At the dome service, only the rice is served by waiters at the beginning with juice flowing throughout. A sample menu might look like this:

Vanaspathy Briyani Rice, Vegetable Kurma, Mutton Peratal (wet consistency), Chicken varuval (dry consistency), Prawn Sambal, Eggplant kootu (stew), Cucumber Salad (pachidi), Sweet preserved fruit acchaar, Payasam (sweet desert).

The usual Malay kenduri consists of piles of nasi minyak (Ghee rice), or briyani rice (Nasi Beryani), sweet corn rice (Nasi Jagung), Arabian fragrant rice (Nasi Bukhari) and tomato rice (Nasi Tomato). Out of these, 'Nasi Minyak' is the popular choice, and you will more often than not hear your friends hinting when they say 'I'll be waiting for your Nasi Minyak'. It is a simple yet fragrant rice that is cooked with spices and a generous dose of ghee or clarified butter.

The must-have main course in any typical Malay wedding (Sanding) are rendang daging, sambal goreng pengantin, ayam masak merah and dalca. Other popular additional dishes can range from sweet sour fish, sambal prawns, sweet sour prawns, black pepper prawns, kurma, daging gulai kawah.

The customary desserts chosen to end the meal are endless – from bubur chacha, bubur terigu, bubur pulut hitam, kuih talam, kuih kaswi (rice cake with palm sugar), kuih koci (of glutinous rice flour), kuih keria (sweet potato doughnuts), kuih lapis and sago gula Melaka (palm sugar sago)

Other than these main courses, some side dishes that go well may also include delicious rojak petis, tahu telor, satay, acar buah, ulam and acar timun.

Using a small bowl with water or ketor (a jug with cleaning water, together with a big bowl to catch the wash), you dip the tip of all your right fingers for cleansing.

Eating Out: Kopitiam, Warung, Curry House

As food goes, eating out is easily over fifty percentile of the working person's gastronomic activity. Do this math. Say, half of our breakfast is at the office canteen. All of our lunch is at restaurants, cafeterias or seminar rooms. Count a fifth of dinnertimes as taking place outside the home. Factor in the occasional midnight Mamak teh-tarik nightcap, and lo! No wonder Malaysia is said to be a foodie's fantasyland. Food in chic restaurants. In push-carts and peddle-carts, and in converted mini-vans. Food in restaurants and roadside stalls. Food in baskets balanced on kandar poles, like the oldtime Indian guy who peddled nonya kueh's out of those. Food sold out of a box on a bicycle rack or a box balanced on the head, like the Indian kacang putih seller of yore. Only thing we don't have, is food out of sampans, as they do on Bangkok's klongs or canals.

The original Chinese eatery is the coffe shop. They were (now on the endangered list) mom and pop operations, serving roti kahwin/roti bakar (bread toast) and black coffee. And a side of twin half boiled eggs. Some specialized in noodles and others sold chicken or duck rice. Some had mixed rice. The kind of food court style Chinese places prevalent now, is a fairly new phenomenon. These corner shoplot restaurants, known as *Kopitiams* have the owner running the *economy rice buffet stand* and the beverage services. There can be up to 30 stir-fried varieties of food for self service convenience, evoking the ubiquitous Chinese buffet restaurants of the US. The owner rents out space for about 10-12 stalls in the outer perimeter of the place. The stalls here specialize in anything from chicken/ duck rice, char kuey tiau, mee soup, curry mee, pan mee, clay-pot rice, Hokkien/Cantonese stir fried noodles, rice porridge, Pau (steamed rice buns), satay, nasi lemak, roti canai/dosai, rojak/pasembor, bakso, chee cheong fun/yong tau foo, Thai food, Vietnamese food and what have you. You make your order with the respective stallholder and have your food brought to you in the jungle of tables and chairs.

A popular family restaurant, the darling of sundown dining, is the seafood restaurant. That would count as the common man's equivalent of fine dining. Air-conditioned comfort and full service (beverages) is what you avail. You sit down at a red linen attired round table with your family, and wait in anticipation of your favourite course of steamed fish, sweet 'n sour pork, drunken chicken, braised in brandy, whisky, red wine, beer, marmite something or other etc. Kai Lan or asparagus sautéed in garlic, or kangkong in sambal belacan, are some of the popular vegetables in the menu. All the items are fresly cooked to order, unlike the economy rice deal.

The popular Malay eatery is the Tom Yum *warung.* A spacious, well laid out, place with an ethnic Malay look. Usually built on state land, bamboo railings and attap roofs lend that kampong feel. The instant giveway, is the assortment of pink, blue, red, yellow, green fluorescent tubes arranged every which way. It is visually vehement and optically obtrusive in the evening twilight. That's as it should be – a loud welcome call to the joint. As per its eponymous calling card, the warung's main menu is the Tom Yam – a spicy, stand alone, sweet and sour seafood soup with plain white rice. Sides of meat sauces and vegetable stir-fries are often ordered to glam up the family group's dining experience.

A recent development on the restaurant scene, is the appearance of the Chinese Muslim restaurant. More and more places with names like Mohammad Chan, Rahmat Tan, and Mee Tarik Warisan Asli, speak of this niche market run by Chinese Muslims. Like the Indian Muslim places, they are frequented by all. Muslims, who previously could only wonder what Chinese food was like, can now safely indulge.

The Indian or Indian Muslim (Mamak) establishment is a single owner-operator who also likes the corner shop-lot. Apparently, its an Indian trait in New Zealand too. My Kiwi brother-in-law says that they have a saying there – a football metaphor. "Give an Indian a corner, and he will built a store there".

The Indian restaurant or *Curry House,* too, has a teh tarik barista, mamak mee/mee rebus stall, dosai/chapatti/roti canai counter, a mutton/chicken soup spot, a nasi kandar/mixed rice corner, etc. Only difference, all the stalls are sole-proprietor owned. While the Chinese and Malay places are oases of quiet, especially of the waiters, the Indian waiters shout out their orders from whichever table they take orders at. Together with the Tamil music videos on the TV screens, this shouting of orders adds to the quaint cacophonous ambience of the place. A kind of merry atmosphere, if you add the conversations of the diners. You wonder how the cooks who man the stalls can keep track of the shouted orders while doing their stirring, flipping and and tarik-ing. This may change too. There is already a place in Klang where the waiters key in their codes on a handphone-like device, that appears on a receiving thingy at the appropriate stall. It may be an improvement for the workers, but may not be so for the patrons who want the old atmosphere.

A few of the restaurants will also have an upper room. Or side rooms for private parties. You have air-conditioned privacy in addition to your favourite food.

Malaysia is especially conducive to dine-outs, as the great variety of food cannot be duplicated at home. Besides, why go to the cookbook when its readily available by the pros? Besides, doesn't Mama need a break? Besides, don't you want a change of – OOPs! – scenery?

Soup du Jour: Mulligatawny, Wan Tan, Tom Yam

The easiest to prepare, one pot, most fluid of foods as well as the most comfort foodish, is the savoury soup. It exists in all cultures and probably was the first concoction cooked over a fire, after early man threw a tubby tuber into the shimmering embers. Not only is it the standard sustenance for your common cold, it is also a prime prescription for the sunken psyche – read, *"Chicken Soup for the Soul"*. It can be an entire meal on its own and comes in sweet, sour, sweet'n sour, savoury, bitter and a combination. What would life be without it on a cold snowy or a wet rainy night?

Thanks to Queen's English, many foreign words have entered universal usage. With the British fondness for curry, is that to be construed as a cultural appropriation of the Indian cuisine? Another Tamil item that has become solely identified with the British, is *Mulligatawny*, litt. "pepper water". (Tamil: Milagutannir. *Milagu* (pepper) + *Tannir* (water). It is a popular London pub mainstay that was originally pirated and perfected by the Britishers of Madras Presidency from the local concoction. The original base of it is the *rasam*, a thin spicy sour soup taken as an aperitif in Tamil homes and in restaurants to aid digestion. The British added meat and extra items. The closest we have here, to the tangy tawny is the mamak mutton or chicken soup. You certainly want that milagu marinated Mamak mélange when your'e having the sniffles or wanting comfort. Rasam ("juice" in Tamil), is a simple brew with chopped onion, garlic and curry leaves sauteed, with crushed pepper, fennel and fenugreek, turmeric and asoefetida and boiled in water. A refreshing drink equal to Tom Yam in flavour and tongue awakening tang.

Chinese soups are usually clear and thin compared to western, aka french soups, which are blended thick and creamy or, loaded, as in minestrone or French onion. The exceptions are the *hot 'n sour* and *egg drop* soup of the US Chinese buffet. Locally, you might consider the *bird's nest* and the *shark's fin* as non-thin soups. Naturally, these last two belong at the *haute cuisine de Chine* fine dining table and cost you an arm and a leg. No, not literally! The base of the common chinese soup is pork ribs or chicken legs boiled with garlic, ginger and a choice of hairy guard, watercress, or glass noodles (*soo hoon*).

Clear soups with chopped chives floating and submerged fish ball or wan tan usually accompany rice dishes like the hailam chicken rice and the wan tan noodle. They also act as the liquid medium for soup noodles. As with the rasam, chinese soups are meal starters and appetizers. Eventhough Tom Yam is a Thai soup, in Malaysia it has become synonymous with Malay eateries, which feature seafood and tom yam in their menus. A brazen bunch of hot, spicy, savoury and soury is what makes the tom yam a celebrity among soups. Add to this, loud layers of lemongrass, kaffir lime leaves and sexy seafood, and voila! Mummy Mummy! Tom Yam is Yummy in My Tummy!

Somehow, chilli, sour, and salt, make for quite a culinary experience, as evidenced by the the Tom Yam soup. Speaking of souring agents, the Malay sour of choice is the *assam jawa*, which are thin coins shaved from the *gelugor* fruit (Garcinia atroviridis). The *belimbing*, (Averrhhoa bilimbi) is also another popular souring agent, also used by some Indian families in their fish curries. The Chinese use lime juice or black vinegar to kick things up. In Chinese Haute Cuisine (ten course dinners) you sour your bird's nest or sharksfin soup by drizzling a balsamic type of vinegar on it.The Indian sour, which goes without saying, is the Tamarind. Tamarind, of course, is the Arabic, Tamar Al-Hind, or, "Date of India." It is the mainstay of South Indian cooking, for fish curry, rasam etc. North Indian cooking prefers dried mango slices or powder, called *amchoor*. The rasam is the is the meal accompaniment of Tamil cuisine, and digestive aid. Doesn't the mere thought of sour open the floodgates of digestive enzymes in the mouth and stomach?

A common Malaysian soup with a healing attribute is one made from the *haruan* (Snakehead Murrel) fish. It is traditionally given to women in *pantang* (post-delivery convalescence) and those recuperating from surgeries). It is a difficult to dissect, die hard creature. You stun it by knocking its head with a hammer. Perhaps that is the reason for its supposed palliative property.

The heaviest food you can eat is actually the lightest meal. *Wan Tan or Wonton* (One Ton ?) soup is a thin, savoury stock swimming with wan tan, or little dumplings. The broth is brewed by boiling together dried anchovies, garlic, ginger etc Wan Tan means, "Cloud Swallow" in Cantonese because as the dumplings cook in the soup, they rise to the surface. Minced pork is wrapped in a 2 inch by 2 inch eggroll wrapper, and boiled in water. This is not unlike the Italian ravioli, which is a cheese mixture sandwiched between two sheets of dough and cooked in water. Knowing Italian cuisine's imitation of the Chinese noodles (spaghetti etc), the ravioli is quite likely a wan tan wannabee, by way of Marco Polo (?).

Bak Kut Teh, is a light soup of pork bones and meat simmered for hours, in five spice powder and garlic. Meaning,"Pork Rib Tea", it is an eminently drinkable soup that, accompanied by white rice and yu char koay (*you tiao),* can be a wholesome meal by itself. In fact, it was what gave the Hokkien harbour coolies of Klang, Singapore and Penang their sustenance and energy. A morning pick me up, if you will. Well, come to think of it! Is that why Bak-Kut Teh shops mostly sell in the early mornings?

The *Teh* in Bak Kut Teh, could very well refer to "Tea" or broth. However, just as most would nominate the coastal town of Klang as the founding site and world capital of the soup, so would the descendents of Lee Boon Teh, claim that the soup is named after him. Someone should also check out the claim that most Bak Kut Teh operators in Klang are Lees. While the Malaysian bak kut teh are Hokkien, with its stong herbs and dark soy sauce, Singaporean, Teochew bak kut teh is clear and only pepper infused.

Another big entry in the Malay restaurant menu, besides Tom Yam, is *Sup Utara,* or "Northen Soup." *Ox-tail soup,* besides being pub and hotel fare, is also asoociated with Malay restaurants. It can be stew-like. *Gear-box soup*, is also more common in northern states like Kedah and Kelantan. Bye the bye, why do all these soups have a northern incidence or origin. What gives? Could it have anything to do with their bordering Thailand, the land of Tom Yam?

The name "gear box", for a food is head turning and interesting. I have been aware of it for years and thought it referred to the animals gut – which I associate with the vehicle's gear box. However, it turns out the gear reference is to the bovine's kneebones, due to its size. I still don't get it. The gear-box is inside the vehicle, not in the wheel well. Anyhow, it's a spicy sour, stew like soup with the gear-box (big bone) stuck upright in the middle of the bowl. Sometimes, it comes with a drinking straw, to suck out the marrow. From my experience with bone marrow in dalcha (bone sambar), there's not a great chance of finding marrow, if it had melted out in the long boil. However, all these northern soups, sound attractive and inviting.

Unlike *soup du jour* (soup of the day), Malaysian soups are standard, daily fare in the respective cuisines. Each shop will specialize in one soup only. It works for the customer, since you can't expect much from a jack of all soups. A soup specialist, even if he is a soup Nazi (Seinfeld character), will have patrons lining up.

Peace Porridge: Bubur Lambuk, Congee, Kool(u)

Bubur Lambuk, is a specialty Ramadan preparation in Kampung Baru (Litt: New Village), in KL. Kampung Baru, like the Chinese New Villages everywhere, are actually aging, run down places. The Chineese New villages were a British effort to contain the communist threat.

Bubur Lambuk (dumpling porridge?) echoes The *Nonbu Kanji* (fasting porridge) of Tamil Nadu that makes its appearance during Ramzan (Ramadhan). It is a porridge made in an elaborate process and served as *iftar*, or breaking of fast meal due to its fast breakdown in the stomach. In fact, it is already pre-broken down.

About the Bubur Lambuk – *"However, the more commonly accepted claim is that this iconic Ramadan recipe was created in 1949 by the late Said Benk. He was a Pakistani immigrant, and a congregant of the old Jamek mosque (Masjid Jamek) in an area called Kampung Baru, in Kuala Lumpur, the capital of Malaysia.*

One day, during Ramadan, the fasting month, he brought with him a homemade rice porridge for Iftar (breaking of the fast), sharing it with his fellow congregants. It proved to be such a hit, that he was asked to make it for everyone for the rest of the month. I am inclined to believe this story because bubur lambuk has a definite south Asian (Indian, Pakistani, etc) flavour to it.

In fact, I'd even go as far as saying that the precursor of Bubur Lambuk is Haleem, *that South Asian porridge-like stew made of meat and grains. Which in turn, owes its origin to an old, Arabic dish called Harisa."* – Azlin Bloor, Food Blogger.

Congee is the name of the Chinese rice porridge. In Malaysia it is now more commonly called bubur, or Teochew porridge. Coincidentally, that word itself comes from the Tamil word *Kanji* meaning, porridge or starch. The word most likely got to be a descriptor of Chinese porridge when British merchants went from India to China. Kanji is also the Malay word for starch.

Kool or koolu, is a type of poor man's porridge made by boiling broken rice and *kelviragu* (finger millet) flour. The resulting thick purple *kali* (paste) is liquefied by adding yogurt, sambaar, or water and drunk with curry accompaniments or plain old green chilli.

And then there are the sweet porridges like payasam, bubur chacha, bubur pulut hitam, mung bean porridge etc. Payasam is a sweet Tamil gruel, served as desset at wedding banquets, festivals and for high tea. Its ingredients are *semiya* (vermicelli), *javvarisi* (sago), *thratchai* (raisins), *munthiri* (cashew nut), as well as cardamom braised in ghee. The entirety is boiled in milk and saffron for a golden, eggnog lookalike.

Bubur cha cha – a trinity of *keladi* (taro), *keledek* (sweet potato) and coloured tapioca noodles boiled in milk. Likewise, *bubur pulut hitam* (black gelatinous rice) and mung bean porridges are boiled in coconut milk to give the respective desserts.

Reckon you could find a porridge barroom somewhere, serving only porridge, sweet and savoury? It would be like the pizzeria in Twin Falls,

Idaho, where we had nothing but pizzas for appetizer, entrée and dessert. It was a piece of the pizza partisans' promised land.

Pilaf: Puliyodharai, Hainanese Chicken Rice, Nasi Dagang

The full baked truth about Malaysian cooking is that all use rice as their staple, except perhaps the north Indian Punjabis who use atta (whole wheat) flour for their chapattis. The wheat based egg noodle is a northern Chinese food type. Southerners from both India and China do rice, which is the base to which veggies and meats are sides. Although, it should be the other way – rice as "filler" to the main actors of meat and veggies. Chinese use the fragrant jasmine rice aplenty, or some other polished rice, as do the Malays. It is cooked almost aldente, though Chinese often cook it to a sticky consistency to facilitate picking by chopstick.

The South Indians have always differed in their choice of rice. Sometimes known as "Indian rice", the oldtimers prefer parboiled rice. It is shunned by the other races, due to its overly "bloomed" texture and musty smell. Indians have always sworn by its better health index compared to the polished variety. The smell probably comes from its intial steaming in-husk, sun drying, and finally milling. This process supposedly locks in the vitamins of the outer mesocarp, whereas raw milling "polishes" or loses it. The younger set prefer the polished white of Malaysia's rice bowl. Or, the Imported South Indian Ponni rice. Thanks to the North Indian Moghul royalty, the long grained basmati variety is considered the maharani of all rice. It has even become a brand name of sorts, contested by growers in other countries. Having failed the bid to brand basmati, Texas now has texmati.

This is not about rice per se, but about how it is flavoured by other ingredients. The generic word is pilaf or pulao, which describes all kinds flavoured of rice. Nasi minyak – Ghee rice, the Spanish *paella*, the African American *gumbo*, etc. belong in this class.

Biryani – chicken or mutton buried in the rice. Although associated with Indian cuisine, it owes its origins to the *pilaf* of the Middle-East. The biryani sold in your banana leaf restaurant is kind of overrated. I am underwhelmed by the returns in terms of price and nutritional content.

It is mediocre in taste and flavour, high in price, but low in nutritional content. Loads of rice and some meat, but no vegetable. For the price of a biryani, you might buy three claypot chicken rice, another pilaf type dish. The best bet for your money is the world famous Hyderabadi Dum biryani, or as makansutra says, Dum good biryani. It was developed in the royal kitchens of the Nizams of Hyderabad, marrying Moghul and local Andhra cuisines. Richly marinated mutton (or chicken if you'd rather), is layered on with herbs and basmati and steamed in sealed cookers – pressure cooking, really. That's what Dum means – cooking rice and meat together with precision timing and temperature so that both are cooked. Not the shameful shortcut scams of sham biryani where rice and meat are cooked separately and mixed up after the fact. Shame, shame. The Malay version is the Batu Pahat Gum biryani, cooked in the same way, with the dough sealing the pot and lid. The ingredients might vary. The obvious similarities between the two are the references to the town of origin, and the sealing with dough. And not to forget, the Dum and Gum. Dum, we know. What is Gum? Beats me. Gumbo briyani? Sounds like some funny characters – Dumb and Dumber?

A close variant of the biryani is ghee rice, a mainstay of Malay weddings, where it is called nasi minyak. There are no meat or vege included.

The Tamil pilaf is the *puliyodharai*, AKA tamarind rice. It is the all time favorite picnic food of Indians. Something like nasi lemak is to Malays. *Puli* (tamarind) is the underlying flavour. Cooked rice is stirred, together with a paste made of tamarind, *kadalai paruppu* (Bengal gram) for crunch, whole red chilli, and other spices.

CCR, Chinese (Hainanese) chicken rice with roast/boiled chicken or roast pork on the side plus diced cucumber and soup, is a replica of nasi lemak (NL). Only, the CCR is cooked in chicken broth, while NL is cooked in *santan* (coconut milk). Nasi Dagang is a Malay style pilaf, related to NL that is prevalent in Kelantan/Trengganu/Pattani.

A sweet rice preparation that can be a desert or teatime thing, is the *ponggal*. It is the signature item on Ponggal day, the Tamil harvest festival. The word itself means, "boiling over", with joy, that is. The community gathers to cook freshly harvested rice in fresh cow's milk, plus nuts, lentils, and raisins to the consistency of the Southern US grits, or the Chinese *chang.* Nowadays, every day can be ponggal, as ready mixed ponggal rice is sold in packets. Just add milk and boil.

Chang/Zongzi the Chinese savoury glutinous rice, is likewise, boiled or steamed, after being wrapped in little pyramid shaped packets of bamboo leaf. Served especially on the dragon boat festival day. In China, Chang was thrown into the river as a food-offering to commemorate the death of Qu Yuan, a famous poet from the kingdom of Chu who lived during the Warring States period. The people believed that the fish would consume the chang rather than Qu Yuan.

The Malay *ketupat* is a similar cooked rice. Plain white rice cooked in a squarish, trapezoid packet woven out of coconut fronds. An even more suitable comparison to the above dishes, is the *lemang.* Just as creative, if not more, the lemang is glutinous rice flavourd with salt and oil, cooked in bamboo against an open fire. It is the ideal partner to the *rendang*, as the *iddli* or *thosai* are to *chutney*, as Hainanese rice is to *Char Siew* or steamed chicken.

Malaysian born, Malaysian bread: Roti Canai, Char Siew Pau, Roti Jala

Roti Canai (Roti: North Indian word for bread) is the pasta that comes to most people's minds when you mention the confection. Even the tourists seem to ask for it as a preference. Malaysian born and Malaysian bread? Make no mistake about it, it is Indian in origin. It may even be from the Middle-East. Murtabak, an Arab savoury pastry, is made with a dough that is stretched like a roti canai's. You would be right to say that it was the Indian Muslims (Mamaks) who introduced it and still are the main purveyors of it, even though other Indians as well as Malays are making and selling it everywhere. In the Penang restaurant in Chicago's Chinatown, (NYC too), a young Chinese youth can be seen flipping the filo-like dough behind a glass screen. In 1996, I met a Tamil speaking Chinese guy from Sg. Petani selling the stuff in a Malaysian restaurant in Arlington (in Fort Worth/Dallas Metroplex), Texas! He said he had lived in an estate in Kedah and picked up fluent Tamil, and the roti making secret. Roti Canai has gone global thanks to Malaysians! In Dallas, Chicago, Indianapolis, and in Idaho and Iowa, places we have visited or lived in, we found the *Kawan* brand frozen roti canai in Asian stores. This was way before the identical, parathas from India, turned up in the supermarket freezers.

A food website says that Roti Canai was introduced by the South Indians who came as indentured rubber tappers to Malaya. Wrong! The Tamils are rice eaters. They never had wheat as the main item in their diet. Another site says Roti Canai comes from Chennai (→Channai → Canai), the capital of Tamil Nadu state. Guess again. Chennai may be the recently resurrected old name of the city, but it was Madras since British colonial times, when the Indians came over. Canai is Malay for "to roll thinly". And that, is the extent of Malaysia's claim to that most mouthwatering morsel of flat bread. It is actually a North Indian bread, that originated as Paratha ("flat" in Hindi). Roti canai is still called roti prata in neighbouring Singapore. In Malaysia, prata was replaced with canai in the 70's. You wonder how and why.

It was the South Indian Muslims (perhaps more specifically the Malayalee "Kaakaa" tea stall holders and restaurateurs), who brought it into this region. Meaning of, "kaakaa" (crow) – Tamil term for Malayali muslims. Tun Mahathir, would qualify as a Kaakaa, by way of his father? *Roti Canai* is Malaysian bread in the sense that Malaysians have popularized it and even marketed it globally. The way of making it has also been transformed. The Indian Paratha is made by flattening the dough with a rolling pin, and oil or ghee is smeared on top. It is then folded and rolled with the rolling pin, and spread with oil. The process is repeated several times so that flaky layers are created in the rolling process. Our roti canai takes a short cut! The entire dough is flipped a few times on to the table till it becomes filo thin, and then the corners are folded in like a square. Alternatively, the edge of the circular sheet is yanked up like a magician's handkerchief and the limp sheet is swirled onto the table like a coil of rope and pressed into a flat round bread before being grilled on the griddle. The flipping action falls in the range between the rolling pin action of a paratha maker and the UFO-like gyro-technics of a pizza flipper.

The dip of choice for the roti is sambar (dhall stew) the south Indian vegetarian sauce. Malaysians would like a dab of sambal, the Malay spicy condiment, in the sambaar.

Like anything in the business world, the roti canai has gone through many innovations. Eventhough the original plain prata is the all time bestseller, the ones with fillings have their own clientele. The oldest filled roti canai is the *murtabak*. Roti that is filled with a savoury spicy meat and wrapped into a flat round medallion. The accompaniment for this is chicken or mutton kurma and sweetened sliced onions.Take your pick on these latter day fillings – cheese, banana, apple. I have seen (a picture of) a Singapore square prata loaded with three scoops of icecream, rolled into a burrito (Mexican wrap), topped end to end with ice cream, and drizzled with rose syrup!

The roti canai may get a two thumbs – up for taste, but sorry, it may not be the most wholesome food on your menu. Its nutritional value is questionable. The dough marinates in margarine and condensed milk, and it is toasted on the griddle with a genereous sprinkling of oil. Along with the condensed milk infused *teh tarik* as refreshment, the bread-tea combo seems a collossal collocation of cholesterol and coronary carelessness. The doctor will tell you that an occasional helping of it wouldn't kill you. Just, to avoid making it your daily staple.

The Chinese make a similarly sheet-like wheat product called a spring roll skin. A sibling of the filo dough. A filling of stir-fried jicama (watercress) and carrot is rolled in the skin. The *poh piah*, is fine finger food serving for evening tea.

Besides the roti paratha/roti canai, the other Indian breads include the *capati*, an unleavened flat bread that is similar to the Mexican tortilla. The *naan* is the leavened equivalent of the Greek *pita*, a baked, leavened flat bread. It is curiously baked in the in – sides of the *Tandoor*, basically a large *Stamnos*, wide bellied Greek water jar.The *thosai* wouldn't qualify as a bread. It is more a crepe, made from a batter of rice and urad dhall.

Heard of fried bread? The Hispanic people of New Mexico have fried bread as their specialty. It is actually deep fried flat bread, and Malaysia is not short of it. Firstly, Indian restaurants and homes make a deep fried Punjabi bread called the *poori*. It is actually a *chapatti,* fried such that it balloons into a spheroid shape. Press the dome of dough and its papery skin breaks off easily, as you prepare to dip it into a mashed potato curry dip. The Chinese breakfast favorite, the *yu char koay/youtiao,* is a savoury, foot long 'twin' log bread, tasting something like what a fried roti canai would taste like. The glutinous rice filled and the bean paste filled breads, are also fried doughs, and *char koay*'s companions at the breakfast bread basket. The *yu char koay* (Cantonese: "oil-fried devil") – dipped in thick black coffee is the way oldtimers relished it. It supposedly represents a husband and wife conspirators against a Song dynasty official. By the by, *koay* is the origin of the Malay word, *kuih,* which is a generic term for Malay savouries and sweetmeats. You might consider the Malay *cecodok* a kind of fried bread too, as it has wheat flour as a primary ingredient. A mixture of self-raising flour and mashed ripe bananas (cooked quick oats consistency) is deep fried for a sweet, tea-time good time. *Cucur udang,* is a similar fried dish with prawns (shrimp) and a sweet chilly dip.

For a long time, we had to thank the North Indian Muslim and Pakistani breadmen for our daily bread, the loafy kind that is. The roti bhai would come around in the evenings with his big cylindrical basket on a bicycle and children would scream, "Roti bhai has come!, roti bhai has come!" Our reward for the advertisement would be a sandwich of bread with margarine and kaya. Even today, the Tamil Muslim breadman comes around the city flats and kampongs on his Honda 70 cc motorcycle, the metal basket and the steering wheel strung with breads, buns, and keropok. Roti Kahwin, or "conjugal bread", refers to two slices of bread slathered with margarine and kaya, a caramel custard-like spread made of beaten eggs, coconut milk and sugar. Up until Gardenia came along, the Indian Muslim owned Federal Bakery was the premier league champions of the bread fraternity.

Speaking of Malaysian born bread, there is the once upon a time, all time tea-time favourite of coconut bun, and the later addition of kaya bun. Ah! the sweet smell of fresh made coconut bun at the Chinese bakery in Kampung Kuantan, Kuala Selangor, where we adjourned after school while waiting for the car commute back to Bukit Badong Estate some 11 miles away! The memory of that enchanted childhood, the charcoal fired oven, and the snout awakening smell of baking coconut bun is vivid. My one term school life at the Sekolah Kebangsaan Kg.Kuantan included more than a few air raid drills during the "Confrontation" with

Indonesia, when it threatened to annex our Sarawak state. At the school siren, we would line up in the corridors, march into the adjacent rubber estate, and lie flat in the dry drainage ditches. What fun! The springy bed of dried rubber leaves crackled and crinkled under our weight. What did we know then, of the historical significance of that diversion? Happening during the mid 60's, it was contemporary with the US – USSR face off in Cuba, at the height of the Cold War. Our own "Bay of Pigs".

On our recent trip down there, we found the tiny village, tinier still. The bakery and the entire row of wooden shops is missing from the map. The only big thing to bray about there, is the fire-fly light sans sound show. Like many enterprises undertaken by local governments in Malaysia, this one too is losing steam, it seems. The place seems abandoned.

Small, local, Chinese run bakeries today provide western breads, confections and pastries. Traditionally, a type of Chinese bread, the *pau* or *pao* is a steamed rice bun stuffed with sweet black bean paste, or the savoury *char siew* (fried minced pork). Speaking of *Pao*, there is a Portuguese inspired Goan dish, called *Pav Bhaji*, that is their national dish. *Pav* looks like our own plain bun. Bhaji is a dipping sauce/curry that goes with it. So I am thinking: Pao/Pav. Is there any more to it than similarity in name and sound? Did the Portuguese get the name from their contact with the Chinese language in Macao, or their trade in Shanghai ? My first thought, before further research is done, is *Pav* may be the Indian spelling of the Portuguese *Pao*. *Bhaji* is decidedly Indian sounding, so set it aside. The Portuguese pronunciation of "-*ao*", is "-an". Sao Paolo, is said San Paolo. *Christao,* the name of the Malacca Portuguese language, sounds "Kristang." So, I assume that Pav/Pao is actually Pan. Bun? Perhaps the *puff* in curry puff is related to *Pav*. If you have a pav bhaji, why not a curry puff, since both are pastries with curry.

The Malays do the *roti jala* ("net bread"). It is a take on the crepe, made by swirling a runny batter of wheat flour criss-crosswise through a dipper with holes. The griddle is similar to the dosai or roti canai one. The effect is that of a net. The cooked roti is then rolled like a chain-link fence and served with chicken curry. It is reminiscent of the *rava thosai*, where the watery batter is poured into crepe shape and served folded.

High Spirits: Tuak, Kallu, Samsu

It seems that you cannot escape the notion of spirits as fuel for lively company at dinnertime. Invitations to indulge in the imbibing of the intoxicant are made and accepted in all cultures, unless it is prohibited by religious injunction.

Tuak is fermented rice, yeast and sugar and drunk in parts of Indonesia such as Sumatra, Sulawesi, Borneo and parts of Malaysia such as Penang Island and East Malaysia. It is also referred to as rice wine. The beverage is a popular drink among the Ibans and other Dayaks of Sarawak during the Gawai festival, weddings, hosting of guests and other special occasions. The same word is used for other drinks in Indonesia for example the palm wine of the Batak people of North Sumatra. Tuak is is brewed from glutinous rice from a recent harvest mixed with home-made yeast called *ciping* produces bitter Tuak. For sweet Tuak a smaller proportion of ragi (semolina) is added. The yeast is pounded into powder and mixed with the rice after it has cooled and the mixture is left to ferment in jars for anything between 3 and 10 days During this time the solids separate from the liquid and float to the top. Sugar is added to boiling water and the cooled syrup is added to the fermented mixture. The Tuak is ready to be served or as with the locals, it is preferably left to stand for another 10 days for the taste to mature. The longer the Tuak is kept the more mature. Depending on its sugar or alcohol content, It can be stored for years in sealed bottles, and over time, the colour darkens and assumes the aroma of honey.

Tapai (also tapay or tape), is a traditional fermented preparation of rice, tapioca or other starchy foods, and is found throughout much of Southeast Asia, especially in Austronesian (island) cultures, and parts of East Asia. It refers to both the alcoholic paste and the alcoholic beverage derived from it. It has a sweet or sour taste and can be eaten as is, as ingredients for traditional recipes, or fermented further to make rice wine.

Kallu is Tamil for *Toddy* (Hindi), which is the sap of the coconut blossom. A "one tree kallu" is said to be especially sweet, refreshing, and cooling to the body. Malays, who call it *nira,* have medicinal uses for it. Interestingly, *neer,* is Tamil for water. *Tanneer,* is plain water. *Venneer*, hot water. *Ilaneer* (litt: "young water") is coconut water. When an Indian invites you to a *tanni(r)* session, he is actually inviting you for a "drink". And not for high tea, but high spirits.

So, fresh kallu is innocent, it seems. It is a little tart and sweet, but not stinky, fizzy, or "tipsy". However, when the product of many trees get mixed in the vat, and after a few hours, you begin to notice sourish ferment. It has the potency of perhaps beer. Without industrial fermentation, and fresh from the tree, the potion even has fizz. The appearance and experience of it evokes the look and taste of 100 Plus. Kallu also means "stone", in Tamil. So it is quite foreseeable that the kallu gulper might get "stoned" after a few too many jugs, rather mugs. To be "stoned" is the Americanism for being, "dead drunk".

The toddy tapper slices the stem of the coconut blossom, which is about two inches in diameter, and discards all the flowers. This is the tap which drips the sap, drop by deliberate drop into a small pot tied to it. Thereafter, he shaves a thin slice every day, to release the juices. A single tree can yield a pot, about 1-1.5 litres, depending on the number of blossoms.

Samsu is Chinses sake, or rice wine. *Mijiu* is a Chinese rice wine made from glutinous rice. It generally looks clear with balanced sweetness and acidity, similar to its Japanese counterpart *sake* and Korean counterpart *cheongju*. The alcohol content ranges between 15% and 20%. Rice wine was made around or before 1000 BC by ancient Chinese, and then the practice spread to Japan and other East Asian countries. Since then, it has played an important role in Chinese life. In most Chinese supermarkets there are various kinds of rice wines. It is a traditional beverage to the Chinese and some of the families still follow the custom of making rice wine by themselves. The rice wine is made using glutinous rice, Chinese yeast and water. It is also served as an appetizer and is believed to be beneficial in improving metabolism and skin.

Mijiu is usually drunk warm, like the Japanese sake and Korean cheongju, and is also used in cooking. The cooking mijiu available in Asian grocery stores are generally of a lower quality, and often contain added salt to avoid an alcohol tax. Mijiu is produced both in mainland China and Taiwan. A clear liquor called rice baijiu is distilled from mijiu.

Vistors to Malaysia are advised – strictly warned – not to mix alcohol with durian. Scary stories will be told, of how cerebral haemorrhages are likely. Experts give a range from dizziness to cardiac arrest, that can happen.

Credible Crepes: Paal Appam, Apam Balik, Jian Bing

While the more common Indian crepe is the *Dosai*, *Appam* is the Tamil word for a crispy crepe with a fleshy center. The Dosai is a savoury thin crepe, a breakfast item eaten with saambaar and coconut chutney. Ingredients: soaked rice, cooked rice, urad dhall and salt. The dhall acts as a dough raiser or fermenter. It is folded back like an omelette. Once less well known among non-Indians, it is now enjoying a good eat with them. As in any industry, the dosai has undergone many innovations, from the pancake like *oothappam*, paper thin *cone dosai*, to "turnover" *masala dosai*.

The *appam*, or *thengai paal appam* (coconut milk crepe) is also a breakfast favourite but sweet. It takes the shape of the little "wok", so it is basically a bowl with a fleshy bottom and crispy brown rim. Latter day innovations include a lady in Bangsar who breaks an egg into the centre. And then, there is a version with brown sugar stirred in, or cheese, or whatever you please.

The Malay take on the crepe is the tea-time treat called *apam bailk*, literally, "the returning crepe". It is not that difficult to figure out the funny name. Definitely not a boomerang, or worse, a flying saucer. The crispy thin crepe is folded back on itself. Just think of the American apple "turnover", though the turnover is not a crepe. There are two types of apam balik, the thin (crepe) and the thick (pancake). The thin one qualifies as a crepe. The thick one, which is about foot in diameter and about half an inch thick, can consider itself the cousin of the apple turnover. Ingredients of apam balik, being a sweet preparation, are pourable self raising flour for the base. It is dabbed with margarine, sprinkled with sugar and crunchy peanut powder and folded over – after the base gets browned.

The *po piah* can be considered a crepe, eventhough it is a roll, like the Chinese egg-roll or Vietnamese springroll. It begins as a flat thin rice crepe and ends up like a French crepe, rolled. It is a finger food without a need for dipping sauce, as its all inside – smeared sauce, julienned jicama, cucumber, scrambled egg, crushed peanuts etc. A kind of snow white rice crepe is made in Dim Sum places, where prawns are placed in, rolled and steamed. A fine breakfast indeed, accompanied by a spicy prawn paste.

A savoury Chinese crepe is *Jian Bing*. The batter is made of millet flour, soy milk and oil. An egg spread and cooked over the crepe. Chinese blackbean paste thinned with water, and chilli sauce and water. These will be spread on the crepe like you would a pizza sauce. The toppings can include anything from spring onion/cilantro, crackers, crispy wonton, pork rind or char koay (yu tiao). The whole deal is folded twice over to make a quadrant.

Steamy sets: Char Siu Pao, Kozhukattai, Kuih Kaswi

Char Siew Pao, "roast pork bun", is a kind of steamed Shepherd's Pie. Sold in the mornings and evenings, it can either be breakfast or after dinner (suppertime) snacks. Pao is a mainstay of the Cantonese Dim Sum dining space. There are sweet and savoury pork paos and the blackbean paste and kaya filled paos. There might even be an anchovy sambal bun. The base or wrap of the pao is plain rice flour, which is rather bland or totally tasteless.

Chinese steam many items. The popular Malaysian mainstay is steamed fish, in a variety of sauces. Then you have steamed bak choy with a drizzle of oyster sauce and fried onions. Yum.

Bak Chang, is savoury glutinous rice embedded with pork, nuts, eggs, mushroom etc, wrapped in bamboo leaves into a pyramidal packet. It is steamed or boiled. It is ideal as a snack for the long trail hikes – savoury, carb heavy, no plates or forks!

The Tamil steaming seems exclusively breakfast oriented. *Idli* is a steamed rice medallion made with thick rice batter. *Idiyappam* ("thunder cake") is a rice paste pressed through a multi holed mould to make a neat nest of thin noodles. *Idli* is eaten with coconut chutney and saambaar just like dosai. Whereas, idiyappam is accompanied by coconut scrappings and molasses, or for savoury, *sothy*, a watery coconut milk gravy with the usual *thaalippu* (tempering agents), onions and fenugreek.

Also on the breakfast menu is *kozhukattai*, a kind of curry puff/ empanada. The difference is kozhukattai is rice skin, filled with cooked a Bengal gram, scraped coconut and molasses mixture. Curry puff is wheat flour skin, filled with curried potato and meat. The former is steamed while the puff is deep fried in oil. Another steamed breakfast best bet is *puttu* which is moistened coarse rice flour mixed with coconut scraping and steamed in a stainless steel steaming tube or bamboo, or steamed on a tray. It is eaten with molasses. Malays have a take on the puttu and call it *putu piring*. The process and ingredients are the same, except that it comes in springy 3" diameter discs and can be handled like finger food. Idiayappam, puttu and kozhukattai collectively come under *"putumayam"*. Hence, the putumayam man, who comes around when you are still in bed, harassing and hounding you, honking his high pitched rubber ball bicycle horn. Notice that Tamils seem to be able to survive on rice alone, going by the variety of dishes using only rice as a main ingredient.

Malay steamy items are many. *Kuih kaswi, kuih kochi, kuih talam, bengkang/bingka ubi, kuih lapis, onde onde, seri muka, kuih lompang* etc. Some of the above can also be attributed to the Nonya cuisine. But we can give them malayness, as the nonya culture is a fusion of the Malay and the Chinese.

Kuih kaswi is of two types – the gula Malacca and the pandan (green colour). The taste is like that of kuih lompang. The difference between the two is: Kaswi is made from wheat and tapioca flours, Lompang is made from rice flour and tapioca flour. While kaswi is cut into squares and sprinkled with coconut shaving, lompang is shaped like a litte bowl with a subtle dent (lobang/lompang) in the centre.

Wow. Our Mal-Asian foremothers really knew how to cook healthy. What with steaming (incl. boiling, blanching, poaching, simmering and stewing), as opposed to frying (grilling, broiling, braising, baking and sauteing). Kudos to them.

Hot pockets: Wan Tan, Bonda/Samosa, Karipap

While steamed items are aplenty, there are certain kinds that come in containers. Kueh Chang (Zongzi, Joong) is a savoury gelatinous rice dumpling that has a filling of stirfried candle nut, meat, shiitake mushroom, spices plus full boiled eggs. The preboiled rice is packaged into a conical pouch of bamboo leaves. The base of two leaves are folded into a cone (ice cream, or kacang putih like) and the fillings added. Sometimes, the tip is filled with rice dyed blue, from the butterfly pea flower – a common fence climber in these parts.The remaining 'tail' of the leaves are skillfully pleated over each other to form a perfectly pyramidal cone, and steamed in boiling water to complete the cooking process. Unwrapping the 'gift' and eating it hot, with a cup of coffee or Chinese tea is the way to go. Ideal as an evening munchie, it can be had anytime of the day too. A perfect, energy pack for a trek in the outback, or a sumptuous snack during an unexpected hunger attack.

Though there are many variations of the Chang around S.E Asia, such as Machang (Phillipines), Bachang (Indonesia, Thailand) etc, similar styles are found in the Americas such as Tamales (Mexico), Pomonha (Brazil) using corn.

Even if, given that there are some Indian dishes that employ banana or lotus leaves to wrap and steam food, it is quite rare in Malaysian Indian cuisine. However, an invariable item in the steel "trunk" of the Puttumayam man, besides the Idiayappam, Thengaai Paalappam, and Kozhukattai, is the Puttu. A favourite breakfast item, it is moist rice flour, scraped coconut, and sugar steamed in a tray or in a banana leaf-lined bamboo tube. These days, special eversilver steaming pots with a chimney-like steel tube attached atop it, are used. The white (rice, sugar, and coconut) concoction is mashed like powder and eaten with fingers or spoon. Most flours can be used for puttu, such as atta (whole wheat), rava (semolina) and kelviragu (finger millet). Tamil dishes are often descriptive of the process of their making, like *puttu* ("to break up"), *murukku* ("to twist"), *pongal* ("boiled") and *sundal* ("reduced") *peratal* ("stirred") and *varuval* ("distressed").

Ketupat is different from the above two dishes in content, consistency and flavour, but steamed, nevertheless. Plain rice is half filled in little purses woven from strips of coconut frond. They are boiled in water, just like chang. As the rice bloats and compacts inside the bags, the result is a solid rice cake. It is cut into little cubes, to accompany the satay. Unlike chang and puttu, which are stand alone, ketupat is a second fiddle to satay, and being bland, needs the satay sauce to dress it up. Just like *lemang* and *rendang, satay* and *ketupat* make a regular couple on Ramadhan. As a matter of fact, the image of the ketupat is the enduring symbol of Hari Raya on any banner, 3-D ornament, or media. The inevitable Raya food, the lemang, is enclosed and steamed in a banana leaf inside a 2 foot tube of bamboo.

In Cantonese, they are called *wantan*, which literally means "cloud swallow" because when they are cooked, the dumplings float in the broth like small clouds.They are similar to the Italian *ravioli, tortellini*, or the polish *pierogi*. Again, this coincidence may be attributed to Marco Polo, the Venetian visitor to China. Spaghetti = egg noodle; fettucini = koay teou; ravioli = wan tan; linguini = udon; capellini = wan tan noodle; vermicelli = mee hoon, and what have you.

Back to hot pockets. The wan tan is a teaspoon of marinated mashed pork encapsulated in a wee sheet of wheat, and boiled in bone stock. It often goes (comes?) with wantan or kicap mee, or floating in broth.

Bonda is a round south Indian fried snack, with potato filling. It is mentioned as *parika* in Manasollasa, a 12th-century Sanskrit encyclopedia compiled by Someshvara III, who ruled from present-day Karnataka. The process of making a spicy bonda involves savoury potato balls dipped in gram flour batter. Bonda has a sweet and a spicy variant. Keralites prefer the sweet one called *Sugiyan*, while the savoury version is common in the rest of India.

Another indian hot pocket is the *samosa*, deriving from the Persian *sanbosag* ("triangular pastry"). Exactly descriptive. The filling and cooking are the same as curry puff's, except for the shape. Its dip is is a chutney, either tamarind or mint. Now, *Hot Pockets* is an American brand that produces a rectangular stuffed dough, that resembles the empanada, pirozhki, calzone, samosa, knish, kreatopitakia, Khuushuur, and our own karipap (curry puffs).

A *curry puff* is a teatime snack of Southeast Asian origin. It is a small pie consisting of curry chicken and potatoes in a deep-fried or baked pastry shell. The curry is quite thick to prevent it from oozing out of the snack. A common snack in Malaysia and Singapore, the curry puff is one of several "puff" type pastries with different fillings.

Another Malay version of this snack is known as *epok-epok* and *teh-teh* which is smaller than the curry puff. The curry puffs from Indian bakeries differ from epok-epok in the use of 'layered' pastry that creates a flaky crust. Other varieties of the epok epok are filled with a half boiled egg instead of chicken. Another alternative is tinned sardines.There are also vegetarian curry puffs that are in fact not spicy and made from shredded radish, tofu, potatoes and grated carrots. They are often eaten with sweet chili sauce. There is also relatively large and nice looking version of curry puff called shell curry puff sold in shopping malls of Isetan and AEON and others in Malaysia.

Oodles of Noodles: Kuey Teow, Laksa, Idiappam

Noodles, as we know them, are China's gift to the world. Actually, the Italians, Marco Polo and Co., smuggled it out and spread it to the West. We in East and South-East Asia, have it direct from the source. The cuisine has noodles ranging from fat and long (Hokkien Egg noodles), thin and endless (*mee hoon*), short and wormy (*Loh See Fun* = "rat's tail"), long and ribbony (*kuey teow*), and angel hairy (*mee suan*). It may not be their *raison d'etre,* but knowing the Chinese preoccupation with longevity and eternity, you guess that they probably invented it to psych themselves up. In fact, birthday celebrations must include a noodle dish, for long life and to have "many more". The shape of food represents the idea it conveys in the culture.

People who live in an environment have innumerable and innovative ways to adjust to it. The Eskimos are said to have sixteen words to describe every grade and shade of snow. The Chinese, needless to say, have umpteen types of noodles and ways of preparing them. Stir fried kuey teow, mee floating in hot soup, Wan Tan mee blanched and tossed in soy sauce.

Proof of the pudding (er, mee), speaking of adaptation, is the Nyonya dish called laksa, which can be of two types. The *Penang assam laksa* is a translucent, chewy noodle in a sweet sour, fish soup. The *curry laksa,* is regular egg noodle in a coconut curry soup. It is something that comes to your mind on a cold rainy evening, for a "wake me up". Salivating already?

The name comes from the Hokkien *luak sua*, meaning "spicy sand", which refers to the taste and texture of ground dried prawns.

Mee Hailam (Hainanese cuisine) may sound Chinese alright, but over a dozen recipes on the web/net feature Malay cooks and not a single Chinese. Wherefore? Methinks its because Hainanese cooking doesn't use pork, and Malays freely fondly frequent there. It is similar to Hokkien mee, but runnier gravy and sweeter with the addition of chilli, tomato and oyster sauces.

Mee Rebus, is the Indian muslim innovation. The name means "blanched noodles". It is your regular egg noodles, smothered in a yellow stew of potatoes and stuff in coconut milk. And who can deny the draw of mamak mee goreng, another Indian muslim master class. It is a dry fried egg noodle, with heat and spice and other things nice. It goes well with a drink of the teh tarik (Litt: "stretched tea"), also a Mamak original.

Idiappam literally means "thunder crepe", in Tamil. It is a kind of stringy noodle. In fact, the English term for the Idiappam is "string-hopper", probably because it resembles a basket (hopper) of strings? Eventhough it is more of a nest-like mess of entangled strings, Idiappam begins as strings of moist rice as it comes out of the multi-holed idiappam/murukku press. A circular motion during the pressing results in its nest shape. In Tamil cooking, it is one of the steamed food, along with the Idli, kozhukattai, and puttu.

Laksa utara ("northern laksa") or laksa kedah, is the Malay version of the assam laksa. Like the assam laksa, the soup is made by boiling sardine or kembong (spanish mackeral) with red onions, bunga kantan (ginger flower), daun kesum (vietnamese coriander), asam keping (gelugor slices), belacan, salt and sugar for taste. Unlike the assam laksa, mee utara is egg noodle instead of the chewy glass noodle.

Another Malay mee, is the mee Bandung. It is said to be close to mee Hailam. Excerpt – *"The spicy gravy made from tomato paste and beef broth gives a variety of taste of spicy, sweet, sour and salty! With the perfect combination of beef, prawns and vegetables, no wonder this delicacy is a popular balanced meal. Of course, the ingredients are not limited to beef and prawns. You can also add in fishcakes, fish balls, chicken or squid"*. But why Bandung, which is way over there in Indonesia's West Java? Could it be because Muar, Johore, is touted to be the capital of mee Bandung. And them Javanese are plenty there? If the mee is Bandung, should it be paired with air Bandung, another Malaysian refreshment unrelated to Indonesia?

Ah, there! The writeup on air bandung reveals that Bandung actually refers to bandung, meaning "pairing". My Bahasa kicks in with "banding" — compare!, or "ganding" – join. The drink is actually a mixture of evaporated milk and rose syrup resulting in a pastel pink drink. Favoured mostly by Malays, it can be kicked up further with the addition of cincau (grass jelly), ice cream, a soda or even milo. Psst! The soda added air bandung found in its namesake city, Bandung, Indonesia, is called Soda Gembira – "happy soda". I had always thought that mee and air bandung originated fron Bandung. Now, it all adds up.

In a pickle: Urukai, Haam Choy, Jeruk

Pickling, as a culinary process, began with the necessity for preservation of excess food. Before refrigeration, salt was found to be an effective preserving agent. Later, vinegar was discovered. The combination of both substances further enhances the curing action. The operative word these days when discussing pickles, is probiotics. It seems like them gut bugs do love sour.

Chinese salted veggies are different from Korean *Kimchee* only in that, the latter is pickled in vinegar and chilli paste. While the kimchee can be eaten as is, on its own, salted greens have to be soaked in water to remove the salt, like you do the Spanish salted cod, and then added to stir-fries.

Haam Choy is a Hakka pickle from *bok choy* (mustard green). The thick stemmed greens are blanched in hot water. It is then slapped with salt and kneaded. Slice some ginger and boil it. Add the ginger water to the vege and keep covered for 24 hours. Next day, squeeze the water out and stuff it (really cram it) into a Mason jar or similar bottle. Top it with the ginger pieces. Sprinkle a few tablespoons of sugar and then, a few tablespoons of salt. Pour a small bowl of vinegar, top up with the remaining ginger water and refrigerate. It should be good for cooking after two days. Better still, after 10 days. The above is lifted straight from a video of its production by a 101 year old Hakka grandma. Haam choy 101.

This condiment adds 3 S's (sweet, salt and sour) to any stir fried dish or soup.

Urukaai is the relish (appetizer, aperitif, digestif) in a Tamil meal. *Ooru* ("to soak") + *Kaai* ("unripe sour fruit"). "Soaked fruit" decribes a pickle quite well. Salt and vinegar are great for pickles. What if you add chilly and spice? That is exactly what that little bottle of Indian pickle (mango, lime, garlic, ginger, mixed vegetable, or mint etc) is. It opens up the taste buds to receive non-spicy food such as curd (yogurt) rice, or saambaar. During my single digit years, I remember my father asking for *bojana korada*. It sounded very foreign, more like Kannada. Bojanam means meal and korada? Korada in Tamil referred to a plumber's wrench. So, appetite opener? Punjabis use pickles as a dip for their chappati.

Jeruk (urukaai?), is the Malay pickle. Differing from haam choy and urukaai, the jeruk leans more to sweet and sour, and is exclusively a tit-bit/snack item. Jeruk Madu Pak Ali, is a large scale producer of jeruk, out of Penang. Madu or honey is the additional additive. Pak Ali pickles orange (?), *chermai* (star gooseberry), *buah pala* (nutmeg), *rokam* (runeala plum) and *salak* (snake fruit*), kelubi* (forest salak, a smaller sibling of salak).

A sweet pickle that is served as an accompaniment in briyani or wedding dinners is the *preserved fruit achaar*. This is basically a sweet compote of preserved berries, cherries of many colours. A cool complement to the heat of a meat dish. A less expensive, less time consuming preparation is the plain achaar that is somewhat of a vegetable rojak (salad). It is julienned papaya, cucumber and carrot stirfried in vinegar and sprinkled with sesame seeds. It is found on Indian and Malay wedding menus.

Speaking from experience, the southern United States like Texas, are big on chilli and cucumber/dill pickles, perhaps from proximity to Mexico. The sour cucumber is especially good to be slapped on burgers. We have our own sliced chilli pickles that go as sides to your steaming bowl of soup mee, or wan tan mee.

Aside from the regular vegetable or fruit pickle in brine, there is a type of fish preserved in oil. It is a Chinese style. Sliced mackerel in briny oil functions as appetite enhancer and sodium additive.

Leave it to man's devices and he'll devise diverse designs and variants. A strange drink in a seafood place in Ijok caught my fancy and it turned out great. They had crushed a pickled kumquat in warm water and added the needed sugar. A little bit salty lime, a little bit sweet tang and whole lot of refreshment.

Condiments: Sambal, Thuvaiyal, tiáo wèi pǐn

A condiment is a spice, sauce, or preparation that is taken with food to impart a specific savour, to enhance the flavour, a relish to burnish the dish. The most common is the enduring pair of table salt and pepper. These days there is a whole lot of sprinkling "things" like parmesan cheese, chilli flakes, and garlic powder.

Sambal ("Sauce") is Javanese origin relish (condiment, dip, chutney, pâté), that has dozens of variations in Indonesian cookery. In Malaysia, sambal ikan bilis (anchovy) is most associated with the *nasi lemak*, the awowed national breakfast of Malaysia. The *sambal belacan/sambal tumis* is a good standby at Malay meals, especially as a dip (not dressing) for *ulam* (herb salad). The headliner in sambal is the *belacan* (shrimp paste) that delivers a punch and potency that awakens the taste buds. There is also a dry version of sambal sold in bottles, that adds powdered dry shrimp.

Now, sambal is also known as sambal in Sri Lanka (sambol), South Africa, Netherlands, and Suriname, by way of Indonesian migration there. For our part, we have failed to popularize in it Britain or elsewhere in the commonwealth. Even more sadly, Americans know bottled Sriracha from Thailand as equal to sambal. (Sigh!) If only they knew the real thing.

The Tamil version of the sambal or chutney is *thuvaiyal* ("mashed")/ *Thogaiyal.* Coconut thuvaiyal is associated with the breakfast idli or thosai. *Pudina* (mint), curry leaf thuvaiyal and *paruppu* (lentil) thuvaiyal etc go well with rice. Paruppu thuvaiyal matches rasam, especially after a fast or brooklax colon cleanse and a shower, when you are feeling *kolai pasi,* (Litt: "killer hunger") or angry hungry. In thuvaiyal, unlike in a sambal, chilli plays a supporting role. It includes pepper, coconut, *perungaayam* (asoefetida), and a herb of choice as main ingredient. These are sauteed and blended into a thick savoury paste. *Thottuke,* is a colloquial rendering of thuvaiyal simply meaning, "something to dip in."

All kinds of Chinese sauces come readymade in bottles. Consider this – Soy sauce (Thin and thick), hoisin sauce, plum sauce, duck sauce, oyster sauce, fish sauce (Thai), hot (chilli) oil, yada yada yada. If you want a kicked up version, here goes. To a small bowl add equal amounts (1 tablespoon) of premium soy sauce, vinegar and water and add a ¼ teaspoon of sesame seed oil. This is the base. Add a tablespoon of chilli oil, with sesame seeds. Throw in a pinch of finely chopped green onion and cilantro. Voila! A petit appetite pick me up. Naturally, you can waltz around with a variety of versions and perversions of this provision.

Raising a stink: Budu, Soy sauce, Worcestershire

In Malay home cooking, *Tapai*, *Budu*, *Cincalok*, *Tempoyak*, Fish sauce, might be candidates for Mark Zimmerman's *Bizarre Foods* show on the Asian Food Channel. These are cured and fermented liquid condiments to enhance favours. *Tapai* (also tapay or tape), is a traditional fermented preparation of rice or other starchy foods. *Budu* is a fish (anchovy) sauce, traditionally found in the east coast states of Kelantan, Trengganu, Southern Thailand and Sumatra, Indonesia. *Cincalok* is a Malay dish that originated in Malacca, and consumed by Malay, Peranakan and Kristang. It is fermented whole minute shrimp known as udang geragau (acetes) or krill. *Tempoyak* is a Malay creamy condiment made from fermented durian, comparable to sour cream, blue cheese dip, or mayonnaise. These can all be consumed either as dips or seasonings. These are Malay centric, and for the others, is an acquired taste due to their stink and rot. Umami, is the general name for such a taste, the fifth in the series of (sweet, sour, salt, bitter, and …….).

Hoisin sauce is one of the Chinese condiments listed in the preceding article. It is based on fermented soybean paste with other flavors and spices. *Kicap* (Malay), *ketjap* (Indonesian), *ketchup/catsup* (English) all derive from the Hokkien *kôechiap/kê-tsiap*, a fish sauce. Kicap here refers to fermented soy bean, or soy sauce. It is both of the thin salty, and the thick sweet varieties.

Soy sauce in its current form was created about 2,200 years ago during the Western Han dynasty of ancient China. The 19th century Sinologist Samuel Wells Williams wrote that in China, the best soy sauce was "made by boiling beans soft, adding an equal quantity of wheat or barley, and leaving the mass to ferment; a portion of salt and three times as much water are afterwards put in, and the whole compound left for two or three months when the liquid is pressed and strained".

"The Lea & Perrins brand was commercialised in 1837 and was the first type of sauce to bear the Worcestershire name. The origin of the Lea & Perrins recipe is unclear. The packaging originally stated that the sauce came from the 'recipe of a nobleman in the county'. The company has also claimed that Lord Marcus Sandys, ex-Governor of Bengal encountered it while in India with the East India Company in the 1830s, and commissioned the local apothecaries to recreate it, (the partnership of John Wheely Lea and William Perrins of 63 Broad Street, Worcester). Michael Portillo, the presenter of the BBC documentary series *Great British Railway Journeys*, visited the Worcestershire factory where the gentleman he interviewed stated the original recipe was from Bengal. Then, the British added fermented fish to it.

According to company tradition, when the recipe was first mixed there. the resulting product was so strong that it was considered inedible and the barrel was abandoned in the basement. Looking to make space in the storage area a few years later, the chemists decided to try it again, and discovered that the long fermented sauce had mellowed and was now palatable. In 1838 the first bottles of "Lea & Perrins Worcestershire sauce" were released to the general public.

In 2009, Lea & Perrins accountant Brian Keogh found notes from the 1800s dumped in a skip. The documents were to be placed on display at the Worcester City Art Gallery & Museum".

Since Indians don't seem to bottle and market watery sauces, the Worcestershire "(woostersure"?) sauce should at least partially count as Indian. Afterall, the original spark was from India. Does the original Bengal sauce exist still? People who are into these things say that it is a commercial myth. Some say it was not Lord Sandys, but his lady. They also say that *The Gambler's Wife* author, Mrs. Grey passed on a curry powder recipe from her uncle (Sir Charles, Chief Justice of India) to Lady Sandys.

The familiar chilli sauce is like the asian take on the western tomato sauce. We like it on everything from fried chicken to burgers and burritos.

High 'n Dry: Ikan Bilis, Vaththal, Bak Kwa

You could always pick fresh vegetables in the backyard, but excess meat had to be preserved, in those non-refrigerated days. The result of that necessity is today's dried delicacies.

Ikan bilis (dried anchovies) are a much loved South East Asian ingredient. They are pungent, smell of the sea and packed with umami notes and flavour. You'll find them in a few different sizes too, from the really tiny 1 cm ones to the ones that are as long as your fingers. They range from the 2 cm long "blue eyes", the *mata biru, si kang*, to the 5 cm *hitam, pek pak, jalur emas* ("gold stripe)", to the in between *buntiao halus.*

They shine in the kitchen in many ways. "One of my favourite methods of livening up an Asian meal is to serve it with some fried anchovies. All you do is fry a handful or two in half a cup of hot oil for about a minute until they turn a mid brown colour. They add a deep, salty flavour and a fantastic crunch to any meal. If you happen to have peanuts lying about, fry those up too and be amazed at the affinity between these 2 very humble ingredients". – a quote.

While dried anchovies are quite commonly used as a garnish or as a side, they can also be cooked more elaborately, as in fried rice. Sambal Ikan Bilis is a spicy side dish made with chillies, that is a regular accompaniment to many meals and a staple chilli paste or condiment to Nasi Lemak, a coconut rice dish traditionally eaten at breakfast. It acts in the same way that crispy fried bacon lifts boring sandwich, or bacon bits plain mashed potatoes. Dried anchovies are also used to make stock for various dishes, like the Korean sundubu-jjigae, or our own wan tan soup.

The Tamil jerky is the *Vathhal* ("reduction"), slices of dried mutton that Malaysian Indians have largely forgotten. Back in the early sixties, relatives visiting from India brought dried *vathhal* as gifts. That was perhaps the last time I had tasted mutton jerky *kuzhambu* (aka curry). The smell and taste has almost gone from my memory.That recipe has joined the list of extinct things, as far as Malaysian Indian cooking is concerned, although in India it still exists in the villages. The Indian sundry store still carries varieties of vegetable vaththal, such as *koth-avarangkai* (cluster beans), *manathakkali* (black nightshade berries) etc. I suppose sun dried vegetables (or meats) gain and impart a stronger flavour to the cooking.

While we appreciate the Europeans for introducing Asian food terms to the English language, they sometimes committed big bad blunders. Take curry for instance. Curry, in Tamil refers to meat or vegetable (*mara kari –* Litt: "tree meat"). The actual Tamil for sauce/stew is *kuzhambu*. It is not so uncommon to hear the term *kari kuzhambu* or "meat stew", when indians speak of meat curry.

Bak Kwa is the Hokkien (Fujianese) word for "dried meat". It is actually more like wafer thin slices of barbecued pork jerky. Unlike beef jerky, which is tough, and dehydrated to remove the moisture in the meat, Malaysian Chinese style pork jerky is moist and grilled to perfection over charcoal fire. Whereas jerky is a strip or slice of whole meat, bakkwa is a thinly spread ground meat preparation. And hence, its softness as opposed to the toughness of beef jerky.

"When Chinese immigrants brought this delicacy over to Singapore and Malaysia, it began to take on local characteristics. A notable example lies in the preparation of bakkwa, where the meat is grilled over charcoal rather than air-dried, imparting a smokier flavor to the meat. The Singaporean and Malaysian versions of bakkwa are also sweeter than their mainland China counterparts with many different variations having developed to suit local palates, such as chili bakkwa." – quote

May we not forget that jerkies are not that uncommon in our kitchens. Besides the above items which are quite scarce and seasonal, excepting the ikan bilis, what about our spices? Sun dried chilly, dry spices, seasonings, sun dried tomatoes, fruits (raisins, figs, apricots) and what have you.

Salads: Yee Sang, Pachidi, Ulam

In the evolution of cooking, salads are the one concession, it seems, to our ancient raw vegetable diet. Our cave dwelling hunter-gatherer ancestors were probably familiar with our salad leaves, snacking noisily on them to stave off growling stomachs, while hoping to hook a meat dinner.

Chinese New Year is not complete without the traditional practice of 'loh hey', also known as 'loh sang'; i.e, tossing of the 'yee sang' on the seventh day of new year as an act to welcome prosperity, luck and vigour. *Yee Sang* is the salad itself. This practice is more of a Cantonese community custom, as 'loh hey' in Cantonese means 'to toss upwards', the higher, the better. The celebrants gather around the table armed with chopsticks, and work it in unison.

In the ancient days, a legend (Chinese always have an origin story to anything in their culture, don't they?) was told about how the female deity, Nuwa made animals out of clay and mud, and on the seventh day she created human beings. Hence, 'yee sang' was a dish made to celebrate the birth of mankind. This parallels the monotheistic faiths' account of God creating man and woman on the sixth day, before resting on the seventh (the Sabath).

"'Yee sang', also in Cantonese, means 'fresh fish' and snakehead murrel (ikan haruan) was commonly used as the main ingredient. Julienned carrot, cucumber, jicama, and pickled vegetables and crunchy crackers are also part of this dish. Lastly, plum sauce is the condiment used to enhance the flavour of 'yee sang'. If you have never tasted 'yee sang', this dish is crunchy, sweet and sour." The act often ends with a combined shout of "Yeeeeee Sang! Well, they also shout out "Yaaaaam Seng (drawn out form of yam seng, or "cheers") at the drinking table.

The word salad, itself denotes a mixing of vegetables. The Indians have a mixed salad that's not unlike the potato salad. Only, there is no potato. The South Indian *pachidi* (North Indian *raita*) is chopped or julienned carrots, cucumber, onions tossed in yoghurt and salt. It is the cool antidote to a spicy hot curry or briyani.

Mango strips drawn through a mandoline slicer can also be served as pachidi. Sprinkled and tossed with dried prawns, it becomes a Thai/ Malay relish. Raw mango *kerabu mangga* is similar to the Thai *Som Tum Mamuang.* The addition of julienned onion, lotus flower, cili padi (bird's eye chilli), dry prawn powder, fish sauce, lime juice, and peanut powder completes the packing for a sensory bomb in the mouth.

Rojak ("mish-mash") or Pasembor (the Penang appellation) are Indian Muslim street food, alongside the *cendol*, a dessert item. Ingredients are cubed firm tofu, fried prawn fritters, boiled egg, bean sprout, julienned cucumber and *sengkuang* (jicama), slathered with peanut/sweet potato sauce. This salad with a Malay name, is an anytime, anywhere meal. Like the Mamaks' *roti canai* and *teh tarik*, the Rojak/Pasembor pairs perfectly with the *cendol*, a shaved ice desert. A cool and sweet accompaniment to a hot and savoury dish.

The Malay salad, *kerabu,* is a healthy dose of herbs. The standard salad is the *kerabu ulam raja*, (litt: royal or king's salad). This list of ingredients makes for a zesty tossed salad. Shredded ulam raja (Cosmos caudatus) leaves, roasted shaved coconut – *kerisik*, (pounded ginger, *serai*/lemongrass, chilli), blanched prawns, tamarind juice, 1 inch pounded belacan, thinly sliced large onion, thinly sliced *bunga kantan* (lotus flower), salt, sugar and flavouring powder. TOSS!

Rojak buah, or fruit salad, is sliced fruits like mango, papaya, jicama, pineapple, and cucumber tossed in thick soy sauce, sugar and belacan syrup. The American fruit salad is chopped apples and grapes in mayonnaise. Both are after meal desserts or stand alone snacks.

Just Desserts: Lin Chi Kang, Bubur Cha Cha, Paal Payasam

With the main entrée mainly savoury (salt, hot, sour etc), the taste bud craves sugar to assure itself that it has gotten the entire gamut of the gastronomic senses. That is perhaps, why dessert is last and sweet. Somewhat like a sweet beverage. True deserts are more substantial while not overly voluminous like the entrees. They can be semi-solid custards like flan or pudding. They can be semi-liquid, like a sweet porridge or yoghurt (moru/lassi). Or, they can be soft and spongy like cake, brownie, fudge. Or, creamy like ice-cream and mousse. Or, crisp and succulent like jelly or jello. Or, they can be natural, like fruits and their juices.

In some Indian restaurants and old timers habits, dessert is followed by yet another munchie, the betel leaf (North Indian *paan*). The juice is ingested and supposedly aids digestion. Betel comes from Portuguese by way of the Tamil *vettrilai* ("victory leaf"). Why victory? Beats me too, except perhaps, that is shaped like lord Murugan's broad spear, which is known as *vetrivel*, or "victorious spear".

Malay desserts are called *pencuci mulut*, or Litt: "mouth wash". They include the gamut of Malay/Nonya kueh listed in the section, "steamy sets". Older Malays also indulge in betel leaf chewing, or *kunyah sireh*. It adds another layer of something to the conversation. Don't westerners chew gum or mint after meals? Now, smoking after a meal is a bitch. Why please? The tastebuds have just had a party of flavours. And you want to assault it with bitter and dry smoke?

Lin Chi Kang or lotus seed dessert, is mildly sweet and watery. Iced, it is rather cooling after a hot meal. The ingredients include white fungus/ snow ear fungus, red dates, dried longan, lotus seeds, goji berries, lily bulbs, rock sugar, and water. Except for the fungus which is chopped, the rest are whole and munchable. A similar Chinese dessert is canned longan or sea coconut swimming in H2O with ice cubes.

Bubur cha cha, is a south east Asian porridge containing a choice of sago pearls, sweet potatoes, yams, bananas, coconut milk, pandan leaves, sugar and salt. In Malaysia it is commonly cooked with coconut milk, sugar, and cubes of yam (purple), sweet potato(orange, yellow). It is a hot porridge that is savoured slowly. A common Malay porridge is the *bubur kacang hijau*. The Tamil version, *paasi payir kanji* has added *javvarisi* (sago pearl). During durian season, the durian flesh adds flavour and thickness to it.

The quintessential South Indian dessert is *payaasam*. This ancient recipe has only 3 ingredients – milk, rice, and sugar. These days, rice is replaced with vermicelli and sago pearl, and milk with coconut milk. Raisins, cashew and cardamon are the other additives. Everything is boiled, for a hot sweet stew. The north Indian *kheer* (just a name change) retains the three original ingredients. Some Indian restaurants serve *kesari* (a pudding made of semolina) in place of paayaasam.

Stand alone desserts served by the roadside, are chendol, ABC (shaved ice/snow cone-like concoction). They can be had anytime, tea time, snack time, dinner time – in your own time.

Time was, in my 15 years in America, my taste buds would say, "Donuts? Do not!" It rather yearned for the Malaysian doughnut. American Donuts get into your teeth, stick to your palate, are too sweet even without the chocolate, jelly layers and toppings. They drink like sponges and disintegrate immediately into the cuppa. Malaysian ones are just right in sweetness, and you just dust off the powdered sugar if they are too much. It is safe to dunk and the slight chewiness is welcome. It stands right in the mid-range of a donut and a bagel. So you get the best of both rings. Another Malaysian doughnut is the sweet potato doughnut (*kuih keria*). Excellent teatime treat. The Indian fried savoury, the *ulundhu vadai*, may be considered a doughnut because of its ring shape.

Just for a place to park, let's place these here. In terms of lentils or beans, while the Indians have the dahl (paruppu), green, ulunthu, and other "grams". The Chinese have the fermented black bean paste that raises a stir fries' appeal. The Malays have the biggest beanie of them all – the Petai. The delicious, crunchy, beans are a good diuretic (kidney cleanser) but have a stinky side effect, when you take a leak!

Crispy crackers: Keropok, Zhizha, Appalam

An accompaniment to the main rice course in Malay meals, is a crispy cracker called *keropok*. Good as side dish or as snack in itself, the keropok is made by thoroughly pulverizing seafood (fish, prawn, etc), adding flour, water, and salt. The goo is then rolled into sausages, boiled, sliced into thin coins and sun dried. Deep fried, the coins expand like a flower opening up to the morning sun.

In Indonesia, the term *krupuk* refers to the type of relatively large crackers, while the term *kripik* or *keripik* refers to smaller bite-size crackers; the counterpart of chips (or crisps) in western cuisine. For example, potato chips are called *kripik kentang* in Indonesia. Both terms, krupuk and kripik, sound like the crackling and crumbling of this crispy canape in your carefree clapper. Thus, the etymology of the term krupuk is an onomatopoeia in Indonesian, of the crunchy sound of this crispy snack. Crack-crack, crick crick. Crikey! (British exclamation).

In Malaysia, it is known as *keropok*, and associated with fish and other seafood. *Kerepek* are chips made from plants, such as plaintain, yam etc. The three types of keropok in Malaysia are Keropok kering, Keropok lekor and amplang. *Keropok Lekor*, a chewy type, originated from Terengganu and *Amplang* from the coastal towns of Semporna and Tawau in Sabah which is also can be found in Kalimantan. *Keropok kering* can be found in most Malaysian states. Mukah town in Sarawak, a fishing hamlet is also known for keropok production.

Zhizha is made from pork rind, popularized in Qingdao, Shandong. It is a byproduct of lard. The skin is removed and sliced as thin as a gold coin.

After the extraction of lard, the rest is hard and tastes like a salty cracker, seasoned with salt and MSG while it is hot. *Huazhi,* is made from intestines, chopped and deep-fried twice, and used in stew or soup. These are also known by the Spanish name, *chicharron.*

The Indian cracker is the *appalam,* aka *pappadom*. It is an indispensable part of the Indian banana leaf meal. It is made by mixing powdered *ulunthu* (black gram), salt, and water. The dough is rolled into thin circular sheets and sun dried. It is fried, like the keropok, and behaves the same way, in the hot oil. Some take straight bites of it in between mouthfuls of the rice. Some crush it onto the entire meal. The purpose is to add salt or savouriness, much like a dip in the pickle.

Like the keropok, the zhizha and appalam are deep fried in oil. All can be eaten as snacks or with meals.

A most fine cracker is the sweet, colourful, 10 inch diameter disc called *biskut piring* ("plate biscuit"). It was a favourite of our childhood and now rare. The melt in your mouth wafer recalls the holy communion served at Catholic masses. A somewhat similar material is the vanilla or chocolate filled wafer sandwich. And then, there is our own *love letters*, a CNY staple. A version of it is, the choc filled rolled wafer tube, which we used to pretend smoke as cheroot or cigar.

Crackly Snackies: Yee Chai Peng, Omappodi, Kerepek

Between meals, you sometimes want to snack on/sneak in something. It usually has to be crispy, crunchy, a little salty and a little sweet.

Malaysia has its own dry peanut snack called *kacang menglembu* named after the Ipoh suburb where it is produced. It is the favourite at Chinese New Year and beer parties. Shangtung peanuts are bigger beaned and sweeter, named after the eponymous city in China.

The Ngan Yin factory in Menglembu produces the hand brand peanut and is a favourite. There are other brands too, such as Pagoda from nearby Sungai Siput.

Yee Chai Peng (Cantonese) – Ear biscuit, Pig's ear biscuit. It is a 2" diameter disc, with a white and brown swirl. A sheet of bland white dough is placed on top of a savoury brown dough and rolled (think swiss roll). The log is sliced into thin coins and deep fried. The ear lobe biscuit or cow's ear is similar but slightly bigger and shaped like an actual ear.

Murukku, "twist", is a common Tamil snack that is served at Deepavali, but eaten at other times too. *Omappodi* aka "mixture", is an alltime snack of tiny or broken murukku, peanuts etc. There is a Chinese snack that looks like a twisted six inch length of rope called *mahua.* It is sweet and has a hard crunch.

Then, there is the *Acchu Murukku,* "mold murukku", a mainstay of Deepavali. It is made by coating a flower shaped mold into sweet rice batter and dunking in hot oil. Due to its floral appearance, Malays, who have taken a fancy to this sweet stuff have rechristened it *kuih rose*, or *kuih loyang*. The Chinese too, have jumped on the bandwagon and market them under the name, *honeycomb crisp*. Perhaps they like it because it's taste reminds them of their own melt in the mouth wafer called *love letters*. How confused can people get?

Speaking of hijacking and renaming foods, the Indian *athirasam,* is now packaged for Central Market visitors as *telinga keling,* "Indian ears". Well, at least due credit is given the Indian, keling being the old appellation for South Indians. But to lift an idea as in the case of the *acchu murukku* and not give due credit to the source, seems the height of cultural appropriation. Even the brass *acchu* ("acuan" in Malay) or mold, is from India and can only be found in Indian stores. And yet we have food wars with Singapore over its nominating hawker food to UNESCO's list of intangible cultural heritage. Indonesia is up in arms over Malaysia claiming *rendang* as its own. I am only saying, "take all you want, but keep the original name." Copycat, if you must, but isn't it polite to cite the copyright? Rendang and Nasi Lemak are still that the world over, aren't they? Supposing somebody in the west starts marketing rendang as beef ragout and nasi lemak as coconut milk pilaf? As Malaysia is a multicultural space, appropriating another's without giving due credit is like stealing your neighbour's clothes right under his nose.

Chewy, Gooey 'n Oh Goody!: Halwa, Dodol, Ang Koo

Sticky sweet stretchy stuff seems to be special favourites with Malaysians. Why not, if a cuisine is to embrace the whole range of tastes and textures? Our cuisines pass the test.

Halwa is a sweetmeat that is of Middle Eastern origin, at least namewise, but has been adopted and perfected by Indians. Indian banana leaf restaurants display the varieties in glass showcases at the front of the shop, along with other Indian sweets. The Tirunelveli (Tamil Nadu) halwa is reputedly the best and the priciest. The glossy glob of goo literally glides in ghee. There is even a Tamil saying that mirrors the English, "sending coal to Newcastle." "Giving halva to Thirunelveli?" "Giving halva", also means to sweet talk, or flatter.

Halwa's stick to the roof of your mouth quality, is probably thanks to the gluten in the wheat. Halwa makers often take the easy way by using wheat flour. My aunt made the most translucent, melt in your mouth halwa by using the milk extracted after grinding wheat grains that had been soaked overnight. With cardamom, saffron, and sugar in heated ghee, the wheat juice is stirred and reduced to a bubbling pasty consistency. When cooled, cut, and garnished with almond slivers and cashew nuts, it is a sweet toothed Maharaja's delight, a king among Indian sweets.

Halwa proper is rarely done at home, as it is readily available in restaurants and sweet stalls. Besides, making it is a bother, requiring hours of stirring. The carrot halwa, is a poor imitation that is done at home.

The Malay version of the halwa, the *dodol* (Sundanese) is an occasional sweet. And, unlike the halwa, it is made at home as a community event. On Hari Raya eve (Puasa or Korban), the extended family members gather around a huge outdoor *kawah* (cauldron/wok) and take turns stirring. The process can take don't know how long (pardon the Manglish). 9 hours?! Glutinous rice powder, rouxed in coconut oil, stirred with coconut milk and gula melaka (molasses), yields a dark chocolate looking, liquorice textured, confection.

Durian is the favourite flavor, and it is seasonal just like the dodol. The elasticity and stickiness (not unlike gummy bears) comes from the gluten in the glutinous rice flour. The flour, coconut milk, and *pandan* (screwpine) leaves are stirred together over medium fire. As the mixture begins to bubble and sputter like the sulphurous mud of Rotorua, New Zealand, brown sugar and durian pulp is added. Stirring is continued till glossy and phlegmatic. The brown sugar gives it a chocolaty darkness. Indeed, as the dodol stubbornly sticks to the roof of your mouth, you are sometimes reminded of milk chocolate. Gummy bear texture and liquorice taste, is an approximate comparison to dodol.

The "Straits Chinese" or *Baba Nonya*, refuse to be outdone. Their contribution to the chewy challenge is *Kuih Ang Koo*. It means, "red tortoise". The texture of the round cake is closer to the liquorice stick. Again, glutinous rice is the culprit. That, a tiny amount of cornflour, and a few drops of red colouring, are kneaded and small portions rolled into circular sheets. A filling of cooked and mashed mung bean, and sugar is placed in the centre, folded, and pressed onto a mold. The cake is placed on a circular cut banana leaf and steamed until cooked.

Ang Koo is a strictly home production and served on festive seasons. Remember the red colour – auspicious? These days, it is common to see ang koo being sold at the market place by the Nyonya Kueh vendors. It is usually associated with the worship of Chinese deities, particularly the Jade Emperor. Ang Koo also features prominently in the Baby's Full Moon Celebration (*Muah Goay*), an offering made by parents after their new born child has passed a full month of age. The Baby's Full Moon is both a thanksgiving celebration and a proclamation to friends, relatives, as well as to the deities and long-departed ancestors, that a new member has been added to the household.

Halwa, Dodol, Ang Koo. Saffron, Brown, Red. Indian, Malay, Chinese. Sweeeet!

Oven and Grill: Satay, Char Siew, Tandoori

Shall we take the fact that Malaysians use the grill much less than the other methods of cooking, as proof of our culinary advancement? Haven't we come a long way from those cave dwelling days when grilling was the high tech cooking method? We are the more progressive society. Take the Americans (BBQ) and Australians (Barbie). Every one of their homes has a grill and grilling is a weekend necessity. Their womenfolk would be the first to tell you that the men revert to their hunter-gatherer, cavemen mode at those times. Grilling is almost exclusively a male activity. A man who wouldn't know how to boil an egg, takes to the grill like a duckling to water. The oven, which has its origins in the pit cooking of earlier times, is in almost every Malaysian home. If not a convection oven, at least a microwave? I remember those days when my lower middle class mother cooked sponge cakes in an aluminum *paanai* or soup pot. Hot coals below and on the cover. The method is Dutch Oven. Only, Dutch ovens were made of cast iron rather than aluminum.

I said grilling is rarely done in the home, but it does happen outside. Not out on the the lawn, but in eating centres. Here too, its a mostly male activity. The grilled item that has instant recognizability is the satay. Food historians might trace its origins to the kebab of the Middle-East. Whereas, the kebab is rather unwieldy, and its meat needs to be scraped onto the plate first, the satay is a finger food. Ice-cream-like, it can be eaten right off the stick. The food itself has become entrenched as a Malay dish. But its name is a different thing. Satay doesn't sound Malay. Indonesians spell it, *sate*. I heard a tour guide say that it is from the Chinese, *sa tai*, meaning "3 pieces". The stick does have about three pieces of meat on it, if you had noticed. The indian wants to get in on the act too. One of the Tamil words for "flesh" is *sathai* and *thasai,* for *"muscle".* Go figure.

If Penang is the capital of the laksa, and Trengganu the birthplace of nasi dagang, Kajang claims bragging rights for satay, even if it originated in Java. An Indonesian publication traces the word to *sak beteng* ("skewer") from ponorogo regency of East Java.

A meat of your choice is marinated overnight in a paste of blended Lemongrass, Galangal, Garlic, Shallots, Turmeric powder, Coriander powder, Chili powder, Salt and Sugar. Three, inch thick pieces are strung on a bamboo skewer, and grilled on charcoal flames. The dip is a sweet hash of, Roasted pounded peanuts, Palm sugar, Tamarind, Dry red chilies, Garlic, Shallots, Galangal, Lemongrass.The meat can be eaten as is, as it is already marinated. Dipping into the sauce is double happiness. The accompaniments are diced onions, cucumber, and cubes of *ketupat* or *nasi himpit* ("compressed rice").

Ikan bakar, or grilled fish is another local food of the gods. Pinching crispy fish flesh and dipping in a tamarind sauce, is a great side to plain rice. The curry sambal smeared fish can be grilled naked or wrapped in banana leaves/aluminum foil, for a wet texture. The common fish for the grill are *cincaru* (torpedo scad), *selar* (oxeye scad), *or pari* (stingray).

The Chinese BBQ is the *char siew* ("fork roasted"), a Cantonese dish. Pork belly, cut into strips along the grain, is marinated overnight. The marinade consist of, *nam yue* or fermented red bean curd, maltose or honey, soy sauce, oyster sauce, five spice powder.This is a sweet, savory, sticky sauce that gives the pork a natural glaze when baked in the oven at 400F for 15 minutes.

It is a compatible companion with chicken rice (Hailam dish) and want tan mee (Cantonese dish). Fine chopped char siew is also used in Chinese fried rice.

What do you call something that is both a grill and an oven? Grilloven? Naah! The *tandoor* ("clay oven") might qualify, because it has direct convection heat from charcoal embers plus thermal radiation from the heated tandoor itself.

Tandoori chicken is a chicken dish originating from the Indian subcontinent and is popular the world over in Indian restaurants. Raw chicken (breast or leg) is marinated in a mixture of yogurt and tandoori masala, a spice blend. It is seasoned and colored with cayenne pepper, red chili powder, or Kashmiri red chili powder as well as turmeric or food coloring. The skin is generally removed before the chicken is marinated and roasted.

The marinated chicken is placed on skewers and cooked at high temperatures in the tandoor, which is heated with charcoal or wood, which adds to the smoky flavour. The dish can also be cooked in a standard oven, using a spit or rotisserie, or over hot charcoal. The pasta partner is usually the naan, a flatbread that is slapped onto the hot insides of the tandoor. The accompaniments are mint chutney, onions, cucumber and a wedge of lime.

I do remember as children, when in a moment of monotony, we would pull up a tapioca tree and throw the tubers into the embers of an open firepit. The sweet taste of the starch was quite something, on a boring afternoon.

Tapas: Dim Sum, Thaali, Nonya Kueh

Little bites. Mouth sized morsels. A childrens' riddle goes: "what is smaller than an ant's mouth?" It's food, of course! Tapas are a Spanish culinary style where you get to sample a variety of foods in a single sitting, giving you the feeling of having tried them all. Basically, its finger foods. Been at a hotel buffet, and wondered how you are going to sample everything on display? You take a bit of everything.

"The story is, the original *tapas* (fr. Spanish *tapar* "to cover") were the slices of bread or meat which sherry drinkers in Andalusian taverns used to cover their glasses between sips. "This was a practical measure meant to prevent fruit flies from hovering over the sweet sherry. The meat used to cover the sherry was normally ham or chorizo, which are both very salty and activate thirst. Because of this, bartenders and restaurant owners began creating a variety of snacks to serve with sherry, thus increasing their alcohol sales. Tapas eventually became as important as the sherry itself" – quoted

Asians have such traditions, born of such needs. "The Cantonese *Dim Sum* is one fine example. Dim Sum means, 'to lightly touch (your) heart'), i.e, "to barely fill (your) stomach". It refers to a light meal or brunch. And then, there is the Japanese innovation of the sushi bar, where you sit by the tracks of the snaking sushi trolley, and pick off the plates like a grizzly bear does as the salmon valiantly swims upstream for its annual spawning at the place of its birth.

"Dim sum is usually linked with the older tradition from yum cha (drinking tea), which has its roots in travelers on the ancient Silk Road needing a place to rest. Thus, teahouses were established along the roadside. An imperial physician in the third century wrote that combining tea with food would lead to excessive weight gain. People later discovered that tea can aid in digestion, so teahouse owners began adding various snacks." – (Wikipedia). Among the various titbits in the dim sum basket are *lo mai kai* (steamed glutinous rice), *char sie pau* (steamed meat buns), *siu mai* (steamed dumplings), *guo tie* (potstickers), spring roll, and congee (rice porridge)

The unique culinary art of dim sum originated with the Cantonese in southern China, who over the centuries transformed yum cha from a relaxing respite to a loud and happy dining experience. In Hong Kong, and in most cities and towns in Guangdong (Canton) province, many restaurants began serving dim sum as early as five in the morning. It is a tradition for the elderly to gather to eat dim sum after morning exercises. For many in southern China, yum cha is treated as a weekend family day. More traditional dim sum restaurants typically serve dim sum until mid-afternoon. However, in modern society, it has become commonplace for restaurants to serve dim sum at dinner time; various dim sum items are even sold as take-out for students and office workers on the go.

Though there is no specific cuisine that is tapa-like in Malay and Indian cuisine, one can easily be assembled. Just collect all the bite size morsels of Tamil food out there, and Voila! A sampler plate of Tamil tapas might have *masala vadai, ulundhu vadai, adai, akkaravadisal, athirasam, bonda, bajji, boli, cheedai, cutlet, kolkattai, kesari, puttu, pakoda, paal khova, paniyaaram, paayaasam, paal appam, idiyappam, samosa, sundal, sukhiyan, halwa etc.*), bite sized savouries and sweets, all.

The same can be said of Malay tapas – *bahulu, bingka ubi, bengkang, checodok, cucur, dodol, keledek, keladi, keropok, pisang goreng, kuih lapis, kuih lompang, kuih ketayap, kuih kaswi, kuih kochi, kuih talam, onde onde, serimuka*. These are mostly on the sweet side, and would fit more in a teatime tapas bar.

The Indian and Malay tapas are, as a rule, only high tea treats, whereas, Dim Sum can be had for breakfast, lunch and dinner, in that order of regularity of eating.

Teatime Titbits: Checodok, Char Koay, Chakkarai Ponggal

The English have own their afternoon tea ritual. The Japanese have their solemnly ceremonious tea sessions. The Malaysian tea-time is not so formalized or ritualized, but pervasively prevalent. There is no fixed time of day, or particular place for imbibing the beverage. Any time can be teatime. Any place, a tea parlour. Breakfast time, or break time; lunchtime, or lepak time; dinnertime or donowhat time; suppertime, or soccer time.

It may not be surprising if even Tee time (on the golfing greens) turns into teatime. Just bring along your own thermos flasks, eh?

While teatimes are not fixed, so are the snacks that go with it. Depending on the time of the tea, the accompaniments can be anything from nasi lemak, char koay (*youtiao*), chapatti to fried noodles, mixed rice, or satay. There is, however, a special teatime between lunch and dinner, about 3.00 to 4.00 pm, which is a legacy of the British colonial time here. It is the happy hour of tea, if you please. This is what is under discussion here, and the titbits that are common accompaniment.

The cuisine of tea is not as rigid as the English or Japanese tea occasions, which are hung up on a particular way of making and serving. In Malaysia, the forms of preparation vary from Chinese to chai, to herbal to halia, to mamak to masala, to green to ginseng. To the man on the street, tea generally refers to the signature Mamak, or *teh tarik*. Mamak cuisine is everybody's child. The *teh tarik*, or, "stretched tea", is tea mixed with sweetened condensed milk and poured alternately into two large eversilver mugs or *koleh*s (Tamil, *kuvalai*). The mid-air refueling action of transferring the caramel coloured concoction, and the alternate raising and lowering of the Mamak's arms, like a ship captain's at the wheel, is itself a circus performance that is gleefully publicisized abroad by the Tourism Ministry fellers. That, and the Mamak's hand coordination when flipping the roti canai, adds visual interest to the savouring of roti canai and teh tarik. It is a pairing, which most Malaysians consider a match made in heaven.

The frothy foam that forms in the turbulent tumult of the tea tumblers, is a true topper. It predates the creamy crown on the modern mocha or latter day latte. The Indians, especially, have always drunk a more lukewarm tea or coffee, cooled this way. The Chinese prefer drinking straight out steaming hot, although the old *Ah Pehs* ("uncles") like to cool theirs by pouring it into the porcelain saucers and sipping luxuriously from it. That is the scientific principle of larger surface area equals faster cooling. In homes in Tamil Nadu, they serve your tea in an eversilver tumbler that sits inside a slightly wider mug *(davarah)* that comes up half way to the tumbler's height. The idea, as you guessed it, is for you to do your own teh tarik theatrics. Guests, though served the same way, would have their tea or coffee already "pulled" and cooled to save the bother.

The British and some of us prefer the plain tea, i.e, without milk. Some even like it hot and without sugar. It is an acquired taste. Brings to mind the cowboy in old westerns, on his break from horse riding. I never noticed a cowboy adding sugar to his coffee.

The strong flavor and smell of the mamak stall tea, is something not duplicated at home with your BOH or Lipton sachets. Someone said long ago, that the secret was in the fact that they used the leaf stems and other remnants of the milling process. Basically, the floor dust. Why not? If fish heads, which used to be discarded are now highly regarded, why not the tea factory throwaways. That is, so long as they are not literally swept up off the floor. Hoohh!

The preferred tea break things are the Malay Pisang Goreng, Keledek (sweet potato), Keladi (Yam), cekodok, Cucur Udang. Indian vadais — masala (paruppu) and ulunthu (urad) vadai). Chinese char koay, char siew pao. The all Malaysian curry puff, coconut buns, as well as the the usual sweet kuih-muih.

Added to the above, there is the tea-set set known as the Nonya Kuih. A dozen or so steamed sweet cakes.

Banana bon bons: Vaalaikai Kootu, Chekodok Pisang, Fried Caramel Banana.

Ah, the banana! Beauteous, bounteous, beneficent banana. Its name is versatility. I remember my childhood days in Bukit Badong Estate, where my father was headmaster of a one-room schoolhouse. One day, my mother decided to do a banana lunch, meaning only banana on the plate...er, leaf. She went out to the backyard, slashed a banana tree and proceeded to harvest its parts — the tree being a veritable grocery store of goodies. The raw banana, ripe banana, the jantung or flower bunch, the heart (*vaazhai thandu*) in the centre of the trunk,

A single banana leaf (frond?) yields about 7 'plates'. Plate, as in container for food.

First, the tip of the leaf is cut and reserved for the head of the household or the chief guest. It is called the *Thalai vaazhai* or, "head banana leaf". The rest of the leaf is split lengthwise along its central rib, and dissected into smaller pieces. The family sat down cross – legged on the floor.

Next, came the plating. Possibly the only item not from the tree was the rice, which is a staple. Many people still haven't gotten the notion that rice should only be a vehicle to facilitate the intake of the nutritious stuff, not the "main" food. The way many Malaysians pile on their rice and reduce the veggies, scares the doctor.

With the rice that day, we had *sambaar* (lentil gravy) made of – good guess – unripe plantain (a banana variety). Plantain was also thin sliced and deep fired like banana chips. It was a crunchy accompaniment, that functioned like the ubiquitous *appalam* or *pappadom,* the Indian *keropok.* She also stirfried cubed plantain in masala spice for a hot *peratal*.

Mum made a *kootu,* or stew, out of cubed plantain with saffron, blended coconut paste, and the usual spices, for an entirely different taste. With the flower – *vaazhai poo* or *jantung pisang,* she stir-fried it, after marinating it in salt and squeezing it to remove bitterness and tepidity. The *vaazhai thandu* is the cylindrical, ivory tusk-like, "heart of palm" in the centre of the banana stem. This, she finely sliced, diced and stir-fried with turmeric, lentils and the usual seeds and bulbs (mustard, cumin, fenugreek, plus onion and garlic).

For dessert, we had green gram *kanji* (congee/porridge) cooked with sweet ripe banana. There was also a ripe comb of banana, if you still had a stomach space for it. A little later, for tea, we had banana fritters. Now, that was what you call a meal-in-one. With the different tastes, smells, and textures, you'd never know the entire entrée and cutlery came from a single tree! The crunchy, tasteful thandu, the meaty chewy flower, the creamy kootu, piquant peratal, crispy chips and the sumptuous saambar. With such versatility, is it any wonder that you would probably go bananas trying to find an Indian home without a clump of banana trees in their backyard?

They tie the trees at wedding *pandhals* (tents) to form arched entranceways. The dried bark yields a *kayir* (coir/string) that can be used to tie food bundles of banana leaves as in *nasi lemak* (a popular breakfast of coconut rice and sambal). The only difference in the Malay and Indian way of using banana leaves as wrapping paper is, Malays use the underside of the leaf. Chinese prefer to to wrap their food in lotus or yam leaves or in bamboo leaves as in steaming *chang*.

Apparently banana's fame had spread far and wide beyond its tropical turf, even to China's forbidden city. Back then, when I was in Hydrology in the Selangor Drainage and Irrigation Department, we used to guage the Selangor river at the Rantau Panjang bridge. The Malay mandor, a refined raconteur, regaled us with a tall tale about how a Chinese traveler (Fa Hsien? I-Ching? Xuan Zang?) returned from India with incredible intimations. He told how the Indians were so rich, they threw away their plates after every meal. Someone wanted to verify the story, and found that they were indeed throwing away their plates. But, you'd have already guessed what it was!

Cekodok pisang, is a Malay croquette. The *pengat pisang bersagu*, is a sweet banana porridge cooked in coconut milk and sago. Fried banana or *pisang goreng* is another teatime must have. Vacuum packed banana chips is a popular Malay cottage industry.

A Chinese 'native' banana item is difficult to come by. However, there is a a version of pisang goreng (fried banana) that they do by smearing it with caramel and sesame seeds. It is called toffee banana – slices of banana dipped in batter, deep fried, coated in toffee and sprinkled with sesame seeds. Rich! Typical of them, ain't it?, to do a sesame chicken on fried banana!

Who doesn't enjoy banana bread. The creative award for that goes to America, a country that does not grow the nanas. Apparently, during the depression of the 30's, people used about to rot bananas in breads. The baking powder/baking soda was just making its entrance at the same time. And hence, was born a favoured tea pastry. Another one of those children born of necessity, the mother of invention, innovation, inspiration, and imagination.

With such a soft, creamy, sweet, and fragrant flesh, it is a wonder someone hasn't come up with a banana jam or spread. But not not worry, a peanut butter sandwich inlaid with sliced coins of banana, is a sure thing. Nature's own cream to match the darling durian.

Trees and Herbs: Veppilai, Belimbing, Pomegranate

Aside from door decorations, one way of identifying the racial identity of a household as you move around the neighbourhood, is to observe the kind of tree that grows within the gates. For instance an Indian home is easily recognizable by the presence of the *veppilai, or neem* tree. That is the tree that gives you castor oil, the old time yukky stuff that Indian parents forced down their children's throats for laxative. The stuff is banned these days, but in those days, it was a much dreaded monthly exercise in bowel cleansing. You were held down on father's lap as he pinched your nose and sent a *sangu* (spouty infant feeding spoon) of the stuff into your mouth. It was a battle lost, but your body wretched and stretched to eject it.

The veppilai leaf extract is now being marketed as a natural insect repellent and insecticide. The science and technology is new, but Indians have always known its curative and preventive properties. They have, since time immemorial used its leaves as a bed for chicken pox patients to lie on. They bathe in water soaked with these leaves and tumeric and warmed by the sun, to ex the pox. Mariamman, the Hindu goddess is always associated with the veppilai leaves, its devotees carrying bunches or she herself holding it. Indians consider that air that has brushed a veppilai tree is fresh and healthy.

Another sure giveaway is the *kari veppilai*, a veppilai lookalike, that is none other than the indispensable curry leaf. Hence, the origin of the Malay, *karipulai.* Used in curries, sambaars and stir fries, they are a flavor enhancer, similar (yet different) to the basil in western cooking. These days however, the curry leaf tree is in almost any house. Even some Chinese homes grow these, as they have learned to use it in their cooking, especially deep frying it and sprinkling on fried prawn etc.

An even surer identifier is the *murungai* (moringa) tree, used in murungai leaf stir fries, *thanni saar* (a watery sambaar) and drumstick kootu. When an Indian purchases a house, the first tree he plants, is generally a mango.

The Malay house is often identifiable by the belimbing tree. Its thumb sized, thumb shaped fruits are added to fish gravies to give sourness. Other souring agents in Malaysian cooking are: *asssam Jawa* used in Tom Yam, and Tamarind, from the Arabic *Tamar al – Hind*, "date of India".

A turmeric, lengkuas (galangal), or ginger bush nearby can be a giveaway. They use lots of those in the cooking.

The Chinese house is characerically planted with the pomegranate bush/tree. I have never seen a Malay or Indian residence that had that. Significance? The dense seeds might signal fertility. One might also find a stand of thin bamboo, or a cherry blossom tree. *Kumquat* (tangerine) is tiny oranges that grow to a large bush and can be found in large pots either in or outdoors.

The many buds of the *māo liŭ* (pussy willow} make it a favourite flower for Chinese New Year. The fluffy white blossoms of the pussy willow resemble silk, and they soon give forth young shoots the colour of green jade. In Chinese tradition, this represents the coming of prosperity. Towards the Lunar New Year period in spring, stalks of the plant may be bought from wet market vendors or supermarkets.

The mango tree (Webster: Tamil: *Maan kai = Deer fruit*) is a universal favorite in most Malaysian homes, regardless of ethnicity. Handsome looking, shady, easily maintained, and easy fruiting, the mango tree is a common sight in the neighbourhood. So is the fast growing, fast fruiting papaya. Papaya can be found in anyone's garden. Chuck the seeds and care less. Low maintenance. The fruits are a welcome dessert at mealtimes. Malays also stir fry the half-ripe fruit for a delicious entrée, or they will "Jeruk" or pickle it in sugar n' vinegar.

Don't forget the near banal but never bland banana. They may be found in everyone's backyard, drain reserve or road shoulder.

Sukun (breadfruit) is a cousin of the *nangka* (Jackfruit). The sukun is smaller and spherical, while nangka is bigger and elongated. They are ideally cooked in saambar, curry, or stirfries. Say you want to prank your vegetarian friend by serving him meat. Sukun/Nangka are the ideal meat cheats, based on their look and texture.

The coconut is another common ornamental as well as all purpose tree. Malays of old used to plant a tree at birth, and at weddings. A man builds his own home after the birth of 1st child and plants a coconut tree. The child and tree grow up together. And enjoy each other for life.

Eventhough Indians have an age old tradition with cooking with coconut milk, making brooms, and roof thatches, not to mention toddy tapping, the Malays, by reason of living in kampongs and river banks, have other creative uses. Rafts, footbridges across drains and canals, and stairs as in Iban long houses.

Speaking of coconuts, this writer recalls a time when still schooling, and part-timing as a banquet waiter in the old Equatorial Hotel in KL. The Minister of Agriculture was the featured dinnertime speaker. As we floated between tables with our trays and between kitchen and banquet hall, I heard some snatches of the speech. True to his glamourous gift as a glib gabber of the gossipy kind, gleeful giggles and guttural guffaws engulfed the gallery.

At one point, the Honourable (Yang Berhormat) minister mentioned something about a coconut trunk standing upright and tall, with big nuts shaded by ample fronds. I was busy at the table, so my recollection is not so accurate. Next, he seemed to say something about a pineapple bush, with a spread out bed of thorny fronds, out of which rose an ultra short and thin stem, holding aloft a big pineapple. The fruit was as big as a coconut. Finally, he brought out about a plant which had an elongated and threadlike stem that drooped on the ground and couldn't support its coconut-sized watermelons. By this time, I had gone to the kitchen to pick up the next course. From, the explosive hoots of laughter that came from the dining hall, it must have been one funny story, that the minister had told.

Spice of Choice: Empat Beradik, Yuxiang, Thaalippu

Spices are categorized into dry spices and wet spices. Dry as in powder, and wet as in paste.

The Malay spices are well known as *rempah empat beradik,* meaning the "four siblings" i.e. *bunga lawang* (star anise), *kayu manis* (cinnamon), *buah pegaga* (cardamom), and *bunga cengkih* (cloves). They go into most cooking. The wet spice is actually all the above blended or ground with a little water. Sauteing in hot oil releases the fragrance and the flavour of the fare. Rempah ratus ("100 spices") is a general term for all spices. Not allspice.

Tom Yam paste is another popular blend that is used in stir-fries and the eponymous soup. The ingredients are are herbs like lemongrass, galangal, kafir lime leaves, chilli etc

Yuxiang (lit. 'fish fragrance') is a famous seasoning mixture in Chinese cuisine, and also refers to the resulting sauce in which meat or vegetables are cooked. It is said to have originated in Sichuan cuisine, and has since spread to other regions. A more-or-less equal portions are mixed, though some prefer to include more scallions than ginger and garlic. The mixture is then fried in oil until fragrant. Water, starch, sugar, and vinegar are then added.The yuxiang seasoning includes finely minced *pao la jiao* (pickled chili), white scallion, ginger, and garlic. These form the basic sauce.

An even more famous Sichuan dry blend is the five spice powder (5 sisters?). Here, the star anise is the (duh!), "star"! The others are: cinnamon, fennel, cloves. The fifth factor can be a toss up between white pepper and *da hong pao* (Sichuan peppercorn). This is the blend that boosts the beguilement of *bak kut teh* (Hokkien: 'Pork Ribs Tea.'). Star anise is said to be a key ingredient (shikimic acid) in Tamiflu (Roche), the flu drug.

In Indian, especially Tamil cooking, there is no one favoured spice. Everything, from saambar and curry (kuzhambu) to stir fries is preceded by a preamble called *thaalippu* or tempering/sautéing, whereby a "pluck" (bigger than a "pinch", much smaller than a "grab") of a spice combo is added to hot oil. The spices are roasted briefly in oil or ghee to liberate essential oils and enhancing the flavours. Although the tempering is the first step in most cooking, the sautaed spices can also be done separately and added later to dishes like sambhar or chutney.

The ingredients (the favoured 5?) typically used in tempering include *seerakam* (cumin seeds), *kadugu* (black mustard seeds), *sombu* (fennel seeds), *perungaayam* (fenugreek seeds), and *ulunthu* (black gram). After the tempering, it is joined by the curry leaves, onions/garlic, fresh or dried chillies, the pastes – ginger/garlic, chilli, turmeric, cumin (for colour and flavour). Those requiring longer cooking are added earlier, followed by the fast cookers. The final grand entry is, of course the star of the show— your meat or veg of choice.

The definitive spice of the Tamils is *manjal*, or tumeric. It is also the word for the colour yellow. Its praise is crooned in the multi millennium old Tamil Sangam literature. Nowadays, it is also sung by international scientists and nutritionists – for the curative efficacy of its key ingredient, curcumin. In the Tamil spice chest – a "five compartment box" (*anjarappetti*) – the turmeric compartment has pride of place. The other compartments have *kadugu* (mustard), *malli* (coriander), *seerakam* (cumin), and *milagu* (pepper).

Is it any surprise that turmeric is used in every Tamil recipe? It is in curry powders, sprinkled in vegetable stir-fries and what have you. Just as you are concluding that turmeric is the all purpose cooking spice of the Tamils, "all-purpose" takes on an added dimension. Turmeric – *manjal* ("yellow") – is an auspicious thingy and colour. Matter of fact, it sounds similar to *Mangalam,* "auspiciousness", or *Maangalyam,* the *thaali* (chain and pendant) that identifies a married Indian woman. A plain thread dyed with the turmeric and attached to a simple turmeric tuber is as precious as a gold one in terms of significance. The paste of the *kudamanjal* (rounded, "pot" turmeric) is smeared on the top right corner of wedding invitations; documents; at the entrance posts of the main doorway; on mango leaves festooned across the front door etc. At the end of Mariamman temple festivals, the devotees play the *manjal neeraattu,* or splashing each other with turmeric water. Is it for disinfecting purposes?

The days of this may be bygone in Malaysia, but the women of Tamilnadu, India still apply the paste of the fragrant *kasturi manjal* to their faces and bodies, before bathing. Supposedly, it is a beauty as well as health treatment. They have identified about eight other varities of turmeric. The cooking turmeric is the *virali manjal,* or "finger" turmeric.

Push-Cart Blanche: Rojak & Chendol, Popiah, Pisang Goreng

Alfresco dining was possibly the only mode of "eating out" in those days of yore, before diners and gourmet restaurants. Long before food trucks, there were the itinerant hawkers with their three-wheeled bicycle carts and push carts vending their snacks and refreshments in the the shade of raintrees. The vendors would also paddle around neighbourhoods peddling their palatables. These days, the local councils have herded these vehicles and corralled them along certain streets, for the convenience of lunchtime crowds and street foodies.

One could avail oneself of mamak mee goreng, chee cheong fan, pisang goreng and other fried tit-bits, nasi lemak, vadai varieties, kacang putih, apam balik, putumayam, putu piring, popiah, char siew pau, bubur, fruit juices, cut fruits, cendol, ABC, rojak, nonya kuih, burgers, roti john, roti canai, fried/soup noodles, fried radish cake, satay, sausages. There are food which don't occur here, like economy rice or banana leaf meals because of portability issues.

Here are some representative (ethnic) food. Now the rojak, meaning, a "jumble" or "mish-mash" is a salad from Indonesia where there are 2 dozen varieties. Malaysia has the mamak rojak and fruit rojak. "In Malaysia, mamak rojak (also known as Indian rojak or Pasembur) is associated with Mamak stalls, which are Muslim Malaysian Indian food stalls where *rojak mamak* is a popular dish. It contains fried dough fritters, tofu, boiled potatoes, prawn fritters, hard boiled eggs, bean sprouts, cuttlefish and cucumber mixed with a sweet thick, spicy peanut sauce.[

Now, the accompaniment to the rojak, is the "Cendol./ˈtʃɛndɒl/is an iced sweet dessert that contains noodles of green rice flour jelly, coconut milk and palm sugar syrup. It is commonly found in Southeast Asia and is popular in Indonesia, Malaysia, Brunei, Cambodia, East Timor, Laos, Vietnam, Thailand, Singapore, and Myanmar. Next to the green jelly, additional toppings might be added, including diced jackfruit, sweetened red azuki beans, or durian.

Earliest written records of the word *cendol* or *tjendol* (Dutch spelling) can be traced to dictionaries and books of the 19th century in the Dutch East Indies (now Indonesia). One of the oldest known records of the word *tjendol* is listed in the 1866 *Oost-Indisch kookboek* or East Indies recipe book. This book includes a cendol recipe with the title *Tjendol of Dawet* which indicates that cendol and dawet were already used synonymously at that time. In the dictionary *Supplement op het*

Maleisch-Nederduitsch Woordenboek (1869) by Jan Pijnappel (Gz.), tjendol is described as a kind of drink or watery paste made from sago, coconut milk, sugar and salt."

They may also have persian roots. "A *falooda* is a Mughlai cuisine version of a cold dessert made with noodles. It has origins in the Persian dish *faloodeh*, variants of which are found across West, Central, and South Asia. Traditionally it is made by mixing rose syrup, vermicelli, and sweet basil seeds with milk, often served with ice cream. The vermicelli used for preparing falooda is made from wheat, arrowroot, cornstarch, or sago." A further variation of the chendol/falooda, is the ABC, abbreviation of *Air Batu Champur*, or your shaved ice desert, which has grass jelly, sweet beans, groundnut, sweetcorn etc, instead of coconut milk.

The Chinese item is the popiah, a kind of springroll/eggroll. "**Popiah** (Pėh-ōe-jī: *póh-piáⁿ*) is a Fujianese/Teochew-style fresh spring roll filled with an assortment of fresh, dried, and cooked ingredients, eaten during the Qingming Festival and other celebratory occasions.

It is eaten in accompaniment with a sweet sauce (often a bean sauce), a blended soy sauce or hoisin sauce or a shrimp paste sauce (hae-ko, Pėh-ōe-jī: *hê-ko*), and optionally with hot chilli sauce before it is filled. The filling is mainly finely grated and steamed or stir-fried turnip, jicama (known locally as *bangkuang*), which has been cooked with a combination of other ingredients such as bean sprouts, French beans, and lettuce leaves, depending on the individual vendor, along with grated carrots, slices of Chinese sausage, thinly sliced fried tofu, chopped peanuts or peanut powder, fried shallots, and shredded omelette."

A couple of rolls with tea, is the way to go.

The Malay teatime treat is commonly, the pisang goreng – banana fritters. Or fried banana slices. The pisang goreng stall is an all inclusive term for for items like curry puffs, fritters, and varieties of kueh like pulut inti, pulut panggang, wajid etc.

Hence, the pushcart, which preceded food stalls and restaurants.

Green leafies: Ponnanganni, Pak Choy, Pucuk Paku

I suppose our hunter-gatherer ancestors were quite used to munching leaves while they waited to snag a meat or hook a fish. Even today, its in our genes to eat the greens in the form of salads (already discussed under the section: Salads).

Ponnaanganni (litt: "golden virgin") or, "dwarf copperleaf" in English, is a spinach-like leafy that grows wild in the countryside. As its name suggests, regular eating will give glowing skin, according to the ancient Siddha medical texts. Another green that grows at the edges of burn pits, is the *kuppai keerai* ("rubbish green"). But not at all rubbish in taste. Perhaps it likes the ash. Stir fried with scraped coconut, it is a specialty item in Tamil cuisine. Standing up to 3 feet bushes, are two leafies that have completely different tastes. The *thavasi murungai* is a sweet, 2 inch long leafy and stirfried with scraped coconut. The *pulicha keerai* ("sour green") is cooked with garlic and onions, and mashed for a pickle-like dip.

Those are ground covering greens. The type that grow as trees are the *murungai keerai* (moringa) and the *ahaththi keerai* (august tree leaves). The former (2 cm coin leaflets) and the latter (3 cm) leaflets on a bunch, are stirfried the same way with scraped coconut, but taste very different. Both can be made into *thanni saar* or, watery saambaar. All these Tamil greens carry the surname "keerai" which simply means "leafy veggy", similar to the Chinese, "choy" and the Malay, "sayur".

Pak choy or *bak choy* is a type of fleshy stemmed green that is steamed and drizzled with oyster sauce and sesame seeds. An excellent, crunchy companon to plain rice. It is also pickled. *Choy sam* (Cantonese: "heart of the vegetable"), is also known as Chinese flowering cabbage. Similar to *kai lan*, it also has great crunch. *Gai choy* (mustard green), or *Sawi* in Malay, is a very common vegetable and the most familiar to the non-chinese population. It can be used in stir fries (rice and noodle), on its own, in soups etc. Watercress is a fast growing water friendly green used in soups.

Chinese cabbage (da bai cai) or Napa cabbage has multiple uses in soups, stir fries, pickles and kimchi. Other "white" veggies include bean sprouts, which is said to contain all the benefits of the full grown bush itself.

A fully Malay green is *pucuk paku* (fern shoot), used raw in *kerabu* (salad). It is also stewed in coconut milk and turmeric for a cool sauce for rice. The fern grows wild in the shade of the forest and oil palm trees. Tapioca and sweet potato leaves, are also cooked in coconut milk, like the ferns.

Bunga kantan (bud of the torch lily) is another ingredient along with *ulam raja* (wild cosmos), *petai* (stink bean), *pegaga* (pennywort) in the traditional Malay salad. It is not chopped and tossed, but each of it is taken individually, folded, dipped in *sambal belacan, chincalok* (fermented krill), or *tempoyak* (fermented durian) sauce. Since most of the ingredients can only be got from the forest, this is as "wild" as you can get with salad. Wanna get back to the wild side of things?

Okay, okay. Confusion understood. *Kerabu* apparently, is julienned vegetables tossed as salad. Tossed in kerisik (dried coconut scraping), Lime juice, sugar and chilli flakes etc. Mango kerabu is the favourite. *Ulam* is herbs eaten independently with dip. *Rojak mamak* is julienned senkuang (jicama), cucumber, chopped fried tofu, prawn croquets, and boiled egg, slathered with sweet/savoury peanut sauce. Often accompanied by a bowl of *cendol* dessert for thirst quencher. *Fruit rojak* is many kinds of local cut fruit drizzled with a thick, spicy, belacan infused dark soy-like sauce.

Speaking of leaves, a not very edible but flavour enhancing leaf is the Malay kaffir lime leaf. The Tamil *kariveppilai* (curry leaf) is usually set aside, unless blended as thuvaiyal (chutney). And the Chinese generally use bayleaf in their slow cooked dishes.

Root of the Matter: lián ŏu, Lengkuas, Manjal

Not only man, even animals such as wild boars, have discovered more than met the eye. Below the green shoot were a treasure trove of roots. And tubers. And bulbs, pods, and rhizomes. The potato, sweet potato, yam, yucca are well known, world over.

As for local ethnospecific roots, the *lián ŏu* (lotus root) is a typical Chinese mainstay. They use it in soups, stews, and stir fries and prefer it for their crunch factor. Funny! The root grows with 3 to 5 tubers attached, very much like a string of sausages. A root has either 7 or 9 inner tubes which, when sliced cross-sectionally, displays that many holes, resembling a spoked wagon wheel. Believe it, there is even a small hole in the center, like a hub! I wonder, considering the Chinese propensity for seeing health benefits envisaged by the shapes of food, what this means?

The *lengkuas* (galangal), is a rhizome (continuously growing horizontal root) that adds flavour to many South-East Asian foods. A family member of ginger, lengkuas is peppery, spicy and more citrusy. It is the zing in the Malay dishes, assam laksa, rendang, satay dip, meat sauces etc. Tom Yam and its cousins, khao tom, tom kha gai etc.etc, and most Thai dishes add this root. Nyonya cooking, deriving from Malay-Chinese fusion also subscribes to it.

Lengkuas has quite a list of health benefits as does, the *serai* (lemongrass), another South East Asia specific herb. Although not a root (it is a grass), serai's thick base is just above ground. It is a constant companion of lengkuas, on their culinary journies. Its popularity abroad is attributable to Thai cuisine's worldwide reach. It has gained a good report card as a cancer fighting agent. In fact a Jewish farmer in Israel is reportedly cultivating it in a desert on a commercial scale.

Manjal (turmeric) is another one of the rhizomes of the ginger family. Its greatest use is in Indian cooking, where it is also an ingredient in siddha medicine of Tamil Nadu. As noted in the earlier section on spice of choice, it has a variety of uses from spice, dye, medicine, cosmetic and antiseptics. Reasearch has uncovered its anti-carcinogenic properties.

Besides the above Asian roots, Malaysians also freely use transplanted tubers such as *ubi kayu* (tapioca, cassava, yucca, manioc) from Brazil. Yam (Taro) from West Africa. Potato (continent America). Sweet potato (central America). Many creative concoctions of these have come forth, aside from the plain fire roast, or boil.

Fruit Basket: Durian, Longan, Mango

Malaysian tropical fruits have enriched the English lexicon with Malay words. Durian ("thorny one"), Rambutan ("hairy one"), Mangosteen (Manggis), Pulasan ("twisted one").

If there are wine tastings in wineries, there are free fruit tastings in Malaysia, which you do during durian season. The seller splits and exposes a choice morsel and you pinch a piece to sample it. Like, and you purchase it. You are also allowed, almost expected, to sample mangosteens, rambutans and dukus before buying your kilo or so.

Fruits can be fabulous factors in food preparation, none being bland. Durian especially, can hold its own due to its flavor and. When in season, it commands the allegiance of the crowds, being the "King of Fruits". They don't call it King of Fruits for nothing. Along with the egg, the durian is natures's perfect packed food – in-flight microwaved "lunchboxes" be dammned. For starters, the entire package is hermetically sealed and secured by a body armour of thorns and underwritten by heavenly stink! It has three or four discrete chambers, each harbouring three lushious globs of gold pulp. Mature sizes can range from rugby ball to basketball size.

The durian flavoured "potong" or stick ice-cream retains its smell (odour, stink, fragrance, aroma) despite being cold stored in deep freeze. The quientessential Malay dip, sour durian *tempoyak*, already starts you drooling. Who will deny the dreamy delight of durian infused dodol? Durian sweets already exist. With the fruit's natural creaminess, durian milkshakes are a possibility and will probably resemble a kicked up eggnog, the yuletide (Christmas) concoction. The pineapple, mango, due to their tanginess, are also suitable in salsas, salads and other snappy savouries.

The longan (from Cantonese *lùhng-ngáahn* 龍眼, literally 'dragon eye'), is so named because it resembles an eyeball when its fruit is shelled (the black seed shows through the translucent flesh like a pupil/iris). The seed is small, round and hard, and of an enamel-like, lacquered black. The fully ripened, freshly harvested fruit has a bark-like shell, thin, and firm, making the fruit easy to peel by squeezing the pulp out. Speaking of eye, longan's smaller cousin is the *mata kucing* (Malay: "cat's eye"). A more famous, more succulent, zestier fruit in the same soapberry family is *lychee*. Our own *rambutan* is also a relative.

Longan and lychee come preserved in cans or dried. Dried longan is used in desserts like *lin chi kang.*

In Tamil tradition and culture, the mango, jackfruit, and banana constitute the *mukkani* ("fruit trio"). It is an auspicious combo. A mixed juice (*saaru*) of these fruits is served to a newlywed couple on their first night. It can be a VIP welcome drink. Used to be a royalty refreshment. All three are in season during summertime. Interestingly, both the mango and jackfruit are etymologically Tamil, and entered English thanks to the Portuguese. Banana is West African namewise but originating in S.E.Asia. Mango is *maan kai* (deer fruit) and jackfruit is *sakkai* ("fibrous") *pazham* (fruit).

When talking fruit, we are referring to the ripened, sweet ones. Any number of these fruits (such as mango, jackfruit, and banana) in a raw state, are cooked as savoury side dishes in so many ways.

Slow Cooked Sure Things: Bak Kut Teh, Beef Rendang, Mutton Soup

Nutritionists will frown at overcooked food, but you cannot argue with the fact that such food tastes better. Soups, stews and curries get their full potential when the slow cooking coaxes the essences out of the ingredients. Fish curry is even better the day after! And haven't we heard the old saw about aged wine?

In Chinese meals, soups are a given. Bones and melon vegetables simmering for hours are the perfect pairing for the economy rice dish. Unlike in Western culinaire, where the soup is appetizer, the Chinese soup is an accompaniment.

Mainly thin and clear, Chinese soups have been treated under the soup section. But lets focus on a soupy meaty meal that is the *bak kut teh* ("pork bone tea"). As it steeps ceaselessly in the cauldron, the soup and meat are an aromatic accompaniment to plain rice. The five spice powder and smoked garlic are the magic potion to effect it. Another overcooked Chinese concoction is the *congee* (rice porridge). The rice is boiled with bits of meat until it breaks down into a gastronomically goody, gooey mush.

Fishball soup is sipped as is, or as a base for noodles. And then, there is the higher class of soup served mainly at grand occasions – the shark's fin soup and the bird's nest soup. The fin is real, but the nest actually the dried saliva of the swiftlet. The little birdie builds its nest in the ceiling of dark caves, using its gummy drool. The astute little swiftlet's brittle spittle forms a veritable crucible-like snuggle space, in the absence of any other building material. Why fins and nests? Why not, if one can have foie gras, caviar, and escargot? Isn't it a matter of taste? And deep pockets!

While Chinese restaurants are adept at made to order, fresh cooked meals in minutes, there are also such things as slow cooked spare ribs and BBQ pork.

Malay soups also have similar main ingredients as the Chinese. Sup tulang, gear box soup (knee bone soup), oxtail soup, are some of them. These are decidedly northern Malaya fare and very savoury and salutary. The rendang is the quintessential Malay meat dish. The melt in the mouth meat is due to its simmering action. Stirred steadily in coconut milk, serai, and rhizomes like ginger and galangal, the finale is finesse.

As observed elsewhere here, the Thai Tom Yam, from across our northern border, is Malaysia's most identifiable "native" soup, full of tang, zing, zest, fizz, buzz, craze, doozy. It wins on smell, savour, salubriousness and satisfaction.

Mutton soup or chicken soup? It is not a major part of the everyday Indian diet, except for the vegetarian *rasam*, a thin pepper soup. On the days they are made, it is comfort food. The Mamak restaurateur has perfected the Indian meat soup, a super savoury (spicy, salty, peppery, piquant) meal in itself. Good for a cold rainy day, or a stuffy nose cold. The British, who adapted this recipe from the *milagu rasam* (pepper juice) on their colonial outing in India, call it Mulligatawny. The Irish sounding (Mulligan's tonic?) stew is the Mamak soup doppelganger. Mulligatawny is from the Tamil *milagutannir*. *Milagu* (pepper) + *tannir* (water) = pepper water.

Of course, Indian meats and lentils are generally slow cooked, or pressure cooked, for the best effect.

Festive Features: Lemang, Yee Sang, Athirasam

There are certain food items that, like termites after a monsoon shower, or mushrooms after a lightning strike, appear only seasonally. They are identified with a particular festival. Think of an ethnic holiday, and which food comes to mind? Think Hari Raya, and *satay – ketupat* jumps into view, sure. Nasi kunyit, nasi tomato and nasi minyak will be spread out on the mat too, as well as the usual suspects such as kuihs and cookies. However, they are year round food, available in Malay warongs and residences. The *lemang – rendang* combo is the most likely candidate for the honour. Although the *rendang* is a year round menu item, the *lemang* comes with

Ramadan, the month of the fast, and lingers till Shawwal, the month of the festivity. After that, it practically disappears from consciousness.

Gelatinous rice and coconut milk are cooked in bamboo internodes, for a texture that matches well with the beef rendang. The inside of the woody cylinder is lined with banana leaf so that, when split after cooking, the cooked rice appears as a neat package. Although cooking meat in the cylindrical tubes is common among the native tribes and aborigines of South-East-Asia, the lemang differs, with its carb content.

The signature food of Chinese New Year, it seems, is the *Yee Sang*. On CNY eve, as the family gathers at the reunion table, everyone tosses the julienned raw vegetables, raw fish, preserved fruits, sweet sauce etc, while shouting, "yeeeeee sangg!" It's a kind of cowboy whoop. "yeeeeee haaaa!" That's a real community, right there.

Aside from that, *Nian gao* (kuih bakul) is a sticky rice cake usually served during the Chinese New Year. As its name is homonymous to "Prosperous New Year", Nian Gao and is a signature dish just as the mooncake (mid autumn festival), *chongyang* (chongyang festival), *tangyuan* (lantern festival). Its literal meaning is *'nian'* (sticky) and *'gao'* (cake). The only ingredients are – glutinous rice flour, sugar and water. It is almost a *dodol*, the Malay Ramadan delicacy but unlike the stirred dodol, the gao is steamed.

The iconic indian eat during during Deepavali is hard to pin-point. *Idli, thosai, puttu, idiappam, biryani* etc ? They are perennial. *Murukku* is something people generally associate with the Deepavali season. However, it is widely marketed in supermarkets and by the kacang putih man (vendor of snacks). The *Acchu Murukku*, which is also a regular at Deepavali is now made and sold by Malays under the name of *Bunga Rose*. Even the essential Deepavali sweet, *athirasam* is made and sold year round by Malays as *Telinga Keling* (Indian Ears?). Well, at least the name is an accreditation to its Indian origins. If Indians have allowed the loss of their cultural markers, you don't blame others for appropriating them. Roti chanai (Roti paratha, actually) is marketed the world over by Malaysian Chinese exporters as the Kawan brand. A clear example of Indians losing their cultural markers is the *Ketti Urundai* (Litt: "Hard Ball"). Where has it gone? Swallowed whole by modernization. Remember that rock hard, golf ball sized thing that today's Indian grandmothers used to watch their mothers make when they were young? Children used to play with it by throwing at each other and at the wall, to disintegrate it. It was the last of the Deepavali sweetmeats to be finished after the festival, may be six months later when there was nothing else in the cookie jar. By then, it had become a desired delicacy. Well, if they still make it at all, the *Ketti Urundai* would be the quintessential festive food at Deepavali. As far as I can remember it was made only during Deepavali, and Christmas.

The ingredients are: Green Gram flour. Parboiled Rice flour. *Pottu kadalai* (split chickpeas). Coconut flesh – cut into small bits. Cardamom powder. Dry Ginger Powder. Jaggery (palm sugar).The flours are roasted and mixed with the spice powders and other bits. A molten jaggery lava is poured on it and mixed thoroughly. Balls are formed while the dough is still warm/ hot. And you are in for a jaw breaking time.

Christmas cuisine in Malaysia used to be centered around the turkey. It was baked, cooked as curry, or any way you would, depending on whether you were Eurasian, Indian, or Chinese. These days, you would be hard pressed to find a unique eat on the 25th of December, except perhaps the "Christmas" or fruit cake. The fruit cake is a British essential at Christmas time, and hence Malaysians have adopted it. In America, it has become a joke. There, when you present it to some family at Yuletide, they use it as a doorstop. Another joke is that, when it is so presented, expect the cake to come back to you the next year or the year after. What goes around comes around. It is all a joke of course. Not all fruit cakes made by American housewives are that hard or unappetizing. Reminds you of the Deepavali *Ketti Urundai*, doesn't it? It is probably the Americans' rebellious attitude to all things British. Like they have their own word for a British word. Like they prefer coffee to the British taste for tea, they look down on the fruit cake.

Seasonal Servings: Moon Cake, Bubur Lambak, Ponggal

As festivals, by definition are seasonal, so too are certains foods associated with them. Fruitcake evokes Christmas, as does eggnog in America at yuletide. These foods, joy-giving and enjoyable as they are, only make their appearance once a year. But why? Perhaps, a case of absence making the heart grow fonder? So, the annual arrival is greeted like a long lost relative on the special day?

How nice it is to have a Chinese friend, especially in the eighth lunar moon! The 15th, known as Mid-Autumn is celebrated as the Mooncake Festival. You'll likely get a gift of the delectable, desirable, once in a year, pastry. The specialist bakers pack them in nice little gift boxes and going by the price of some of those, the baker could possibly take a vacation for the rest of the year. Perhaps the moon in the cake refers to the golden egg yolk embedded in the black bean paste. It does resemble a full moon in a pitch dark night sky.

Mooncakes are constructed of a thin, soft pastry surrounding a sweet, pate-like filling, and of course, the yolk. Mooncakes generally have a 3-D embossing of Chinese characters for "longevity" or "harmony", as well as the name of the bakery and the filling inside.

The festival is connected to the lore of Chang E, the mythical Moon Goddess. According to tradition, the Chinese Emperor was to offer sacrifices to the sun in the spring and the moon in the autumn. Another folk story relates the revolt of Han Chinese revolutionists against the Mongol (Yuan dynasty) rulers. Someone by the name of Zhu Yuanzhang had spread a rumour of a deathly disease that could be only be eleviated eating mooncakes that contained contained messages hidden within. The coded cake communique was a complete *coup de maître* (stroke of genius) and the Mongols were driven back over the Wall. Great. Just like today, the Han (not Hun) distribute the cakes in packages of four. They were to quarter all the cakes, which had characters baked in on top. The resulting sixteen pieces were moved around like mahjong tiles to reveal a message. Some suggest that the American fortune cookie may be take-off of the moon cookie.

The Malaysian version of the seasonal savoury, is the lemang. Like the mooncake, which is usually consumed over a few days, the lemang is eaten during the the month long Ramadhan fast. Therefore its consumption occurs at iftar, the breaking of the fast.

Glutinous rice, coconut milk and salt are cooked in bamboo tubes lined with banana leaves so that the rice wouldn't stick to the sides. The cooking method is similar to roasting over a spit, i.e indirect heat. A bed of red hot embers is built, and the bamboo tubes are lined up upright at about a 60⁰ angle against the heat source. Like spit roasting, the tubes are regularly rotated for even cooking. Again, like slow roasting, the process takes about 4-5 hours.

Lemang cooking is common in the Nusantara region – Brunei, Indonesia, Malaysia and Singapore. The Iban prepare this for *Gawai* or harvest festival, as do the *Orang Asli* of Peninsula Malaysia. In the Phillipines, meat and gravies are cooked this way. The Dayak call meat cooked this way, *pansoh*.

What is lemang without the *rendang*. They are made for each other. The beef rendang is a dry dish that is cooked in ground coconut and a paste of ginger, galangal, lemongrass, as well as turmeric, garlic, shallots, chillis etc. Because of the antimicrobial qualities of the ingredients, it can keep for a quite a while, too.

Ponggal is sweet dish that appears only during *Thai Ponggal*, the harvest festival of the Tamils. It is celebrated on the first of the month of *Thai*, corresponding to the 15th of January, as a vote of thanks to the Sun, which enabled the crops. This is when the harvest is over, and the farmers heave a sigh of relief and chill out. The festival is celebrated over four days, as follows: *Bhogi* (burning old stuff), *Veetu Ponggal* (household celebration), *Maatu Ponggal* (cattle appreciation), and *Kaanum Ponggal* (sightseeing).

Ponggal is cooked on the second day, where the neighbours get together to cook the first fruits of the rice harvest in fresh cows' milk, fresh pressed sugarcane juice, lentils, cashew and raisins. There is a contest to see whose pot froths and boils over first. Ponggal, afterall, means "boiling over". A metaphor for the boiling over of joy, happiness, hope, prosperity. As the rice gruel boils over everybody exclaims "ponggalo-o-o ponggal!", meaning, "Boy oh boy, what a boil!" There is mutual sharing of their steaming sweet ponggal and goodwill distributed all round.

Ponggal is quite a pudding or thick congee.

The Wedding Banquet: Kenduri, Virunthu, Yàn Huì

Considering that the last but not least of dining experiences is the best, this is last in the chapter on food – like a delectable desirable dessert. The wedding feast is the height of any food affair, even above five – star fine dining, for most people. You count down the days with drooling, after receiving your invite. This is because, only the best of a culture's cuisine is on display, after allowing for budgetary deliberations. You would rather splurge on the menu and skimp on the secondaries. It is the climax of the event. The one that stays in your memory the longest.

Weddings ceremonies get their own page under the LIFE AND DEATH section. Here, we'll have a look at the menus and other activities of reception (entertainment, music etc)

A menu from a Malay wedding planner goes as follows. You make a choice from each section. (*Main Course*) Mee Goreng/or, Nasi Briyani, (*Vegetable*) assorted veggies *with mushroom, (Chicken) Ayam Masak Merah,(Fish) Assam Fish, (Dessert) Nonya Kueh, (*Beverage) Fruit Punch. The guests serve themselves from the "spread" on the table. Cutlery consists of your right hand. Every table is provided with an aluminum tea-pot and basin (*ketor*), or a basin of water with rose petal for handwashing.

While the kompang (hand held single face drum) accompanies the bridal procession during the wedding ceremony, it can also be a part of the entertainment at the reception. Singing of nasyid (religious) or pop songs may be part of it too.

Indian receptions are usually held in rented halls or ballrooms. The program includes full orchestras belting loud movie music and dance performances facilitated by an amateur MC/DJ who fancies himself to be be the world's greatest stand-up comedian. A social dance at the end of it, mostly with family and friends, after most of the guests have left. There may be a combination of on stage cake-cutting, bottle popping, candle lighting ceremony somewhere in the program. Live bands with local singers and dancers are a given.

Somehow, Indian wedding planners are still sticking to decades old schtick. One (in) famous one is the grand march – in, to the accompaniment of martial music, of waiters bearing platters of rice, led by two of them carrying flaming swords. The spread is quite comprehensive. This menu is an actual sample from Rubben Caterers, a very long time provider. It goes top down: Ghee Rice, Mutton Ribs Dalcha, Chicken Varuval (dry stir fry), Mutton Peratal (wet stir fry), Sweet Sour Prawn, Mixed vegetables with Taufu, Preserved fruit achar, Ice cream (cup) and Root Beer cordial.

The service can be either at the table (Serving Domes) or buffet line. The eversilver domes are actually lazy susans (turntable, dumbwaiter, rotary tray) that have the main entrées resting inside like seeds in a lotus pod.

Chinese dinners are elaborate, without saying. 10 to 12 course dinners are the norm. In the course of the dining, there will be interludes of music, speeches by representatives of the in-laws, toasts, roasts, boasts, cake-cuttng etc. By far the most elaborate, austentatious, and personal of dinner services, Chinese wedding dinners are served personally by a waiter for every table of 10 to 12 guests. The entire thing is orchestrated with military precision, as the food arrives at every table at the same time. With such sumptuousness, formal entertainment seems almost unnecessary. Fine food and free flow of libations certainly fuel frisky frolicky fraternizing. Besides, the method to the seating madness is, to place people in family or familiar groups. Thereby eliminating stranger discomfort and awkward moments.

As per the Chinese predilection for perceiving meaning in menu items, the meals have merry messages for the couple. The below list, which can be taken as a complete menu, gives a rundown of the matrimonial meaning of the dishes. All are auspicious, propitious, delicious, gracious, melodious, judicious yada yada yada and not outrageous, audacious, or presumptuous.

1. Abalone (Mandarin meaning similar to *"abundance"*) and Sea Cucumber – (Homophonic to Cantonese *"good heart"*).
2. Roast suckling pig – symbolizing virginity and bride's purity. Rose(d) red colour also shouts good luck.
3. Fish sounds like *"abundance"*. The whole fish, with head and tail attached represents the couple's marital success from *"I do"* to *"till death do us part"*.
4. Roast (Peking} Duck – Fidelity
5. Scallops – fertility, homophonic of *"raising children"*
6. Chicken – representing the mythological phoenix.
7. Noodles – served at the same time as fried rice, it represents longevity of the marriage.
8. Dessert – sweetness of the marriage, especially the hot red bean soup, with lotus seeds representing fertility.

Exercise: Yoga, Sema, Chiqong

Malaysians have a good repertoire of mind-body meditative exercises. Yoga, Chigong are the main forms, thanks to Indian and Chinese cultures. The Bumiputra society does not seem to posess a specific exercise with a physical – mental nexus. The *Ruku* during prayertime can pass as exercise. While focussing their minds on the creator, they also do physical flexes and folds of their arms and legs in the Ruku – note section on religion ("the shape of religion"). So, we will go further afield to a form of Islamic discipline called Sufism for that, especially the trance-like swirling (*Sema*) that they do. The swirls demand balance, concentration, and more as the passive observer feels giddy just watching.

There are certain elements of meditative exercise preceding malay dances such as the Javanese Kuda Kepang.

All three place emphasis on breathing and slow movements, which equals meditation and mindfulness.

Yoga *asanas* ("seat" or postures), involve contorting and twisting the body "out of shape", that is supposed to get you physically pliable and in shape. Some of the asanas remind you of those young Chinese acrobats, who are always touring some part of the world at any one time. Chigong movements are like a slow motion of someone fighting off a swarm of mosquitos. While silat itself, is remiscent of the above exercises, the warm-ups are akin to yoga and qigong. All these exerscises can be considered as under the category of stretching and breathing. The others being aerobic and weight exercises.

The practice of yoga is thought to date back to pre-vedic Indian traditions; possibly in the Indus valley civilization around 3000 BCE – as a seal depicting a yogi-like figure is one of the the Harappan finds. Yoga is mentioned in the Rigveda, and also referenced in the Upanishads, though it most likely developed as a systematic study around the 5th and

6th centuries BCE, in ancient India's ascetic and Śramaṇa movements. The Yoga Sutras of Patanjali date from the 2nd century BCE, and gained prominence in the west in the 20th century after being first introduced by Swami Vivekananda.

The Sanskrit noun योग yoga is derived from the sanskrit root *yuj* (युज्) "to attach, join, harness, yoke". It is cognate with the English, "yoke". There is a Tamil word *"Oham"* that equates with yoga, found in the classical era writings of the Siddhars (early Tamil savants). Now, if one were to consider that the inhabitants of The Indus Valley civilization were indeed Dravidians, as most scientists believe, and who also believe that yoga was present in that civilization, then might it not be reasonable to expect that yoga existed in Dravidian literature much before the Sanskrit? A simple syllogistic logic.

Yoga consists of *asana* or posture, *pranayama* or breathing, *Pratyahara* ("Abstraction"), *Dharana* ("Concentration"), *Dhyana* ("Meditation"), *Samadhi* ("Liberation").

"In the early 11th century, the Persian scholar Al Biruni visited India and translated Patanjali's Yogasutra. Al Biruni's translation preserved many of the core themes of Patañjali 's Yoga philosophy, but certain sutras and analytical commentaries were restated making it more consistent with Islamic monotheistic theology. Al Biruni's version of Yoga Sutras reached Persia and the Arabian peninsula by about 1050 AD. Yoga was, however, not accepted by mainstream Sunni and Shia Islam. Minority Islamic sects such as the mystic Sufi movement, particularly in South Asia, adopted Indian yoga practises, including postures and breath control. Muhammad Ghawth, a Shattari Sufi and one of the translators of yoga text in the 16th century, drew controversy for his interest in yoga and was persecuted for his Sufi beliefs."

Malaysia's National Fatwa Council in 2008 passed a decree, prohibiting Muslims from practicing yoga, saying it had elements of Hinduism and that its practice was blasphemy, therefore haraam. Some Muslims in Malaysia who had been practicing yoga for years, criticized the decision as "insulting." Sisters in Islam, a women's rights group in Malaysia, also demurred, saying yoga was just a form of exercise. This fatwa is legally enforceable. However, Malaysia's prime minister clarified that yoga as physical exercise is permissible, but the chanting of religious mantras is prohibited.

Sema or whirling dervishes are a part of the practices of the Mevlavi Sufi order of Turkey. The physical-spiritual act of whirling is supposed to facilitate closeness to God. If Sufism is an attempt to get up close to God through austerity, why wouldn't it be pro – Islam? If that is against islam, wonder what is fasting during Ramadan or the Shiite practice of *Ashura* (self-flagellation)? Perhaps, with the growing incidence of materialism and corruption everywhere, the Sema might just be the medicine this world needs.

Qigong is another mind-matter discipline that has received international acceptance.

"The origin of qigong is commonly attributed to the legendary *Yellow Emperor* and the classic *Book of Internal Medicine*. Archaeological evidence such as the *Mawangdui Silk Texts* (168 BC) shows a series of *Tao Yin* (導引) exercises that bears physical resemblance to some of the health exercises being practiced today." The Taoist writings of *Laozi* (~ 400 BC) and *Zhuangzi* (~300 BC) both describe meditative and physical exercises to extend one's lifespan and as means of accessing higher realms."

Buddha himself is seen "enlightened" in the padmasana, or lotus posture. "On reaching China, Buddhist practices mixed in with the Chinese forms, birthing the Chinese Buddhist qigong tradition. Chinese Buddhist practice apexes with *Chán* (禪) Buddhism in the 7th century AD. Meditative practice was emphasized and a series of qigong exercises known as the *Yijin Jing* ("Muscle/Tendon Change Classic") was attributed to Bodhidharma, the Tamil prince turned missionary to China. The Chinese martial arts community eventually identify this Yijing Jing as one of the secret training methods in *Shaolin martial arts*."

Tai chi chuan is often described as being Taoist in origin, while *Shaolin* martial arts is named after the famous Buddhist Shaolin temple. Qigong is not just a set of breathing exercises as it encompasses a large variety of both physical and mental training methods designed to help the body and the mind based on Chinese philosophy.

Court Games: Sepak Raga, Sadu Gudu, Wushu

Sepak takraw, or kick volleyball, is the indigenous pastime of Southeast Asia, being the national sport of many SEA countries. While its exact origin is uncertain, sepak takraw is thought to have been introduced by the Chinese by way of the traditional games, *cuju*, an ancient chinese military exercise, where soldiers would try to keep a feathered shuttlecock airborne by kicking it back and forth between two people. As the sport developed, the animal hide and chicken feathers were eventually replaced by balls made of woven strips of rattan.

Sepak takraw differs from the similar sport of footvolley in its use of a rattan ball and only allowing players to use their feet, knee, and head to touch the ball. In Brunei, Indonesia, Malaysia, and Singapore it is commonly called sepak takraw. It can be known as sepak raga as well in Indonesia and Malaysia. In the Philippines, the sport is also called "sepak takraw", resembling the related native sport known as sipà. Sepak, or "to kick", is Malay, while Takraw is Thai for "rattan ball".

The earliest historical records in Malaysia occur in the *Sejarah Melayu* ("Malay Annals") as played in the 15th century Malacca Sultanate. It details the incident of Raja Muhammad, a son of Sultan Mansur Shah who was accidentally hit with a rattan ball by Tun Besar, a son of Tun Perak (the Prime Minister), in a Sepak raga game. The ball hit Raja Muhammad's headgear and knocked it down to the ground. In anger, Raja Muhammad immediately stabbed and killed Tun Besar, whereupon some of Tun Besar's kinsmen retaliated and wanted to kill Raja Muhammad. However, Tun Perak managed to restrain them from such an act of treason by saying that he would no longer accept Raja Muhammad as the Sultan's heir. As a result of this incident, Sultan Mansur Shah ordered his son out of Malacca and had him installed as the ruler of outlying Pahang.

International play is now governed by ISTAF, the International Sepak Takraw Federation. Major competitions for the sport such as the ISTAF SuperSeries, the ISTAF World Cup and the King's Cup World Championships are held every year.Sepak takraw is now a regular sport event in the Asian Games and the Southeast Asian Games, in which Thailand has won the most medals.

Sepak takraw sport is played on a court similar to a badminton doubles court. Area of 13.4 by 6.1 metres (44 ft × 20 ft) free from all obstacles. Sand and grass court not advisable. The width of the lines bounding the court should not be more than 4 centimetres (1.6 in) measured and drawn inwards from the edge of the court measurements. All the boundary lines should be drawn at least 3.0 metres (9.8 ft) away from all obstacles. The centre line of 2 cm (0.79 in) should be drawn equally dividing the right and left court. The net is similar to badminton's.

A match is played by two teams called 'regu', each consisting of three players. On some occasions, it can be played by only two players (doubles) or four players (quadrant) per team.

One of the players shall be at the back; he/she is called a "Tekong" or also known as the "Server". The other two players shall be at the net, one on the left and the other on the right. The player on the right is called a "feeder/setter/tosser" and the player on the left is called a "attacker/ striker/killer". The feeder tosses the ball in a low arc to the tekong's foot, who lifts the ball towards the net, whereupon the killer executes a kind of bicycle kick (aka scissor kick, overhead kick). It is supposed to stun the opposition with its force and sneaky stealth. The opposition is on to your schemes and its killer waits at the net with his own back flip. And so the back and forth goes on till the ball hits the court, or goes off it, like in volleyball. A far cry from solo footbag.

Sadu Gudu, as we played in childhood, is now officially Kabaddi. There is even a thought that kabaddi itself may have a Tamil origin, namely *kai pidi* or Kai (hand) + pidi (hold). It is a contact team sport, a mix of tag and wrestling. Played between two teams of seven players on opposite courts, the objective of the game is for a single player on offence, referred to as a "raider", to run into the opposing team's half of a court, tag out as many of their defenders as possible, and return "home" to his own half of the court, all without being tackled by the defenders. Like a deep sea diver seeking pearls, the raider has to finish his mission in a single breath. Lose your breath, lose your play and sit it out. To satisfy the referee that you are on the single breath, you are required to chant "kabaddi, kabaddi", "sadu gudu, sadu gudu", or some other phrase. It is obviously difficult to steal a second breath. Reminds me of a caregiver administering pills to a delinquent resident. She makes conversation during the process. You just can't hide the pill under your tongue while having to talk, hee heeee!

The team being "raided" hold hands to form a chain to encircle and ambush the intruder. You attack the fringes and if tackled, struggle home even if you barely touch your boundary. Points are scored for each player tagged by the raider, while the opposing team earns a point for capturing the raider. Players are taken out of the game if they are tagged or tackled, but are brought back in for each point scored by their team from a tag or tackle.

If Sepak Takraw has South East Asian nativity, Kabaddi has a South Asian habitat. It is played in India, Pakistan, Sri Lanka, Bangladesh, Nepal and Maldives.

In the international team version of kabaddi, two teams of seven members each occupy opposite halves of a court of 10 by 13 metres (33 ft × 43 ft) for men, and 8 by 12 metres (26 ft × 39 ft) for women. Each has five substitutes. The game is played with 20-minute halves with a 5-minute half break in which the teams exchange sides.

Wushu, or Chinese Kungfu, is a hard and soft and complete martial art, as well as a full-contact sport. It has a long history in Chinese martial arts. It was developed in 1949 in an effort to standardize the practice of traditional Chinese martial arts, yet attempts to structure the various decentralized martial arts traditions date back earlier, when the Central Guoshu Institute was established at Nanking in 1928.

"Wushu" is the Chinese term for "martial arts" (武 "Wu" = military or martial, 術 "Shu" = art). In contemporary times, Wushu has become an international sport under the International Wushu Federation (IWUF), which holds the World Wushu Championships every two years. Wushu has become an official event at the Asian Games, Southeast Asian Games, and the World Combat Games among other multi-sport events.

Competitive Wushu is composed of two disciplines: *taolu*, which is a kind of individual, exhibition style and *sanda* sparring and actually resembles Thai kickboxing. But it has other disciplines, like self defense, breaking hard objects with fist, and other related practices, that are not performed in competitions. Aside from barehand combat, including the long fist, Tai

Chi Chuan, weapons are also used like swords (broad and straight) as well as cudgels and spears.

Board Games: Mahjong, Thaayam, Congkak

Mahjong is a Qing era table game that has internationalized. Though not exactly a board game, it is a tile game similar to dominoes, which in turn, is traceable to the Song dynasty of China. It is commonly played by four players and is akin to rummy, the western card game, requiring strategy and serendipity.

"The game is played with a set of 144 tiles based on Chinese characters and symbols, and each player begins with 13 tiles. In turns, players draw and discard tiles until they complete a legal hand using the 14th drawn tile to form four melds (or sets) and a pair (eye). A player can also win with a small class of special hands. There are fairly standard rules about how a piece is drawn, how a piece is robbed from another player, the use of suits (numbered tiles) and Honors (winds and dragons), the kinds of melds allowed, how to deal the tiles and the order of play. Despite these similarities, there are many regional variations to the rules including rather different scoring systems, criteria for legal winning hands, and even private table rules which distinguish some variations as notably different styles of mahjong."

In Chinese, the game was originally called 麻雀 (pinyin: máquè)—meaning sparrow—which is still used in some languages in southern China. It is said that the clacking of tiles during shuffling resembles the chattering of sparrows. Suffice to say that that it can take whole book to explain the intricacies.

Chinese checkers is a board game that is not even Chinese! It belongs to Germany, where it is called *Sternhalma*. *Stern* ("star") refers to the star shaped board.

Thaayam or dhaayam, is a Tamil game that is comparable to the North Indian pachisi. It is a lesser known board game compared to its more famous India export, chess or sathurangam. The thaayakattam or board can be standard chessboard size, or drawn on the floor with chalk or charcoal. The thaayakattam is of 3 concentric squares (7x7, 5x5, and 3x3) for a total of 83 squares (Chess has 64). The central square is called *manai*, or home. Interspersed around the perimeter "bends", certain squares are marked with an X called *malai*, or "hill" which are safe zones where you cannot be kicked out by a pursuing opponent. The clear squares are the risk areas where collisions happen and chips get hurled over.

Thaayakattai, or a pair of elongated 4-sided metal dice. The sides have from zero to 3 indentations, making a maximum number of 6 advances per throw.

4 players can play at one time, and each will enter from the middle peripheral square on their side. The basic rule of this game of chance is to get a zero on the dice throw to get a chance to begin. Proceed to complete the outer perimeter before attempting to move in to the inner perimeters and on to home. Each player, with his own coloured set of 6 chips or *kaai* ("unripe fruit") must herd it all to the manai where it becomes *palam* ("ripe fruit"). The first to complete the process is the winner. One who loses all his kaai will have start over again. Naturally, there are further rules and complexities that enhance the thrill factor.

The board game of Chess, or Sathurangam, or Anaikuppu is also touted a having origins in Tamil land. *"The ancient 'Sathuranga Vallabhanathar' temple at Tiruvarur in southern Tamil Nadu is often cited as proof of the game's local provenance. The name of the presiding deity, Sathuranga Vallabhanathar, means one who is an expert chess player.*

According to legend, Lord Shiva was named so after he defeated the local king's daughter Rajarajeshwari, an incarnation of Goddess Parvathi, in a game of chess and won her hand in marriage. Temple records show that the game was being played in the region nearly 1,500 years ago". – The Hindu newspaper

"Congkak is a popular game of logic played throughout Asia, Africa and the Americas, with many adaptations. Known elsewhere as mancala, the version commonly played in the Malay Archipelago requires two players to share a wooden board with one row of seven holes along each side, and one bigger hole at either end. The two rows of seven holes are designated as "houses" in the "village" (kampong) while the last two larger holes serve as "storehouses", although there are variations. Seeds are placed in each hole, and then redistributed according to the rules of the game. The objective is to gain as many seeds in one's storehouse

as possible. A popular game in the past, the attractiveness of congkak began declining in the 1980s as Singapore became more urbanised." – extract

"The game is believed to have originated from the Middle East, where it was known as mancala (Arabic for "move") in Arabia. The earliest discovery of the board game was made in Jordan, dating between 7,000 BC and 5,000 BC. The game was probably brought by Arab or African traders travelling to China and beyond on their trade travels. The game is believed to have spread throughout Southeast Asia, similarly through merchants via the trading post of Malacca. The game became popular among the wider population, particularly among Malays and Peranakans or Straits-born Chinese. There are thus unique Malay terms for the rules of the game." – quote. The game is known as *pallaangkuzhi* or (pathinaalaam kuzhi – "fourteeth pit") in Tamil. It is a game from Chola times, whose merchants were here some milleniums ago.

Board games anyone? Sorry, even modern ones such as scrabble and monoploy seem headed for oblivion. That is, on a personal, individual to individual interact. Sure, there is a ton of new games coming up on the computer and phone screens. They don't count as they are often played solo. Old is gold, but it is also gone.

Ethnic Games: Kavanda Kavandi, pīng pāng qiú, Gasing

How many scores of childrens' games have become extinct due to modernization and shrinking public spaces! With children confined to rooms and friendless, electronic games are their sole entertainment. Pastimes like kite flying, marbles, hopscotch and 'police and thief' needed open space. And the equipment were simple, or none, without need for electrical plug-ins.

Kavanda-kavandi (kaunda kaundi) was a childrens' game till the sixties, of unkown etymology. It was played with a foot long stick with which to hit a shorter, 4 inch stick, like a cricket ball. Accompanied by a meaningless sing-song phrase, *"kavanda – kavandi kavandikku lavandi"*, its exact rules are lost. I remember that a little hole was scratched in the ground and the shorter piece placed across it. It was flipped as far as possible, with the longer stick. Like in cricket, the opposing team had to catch the airborne little stick and throw it back at the hole. Failing to catch meant that the other team would continue hit it further afield. When it finally manages to catch it, the opposing team would then have to return the stick to the starting point while singing the above tune, "kavanda kavandi kavandikkku lavandi." In the absence of any specific ethnic origin to the sport, the "Tamil-ness" of the phrase, as we played it, would probably make Indian.

Chinese folk games are not to be found in Malaysia, at least not in these modern times. Hence it would be fun to describe a game or two that the Chinese love and dominate in, but cannot claim as theirs. *Although the game (yǔ máo qiú) may have originally developed among expatriate officers in British India, where it was very popular by the 1870s, yet China regularly takes home the gold in badminton during the Olympic Games. It is often played casually in the park or in local or national competitions. Casual badminton players have no problem playing outside, but more serious players prefer to play inside to avoid possible disruptions by the wind."*

"In the 1930s, Edgar Snow commented in Red Star Over China that the Communist forces in the Chinese Civil War had a "passion for the English game of table tennis" which he found "bizarre". Probably, this sport doesn't need much introduction. Not only is pīng pang a national sport of China, but it is also fairly cheap in terms of setup and supplies. You don't need to construct or pave a court. The tables used in ping pong are portable, and they can fold up to save space. Ping pong is the most played recreational sport in China, with over 300 million players."

Boy, talk about not claiming it, but owning it!

While kite flying and top spinning are simple and universal enough pastimes, the Malays have turned these into art forms. The *Wau Bulan* ("moon kite") is an elaborately built big bird in the sky, complete with sound effects made by a built-in vibrating bamboo sliver.

Likewise, top spinning, has graduated from a kid to an adult game. "Giant top spinning is no child's game! Each gasing or top weighs approximately 5kg and the wooden tops are as big as the size of dinner plates placed mouth to mouth. It calls for strength, coordination, and skill. The gasing, if expertly hurled, can spin for as long as 2 hours. Top spinning competitions are an annual feature in the east coast of Peninsular Malaysia especially Kelantan and Terengganu."

The winner is determined by the length of time it takes till the top's tilt, wobble, and final topple. Whereas adult top spinning has survived as a cultural and tourist exhibit, regular tops have bitten the dust of modernity. Requiem.

Word Games: Berpantun, Paatukku Paatu, ...

Call – response games are usually of a verbal nature, including exchanges of poetry, song lyrics, drums, etc

Main pantun (poetry play) is a type of call and response in traditional Malay society, probably from the time of the Malacca Sultanate – which explains why Baba-Nyonya are/were also great practioners of it. Pantun is a poetic quartrain, with the top two lines being *pembayang* (precursor) and the bottom two, *maksud* (crux). An example follows: Excuse the amateur translate!

Jual ("Sell")	Beli ("Buy")
Panas-panas makan semangka	Daun jambu tertiup melambai
Makin segar jika ditambahkan gula	Jatuh tertimbun bagai sampah
Apabila engkau tahu jawabnya	Ekor itu saperti belalai
Binatang apa yang ekornya ada dikepala?	Belalai milik si hewan gajah

Translation:

Call	Response
Watermelon eaten in hot weather	Guava leaves in wind billows
Fresher yet with sugar added	like a thrash heap a'fallen
When you do know the answer	The tail a trunk mirrors
What animal has tail on its head?	Belongeth to the elephant

When professional bards go at each other with this style of entertainment, you definitely feel the artistry, romance, humour and class. It was in the realm of the upper class, and has now been relegated to the performing stage. In a romantic type of call-response, it is between a male and female in a sing-song courting format, praising the partner's beauty, and virtue.

In the 60's and 70's radio and live performances and S.M Salim ruled the airwaves. It was a standard part of any dinner gala.

Paatukku-paatu ("song for a song"), is a latter day tamil brain game similar to the hindi *antakshari* ("last letter"). It is a parlour game, or road trip entertainment (remember "I Spy"?), where two teams or two people try to come up with popular song phrases.

When the first person stops a line of song at any point, the next person will have to come up with another song beginning with the first letter of the last word. Lets try one.

A: "By the the rivers of Babylon, where we sat down ...."   (Boney M)

B: Daddy doesn't pray anymore
    I guess he's finished talking to the Lord
    He used to fold his hands and bow his head down to the floor
    But daddy doesn't pray anymore   (Chris Stapleton)

The other team should sing a song beginning with "A", and so on. Hours could be spent in such activity.

Although an ecquivalent activity is yet to be found in Chinese culture, the Baba-Nonya (A Chinese people) have a history of excelling in the Malay tradition of berpantun. Shaped by Chinese folktales and unique legendary characters, they gave rise to a unique Sino-Malay literature.

There exists a database of 11,204 pantun, syair and dondang sayang written by babas over 100

Years. However, the practice of spontaneous, extemporaneous, impromptu delivery of the pantun and dondang sayang has slowed, except for literary programs organized by Baba associations in Penang, Malacca and Singapore.

"The Telephone game, aka *Chinese Whispers,* is a game where a message is passed along (as a whisper) from one player to the next, until it reaches the end of the line of players, and the message is repeated. While the point is to transmit the message without errors, a lot of the fun of the game lies in the message becoming distorted, often hilariously, by the end." While it is not Chinese in origin, the game is mentioned here owing the Chinese reference.

The Last of the Malaccans: Baba, Chitty, Serani

Isn't it the nature of things, that the majority culture ultimately subsumes the minority? It seems as if even nature detests variety and ultimately gears towards uniformity. Like one chemical titrated into another, the resultant is a whole new blend or compound. However given the right environment and nurture, some communities survive and flourish. Eventhough the Jews, diffusely dispersed worldwide as they are, have maintained their identity with vitality. The "Black Jews" of Kerala, South India have mostly disappeared there in recent times, only because they have migrated, like many others, to Israel. Countless centuries out of India, groups of Romani (gypsies) still roam parts of Europe, a very discriminated but discrete group.

In Malaysia, three tiny communities still survive in the state of Malacca, a remnant from 600 years ago, since the days of the Malacca Sultanate and Portuguese occupation. The Babas are considered to be the descendents of a 15th century bridal entourage of the Princess Hang Li Poh, who intermarried with the locals. Hang Li Poh herself, was married to Sultan Mansur Shah, 2nd Sultan of Malacca, in a political arrangement between the royal houses of China and Malacca.

The Malays are a different situation. Like one of their Malacca sultanate generals Hang Tuah is said to have said, *"Takkan Melayu hilang di dunia"* – "Never shall the Malay disappear from the face of the earth". But is there a vestige of the Malaccan Malay? They had already moved and emerged as the Johore sultanate along with the last sultan of Malacca. Traces of their settlements can be found near Muar and Batu Pahat in North Johore. The question as to where are the Malacca Sultanate Malays, is a difficult one, as they have assimilated into the broader malay community, just as the peranakan Malays of Penang (P.Ramlee et al) and other Nusantara people (Bugis, Minangkabau, Javanese etc) have blended with the Malay ethicity. In fact, anyone can become

Malay – "*Masuk Melayu*" – if they will convert to Islam and adopt Malay customs.

The Indian and Chinese peranakan have largely distinguished themselves from the larger community of their Indian and Chinese brethren, although still considering themselves Indians and Chinese respectively. The Malacca Portuguese community, separated by two oceans and two continents from Portugal, never had that choice – to merge, or not, from the mother community. All three are afforded some of the perks of Bumiputraism – ----("sons of the soil").

The Chitty's are descendents of the Tamil business community during the same period. They get their name from the Chetty or Chettiar community, a caste of moneylenders and financiers. However, the present crop of Chitty's will be the first to protest that they are not Chetty. They are in fact a hodge-podge of many castes, with family names like Chetty (banker), Pillai (accountant), Padayachee (army oficer), and Naicker (political administrator). They claim to being around longer than the Baba's, possibly arriving during Parameswara's time itself. Parameswara's ancestral home of Malayur, on Sumatra had already been Indianized many centuries earlier. There is an existing Malaiyur in Tamil Nadu, meaning "Hill Town" (Hilton?). *Malai* (hill) *Oor* (town or village).

The Portuguese, with their patron saint Apostle Peter, are Roman Catholics, but an ethnic polyglot of Portuguese, Dutch, English, and local native bloodlines. With names like D'Costa, Oliveiro, Lazaroo, Texeira, and Santa Maria (Portuguese); Danker, Kraal, Zuzartee, Van Huizen, Goonting (Dutch) and Scully, Pedley, Boudeville (British), they are a mingling of many nations, unlike the Chitty's who are a cauldron of many castes within the Tamil community. Portuguese are sometimes referred to as Serani (fr. Nasrani = Nazarenes = Christians). The town of Jesus Christ's birth, is Nazareth in present day Palestine. Another old appellation for the Portuguese is, Eurasian. Sometimes Kristang (local for Christian) is used.

Baba folk, are basically Chinese in terms of culture and religion. They are Toaists, though many are now Christians. The language and couture, especially of the older generation, is Malay. They have also evolved a distinct fusion cuisine of Malay and Chinese styles, called Nyonya cooking.

Sample speech (Baba):

<u>Baba</u>		<u>Malay</u>		<u>English</u>
"Taci sudah sampei."	—	"Kakak sudah sampai"	—	"Elder sister has arrived,"
"Cangkir ni pane."	—	"Cawan ini panas."	—	"this saucer is hot"

Like Malay, Baba Malay has many loan words: taci (from Tamil), cangkir (Chinese) and pane (Malay).

The Chitty, likewise, have maintained their Hindu faith, personal, and family names in the mother culture. Their temple, the Sri Poyyatha Vinayagar Temple, means Temple of the Never Lying Ganesha (Elephant-headed God). It is the oldest in the country, naturally. Like the Baba's, they have lost their language, except for the Tamil ceremonial and cuisine words which still enjoy currency. Like the Baba, Chitty Tamil is virtually Malay.

Sample Chitty talk:

<u>Chitty</u>		<u>Malay</u>		<u>English</u>
"Ayyah, saya mau arshaneh"	—	"Pendita, saya mahu menyembah"	—	"Priest, I want to make an offering"
"Swami sudah dating"	—	Sami sudah menjelma	—	The lord has appeared

Interestingly, there is a Chitty group in Sri Lanka, who have nothing to do with our Chitties. They are the Colombo Chitties, who are descended from the Chettiars who settled in that area. Michael Ondaatje, author of the Booker Prize winning *The English Patient,* is of Chitty descent. His ancestors were advisors to the Tamil (Pandyan) Kings of Madurai. Our Chitties have no such claim to fame in modern times.

Baba's are usually paired as Baba-Nyonya in a male – female form, somewhat like Yin and Yang. (Hokkien: *Bā-bā Niû-liá*). Interestingly, this title has no Chinese origin."Baba" is an honorific used in several North Indian and Middle Eastern cultures, being of Persian etymology. It refers to "grandfather", or to a sainted person. E.g "Sai Baba." "Nyonya" comes from the Javanese for mistress from the Portuguese, "Nona" (dame). The Nyonya matron is usually called "Bibik", which sounds suspiciously like the

"Beevi" or "Bibi" attached to the first names of Tamil Muslim women. e.g, "Aayeesha Beevi". Bibi, is also North Indian for a sister-in-law. So, is there a case for *Baba – Bibi*, you think? As long as you don't constrict it further to *Babi*. Bad idea.

Indians too, have the equivalent to the Yin-Yang, male and female forces, i.e., *Shiva* (judgmental force) and his consort *Shakti* (power source). Shiva-Shakti – one completes the other. So, perhaps, like the Baba-Nyonya, with the Chitty community's permission, they might be called Chitty-Nachiya. "Nachiya" is the common appellation in India, for a Chetty matron or matriarch. The Portuguese pair could be "Senhor-Dama" – Gentleman – Lady in Portuguese.

The Portuguese have retained their western cultural "face", while their physical face is certainly Malay or at least, Malaysian. They speak English and dress in modern attire. Like the Baba's, they have settled in other parts of Malaysia, unlike the Chittys, who have generally stayed put in Malacca.

Their mother tongue, Papia Kristang (Christian Language), is an archaic form of Portuguese that has many Malay, Chinese and Tamil loan words. It is the oldest extant Portuguese dialect anywhere in the world. It has a branch in the Portuguese family tree, at the Portuguese Language Museum in Sao Paolo, Brazil. However, it is spoken by only small group of older residents in the Portuguese Settlement in Ujong Pasir, in the outskirts of Malacca City. It is also referred to as Cristâo (pronounced, "Kristang") or Portuguese de Malacca.

It is an interesting fact that all these communities, have retained their religion and culture but lost their language. Perhaps there is a practical reason for this. Religion, being their personal and private domain, always sticks with them, whereas language being a tool of trade with others necessitates communication in the Lingua Franca. So, you use it or you lose it.

One way out of the above situation, that is to try to retain your language while using the Lingua Franca, is assimilation – keep as much of your words as possible. The Baba, Chitty, and Portuguese have done these. The Portuguese words while clearly Portuguese, have lost their phonetic shape and become more like Malay.

Portuguese		Kristang (Christao)		English
Muitas Mercês !	–	Mutu Merseh!	–	Thank you!
Estâs Bom?	–	Teng Bong?	–	How are you?
Boa Manhâ		Bong Pamiang		Good Morning

The Baba, who originally sprung up from Chinese and Local Malay ancestors, have moved into, and interacted with the larger Chinese community that arrived only in the 19th and 20th centuries as tin mine coolies and petty traders. Even before the coming of the latter immigrants, Baba's went back to China to get brides and husbands. This was because marriage to the Malay locals would result in islamization. Islam had, by this time, become entrenched in the Malay consciousness. It effectively put a stop to the widespread intermarriage with the Malays, not only of the Babas, but also the Chitties, and Portuguese. The Chitties and Malays did intermarry during the period when both were Hindus.

Even today, an Indian or Chinese who converts to Islam, either by marriage, or by choice, generally becomes enculturated as a Malay. This is not through coercion by the Malays, but because of their alienation by their own culture, family, society etc. Their children, of course, become Malays in every sense.

The irony in this is, the Indian Muslim has managed to keep his indianness intact. Any Tamil will tell you that the Indian (Tamil) Muslim speaks a purer, classical Tamil than most other Tamils, eventhough they use an appreciable number of Arabic or Urdu words. He tends to pray in his own Masjid India, and hears Friday sermons (*khutbah*) delivered in scintillating Tamil. He has a long history stretching back to Bendahara (Prime Minister) Tun Kudu and the great Munshi Abdullah (an early writer in Malay). Even the recently retired Prime Minister, Tun Dr. Mahathir Mohamad, is patrilinearly Malayali and Matrilinearly Malay. Malayalam (the language of his grandfather) is a fairly recent offshoot of Tamil, as Italian is, of Latin.

The Chinese Muslim community in Malaysia, if there is indeed such a thing, probably looks more like the Malay community. Chinese individuals who convert to Islam tend to assimilate into the majority Muslim community of Malays. For a true Chinese Muslim community you may have to visit the Uighur (Sinkiang) or Yunnan areas of China.

There is no evidence of the Chittys mingling with the larger, latter day Indian community which came in as indentured labourers and petty clerks. Not even in Malacca. Why would they? The way I see it, if you were a Chitty with a 600 hundred year history and an impressive pedigree dating to the 14th century, as international traders, would you marry the rubber tapper? The Portuguese, of course have no larger community nearby in which to integrate, so they are gradually marrying into other cultures.

The Babas are said to have been very thick with the British colonial machinery, loyal to the Queen, as indeed they must have been to the Malacca Sultan, and to the royalty of Portugal and Holland. The Chinese are adept diplomats, surviving in changing political environments in win-win business and political affiliations with the government of the day.

In the midst of these, the local population of the Malays, being the host community, has carried on as usual. In a way it may not be business as usual, afterall. In a way, the Malay community may be the one that has changed the most in the last 500 years. In no small irony, the majority community has lost much of its original cultural sheen.

The Malay society of the 1400s retained its thick layers of Hindu/Buddhist undercoating until getting a final application of Islam. The Hindu influence survives in the terminology and ceremonial rites of the installation of the Agong and Sultan. But the modern Malaccan Malay has no hereditary ruler today, as his liege. So there! Doing a cultural archeological dig beyond the Hindu/Buddhist layer, you would encounter an animist, indigenous social strata that exists in his beliefs about spirits.

In addition to losing its pre – 14th century identity, the Malays as host had a two way barter of culture, cuisine, couture etc. So, in as much as influencing Baba, Chitty and Portuguese culture, the Malacca Malay society (and by extension Malays generally) has itself been greatly influenced by them. Let's not forget that Baba, Chitty and Serani all have Malay biological and cultural genes. The Malay is a supreme example of someone who has thoroughly reinvented himself in different phases of history. Like universal English, his language is the lingua franca of the region, including Indonesia.

Receptivity, not originality, is the characteristic of the Malay races.But the importance of Malay, when the traveller heads eastward from the Bay of Bengal, has been recognised by Europeans since the sixteenth century, when Magellan's Malay interpreter was found to be understood from one end of the Archipelago to the other. It is the strong and growing language of an interesting people, and (in the words of a recent writer on Eastern languages) "for Malay, as for Hindustani, a magnificent future maybe anticipated among the great speech-media of Asia and of the world. They manifest that capacity for the absorption and assimilation of foreign elements which we recognise as making English the greatest vernacular that the world has ever seen."

English is now, the largest donor of words to Malay. In a circuitous way, we had arrived at a place where English, which osmotically absorbed from Greek, Latin and other languages, passed it on to Malay as a colonizer's language. The linguistic colonization continues unabated. Today, technological terms are appropriated into Malay as fast as it enters the English lexicon. English and Malay are similar in the way they have prospered (as lingua franca) by unabashedly borrowing from whomever they came across. They present a model of linguistic survival and success by adaptation. It is a model of survival of the fittest, of embracing foreign concepts and making it your own. Whereas, on the other end of the continuum, Tamil claims an unbroken tradition of linguistic chastity, unmarred by foreign borrowings. Its poets have designated it, *KannithThamil* ("virgin Tamil"). Even the latest scientific and technological terms are coined by mining ancient words from the millennia old classic literature. In fact, Tamils like to boast that *ThaniThamil* ("stand alone Tamil") is ever young because of its unchanged state over several millenia. If there is such a thing as a living dinosaur, this must be it! Its contemporaries (like Latin, Greek, Sanskrit and Pali) they point out, have long since become extinct, or mutated into a myriad of other languages.

After the fall of Malacca to the Portuguese, the Sultan escaped to Johore Lama and started the Johore Sultanate, which continues to this day. No semblance of the glory days of the Malacca Sultanate exists today. There are no more *Hangs* (Tuah, Jebat, Lekir, Lekiu, or Kasturi), Malay knights in armour. The only one we know is William Hung. But he is a mainland Chinese, American Idol wannabe. Recent genetic analysis has brought forth that these *Hangs* are actually not Malay, but Chinese warriors who accompanied Princess Hang Li Poh. The Chinese are Han, by race. Hopefully, they are not the same as the Huns of Hungary, known in history as barbaric invaders of Eastern Europe, who appeared from the Orient. Anyway, some local Chinese historians discount even the royalty of Hang Li Poh. They say that Hang Li Po was never a Princess and the *Hangs* were never warriors, just some slave girl and her companions. The Chinese emperor, they say, would never give his daughter away to an obscure local chieftain, of a distant foreign land, that was a vassal state.

We do have cultural holdovers from the past such the *Joget* music and dance with its graceful moves, the *Pantun* bartering (a kind of conversation in rhyme and riddle).

The *Baju Melayu* has Chinese collars, and sleeves, The *songkok* is Turkish Fez evidently, and *kopiah* (scull cap) is Arab. The practice of chewing betel leaf (sireh) may be from the Chitty. Betel itself is a Tamil word by way of Portuguese and then English. Vettrilai → Betelle → Betel. Vettrilai: composite of *vettri* and *ilai* (victory + leaf). The *ilai* part, meaning leaf, has entered into Malay as *helai*, which refers to a sheet or leaf, of paper or cloth.

Unlike the Portuguese community with its mother country so far away, it is easy for the Malacca Malays to integrate into the larger Malay society of Malaya. The Malay racial/ethnic/cultural makeup has been vastly altered by the infusion of Bugis, Boyan, Javanese, Minangkabau, Pattani and Cambodian strains, as well as by the even earlier inter-mixing with Indian, Chinese (in pre-islamic times) and Arabs.

The Jawi Peranakan ("jawi pekan"). *"One of the greatest manifestations of the fusion of the culture of the Indian peninsula and local Malays, has been the birth of the Jawi Peranakan community--a community of mixed Tamil (or Malayalee) Muslims and Malays--that has played an important role in Malaysia' s economic, social and political life. In this case it was not a mere borrowing, but a total fusion between the heritage of Tamil and Malayalee Muslims and that of the indigenous Malays. The Jawi Peranakan have evolved their own cultural traditions including a unique dialect and even a manner of speaking, later popularized by P. Ramlee. Even Tamil Muslims who have not assimilated with the Malays have adopted some of the practices of the Jawi Peranakan. This is one of Penang's most interesting subcultures.*

The original Jawi Peranakan have increasingly returned to calling themselves "Malays" except where "clan pride" restores a strong desire to belong, in particular, to the Mericans". – Prof. Ghulam Sarwar-Yusof

Origins: Kumari Kandam, Yunnan, Sunda Shelf

The stories of origins are in all of us. Like the child who asks her parents, "where do babies come from?", human societies have pondered their origins and genealogies. Where did we originate, as a people? The simple answer would be, "Adam and Eve!" But, that is too easy and simplistic an answer. We want to know where our "social/political" race originates from, not the collective human race.

At this point in my ramblings, in deference to the subject matter, I shall strive to be move "scientific" and make voluminously verbatim quotes from scholars and bloggers alike. This is because the question of human origins is in the realm of historians, anthroplogists, geneticists, and the member of the particular race. I take the liberty of quoting these in their entirety, and believe that printing the URL will function as full citation of the original writer. The blogs are by members of the races they write about.

Here is a couple of blogs that claim to explain the origins of the Tamils.

"Who are the Original People of Malaysia? The scientists have made it clear. By studying DNA, they have established that the chromosome marker labeled M130 as the evidence for the first ever settlers of modern humans who emigrated from Africa into the Asian coastal land along the Indian Ocean, South China Sea, all the way to Australia and the Americas. The first such migrations has been calculated to be about 70,000 years ago.This genetic study also dispells any myth about the creation of modern humans independently in lands outside Africa. In other words, there is no such thing as sons or daughters of soil in lands outside Africa from at least from the scientific view point. Everyone everywhere outside Africa is a migrant or emigrant, except that some came in earlier than others.

Genetic studies have also clearly established that all modern humans came from the same source in Africa and that the differences in looks are due to local adaptations of the human body in response to environmental differences. Typically one would find darker skin in hotter climates and lighter skin in colder climates with a whole lot of intermediary stages reflecting the multitude of environmental variations in the world. Over the years human beings continued to evolve with different genetic markers signifiying some changes along the line.

In South India among one group of Tamils, the genetic marker M130 has been found showing them as direct descendents of the first humans who first emigrated out of Africa about 70,000 years ago. The interesting thing about the marker is that the same genetic footprint is also found among certain groups of orang asli in Malaysia and in larger numbers among the Australian aborigines.This marker is present in 10% of Malaysian aborigines, 15% of New Guineans and 60% of Australian Aborigines. This confirmed the first coastal migration from Africa to Australia, through India: an evidence that could not be obtained by archaeology has been obtained by genetics.

Therefore it is clear that the first settlers in Malaysia, Indonesia and in Australia were the migrants from South India about 40,000 to 60,000 years ago.

But Malays who claim to be "sons of soil" in Malaysia had not exhibited this ancient marker as have a few of the Orang Asli discendants. One needs to remember that Orang Asli is not a single racial group but comprise more than 14 different tribes in West Malaysia alone. A few of them look very much negroid.

Malays share their gene pool with those from Yunnan of Southern China. Moreover, their skin colour is not similar to those indigenous people of South East Asia which was dark like the Australian aborigines.

On the other hand a typcial Malay's skin colour and facial features are closer to Southern Chinese. Evidently they are later day migrants, but not more than over a period of a few thousand years at the most. Today's aborigines of Malaysian forests too have extensive mixed blood as a result successive inter-breeding with various racial groups.

Technically in Malaysia, a Malay came into existence only after conversion to Islam because the political and legal definition of Malay is that the he or she must be a Muslim. On this token alone, one can argue that there were no Malays in Malaysia before about 1400, which gives them less than 700 years tenancy in Malaysia as compared to the carriers of M130 marker that goes beyond 40,000 years ago. The Malays were created only after conversion to Islam started on a massive scale following a palace coup by Muslim half-brother against his Hindu Malay half-brother in the Malaccan Hindu Kingdom and subsequently through engaging war over the other Malay Hindu Kings in the peninsula then. Moreover, in Islam, no Muslim can be allowed to renounce his religion. It is interesting to note that the Malays were referred to as Islamised Javanese and not even by the term Malays in the years 1400 by traders."

Source: http://haplogroup-i.com/2008/04/04/dna-shows-70000-year-link/ DNA Shows 70,000 Year Link

This next one is more to the point and expands on the origin theme.

"April 4th, 2008

A 30-year-old systems administrator from a small village close to Madurai in Tamil Nadu has been identified as one of the direct descendants of the first ever settlers in India, who had migrated from the African coast some 70,000 years ago.

The DNA of Virumandi Andithevar, one of the circa 700 inhabitants of Jothimanickam village, matched the white chromosome marker scientifically labeled "M130", which is a gene found only among the descendants of the African migrants who had spread across the world tens of thousands of years ago. "This young man and 13 members of his nine-generation clan carried the same marker in their genes. It means that his ancestors in all probability settled in this village several generations ago," said Prof. Rm Pitchappan, who led a team of scientists tracking the "M130" DNA.

"M130 is actually present sporadically among the population along the Western Ghats and around Madurai," said Dr Pitchappan, who heads the School of Biological Sciences at Madurai Kamaraj University. His research was part of the "Genographic Project", a global initiative launched by National Geographic and a team of reputed scientists for unraveling the mystery of human migration. "The genetic studies carried out using M130 told us about the first human migration to India. We identified the marker of the first coastal migration in our Madurai samples. The search took us to Virumandi, who belongs to the Piramalai Kallar community, whose DNA matched M130, establishing him as one of the direct descendants of the first migrant from the African coast, who must have come here some 70,000 years ago," Dr Pitchappan said.

Virumandi is elated with the news. "This is God's gift to me, to be told that my roots go back to 70,000 years. They used to say that our village of 700 people had spawned from just three ancestors and I had often wondered from where and when they came. Now I have the answer — they came 70,000 years ago from Africa," Virumandi said.

It took five years to establish the DNA link between Virumandi and the first migrants to the subcontinent. The studies also proved that though the migration to India took place some 70,000 years ago, the first settlement in the South happened about 10,000 years later.

"More than half of the Australian aborigines carry this M130 gene. The marker is also present among some people in Philippines and the tribals of Malaysia," said Dr Pitchappan.

The Genographic Project will gather all data in collaboration with indigenous and traditional people around the world. The public is invited to join the project by purchasing a Genographic Project public participation kit. The proceeds from the sales go to further field research and the Genographic Legacy Fund, which in turn supports indigenous conservation and revitalization projects.

from The Asia Age

Posted by Sathia at 05: 07 ✎ "

Editor's Note: Does this mean that the Tamil has had a continuous contact with the Malay land since 60,000 years ago? Even beyond this modern genome based results, the Tamils have their own estimation of their existence. The circa 9th Century CE Tamil grammar classic, *Purapporul Venba Maalai* (author: Iyyanarithanar) has this to say about the race.

"Kal thondri man thondra kaalatthey, vaazhodu mun thondriya mootha kudi." Which means, "The elder tribe which appeared with a sword, at a time when rock existed but soil did not exist." How old is that? The Tamil scholar (*Pulavar*) will tell you that Rock refers to the hills where man first appeared, and soil refers to the alluvial lowlands he later came down to cultivate, and the sword was actually the staff he used to protect himself from wild animals in the hills.

The following is a blog about a similar study in China.

"African Origin of Modern Chinese

Posted By: <u>Oba</u>

Date: 5, December 01, at 5: 06 p.m.

Saturday, July 15, 2000

http://english.peopledaily.com.cn/200007/15/eng20000715_45573.html

Modern humans, or Homo sapiens, might migrate from Africa into China by way of Southeast Asia between 18,000 years and 60,000 years ago, researchers say.

This latest research finding by Chinese scientists and their international colleagues concluded that modern humans might have moved from Africa to China replacing Mono erectus (archaic upright – walking human beings) there to become the ancestors of the country 's modern humans.

The conclusion is based on the comparison and analysis of Y – chromosome DNA using samples of the extant 88 populations living in East Asia, Southeast Asia and the Oceania, says Li Jin, one of the Chinese researchers of the study "Chinese Human Genome Diversity Project."

Li Jin is a professor of both the National Human Genome Center in Shanghai and the Institute of Genetics of Fudan University.

Scientists found that the variations of Y-chromosome in north China are derived from those in south China, a result proved as that a small number of settlers of African origin moved to northern China due to the hurdle of the mighty Yangtze River. And Polynesians, who live in the islands in the

Pacific Ocean, are found to have different Y-chromosome to Taiwanese, forcing scientists to reconsider the hypothsis that Polynesians were descendants of ancestral Taiwanese aborigines.

As a whole, nearly all Y-chromosome variations in East Asia and the Oceania could be found among those in Southeast Asia, adds Li Jin.

So, the findings also indicate that modern humans migrated from Africa to Southeast Asia nearly 60,000 years ago.

Subsequently, the migrants were believed to have headed for two directions: one moved northwards to south China and then spread to the country's northern areas by crossing the Yangtze River, and the other went to Indonesia and ultimately reached the Oceania.

The Y-chromosome research is an important method for tracing the human migration patterns and the findings make clear the relationships between people groups in Southeast Asia, and East Asia and the Oceania, says another major Chinese researcher Jiayou Chu, who is a professor of the Chinese Academy of Medical Sciences.

This latest research result was published in today's issue of the Proceeding of National Academy of Sciences, a U.S. journal.

The finding means that scientists have made headway in the pursuit of human origin, though the conclusion that modern Chinese human beings migrated from Africa still remains controversial, says academician of the Chinese Academy of Sciences Zhu Chen, who is also the director of Shanghai's National Human Genome Center.

In 1987, the U.S.'s scientists brought forward a theory based on mitochondrial DNA evidence that all human beings originated in Africa and later migrated to other corners of the globe. In the intentional (sic) academic circles, few arguments were raised about the theory that all palaeoanthropic mankind originated in Africa. Meanwhile, the scientists note that fossils of Peking Man who lived 500,000 years ago and Yuanmao Man over 1.7 million years ago were found in China, but both lack any direct hereditary connection with modern Chinese man.

There is a disconnection or "faultage" in fossils of palaeoanthropic Chinese who lived some 60,000 to 100,000 years ago, researchers say.

Coinciding with the fossil record, Chinese scientists discovered last year that primitive elements of DNA found in modern Chinese are identical with those found in Africans.

The discovery has provided weighty evidence on the genetic basis for the theory that modern Chinese were not evolved from the archaic upright-walking human beings in China but originated in Africa."

Here is a blog on the origin of the Malay,

"The origin of the Malays has always been a dispute in the academic circle. There are three primary possible theories of the early history of the Malays existence. The first earliest theory is based on the Mekong river migration called the "Yunnan Theory" published in 1890. The second most latest (sic) published theory in 1965 was the "New Guinea" theory where the Malays ancestor seafarers served as scouts and laborer to traders for 2000 years, and the most latest theory (sic) is the "Taiwan Theory" published in 1997 where it states that Malay descendants are sea migrants originally from Taiwan."

Ed: Mon are Austroasiatic (Mainlandic), Malayu are Austronesian (Islandic).

"Currently the Malays are an ethnic group of peoples who are primarily found living around the Malay Peninsula region, which covers the extensive vast Sumatra/Borneo areas and small low-lying islands. It is estimated there are some 23 million Malays in total population. The breakdown in general which are based on geographical locations is as follows. Malaysia has 12 million Malays, Indonesia numbers stands at 7 million, while Thailand has 1.9 million, Singapore around 450,000 and Brunei in the region of 260,000.

They're a member of the Austronesian family of languages and the Malays can be found speaking the various languages of Malay, Indonesian, Yawi and Thai. The latest census indicates that about 99% of the Malays are Islam and the Malays as an 'ethnic group' which is discussed here, are not to be mistaken with the Malays as a 'race'. That area of topic covers a wider group of people in the South East Asia and even the Pacific Islands.

Despite the varying theories of the origin of the Malays, the academics do agree on a few fact finding discoveries. The Malays although almost all are Muslims currently, they are originally Buddhist. The practice of Hinduism during the golden age of Srivijayan times was a result of influence coming from the Srivijaya Kingdom. For a millennium the Malays practiced Hinduism/Buddhism before they embraced Islam in the 15th century of the second millennium.

Archaeologists have found numerous ancient artifacts and architectures of the existence of Melayu Kingdom in Indonesia and Malaysia. The Malay kingdom have also been mentioned and etched in various early sources and records from the Tang, Mongol Yuan and even Ming Dynasty; who often referred the word Ma-La-Yu to a kingdom from the southern sea.

The origin of the Malays may not be conclusive as of now, but generally at least we have an idea of the existence of the Malays. This ethnic group now makes up a majority in the archipelago and speaks various dialects of Malay language. The Malays cultural influences are continuing to be a main stay in this region.

{{The Sejarah Melayu = Malay Annals (Ed: – Also referred to as Sulalat Al-Salatin): – "Here now, is the story of a city called Palembang in the land of the Andalas (Sumatra). It was ruled by Demang Lebar Daun, a descendant of Raja Shulan, and its river was Muara Talatang. In the upper reaches of Muara Telatang was a river called Melayu and in the river was a hill called Si Gunung Mahameru." It is for this mystical hill that Sang Utama descends upon a white bull and later becomes Sri Ti Buana. Sri Ti Buana leaves Palembang to found a new city (Simgapura). His descendents rule it for the next 5 generations until a major offensive by Majapahit. Its last King was Parameswara who escaped to the Malay peninsula to found the Kingdom of Malacca.}}"

Ed: – The Raja Syulan/Chulan is most certainly Rajendra Chozhan (Cholan with "lan" well inflected) who sacked Srivijaya in 1023 CE. Or he could be the great Rajaraja (King of kings") Chozhan, and Rajendran's father and Paramount ruler of the Tamil Chola empire.

The Sejarah Melayu talks of "Raja Syulan of benua Keling" (Tamil country). Mentions Naga Patam (Nagapattinam, "Snake town" the major seaport in Tamil Nadu. Other Tamil names mentioned include, Adiraja Rama Mendeliar (Mudaliar = owner of capital and property), Uwan Malini, Uwan Sundari, and Jambunga Rama Mudliar. Hence, like it or not, the Malay is linked, if not genetically, at least historically with the Tamil.

Of course, the Malay royalty also seek to claim lineage to Alexander the Great (Iskandar Zulkarnain). This is by way of Persian influences. Although why Persians will claim Alexander as a forefather is beyond understanding, since Alex is the one who routed their Cyrus the great. The Malays also embrace Solomon (Sulaiman) as a link to their past.

"@@@ One history says Malays from Borneo. The Bugis did. They controlled the Malacca Straits. Orang Laut "Sea People" may have traded wih Japan.

Anthropologists trace the original home of the Malay race to Northwestern Yunnan in South-East China. This Proto-Malay (Jakun) were a seafaring people. Orang Selat (Portuguese historian Gordinho Eredia refers to them as Saletes). Eredia = "He who controls Malacca has his hands on thethroat of Venice."

The present day Malay of the Peninsula and coasts are descendents of the Proto-Malays mixed with modern Indian, Thai, Arab and Chinese bloodlines.

For nearly 2,000 years unremitting trade traffic between the Archipelago and India resulted in frequent (Websight: Sejarah Melayu) intermarriages with Tamils and Gujaratis. In Perlis/Kedah you have social intercourse with the Thais.

East-Coast Kelantan has strong traces of Javanese culture that date back to Majapahit empire (Sumatra) of 14th century. The north Sumatran kingdom of Acheh (Malay people) dominated Perak state for over a century, the Bugis from Celebes island colonized Selangor, The Minangkabau of Western Sumatra (Padang) had their own chieftains in Negeri Sembilan ("Nine States"). This mix of races can be seen in modern Malay lineage of Malacca royalty. Sultan Muhammad Shah marries a Tamil woman from South India, Sultan Mansur Shah married a Javanese, a Chinese, and a Siamese wife, who bore two future Sultans of Pahang state."

Ed: – Though all the above studies and other studies about migration indicate our ancestors came from Africa, it shouldn't contradict Judeao-Christo-Islamic teachings about our Adamic origins. For one, neither the Torah, Bible nor the Koran clearly pinpoint the exact location of the Garden of Eden. It could very well have existed in Africa, which is in the vicinity of the holy land.

Conclusion: Even to the, "people of the book" (i.e. Jews, Christians, Muslims), the idea that we are all "Out of Africa" seems plausible. Afterall, the Garden of Eden has not been positively identified, as to its exact location. Even the popularly assumed site of the Garden, Mesopotamia, is not too far from the borders of present day Africa.

What about the Indian sub-continent detaching from Africa and slamming into Asia's underbelly? Even then, the original inhabitants of India may be said to be out of Africa, in an unintentional sort of way. There is an unconfirmed Tamil myth that that they originally lived on a continent touching Madagascar, Western Australia and South India, known as Kumari Kandam (Virgin Continent"). It talks of the first two of three Tamil Academies. The present day Tamils apparently are the ones who escaped to South India after a colossal *"Kadal Kol"* (continental subsidence) sunk the continent.

B.O.Stoney (Hon.Sec. of the Malay Settlements, Kuala Lumpur) wrote that among the various theories of origin that (they) be "from the same stock as the Mongol of Central Asia. Others have asserted that he is of Indonesian origin." He also quotes Sir Frank Swettenham's, "British Malaya" that the "Malays are the descendendents of people who crossed from the South of India to Sumatra, mixed with a people already inhabiting that island, and gradually spread themselves over the most central and fertile States – Palembang, Jambi, Indragiri, Mengangkabau, and Kampar."

Stoney adds that "The Malays themselves are not much given to speculation on the subject of their national ancestry and they are, for the most part, quite ready to accept without demur the account contained in the books of Malay Annals of the conquest and colonization of the Malay Peninsula by a people who came from Palembang, in Sumatra.

Malay royalty claim descent from Alexander the Great (Iskandar Zulkarnain). How that works, is unclear. We only know that Parameswara assumed the Persian title, Iskandar Shah, after he married the Princess of Pasai. Persians were brutally suddued by Alexander. Why would they claim Alexander as their hero? Go figure. So do the Rajputs (Rajaputra = Children of Kings) of Rajasthan, India, claim Alexander (Sikander). That is rather strange too, because Alexander never conquered India. He was soundly defeated/or held to a draw at the border by King Porus (Purushotthaman) of the Paurava empire. Why would Rajputs claim descent from a loser? It would be more logical for a present day Greek to claim Alexander as their forebear, eventhough he was Macedonian, not Greek. Perhaps every royal family wants to own the Alexander brand because he was a world dominating hero. However, in the conquered lands of the Middle-East, Persia, and Parthia (border of India), he left behind his generals as *satraps* or governors, to rule the lands. He himself never lived long, after the India imbroglio, nor married or had children. So, whence the claim that Alexander is their forebear? Fantastic fable, mysterious myth? outrageous "outta" (bullsh--)?

Global Travelers: Rajendra Chozhan, Zheng He, Enrique

The famous Greek traveler Megasthenes (c. 302 BCE) mentions the "Pandae" kingdom and refers to it as "that portion of India which lies to the southward and extends to the sea". The Roman historian Strabo (c. 1st century BCE) mentions the embassies sent by the Pandyas to the court of Augustus Ceasar.

Chinese writer Pan Kou, who lived before the 1st century CE, refers to the city of Kanchipuram in his work *Tsien han chou*. The Chinese historian Yu Huan in his 3rd century text, the *Weilüe*, mentions The Kingdom of Panyue (Pandya): *"...The kingdom of Panyue is also called Hanyuewang. It is several thousand li to the southeast of Tianzhu (Northern India)........... The inhabitants are small; they are the same height as the Chinese..."*

The Chinese records of the Song Dynasty show that the first mission to China from Chu-lien (Chola) reached that country in 1015 C.E. and the king of their country had been Lo-ts'a-lo-ts'a (Rajaraja), Rajendra Cholans's father.

Greeks, Romans and Chinese interacted with the Tamils as early, or earlier than the beginning of the Christian era. They visited the Tamil country and were themselves visited by Tamils. No name is recorded, of the travellers as Tamils, unlike the Chinese were not keen historians or chronichlers of their travels. Their ancient literature was more focused on love and war poetry and moral/spiritual themes. Besides, they were all traders, rather than tourists. Their kings did leave behind lots of stone stele and copperplate inscriptions.

Much is known about the Chola King, Rajendra I because he had generously inscribed his exploits in India, Ceylon, and South-East Asia on copper and stone. This is a highlight of his martial exploits:-

Year	Event
1002 CE	Ransacked the Rashrakutas (Karnataka/Maharashtra)
1018 CE	Sacked Sri Lanka
1018 CE	Parried with the Pandyas/chased away the Cheras (Fellow Tamil kingdoms)
1019 CE	Conquered the Kalingas (Orissa) and gained over the Gangas (Bengal)
1021 CE	Chastened the Chalukyas (Central India)
1025 CE	Swooped and swept over South East Asia

Rajendra's overseas maritime exploits in South East Asia (1025) is what interests us. It is to date, the only maritime conquest by an "Indian" naval force.

Up to the 14th year of Rajendra's reign, relationships were good with the Srivijaya empire in Palembang, on Sumatra. Both the Cholas, and Sailendras (Srivijaya) had had good understanding on Chola – China trade. The Cholas were intermediaries (middlemen) in the movement of goods between the west (Rome, Arabia) and the east (Vietnam and China).

From Rajendra Cholan's own inscriptions, It seems that the Khmer king Suryavarman I of Khamboja (Cambodia) requested aid from Chola against Tambralinga kingdom. After learning of Suryavarman's alliance with Rajendra Cholan, the Tambralinga kingdom requested aid from their suzerain, Srivijaya king Sangrama Vijayatungavarman.This eventually led to the Chola Empire coming into direct conflict with the Srivijiya Empire. The war ended with a victory for the Chola – Khmer collaboration, and major losses for the Sri Vijaya – Tambralinga side. No lands were taken, except spoils. The defeated Sangrama got back his throne in return for promise of future good behavior and tribute.

The list of places conquered by Rajendra in his own words taken verbatim from the stele he erected at Tanjuvur, his capital:

"(Who) having despatched many ships in the midst of the rolling sea and having caught Sangrāma-vijayōttunga-varman, the king of *Kadāram*, together with the elephants in his glorious army, (took) the large heap of treasures, which (that king) had rightfully accumulated; (captured) with noise the (arch called) Vidhyādharatorana at the "war gate" of his extensive city, Śrī Vijaya (Palembang) with the "jewelled wicket-gate" adorned with great splendour and the "gate of large jewels"; Paṇṇai (Panai) with water in its bathing ghats; the ancient Malaiyūr (Jambi) with the strong mountain for its rampart; Māyuriḍingam (? ?), surrounded by the deep sea (as) by a moat; Ilangāśōka (Pattani) undaunted in fierce battles; Māpappālam (Pegu) having abundant (deep) water as defence; Mēviḷimbangam (Palembang/Ligor) having fine walls as defence; Vaḷaippandūru (??); Talaittakkōlam (Takuapa) praised by great men (versed in) the sciences; Mādamālingam (Tambralinga – Southern Thailand), firm in great and fierce battles; Ilāmuridēśam (Lamuri/Aceh), whose fierce strength rose in war; Mānakkavāram (Nicobar), in whose extensive flower gardens honey was collecting; and Kadāram (Kedah), of fierce strength, which was protected by the deep sea"

This far distant from the historical happening, things become subjective, but Rajendra Cholan's exploits in this region raise questions about his continuing impact. Certain royal families, like the Perak royalty, still carry names like Raja Chulan ibni Almarhum Sultan Abdullah Muhammad Shah II Habibullah KBE. A major roadway in Kuala Lumpur, Jalan Raja Chulan, is named after him. The name Chulalongkorn the 5th (son of King Mongkut), of the Chakri dynasty, likely reflects Rajendra's visit to the neighbourhood.

In Malay culture, the *Malay Annals* (15th/16th centuries) begins with the story of a king named Raja Shulan who was a descendant of Iskander Zulkarnain (Alexander the Great) and his son, Raja Chulan. In this account, Raja Shulan is setting out to conquer China! Details may change, but memories die hard! Historical fact: Cholan and China were all time trading buddies.

Zheng He (Cheng Ho)

Not to be confused with <u>Zhang He</u>, a general of the Three Kingdoms, Wei, Shu and Wu (from 220-280 AD). **Zheng He (Cheng Ho)** (birth name Ma Sanbao – 1371-1433 AD) was the most famous Chinese maritime explorer whose expeditions are known as the travels of the *"Eunuch Sanbao to the Western Ocean.* Cheng He was descended 6 generations down from Sayyid Ajjal Shams al-Din Omar, who was a governor of the Mongol province of Yunnan. When the Ming dynasty finally captured Yunnan, eleven year old Cheng He was taken and made a eunuch at the Ming Court, where he made an impression on the emperor.

He would grow to be a powerful admiral in the Ming fleet, and establish the Indian ocean trade outposts for China. This a list of his ambassadorial hits.

Voyage	Travel Period	Regions visited
1st Voyage	1405-1407	Champa, Java, Palembang, Malacca, Aru, Sumatra, Lambri, Ceylon, Kollam, Cochin, Calicut
2nd Voyage	1407-1409	Champa, Java, Siam, Cochin, Ceylon
3rd Voyage	1409-1411	Champa, Java, Malacca, Sumatra, Ceylon, Quilon, Cochin, Calicut, Siam, Lambri, Kaya, Coimbatore, Puttanpur
4th Voyage	1413-1415	Champa, Java, Palembang, Malacca, Sumatra, Ceylon, Cochin, Calicut, Kayal, Pahang, Kelantan, Aru, Lambri, Hormuz, Maldives, Mogadishu, Barawa, Malindi, Aden, Muscat, Dhufar
5th Voyage	1416-1419	Champa, Pahang, Java, Malacca, Sumatra, Lambri, Ceylon, Sharwayn, Cochin, Calicut, Hormuz, Maldives, Mogadishu, Barawa, Malindi, Aden

Voyage	Travel Period	Regions visited
6th Voyage	1421-1422	Hormuz, East Africa, countries of the Arabian Peninsula
7th Voyage	1430-1433	Champa, Java, Palembang, Malacca, Sumatra, Ceylon, Calicut, Hormuz... (17 states in total)

Since Cheng He visited the Arabian Peninsula and the vicinity on the 4th to the 7th trips, it is quite likey that he went to Mecca. Both his father, Mir Tekin, and grandfather, Charameddin, had made the pilgrimage to Mecca and that might have inspired the lad's wanderlust. He is credited with settling many Chinese muslims in the Nusantara region, and is revered by both Muslims and Chinese. The Muslims had erected many mosques in his memory while Taoists erected temples for him.

In the Malaysian context, Cheng He's visit to Malacca coincides with the reigns of Parameswara (1414-1424) and Muhammad Shah (1424-1444). Note that Cheng He on his first 3 Journeys (1405-1411), actually predates Parameswara's founding of Malacca (1414)! About 30 years after Cheng He's last voyage Sultan Mansur Shah sends his emissary, Tun Perpatih Putih to the Ming Court, requesting a royal bride for the Sultan. The *Malay Annals* (Sejarah Melayu) reports that Princess Hang Li Po arrived in 1459. Her entourage of 500 young people, were the beginning of the *Peranakan* Chinese, or the *Baba-Nyonya* community of Melaka,

Just as much as the earlier Indianization of South-East Asia is for Indians, the exploits of Cheng He in this region provide the valid case for their claim to Malaysianness. Chinese, Indian and Malay were all here at the same time. Unless one is willing to claim oneself as Orang Asli, none has the case to brand another as immigrant. To brand Chinese and Indians as immigrants (*pendatang*) is the favourite game of Malay opposition politicians. Afterall, race biting is the standard ploy of any party in the opposition.

In the 1950s, historians such as John Fairbank and Joseph Needham popularized the idea that after Zheng He's voyages, China turned away from the seas due to the Haijin edict and was isolated from European technological advancements. Modern historians point out that Chinese maritime commerce did not totally stop after Zheng He, that Chinese ships continued to participate in Southeast Asian commerce.

The two-way cultural interchange between the Indian Ocean and the China Seas is exemplified by two archeological finds in the respective regions. The common thread is the Tamil and Chinese languages and their scripts. For one, a Tamil stone tablet has been unearthed at the site of an ancient Hindu temple in China. It was located in Guangzhou (near Canton). The bilingual Tamil and Chinese inscriptions on it are a prayer to Shiva for the good health of the Yuan (Mongol) emperor Kublai (Chekachai) Khan. It was commissioned by a certain Tavachchakkaravarttigal Sambandhap-perumal (Saivite leader). Year of inscription is 1281 A.D.

Going the other way, a stone tablet in Chinese, Tamil, and Persian was dedicated to the Buddha (Chinese), Shiva (Tamil) and Allah (Persian) by the great admiral Cheng He. He had commissioned it in Nanjing (1409) and taken it on one of his 7 excursions to the Indian Ocean. He had installed it in Galle, southern Sri Lanka. The stele was accidentally uncovered in 1911 by S.H.Thomlin, a British engineer while repairing a ditch. The slab had been used as a bridge for over 500 years!

Chinese had business with kingdoms up and down the Indo-Chinese peninsula, Phillipine islands and Borneo and Malay peninsula. They rounded the peninsula to trade in Malacca, Java, Sumatera and even to Africa and Arabia.

Enrique, aka "Black Enrique"

Malays and their Austronesian kin are known seafarers. The "orang laut' (sea people) ruled the waters of the Sunda shelf, and they have long ago settled the island of Madagscar, on the other side of the Indian Ocean. However, not many realize that The Malacca Straits, being the artery that connected the two great waters (Indian Ocean and South China Sea), has enriched the region as the confluence of cultures. Malaysian culture, then, can be described as a soup that has a Malay base, with generous infusions or Indian, Chinese, Arabic, and European meats and spices.

A Malay was the first to circumnavigate the globe.

He gets the distinction not from active enterprise but by being a passive passenger. His being a favourite slave of the admiral of the fleet, explains the obscurity of this historical fact.

The story begins in Malacca in 1511. This is the only date from Malaysian history I know by default, other than 1957 – independence. Did you imagine this? The famous Ferdinand Magellan was part of the Portuguese invasion of Malacca under Alfonso D'Albuquerque. In Malacca, Magellan had bought a Malay youth, captured from Sumatra. He is known to us as Enrique, aka Black Henry. In a fateful twist, he became Magellans's shadow around the world. Enrique was with Magellan when he was in the service of the Portuguese king (Manuel I). After the Malacca, and later India and Africa postings, Magellan had the idea of finding a western route to the spice island (Maluku), going around South America. With some negative report preceding him, the Portuguese king did not grant his plans. Turning to the Spanish king (Charles I) Magellan got 5 ships with 265 crew for the project. And Enrique was on board.

Historical context: The Portuguese sailing around the Cape of Good Hope (Eastbound) and Spanish eagerness to sail around the Cape Horn (Westbound) can probably explained by the division of South America into Portuguese (Brazil) and Spanish (west) by the Treaty of Tordesillas (1494). They extended the division to the rest of the world by the Treaty of Zaragoza (1529). So you have Portuguese Brazil, Angola, Mozambique, India, Ceylon, Malacca, and Timor. And you have Spanish South/Central America, Caribbean, and Phillippines. Going by the demarcating lines, Taiwan (Formosa) and Macao shouldn't be Portuguese, but they were!

This an abridged time-line of Enrique's sojourn.

Date	Event	In Service of
1511	Enrique acquired by Magellan in Malacca	Portugal
15 11-1516	Follows Magellan to India, Africa, back to Lisbon	"
March 22, 1518	Starts Journey from Valladolid, Spain	Spain

Date	Event	In Service of
Nov 1, 1520	First ever ship through the Straits of Magellan	"
Nov 28, 1520	Out of Magellan Straits into Pacific Ocean	"
March 16, 1521	Sighting of Samar, Phillipines' easternmost island	"
April 27, 1521	Magellan dies in battle on Mactan, near Cebu	"
Sept 6, 1522	Magellan's ship, "Victoria" reaches Seville, Spain	"

History records that Magellans's home ship, and the only surviving of the original flottilla, the *Nao Victoria*, limped home to Seville, Spain. It was led by Juan Sebastian del Cano, and seventeen crew. He is the first European to have circumnavigated the globe. We get the story from Antonio Pigafetta, the Venetian scholar, who paid his passage with Magellan and chronicled the journey in "A report on the First Voyage Around the World" (Italian: *Relazione del primo viaggio intorno al mondo*).

Juan Sebastian may have been the first European around the world but Enrique is very possibly the first human. Magellan's journey ended at Mactan/Cebu and it is unknown if Enrique continued the trip to Spain, since he was in home territory. If he had continued to Malacca, it would have been a rightful round trip. Eventhough Juan (and crew) and Enrique were on the same quest, Enrique had had a head start in Malacca. Juan still had another halfway around the world to go to finish line.

The support for Enrique as the first circumnavigator comes from Stefan Zweig, author of 'Conqueror of the Seas, a biography of Magellan'. *"What an amazing moment, one of the most remarkable in the history of mankind. For the first time since our planet had begun to spin upon its axis and to circle in its orbit, a living man, himself circling that planet, had got back to his homeland. No matter that he was an underling, a slave, for his significance lies in his fate and not in his personality. He is known to us only by his slave-name Enrique; but we know, likewise, that he was torn from his home upon the island of Sumatra, was bought by Magellan in Malacca, was taken by his master to India, to Africa, and to Lisbon; travelled thence to Brazil and to Patagonia; and first of all the population of the world, traversing the oceans, circling the globe, he returned to the region where men spoke a familiar tongue. Having made acquaintance on the way with hundreds of peoples and tribes and races, each of which had a different way of communicating thought, he had got back to his own folk, whom he could understand and who could understand him."*

In the Malaysian context, the lives of Rajendra Cholan (1025), Cheng He (1405), Enrique (1511), are inextricably linked physically in the Straits of Malacca. Rajendra Cholan had aimed his armada against Sri Vijaya on Sumatra and Kadaram on the Malay Peninsula. Cheng He had sailed up and down the straits multiple times, and Enrique had started his round the world tour from Malacca. How's that for a historical choke point for three different people groups originating in diverse parts of Asia? Rajendra and Enrique didn't reach China, but Cheng He and Enrique did visit Rajendra's land in Southern India. This "meeting" still plays out in the daily lives of Malaysians, *Truly Asia*.

The Malacca Straits, being the artery that connects the two great waters (the Indian Ocean and the South China Sea), has enriched the region as the confluence of cultures. Malaysian culture then, can be described as a soup that has a Malay base, with generous infusions of Indian, Chinese, Arabic, and European meats and spices.

Lest we think that these are the only Asian explorers/travellers, there are others with a "softer" agenda. The Tamils, *Bodhidharma* (5th/6th century AD) and *Bodhisena* (700 AD) who enhanced Buddhism in China and Japan respectively, are countered by the Chinese, *Faxian* (405-411 AD), *Yuan Zhuang* (630-645 AD), *Yijing* (671-695 AD) who went the other way to India to learn Buddhism. Both crossed two oceans to get to the other's place. The Malays of Sumatra/Java had sailed across the Indian ocean to settle Madagascar on its westen edge (1st century AD). Their Polynesian cousins had settled New Zealand and other islands in the Pacific.

The Ancestral Village

As a nation of immigrants, Malaysia is not unlike the United States, or Australia. Step back a mere 600 years and all the major races in Malaysia had a home elsewhere. Like the native Americans and Australian aborigines, our Orang Asli were the only inhabitants of the peninsula at a point in time.

Eventhough the US is mish mash of ethnicities, they still look back to their original counties, burroughs, shires and villes in Europe with fondness. Many Caucasians also wear Native American and African bloodlines as badges of pride. Likewise, Malaysians, as immigrants, look to our foreign soils with pride.The Malays look to Palembang (Minangkabau), West Borneo (Bugis), and Jambi (Malays) with attachment and affection. However, having lived as natives of this land for this long, many have lost complete knowledge of their ancestral villages. Their ancestral villages (kampong halaman) are now here.

The Chinese identify themselves with the southern Chinese regions of origin such as (Cantonese) Guangdong, (Hokkien) Fujian, (Hakka), origin – Central Plains, (Teochew), origin – Central Plains, (Hailam), Hainan island, etc. If not to visit their ancestral villages, Malaysian Chinese do make it a point of visiting China as a whole. Even the local dialect might be a problem, as even Malaysian Mandarin might sound different to the mainland Chinese.

The Indians are mainly from the Southern states of Tamil Nadu, Kerala, Andhra Pradesh, and the North Indian state of Punjab. They still remember and do visit their ancestral villages. In the the "great grandparents" generation, the typical question upon meeting another Tamil, was *"Entha oor?"*, or "What's your village?". The Malayali would say, *"Enthe Rajyam?"* Same thing. The *oor*, of course, was in India. The present adult generation would more likely answer, "Air HItam Estate", instead of, "Aavichipatti", or "Tanjung Malim", rather than, "Tanjavur". They do know their ancestral Indian village and make it a point to pilgrimage there sometimes, having increasingly distant kinship ties.

Malays might visit the general areas of their old country origins, but are more likely to "balik kampung" (return to hometown) during public holidays. With the Malay sub-groups assuming a more 'standard' ethnicity, shades of Malay, Javanese, Bugese, Minangkabau – ness may be blurring altogether. The Chinese and Indians, thanks to technology, are still able to touch base with the mother culture through mail, movies, music, and mass media.

Like the Irish of America still link with their counties in Ireland, all Malaysians except the originals of Peninsula and East Malaysia, do have an "old country" to reminisce about.

Naturally, as some settle abroad in places like Australia and New Zealand, or US and Canada, Malaysia will be their ancestral home. Familiar sights, sounds, smells, tastes, social times, significant times will come to mind. They will yearn fondly about roti canai, nasi lemak, or asam laksa. Desperation will lead them to try recipes from the web.

Malaya: African Arrival, Proto-Malay Settlement, Indianization, Islamization, European Colonization, Japanese Occupation, Independence.

South-East Asia's history for millenia is broad strokes of many colours, constantly repainted many times over, like a psychedelic modern art. The original canvas was an emerald expanse of tropical jungle. The first line drawings or outlines were the march-in of early man out of Africa roughly 40,000 years ago. To this day, they form little dusky dots here and there, of Negritoes, Melanesians, Veddoids and Australoids. Then came the broad sweep of mongoloid people out of Taiwan and southern China – the Mon-Khmers, Thais, Malays, Austronesians, and Micronesians. These consider themselves natives or sons of the soil.

To this bland base, came the overarching tinting of the canvas with Indianization, around two millenia ago. It was not so much occupation, but cultural colonization by Tamil traders. This process spurred the upgrading of local society from village or tribe based, to nation centric. The Indianization spanned like a proper "U", from Burma in the far north west of SEA to the Nuasantara (Malaysia/Indonesia) to Indochina and the Phillipines in the far north east. It gave rise to a Hindu/Buddhist culture and to grand archi-structures such as the Buddhist Borobodur and Hindu Angkor Wat and Prambanan.

Next came the localized application of shamrock green in the 11th century CE. Though not as broad and monochromatic as the indianization, islamization came to colour what is the under belly of SEA, the Nusantara and Mindanao. Europeans tend to think this was along the lines of Indianization, as it was propagated by Indian Muslim merchants. Unlike Indonesia, which has a more syncretic concept of religion, Malaysia, and Acheh have chosen to adopt a more absolutist stance to the extent of scrapping and scraping away of previous cultural underlays. Many Malay cultural layers have gradually disappeared over the years, and what remains is a completely foreign middle eastern façade.

Another half millenium passes. Now it is the 16th century. As if on cue, a whole new multicoloured strokes are done. The Portuguese colonize Malacca and Flores, the Spanish conquer the Phillippines. The Americans added their tint there after the Spanish-American War. A century after the Portuguese, the Dutch painted Malacca and later Indonesia, orange. Then in the 1800s the British add their blemish to Burma, Malaya, Sarawak, and British North Borneo. The French smeared Indochina with their tricolour. Only the Thais escape the grasp of those itchy fingers of the Europeans. Thank you Thailand, for saving our collective face. All is not lost, afterall.

Wait! Its not over. Japanese occupation is sandwiched between two British colonial periods that were split by the WWII, i.e (8.12.1942-2.9.1945). They managed to shade SEA and China/Korea in Nippon paint (☺). Again, though Thailand was unscathed, the Japs did purloin Siamese territory to build the infamous Death Railway.

What about China in all this? The giant was not entirely sleeping all this time. About the time Malacca was getting up to be a nation state, the Middle Kingdom was accepting tributes from states around here. How's that for a steady passive income, without having to step foot outside the house, huh? It was entirely diplomatic. When Cheng He first came around sailing here in 1405, it was just trade, just like the earlier Tamil merchant guilds. Looks like the tide is turning again, accompanied by rough winds. The giant is now fully awake and romping all over like a Chinese New Year dragon. With its Belt and Road intrusives across Asia and Africa and its snarly clutch on the South China Sea, is this gonna be another round of colonization, er colorization, of South-East Asia? Somebody sees red.

The Japanese Death Railway aka Siam-Burma Railway

Of all the colonists who infested here, the most virulent and vicious strain surely, was the Japanese one. While the others came to trade, enculturate, dictate, confiscate, expropriate etc, the Japanese were in such a haste to orchestrate their, *"Greater East Asia Co-Prosperity Sphere"*, that they perpetrated hell on humankind. Like a Johnny come lately and finding ready pickings, they rushed through restarting the abandonded administrative and business structures. Locals who were not up to their speed or suspected of British bias were dreadfully dealt with, including on the spot decapitation.

Sometime during the war, their sea route through the Malacca Straits to Burma and their end goal of India, became untenable. They planned to revive an abandoned British idea to build a railway from south of Bangkok to Tyanbyuzat on the Burma side to link existing lines on both sides. That seemed the only option to achieve their goal. Here is where their already observed seriousness and dedication to imperial orders really shone through. Where would they find the labour for it, as the Thais were not easily cowed, being not under their rule. They turned to Allied POWs in Singapore. Later, they would entice the recently abandoned and jobless Tamils in the estates with good pay, housing and the usual sops. Word soon got back that it was basically slave labour and a death sentence, and they resorted to forced conscription. While they were particularly brutal to the Chinese back in Malaya, the Japanese also conscripted Chinese artisans from the tin mines for their mechanical skills, and Malays of the northern states.

Driven by imperial allegiance, they daily drove scores to death. A total of 250,00 Asian and 60,000 POWs were engaged. About half of the Asian forced labourers, or *Romusha*, were Tamils lifted from the estates and 90,000 of them died in situ. The other half of the Asians included Javanese, Burmese, Malays, Chinese. Of the POWS, 12,000 perished.

The British had wisely given up the the idea of cutting a railway through the Tennaserim Range and hugging the Mae Klong (aka River Kwai) Valley, as undoable. The Japs, with stolen rail parts from Malaya and stolen labour, finished it in 16 Months. Who paid for it? The Asian conscripts and POWs paid with their blood and lives. They were marched from work camp to work camp, overworked, denied health care, exposed to the elements, irritants and ailments. No human experiments or extermination occurred (viz Auschitz), but would this qualify for genocide?

It was a mission impossible successfully accomplished but never commissioned. Bridges were constantly bombarded by the Allies. All for what? And then, the Brits who had absconded with their tails between their legs, returned after the Japs lost, and sold the rails to the Thais for scrap. The Japanese, for their part, repented their foolishness and supposedly paid the Malaysian government a huge monetary reparation. That money, was never ever sniffed by the real victims and their survivors. According to Malaysian magnate Robert Kuok, that money was used to set up the Malaysian International Shipping Corporation (MISC), to be run by the political cronies of the government of the day. The government didn't allot a decadent cent of it on a decent monument. This is in stark contrast to the grand war cemetary of the Allies and the cenotaph erected by the Japanese in Kanchanaburi. A Malaysian group of survivors, survivors of survivors and the fallen of the railway (DRIG: Death Railway Interest Group) has taken initiatives towards erecting a modest monument.

All these shenanigans at the political level by the British, Japanese and Malaysian governments, goes to prove that in wartime or anytime, the poor are the ones who get kicked and dribbled round the field by both sides. The ruling class shakes hands with the erstwhile enemy and makes deals. This has been the trajectory of history, the trajedy of politics, and the travails of the poor – what a travesty of the human condition!

Discoveries: Singapore, Penang

Things are gradually turning. What the colonist took is slowly being returned. Archeological artifacts in foreign museums are asked to be returned. The British crown is yet to return its crown jewel, to its one time political crown jewel, India. But history books are still not fully revised to reflect the truth of world histories.

They still hold to a Eurocentric view of world discoveries. Even non-European history textbooks mention that America was discovered by Columbus, Australia by Cook, New Zealand by Tasman, and that Magellan discovered the Phillipines, and so on. Yet, there is a double standard regarding other regions. They don't say that Vasco da Gama discovered India or Marco Polo discovered China. Probably because they already had age old civilizations there? Going by that, Aeons before, and at the time of Columbus, the great empires of the Incas, Mayas and Aztecs were in full throttle weren't they?. They qualify China and India by, "First European to reach" those places. Or, "founding". Francis (Light) and Stamford (Raffles) did found Penang and Singapore as we know them, although they didn't discover them. In our history books, that distinction belongs to Sang Nila Utama of Malayur (Jambi), who renamed the island of Temasik as Singapura. Temasik too, was most likely, already inhabited then.

European astronomy may have speeded up our discovery of the stars and outer space. But their knowledge was initially borrowed from the Indians and Chinese by way of the Arabs. Indian *sutras* and Chinese analects have recorded celestial happenings like total eclipses that coincided with earthly happenings; rare configurations and conjunctions in the constellations that caused much consternation here in the third rock from the sun.

Why is America still discovered by Columbus, or Vespucci, or Erikson, when there were flourishing civilizations already there, who welcomed them? We are reminded of the story of the Arab and his camel. On a cold night, the camel gradually gets into the tent and kicks its owner out. Couldn't our own explorers mentioned in the preceding chapter on Global Travellers (Rajendra, Cheng He, Enrique) be accorded the same distinction as discoverors? In fact Malay mariners did settle the island of Madagascar that long ago. And the Maori and other Polynesians, and the Australian aborigines.

If we buy the out of Africa theory, it's the African who was the first!

Door Décor: Red Lantern, Mango Leaves, and Khat

The first time visitor to Malaysia, whether he gets off main street and into the residential areas or not, will not be at a loss finding his way around. You see, as in almost everything else, Malaysians tend to festoon their homes in ways that advertise their ethnicity.

If the visitor wishes to locate a Malaysian Chinese pen-pal (or, facebook pal), all he has to do is to look out for houses with awnings (anjung) that have a couple of bright red, beach ball shaped lanterns hanging from the ceiling. However, red colour identifies only the Taoist resident. Red, as anybody who has been to Chinatown, www, (whole wide world), is the colour of wealth and prosperity. Chinese New Year is always awash in a sea of them beachballs, with every home, business, temple, and community association getting into the fray.

There are other Chinese homes, that sport yellow, pineapple shaped hanging ornaments, with green crown and leafy base. These are more likely, your Chinese Buddhist friends, as saffron is the identifying colour of Buddhism. However, the pineapple is not specifically a Buddhist item. I have seen the red altars of Taoist homes, that have 5 or 6 green pineapples as offering for the resident deity.

Walking along, our foreign friend will notice a bunting of green mango leaves (*maavilai thoranam*) strung out across the top of the main doorway of Hindu homes. Each leaf is streaked with three horizontal turmeric stripes across the centre (≡). The centre of the middle line will have a red curcuma dot or *Kunkuma pottu.* These days, they are made of plastic for long lasting "freshness." Aiyyo – Aiyohh! (Oh Woe!)

The mango leaf markings are actually the *Pattai* or caste mark of Sivaa. In India, the above mentioned horizontal markings of white holy ash (*thiruneer*) identify the Saivite, a devotee of Shiva. The Hindu of the Vaishnavite persuasion (Vishnu devotee) advertises his loyalty on his forehead, with an elongated U and a red line in between the two prongs. That is called a *naamam*.The Malaysian Hindu generally opts for a much simpler smear of holy ash at Friday prayers. That is the Hindu home for you.

Interestingly, many Hindus also still nail a horse-shoe in the shape of a U at the cross beams of the doorway. Is it because of the similarity to the Vaishnavite *naamam*? This is difficult to say, because Europeans have long done this, for protection and luck. I had long wondered if the Hindus just wanted to mimic the Europeans. But if that were the case, why wouldn't the Eurasians do it? It is quite likely that horseshoe U resembles the vaishnavite trident Ш.

Chinese homes also display reflecting mirrors in the shape of an octagonal *pa qua*. The mirror is apparently to drive away evil spirits. The belief is, that the demon or devil, or dragon will be scared off by its own image, as it tries to enter the front door. Some Chinese keep aquariums at home for a similar purpose. The fish, with its unblinking eyes, is said to be the perfect watchman, not giving a wink of time for the devil to get inside.

Christians, especially the Catholic kind, will hang a crucifix on the front door or wall or on their necks. Oftentimes you will notice a cross fashioned out of a single blade from a coconut frond. Often it is a dried shriveled leftover from the last Easter celebration. Some Catholic homes still hang a framed picture of St. George slaying the dragon, St. Michael (archangel), or some patron saint. They are also prone to having an image of St.Christopher, the patron of travelers, on their car dashboards. The non-Catholic Christians are more likely to display a verse of scripture in their entrance-way. A popular one is the verse from the book of Joshua that reads, *"As for me and my household, we shall serve the Lord."*

The Muslim home will usually have a Koranic verse in Arabic script. I have never seen a Malay Muslim home sport the Islamic emblem of the crescent moon and star. That, apparently is reserved for mosques and suraus (Muslim chapels). The Indian Muslim, however, is uniquely identifiable by his display of a upturned crescent with the number 622 between the horns denoting the *Hijrah,* date of Muhammad's flight from Mecca and Islam's founding.

If you think the ethnic/cultural/religious showcasing is only outdoor signage, wait till you see the indoor exhibits. The unwary foreign visitor had better be prepared for an onslaught of bright red and be assailed by religious paraphernalia of the same shade.

Many Taoist Chinese homes have huge altars positioned in the main living room, where you will never miss it. The red painted altar is accentuated by red lights, red candles and more red lanterns, in an assault on the senses. Sometimes, a big shrine is erected in the front yard or outside. Or it might be a pre-fabricated shrinette replicating a Taoist temple, replete with rooftop dragons. Sometimes, along with the Chinese Taoist deity, you might find a Hindu idol co-habiting there. Often, cylindrical incinerators are built, for burnt offering of yellow napkin sized joss paper.

The Hindu home used to have a modest altar in the living room, usually a piece of plank on two brackets. On it rested a picture of the resident family deity (*Kula Deivam* in Tamil or *Ishta Devata* in Sanskrit), and worship objects like incence (*Saambrani*) burner, camphor (*Soodam*) and joss sticks (*Oothuvaththi*). All these items are burnt to produce fragrance. Aside from the main deity, you also frequently found pictures of Jesus, Buddha, and a mosque to signify Islam – very egalitarian and syncretic. Some even had a picture of Mahatma Gandhi in the mix!

Modern Hindus are going for elaborate wooden altars in special prayer rooms or in the living room. Some have opted to construct virtual temples in the front-yards, where they will do their daily worship to the chanting of mantras, and ringing of bells that evoke the ice-cream man of childhood. Why do they exile the god to the yard and not retain it in the house? Perhaps, it is due to a sense of unworthiness sharing your space with the deity?

The Hindu would shower the deity with white flowers, usually jasmine. White signifies purity of heart and soul. The flowers must not have come from a thorny bush. The flowers, *poo* in Tamil lend their name to worship or *pooja*. Hence the Malay word for idolize, *puja/memuja* or the word for praise, *puji/memuji*. By the by, the Malay word for flower is *bunga*. And the Tamil word for a flower garden is *Poonthottam*. A flower park is *poonga*. The word *poonga-vanam,* means a meadow of flowers.

15 years ago when I left these shores, I did not see these many sparkling new, grand Hindu temples. There were no private shrines in low cost terrace houses taking up half the compound. The tying of yellow/maroon

strings on the wrist was unheard of, although they did have the talisman (*thayitthu*) tied to their biceps. In the 60's and 70's, the social reformer and rationalist E.V.Ramasamy (Periyar) partially succeeded in stamping out superstitions in the guise of religion. He was not against bona fide religion. If alive today, he would probably be plucking out the hairs on his head or his Moses-like white beard.

It is as if the simple Hinduism of the forefathers has dissipated, and a wholesale importation of the convoluted brahminical forms of it is firmly entrenched. This probably illustrates the fact that when people perceive their culture or religion under attack (case in point, the spate of Hindu shrine demolitions in the early 2000s) they would swing hard to the right, in the direction of extreme conservatism. It's a kind of defense mechanism, or self preservation, if you will, that is found in all cultures.

There is an ancient Tamil saying which goes, "Don't inhabit a village that does not have a temple." Our Hindu friends have always lived by that precept, building temples in any estate or neighborhood they lived. They seem to have overlooked an important point in the axiom. It says temple (singular) in the village, not temples on every street or corner. That kind of thing does happen in Tamil Nadu, India, where there are streets named after each caste, and each street has its own caste-based temple. Religion in general, and temples in particular, ought to be reasons for the unity of believers, not their segregation. There is a grouping of temple buildings in the vicinity of the old Sivan temple in Sentul, Kuala Lumpur, that is a puzzle. There seems to be about five different temples to different deities, under five different managements, all within a stone's throw distance of each other. If that be the case, it would be an absurdity and an obscenity in itself. Religion as a divisive, rather than cohesive force.

About the practice of tying strings on the wrist, The Buddhists do it too. The Sikhs wear something that looks like an amulet, but is actually a braclet (*Kara*) signifying unbreakable attachment to God and to the Sikh brotherhood. This, along with the *Kes* (unshorn hair), *Kangha* (comb), *Kachh* (soldier's shorts), and *Kirpan* (sword), are their 5 K's (or *Kakkar*). Except for the the first 3, you wonder how they have them all on their selves at all times. The sword and shorts are said to represent battle readiness anyway.

Cultural identifiers: Kris, Kolam, hóng dēng long

Every group has its mark or symbol to identify itself. In terms of the religions, there different colours. Green is the colour of Islam. Apparently the prophet liked it because it is a welcome change from the sandy hue of the surrounding desert. The colour of Taoism is bright red, representing prosperity and vibrancy. The Hindu colour is sandalwood paste, while the Buddhists opt for saffron or bright yellow.What is the Christian hue? Likely sea blue, representing sky and water (heaven, baptism).

The symbols are also descriptive. Islam has its crescent moon and star. The Hindus identify with the *Aum* symbol, ॐ or ௐ. The Buddhist has the chakra wheel ☸. The Taoist Yin Yang. The christian has the cross, though others prefer the fish ΙΧΘΥΣ. Ichthus, being a Greek acronym for Iesous Christos, Theou Uios, Soter (Jesus Christ, son of God, saviour).

When it comes to cultural symbols one may have to choose from many. When you think Malay, the image of the *Kris* crops up. It has become so integrated with the Malay notion, that a when a ultra-manic UMNO politician stabbed it in the air during a party convention, it sent a shockwave of jitters and shudders amongst the general public. It is located in the centre of *Sang Saka Bangsa,* the official flag of UMNO, the Malay nationalist party. The wavy form dagger is original to Java and takes its name from the Javanese *ngiris*, "to slice". It aslo occurs in cultures from Cambodia to India.

The Indian evokes the *Kolam*, a flower flavoured, rice flour floor painting with a flair for flourescing the vicinity. It is drawn in front of the house to brighten it up. In India, The Good Wife is expected get up early in the morning and do the kolam after a bath and prayer. At other times, the *kutthu vilakku* (oil lamp stand) that is lit on auspicious occasions, does the job. Made of rice flour, kolam is environment friendly, biodegrable and acts food for ants and bugs. Indian women also identify themselves with the *pottu*, or forehead mark. Hindu men occasionally smear ash on their forehead.

Red lanterns (h*óng dēng long*) adorn most Chinese homes, and are the instant indicators of the culture. Note the etymological affinity to the Malay, *tanglung*. What started as simple hot air balloon contraptions in the Eastern Han dynasty (25-220 CE), Buddhist monks popularized it in the worship of Buddha. Of the flying, floating (on water), and hanging lanterns, the latter are the most common in Malaysia.

"Each of the various types of Chinese lanterns comes with its own set of meanings, but generally speaking, all of the lanterns signify a wish for a better and brighter future".

The Chinese is known by the dragon, the Indian the cow, the Malay..? Camel, perhaps? China, India, and Malaysia are symbolized by the Great Wall, Taj Mahal, and the Twin Towers. The respective cultures are recognizable by the Bagua, Aum, and Crescent Star. The bagua is a hexagon (aka 8 trigrams) that permutates to 64 qualities of nature. It is used in Taoism for feng shui purposes. In the centre of a nest of (8x8) trigram "figures" lies the *taijitu* (yin-yang symbol). The Hindu symbol is the Aum or Ohm – supposedly the first sound heard at creation and thus divine. Muslims are recognized by the crescent and star symbol, even if it was popularized during the Turkish Ottoman Caliphate of the late medieval period, a thousand years after the dawn of Islam.

Kitchen: Lesong, Ammi Kal, Caido

It doesn't apply so much today, but time was, when each ethnic kitchen had a distinctive equipment. All that has mostly disappeared with the appearance of the the almighty food processor and blender.The

Malay home was never without the *batu lesong*, a *mortar* and *pestle* made from granite. It was the all purpose machine to grind spices and herbs, as well your favourite sambal belacan. The almost bell like metallic sound of granite against granite is an indication that mom is up to something, and sends off dinner bell signals to your stomach.

The Tamil home was never without any of these items. Now, they are mosly museum pieces, or garden ornaments. The *Ammi kal* is a regular 1 foot by 1 ½ foot, 8 inch high granite grinding stone. It comes with a 4 inch diameter tubular granite roller which is the moving, grinding part. The *Aattu kal* another 2-piece granite wet grinder for thosai dough, similar to a large mortar and pestle. *Ural/ulakkai* another combo that is similar to the wooden lesong, for dry pulverizing rice or other grains. Different from the other two, this one is operated standing upright and pounding with the ulakkai, alternating arm action. Great shoulder workout! Battle ropes be damned.

Although butchers everywhere have used heavy meat cleavers for their business, every Chinese home had a cleaver. Chinese cleavers are a few kinds. The heavier bone breakers are called *gudao*, and the lighter *caido*, are used for chopping, slicing, mincing and dicing. Even today, homes and restaurants use these broad and square knives – a real multipurpose tool-in-one indeed.

A manual coconut scraper found in Indian and Malay homes has also completely absconded a long time ago. Alas, or At last! Depending on how you see it, these changes in the kitchen environ are strongly felt, one way or the other. Going for the old utensils is the workout, unlike the push button sluggard's appliance. You got the 2-in-1 benefit of food milled and body drilled to perfection. Opposing the motion, you get convenience, efficiency, lack of sweat.

Language in Malaysia can be of three types: Vernacular (Chinese, Tamil, Iban, Kadazan etc); National (Bahasa Malaysia); and international (English). While each has its own unique characteristics and qualities, I see two basic types – English and Malay as one category, and Tamil and Chinese as another.

English and Malay originated on islands. They both were influenced by outsider languages. Just as England was physically conquered by the Romans (Italy) and the Normans (France), so was the Malay zone physically come upon by the Portuguese, Dutch and British. And prior to that, English was culturally influenced by Greek. So was Malay priorly influenced by Tamil, Sanskrit, Chinese, and Arabic. In this sense, English and Malay can be said to be well sought out and well behaved children raised by a village. They were good students, and learnt fast from their elders. In fact English and Malay have most of their vocabulary borrowed. English has most legal and religious terms from Latin, scientific terms from Greek, and cultural terms from French. So too, does Malay have religious terms from Arabic, legal/political terms from Sanskrit, and trade/day-to-day terms from Tamil and Chinese.

Chinese and Tamil on the other hand, are their own category, not raised by a village, nor even a family. As with Adam, they claim no mother. As my grandmother wisely said, "If you feed and raise another's child, your own will grow up by itself." Sanskrit, Latin and Greek can be included with Tamil and Chinese. All of the latter category are teachers to the former, as they have longer histories and older literatures and thus all are, unsurprisingly, considered classical languages.

Here we begin our examination of the uniqueness, quirkiness, queerness as well the connectedness of our languages.

Manglish: Of Ahs, Os, Lahs, and Nahs

Manglish (Malaysian English) or its Singapore equivalent Singlish (alaa, same thing lah!), is the colloquial pidgin, patois, brogue, or barstardized, creolized English that is unintelligible to the English ear. It is not a dialect, like London's Cockney, because the difference is not only in the accent but in the vocabulary and grammar. Manglish is the preferred mode of speech for Malaysians to convey the ideas, intimations, idioms, and idiosyncrasies of their indigenous experience.

Shakespeare would squirm in his sarcophagus and his Royal Highness Charles III would choke on his Earl Grey, were they told it was English. But to the native speaker, it is the most natural thing. It is akin to a comfort zone, where you can hang out humourously, hilariously and unabashedly with your pals or gals, without having to answer to the grammar-schoolmarm. Besides freedom of expression, it affords a wider vehicle to carry local jokes and nuances of meaning.

Pidgin English (not to be confused with Pin-Yin, Mandarin written with Roman alphabets), has long been spoken in British Malaya. It does not derive from "pigeon" or "prison" although it could be spoken there. The word is apparently a sinofied form of "Business" English. Business → piginess → piginis → pidgin. Some countrified Americans have a way of saying "bidness" for business. Pidgin was indeed, the hodge-podge English that the Chinese retailers used when doing business with the British wholesalers of colonial times.

Another old nomenclature for this is "Broken English." – (brogue English?) Could there be another explanation of Manglish, namely, "Mangled English", properly mauled, masticated and spat out in rapid rat-tat-tattle? English, not as she is spoken, but as she is broken. It can't refer to "Mandarin English" because most of the words and syntax are obviously of the Hokkien dialect. It certainly cannot denote "Mangala English", "mangalam" being Tamil for "auspicious". Far from the elegant English of the British gentry, mongrel Manglish is the domain of the Malaysian middle and lower classes.

Manglish appeals to the speaker who wants a parsimony of sounds and grammar. Afterall, isn't poetry that way too – to express the most (complex thought) with the least (words)? Mrs. Reginald Sanderson, writing in the twentieth century, says Hokkiens are known for their curtness of speech. "*Hokkiens, though living in China in Amoy, six hours by sea from Foochow, have very few similar words in their dialect. Take, for instance, the word "our." Men from Foochow say, "nguai-gauk-neng," while a Hokkien enunciates clearly, 'goa' – that is all."* Interestingly, Malays of old used "gua" instead of "saya" or "aku" ("I") when speaking to Chinese.

The native speaker of Manglish will take great pride in being a connoisseur of it and even employ it as code language to befuddle the unsuspecting non-speaker. In fact, the debauchery is taken to great lengths in Singapore, where its alter ego, Singlish is celebrated on the net and word lists are published and distributed to tourists, to enable them to get around the local scene. Whole mega drama series are produced in Singlish to large swooning audiences. To the uninitiated, Singlish could be Singhalese (one of the languages of Sri Lanka) for all they know, or jibberish from the land of Jumaanji. To the linguistic purist or puristic linguist, Manglish/Singlish is a stain that just won't go away.

You would think that such creolization of languages happens everywhere. While there is no chance of a pidgin patois forming in mainland China due to a shortage of English speakers there, India with its large English speaking population has "Inglish." It has no currency among Malaysian Indians, who use adaptations of Manglish. Inglish varies from region to region in India. Mixed with Hindi, it becomes Hinglish, with Tamil, it is Tamlish or Tanglish, and so on.

[One noted feature of Singlish is the use of words like *ah*, *lah*, or *wah* at the end of a sentence to indicate a question or get a listener to agree with you. They're each pronounced with tone — the linguistic feature that gives spoken Chinese its musical quality — adding a specific pitch to words to alter their meaning. (If you say "mǎi" with falling and rising tone, you want to "buy"; "mài" with a descending tone it means to "sell"; "mái", with an ascending tone means you want to "bury"! According to linguists, such words may introduce tone into other Asian-English hybrids.]

Not only is Manglish distinguished by its sound and syntax, it is also loaded to the hilt with mostly Hokkien contractions, in addition to some Malay. Some examples:-

"Eh, eek ordi ahr?" — "Have you eaten yet?"

"Nor Check" — "Not Yet"

"Nor chek ahr? Aaaiyyaa, cannot like that one O." — "Not Yet? Sheesh, That's not good!"

"Nemine, I buy something for you Lo." — "Never mind, Let me buy you something"

In the above conversation, "already" becomes "ordi", "never mind", transforms to "Nemine." Notice that the suffixes "ahr", "lo" and "o". They are Hokkien derived and serve as emphases to what went before. Perhaps there is a connection here, to the American "Huh" or, "OK?" The "o" is likely a shrinked up "lo", which in turn is a version of the Malay, "Lah".

"Today school, lousy time ahr? – "Tough day at school, huh?"

The "a" ending is also common to the native Tamil speech and consequently carries into Manglish conversation. The "aa" is joined to the last word, not stand alone, as with the Hokkien "ah", and denotes a question, just like the Hokkien version.

e.g:

"Ey, You heard the newsaa?" — "Have you heard the news?"

"No lah. Why, anything importannaa?" — "No. Anything important?"

Another suffix possibly supplied by Tamil is "What?"

"You Donnowaa? Big commotion in town what?" — "Didn't you know? There was huge commotion in town."

"Yessaa?" — "Is that so?"

The "aa" ending in Tamil is the colloquial constriction of the classical form, "...iyaa?" "...aayaa?", meaning, "have you .... ?" It is added to the end of verbs to denote the question "have you ....?" The classical Tamil "Saapittaayaa?" (Have you eaten?) shrinks to colloquial, "saaptiyaa?"

An aberration occurs with the English word, "One". In the following example, the word has two meanings.

"Oh, that one ah? Very kedekut (stingy) one O."

The first "one" is simple enough, referring to a person or thing under discussion. The second "one" is more challenging, perhaps serving as an emphasis like, "(stingy) indeed.".

The Tamil Manglish uses "one" as an article, instead of the usual "a", "an", or "the". "*One day, I saw one eagle sitting on one branch.*" The Tamil equivalent of "a" or "an" in Tamil is "ohr", short for "oru" = one. Similarly in Malay, *satu* (one) becomes *se* (a). The Tamil tendency to use "one" may be due to direct translation with Tamil syntax. "*Once upon a time, there was a King.*", in Tamil is translated thus: "*Orey oru ooriley, orey oru raja irunthaar.*", meaning, "In one and only one city, there was one and only one king." An Indian overheard speaking Manglish in a government clinic: "*Come out only, one Indian feller slammed the door*" – "As soon as he came out, an Indian guy slammed the door behind him."

Strangely, the Malay suffix "Kah?","Ke?", that is affixed to the last word in a question, does not figure in Manglish. So a phrase like,

"*You see Harry Potter 4 orredi kah?*" sounds rather jangling, to the mad Manglishman.

"Got" is from the Malay word "ada". "Got Milk?" – "Ada Susu?" It finds frequent use in Manglish.

"You got one dollar change ah?" – "Do you have change for a dollar?"

"Dohn have lah!" – "Sorry, I don't have any."

"*Nah! Take some more lah. Don't be shy ah?*" – "Here, do take some more. Don't be coy now, OK?"

The Malay verson of "ok?" is "ya?". *Nah!* – "here!" – is Malay.

A by product of the ascendance of Mandarin as lingua franca among Malaysian Chinese is the suffix, "Mah". It functions the same as "Lah", to lend emphasis to a statement, albeit in a softer tone. "Make sure you take this route. It is faster, mah!" It is also used as question in Mandarin proper. *Ni hao Ma?* – You fine or not? Ma – "or not" requires a Yes or No, hence not a open question.

The Tamil, "Dah" is also an emphatic ending. *"Po dah!"* means, "Bugger off!", "Get lost!" or, "Get outta here!" depending on the tone employed. There is a colloquial Malay version, *"Peegi dah!"*, which means the same thing.

Another Malay or Chinese derived suffix is the "O!" It denotes a sense of respectful admiration, or appreciation.

"I see Nicole David yesterday. Man, Very cchhoon O!" – "I watched Nicole David's game yesterday. Boy, is she's sharp!"

A common English word that has been (mis) appropriated by Manglish is "only" or "onni", for emphasis.

"Just now onni I senn it" – "I only just sent it."

Notice that Manglish does not have a sense of the past tense – "send" or "senn" for "sent". Neither is there a present or past simple. *"My father drive me to school"*. "shop close"

Manglish, as she is spoken by the Chinese, generally lacks consonants like "t", "r", and "l" or tenses. "That" sounds like "there", "what" becomes *"wha."* "About it" morphs into, *"Abourit"* and, Fried Rice cooks down to, *"Fly Lice."* French Fries is "Flench Fly". "No problem" reduces to *"No poblem"*

"There one no poblem wha, dohn worry abourit. Ingineering never ask for Bahasa distinction."

"Not to worry, that shouldn't be a problem. A distinction in Bahasa Malaysia is not needed, for admission to the Engineering course."

The letter V assumes the W sound (upper teeth touch lower lips in V, Both lips form the "O" in W).

"Oo Yoh! So young onni, he all lady drive new Woh Woh to schoo Oh!"

"Great guns! he's already driving a new Volvo to school at such a young age!."

Chinese, being a tonal language, omits a lot of complex sounds, preferring the terse and clipped single consonant soundbites. "Th" becomes "T", ……… You ask for directions to an office, and, "Turd flor", comes the curt response, sounding like, "dirt floor." But if the Chinese palatte is parsimoniously unpretentious with the phonics, the Tamil tongue is audaciously ostentatious with it. Your ears will be assaulted by, "Tharrdu Flaarr", vowels and consonants growling. To be fair, today's young Malaysians all enunciate their English much better, even if they still trip over their tenses and skip over syllables.

"never", always means to "don't", "doesn't", "didn't". *"The air-con awhways (always) never work one o."*

"Sorry" has become an all round, all-purpose, all-in-all word. You will hear Malaysians use nothing but *sorry* for everything from a simple apology to profuse remorse.

"Excuse me!"	– "Sorry!"
"I beg your pardon?"	– "Sorry?"
"Uh Oh!, My bad!"	– "Sorry! Sorry!"
"A thousand apologies!"	– "So, so sorry!"
"My deepest condolences"	– "I am so sorry!"

What a sorry story.

"Action", denotes haughtiness or showing-off, probably echoing the on-stage action of thespians, or catwalk models. "Action", as in acting the big shot, or pretending to be somebody else.

"Waah! nowadays you very action ah, bugger? Can't see you at all."

"Having airs lately, are you? You seem so scarce these days." This is a typically Indian style, though others are likely to use it too.

"Don't bluff me, ah?" = "Don't pull my legs, will you?" Nouns become verbs easily. "Friend" means to be friends with as in, *"I dohn friend you any more"*

Check out these words that are quirkily used.

"Put", also means "to place" or "set", "pour" besides storing something in a container. *"Ah Moi ah! Don't forget to put this back in the drawer. And*

*put the plates on the table, ah! And put the juice in the cups. Aaaiyaa!
Who put the flowers over there?"*

"Stay" always means to "live".

"Where do you live?" – *"Oh, I stay in Bandar Botanic, Klang".*

The Queen's English, we know, differentiates between long term accommodation (live) and short term (stay).

If you thought spoken Manglish is mind-boggling, check out the written version. I found this on a toilet door in the Fitness First gym at Aeon Bukit Tinggi, Klang. Smartly typeset, in a smart frame, you read it and almost pass it over.

Dear Our Value Customers,

*Please insist for a receipt for payment of all fees
Thank You*

Fitness First, Aeon Bukit Tinggi

I see at least 4 mistakes. It looks like a grammatically true direct translation from a Chinese original.

Malaysian Chinese travelling to China have been confounded by their inability to make the Peoples' Republic people understand their Mandarin. Perhaps, it has to do with intonations and stress. Mandarin with a Cantonese or Hokkien (twang?) Would surely be confusing.

Tamils who tavel to Tamilnadu have been surprised to notice, and to be told by the Indians themselves, about their superior command of the language, especially the purity of words. The Indian Indians, be it Tamils, or Hindi speakers are notorious for their uninhibited use of English words and terms in their local languages. Malay youth went through a similar phase in the 70's, injecting English into their casual interjections. like "I", "you" in the daily conversations. It was a kind of fad, with the celebrities of music and stage. "I jumpa you nanti, OK? Boyfriend I tunggu I kat Odeon."

Finally, to put Manglish into context, to understand the source of its syntax, and to trace its grammatical pretext, here is a simultaneous translation of a simple English sentence. I asked form 1 students to translate this into their own languages. From the mouth of babes, parse this.

English:	What time did the film begin?	
Malay:	At time what began film that?	— *"Pada Pukul berapa bermulanya filem itu?"*
	Or, Film that began at time what ?	— *"Filem itu bermula pada pukul berapa?*
Mandarin:	Movie at what time begin?	— *"diàn yǐng shì shén me shí hòu kāi shǐ de?"*
Tamil:	That film at what time began?	— *"Antha padam eppo aarambithathu?"*

Herein lies the genealogy, etymology, physiology, confoundology of our unofficial national language (!) of Manglish. When locals speak a foreign language colloquially, a pidgin is born. Dialects are born in the same way, when local ingredients and environments shape a regional style. Some savour the new flavour, while others figure it's such a bother. However well you speak the Queen's English, when you lose your composure, or need comfort, you <u>will</u> revert to Manglish. Research bears out the fact that when you are vulnerable, the mother tongue is what comes to your lips (!). When I stub my toe I don't cry, "Mother!" I yelp, *"Ammaaa!"* (Tamil), or *"Aduh Maak!"* (Malay), or "ma maa!" (Mandarin).

One common Sinicism in Manglish, is the absence of tenses. For instance the notice, "Bank is closed on Mondays" – (*Present Perfect*) renders, "Monday bank close." "Opens at 7.00 AM" – (*Present Simple*), is "7.00 AM open. Manglish is no help when trying to make sense of the tense and the linguist is likely to get a sensation of tenseness at the back of his neck.

If **HRH Q E 2** can condone confounding Cockney in her royal capital (London), couldn't we maintain our Manglish?

English: Inglipees, yīng yǔ, Inggeris

How she shifts accents

Just as a language (In this case English) will change syntax without pretext to change the context, depending on the speaker, the accent and intonation could also change its subtext.

While the Malay form for "English" is Ingerris, and the Chinese, Ying Yu, the correct Tamil form is *Aangilam. Inglipees* is a colloquial way of saying it. The Tamil tongue, while able to handle all sounds and syllables, has a problem overeaching it. While overemphasing the sound, it changes the sound itself. As with all Malaysian speakers of English, this is a problem of the older folks. Like the (in) famous Tamil head swivel, this has generally dissappeared. In the soundbox of the non English speaking Tamil person, the letter "A" is heard as "Yay", and "Yem", "Yen" and "Yex" etc, for, you guessed it. I faintly remember my father, a Tamil school teacher, coaching English to a 3 year old me:

"what is your name?"	— *"Vutt-eese yoovar name?"*
"Say, 'My name is Pannirselvam. I am a boy'."	— *"Say, 'mye name is Pannirselvam. Aie yum yay bhaai."*

Even in these times, where misplaced stresses on words is long gone, young Indians are still prone to mispronounce certain words. The Tamil spoken in Tamilnadu has been overrun by English words. Yet the speaker often trips over the prononciation. For instance, the word propeller, comes out sounding as fropeller, and fan becomes pan. A swap of F and P. This is not unlike the East Asian tongue trip over L and R, as we shall soon see. Trouser comes off as Douzer.

@Louis Rhys: *"In his excellent book* Japanese in Action, *at the end of the 'Fractured English' chapter, Jack Seward writes that when Douglas MacArthur was being promoted as a presidential candidate, 'his Japanese well-wishers arranged for a mammoth banner to be displayed in downtown Tokyo... [which] read: 'We Play for MacArthur's Erection.'"*

Robusto Jan 20 '11 at 2.30 pm

"As I understand, in at least some major dialects of Chinese (maybe all, I don't know), the/L/and/R/sounds exist but are prosodically restricted. The/l/can only appear syllable-initially while the/r/appears syllable-finally. This means that a Chinese speaker would have more trouble with an/l/sound at the end of a word and also with an/r/sound at the beginning of a word. This means that a speaker should be able to pronounce the/l/in "ladder" but have difficulty with "red". This agrees with Jon Purdy's examples of yimier for "email" and luōqièsītè for 'Rochester'."

"Korean has the opposite going on; that is, their/l/and/r/are in allophonic variation such that/r/shows up syllable-initially and/l/syllable-finally, meaning they would have more trouble saying the/l/-sound in "ladder" than in "feel"

I believe the reason is that, in Japanese at least, there is no Western L sound, therefore a native Japanese person won't learn to pronounce it (at least the Western way) at an early age."

Perhaps because this word features several difficult sounds – the "L"/l/ sound, which is sometimes pronounced by Chinese-speakers to sound more like an "R," (usuarry) the voiced fricative/ʒ/sound represented by the "s" in this word, and the various vowel sounds in the word."

Ed: the Malaysia king of fruits is *Liulian* in Mandarin, which is equal to the western *Due-riyan*.

Neither the Malay language nor Malay speakers have much of a problem with English phonetics. Their problem, rather, is with the placement of emphasis. The case of former DPM Ahmad Zahid Hamidi's address at the UNGA is a textbook example, which became an infamous in-depth internet interlocution. Emphasis of words mirrors the speaker's native language. Even speakers of the same language can fall into the problem. An Englishman says "PHO-to-grapher", while an American says "Pho – TORE – grapher". The stress or accent is on the capitalized letters. And then there are other sonic differences. The British drink "WOHter". The Americans drink "WAHder". The Indian is likely to say "Waaaterrr". They both misunderstand each other. So, its up to your imagination if Ahmad Zahid made his point to the UN audience, although Malaysians would have easily got it. I thought it was quite well enunciated and executed, except for a bit of what seemed like nerves, some tripping over consonants, and an overdependence on the teleprompter. Some of Zahid's typical "Malay traits" in his speech were, "sustain_ble dev_lopment", the missing vowels.

Exclamations: Aiyyoh! Aaaiiyaa! Adohai!

Three different expressions in three different languages, Tamil, Chinese, and Malay respectively, and they all sound alike. They mean, "Oh Woe!", "Oh Crud!", and, "Oh Boy!" in that order.

All three are non-words (not found in any dictionary. They are not neologisms, but silly guttural utterances but have been around a long time in common usage. They are sounds that mean something and nothing at the same time, being very much a part of our language and yet not accepted as valid words. English too, is not short of these either. Consider, ughh, ohhh, ouch, oops, yikes, yowzer, yahoooo, yoo-hoo, woo-hoo, yippee-yay, yeee-haaa.

Aiyyoh! Is expressly Tamil and is commonly used in laments, as when hearing bad news like a death, or loss of property. The emphasis is on the "Y" but a long drawn out "o" as in *"aiyyo-o-o-ohh"* is often used by mother's freaked out by children messing up a newly a cleaned space or doing some other mischief. "Some young Indian females often reduce it to, "Yo-o-o-o-oh!", to communicate irritation with something or somebody. *"Ayyoh!"* said in a short undertone, conveys the sense of "Uh-Oh!" or "Ooops"!

"Aiyyoh" appears to be a corruption or dimunitive of the classical Tamil form, *"Aie – ya – hoe!"*. I remember watching those black-and-white Tamil historical movies, in which the king expresses his dismay in such fashion." The commoner parts always did the *"aiyyoh!"* *"Aie-ya-hoe!"* sounds very much like the battle cry, *"Ivanhoe!"* in the late 50's TV series of the same name and portrayed by no less than Sir Roger Moore. Remember James Bond, The Saint, The Mavericks?

There is a similar sounding word of Chinese etymology, *"aai-yo!"* which is equivalent to, "oh my!" in American English usage, or the Cockney, "blyme!", to connote mild frustration. A variation is, *Ai Yerr!,* which said with aversion – meaning, "yukk!".The Malay/Indonesian *"Ayuh",* though phonetically similar is lexically different (a heteronym), meaning "let's go" or "come on!" A variation of the *"aai-yohh!"* which expresses awe rather frustration, is *"fuu-yohh!" or "Ooo-yohh!"* On a KTM commute, two little Malay boys were observed "ooh"ing and "aah"ing their excitement with "ooo-yohh"s. They were tickled by something that caught their fancy outside the moving train. Primary school age boys might say, *"fuu – la mak!"* in a variation of *"alamak!"*

"Aaai-ya!", or"ai̲i-yaaah" is manifestly Chinese and is someone showing major impatience at something or someone. It may be akin to the

American "crud!" or "damn!" Indians are more likely employ this word (sound, neologism etc.) as *"hai-yaah!"*, like a Kung Fu fighting movie hero. A website claims that *"Aiyo"* in Mandarin is actually an expression of pain, while *"aiya"* is Cantonese for indicating displeasure, disappointment, or exasperation.

"Aiya!, we didn't qualify for the World Cup again"

"Eeyaaah!" is the Kung Fu war cry, which has its echo in the cowboy whoop, *"Yeeehaaah!"*. The Tamil counterpart – "H<u>ai</u> <u>Ya</u>hh!". The emphasis is on the underlined portion. It is usually voiced by children under six years of age and conveys the sense of "wow!" as when opening a present. It could also mean, "Eureka!", as when discovering a lost memento.

The <u>Urban Dictionary</u> has only this entry under "Aiyyo." It explains that it "expresses something or nothing, often used by Eminem", the singer.

"Aiyyo, turn the beat up a little bit."

"Aiyoh" and *"Aiyah"* are now in the English language, thanks to Oxford English Dictionary (OED). The dictionary attributes aiyoh as originating from Mandarin and aiyah as coming from Cantonese. Still, they don't carry meaning, only express feeings.

Desi Arnaz, who loved Lucy, used to famously utter *"Ah-yai-yai-yai-yai-yai-yai-yai!"* in Spanish, which roughly translates as, *"Boy-o-boy, boy-oh-boy-oh-boy-oh boy!"* He was saying without saying, that Lucille Ball, his onscreen and real life wife was "loco de cabeza" – "crazy in the head".

The Malay cousin of the expressions under consideration is, *"adohai"*, or its variant, *"adoh!"*. The former expresses a big nervous sigh like, "Oh Boy!", while the later conveys mild pain such as, "Ouch!" Another version is, *alahai !*, which is a big sigh of resignation.To connote surprise or sudden realization, the Malay may use, *aikk !*, which looks like,"what the..!", "woops!"

"Alamak!", is another sound bite in similar vein, that is close in meaning to, "Oh my God!" It may be accompanied by the tapping of the palm to the forehead. It has nothing to do with Allah or Mak (mother). Or does it? However, *"Allah!"* or *"Maasha Allah!"*, is a common expressive utterance of Muslims (and Arab Christians). The latter, is a word of wonderment and appreciation of some positive event such as a birth, meaning "God has

willed it!" Alamak may often reduce to *Alaa* or *Alahaai !*. The adolescent Malay male is likely to gush, "Hoo – lamak!" to convey the sense of, "woo – ho-o-o!" or "woww!" *Astaghfirullah al-azi-i-i-m* is actually etymological and has meaning.

'Astaghfirullah al Azim' (Arabic for "I seek forgiveness from Allah the Almighty". "What have I done! Astaghfirullah!" Or, it might be used in conjunction with expressing dissappoinment at someone.

To say *Aloha!* would be entirely different in meaning and language of origin because that, rather than a moan or groan, is a joyful sound of Hawaiian welcome. A similar sounding word, to *"alaa",* used in disputing another's statement or claim, is to begin with, *"ehllehh!"* It may mean something like, "rots!" or the modern, "you wish!" When expressing admiration of someone's tall story or smooth move, you may respond with, *"Che-ehh!"* or *"Che Waah!"*

"In trying to figure out the origins of *Alamak*, many have laid claim to it, including the Babas, and the Portuguese. One Malay blogger postulates in his web posting, that *Alamak* may actually be of Sanskrit etymology. He points out the historical fact that the Malay language has been influenced by Sanskrit since it first attained viable literary wings. *Alamak*, parsed into its parts, yields *Ala* (Skt: *Allaa* = God) and *Mak* (Skt: Maatr = Mother). The resulting, *"God! Mother!"* is a likely equivalent to *Alamak. Alahai!"*

Sathia

July 5th, 2008 at 9: 11 pm

Back in the early 80's, there was a popular tune that started with *"Aloimak, Kuliwak, kuliwak, kuliwak. Aloimak kuliwak."* It went on for several repetitions throughout the song. Not to worry about its similarity to *"Alamak!"* Even as a reasonably young'un then, I knew it was not Malay, but some sort of African Lingo. Anyway, there is a variation of that utterance, *Ailamak!* We can parse it thus, *Hai la mak* – Oh, mother!

Another religious utterance that Hindus make, is *"Haro-o Hara!"* Hara being another name for Shiva. Vishnu, the preserving one gets, *"Govindaa!".* Even though both phrases are exclamations of devotion, they also have negative meanings in certain circumstances. *"Haro Hara!", and "Govinda,*

Go-o-vinda-a!" sometimes mean a desperate, "gone! Its all gone!" in colloquial speech.

Ecstatics: Halleluyah!, Alhamdulillah! Arohara! zàn měi shàng dì!

Everyone gets ecstatic once in a while. The believer over the almighty. The naturalist over the vista. The gambler over the struck pot. The above list, meaning respectively,: Praise Jehovah!, Allah be praised!, Oh Lord Shiva!, Praise God!

"Hallelujah, is a frequent and autonomic utterance by Christians when in deep devotion to the divine. In the Hebrew Bible hallelujah is actually a two-word phrase. The first part, *hallelu*, is the second-person imperative masculine plural form of the Hebrew verb *hillel*. However, "hallelujah" means more than simply "praise Jah" or "praise Yah", as the word hallel in Hebrew means a joyous praise in song, to boast in God (Yahweh/ Jehovah)."

In contemporary worship among many Protestants, expressions of "Hallelujah" and "Praise the Lord" are acceptable spontaneous expressions of joy, thanksgiving and praise towards God, requiring no specific prompting or call or direction from those leading times of praise and singing.

In modern English, "Hallelujah" is frequently spoken to express happiness that a thing hoped or waited for has happened. Hallelujah is also used together with Amen ("So be it"), or in liew of it.

Alhamdulillah (Arabic: ٱلْحَمْدُ لِلَّٰهِ, al-Ḥamdu lillāh) is an Arabic phrase meaning "praise be to God", sometimes translated as "thank God". This phrase is called Tahmid (Arabic: تَحْمِيد, lit. 'Praising') or Hamdalah (Arabic: حَمْدَلَة). It is also commonly used by Arab Christians, and other non-Muslim speakers of the Arabic language.

The phrase has three basic parts:

al-, the definite article, "the".

ḥamd(u), literally meaning "praise", "commendation".

li-llāh, preposition + noun Allāh.

'arOharA' is a shortened form of the phrase 'ara harO harA'.

"This was first used by Saivaites (followers of Saivam – worship of Shiva), at the time of Thirunjanasambandhar. During Thirunjanasambandhar's journeys, the bearers of his 'pallakku' (Palanquin) and followers had the habit of chanting (meaningless) phrases – like 'yElEloh yElEloh', as a form of stress relief. Thirunjanasambandhar taught them to replace these with the meaningful 'ara harO harA'. Over time, the use of 'ara harO harA' faded among the 'Saivaites' but lived on with the 'Kaumaras' (Murugan Devotees). It was further shortened to the present 'arOharA'."

The phrase is most heard at Kaavadi processions during Thaipusam. When one party says, 'vetrivEL Muruganukku' (*to Lord Muruga – the Bearer of the 'vetrivEl' (victorious spear)*), the other party responds with a, "arOharA" (*Praise the Lord!*)."

zàn měi shàng dì! (Praise God). Taoism or Daoism is a religion that originated in China in approximately the fourth century BCE. It is polytheistic with many deities and ritual practices. Hence, not having a personal relationship to God, but a ritualistic/mechanistic one, praises are non-existent in Taoism. The above phrase is more likely to come from the mouth of a Chinese Christian. Chinese Muslims would most likely use the Alhamdulillah. Chinese Buddhists don't have an idea of a personal God either. Buddhism doesn't have an almighty.

The closest Sikh utterance in praise of God, is the social greeting, "*Sat Sri Akal*", (God is the Truth). *Waheguru* (wondrous enlightener), is one of the titles of God.

Fascination: Waah!, Hoah! Adeyappa!

Fascination with anything is the realm of children, although adults sometimes do experience it. Everything is jaw-drop awe-some and wow worthy wonderments to them. As adults, the grown up kids still use the same terms for even lesser amazements.

The Malay "*Waah!*" is similar to "wo-ow!", appreciating someones's prowess, dress etc. If it is even more appreciable, it is reduplicated as, "*Waah – waah – waah!*" and is along same line as the Hindi/Urdu, "Wah Rey Wah!", "Wow!". *Amboi!* Is another wow-like response but more sarcastic like "my my!". *Amboi, sombongnya!* "My, my! What a stuck up!".

The oldens were often heard muttering under their breath, *oomh, oomh, ooomh!* – basically meaning, "oh boy, oh boy, oh boy!"

The Chinese whoop is, *"Hoa-a!"*, an exclamation of amazement. *Wāwā jiào – something like Wow Wow! Ha!* – Huh! gosh! – Tian Na!, *li hai* = "awesome", *wa sai* – "wow!",

A Tamil interjection (and there many) is, *Adeyappah!* (Oh Father!) = Oh wow!, or, *Yammaadi!* (Oh mother!) = "jeepers creepers!". *Adadah!* (Uh Oh!), when you realize you have forgotten your purse. *Adi Aaathi !* or *Aaathaadi!* (Oh, Grandmother!), can mean anything from *Huh!?* to *goodness gracious!*.

Wunderbar! Is German for, "wonderful!." It is present as, *Syabas!* in most languages. Likewise, *Eureka !* ("I found it !" or "got it!"), is used by everyone, but I find it difficult to find a likely local locution. Perhaps we should stick with it, as it is already in use and an easy sound bite.

Revulsions: Cchihh!, Chisss! Sueiyy!

Another group of sound bites as in the previous article, that are not in the dictionary but convey various nuances of meaning, are Cchihh! (Tamil), Chiss! (Malay) and Sueii! (Chinese). You wonder why these are not in your dictionary. Perhaps, as the expression goes, when words cannot express how you feel, you come up with non-words.

Ccheehh! or chihh! Is Tamil for "horrors!" or "yuk". Note that the double cc and double hh are for emphasis so that it sounds like the blast of an air break or a serious sneeze. It can sometimes take the form, *"Cchit –tey – ree !"* (eeeyewwww!), as when witnessing an insolently obscene scenario. Equal to the Malay, *"jijik!"*

Chee – cheeh! or, *Chich – che-e-h!* (nonsense!) Adamant denial of one's culpability. "Chich-cheeh! Why would I do that." Chee – chee – chee! (naughty naughty naughty!). Usually said in a drawn out montone, it expresses a mild disgust, as when an infant messes up on itself.

Chehh! Sounds like an explosive 'chair!' (damn!) expressing disappointment, like when you can't locate your glasses. *Cheh – chehh!* (not at all!) denial that someone may have committed a misdeed. Or denial that something may have happened. "Cheh-chehh!, I don't think it happened that way, or that he did it."

The Malay hiss would be, *Chisss*! (bite your tongue!) – something Hang Tuah might have said as he accosted an enemy of the Malaccan throne. When you want someone to shut up, you just catapult it out. A more modern and commoner version would be "chit!" conveying the sense of "nonsense!" Because of their similarities, chiss and ccheeh could be of the same source. The Tamil *chee – chee* (yuck!) can also manifest in Malay as "*Eee* !, *Jijik* !" (yucky!)

Sometimes, a mild frustration or surprise produces, "*Eeesh, eesh, eeeesh*!" (my, my, my!).

Chinese: "*Suieyy yer*!" – "shameful!" or, "damnation!" *pēi,* in Mandarin describes bah!", or "pooh!". ai yaa – "oh no!", zhen tao yan – "gross!".

English: Yield! Fie! Get outta here!

Terms of Endearment: Abang, Atthaan, Băobao

After marriage, Malays address their spouses as *Abang* (older brother) or *Adik* (little sister). Even if the wife is older than her husband, she calls him her abang and the young husband calls his older wife, his adik.This is an example of how language can surprise, rendering its uniqueness and cultural cuteness. The cuteness comes from the fact that it is illogical, as often happens in poetry. Brother marry a sister? We know for certain that this usage is not a case of incest. In context, it is a perfectly poetic endearment. The origin of this may reside in the deep recess of the past. I reckon that it probably goes back to Adam and Eve. Afterall, wasn't she flesh of his flesh and bone of his bone? He might probably have called her "hey, I'l sis" and she, "hai, bro".

The African-American male commonly calls his wife, or any young woman sister. But not the other way round. The women don't go around calling men brother, at least, to strangers. Men call other men bro, or brother. Women call other women sisters. Again, this has to do with language.

The Tamil wife might call her husband, *Atthaan,* also referring to elder sister's husband. The man simply calls her by name, or deer, peacock, uhhmm, you there etc. Take your pick. Many wives of the older generation get their husbands' attention with a *ungalatthaan*, which roughly means, "ya, you." The male version, which means the same, is *unnaithaan* ("yes you). That should be the response after she had first drawn his attention with a decent address and he turns his head and says, "did you call me?". In this case the later, "yes, you" has become the initial address. Some other wives say, *ennenga,* literally meaning, "what is it?" The context, of course, is it is an attention getting device, and very polite.: "Did you call?" It is an even more polite and formal form of address than, "Dear" or "Darling" as many of the modern wives are doing. But how are "yes, you" and "what is it?" more preferable than "Dear!?" Again, it is the peculiarity of the particular language, like the Malay abang/adik dichotomy. Others use Kanna (for men), Thangam (gold), Chellam (love) for women etc. The context of all these usages is due to the old custom where a wife is not supposed to refer to her husband by name. Nowadays, these are out the window and anything goes.

There is a class of Tamil, the Brahmin women, who address their husbands as *anna,* meaning, guess what?. Older brother! However, the etymology of it is very different. "Nna", suffixed to a verb conveys, our "lah". *Vaango* (Brahmin for "come") plus *nna* means, "come on", "come lah". *Yen,* means "why?. *Yennaa,* should be "why lah!", but conveys, "Dear".

Chinese: Some say that Chinese don't normally express endearments in words and that when it happens, it sounds like an insult. (*zhū zhū*) piggy, (*dà huàidàn*) big bad egg, (*xiǎo bèndàn*) little bad egg, (*xiǎo shǎguā*) little fool, (*xiǎo xīngān*) little darling, (*chòuxiǎozi*) stinky boy. Some are positively descriptive according to international standards – (*Wǒ de xiǎo jiaozi*) my little dumpling!, (*bǎobao*) baby.

Terms of Affection: Ah Moi, Ammoi, Sayang

Amoi is Malay for a Chinese lass. Malay and Indian men mention the Ah Moy when referring to the pretty little Chinese missie, usually with an undertone of romantic interest. You may, perhaps want to flatter an older Ms by calling referring to her as a Ah Moy. Considering that everbody loves the Amoi, could she be any relation to Amy, from the French for "beloved" ? Mon Ami (My friend). Ah Moy, is actually a very common Chinese female first name, of uncertain meaning.

Ammoi or Appoi, are for a young Tamil missie or master respectively. Ammu is a diminutive for Amma (mother). And Appu for Appa (Father).

Ammoi and Appoi are diminutives and a little extra effusive. Tamil parents are fond of addressing their children as Appa and Amma. Again, its one of those linguistic quirks, similar to a Malay husband calling his wife, adik (little sister). Some of my grandmothers used to greet me, *enna peththa raasa!* ("The king who gave birth to me").The birth order is reversed. Ammayee is Telugu for young woman.

Malay family members use sayang by default – among couples, parents to children etc, conveying, "dear".

Malaysians are likely to call the older Chinese person as *Ah Peh* (uncle), *Ah Soh* (Auntie). Indians, besides their formal addresses, also do other name calling. For example, *Perisu* ("the big one") enjoyed a brief currency directed toward the family elder. *Sirisu* ("the smaller one") refers to the younger elder/junior elder. Malays refer to their father's brothers as Pak Long (elder), Pak Ngah (middle), and Pak Su (youngest). Similarly, with mother's siblings.

When it comes to significant others the language (slang) has changed over time. Malay youth used to refer to their girlfriends as *mak we* or, *awek*. As for Tamil boys, *sarakku* ("cargo"), had a good run in the 80's. Currently, its *figaru* ("figure"). Go figure. A "suitable", Chinese hunk is *Leng zai* (beau/handsome). A "woo-able" girl is *làmèi*: hot chick; sexy girl (literally, "spicy little sister"

Grans: Nenek, Aayah, Nai Nai.

The common Malay appellation for grandma is *nenek*. Note the similarity to the Mandarin, *nai nai* (paternal grandma). *Opah,* is another way of saying grandmother. This is counter to the German/Dutch *Opa* for grandfather and *Oma* for grandmother, which leaves me wondering whence the Opah? Is she from here, or someplace else? Oppa, Gangnam Style? For a long time, I thought that it was from Indonesian by way of Dutch. No. No such usage there. The Japanese granny is *obaasan*. Could she be from there?

While you won't find the etymology (word genealogy) of opah, neither is nenek that straightforward. *Nana* (nanny) is common in America. In Italy, she is *nonna*. In the absence of a clear etymology, *nenek* could be from anywhere.

Very commonly, *Paati* is used indiscrimately in Tamil. Since *Amma*, *Aaatha*, and *Aachi* all convey "Mother", You will hear Tamils employ, *Ammachi* (Amma's Aachi), *Ammamma* (Amma's Amma), etc. The latter being very frequently used by Malayalis, or those with Malayali relatives. Paternal grandmas are also interesting: *Appattha* (Appa's Aattha), and, don't laugh, *Appachi* (Appa's Aachi). My wife refers to her maternal grandmother as Ammachi, but thinks I am pulling her legs when I say that my paternal grandmother was referred to as Appachi (Upper-Chee). Do I look like I belong to an American Indian tribe? Only a South Indian one. Though I used the standard, *Paati,* I have heard older folk ask me about the whereabouts of my *Appachi*. "Is your *appachi* at home?" *Aayah*, is another designation for grandmother in Tamil, commonly heard in rural Tamil Nadu. It is parsed this way. *Aai* is ancient Tamil for Mother. So what is mother's mother? Why *Aai Aai*, of course. Over time it has become *Aayah*. (significantly, *Uai* is a synonym for mother in Malay).

Somehow, grandad's don't have the luxury of many forms of address. If it is Nenek, Paatti, Nai Nai, then, their spouses are: Datuk, Thaattha, Ye Ye respectively. *Datuk*, Atuk, or *Tok*, in Bahasa, is a title freely conferred on grandfathers and senior men by the third generation. You don't have to be senior civil servant, businessman, or ruling party politician to earn it. *Thaattha*, is grandfather in Tamil and in many other Indian languages. *Paatan* (male form of *Paati*?), is used in the third person, for great grandfather. *Pootan or muppaattan,* is great – great-grandfather or an ancestor, also used in the third person. If there is an *Ammamma,* shouldn't there be Appappa? Never happens. In fact, as we have seen in the section on exclamations, *Appap-ppahh!* Stands for "boy-o-boy!".

The Chinese paternal grandma is Nai Nai as opposed to the maternal, Wai Po. The Hokkiens say *ah ma*, and the Cantonese say *popo* (maternal) and *maa maa* (paternal). You'd think it'd be the other way round. Mother's Maa not Maa Maa? Father's Po, not Po Po? Interestingly, Hokkien for mother is *ah bú/ah bó*. Similar to the Malay *ibu?* Aren't we all speaking the same language, or what? Except for the politicians, of course. Divisiveness and opposition is their bread and butter.

We address a non-relative senior as Uncle/Aunty, Pak Cik/Mak Cik, Ah Peh/ Ah Soh and, Ayyaah/Aachi, depending on the ethnicity of the addressee. Everyone is a relative of some sort in Asia.

Hypocorism: Matt, Mat, Mani, Mah

Hypocorisms are a daily usage, although the same cannot be said of the word itself. Dimunitives like the names above, are constrictions of proper personal names for convenience,, affection, or plain laziness. Also coming under the category of pet names, name calling usually starts when the owner is still toddling in his pampers. No wonder, hypocorism is the Greek for "to use child talk". The only occasions when the whole enchilada is employed, is during formal settings, or very informal parental reprimands. Sometime, the kid gets his full name, with honorific – "Mr. William Archibald Parker, stop that right now!!!" Compare that with the soft and loving, "Bill..y!" Same message. Same effect. Most European names lend themselves to hypocorize, Matt, for Mathew, Tom for Thomas, Tim, Timothy etc.

Malays tend to abbreviate well. Even the already short Ali becomes *Li* among close friends. Hanapi can be *Pi*, Rahim *Im*, Rokiah, *kiah or Ya* and so on. These bits are the last syllable of a name. Even Mat or Mamat, is the end syllable of Muhammad, a most popular first name that precedes the identifying name. Latif, is the identifier in Muhammad Latif, in answer to the question, "Which Muhammad"?

Modern Malay names are like ETS coaches on KTM's JB – Padang Besar route. Unlike the Indonesian tendency for single name (Suprobo, Widodo), or, even our own Musa Hitam, Badul Tompel, Malaysians tend to be ostentatious about it. Some do carry it to silly extremes. In October 2018, the longest recorded name for a Malaysian is *Princess Aura Nurr Ermily Amara Auliya Bidadari Nawal El-Zendra* – 78 letters, 2 letters short of the total allowed by the National registration Dept. Have a heart for the child, when it has to fill out a form. Mind you, that does not include the *patronymic,* the compulsory father's name after adding *"binti"*

Some have found it useful to have the trundling train truncated and transformed by coupling initials or acronym. *Zaaba* is a self-naming by Zainal Abidin bin Ahmad, a famous Malay literateur and Linguist of yesteryear. *Princess Aura* might not be so lucky – her acronym would be *Paneaabnwz.*

Indian dimunitives can be pieces taken from the whole, or a portion with a "u" attached at the end. *Mani* is a common one, plucked from Subramaniyam. The female *kala* is easy enough, from Chandrakala or Kalaivaani etc. *Subra*, *Chandra*, and *Vaani* is also extracted from the above. The addition of "u"at the end of a hypocorism endows a sense of endearment to it, such *Ramu* (Ramanathan), *Somu* (Somasundaram), *Meenu* (Meenakshi, *Paaru* (Parvathi).

Another way of hitting all the notes of a long name into a short burst is to combine little parts together. For instance, how to do justice to the lengthy (aren't they all?) Ramakrishnan? *Ramki*. Balakrishnan will be *Balki*, *Maali* (Mahalingam). Mindy Kaling, the American comedienne, shrank her father's name Chockalingam, by plucking out the middle. Nobody has yet tried to shrink a crazily long name like Sivaramakrishnan, Vinayagamoorhy or, Srishanmuganathan.

Though Chinese names don't need trimming as they already come in three neat, bite-sized pieces, I can see a hypocorism when only the first part (the clan name) is used. Or rather, The latter two should be the more informal. Ng May Ling – Ng, May or Ling ? How about Ng for the formalities, May for family and friends, and (dar) Ling for the significant other?

Hypocorism can occur with whole sentences too. Exempli gratia: – the word *goodbye*, or even *g'bye*, is a condensation of "God be with you". The Spanish version of it, *Via Con Dios,* "Go with God", is similar. Both are blessings for the journey.

Euphemisms: guī shāndào, Meninggal Dunia, Kaalamaanaar, Passed On,

A Euphemism is to a sensitive subject, what mango lassi is to chilli chicken, if that makes sense – a coolant. Matters of death are especially prone to euphemization (!). So you say, "kick the bucket" for "drop dead", "pass away"

In Chinese, *Sei* means "Die or dead." Hokkien, *Sei Kh'iau Kh'iau* means, "Dead trough and through", Presumably after turning over the body of your dead antagonist. Cantonese, "Hei Chaai Mai Ku" – "gone to pick mushrooms." It is similar to the English or German "to enter the eternal hunting grounds" An interesting one in Cantonese, 'He has gone to sell salted duck eggs' (他去賣鹹鴨蛋 *Hei Hwei Mai Haam Aap Daan*). Mandarin, *guī shāndào* – "to return to the mountain path." Cantonese, *pūk gāai*, literally means, "fall on the street"/"bankrupt", "drop dead", from whence Malay picks up *pokai* (bankrupt).

In Tamil, "he has dropped his head" – *Mandaiya pottaar* – died is crude. *Iyarkkkai eiythinaar* – "he's attained, or become, nature" (more subtle). *"Thavarittaar"* – "he's slipped" – is a common and sensitive way of announcing a death. *Marainthaar* – "Has faded", usually in writing. A more common way of putting it, is *"kalamaanaar"* – "He has become time", the import of it being, "He has become timeless". Time, afterall, is timeless, in and of itself. The very antagonistic, *"Poi Tholainthaan"*, means, "He's got lost/a goner." *Seththaan*, "he dieded". The last two as you guessed are reserved for enemies or a most hated person. There is a host of words for "death" – *irappu, maraivu, maranam, saavu, maaippu, Iraiyadi eiythal* and the Tamil Muslim, *mavutthu* (maut). For a more sombre and serious note, you say that the deceased has reached Lord Shiva's feet or *'Paramapadham adaithal'* ; has reached the abode of Vishnu or *'Pallipadi Yethinam'* or *'Iraiyadi Eithal'* – *reaching God's feet.*

In Malay, *Meninggal dunia* – "left the world", is most common. More religious, *pulang ke Rahmatullah – "returned to heaven".* Or, Returned to *Alam baqa* (afterlife). *Or* "maut". *Mangkat* is reserved for royal deaths. *Mati, mampus* (very unfriendly) – "gone to damnation".

Similarly, references to the dead (more politely, the deceased), are couched in fuzzy terms. The common English reference to a dearly departed, is as, "the Late So 'n So". Why are they late? Most religions refer to the death of a believer as winning a berth on the boat to heaven. Those who died outside the faith are considered to have missed the boat, so to say. So wouldn't it be more appropriate that, the dead in the faith are "on time" to keep their "appointed time" with their maker? That would make those who died faithless, in apostasy, or in sin, to be the truly "late" in meeting their destiny. With a thunderclap thud of finality, death closes the door for a change of heart. Too bad.Too late.

One certainly can't be late for one's own funeral. Obviously, you are the first one there, being the reason for the gathering of friends and family. Perhaps we are still adhering religiously to the British tongue-in-cheekism (euphemism) about Mr. Soh 'n Soh missing or absent from our latter day events and functions. When talking about the deceased, you don't want to say, "Mr.Soh 'n Soh who cannot be with us today". That would be too depressing. Why not lighten it up a touch with something like, "Mr. Soh 'n Soh, who is still on his way to join us." Or, even more poignantly, "The late, Mr.Soh 'n Soh." But again, that would only be applicable to later events, after the fact (of the funeral). Remember, he can't be late for his own funeral? Reminds you of Marilyn Monroe who was late for (the late) President John F. Kennedy's birthday party. As she rushed in to the party venue, she was announced (facetiously) as "the late Marilyn Monroe". As it turned out, 3 months later it was not funny at all. She literally became, "the late". It is perfectly alright to address the deceased as if they are stil living. Mr. Soh 'n Soh is still Mr. Soh 'n Soh. Not, "the Ex-, or the former Judge Soh 'n Soh", as you would speak of his professional status or office, after retirement.

A search for the origin and meaning of "late" as applied to the dead, yielded this:

"In the 13th century, the word bears the meaning: *"occurring in the latter part of a period of time."*, which then was derived to *"being or occurring in the near, or not too distant, past; recent" (of late)* in the 14th century.

Then in the 15th century, the meaning of the word *'late'* was derived further to be an adjective that indicates that a particular person was alive in the past recently, but not anymore."

The Tamil euphemism for the departed is as puzzling as the English. *"Kaalam Sendra* Mr. So 'n So", roughly renders,"Mr. So 'n So whose time has passed, or, "who has gone to time." *"Kaalam Vendra"* would be more appropriate, as it means, "He who has overcome time." Someone who has lived well and died just as well, can be considered to have fulfilled the expectations of his time on earth.

In Malay, the deceased is referred to as *mendiang* or, *arwah* (the departed soul). Royalty are *al-marhum*. The Chinese deceased are *Yǐ gù de mǒu mǒu* (deceased person). Tamil departed are addressed as *Amarar* ("The

Immortal"), especially in reference to a well respected, pillar of society. Others get a *kaalam sendra* (late), or *maraintha* (faded). As they say, *"Soldiers never die, they just fade away."*

English euphemisms are aplenty. *Passed away* (most common euphemism for death), *No longer with us, Kicked the bucket* (a phrase with a flippant tone), *bit the dust* (also with a flippant tone), *pushing up daisies* (facetious), *gone to meet his maker* (humorous), *in a better place now*, (comforting), *gone to buy the farm, cash in one's chips.*

Euphemism (Greek for: good speech), is often confusing, as it is meant to be. Clear and direct speech can be awkward and non-PC. But how do you parse, *"kick the bucket"*? No clear picture, even if the phrase goes back to 1785. And, what is a *bucket list*? A bucketful of lists? Why not, with our tendency to put off so many projects till kingdom come.

Greetings: Amacam?, Sowkiyama?, Ni Hao Ma?

Greetings among acquaintances and neighbours tell a lot about the community and its priorities and values. While English greetings revolve around small talk such as the weather, "nice day!", "what a day!", "good morning!", "whazzup?"etc., Malaysian ones tend to emphasize personal concerns, such as, "have you eaten?", or, "how are you doing?", "How's your family?" Food always figures prominently in greetings. Malay – *Sudah Makan?* Chinese – *Ni chi le ma?* Tamil – *Saaptiyaa?* They all mean, "Have you eaten?" This is not being a busybody nosey poker or a half hearted invitation to a meal. It is a intellectually ingrained, instinctive interest in the other's needs. Hunger, being the Asian metaphor for neediness or distress.

The old English formality, "how do you do?", and its American counterpart, "Wazzup?" have their counterpart in the Malay, "Amacam?" or "Apa macam?". The Chinese form is, "Ni hao ma?" (You good or not?), which should be used only when you seriously want to know your friend's health. Otherwise you might likely get a response like, "What makes you think I was sick? ". The Tamil salutation is commonly, "Sowkiyama?" or "Nalamaa?" both meaning, "All going well?"

"Whats up?" For the longest time, I was at a loss as to how to respond to that Americanism. The sun's up. Surf's up. The birds are up. I am up. Cuz, if I ain't, I'd still be in bed, no? The Brit would probably answer that with, "The weather's up."

Taking leave: Goodbye, as we have seen in another section, is actually from the Old English "God be with ye", similar to the Spanish *Vaia con Dios*, "Go with God". The Malay promises *Jumpa Lagi* or "We'll meet again." The Chinese has a similar, *Zai jian*, or "meet again". Tamil similarly, has *Poi Varen* – "I'll go and return". It also has a unique, *Varattumaa?* – "Shall I return?" it is rhetorical, not a request for permission with, "shall I leave?", implied. The English equivalent is "see you soon," to which the response would be, "Bye, see you." French "adieu" and German, "auf wiedersehen" are also in that class.

Naturally, among friends you don't want to just take off, without a promise of meeting up again. Otherwise, it would be,"good riddance" or worse, "go to hell!" or, "hit the road, Jack!". And don't you come back no more, no more, no more, no more. Hit the road Jack!

Scripts: Rumi, Kanzi, Vattelutthu

Multilingual storefront signs are a sight unique to Malaysia. Whereas you get bilingual at best, like French/English in Canada or Chinese/English in Chinatowns around the world, a Malaysian storefront will often display in Bahasa Malaysia, English, Mandarin and Tamil. At the least, it will be in three, Malay, English and the additional language of the shop owner or the community being served by the business. It is a business's nod to the international, national and vernacular lingos.

This is not to say that street signs are in all languages. Street names are neutral, in the sense that that they don't need translation and they are all in Roman script for good reason. I imagine that it would be a blithering babel of befuddling bedlam and maddening mayhem, akin to a silver screen that has sub-titles in four different scripts, blocking half the screen.

Going along with the theme of Malaysian unity in diversity, the major representative groups have their own scripts with their unique forms and functions.

Chinese script is a class act by itself, in the sense that it does not have alphabets per se but literally, word pictures. Each 'alphabet' is a pictograph that tells a story. No wonder they call it "characters", having personalities rather than alpha-beta, which are sound bits that make up the abugida style of script.

Despite recent modifications to the script, Chinese characters still retain the basic shapes/forms of what they want to convey. Older versions of the script had a character for every word. Imagine the gigabytes of memory needed to store that information. The Chinese characters (Kanzi) borrowed by Korean (kanja), Japanese (kanji), Vietnamese (kan tu) characters are probably the only surviving form of this type of writing. The extinct Egyptian Hieroglyphics is one such writing form that is still being deciphered as it is discovered.

The Malays don't have a native script of their own, although their Javanese cousins have a rarely used script (the *Kawi*) that resembles Tamil's circular scribbling. Malay's ancient script was similarly rounded, found on stone scriptions found across Sumatra. The closest indigenous script found in our area is the historic, *Singapore Stone*. That too, has been identified by epigraphists (pundits of scripts) as derived from Tamil, Javanese or Sumatran. It was found at the mouth of the Singapore river (original location of the Merlion) in 1819. It was a 10 feet by 10 feet slab of sandstone rock, before it was recklessly destroyed by a clueless, artless (heartless?) British civil servant.

Munshi Abdullah has recorded it in his travelogue. *"Mr. Coleman was then engineer in Singapore and it was he who broke up the stone; a great pity, and in my opinion a most improper thing to do, prompted perhaps by his own thoughtlessness and folly. He destroyed the rock because he did not realize its importance. Perhaps he did not stop to consider that a man cleverer than he might extract its secrets from it, for I have heard it said that in England there are scholars with special knowledge who can easily understand such writing, whatever the language or race. As the Malays say, "If you cannot improve a thing, at least do not destroy it."* – Hikayat Abdullah, at pp 165-166 (1849). Way to go, Munshi.

It was dynamited for gravel! Fortuitously, Sir Stamford Raffles, the enlightened founder of modern Singapore had pieces of it redeemed and sent to the Royal Asiatic Society's museum in Calcutta, India, for study. Only a small (26 inches long) piece remains, now on display at the Singapore National Museum. By the way, Raffles was also the administrator(albeit short term) of Java when his surveyor, Colin Mackenzie made a full assessement of the Prambanan Hindu complex outside Jogjakarta.

There is one rock inscription in the compound of the St. Anne's Church, in Cherok Tok Kun, Bukit Mertajam. Translation: *"I acknowledge the enemies of the contented king Ramaunibha (of Kadaaram kingdom) and the wicked are ever afflicted."* It was discovered by colonel James Low, a British army officer, in 1845

The script that Malays universally read and write in is the Romanized or Rumi script, while the lesser used Arabic derived Jawi script is sometimes used in religious texts, and store front signage. Jawi is dying out, with the passing of the older generation, as seen in the discontinuation Jawi newspapers such as *Warta Negara* (3 September 1945-13 July 1969). It currently resides in Malaysian banknotes and some city street signs.

In Indian businesses, Tamil features next to the Rumi Malay, and is especially prominent in the Little India enclaves of the large cities. The writing is left to right and descending down the page just like English. Arabic or Jawi script, travels in the opposite direction, from right to left and down the page. It is much like the British and American left-hand and right-hand drive respectively. The Chinese script descends from top to bottom in a column, and then plummets down similarly in a new column on the left. Lots of head bobbing, rather than head turning. The exception to the descent is storefront signages, which are horizontal left to right. This style appears to be the current norm, especially in China.

The Chinese characters are angular and squarish in shape, like picture frames in which are lines that make up images. The total effect is like a storyboard, similar to cartoon frames. A novice may see it as resembling random chicken scratchings.

電腦	飛機	大學	收音機	貓頭鷹	精神分裂症
computer	aeroplane	university	radio	owl	schizophrenia
(electric brain)	(flying machine)	(great learning)	(receive sound machine)	(cat-headed eagle)	(split mind disease)

When put together in picto or ideo graph thusly, the word remind me of the Red Indian trying to speak English. "Sitting Bull", "Dances with Wolves"

Arabic letters flow in a line, resembling a river-boat procession, the boats are laden with people and things..

e.g., أنا كسَرت الأصنـامَ ("oh my goodness!").

Tamil writing is called the *Vatteletthu* ("circular writing") and consists of circular and semi-circular curvy lines that form shapes like eyes and tails. It evolved because that was the form best suited for the prolific stone inscriptions in Tamil, throughout history.

வானூர்தி	பழ்கழய்க்கழகம்	வானொளி
Aeroplane	University	Radio
(Sky Crawler)	(multi Arts Movement)	(Sky sound)

Thai writing can be found in parts of northern West Malaysia and resembles a mix of Tamil, Hindi (Devanagari), and Hebrew.

เราทุกคนเกิดมาอย่างอิสระ เราทุกคนมีความคิดและความเข้าใจเป็นของเราเอง เราทุกคนควรได้รับการปฏิบัติในทางเดียวกัน.

Hindi writing, called the *Devanagari* (litt: City of God) script looks like pots and pans and odds and ends hanging on a clothesline. *Gurmukhi* is the Punjabi version of Devanagari. This a sample: – ਤੁਹਾਨੂੰ ਮਿਲ ਕੇ ਚੰਗਾ ਲੱਗਿਆ [tuhānū mila kē cagā lagi'ā], "Nice to meet you."

Writing the Devanagari script seems as arduous as writing in Hebrew or Chinese, compared to the flowy style of Tamil and other derivative South Indian scripts. Being circular means, it is the most time-saving and easy on the wrists of the scribe. A naturally cursive character.While Chinese script may take three to 15 separate moves to complete a character, all Tamil letters although looking very complicated, can be completed in a single stroke, or 2 at most. It stands to reason that the first shape children learn to draw, at ages 3-4, is an O and an X. This is followed, at ages 4-5, by the square and triangle.

English, or Roman alphabets, also take up to 4 strokes (e.g. E), especially when written in capitals. With its largely vertical strokes, it is liable to look like a picket fence., e.g: **THE SILLY LITTLE BILLY GOAT LEAPT OVER THE RICKETY PICKET FENCE.**

Proverbs: Yànyǔ, Peribahasa, Pazhamozhi.

Proverbs: "A short, well-known pithy saying, stating a general truth or piece of advice" – Google. It is in all languages. Like old wine, they are distilled from years of folk wisdom, life experience, humour, and poetry and enrich even a primitive language.

Bahasa Malaysia: *Peribahasa* – (fr. Sanskrit: *Paribasha* – "maxims"). Tamil: *Pazhamozhi* (pronounced ; Palamoli). It means "old language" or, "fruity language", both of which are appropriate. Mandarin: *Yànyǔ* ("sayings and quotes"). Corresponding to the gist of the Chinese proverb, "*A journey of a thousand miles begins with a single step*", a crisp proverb should speak for itself. Much like a good joke, great proverbs should light up at the switch on and self-explanatory. In other words, they are the polar opposite of riddles.

Chinese idioms are mainly composed of four characters. It is rare that the idiom has more than four characters, such as "*Wu Shi Bu Xiao Bai Bu*" – the pot calls the kettle black ; "*Yi Shu Ze Bu Da*" – Haste makes waste ; "*Zhui Wu Zhi Yi Bu Zai Jiu* – having ulterior motives. It has something to do with the Chinese syntactic structure and single-syllable Chinese words.

The following is but a shortlist of a long list of Chinese proverbs.

He who asks a question is a fool for five minutes; he who does not ask a question remains a fool forever.

To believe in one's dreams is to spend all of one's life asleep

If you are planning for a year, sow rice; if you are planning for a decade, plant trees; if you are planning for a lifetime, educate people.

Parents who are afraid to put their foot down usually have children who step on their toes – Hear! Hear!

A bit of fragrance clings to the hand that gives flowers

He who strikes the first blow admits he's lost the argument

If you want happiness for an hour – take a nap. If you want happiness for a day – go fishing. If

you want happiness for a month – get married. If you want happiness for a year – inherit a fortune. If you want happiness for a lifetime – help someone else

He who is drowning is not troubled by the rain

The Malay saying, *Memberi Belanda means,* "Dutch giving". Give and then take back. The English, "Dutch treat" or to "Go Dutch" means each pays for himself. The following is a list of Malay proverbs, no explanation needed: –

A diplomat should be yielding and supple as a liana that can be bent but not broken.

A fool is like the big drum that beats fast but does not realize its hollowness.

An ox with long horns, even if he does not butt, will be accused of butting.

Don't think there are no crocodiles because the water is calm.

He that can see a louse as far away as China is unconscious of an elephant on his nose.

However big the whale may be, the tiny harpoon can rob him of life.

One can pay back the loan of gold, but one dies forever in debt to those who are kind.

The turtle lays thousands of eggs without anyone knowing (buries in sand), but when the hen lays an egg, the whole country is informed.

Though a tree grows ever so high, the falling leaves return to the root.

To depend on one's own child is blindness in one eye; To depend on a stranger, blindness in both eyes.

Where does the ant die except in sugar.

Where there is wind, there are trees.   (Not the other way round?)

In terms of empathy and hospitality, Tamil has a saying, *"Its like the crane and the fox inviting each other to a banquet."* Apparently, the fox served the crane water in a broad dish. It was convenient to the fox, as it could lap it up off the wide, shallow surface. The crane couldn't get a drop in. The crane served the fox water in a long necked jug. It was convenient for the crane, but as you can imagine, the fox couldn't get its mouth past the jugs's narrow mouth. This proverb speaks to the idea of diplomacy and empathy – to stand awhile in the other's shoes.

What won't bend at five will not bend at fifty. When the tongue says "five" (*ainthu*) it bends, when it says "fifty" (*Aimbathu*), it doesn't. The extended connotation, of course, to train onself at a younger rather than later age.

Fire lasts only as long as it heats. The earth lasts only as long as it revolves. Man lasts only as long as he tries. You are a man

Pull a mountain by tying your hair to it. If you succeed you will get a mountain, if you lose you will lose hair

If the mother-in-law breaks it, it is a mud pot. If the daughter-in-law breaks it, it is a golden pot.

A single tree doesn't make an orchard

Only when out in the sun do you miss the shade

Even elephants' feet do slip

Even ants can wear out a rock

Even if the tiger is hungry, it wont eat grass

Even water can be held in a sieve, if you wait till it turns to ice

There is no such thing as empty hands. You always have 10 fingers on them

When (you) dress up as a dog, be prepared to bark

(He) uprooted a mountain to catch a mouse

Some proverbs fade off into disuse due to their insensitivity or illogicality. One such is the Malay proverb that some irresponsible schoolteacher recently resurrected and caused a stir. The saying goes thus, *"If you come across a Keling* (i.e. a South Indian) *and a snake, kill the Indian first."* Now, that in itself, might even be acceptable if it had a valid meaning or logic. None is profferred. Indians say that it is their proverb which has been appropriated from them and turned back against them, in a case of plagiarism cum mischief. The Tamil original goes, *"When you come across a double-tongued person and a snake* (with a forked tongue, naturally)*, kill the two-faced human first."* The rationale goes, the fork tongued human is more dangerous than a snake because he can destroy a whole community, whereas the snake only affects its victim. Now, if the Malay copycat is saying that the Indian is a double tongued person, it needs to defend its thesis. Using the scientific approach, every theory that cannot be proven remains just that, and does not progress to law status. The Malay interpretation, if one remembers correctly, is that the Indian tends to raise a ruckus when he sees a snake. So, kill the the noisy one instead of the poisonous one. So the question that arises is, "what is your point?" So, doesn't anybody else go berserk when a snake enters their personal space? So, are all Indians jumpy around "long johns"? So, would that make the popular western image of the turbaned Indian snake charmer, a figment of the colonial British imagination? Now, there's a funny picture for you. A hysterical Indian snake charmer hopping helter-skelter whilst lovingly handling a hissing snake in his hands!

Idioms: Hairless, Green Hat, Wok Ears

An idiom is a phrase that cannot be understood on its own, except in the context of the culture wherein it was born. In other words, it is idiosyncratic. It may be incomprehensible even among speakers of the same language (English), such as American or Australian. Examples: "over the moon" is a feeling of ecstacy, but you get it from the words in the phrase. Quite similar to a metaphor. Even so, there are similar idioms among vastly atypical culture groups such as Malay, Chinsese, and Indian.

Take the word *hair*, which has both different and baffling connotations. In Tamil, the word has assumed expletive proportions, but not to the level of obscenity. *Mayir* is genteel Tamil for a headful of hair, although its colloquial version, *mayiru/masuru,* has assumed meaning as pubic hair. *Aandi* refers to a pauper, beggar, mendicant, fakir or bankrupt – someone with no worldly possessions. Consequently, the notorious Tamil cuss word, *Mayiraandi,* or *Masuraandi,* simply means "the hairless one". This is where the idiosyncracy of idiomatic language comes into play. This Tamilism does not denote a bald person, but rather, an immature person or even questions one's manhood. You see, mayiraandi here means, he who has no pubic hair – basically a pre-pubescent child. When a feller tells you to, "go, pull out your hair" in Tamil, he wants you to become "hairless" or, immature. Hair, as four letter word, can you imagine? What a bad hair day for the harried person!

The Americanism, "to pull hairs" can mean tugging at your head hair, out of frustration, or to a female catfight.

"Wear a green hat" (戴绿帽子 or dài lǜ mào zǐ) is an expression that Chinese use when a woman cheats on her husband or boyfriend because the phrase sounds similar to the word for cuckold.

One theory is that back in the Ming Dynasty. Emperor Zhu Yuanzhang enacted a law, which required men who worked in the prostitution trade to wear green hats. Later, it became common to say about a man whose wife had an affair, that she made her husband wear a green hat.

One other theory suggests that the families of prostitutes were forced to wear green hats during the Yuan Dynasty. Another says that male brothel workers wore green hats during the Tang Dynasty. The only green hat we know, is that worn by the likable leprechaun of Gaelic fable.

Just like my siblings used morse code in the 80s when talking about certain Chinese pork noodles, Indians are prone to use digital messages. They (siblings) used 1.20 or 2.50 based on the price of the *tapaus* ("takeaway" packets), in order to spare the sensitivities of our Indian Muslim neighbour. Indians use "9" to euphemously refer to gay/"girly" types. It likely derives from femiNINE. 108 and 1008 are used as adjective for a large number. "I have 108 chores to finish" means "My job is NEVER done". "Why the 1008 questions", means "Stop nagging me!" Its origins lie in the distant past. We know from the Tamil classical writings, that they were astute astronomers and masterful mathematicians – the *Kaniyans* ("one who calculates"). 108 and 1008 are divisible by 9, a supposedly lucky number, and hence auspicious.

Telinga kuali – "wok ears" – a stubborn person who doesn't heed advice. Panjang Tangan – "long arms" – One who tends to steal. Mulut murai – "thrush (bird) mouth" – a babbler. Muka tembok –"brickwall face" – A shameless/unrepentant person.

There are many idioms that in hindsight, smack of racism. Examples of such idioms "Cina Buta" (Blind Chinese), "Kling Mabuk" (Intoxicated Indian). Like a good joke, proverbs and idioms shouldn't be personal attacks and unfounded characterizations. They cannot be generalizations, unless the traits continue into the present. These are almost tantamount to racial profiling. Most often, racial jokes like the Jewish or Irish jokes are created by the "butts" themselves. It is similar to the situation where it is OK for an African American to call another, a "nigger", but not OK for others. It is A OK for a group of people to make fun of themselves (called an insider joke), and not enjoy it at the expense of others.

<u>Oxymoron: Muran Thodai, Maodu Xiushi, Oksimoron</u>

Oxymoron is from the Greek compound "Oxus" (Sharp) and "Moros" (Dull). An odd couple. Seriously funny. Found missing. Clearly misunderstood. Act naturally. Pretty ugly. Accurate estimate. Calculated risk. Conspicuous absence. Fine mess. Exact estimate. Minor crisis. Old news. Only choice/option. Original copy. Surely, by now you have gotten the idea of an oxymoron. Unless an oxen headed moron comes up with, "I think it refers to more on oxygen".

While some oxymorons may be oral flukes, some are deliberate creations. "Deafening silence" is definitely that, serving to emphasise the silence. "Social distancing", a new moron thanks to the Covid-19 contagion, must be of the former class. Sociable while distant? Distant sociability? Which is which, do make up your mind. I would have said, just physical distancing or plain distancing. Health professionals coming up with labels such as Covid-19, are not expected to be grammatically accurate. Not their focus.

Oxymoron in Tamil, is met by *Muran Thodai* ("Contradictory Sequence"). It is actually a poetic device, in which a set of rhyming antonyms is placed in a verse for effect. However oxymoron in everyday usage is rare. An example may be, *nandriketta naai* – "ungrateful dog". The Thirukural ("Sacred Voice") has oxymorons aplenty, of the muran thodai kind.

Baik buruk (good and bad), *suka duka* (sadness and happiness), *perang saudara* (civil war), *pahit manis* (sweet and sour), *hidup mati* (life and death), *kiri kanan* (left and right). Malay considers the above list as oxymorons, although English grammar won't recognize it as such, except for *perang saudara* (civil war). An oxymoron like *social distancing,* refers to a singular noun, whereas *baik buruk* refers to a couple of opposite things – a mere list which fails to elicit irony or satire. You don't go – "ughh?"

<u>Lost in translation: How English loses it?</u>

The difference in languages lends itself well to caricatures in movies, teevies and stand-up comedies. And many a time, translation from one to another also gives ample subject matter for comic relief. In all the the following, the humour generating factor is straight application of native grammar, idiom, and misspelling. It is the direct result of employing non-agency, non-professional, DIY translation. Unsurprisingly, these are mostly small business, mom 'n pop establishments with hand written signs.

These samples from Mainland Chinese

"Fresh Crap" – *Live carp.* The Indian would say the same for "Live Crab".

"All is not a real value, you cannot through hard work and hard to get"

(Thomas Alva Edison) – *Nothing that has value in the world, can be had without effort*

"Slip and fall down carefully" – *Be careful not to slip and fall down.* A full stop after "down", would have saved it.

"Garden with curled poo" – *Garden with curved pool.*

"Please don't touch yourself, let us help you try out." – *Please let us help you try it on."*

This one from India, suffers the same malaise with several clauses clumping together.

"please don't share two persons in one plate" – *Eat from your plates, please*

"Super Saloon: Die, Fachial, Messes, and children cutting here" – *(Hair) dyeing, facials, Massage, and kids' haircut*

"Branded Gent's: All Sizes Large To TXL" – *Branded male items from size L to TXL*

"Credit Card Swapping at Reception Counter Only" – *Swipe credit cards at the reception desk*

These Malay store signs have suffered from a case of misspelling, or creative spelling. Spellcheck unavailable?

"please pay your parking fee before existing" – scary

"Shoplifters will be prostituted"   – scarier

"NOORANI CHICKEN: Hole Sealer"   – scariest (wholesaler)

On luncheon menu: "Scissors Salad"   – A new kind of punishment?

Semantic Change: Cor Blimey!, Poi Solli, Chee Bai, Cerakinan

Being a living and organic entity, language changes not so much in structure (grammar) as in semantics (meanings and spellings of words). Let's see some examples of changes in both meaning and spelling, that have occurred in our languages. Semantic change is not the same as an anachronism, in which a thing is completely outdated and unusable in the present.

Goodbye is a farewell and a parting statement that actually means, "God be with you". An abridgement or corruption. Originating in the 1660's to 70's, Goodbye is said to have begun as, *Gobwye* (Gor be wi ye). *Cor blimey!* (1889) is less universal and reputable, being confined to the cockney speaking proletariat of London. It has corrupted from "God blind me (if I lie)". It is a swear or oath, protesting, professing the truth of one's statement.

Just as words change form, as above, they also make 180° turns in meaning, changing to antonyms. Some examples are as follows:

1. **Nice**: This word used to mean "silly, foolish, simple." Far from the compliment it is today!
2. **Silly**: Meanwhile, *silly* went in the opposite direction: in its earliest uses, it referred to things worthy or blessed; from there it came to refer to the weak and vulnerable, and more recently to those who are foolish.
3. **Awful**: Awful things used to be "worthy of awe" for a variety of reasons, which is how we get expressions like "the awful majesty of God." – Wikipedia

In Tamil, a great number of truisms are quoted daily, which have gone way off the original meaning. Compare these: –

Current:	"Aayiram *poi solli* kalyanam pannu."	(Tell a 1000 lies and get married)
Original:	"Aayiram *perukku pOi solli* kalyanam pannu."	(Tell a 1000 people and get married)

Here, **poi solli** (tell lies) and **pOi solli** (Go tell) change meaning with a single accent on a single syllable. Likewise, the Mandarin word *mai* means both "buy" and "sell", differentiated only by intonation or accent. *Gay*, in this age has a completely different connotation. Not disimilarly, in English you have "flammable" and "inflammable" which mean the exact same thing!

Semantic change also happens when words are borrowed from another language. For example the English word "cool", meaning "nice" becomes *ku* (unfriendly) in Hong Kong Cantonese. A final year study in Singapore finds that Hokken swear words have reduced in taboo(ness) from the the 1st generation to the 3rd – ***Not so "chee bai"*** (vagina) ***anymore: a look at Hokkien swear words in Singapore and how they have changed over time***, By Samantha Catherine Bok Shi Yu.

Malay words have semantically changed as in this list.

<u>Original Meaning</u>	<u>Current Meaning</u>
Ladang (a clearing)	a Plantation
Perenggan (fence)	Paragraph
Injap (opening in a rattan fish trap)	Valve
Cerakin(an) (medicine chest with compartments)	Analysis

Would present day languages be comprehensible in a hundred years or become archaic? They should be manageable, as long as the grammar is maintained.

Coded: OC, ABC, ASK

Don't we all love bite sized bits and bytes of information in our speech? The social media is aflood with this such as LOL, SMS, OMG etc. Before that, the military had an ever expanding dictionary of acronyms such as AWOL, ICBM, JAG etc. It is not that humans are getting lazier, but it is a necessity considering the difficulty writing perfectly grammatical sentences on your smartphones. It harks back to the days of Morse Code or the telegram, where quick read, compact messages, AKA "shorthand", was needful. The same principle applies on the battlefront, the aviation sector and almost any "line" such as engineering, banking, or law.

So, Malaysians are not behind in this skimping on the speaking. ABC (*Air Batu Campur*) is our all time favourite shaved ice dessert, along with the *Cendol.* If you want to call in sick, you'd better have an *MC (Medical Certificate).*

Bahasa Malaysia has *andartu (an̲ak d̲ara tu̲a* – "old virgin") to refer to an old maid. *Pawagam* (pan̲ggung wa̲yang ga̲mbar – cinema), *Cerpen* (c̲erita p̲endek) etc. If you don't have a word, create one by cutting and pasting! I had an Indonesian once ask me the direction to the Waysay (WECE), their way of saying WC. You know, the toilet (WC = Water Closet)

If you have an OJ (orang juice), we have MJ (Michael Jackson), soya milk with black seeweed jelly. Say JFK or LBJ, we have LCW (lim Chong Wei, sportsman), KJ (Khairi Jamaluddin, politician) and MGR (actor/politician).

The Tamil word *kedi,* referring to a criminal, is actually from the English KD (Known Delinquent). It got started during the East India Company days in Madras (Chennai) as a term for habitual offenders. It is part of the Madras Baashai (dialect) similar to London's Cockney. Another such word from that region is Osi (OC) which enjoys currency in Malaysia. The Tamil saying, "Any Osi food, he'll eat without salt.", means a person who'll even eat unsavoury food as long at its free. OC is actually "On Company Service" (OCS) where staff of the East India Company sent letters and stuff postage free. It exists present day in the diplomatic bag embassies use, to send documents free of host country scrutiny. Naturally, anything OC might lead to contraband in the diplomatic bag, as has happened in January 2012, when 40 kg of cocaine from Equador was detained by Italian police.

Borrowing from Singlish, ASK: Ah Sia Kia (Hokkien) = Rich Kid. Mandarin acronym *3Q (San Q)* is an onomatopoeia of "thank you". *1999* in Cantonese sounds like, "lumpy", meaning that a person is incoherent or unclear in speech. By that token, *9* in Tamil refers to a transperson, from the English, femiNINE.

You approach a Tamil at an odd time and he answers, "Sorry lah bro, I have 1008 chores to complete." 1008 – read, "a mountain of ...". Hindu tradition has a 1008, mostly spiritual explanations for this. A more "scientific" explanation may be: *"the distance between earth and sun is 108 times diameter of Sun, and distance between earth and moon is 108 times diameter of the moon. So it's number 9 which appears everywhere in geometry also sum of all angle of a triangle 180, sum of all angles of a quadrilateral 360, I.e. 9 everywhere. The God number 9."* – Wikipedia

"The spiritual answer is based on Hindu mythology with the reference to the 1008 mahayugas, which is one day time in Lord Brahma's lifespan." – Subramaniam Duraisamy. A *mahayuga* lasts 4.32 million years and is made up of a sequence of four different *yugas*

"Sri Sathya Sai Baba went one step ahead of others in explaining the significance of these numbers. A man breaths 21,600 time a day (at the rate of 15 a minute and 900 times an hour). During the day time he breaths 10,800 times." – S. Swaminathan

Not only do acronyms save time, they can also serve as secret codes for those in the "in" group. Even in personal relationships, we tend to create code words. Sometimes, you might even create an impromptu encryption, when someone walks in on your private conversation!

The cockney dialect has gathered a lot of codes that baffled todays listeners as well as bobbies (London cops) of old. An example is the phrase, "I'm going apples", for "I'm going upstairs." You take the first word from the set,"apples and pears." And substitute it for "upstairs". The genius is in not using the rhyming, "pears" which can be a giveway, so use the non-rhyming part. Just to be sure we get the pattern, "wife" becomes *trouble* (from *trouble and strife*). "Bread and honey" shrinks to bread, for money. And there is a ton of it. I have often wondered how "bread" came to mean money in America.

Naturally, codes can be broken after a while. When everybody uses it, as in the smartphone sign language spread out in cyberspace.

Puzzles and Riddles: Vidu Kathai, Teka-Teki, Míyǔ,

"The older brother (Annan) can't reach, but the younger (Thambi) can". It refers to the fact that when the former word is spoken, the lips don't touch, while the latter has both lips pressing. *"A group of horses went down to the river to swim. The black ones were washed away, and only the white ones returned home"*. Answer: Black gram or Ulunthu (Tamil). They are similar in size to the green skinned Mung Bean, but black in colour. When soaked in water the skin softens and is easily stripped to expose the white bean. The black skin swiftly floats to the water surface, while the

white bean stays on the botton, which makes for easy drainage. The black gram, for informations sake, is the chief ingredient in Thosai, Idli, Vadai and Pappadam.

"For one who never brushes his teeth, his whole body is full   – (Comb).
of teeth"

"lighter than feather, but the strongest person on earth   – (Breath).
cannot hold it for a few minutes"

The above are some riddles, or *vidu kathai*, we played as kids, facilitated by our elders. And there were many. It was great fun, as we tried to make a lot of guesses, but never got lucky! They were fun because it was mental exercise and required thinking outside the box. As we saw above, a self-respecting riddle should not be easy to solve.

Here are some Malay riddles (*teka-teki*).

"The fake sells, the original doesn't"   – (Teeth)

"Always entering, but never inside."   – (Button)

"Always approaching but never arriving"   – (Tomorrow)

"Go flying, return swimming"   – (Fly fishing bait)

"Pull, and it goes away. Let go, and it approaches."   – (Flag)

Ancient Chinese riddles, *Mi Yu* ('Secret Talk") usually involved puns on the written characters. Here are some latter day riddles:-

"There is a small vessel filled with sauce, one vessel holding   – (Egg)
two different kinds."

"Washing makes it dirtier; it is cleaner without washing."   – (Water)

"There is a big rooster. When it sees someone, then it takes   – (Tea pot)
a bow."

"When in use, its thrown away, and when not in use its   – (Anchor)
brought back."

"When I go out, I am thick and fat. When I come home, I am meager like
a skeleton.

Then am put in a corner against the wall and my tears   – (Umbrella)
flow freely."

Methinks the second sentence on the last riddle is an unnecessary giveaway.

"What happens when you throw a yellow rock into a purple stream?" – it makes a splash. This is an example of a bad riddle. Or a trick question, which you soon catch on too. It squeezes your brain, nevertheless.

Double-Speak: Kaadu-Medu, Gunung-Ganang, Kow-Tow

If there is a repeat offender in any language, it is a thing called reduplication. It probably arose from humble origins. From baby-talk actually. You hear "mummies" exhorting their tiny-tots to eat their mum-mum, to calm their tummies. They train them to wee-wee or pee pee in the potty. Pee Wee Herman is not involved in this.

People who have limited command of language (vocabulary) often reduplicate to communicate their thoughts. For instance, the Papua-Niugini pidgin for their annual cultural event, is SingSing, meaning a songfest, or tribal Woodstock. To play around, is pilai pilai. Lacking an adjective to offer profuse apology, we fall back on "sorry sorry", instead of "extremely", or "deeply" sorry. Over time, reduplication has acquired literary currency and poetic status.

Some Malay examples: senang-lenang – "easy life", lelaki (laki-laki) – "male", kura-kura – tortoise, gunung-ganang – "mountain range". As with most languages, the redoubling is often for emphasis. For instance, *pukul* 'to hit' becomes *pukul-memukul* 'to hit each other'. *Bertukar* 'to switch' changes to *bertukar-tukar* 'to exchange'. Likewise, *meminta* 'request' and *meminta-minta* 'beg', reveal variation of vigour. *Cerai* 'part, sever' splinters into *cerai-berai* 'disperse'. Some Malay "words" have no meaning unless reduplicated. E.g: *pura* (?) renders as *pura-pura* 'to pretend'.

Tamil echo words occur only in colloquial and conversational situations. E.g. kaasu-keesu – "monies", sambalam-kimbalam – "wages", thoon-thurumbu – "random things." Classical Tamil won't stoop down there, but has exact words to convey exactitudes of meaning. While literary Tamil has the suffix *"gal"* to convey plurality, market Tamil simply adds the prefix *"Ki"* to the duplicate. For example, where the classical plural form for *puli* (tiger) *is puligal,* the local form would be *puli-kili* ("tigers and such"). Sometimes, like the Malay, it may have variation in spelling but retain the rhyme. Exempli Gratia – *lottu losukku* (nonsense, non vocab phrase) meaning "and other random things".

Some common Chinese words include: Lai-lai – "come hither", kow-tow –"obeisance", piāo piào liang liàng – "very beautiful". Piāo liang, is plain "beautiful".

Mandarin (or other Chinese "dialects") are famously fond of photostating verbs, nouns, adverbs and adjectives for emphasis and effect, namely to do something "fully or thoroughly". E.g *hao hao de* (Hao meaning good"). So, hao hao de conveys, "to one's heart's content". Likewise, an *an* jing *jing de* (quietly and nicely). Gao *gao* xing *xing* de (happily and nicely). The second (italicised) *an jing* and *gao xing* are the emphatic. The simple verbs *jang* (rise) and *die* (fall) turn progressive when reduplicated as *jang jang die die* (rising and falling).

In the absence of the plural ending "s" as in English, Malay opts for reduplication. Example: more than one book is buku-buku. On the other hand, hairy is rambut(an) and thorny is duri(an) (?) – no berambut and berduri (having hair or thorn). But many thorns is duri-duri.

A class of reduplication, if it can be so called, is the pair of words in which the second has a different sound (kow-tow) or an entirely different spelling (flotsam jetsam. namby pamby, touchy feely, walkie talkie etc.). That would be a kind of evolutionary linguistic progress. Overall, these repeaters possess a certain poetic ring to it. Remember that *polka dot bikini* song?

The itsy-bitsy teeny-weeny whipper-snappers running helter-skelter are up to some hanky-panky, as they pow-wow and tittle-tattle willy-nilly on tid-bits of wishy-washy rat-a-tat tête-à-tête. The content of the little nit-wits' tall-tales is nothing more than hocus-pocus or mumbo-jumbo, a mish-mash of claptrap chit-chat and humdrum bunkum that is bound to give you the heebie-jeebie collywobbles. Holy moly! What a topsy-turvy, not so hunky-dory world this has come to. (© – yours truly).

Latest Word: Compound Word, Neologisms, Portmanteau, Acronym

It appears that wholesale importation of words from other languages into English has decreased. Most new words entering daily into English are portmanteau (plural portmanteaux) or neologisms.

A portmanteau is a combination of two (or more) words or morphemes into one new word. A portmanteau word typically combines both sounds and meanings, as in *smog*, coined by blending *smoke* and *fog*. "Brunch" is an example of a portmanteau word (breakfast + lunch). Lewis Carroll's "snark" (snake + shark) is also a portmanteau. These new words are also called neologisms.

Interestingly, or naturally, both portmateaux and neologisms are themseleves that. Portmanteau comes from the French *porter* (to carry) + *mantel* (cloak), referring to a large luggage. Neologism is from the Greek *neo* (new) + *logos* (word).

Acronyms and **initialisms** are abbreviations formed from the initial components in a phrase or a word. These components may be individual letters (as in *CEO*) or parts of words (as in *Ameslan – ASL –* American Sigh Language).

Language, as a living organism, continues to evolve, vocabulary being the most obvious part of it. As knowledge continues to expand on all fronts, new words emerge as vehicles to carry it. Different languages may have specific ways of going about creating these words. Some are born naturally to social usage, like comeuppance to describe just rewards or karma. Some are coined by linguists, scholars in their specific fields of science or arts.

Malay, like Indonesian, has largely resorted to borrowing words wholesale from English, as English has done from Greek, Latin, French as well as other languages. Spelling changes are done to reflect local flavour. This is done indiscriminately, not only of technical words but also common words such as, situasi, kombinasi, lokasi, persepsi, variasi. You get the drift, quite easily. The other approach is acrostics, i.e, the fusing of the initial and or last syllables of words to form a new word. *Andartu*, is about five decades old, and is from <u>A</u>nak <u>D</u>ara <u>Tu</u>a, meaning, "old virgin daughter". Old Maid or Spinster, in English. Another one, attributed variously to the super entertainer P.Ramlee, or a Singapore Radio DJ, is *Kugiran,* for **Ku**mpulan **Gi**tar **R**ancak ("Up Tempo Guitar Band"). It is the word for a musical band. Many older words in Malay did not become acrostics, eventhough they came from multiple words. They can sometimes be more descriptive than their English versions. Aeroplane (Air ship) is *Kapal Terbang* – "Flying Ship". Owl is *burung hantu,* or "devil bird". Cockatoo is shanghai-ed from the Malay, *burung kakak tua* – "older sister bird".

Thankfully, Malaysia hasn't followed Indonesia in indiscrimately acrosting. GOLKAR – Partai

Golongan **Kar**ya, is a major political party there. We have UMNO, MCA, MIC, PKR, PAS etc for

our own political parties. Indonesia has Jabodetabek, which might be confused with Dumledore

or Rumplestiltskin of fairy tales. It actually refers to the metropolitan capital (Jakarta and its

surrounding satellite regions). ***Jabodetabek*** stands for **Ja**karta-**Bo**gor-**De**pok-**Ta**ngerang-**Be**kasi.

Basically, that is our Lembah Kelang (Klang Valley). Perhaps we should rename it,

Kulpejsujshalkel (**Ku**ala Lumpur-**Pe**taling Jaya, **Su**bang Jaya, **Sh**ah **Al**am, **Kel**ang). Horrors!

Tamil, in keeping with its boast, *Thanithamil* ("stand alone Tamil") refuses to borrow foreign origin words. In fact their linguists want to get rid of words already in, and have a movement since 1902, the *Thaniththamil Iyakkam*, to flush out all foreign words. Like Greek, Tamil has the advantage of possessing small descriptive words that can be easily fused to admirably convey ideas and meanings. These are not acrostics, just fused extant words. A Tamil from 2,000 years ago, can recognize a modern coined word just as his Malay friend would be puzzled by 50 year-old *Andartu*. An ancient word, now in the English lexicon, is catamaran. It is the Tamil *Kattumaram. Kattu* – "to tie" and *maram* – "tree". A raft-like sea vessel, with pieces of log lashed together. Reversing the order, *marakattu* means a bundle of firewood.

Chinese neologism, likewise are also born of modern needs to coin words for new ideas or inventions. Owl is "cat-headed eagle" – can you get any more descriptive? Chinese, with its picto-graphic script and single syllable sound bites, can easily add multiple words to form new words.

The following is a trilingual sample of some common English nouns, together with native language equivalent and literal translation.

Tamil

Computer	University	Aeroplane	Radio	Television
Kanini	*Pal Kalai Kazhagam*	*Vaan oorthi*	*Vaan Oli*	*Tholai Kaatchi*
("math"ster)	(multi-arts institution)	(sky crawler)	(sky sound)	Distant View

Chinese

電腦	飛機	大學	收音機	貓頭鷹	精神分裂症
computer	aeroplane	university	radio	owl	schizophrenia
(electric brain)	(flying machine)	(great learning)	(receive sound machine)	(cat-headed eagle)	(split mind disease)

Malay

Aeroplane	Owl	Spinster	Cockatoo
Kapal terbang	*Burung hantu*	*Andartu (anak dara tua)*	*Burung kakak tua*
"Flying ship"	"devil bird"	"old virgin daughter"	"old sister bird"

In a way, when we do these neologisms, we seem to revert to our primitive ancestors, as they struggled to communicate with limited sound bytes.

Phonics: Pinyin, Oliyam, Bahasa Baku

Malaysian Chinese parents have begun naming their children in the new way. Pinyin is a modification of the old style of writing Chinese words in English alphabets. A few of the same alphabets have changed. For instance, the G sound is now rendered, X. T is D, Ts is Z, Ch is Q, and S is written Sh. His Holiness, Cardinal Sin of the Phillipines is now Cardinal Xin. That would get him off the hook pretty fast, wouldn't it?. And the jokes can cease forthwith. For the benefit of the non-Catholics, there are two types of sin – Cardinal and Venal. Cardinal sin is the more serious, like murder, blasphemy etc. Venal sin is lesser, like theft, lying, etc.

Mao Tse-Tung is Mao Zedong. Most Malaysians still hang on to the three part name, unlike the China Chinese who now fuse the latter two.

Tamil is a diglossia i.e. two ways of speaking – High and low Tamil, existing side by side. Often mutually incomprehensibe to the uninitiated, it comes naturally to native speakers. Tamil has no H, Sh sound and borrows from Sanskrit. Tamil has three levels of L – La, il, and LL which is rendered in English as Zh – where the tip of the tongue touches the central roof of the mouth.

The other main South Indian languages spoken in Malaysia, Malayalam and Telugu, share many commonalities with Tamil, being all Dravidian. The former two have more Sanksrit admixture, whereas Tamil scholars are fond of weeding out Sanskrit from the vocabulary. Where Tamil has words using *n or na,* Malayalam's equivalent words use *ny.* The Tamil word *Naan* ("I"), becomes *Nyaan* in Malayalam, and *Naanu,* in Telugu. Telugu is called the Italian of the east, because of its preponderance of vowels. While Italian is indiscriminate with *a*'s, *o*'s, and *i*'s, Telugu favours *u.* Like opera's affinity for Italian, Telugu is a favourite of composers of Carnatic cantatas.

The Chinese tongue refuses to say the *R* sound, which often sounds like *L.* Chicken Rice becomes Chicken Lice. The Chinese *L* or *La* sound is very much like the Tamil *Zh* sound which comes about in the retroflex, i.e. when the tip of the tongue touches the roof of the mouth.

Chinese dialects, each also have their own unique sounds.

Hainan   : – "nang bo ti nang, kui bo ti kui"
Manglish : – "human not human lah, ghose oso not ghose lah"
English   : – "Human, yet not quite human. Ghost, yet not really a ghost."

which was parodied by 70's comedian, Hamid Gurkha (?) or Jamali Shadat (?).

Standard Malay or Bahasa Malaysia (aka Bahasa Melayu), is spoken in Malaysia, Singapore and Brunei. It is also the prototype of Bahasa Indonesia. In Malaysia, dialect variations occur in the north and north-eastern parts of the Malay peninisula, namely, the Kedah and Kelantan dialects, the latter related to Pattani Malay of Southern Thailand. These dialects generally differ from Standard Malay, in their contractions. For example, Pergi (go) and *Makan* (eat) renders *Pi Makè* in Kelantanese. The Negeri Sembilan (NS) dialect of Malay, derived from Minangkabau of Sumatra, is an odd island in the standard Malay of the west coast. It reminds you of Hainanese Chinese whose phrase, *Nang Bo Ti Nang, Kui Bo Ti Kui* is somewhat of a mirror image of, *Pi Mai Pi Mai Tang Tu,* the title of a popular Malay sitcom. It's Malay equivalent is, *Pergi keMari, Pergi keMari, Datang Situ Juga.* The translation?: "Back and forth, back and forth, but arriving at the same place." In other words, "what goes around, comes..,"?

Baku (Standardization) was a movement in the 80's, to update the spelling and pronunciation of the Malay language. Hitherto it had a very soft sound. Bahasa Malaysia became closer to Bahasa Indonesia in terms especially, of spelling. The sound of Sh changed to Sy and Y was restricted, leading to confusing situations. For instance, ayer (water) became air overnight. At the petrol station you have water (air) and air (angin) outlets side by side. Suppose you pump air (water) into your tyre? Well we are all OK, even if it took a while to adjust to the new situation. The young people won't know the changes we went through, from catty (kati) to pound (lb) to kilogram (kg). Lucky you.

Since we are on a roll here about dialects and linguistic variants, I remember some of my "members" (colloquial for friends) in primary school engaging in a funny dialect, which I didn't care to master. Do you Boomers remember "F" language? No, Gen-X'ers, its not "Funny" language. It was English encoded with the letter "F", in such a way that it sound like a whole other "Foreign" language. The simple grammar of it, is to place an "f" after a vowel or syllable, as appropriate, or to repeat a syllable by replacing the first consonant with, you know what. Words beginning with "f", like *father,* are not modified or repeated. An example of a "F" language goes thus:-

English : "Yo! What are you doing tonight?"
F'lish   : "Yofo! Whafhat arefar youfou doofing tofight?"
English : "Baskin Robbins. Coming?"
F'lish   : "Basfaskin Rofobbins. Cofoming?"

I didn't get it at all or learn to use it, as it was not dissimilar to understanding Baso Kelaté (Kelantanese). It might as well have been Greek. You suspect that all the

Mother Tongue: Jiwa Bangsa, Huáyǔ, Painthamil

Just as the sweetest sound is that of one's name being uttered, so, it seems, one's mother tongue is a joy to hear. It is the language of comfort. When you stub your toe, you don't cry out "oh father!" Rather, *Aduh Mak!*, *Ma ma!*, or *Ammaah!* Is that why you call it "Mother" tongue, you suppose? Indeed Tamils are probably the only people who literally confer divine status on their language, calling it *Thamil Thaai* or *Thaai Thamil* (Mother Tamil). Living in the UStates, in blue times, I naturally turned to the SBC (Singapore Broadcasting Corporation) streaming Tamil music on the internet. RTM didn't have it then. On shopping trips to Devon Street, Chicago's Little India, the sound of somebody speaking Tamil tickled and tittilated the ears.

If nation, nationality, and nationalism is one's physical body, then language must be the soul. Expunge a language, and you kill the nation. By the same token, you cannot force it down someone's throat. This is well demonstrated by the speakers of Malaysia's major languages.

Malay — "Bahasa Jiwa Bangsa" — (Malay) Language is the soul of the race.

Tamil — "Tamil engal uyirukku nehr" – Tamil is equal to our life. A line from poet Bharathidasan

Chinese — Mandarin, a northern language is overtaking the southern Cantonese, Hokkien, Hakka etc.

Following the imposition of Mandarin in China, under the pretext of "common language", Taiwan, Singapore, Malaysia, and even Hong Kong (Cantonese prevalent), have or are succumbing to it. So, Mandarin is now the new "common tongue", *Putonghua*, of the Chinese and something of pride and value due to its positon as the most spoken language of the world. Nevertheless, Mandarin is often considered an upstart, having a lower view among older speakers of other "dialects" such as Cantonese. Matter of fact, even Confucius is believed to have spoken Cantonese natively, being deemed closer to classical Chinese.

Keeping aside the debate on which of the Chinese dialects is the the most ancient, literarily prolific, poetic, or patently pridegiving, Chinese culture as a whole is BIG on all counts.

While the Malay language has its own unique structure and grammar, its vocabulary is overwhelmingly foreign. A Brunei Malay blogger Roslan Yunus (Brunei Times journalist, and author of "Golden Times"), says that he didn't realize until older, that in a simple Malay sentence, 8 out of 10 words could be Indian (Sanskrit and Tamil). Check these common words. *Saya* ("I") is "sahaya from Sanskrit. Sahaja, sama, cara, belaka, bahawa, mula, nama, pada, sudah, tadi,. *Ada, juga/pun, sangat.* In the context of 1 Malaysia, this is a very positive matter, because everyone has an ownership of it.

I do believe that we subconciously create sentences which contain words from every representative Malaysian language and more. Arabic (A), Chinese (C), English (E), Hindi (H), Malay (M), Portuguese (P), Skt (Sanskrit), Tamil (T),

"Mempelai (T) wanita (Skt) itu (T) kelihatan (M) sangat (Skt) cantik (C?) dan (M) rupawan (Skt) memakai (M) cincin (C) intan (C) baiduri (T) serta (Skt) gown (E) dan sepatu (P) sutera (P).

As a race, Tamils are probably the only people on earth who worship their language as they would their mother or a goddess. This is different from the French love for their language, which is probably that for a paramour. Not every Tamil has this passion, but a sizable number of their "enlightened' ones do. Enlightened in the sense that the community, after the collapse of their last major empires in the 17th century, came to be ruled by small time princes and chieftains as well outsiders who had none of the appreciation of language as oldtime emperors, who were patrons of the old bards and poets. Then, with the "rediscovery" of Tamil classics by European missionaries and scholars, and in coincidence with the Indian independence movement, contributed to the resurgence of Tamil pride. It is not ethnic or cultural pride as such, but rather, linguistic.

University of California, Berkeley, holds a 'Tamil' Conference annually. Its Chair in Tamil Studies, Prof. George L. Hart, writes, *"To qualify as a classical tradition, a language must fit several criteria: it should be ancient, it should be an independent tradition that arose mostly on its own and not as an offshoot of another tradition, and it must have a large and extremely rich body of ancient literature. Unlike the other modern languages of India, Tamil meets each of these requirements. It is extremely old (as old as Latin and older than Arabic); it arose as an entirely independent tradition, with almost no influence from Sanskrit or other languages; and its ancient literature is indescribably vast and rich."*

By the same token, Chinese easily qualifies. They have every reason to be the proud possessors of a treasure trove of ancient literature. It must be the topmost in the list of intangible cultural heritage as per the UN.

<u>Language</u>

Naturalized: Words that have become part of Malay

As Malaysians know and recognize their language cognates in Malay, this section list some of those words that have become part of the national language.

From the Chinese, Bahasa Malaysia has these.

Along – (Ah Long – loan shark)

Amah – (Ah Mah – Nanny)

Ah Moi – (young lass)

Bak Choy – (Baak Choi – a leafy vegetable)

Boleh – *(Bo Liao – Can)*

Cengkeh – (Ceng Keh – clove),

Cap – (Chap – stamp, brand)

Cat – (Hokkien, *Chat* – paint)

Cawan – (Cha Wan – saucer)

Cengkeh – (Ceng Keh – clove),

Cheongsam – (Cheung Sam – ladies' skirt)

Cincin – ?

Cincau – (Chin Chau – grass jelly)

Dacing – (Da cing – weighing scale)

Dimsam – (Dim Sum – dumplings)

Fengshui – (Feng Shui – geomantics)

Gua – ("I", "me" – colloquial)

Intan – (Yin Tan – diamond),

Jong – (………. – Junk)

Kepo (?)

Kuaci – (Kua Chi – dried melon seed)

Kuih – (Que – cake),

Kungfu – (Kung Fu – Chinese martial arts)

Kichap – (Ketchup – "7 ingredients")

Kongsi – ("to share") – (Kong Si – "clan

Laci (?)

Laici – (Lai Chi – Lychee)

Lobak – (Cantonese, Lubba – Carrot)

Longkang – (Hokkien, Long kang – drain)

Loteng – (Lo teng – attic)

Lu – (Lu – You)

Mangkok (?)

Pinggan (?)

Pokai – (Cantonese, Puk Gaai – bankrupt)

Sampan – (Sam pan – small boat)

Samsu – (Sam Soo – liquor)

Samseng – (Sam Seng – Gangster)

Sayur – (Chai/choy)

Sinseh – (Sin She – herbalist)

Taici – (Tai Chi –)

Taiko – (Tai kong – "Big Shot"/ Tycoon)

Taufan – (Tai fong – Typhoon)

Tauhu – (Tau Hu – tofu)

Teh – (Te – tea)

Teko – (Te Ko – teapot)

Tionghua – (Chung Hua – Chinese)

Tokong – (Toh Kong – Taoist temple)

Tonkang – (Tong Kang –)

Towkay – (Tow Kay – Proprietor)

Susu (?)

Wantan – (Wan Tan – Wonton)

Bangku, Senkuang, menkuang, simpang, wayang, wang,

Observe that this wordlist is preponderantly about food items.

From Tamil, these words.

Acuan – (Acchu – mold)

Agung – (Ko, Kohn, king, mountain)

Ajar – (Aasiriyar – teacher)

Alor – (Allur – drain) ?

Alun – (Alai – wave)

Aru – (Aaru – river)

Asal – (Asal – prototype, original),

Amal – (Amal – to implement, enforce)

Apam – (Appam/Aaapam – a rice crepe)

Bagai – (Vagai – "kind"/"type")

Pelbagai – (Pal-vagai – many types/ variety of)

Bamboo – (Moongil – bamboo)

Baris(an) – (Varisai – row) *(Ikan)*

Bawal – Vavvaal (Meen) – "Bat fish"

Benda – (Pandam – thing/stuff)

Bendahari – Pandaaram/Pandaari – Keeper of common property, esp temple priest – holds temple keys)

Belenggu – (Vilanggu – cuffs)

Bunga – (Poonga – flower garden,)

Cabar – (Savaal – to challenge)

Candu – (Sandu opium) ?

Cuma – (Summa – "just" or "only")

Dalam – (Aalam – deep)

Darat – (Tharai – land)

Datuk – (Thaattha – grandfather)

Duit – (Dhuttu – (cash, from Tamil "kaasu")

Emak – (Amma – mother)

Gadai – (Adagu – "to pawn)

Gagak – (Kaakkai – crow)

Gudang – (Kidangu – warehouse),

Gulai (?) – (Kulai – to overcook, stewed)

Harimau – (Arimaa – majestic (male) lion)

Helai – (Ilai – leaf, page)

Ikat – (Kattu – to tie)

Itu – (athu – that/ithu – this)

Kala – (Kaalam – a period of time)

Tatkala – (Tatkaala – current/Tatkaalika – temporary)

Katil – (Kattil – bed),

Kini – (Ini – now)

Kakak – (Akkaal – older sister)

Kanji – (Kanjee – Rice porridge, starch)

Kapal – (Kappal – ship)

Karat (rust) – (Karai – stain; Kaar/karuppu – dark; Karutthal – a darkening, – take your pick.)

Kari – (Karee – Curry, meat stew)

Kawal – (Kaaval – guard, noun and verb),

Kedai – (Kadai – shop),

Keldai – (Kaluthai – Donkey)

Kelawar – Vavvaal (Bat)

Kera – (Kurangu – monkey)

Ketuk – (Kottu – knock, beat (big drum)),

Ketumbar – (Kotthamalli – Coriander)

Koleh – (Kuvalai – mug)

Kota – (Kotai – fort),

Kolam – (Kulam – pond),

Kuil – (Kovil – "House of the Majesty")

Kumpul – (Kumbal – heap, gang)

Kutip – Kooti-perukku ("add and multiply" or Kootu – "sweep up")

Kupang – (kuppam – fishing hamlet) *Kurang* – (Kurai – to lessen, lacking)

Kurus – (Kuru – small. compact/Kurugu – to narrow)

Kutuk – (Kutthu – to poke/punch) or Kuttram Saatru – to accuse)

Laba – (ilaabam – profit)

Malai – (Maalai – garland)

Mangga – (Maankai – unripe mango)

Manik – (Mani – beads) *Melor* – (Malligai – Jasmine)

Mempelai – (Maapillai – Bridegroom, Litt: *Maa (maha) Pillai*, or "great son")

Mempelam – (Maampalam – ripe mango; maankai – unripe mango))

Mendung – (Mandham – dull; Mandaaram – overcast sky)

Misai – (Meesai – moustache)

Modal – (Mudal – "first"/ investment),

Mudalali – (Mudhalali – stock owner/boss)

Mutu/Mutiara – (Muthu – pearl)

Manikam – (Maanikkam – diamond)

Nakal – (Nakkal – snide remark/ prank)

Nelayan – (Ulaiyan – fisherman)

Nira – (Neer/neeru – water; Ilaneer – coconut water)

Pekan – (Paakkam – seaside town),

Perahu – (Padagu – boat),

Perli – (Pirali – to start fake news)

Peti – (Petti – box)

Putu – (Puttu – steamed rice flour)

Ranggi – (Raangi – mischievous)

(Se) *Rasi* – Raasi (suitable/ compatible/lucky)

Satay – (Sathai – *flesh*/Thasai – *muscle*)

Sembahyang – (Samayam – Religion)

Sida – (Seedan – student)

Sekutu – (Kootu – joint/"together")

Sekat – (Sikku – *block/entangle*)

Segera – (Seekiram – quick, instant)

Sorok – (Sorugu – to hide/sheath a sword)

Sungai – (Sunai – mountain stream)

Taulan – (Tholan – comrade/cohort) etc. fr Thol – shoulder

Tadahan – (Thadaaham – *water* catchment area) ; Thadai (n)– prohibition, ban, Thadu (v) – block, Thaduppu (n) – Barrier).

Talam – (Taambulam – tray)

Tairu – (Thayir/Thayiru – Yogurt)

Teman – (Taman – companion) ?

Tirai – (Thirai – curtain/screen),

Tolak – (Thallu – to push)

Uai – (Avvai – mother)

Ucap – (Ucchari – to utter, Uccharippu – pronunciation,

Hurai – (*Urai* – (to make a speech (verb)/a speech – noun) et cetera.

Zat – (Saththu) – Nutrient/Strength

Note that the Tamil list is about daily activities, commerce etc.

Portuguese has donated as follows (notice the number of household items),:

Almari – (Armario – cupboard),

Bangku – (Banco – stool)

Baldi – (Balde – pail)

Bendera – (Bandeira – flag)

Boneka – (puppet)

Beranda – (Varanda – *verandah)*

Bola – (Bola – Ball)

Biola – (Viola)

Bomba – (Bombeiro – Pump"?)

Boneka – (Boneca – doll)

Dadu – (Dados – dice)

Dekan – (Decano – dean)

Garfu – (Rio Garfu – fork)

Gajus – (Caju – cashew)

Gereja – (Igreja – church),

Jendela – (Jannala – window),

Kapitan – (Capitan – captain)

Keju – (Queijo – cheese)

Kemeja – (Camesa – shirt)

Kerbau – (Carabao – buffalo)

Kereta – (Carreta – carriage/car)

Lampu – (Lampo – light)

Mandor – (Mandador – supervisor)

Meja – (Mesa – table),

Mentega – (Mantega – margarine) etc.

Merinyu – (cannon) ?

Minggu – (Domingo – Sunday)

Nenas – (Ananás – pineapple)

Nonya – (Nonha – young maiden)

Padri – (Padre – Priest)

Palsu – (Falso – false)

Pita – (Fita – tape)

Pintu – (Porta – door)

Piun – (Rio Piun – office boy)

Sabtu – (Sabado – Saturday)

Roda – (Roda – wheel)

Ronda – (*Rio Ronda* – Make the *rounds)*

Sekolah – (Escola – school)

Sepatu – (Sapatos – shoes)

Soldadu – (Soldado – soldier)

Tangki – (Tanque – tank)

Tembakau – (Tabaco – Tobacco)

Tempoh – (tempo – time)

Tempoh – (tempo – time)

Tuala – (Toalhas – towel)

Tukar – (Alteracao – exchange)

Vizurai – (Vizurai – viceroy)

Berambus – (Vamos – to go),
periok,, Etc. Etc.

And then, there is the heftier catalogue of Sanskrit, Arabic and English words, in that order of their arrival. Notice that the Tamil wordlist above, like the Chinese wordlist, has to do with trade and mundane matters, whereas Sanskrit and Arabic loans pertain to more ethereal and spiritual matters.

Shurga/Neraka – (*Svarga/Naraka* – heaven/hell)

Dewa/Begawan (Deva/Bhagawan – God)

Agama (religion)

Astana/Mahligai – (palace/ mansion),

Bahagia/Baginda – (Bhāgya – blessed)

Bahtera – (Vahitra – ship/boat)

Belantara – (Vanaanthara – forest)

Cherung – (Churanga – tunnel)

Chahaya – (Chaiya – light)

Manusia – (Manushya – human)

Menteri – (Manthiri – minister)

Merdeka – (Maharddhika – prosperous)

Murka – (Moorka – explosive anger)

Paduka (Paaduka – Sandal/Sole of feet)

Pendita – (Pandita – scholar)

Guru – (Guru – Teacher)

Duta – (emisssary)

Kepala – (Kapalam – head)

Kurnia – (Karunya – (blessings)

Bumi – (earth)

Segala – *(Sakhala* – *everything)*

Singa – (Simha – lion) –

Suami/Isteri – (Svaami/Sthree – Husband/Wife)

Suka/duka – (Sukha/Dhukka)

Suria – (Surya – sun)

Seri – (Sree – holy/esteemed)

Putera/Puteri – (Putra/Putri – son/ daughter)

Pahlawan (warrior) – (Pahelwan – wrestler).

Laksamana – (Rama's brother and aide-de camp *Lakshmana*, but "Admiral" in Malay)

Singgahsana – [Simha (lion) + Asana (seat)] = Lion Throne

Dirgahayu – [Dheergha (long) + Aayur (life)] = Long live!

Malay has even taken these base words and formed its own compound words. Examples are, *Bumiputera, Setiausaha*, etc.

Bumiputera [Bumi (earth/land) + Putra (son)] = Son of the soil

Setiausaha [Satyam (honest/loyal) + *Usaha* (Utsaha → effort)] = Secretary

This (i.e, Sanskritization) is, thanks to the Hindu and Buddhist priests (who were also Tamils) accompanying the Tamil traders, who used Sanskrit (Hinduism) and Pali (Buddhism) as their language of worship. Worldwide, Sanksrit and Pali are still the liturgical lingos of these religions. These Tamil priests were subsequently inducted into the Malay and Javanese royal palaces as personal and religious advisors (*rajaguru*s). Without being too presumptuous, *Bendahara* appears akin to the Tamil, *Pandaaram,* referring to temple priest or keeper of temple property. But it is also quite likely derived from ………., the Sanskrit for …………. *Sembahyang*, sounds suspiciously like *Samayam,* the Tamil word for religion. *Tuanku,* resembles *Tunggan* ("Lord"), although the Malay *Tuan Ku,* "My Lord", is more plausible. Since many words from Tamil and Sanskrit have entered Malay, there is an easy way to find out which is which. Sanskrit derived words mostly have European cognates. E.g: Dewa (*Theos* – Greek), Gua (*Cave*), Kepala (*Cephalos* – Greek), Raja (*Regis* – Latin), Surya (*Sol* – Latin). Indian words without European cognates are more likely Tamil.

This predominance of words from certain languages to particular spheres of Malay life, is similar to the English language, where you find Greek gifts for medical, scientific and philosophic usage; Latin loans for political, legal, and administrative terms; and French freeloads for the arts and cuisine. England, as everyone knows, was ruled by the Romans in an earlier time, and later by the Normans.

Similarly, Arabic words abound in the theological lexicon of Malay. Some of them, as follows:-

Masjid – (mosque)	*Syariah* – (religious law)
Umat (Ummah – humanity)	Khutbah – (sermon)
Maut – (death)	Jenazah – (mortal remains)
Halal/Haram – (kosher/non-kosher)	Hijrah – (migrate) etc;

It has entered business language e.g.

Syarikat – (Sharikah – company)	Surat – (Surah – book chapter)
Faedah – (interest/benefit)	
Nisbah – (ratio)	Makmal – (laboratory)

and daily usage such as,

Muslihat – (Muslihah – scheme)   *Musyawarah* – (consensus)
Miskin – (poor)   *Ziarah* – (visit)
Hakikat – (Hakikah – reality)   *Hal Ehwal* – (affairs)
Khatul-istiwa – (equator) etc.

What with the popularization of Islamic banking, we are becoming familiar with more Arabic words, like, *Muamallat* (Transaction), *Riba* (Interest), Mudharabah (profit sharing), *Takaful* (Insurance), *Wakaf* (Endowment).

English is now, the largest donor of words. In a circuitous way, we have arrived at a place where English, which osmotically absorbed from Greek, Latin and other languages, passed it on to Malay as a colonizer's language. The linguistic colonization continues unabated. Today, technological terms are appropriated into Malay as fast as it enters the English lexicon. English and Malay are similar in the way they have prospered (as lingua franca) by unabashedly, unashamedly borrowing from whomever they came across. They present a model of linguistic survival and success by natural selection. It is a model of survival of the fittest, of embracing foreign concepts and making it your own. Whereas, on the other end of the continuum, Tamil claims an unbroken tradition of linguistic chastity, unmarred by foreign borrowings. Its poets have designated it, *KannithThamil* ("Virgin Tamil"). Even the latest scientific and technological terms are minted by mining ancient words from the millennia old classic literature. In fact, Tamils like to boast that *ThaniThamil* ("stand alone Tamil") is ever young because of its unchanged state over several millenia. If there is such a thing as a living dinosaur, this must be it! Its contemporaries (like Latin, Greek, Sanskrit and Pali), they point out, have long since become extinct, or mutated into a myriad of other mother tongues.

Two ways of surviving. Whichever works.

Lingua Franca: English, Malay, Mandarin, Tamil

While English is practically a universal lingua franca, the Malay language is the medium of communication among the multiple cultures of Malaysia as well as across the archipelago from Sumatra to as far as the

Phillipines. It has been so from centuries back. Perhaps due to its wide "spread" eventhough totalling only 16 million native speakers compared to Javanese's 98 million, it was adopted as indonesia's National Language.

Bahasa Indonesia only differs from Bahasa Malaysia in terms of pronunciation and some vocabulary. While they are only as different as American and British English, Bahasa Malaysia is more English influenced in terms of pronunciation and spelling, while Bahasa Indonesia spells and sounds more like Dutch, their former rulers respectively. While Bahasa Malaysia has retained its cultural identity and ethnic shade of the Malay sphere, Bahasa Indonesia is more open and accepting of influences from the legion of regional languages of Indonesia. This is to better facilitate its role as a lingua franca. So, Indonesian Malay, or Bahasa Indonesia is a neutral tool that does not carry the emotional, nationalistic weight of Bahasa Malaysia. Afterall, It is only the national language, like English is the international language. No worries. No sweat. Wouldn't it be a good study to compare how a single language can have two different treatments and responses in the two neighbouring countries? Not to forget, that Malay is also the national language of Singapore and Brunei, too. In the case of Singapore, its role may be similar to that of Bahasa Indonesia, or of even less sentimental stature.

He (a friend) said Mandarin (aka Standard Chinese) was replacing Hokkien in Kelantan, Terengganu, Penang and Melaka and Cantonese in Kuantan, Kuala Lumpur and Ipoh as the mediatory language of the Chinese populace. Being the language of Chinese education, it has quickly become the mainstay among the younger population. The Chinese dialects (why dialects when many of them are mutually unintelligible?) are gradually beginning to be restricted to the home. Mandarin, beside a universal image and respectability, will be the new mother tongue of the Chinese community. Mandarin is now synonymous with Chinese language. Say, Chinese newspaper, and it has to be a Mandarin one. Not only is it a Malaysian Chinese lingua franca, it is a world Chinese one too.

Tamil has long been the common language since British times, of the South Indians, especially among the Indian and Ceylonese Tamils, Malayalees, and Telugus. Unlike Mandarin which usurped Cantonese and Hokkien as intermediary language, Tamil was a natural choice due to the larger numbers of its native speakers, as well as owing to the Dravidian kinship of the South Indians. Vernacular media, primary education, marketing, and daily exchanges are all in the language. Occasionally, some Punjabis, Malays, and Chinese are known to be conversant in Tamil. In British times, the Mat Salleh *Dorai*, or estate manager, picked up the language in order to communicate with their rubber tapper staff.

By virtue of its position as the national language, Malay is the currency of choice, widespread in East Malaysia as well as being the only language of Brunei. Malay's geographic location on both sides of the Malacca Straits (Riau and Malacca), and the straits' situation at the crossroads of international trade, has long made it the default lingua franca.

Indian couples used to adopt Chinese baby girls who were given up by their birth parents. Chinese adopted Indian boys, as boys were considered more useful to carry the family name. I have seen both kinds. What if the Chinese Indian girl speaking Tamil and the Indian Chinese boy speaking Chinese were to court? And they only conversed in Malay? Won't it be a comedy of errors of Shakespearean shades? Just a thought.

Gone Global: Malay, Chinese, Tamil words in English

The once insular language English, absorbed the language of its conquerors, such as Latin, Greek, and French. As a result, you have scientific and medical terms from Greek; legal and administrative words from Latin; and cultural and culinary words from French. When the British colonized continents and territories beyond their shores, English also appropriated words from those lands, resulting in an exhaustive vocabulary. That is one aspect of colonization that we can be proud of, that while English became our lingua franca, our local lingos have also lent a hand, helping English to fill some gaps.

While most of the words are common nouns of animals, vegetation, fruits and food, important verbs such *Launch* (lanchar) from Malay, *Yen* (to crave) from Cantonese, and *Navigate* (navaai = navy) from Tamil, have also *entered* (latin) English.

Below is a list of "English" words that originate in Malay. Chinese, and Tamil respectively. What a list! A list, some of which, we might not have imagined existed.

List of English words of Malay origin. From Wikipedia, the free encyclopedia

Agar	— (also 'agar-agar') a gelatinous substance obtained from various kinds of red seaweed and used in biological culture media and as a thickener in foods.
Agarwood	— from *Gaharu* tree, a M-alaysian hardwood.
Amok	— (also 'amuck' or 'amock') out of control, especially when armed and dangerous; in a frenzy of violence, or on a killing spree, 'berserk', as in 'to run amok'.
Babirusa	— (also 'babiroussa') from French *babiroussa*, from Malay *babi* hog + *rusa* deer. A wild pig (*Babyrousa babyrussa*) of the East Indies with backward-curving tusks.
Balanda	— (also 'ballanda' or 'ballander') from Makasar *balanda*, from Malay *belanda*, from Dutch Hollander meaning a white person, a European.
Bamboo	— from *bambu*
Banteng	— from *banteng*, 'a SE Asian forest ox that resembles the domestic cow, domesticated in Bali [Bos javanicus.]'
Binturong	— from *binturong*, 'a large species of civet, *Arctictis binturong*, of SE Asia'.
Caddy	— (also 'caddie') from *kati* (a measurement unit, whereby 1 kati = approximately 600 g).
Cassowary	— from *kasuari/kesuari*, 'a very large flightless bird related to the emu'.
Catty	— from *kati* (a unit of measurement)
Camphor	— see Kapur. From Old French *camphore* or Mediaeval Latin *camphora*, from Arabic 'kāfūr', from Malay *kapur*.
Cempedak	— (also Chempedak) from *Cempedak*, a species of tree and its fruit in the family Moraceae.
Cockatoo	— from *kakaktua*, a parrot with an erectile crest. Compound (enclosed group of buildings) by folk etymology from *kampung* or 'village'

Cooties — from *kutu*, 'lice'

Dammar — from *damar*, 'resin; resin obtained from various mainly Indo-Malaysian trees, used to make varnish.'

Dugong — from *duyung*, 'mermaid'

Durian — from *duri* 'thorns', hence *durian*, 'thorny'

Gambier — from *gambir*(the name of the plant), an astringent extract of a tropical Asian plant, used in tanning'

Gecko — from *geko, gekok*

Gingham — from *ginggang*

Gong — from *gong*, a metal disc with a turned rim that gives a resonant note when struck.

Gutta-percha — (a type of tree whose sap is used in the manufacture of synthetic rubber) from *getah*, 'rubber' and *perca*, 'scrap/piece'; hence *getah perca*, 'a scrap/piece of rubber'

ikat — from *ikat*, 'to bind', a style of weaving that uses a process similar to tie-dye to dye the threads. Origin from the Tamil *kattu,* meaning, "to tie"

Jackfruit — generally cited as deriving from the Malayalam *chakka* or *cakkai* via the Portuguese *jaca*, which came from the Malay/Indonesian word *nangka*.

Junk — (type of boat) from *jong*

Kapok — from *kapuk*, 'a fine fibrous substance which grows around the seeds of a ceiba or silk-cotton tree, used as stuffing for cushions'

Kapur — from *kapur* a large tropical tree which yields light brown wood, edible fruit, and camphor [Genus Dryobalanops.]

Komodo — from *komodo*

Kris — (also archaic 'creese') from *keris*, 'a Malay/Indonesian dagger with a wavy-edged blade'

Launch	— from *lancar* (meaning 'swift', 'nimble'; and 'making something moves faster'; and 'doing or held something like an action, attack etc.') and *lancaran* (meaning 'a kind of swift boat' – in old Malay literatures), 'a large motor boat.'
Langsat	— from *langsat*, a species of fruit-bearing tree belonging to the family Meliaceae [Lansium domesticum]
Mangosteen	— from *manggustan*, also known as *Manggis*
Meranti	— from *meranti*, 'white, red, or yellow hardwood from a SE Asian tree (genus Shorea)'
Merbau	— from *merbau*, 'the hardwood of a SE Asian tree (genus Intsia)'
Orangutan	— from *orang hutan* or 'people of the jungle'
paddy	— as in 'paddy-field' or 'rice paddy', from *padi*, referring to the rice plant *Oryza sativa*.
Pandanus	— from *pandan*, 'a tropical tree or shrub with a twisted stem, long spiny leaves, and fibrous edible fruit. [Genus Pandanus.]'
Pangolin	— from *pengguling*, 'one that rolls/curls'
Pantoum	— from *pantun*, 'a Malay poetic/verse form'.
Parang	— from *parang*, 'a Malayan machete',
Picul	— from *pikul* (a unit of measurement)
Proa	— (also 'prahu' or 'prau') from *perahu*, 'a Malaysian or Indonesian sailing boat, typically having a large triangular sail and an outrigger'
Rambutan	— from *rambut* 'hair', hence *rambutan*, 'hairy'
Ramie	— from *rami*, 'the plant of the nettle family which yields this fibre, native to tropical Asia. [Boehmeria nivea.]'
Rattan	— from *rotan*
Sago	— from *sagu*, '(sago palm) the palm from which most sago is obtained, growing in freshwater swamps in SE Asia. [Metroxylon sagu.]; any of a number of other palms or cycads which yield a similar starch.'

Salak — from *salak*, 'a species of palm tree (family Arecaceae) native to Indonesia and Malaysia [Salacca zalacca]'

Sambal — from *sambal*, (in oriental cookery) relish made with vegetables or fruit and spices.

Sarong — from *sarung*, 'wrap/sheath'

Satay — (also 'sate') from Malay *satai*, Javanese/Indonesian "sate", 'an Indonesian and Malaysian dish consisting of small pieces of meat grilled on a skewer and served with spiced sauce.'

Seladang — from *seladang*, a wild ox with a dark brown or black coat with white lower legs, native to India and Malaysia. [Bos gaurus.].

Siamang — from *siamang*, 'a large black gibbon native to Sumatra and Malaya [Hylobates syndactylus.]'

Silat — from *silat*, 'a Malay's martial art'

Tael — from *tahil* (a unit of measurement) meaning 'weight'

Tokay — from *toke* of Malay dialect, means 'a large grey SE Asian gecko with orange and blue spots. [Gekko gecko.]

Trepang — from *teripang/trepang*

List of English words of Chinese origin. From Wikipedia, the free encyclopedia

Bok choy — (Cantonese) 白菜 (baakchoi), a Chinese cabbage: literally 'white vegetable'

Catsup — Ketchup

Char — colloquial English word for 'tea', originally from Chinese 茶 (Cantonese/Mandarin *chá*; Vietnamese *trà* or *chè*).

Cheongsam — from Cantonese 長衫 (cheungsaam), lit. long clothes.

Chi	– or "qi", energy of an object or person, from Chinese Mandarin 氣 (air or spirit). (This word is correctly represented in Wade-Giles romanization by "ch'i," but the rough breathing mark (replaced by an apostrophe in most texts) has disappeared in colloquial English.)
China	– via Latin *Sina,* Persian چین *Cin,* and Sanskrit चीन Chinas; ultimately from the name of the Ch'in Dynasty 秦
Chop chop	– from Cantonese *chuk chuk* 速速, lit. hurry, urgent
Chopsticks	– from Chinese Pidgin English *chop chop.*
Chop suey	– from Cantonese 雜碎 (tzapseui), lit. mixed pieces
Chow	– from Chinese Pidgin English chowchow which means food, perhaps based on Cantonese 炒, lit. stir fry (cooking)
Chow chow	– any of a breed of heavy-coated blocky dogs of Chinese origin
Chow mein	– from Taishanese 炒麵 (chau meing), lit. stir fried noodle, when the first Chinese immigrants, from Taishan came to the United States.
Confucianism	– from Confucius, Latinized form of 孔夫子 (kǒng fūzǐ) 'Master Kong' Cumshaw from Amoy 感謝, feeling gratitude
Dim sum	– from Cantonese 點心 (dimsam), lit. touches the heart
Fan-tan	– from Cantonese 番攤 (fāntān), lit. (take) turns scattering
Feng shui	– from *feng,* wind and *shui,* water 風水; (slang) Denotes an object or scene is aesthetically balanced (generally used in construction or design)
Foo dog	– from Mandarin 佛 *fó* Buddha (from their use as guardians of Buddhist temples)

Ginkgo — mistransliteration of 銀杏 (*ginkyō* or *ginnan*) in Japanese

Ginseng — from Hokkien Chinese 人参 *jîn-sim*, rendered in Mandarin as *renshen*, name of the plant. Some say the word came via Japanese (same kanji), although 人参 now means 'carrot' in Japanese; ginseng is 朝鮮人参 ('Korean carrot').

Go — From the Japanese name *igo* 囲碁 of the Chinese board game. Chinese 圍棋, Mandarin:

Gung-ho — from Mandarin 工合, short for 工業合作社

Gyoza — Japanese ギョーザ, gairaigo from Chinese 餃子 (Mandarin: Jiaozi), stuffed dumpling. Gyoza in English refers to the fried dumpling style (as opposed to water boiled).

Hoisin — (sauce) from Cantonese 海鮮 (hoísin), lit. seafood

Kanji — Japanese name for Chinese characters: 漢字, lit. Chinese characters. Chinese: Hàn zì.

Kaolin — from 高嶺, lit. high mountain peak, the name of a village or suburb of Jingde Town, in Jiangxi Province, that was the site of a mine from which kaolin clay (高嶺土 gāo lǐng tǔ) was taken to make the fine porcelain produced in Jingde.[1]

Keemun — kind of tea, 祁門 Mandarin *qímén*

Ketchup — possibly from Cantonese or Amoy 茄汁, lit. tomato sauce/juice

Koan — Japanese 公案 *kōan*, from Chinese 公案 (Mandarin *gōng'àn*), lit. public record

Kowtow — from Cantonese 叩頭 (Mandarin, kòu tóu), lit. knock head

Kumquat — from Cantonese name of the fruit 柑橘 (Gamgwat)

Kung fu — the English term to collectively describe Chinese martial arts; from Cantonese 功夫 (Gongfu), lit. efforts

Lo mein — from Cantonese 撈麵 (lòu-mihn), literally scooped noodle

Longan	– from Cantonese 龍眼, name of the fruit, literally "Dragon's eye" different from our "Mata Kuching" or "Cats eye)
Loquat	– from Cantonese 蘆橘, old name of the fruit
Lychee	– from Cantonese 荔枝 (laitzi), name of the fruit
Mao-tai	– from Mandarin 茅台酒 (máotái jiǔ), liquor from Maotai (Guizhou province)
Mahjong	– from Mandarin 麻將 (ma jiang), lit. the mahjong game
Mu shu	– (pork) from Mandarin 木須 (mùxū), lit. wood shredded
Nankeen	– Chinese, from Chinese, a durable cotton, buff-colored cloth originally made in 南京 (Nán Jīng).
Nunchaku	– Okinawan Japanese, from Min (Taiwan/Fujian) 雙節棍, lit. double jointed sticks
Oolong	– from Amoy 烏龍, lit. dark dragon
Paigow	– from Cantonese 排九, a gambling game
Pekin	– from southern Mandarin 北京, a patterned silk cloth
Pinyin	– from Mandarin 拼音, lit. put together sounds
Pekoe	– from Amoy 白毫, lit. white downy hair
Qi	– from Mandarin 氣 (qì), air
Qipao	– from 旗袍 (qípáo), female traditional Chinese clothing (male version: cheongsam)
Ramen	– Japanese ラーメン, gairaigo, from Chinese 拉麵 (Lamian) lit. pulled noodle. Ramen refers to a particular style flavored to Japanese taste and is somewhat different from Chinese lamian.
Sampan	– from Cantonese 舢舨, the name of such vessel.
Shanghai	– from Chinese city Shanghai, to put someone aboard a ship by trickery or intoxication; to put someone in a bad situation or press someone into work by trickery. From an old practice of using this method to acquire sailors for voyages to Shanghai.

Shantung — from Mandarin 山東, "shantung" (or sometimes "Shantung") is a wild silk fabric made from the silk of wild silkworms and is usually undyed.

Shaolin — from Mandarin 少林, One of the most important Kungfu clans.

Shar Pei — from Cantonese 沙皮, lit. sand skin.

Shih Tzu — from Mandarin 獅子狗, lit. Chinese lion dog

Shogun — Japanese 将軍, from Chinese 將軍, lit. general (of) military. The full title in Japanese was *Seii Taishōgun* (征夷大将軍), "generalissimo who overcomes the barbarians"

Sifu — from Cantonese 師傅, (Mandarin shīfu), master.

Silk — possibly from 'si' 絲, lit. silk

Souchong — from Cantonese 小種茶 (siúchúng ch'ā), lit. small kind tea

Soy — From Japanese shoyu 醬油, Chinese 醬油, (Mandarin jiàngyóu).

Tai Chi — from Mandarin 太極, "Great Ultimate."

Tai Chi Ch'üan — usually miswritten as Tai Chi Chuan, a form of physical discipline, from Mandarin 太極, lit, "(fist =) Great Ultimate Fighting."

Tai-Pan — from Cantonese 大班 (daaibaan), lit. big rank (similar to big shot)

Tangram — from Chinese Tang (唐) + English gram

Tao — and **Taoism**

Tea — from the Amoy dialect for tea 茶, which is pronounced "tey".

Tofu — Japanese 豆腐, lit. bean curd, from Chinese 豆腐 (Mandarin *dòufu*).

Tong — from Cantonese 堂

tung oil — from Chinese 桐油 tóng yóu, oil expressed from nuts of the tong tree

Tycoon — via Japanese 大官, lit. high official; or 大君, lit. great nobleman

Typhoon	– via Arabic طوفان (Taufan) ; ultimately from 颱風 not to be confused with the monster typhon.
Wok	– from Cantonese 鑊
Won ton	– from Cantonese 雲吞, lit. 'cloud swallow' as a description of its shape,
Wushu	– from Mandarin 武術, lit. martial arts
Wuxia	– from Mandarin 武侠, lit. martial arts and chivalrous
Yamen	– from Mandarin 衙門, lit. court
Yen	– (craving) from Cantonese 癮, lit. addiction (to opium)
Yen	– (Japanese currency) Japanese 円 *en*, from Chinese 圓 (Mandarin *yuán*), lit. round, name of currency unit
Yin Yang	– from Mandarin 'Yin' meaning feminine, dark and 'Yang' meaning masculine and bright
Zen	– Japanese 禅, from Chinese 禪 (Mandarin *Chán*), originally from Sanskrit ध्यान Dhyāna/Pali झन jhāna.

List of English words of Tamil origin. From Wikipedia, the free encyclopedia

catamaran	– from Tamil கட்டுமரம் *kattumaram* ("kattu"=tie up, "maram"=tree/wood) (Source: OED, AHD, MWD)
corundum	– from a Tamil word for 'ruby', குருந்தம் *kuruntham* or குருவிந்தம் *kuruvintham* (Source: OED)
mulligatawny	– from Tamil மிளகுத்தண்ணீர் *milagu-tanneer* from *milagu* black pepper and *tanneer*, water (Source: OED, AHD, MWD)
pariah	– from Tamil பறையர் *paṛaiyar*, plural of பறையன் *paṛaiyaṉ* "drummer". The meaning of "drummer" dates to 1613 (via Portuguese ?), but the current extended meaning of "outcast" for *pariah* is first attested in 1819. (Source: OED, AHD, MWD)
patchouli	– from Tamil *patchai* பச்சை (green), and *ellai* இலை (leaf).[1]
pandal	– from Tamil பந்தல் *pandhal* (Source: OED)

tutenag
— from Tamil துத்தநாகம் *thuthanaagam* meaning "raw zinc" (Source: OED)

vetiver
— from Tamil வெட்டிவேர் *vettiver*; a tropical Indian grass; Botanical name: Vetiveria zizanioides; its aromatic roots are used for weaving screens and baskets and the oil in perfumery (source: AHD)

anicut
— from Tamil *anaikattu*, ("anai"=dam, "kattu"=building/structure) (source: MWD)

candy
— Pers. qand "cane sugar," probably from Skt. khanda "piece (of sugar)," perhaps from Dravidian (cf. Tamil kantu "candy," kattu "to harden, condense"). As a verb, attested from 1530s; hence, candied (c.1600)[2].

cheroot
— via French *cheroute*, from Tamil சுருட்டு *suruṭṭu*, roll or rolled (Source: OED, AHD, MWD)

Cochin-china
— old name of a region and French colony in southern Vietnam, from Fr. *Cochin-China*, from Portuguese corruption of *Ko-chen*, of uncertain meaning; the China added to distinguish it from the town and port of Cochin in southwest India, the name of which is Tamil, perhaps from கொஞ்சம் *koncham* "little," in reference to the river there[3].

Congee
— Rice Porridge, especially Chinese, Hong Kong usage, from Tamil *kanji* "porridge" or "paste or glue"

cot
— *smal*l bed", 1630s via Hindi khat "couch, hammock," from Skt. khatva (Dravidian source: Tamil கட்டில் *kattil* "bedstead")[4].

cowrie
— "small shell", via Hindi and Urdu kauri, from Mahrati kavadi, from Skt. kaparda (Source: Tamil கொடு *kotu* "shell")[5].

curry
— via Hindi-Urdu from Tamil கறி *kaṟi* "sauce" (Source: OED, AHD, MWD)

pagoda

— 1580s, from Port. pagode (early 16c.), from a corruption of Pers. butkada, from but "idol" + kada "dwelling." Or perhaps from or influenced by Tamil pagavadi "house belonging to a deity," from Skt. bhagavati "goddess," fem. of bhagavat "blessed, adorable," from *bhagah "good fortune," from PIE base *bhag - "to share out, apportion"[6].

peacock

— poucock, from M.E. po "peacock" + coc (see cock (n.)). Po is from O.E. pawa "peafowl," from L. pavo (gen. pavonis), which, with Gk. taos said to be ultimately from Tamil tokei

poppadom

— via Hindi-Urdu or Punjabi, from Malayalam or Tamil பப்படம் pappaṭam, ultimately Sanskrit पर्पट parpaṭa "a kind of thin cake made of rice or pease-meal and baked in grease" or "a thin crisp cake" (Source: OED)

portia tree

— ultimately from Tamil பூவரசு puvarasu (Source: OED)

pullicat

— a cotton linen material named after the Tamil Nadu village of *Puliverkadu*, and corrupted into the British, *Pulicat*. Also related to Malay sarong called *kain pelekat*.

rice

— The English word *rice* is **not** borrowed from the Greek word "oruza" ((μαγειρ.) ὄρύζα), as previously thought (and found in older handbooks), nor is it a direct borrowing from Tamil அரிசி *arici*. The relation between Engl. *rice* and Tamil அரிசி *arici* is in fact more complicated, as demonstrated in more recent researches. Although Engl. *rice* is indeed ultimately from (Old) Tamil, the "rice" word has entered English, through several intermediary languages, notably via Church Latin, (Old) French, (Old) Spanish, (Old) Italian and Arabic.[8]

betel	— from Malayalam വെറ്റില *vettila*; Tamil வெற்றிலை *vettrilai*: வெட்ட்ரு "vettru"=plant name + இலை "ilai"=leaf, (Source: OED)
coir	— probably from Malayalam കയര് *kayar*, Tamil 'கயிறு' "kayiru" for rope or thread or to be twisted. (Source: The American Heritage Dictionary)
copra	— from the Malayalam word കൊപ്പറ *koppara*, coconut kernel or Tamil கொப்பரை *kopparai*/ கொப்பறா *koppara* or Telugu word *kobbera*(Source: OED, AHD, MWD)
Malayalam	— from Malayalam മലയാളം *Malayalam*, from Tamil மலை *malai*, mountain, அல *ala*, people, and the appendix அம்-*am* (Source: http://en.wikipedia.org/wiki/Malayalam) or 'malai' - mountain, 'aalum' reigning, 'mozhi' - language.
mango	— form மாங்காய் *maangay* could be a borrowing from Malayalam. Final - *o* of Engl. *mango* is unexplained. (Sources: OED,
teak	— via Portuguese *teca*, Malay *tekka*, from Malayalam തേക്ക് *thekku*, from Tamil தேக்கு *thekku*

[edit] Words currently debated

Major English dictionaries like *Oxford English Dictionary*, *American Heritage Dictionary*, and *Merriam-Webster Collegiate Dictionary*, do not conclusively attribute Tamil origin to these words.

anaconda	— possibly from Tamil ஆனை கொன்றன் *aanai kondran*, elephant killer.[9] OED gives derivation from Tamil *anai-kondra* (*anaik-konda*), meaning "which killed an elephant."[10] AHD, MWD, *New Oxford American Dictionary* give origin from Sinhalese හෙනකඳයා *henakaňdayā*, "whipsnake".
cash	— Of disputed origin. The primary meaning of the word *cash*, "paper money", or "money" in general, may be from French *caisse*, Provençal *caissa*, Italian *cassa* "money box" from Vulgar Latin *capsa* "chest, box".

A secondary meaning of *cash*, referring to any of the various coins used in southern India and China, could be from Malayalam or Tamil காசு *kācu* (Source: OED, AHD, MWD)

coolie — Of disputed origin. OED states Tamil is proposed by some as the language of origin, from கூலி *cooli* a Tamil word for "labour". Alternatively, it could refer to a tribe from Gujarat, whose members were frequently employed as manual laborers.

ginger — The English word ginger is derived from the Middle English *gingivere*, which in turn comes from Old English gingifer and from Old French gingivre, both from Medieval Latin gingiber. The Latin word is derived from Greek ζιγγίβερις zingiberis, of Middle Indic origin (akin to Pali सिन्गिभेरम् singiveram), from Dravidian roots, akin to Tamil இஞ்சி வேர் *iñcivēr* - இஞ்சி *iñci* = ginger (of southeast Asian origin) + Tamil வேர் *vēr* = root.

godown — via Malay *gudang*, from a Dravidian origin, cf. Kannada *gadangu*, Tamil கிட்டங்கி (கிடங்கு) *Kittangi* (*kidangu/kodangu*) "store room" (Source: OED)

Moringa — exact origin unknown, cf. Tamil முருங்கை *murungai*, Tamil word for drumstick (Source: OED, AHD)

Words of Tamil origin occur in other languages. A notable example of a word in worldwide use with Dravidian (not specifically Tamil) etymology is *orange*, via Sanskrit *nāraṅga* from a Dravidian predecessor of Tamil *nartankāy* "fragrant fruit". Popular examples in English are cheroot (*churuṭṭu* meaning "rolled up"),[136] mango (from *mangai*),[136] mulligatawny (from *miḷaku taṇṇir* meaning pepper water), pariah (from *paraiyan*), curry (from *kari*),[137] catamaran (from *kaṭṭu maram*, கட்டு மரம், meaning "bundled logs"),[136] pandal (shed, shelter, booth),[136] tyer (curd),[136] anicut (from *anaikattu*, அணைக்கட்டு, meaning dam),[136] and coir (rope).[138] Tamil words are also found in Sinhala, Malayalam, Tagalog, Thai, and Malay.*[citation needed]* Japanese and

Korean languages borrowed few words from Tamil also has similarities in Tamil.[139][140]

Tamil origin words from dictionaries include, Ayah, Tope, Pallanquin

Wootz (wook) – from Tamil urukku (to melt) – Highest quality steel from the crucible process of steel-making.

Liturgical Language: Hebrew, Latin, Sanskrit, Pali, Arabic

A curious condition in the religious world, is that most religions have their holy scriptures written in an ancient language and insist on using those in their liturgies. This, despite all of them except Arabic being dead! Hebrew was on its deathbed when the Zionists resurrected it as the official language of Israel.

It raises the question, "Does the living God still speak to His people in a dead language?" This was the situation when Latin was the official language of the Catholic church pre and post the reformation. It was the sole domain of the clergy, who thereby dominated the lives of their parishioners. The need for the common people to access the knowledge of the scriptures, aided by Gutenberg's printing press, speeded up Latin's total demise and Christianity's accessibility to all people. Hence, the fact that the Bible is now published in 3,324 languages as of 2017. Translations in more tribal languages are ongoing. All church services are now completely in a living, modern language.

To be fair, some religions like Islam while reading and quoting the Koran in Arabic, have their sermons preached in the mother tongue. For the convenience of the non-conversant in Arabic, the Koran is available in parallel translations. So, that takes care of it.

This is not the case with Hinduism, which has a ritualistic liturgy. That is is say, there is no reading and reflection on the scriptures. That happens outside the worship space, and in the common language. Sanskrit, which is only understood by the purohits, or priests, is chanted while the baktas, or believers are clueless as to the meaning thereof. The situation is akin to a person overhearing a telephone conversation and trying to guess what the person on the other end of the line (i.e. the idol) is saying. Unlike Islam, which specifically instructs its believers to preserve the originality of the koran by official readings in Arabic, there is no such injunction to use incantations or invocations in Sanskrit. The brahmin priests, have maintained their top dog position in the hindu caste echelon (*varnashrama dharma*) by holding on tight to Sanskrit, standing close to the idol inside the sanctum sanctorum, while the devotee stands outside, behind a barricade. Many hindus, especially in North America, are beginning to wonder if English might not be a better medium in worship. This is due the realization that their next generation is losing even its mother tongue, forget about dearly departed Sanskrit!

As it is, rituals are mechanical rather than mindful, how much further the worship distance if the ritual is conducted in an alien tongue? A double bind indeed.

Another religious liturgy that sounds hollow because of its dependence on an unknown, dead language is Buddhism. Pali is a Middle Indo-Aryan liturgical language native to the Indian subcontinent. It is widely studied because it is the language of the Pāli Canon or Tipiṭaka (based on Buddha's sermons) and is the sacred language of Theravāda Buddhism, prevalent in Sri Lanka and South-East Asia. Most of the so-called worship in Buddhism is chanting. Since Buddhism doesn't have a theology or belief in God, the chanting is merely to enable focused meditation, rather than doctrinal rumination. Being so, any language will do, even English, in the west. Since it is only to get into a meditative mood, even gibberish should suffice, as with the *Ohm* word.

Coming to China-centric religions such as Taoism and Confucianism, naturally the chants and worships are in Chinese, as the language itself is modern and living. These religions have extensive texts and commentaries. Being a mother tongue, there is no impediment to the adherent's apprehension, appreciation and adoration of his almighty.

New kid on the block, Sikhism has its sacred text, the Guru Granth Sahib, written in Punjabi. Since Sikhism is entirely a religion of the Sikhs (Duhh!), and they are all Punjabi speakers, and Guru Nanak was a Punjabi, it is as it should be – a people's worship in their own language. The reading of the Guru Granth (Guru Nanak's teachings) is forefront in their worship. It holds central position in the prayer house or Gurdwara, resting on a raised rostrum, equal to a main deity in a Hindu temple.

The message here is that the message (of God) should be pertinent to the current needs of man. The divine has always sought to meet the needs of mankind at all times of history. We have the prophets of the Old Testament, Buddha, Christ, Muhammad, etc coming with messages at critical times in world history. The Hindu *itihasa* (History – Mahabaratha, Ramayana etc) and *puranas* (mythology) tell stories of how the gods took various forms and avatars in various times, to intervene in peoples' problems. Likewise, shouldn't worship – where devotee meets deity – be in an intelligent and intelligible way? Or, is it that the gods only speak and understand Sanskrit or Pali, stuck in the past? Then, what's the point? Again, the priests will never want give up their position as intervenors and intermediaries in the Brahma → Brahmin → Baktha configuration. They forget that even in crowded congregational settings, worship is always a personal encounter between the Lord and the Layman, minus the Liaison Officer.

Just as technology keeps revolutionizing and mechanical models keep upgrading, languages and teachings that fail to keep up with changing needs have expired. Moderns, with their need to understand concepts behind precepts and reasonings behind rituals, will likely move away if those needs are not fulfilled through simple and relevant language.

Sacred, er Scarred language: T** N** Maa, P*** Mak, Ngomma P*****, Mother F*****

There is no doubt that in all cultures mother is held up in high esteem. Mother is held so high that she is often assigned divine status. There is Kuan Yin, Amman the mother goddess, Mary the Roman Catholic "Mother of God". Even in Islam Aisyah, though not deified, is held to be a special and inimitable figure among women.

The most baffling thing about language is, while it places mother on a pedestal when things go hunky dory, she is shot down in moments of anger and rage. She becomes the "mother" of all expletives. What a dichotomy. Father doesn't come into the picture even if you'd gotten the worst of his temper when you were a naughty brat. You would have run to mummy for solace and she would have soothed your pain and massaged your bruised ego. Yet, she is the one used as an object to curse someone. And it occurs in all the languages that I know of! Examined closely, the intended target is never your mother. Neither is it his mother. The intended bullseye is your opponent, but its an insult to mum nonentheless. In colloquial Tamil, older sister is also brought into the discourse. And unmentionable body parts hurled around.

A common blurt in a moment of hurt is the derogatory "Son of a whore", Bitch, and what have you. The target is the mother of the other. The strangest thing of all, is that it hardly gets a decent rebuttal these days. Not even as weak a comeback as, say, "Stupid Moron!" Perhaps that is due to the Patriarchal nature of most communities. The exception seems to be matriarchal societies or those that that idealize mothers. The Latin communities of southern Europe would take offence easily, as happened when David Beckham called the referee, *"hijo de puta"* (son of a whore). He got the instant red card. On the spot chastisement. Latins, being Roman Catholics, revering the Virgin Mary, may possibly explain that.

American black culture has (had?) taken mother smothering in a different direction. Under the cloak of harmless rude banter, they made it into a game. They even had a show on MTV called *Yo Momma*, popular in the US and the UK. *"Yo momma so fat, she's on both sides of the family"*, *"Yo momma so stinky she uses Right Guard and Left Guard"*. You only understand half of it, but laugh nevertheless, because everybody else does. Apparently this kind of exchange is a common daily thing among them.

In Mandarin, one of the worst insults is, *"Nide muchin shr ega da wukwei"* (Your mother is a big turtle). It is thought to be particularly insulting to call someone a turtle egg because a turtle does not know its father and turtles are promiscuous. The term "bastard" as used in other cultures implies the same thing. A very offensive Tamil slur is, *"Appan peyar theriyathavan"* (The fellow who doesn't know his father's name). The Malay version, *Anak Haram* (illegitimate child) is self-explanatory. However, in a liberal thinking, free sex society, there won't be any so-called bastards, or *Bajingan* (Malay), *Kundagan* (Tamil)), *Húndàn* (Chinese)

The reason why it is mothers and not fathers who are the butt of such insults is, the mother is the one who has the answer to the question, "who am I?" She is the closest link to us. Afterall, we came out of her, not out of the guy who went into her. And only she can tell us about our genealogy.

Perhaps even more damning to a man's ego is to call him a sissy or transgender, homosexual etc. the implication is you are feminine. Females in patriarchal societies are often looked down as weak and promiscuous. So, the easiest way to rattle a male is call him something that falls in between man and woman. The Malay *mak nyah*, Chinese *kuà xìng rén*, and Tamil *ponnan* ("girly", pondaan in Malay). In almost all languages, it would be hard to find a male equivalent to, say prostitute, bitch, whore. The closest will be Casanova, Don Juan, Gigolo, but they are almost respectable and badges of honour – as lady conquerors.

The mother, as goddess or concubine, is a dichotomy that disturbs males at different points in their life. The mother is a life giver and life saver to the child who suckles her breast. Yet, a breast also becomes an object that feeds his lust as he grows up. And that breast will in turn feed his child. What a world.

Literature (Classical): Sangam, Shu Yuan, Sejarah (Melayu)

As India and China have produced some of the most voluminous ancient literary texts, Malaysian Chinese and Indians are the proud heirs of a lasting treasure. The Malays have a literary tradition that is years younger and less voluminous.

The oldest extant Indian text is the Tamil *Tolkappiyam*. Some in the Tamil tradition place the text in the mythical second sangam, variously in 1st millennium BCE or earlier. Other scholars place the text much later and believe the text evolved and expanded over a period of time. According to some, the earliest layer of the Tolkappiyam was likely composed between the 2nd and 1st century BCE, (Kamil Václav Zvelebil), Czech scholar in Indian literature.

Sanskrit, which is now a senior member of the dead languages society that includes classical Greek and Latin, has its earliest text from AD 224-383. "The Bakhshali manuscript is an ancient Indian mathematical text written on birch bark that was found in 1881 in the village of Bakhshali, Mardan (near Peshawar in present-day Pakistan). It is perhaps 'the oldest extant manuscript in Indian mathematics.' For some portions a carbon-date was proposed of AD 224-383 while for other portions a carbon-date as late as AD 885-993 in a recent study, but the dating has been criticised by specialists on methodological grounds (Plofker et al. 2017[1] and Houben 2018 §3[2]). The manuscript contains the earliest known Indian use of a zero symbol. It is written in Sanskrit with significant influence from other local languages."

The Tamil language of South India and the mother tongue of the majority of Malaysian Indians, is the oldest of living languages as attested by most scholars. A keyword search for "oldest living (classical) language" brings up Tamil on the top of the chart, although (modern) Hebrew sometimes comes up on top. Then again, Hebrew was practically out of action from 400 CE until the establishment of modern Israel in recent times.

Tamil literature goes back more than two thousand years and was proclaimed a classical language in 2004. Its oldest extant book is the *Tholkapiyam*, about 2200 years old. It is the world's oldest grammar textbook and a most comprehensive one as well. Scholars will tell you that for a language to have evolved a complete grammar, it must have priorly had a long literary history. This agrees with Tamil's claim of the first Sangam (Literary Academy) of 9600 BCE to 5200 BCE.

Tradition and ancient texts allude to the existence of successive Tamil academies called *Sangam*. The corpora of the first 2 academies based in the city of Madurai on the lost continent of Kumari Kandam (Lemuria), are missing in the misty mire of myth. The city of Madurai was lost to a colossal *Kadal Kol* ("engulfed by sea"), or tsunamis. The 3rd and last Sangam is estimated to have spanned from 6th century BCE to 3rd century CE. The precious classical volumes that have survived come from this Sangam.

Sangam was a literal literary club (academy) consisting of poets, philosophers and scholars under royal Pandyan patronage. It was a gathering where literary creations were given a first reading and peer reviewed before being sanctioned as bona fide works. The author was grilled on the logic and grammar of his work.There is also a tradition that the literature was thrown into the lotus pond in the famous Meenakshi temple of Madurai. If it floated, it was a true work! The 2,000 year-old Thirukkural, considered a late sangam work, is said to have passed the test this way. Today, it has been translated into about 41 languages and 57 versions in English alone by 2014 (estimated 100 in 2022) ! It is the most translated non-religious work in the world.

Here is a brief chart of the corpus of Sangam litt.

"The rediscovered Sangam classical collection is largely a bardic corpus. It comprises an *Urtext* of oldest surviving Tamil grammar (Tolkappiyam),

Ettuttokai anthology (the "Eight Collections"), including,

Name	Extant poems	Number of poets
Narrinai (400 Landscape poems)	400	175
Kuruntokai Naanooru (400 shoet poems	402	205
Ainkurunuru (500 very short poems)	499	5
Patirruppattu (Ten Tens)	86	8
Paripatal (Devotionals in the pari-meter)	33	13
Kalittokai (Anthology in the kali-meter)	150	5
Akananuru (400 "Interior"/love poems)	401	145
Purananuru (400 "exterior"/war poems)	398	157

The Pattuppattu anthology (the "Ten Idylls").

Name	Lines	Author
Tirumurukarruppatai	317	Nakkirar
Porunararruppatai	234	Mutattamakkanniyar
Cirupanarruppatai	296	Nattattanar
Perumpanarruppatai	500	Uruttirankannaiyar
Mullaippattu	103	Napputanar
Maturaikkanci	782	Mankuti Marutanar
Netunalvatai	188	Nakkirar
Kurincippattu	261	Kapilar
Pattinappalai	301	Uruttirankannanar
Malaipatukatam	583	Perunkaucikanai

The above two sets (Ettutokai and Patthuppaattu) are only two out of the Paathinenmelkanakku ("The eighteen major collections")! There is also a pathinenkeelkanakku ("eighteen minor collections")! The world famous Thirukural comes under this latter set.

The Tamil literature that followed the Sangam period – that is, after c. 250 CE but before c. 600 CE – is generally called the "post-Sangam" literature. Among the 5 epics of this period, the Silappathikaram ("The Ankle Bracelet"). Written in the 5th/6th century AD, it is foremost for its gripping coverage of a jeweller couple's journey to another country and the depth of details of the life and times of the period.

This latter collection contains 2381 poems in Tamil composed by 473 poets, some 102 anonymous. Of these, 16 poets account for about 50% of the known Sangam literature, with Kapilar – the most prolific poet – alone contributing just little less than 10% of the entire corpus. These poems vary between 3 and 782 lines long. The bardic poetry of the Sangam era is largely about love (*akam*) and war (*puram*), with the exception of the shorter poems such as in *paripaatal* which is more religious and praise Vishnu, Shiva, Durga and Murugan."

Chinese literary tradition goes back – 3000 years to the age of Classical Chinese poetry

"The Tang dynasty (618-907 CE) was a high point in terms of China's cultural development. Therefore, it isn't surprising that this was also a watershed moment for poetry in China. The Tang dynasty poets Li Bai (李白 Lǐ Bái) and Du Fu (杜甫 Dù Fǔ) are some of the most well-known and celebrated poets in modern China.

There is a wealth of early Chinese literature dating from the *Hundred Schools of Thought* that occurred during the Eastern Zhou Dynasty (770-256 BC). The most important of these include the Classics of Confucianism, of Daoism, of Mohism, of Legalism, as well as works of military science and Chinese history. Note that, except for the books of poems and songs, most of this literature is philosophical and didactic; there is little in the way of fiction. However, these texts maintained their significance through both their ideas and their prose style.

The Confucian works in particular have been of key importance to Chinese culture and history, as a set of works known as the *Four Books and Five Classics* were, in the 12th century AD, chosen as the basis for the Imperial examination for any government post. These nine books therefore became the center of the educational system. They have been grouped into two categories: the *Five Classics*, allegedly commented and edited by Confucius, and the Four Books. The *Five Classics* are:

1. the *I Ching*, or *Classic of Changes*, a divination manual;
2. the *Classic of Poetry*, a collection of poems, folk songs, festival and ceremonial songs, hymns and eulogies;
3. the *Book of Rites* or *Record of Rites*;
4. the *Book of documents*, an early Chinese prose collection of documents and speeches allegedly written by rulers and officials of the early Zhou period and earlier;
5. the *Spring and Autumn Annals*, a historical record of Confucius' native state, Lu, from 722 to 479 BC.

The *Four Books* are:

1. the *Analects of Confucius*, a book of pithy sayings attributed to Confucius and recorded by his disciples;
2. the *Mencius*, a collection of political dialogues;
3. the *Doctrine of the Mean*, a book that teaches the path to Confucian virtue; and
4. the *Great Learning*, a book about education, self-cultivation and the Dao.

Other important philosophical works include the Mohist *Mozi*, which taught "inclusive love" as both an ethical and social principle, and *Hanfeizi*, one of the central Legalist texts.

Important Daoist classics include the *Dao De Jing*, the *Zhuangzi*, and the *Liezi*. Later authors combined Daoism with Confucianism and Legalism, such as Liu An (2nd century BC), whose *Huainanzi* (*The Philosophers of Huai-nan*) also added to the fields of geography and topography.

Among the classics of military science, *The Art of War* by Sun Tzu (6th century BC) was perhaps the first to outline guidelines for effective international diplomacy. It was also the first in a tradition of Chinese military treatises, such as the *Jingling Zongyao* (*Collection of the Most Important Military Techniques*, 1044 AD) and the *Huolongjing* (*Fire Dragon Manual*, 14th century AD).

Four classic novels *Water Margin, Journey to the West* (perhaps the most influential of the four classic novels of Chinese literature, and certainly the most widely known beyond China's borders, *Journey to the West* was written in the 16th century by Wu Cheng'en. It depicts the pilgrimage of the Buddhist monk Xuanzang to India, and his resultant travels through the Western provinces of China,), *Romance of the Three Kingdoms* and *Dream of the Red Chamber*; these four novels form the core of Chinese classical literature and still inform modern culture. "

The following time-line serves to show the length (of time) and breadth (of genre) of the total spread of classical literature.

Shang Dynasty (about 1700-1050 BC) — Development of Chinese Writing

Zhou Dynasty (1045-255 BC) — Basic Philosophical and Religious Literature

Qin Dynasty (221-206 BC) — Literary Disaster and Legalism (Warring States period)

Han Dynasty (206 BC – 220 AD) — Scientific and Historical Texts

Tang Dynasty (618-907) — Early Woodblock Printing and Poetry

Song Dynasty (960-1279) — Early Woodblock Printing, Travel Literature, Poetry, Scientific Texts and the Neo-Confucian Classics

Yuan Dynasty – Mongol – (1279-1368) — Drama and Great Fictional Novels

Ming Dynasty (1368-1644) — Novels

Qing Dynasty – Manchu – (1644-1911) — Novels and Pre-modern Literature

The Malay universe isn't short of academic traditions. Srivijaya, on the island of Sumatra, was the ancient Malay empire from the 7th till the 13th centuries CE. It was a Buddhist culture, as opposed to its contemporary Hindu Javanese empire, Majapahit. It was a regional centre of Buddhist studies. Many Chinese Buddhist pilgrims, such as I-Tsing (Yijing) (635-713 CE) had lengthy stays there on the way to Nalanda, India, the oldest university in the world. At an earlier time, not a few Indian Buddhist missionaries had established the Buddhist culture here.

".... many of kings and rulers in the islands of southern seas adore and believed in lord Buddha, in their hearts has flourished (the seeds of) good deeds. Within the walls of Srivijaya capital city lived 1000 buddhist monks, they have studied diligently and performed (the noble teachings) very well.... If a Chinese monk wished to travel to India and seeks the (Buddha's) teachings, it will be better for them to stay here first for a year or two, to deepening their knowledge before continued their study to India.".

– Description of Srivijaya according to I Ching.

"About a millenium later, on November 29, 1929, and in the same neighbourhood (Kedukan Bukit), Dutchman C.J Batenburg discovered a 18 in by 31 in stone inscribed in Old Malay. He found it on the banks of the river Tatang, tributary of river Musi. The Pallava script inscription is the oldest extant specimen of the Malay language. No one today would be able to read it, much less understand. Old Malay is ancient Malay infused with Sanskrit.

The earliest Malay literature derived from Indian literature. Quite naturally, since our zone (South East-Asia) is called Indianized. Indonesia, Indo-China. The *Mahabharata* and *Ramayana* form the core of most South East Asian cultures. *Hikayat Mara Karma, Hikayat Panca Tanderan (Pancha Tantra)*, and *Hikayat Gul Bakawali* are sourced from Indian Tales. These were mostly oral traditions.

And then comes Arab and Persian influences during the Sultanate of Malacca. The *Sejarah Melayu* (The Malay Annals) written during that period, can be considered the origin story of the Malay race, just as everyone else has. More Hikayats were produced during this period. A hikayat corresponds to sagas – tales of exploits of the Malay princes.

Malay classical tradition (14th to 18th centuries) actually begins with the entry of Islam in these parts. The Terengganu Inscription Stone was written in the year 1303. The literary tradition was further enriched with the translations of various foreign literary works such as *Hikayat Muhammad Hanafiah* and *Hikayat Amir Hamzah*, and the emergence of new intellectual writings in philosophy, tasawuf (spiritual formation), tafsir (exegesis), tawarikh (history).

As for Malay classical texts in the peninsula (Tanah Melayu), things get more recent. The *Sejarah Melayu* (The Malay Annals) is supposed to have been written between 15th and 16th centuries. Originally called by the Arabic name, *Sulalatus Al-Salatin* (Genealogy of Kings), it records historical events relating to the founding of the Malacca Sultanate by Parameswara, who escaped from Tumasik (Singapore) when it came under attack from Majaphit. The rise and fall of the Sultanate to the Portuguese. It includes romantic tales of Badang (a Hercules type), Puteri Gunung Ledang (Fairy Princess on Mt.Ophir), Hang Nadim (saved Singapore from swordfish attack) and Hang Tuah's "lancelotic" exploits.

Bridging the classical – modern nexus, was Abdullah bin Abdul Kadir. His paternal grandfather was a Yemeni religious teacher who married a local woman. His mother Selama (Salmah or Sellammah?) was Tamil. Hence, he was multingual – in Arabic, English, Malay, Tamil, Hindi. Hindi, he picked up while teaching religion to the muslim soldiers of the Indian garrison at Malacca. In return they gave him the title of Munshi, "teacher".

Munshi Abdullah (b.1797, Kampong Pali, Malacca – d.1854, Jeddah, Saudi Arabia). Abdullah was known for his work as a teacher, interpreter and writer. He wrote the biographical *Hikayat Abdullah* (The adventures of Abdullah), which was first published in 1849 and became an important source to understand the social history of 19th-century Singapore. Unlike other Malays writing at the time, he avoided fantasy and legend, and recorded true observances of events from personal experience and those of others. A. E. Coope, translator of Abdullah's *Kisah Pelayaran Abdullah ke Kelantan* (Story of Abdullah's Voyage to Kelantan), wrote, "his 'direct reporting' acts as a pleasant cool douche after the lushness of Malay romances". Abdullah is considered as the 'Father of Modern Malay Literature','"

While the Tamil treatises mostly consist of love (*aham/*internal – personal) and war (*puram/*exterior – national) poems, and ethical discourses, Chinese have preferred to record their history and travels. This has been greatly helpful in sketching the history of our part of the world. Their descriptions of kingdoms and naming of kings of old South East Asia states such as Funan and its successor Chen-la, which preceded the Khmer polity, shed much light. Malay classical literature mostly deals with hikayat, or adventures and escapades.

Literature (Contemporaray): Puthinam, xiǎo shuō Novel

The local Tamil novel, which began in 1887 usually had Indian or Ceylonese flavours, written by first generation immigrants. Their lebensraum and protogonists were set in Tamil Nadu or Jaffna. It only began to accrue a local flavour in the 1900's when the next generation began to record their thoughts.

An excellent depository of Tamil work is the *Tamil Malaysiana* collection residing in the Tamil Studies Department of the University of Malaya

(Singapore) since its establishment in 1956. It is all about works relating to Malaysia and by Malaysians, in Tamil. The collection at the UM library stands at 2,500 documents of diferrent types. The first Tamil novel published in Malaysia (British Malaya at the time) was in 1917 by Venkataretnam. *Dream of the Education* was written by Sivagnanam in 1936. More than 500 novels and short anthologiess have been published since.

The earliest translation from Malay (the *Sejarah Melayu*) was in 1946 by Dr. Rama Subbiah, the first Malaysian born Indian to head the Tamil Studies Department at Universiti Malaya. The earliest newspaper was *Muslim Naisen* (Muslim Stalwart) 1882 run by Penang Indian Muslims. *Malaya Mitran* (Friend of Malaya) 1932. *Desa Mitran* (Friend of the Nation) 1933. *Tamil Murasu* (Tamil Herald) – 1935. Many novels have been embedded as weekly (Sunday) instalments in the newspapers.

Current Tamil titles have seen evolutionary improvements in content and quality in genres like social, thriller, historical etc

Chinese in Literature in Malaysia has existed since 1919 (*Mahua Wenxwe*). The Mahua like the early Tamil works mostly dwelled on and depicted mainland China ecology, while the later, *Nanyang Wenxwe* (South Seas literature) captures the Malayan ecology and ethos. Between 1979 and 1981, several reference books came out, discussing the nature of the literature. Ziao Rong's Singapore-Malaysia Chinese Literature Dictionary had four sections. The first two catalogued the Mahua literature, the third listed colloquialisms, and the fourth named literary organizations and titles of reviews. In 1924, it came out in book form. The first part of the catalogue categorized the Mahua (not set in Malaya) literature into the different genres beginning from the first printed book in 1924 till 1977. The second part write-ups of the writers (731 names!). An earlier compilation (1975) by Goh Thean Chye arranges the publication by the author's names – only a namelist, unlike Zhao who provides biodata.

With European colonization came the modern forms of the novel and the short story in Malay literature. Munshi Abdullah pioneered the Malay travelogue with his *Hikayat Pelayaran*.

In the interest of time and print space, we shall briefly record the works of four modern Malay writers (otherwise, it would be a deep sea dive).

With apologies to the rest of the fine authors, here is a list of the 1st four *Sasterawan Negara* (National Laureates) Malaysia.

Kamaludin Muhammad aka *Keris Mas* (Golden Kris). *Pahlawan Rimba Malaya* (1946), *Korban Kesuciannya* (1949), *Anak Titiwangsa* (1967), *Saudagar Besar Dari Kuala Lumpur* (1983) dan *Rimba Harapan* (1985). The jungle (rimba) theme seems prominent.

Shahnon Ahmad. His first short story, *"Bingung"*, appeared in Majalah Guru on 24 May 1956; his first novel, *Rentong*, was published in 1965, almost a decade later. His third novel, *Ranjau Sepanjang Jalan* (Thorns Along the Way), is his better known work.

Usman Awang (nom de plune *Tongkat Warrant*). *Kurang Ajar, Ke Makam Bonda*, and *Pak Utih*

Samad Said. *Salina*, among many others.

Many of these were academicians and staff of Dewan Bahasa dan Pustaka, The National Literary Academy.

The Malay literary world churns out a ton of tomes, including a rash of pulp fiction.

Poesy: Syair, Shi, Sinthu

Malay poesy consists of Puisi, Sajak, Syair, Gurindam, Pantun, Teromba, Talibun, Mantera.

Syair from the Arabic, *shi'r* is a quartrain of narrative or didactic mode conveying theological or philosophical ideas. *Sajak* is a modern free form type. *Pantun* is a rhyming quartrain, usually sung as a call and answer between a couple in love. The whole thing now comes under the umbrella of *puisi* (from the English "poesy")

The Malay dictionary credits the original etymology of Gurindam to Tamil *kurintham or Kirantham. A* search of Tamil dictionaries for Gurindam didn't yield any results. Kirantham or *Grantham* refers to an early form of Tamil script. Merriam Webster Collegiate dictionary and the Oxford English dictionary does have *Corundum* (the unpolished state of ruby) which derives from the Tamil, *Kuruntam.*

Pantun are a unique genre where a couple, or a team, take turns to compose a four line poetry in a call and response type of activity.

Although it may seem like an instantaneous, impromptu interaction, it follows all the rules of poesy. Naturally, the participants need to have a stockpile of words and phrases to pull it off. On the other pole, is the *Sajak*. As lengthy as you want, whatever theme you desire, and structurally freeform, yet oozing poetry. *Gurindam* is a series of couplets with each pair a complete message in itself. Recalls the Tamil *Thirukural*. Whereas, *Syair* is a set of rhyming quartrains that yields full meanng at the end of it. *Teromba* and *Talibun* belong to the Minangkabau community of Negeri Sembilan. The former sings of the *adat* (customs) of the Minangkabaus and is a straight list (no stanzas). The latter focuses on lipur lara (lipur – "comforter" of lara – "sorrows"), and rhythmic repetition of words aimed at lifting the spirit.

"The Classic of Poetry, also *Shi jing* or *Shih-ching*, translated variously as the Book of Songs, Book of Odes, or simply known as the Odes or Poetry is the oldest existing collection of Chinese poetry, comprising 305 works dating from the 11th to 7th centuries BC. It is one of the "Five Classics" traditionally said to have been compiled by Confucius, and has been studied and memorized by scholars in China and neighboring countries over two millennia. Since the Qing dynasty, its rhyme patterns have also been analysed in the study of old Chinese phonology.

One of the characteristics of the poems in the Classic of Poetry is that they tend to possess "elements of repetition and variation". This results in an "alteration of similarities and differences in the formal structure: in successive stanzas, some lines and phrases are repeated verbatim, while others vary from stanza to stanza.

Nearly all of the songs in the Poetry are rhyming, with end rhyme, as well as frequent internal rhyming. While some of these verses still rhyme in modern varieties of Chinese, others had ceased to rhyme by the Middle Chinese period. For example, the eighth song (苤苢 Fú Yǐ) has a tightly constrained structure implying rhymes between the penultimate words (here shown in bold) of each pair of lines:

采采苤苢、薄言采之。　Cǎi cǎi fú yǐ, báo yán cǎi zhī.

采采苤苢、薄言有之。　Cǎi cǎi fú yǐ, báo yán yǒu zhī.

采采芣苢、薄言掇之。　Cǎi cǎi fú yǐ, báo yán duó zhī.

采采芣苢、薄言捋之。　Cǎi cǎi fú yǐ, báo yán luó zhī.

采采芣苢、薄言袺之。　Cǎi cǎi fú yǐ, báo yán jié zhī.

采采芣苢、薄言襭之。　Cǎi cǎi fú yǐ, báo yán xié zhī."

"In the beginning of the twentieth century, the scene was set in China for both socio-political and poetic change, both political and literary revolution; indeed, the "twentieth century has drawn a heavy line across the time-chart of Chinese culture." The New Culture Movement also known as the May Fourth Movement, was a defining time period in the direction of poetic literature in Chinese language. Nominally originating in the socio-politically oriented student demonstrations in Beijing on May 4, 1919, the New Culture Movement May Fourth Movement was associated with a more general "intellectual ferment". The Beijing University (also known as the Peking University) had an important role in this process. Both Hu Shih and Cai Yuanpei are prime examples of those associated with the university around this time who urged a transformation in literary style deprecating the use of Classical Chinese, in favor of embracing written vernacular Chinese. Hu Shih, Xu Zhimo, Guo Moruo and some of poets followed this path towards a more modern literature, through the use of a more colloquial writing style. This, together with a western influence can be seen in other authors, such as Wen Yiduo."

Paa, Pann, Paattu (song), also *kavithai*, refer to Tamil poetry. Tamil poetry embraces all aspects of life literally from birth till death and in between. *Thaalaattu* (Lullaby), *Oppaari* (Lament), when women of old beat their breasts, and wailed in a singsong, poetic fashion. *Pallu* (agriculture). *Sinthu* (Murugan praise), *Thevaram (Shiva praise), Paasuram (Vishnu praise).* These days, Oppaari and Thaalaattu have largely disappeared among Malaysia's Indian community. Thirukkural (couplets = kural = 2 lines) is aphoristic. However, classical and modern forms of poetry enjoy authorships and readeships

Following is poem 40, from the 2 millenia old *Kuruntokai* ("Short Collection").

Yaayum Gnaayum yaaraakiyaro?	Who are are my mother and yours?
Yenthaiyum Nunthaiyum emmurai Keylir?	What kin is my father to yours?
Yaanum Neeyum evvazhi arithum?	How then, did you and I ever meet?
Anbudai nenjam thaan kalanthanavae	Hearts in love have mingled
Sembula peya neeraar	Like red soil and rain water

The *Kuruntokai* (The Collection of Short Poems) is the fifth of the the *Ettutokai* (The Eight Anthologies), which together with the *Paththuppaattu* (The Ten Idylls) comprises the *Patiṉeṉmēlkaṇakku* (The Eighteen Major Collection).There is also a *Patinenkeelkanakku* (The Eighteen Minor Collection!) of which, the famous 1330 couplet *Thirukkural* (Sacred Voice) is one. The 2371 poems of the Ettutokai have been dated by Kamil Zvelebil, Czech scholar of Tamil literature, to 2nd Century BCE till the 5th century CE. Note that all these Sangam works, like classical literature worldwide, were written in poetry form.

The modern Tamil poet, *Mahakavi* ("Great Poet") Subramania Bharati, wrote an article titled *Japaniya Kavidai* dated October 16, 1916, published in the *Swadesamitran* (Friend of Self-rule) newspaper. He introduced two Japanese haiku by translating it into Tamil, which set in motion a new phase in the Tamil literary world of Puducherry (French enclave), his refuge from British police.

The two 17-syllable Japanese haiku published in Tamil created an audience in the freedom fighting era that continued the tryst with haiku through generations.

Retaining the evocation, spontaneity and economy of words, the Tamil version did not follow the metric or syllable of haiku. The richness of local flavour and native language was infused into haiku and it morphed into the Tamil version of 'Tulipa'. Litt. "poetry droplets".

Sages: Valluvar, Confucius, Tun Sri Lanang

Each culture has its own pantheon of cultural icons, who have attained almost deified status. They were philosophers and writers of old, who penned wise sayings and immortal moral dictums.

Tolkaapiyar, was the author of *Tolkaappiyam* ("Ancient Opus"), considered the oldest grammar book in the world. Likely composed between the 15th

up to the 3rd centuries BCE. However Valluvar, the author of *Thirukkural* ("Sacred Voice" – circa 1st century AD), is the one most prominent in peoples' minds. It could perhaps be a manifestation of the human tendency to hate dry grammar and appreciate poetry and flowery language, like we love proverbs and pithy sayings.

Although Thiruvalluvar's biography is sketchy but multi-faceted, he is included in the hagiographies of different castes, religions and traditions. He is claimed by the Saivite and Vaishnavite Hindus, the Jains, Christians and Buddhists. It appeals to all, because of its pure moral tone rather religious rhetoric.

Scholars and leaders from all spectrums have praised the *Kural.* These include Ilango Adigal, Kambar, Leo Tolstoy, Mahatma Gandhi, Albert Schweitzer, Constantius Joseph Beschi, Karl Graul, George Uglow Pope, Alexander Piatigorsky, and Yu Hsi. The text has been translated into at least 40 Indian and non-Indian languages, making it one of the most translated ancient works, after the Bible. Among Tamils, Valluvar commands a status equivalent to Homer, Confucius and Shakespeare.

The *Kural,* Valluvar's sole opus, is the work of a single author because it has a consistent "*language, formal structure and content-structure*", states Zvelebil. The division into three sections (*muppāl*) is probably the author's design. However, the subdivisions beyond these three, known as *iyals*, or chapters as found in some surviving manuscripts and commentaries, are likely later structurings. The *muppal* are Aham (Virtue), Porul (Wealth) and Inbam (Happiness or love) and cover themes from morality, family values, politics, administration, warfare, international relations, and love. If Sun Tzu wrote "The Art of War", Valluvar's work can be called "The Art of Living."

When Valluvar says that while "*disease and cure come from different sources, your bejewelled beloved is the very medicine for the malady that she is*", he is hilarious. The following anglifications are by G.U.Pope ((24 April 1820-11 February 1908)

Kural 1102:   "Disease and medicine, antagonists we surely see;
This maid, to pain she gives, herself is remedy."

Every one of his couplets is rife with rhyme and alliteration.

Kural 12:   *"thuppaarkku thuppaaya thuppaakki,*
                       thuppaarkku thuppaaya thoovum malai."

Key words: *Thuppu* – food, *Thuppaar* – consumer, *Thuppaakki* – make food, *Thoovum* – to rain.

Translation: "The rain makes pleasant food for eaters rise,
                       Itself as food, thirst quenching draught supplies"

At first glance, it seems to refer to someone doing double duty, as when a physician saves his patient by also donating his own blood. Another one of his dualisms.

Here is how Valluvar and Sun Tzu mirror each other, on the subject of diplomacy and warfare.

Art of war: 7: 36 (Maneuvering)

        "When you surround an army, leave an outlet free.
        Do not press a desperate foe too hard."

Kural 773: (Military Spirit)

        "Fierceness in hour of strife, heroic greatness shows;
        Its edge, is kindness to our suffering foes."

"Confucius (/kən'fjuːʃəs/kən-FEW-shəs; Chinese: 孔夫子; pinyin: Kǒng Fūzǐ, "Master Kǒng"; 551-479 BCE) was a Chinese philosopher and politician of the Spring and Autumn period who is traditionally considered the paragon of Chinese sages. Widely considered one of the most important and influential individuals in human history, Confucius's teachings and philosophy formed the basis of East Asian culture and society, and remains influential today.

The philosophy of Confucius—Confucianism—emphasized personal and governmental morality, correctness of social relationships, justice, kindness, and sincerity. Confucianism was part of the Chinese social fabric and way of life. To Confucians, everyday life was the arena of religion.

Confucius is traditionally credited with having authored or edited many of the Chinese classic texts, including all of the Five Classics, but modern scholars are cautious of attributing specific assertions to Confucius himself. Aphorisms concerning his teachings were compiled in the Analects, but only many years after his death.

Confucius's principles have commonality with Chinese tradition and belief. With filial piety, he championed strong family loyalty, ancestor veneration, and respect of elders by their children and of husbands by their wives, recommending family as a basis for ideal government.

Although Confucianism is often followed in a religious manner by the Chinese, many argue that its values are secular and that it is, therefore, less a religion than a secular morality. Proponents argue, however, that despite the secular nature of Confucianism's teachings, it is based on a worldview that is religious. Confucianism discusses elements of the afterlife and views concerning Heaven, but it is relatively unconcerned with some spiritual matters often considered essential to religious thought, such as the nature of souls.

In the Analects, Confucius presents himself as a "transmitter who invented nothing". He puts the greatest emphasis on the importance of study, and it is the Chinese character for study (學) that opens the text. Far from trying to build a systematic or formalist theory, he wanted his disciples to master and internalize older classics, so that their deep thought and thorough study would allow them to relate the moral problems of the present to past political events (as recorded in the Annals) or the past expressions of commoners' feelings and noblemen's reflections (as in the poems of the Book of Odes).

One of the deepest teachings of Confucius may have been the superiority of personal exemplification over explicit rules of behavior. His moral teachings emphasized self-cultivation, emulation of moral exemplars, and the attainment of skilled judgment rather than knowledge of rules. Confucian ethics may, therefore, be considered a type of virtue ethics. His teachings rarely rely on reasoned argument, and ethical ideals and methods are conveyed indirectly, through allusion, innuendo, and even tautology. His teachings require examination and context to be understood. A good example is found in this famous anecdote:

One of his teachings was a variant of the Golden Rule, sometimes called the "Silver Rule" owing to its negative form:

'What you do not wish for yourself, do not do to others.'

Zi Gong [a disciple] asked: 'Is there any one word that could guide a person throughout life?'

The Master replied: 'How about 'reciprocity'! Never impose on others what you would not choose for yourself.'" – wikipedia

Tun Sri Lanang didn't write timeless treatises on ethical living like Valluvar or Confucius. Neither does he continue to be worshipped across the centuries, like them. But, he is the Malay world's earliest named litarateurs, and had quite an extensive political career.

"Tun Muhammad bin Tun Ahmad, better known as Tun Sri Lanang, was the Bendahara (Grand Vizier) of the royal Court of the Johor Sultanate who lived between the 16th and 17th centuries. He served under two Sultans of Johor, namely; Sultan Ali Jalla Abdul Jalil Shah II (1570-1597) and Sultan Alauddin Riayat Shah III (1597-1615) and also advisor to 3 Acheh sultans namely; Sultan Iskandar Muda (until 1636), Sultan Iskandar Thani (1636-1641) and Sultan Tajul Alam Safiatuddin Shah (1641-1675). He had two honorific titles throughout his lifetime; as the Bendahara of Johor, Bendahara Paduka Raja Tun Mohamad, while he was given the title of Orang Kaya Dato' Bendahara Seri Paduka Tun Seberang after settling in Acheh.

Tun Sri Lanang was born in 1565 in Seluyut, Johore, and was descended from Tun Tahir, a brother of Bendahara Tun Mutahir of Malacca. Tun Mutahir himself, was from a line of Tamil Muslim Bendaharas, or Prime Ministers to the Malaccan court. There are not many records about Tun Sri Lanang as Bendahara in Johore. However, during the rule of Sultan Alauddin Riayat Shah III, he shouldered a heavier burden on the affairs of the state as the Sultan was a weak ruler. He shared the responsibility with the Sultan's brother Raja Abdullah (later to become Sultan Abdullah Maayah Shah who reigned between 1615 to 1623).

In 1612, at the request of Raja Abdullah to pen the Malay Annals to ensure, "... *all the adat, the rules and the ceremonies of the Malay Sultans and Rajas to be heard by our descendants and is made known all utterances so that it may benefit them*". At this time, under the orders of Sultan Alauddin Riaayat Shah, Tun Sri Lanang oversaw the editorial and compilation process of the Malay Annals, better known as Sejarah Melayu in Malay.

In 1613, Acheh attacked Johor and in the battle of Batu Sawar, Johore was defeated and the Royal Family and Tun Sri Lanang were captured and brought to Acheh. The Bendaharaship was continued by his descendants. His notable descendants include Bendahara Tun Habib Abdul Majid and the Raja Bendahara of Johor-Melaka.

After a brief "reeducation" in Aceh, the Johor Royal Family was returned to Johor. Tun Sri Lanang elected to stay in Acheh. He became advisor to the third Sultan of Acheh and was bestowed an Acheh honorific title. He was awarded a personal fief in Samalanga, Acheh in 1613 and held the title Uleebalang of Samalanga. He died in 1659 in Samalanga.

His legacy is not only the recording and compiling of the magnum opus "Sejarah Melayu" but also includes the strongly Islamic flavor of Samalanga. Samalanga is also known as "Kota Santri", or "Town of Medrassas" is the centre of Islamic propagation in Acheh until today. Samalanga was also among the last towns to fall to the Dutch during the time of the last Sultan of Acheh, Sultan Muhammad Daud Shah and also one of his strongholds."

Betrothals: Pertunangan, Nitchaiyathartham, guo dàlǐ

This subject is almost archaic and antiquated. "Betrothal" has become "be-what?", "behind-time" or "bygone". Young people consider this a joke and a dinosaur. Marriage is now a direct trade, with the middleman out of the picture. However, address this we must, as it yet exists and carries a heavy cargo of culture, equal to the wedding itself.

While it has lost its standing, it has great qualities. The common denominator in all cultures is the "spying" (Merisik, Thoothu, …..") done by the elders to determine the "suitability" of the bride or groom. With young people choosing their own partners based on emotional draws, suitability suffers, leading to widespread divorces compared to betrothal marriages. Besides, since betrothals were a community project, everyone was invested in its success, and sent friends on spying expeditions to background check the bride and groom. Many modern marriage counselors assess suitability by running self-report "tests" or questionnaires and pre-marital counselling. A prominent public speaker even suggests that women observe their prospective husbands at their workplace, to see how they act towards their superiors and subordinates. If there is a difference in the ways of wooing and working, watch out!

The Malay *pertunangan* (proposal/engagement) is preceded by the *merisik* (surveillance) of the other family.

In the Tamil proposal, after the initial background checks, which includes caste affiliation (on the decline in Malaysia), comes the *porutham* (suitability) "test". This is not a scientific process, but an age old custom of *rasi poruttham* (horoscope compatibility) read by a *jothidar* (astrologer). Some modern ones may consider it as horror scope, as many a girl has been deprived of marriage just because she happened to have a certain *rasi* that would kill her husband or mother in law etc, within a year of marriage. In the earlier generations, dowry (not bride price, but groom price!) is discussed on a commercial scale. *Muhurtham* (auspicious day and time of wedding), is also calculated based on the couples' horoscopes.

When these hoops have been crossed, the elaborate engagement (*nitchayathaartham*) ceremony is held. The engagement is officially announced and culminates in the exchange of the *nitchaya taambulam* ("promissory tray"). The boy has the bigger burden, He will deliver up to 45 *thattu* (trays) of *seer varisai* ("parade of gifts") which includes the wedding saree, gold ornaments, fruits, coocunut, flowers and what have you. It is similar to the Malay, *hantaran kahwin* ("marital consignment"). The girl's side responds with the *maru seer* ("reciprocal gift"). The maru seer tray would contain the grooms's ring, some fruits, flowers, beetal leaves, beetal nut along with some cash which is usually a value ending with 1 viz. 101 or 5001 or 10001.

Manjal (turmeric), *kunkumam* (turmeric + slaked lime = red colour) and *santhanam* (sandalwood paste) are propitious items in both the pre-marriage and marriage phases.

In the Chinese culture, proposals follow the same pattern as above. Only difference is, race, religion, social class do not figure in the choice of partner, except virtuousness. The first step is the selection of auspicious dates for the wedding, the betrothal and the installation of the bridal bed. A Chinese monk or a temple fortune teller selects a suitable date based on the couple's birth dates and times. Some may also refer to the Chinese calendar or almanac for good days. Even numbered months and dates are preferred, and the lunar seventh month is avoided as it is the month of the Hungry Ghost Festival.

After the selection of the auspicious dates, wedding details such as types and quantities of betrothal gifts, reciprocal gifts, bride price (娉金), and number of tables at the wedding banquet provided by the groom's parents for the bride's parents' guests are settled.

<u>Betrothal</u>

Up to three months or earlier before the wedding day, the groom will deliver the betrothal gifts to the bride's family on an auspicious date.送

"The betrothal (Chinese: 過大禮; pinyin: guo dàlǐ, also known as 納彩 or nàcǎi) is an important part of the Chinese wedding tradition. During this exchange, the groom's family presents the bride's family with betrothal gifts (called 聘礼 or pìnlǐ) to symbolize prosperity and good luck. Moreover, the bride's family receives the bride price (Chinese: 娉金; pinyin: pīng jīn; lit. 'abundant gold') in red envelopes. The bride's family also returns (回禮, huílǐ) a set of gifts to the groom's side. Additionally, the bride's parents bestow a dowry (嫁妆, jiàzhuāng, kè-chng) to the bride."

The gifts are often in even number for the meaning of in couple and in pairs. Food items given to the bride include wine, oranges, and tea; while jewelry for the bride includes gold earrings, necklaces, bracelets, and rings. In some regions, they are also combined with some local food, such as peanuts and dates (in Chinese, the word for "date" is a near homonym of "early", while "peanut" is "birth"). This is normally presented on the wedding day, with the wishes of giving birth to a child early in the marriage. Candles and paper cut "Double Happiness" are often seen on a wedding day as well.

After the betrothal gifts and bride price is negotiated and given, the families select a special date for the wedding. The wedding date is announced via invitations about a month earlier, and the invitations are distributed to the friends and relatives about one or two weeks before the wedding day.

In contrast to the Malay dowry (*Mas Kahwin*) and the Chinese dowry (*nazheng*) both paid by the groom, the Tamil dowry (*varathatchanai*) is paid by the bride's family, and demanded by the boy's side as a condition of marriage. Would that make it "groom price"? The cruelty of the system is liable to result in comic situations like when the boy's family asks "how much *ponn* (gold) will you give?", the girl's father replies, "I give my entire *ponnu* (daughter)". Whereas, in the Chinese and Malay culture, the incoming in-law (bride) is inherently precious as gold, the Indian/Ceylonese groom basically sells himself for a quantity of gold.

The Wedding: hūn lǐ, Thirumanam, Perkahwinan

Like it or not, Malaysian weddings usually turn out to be Big, Fat, and Greek. They are expensive propositions, and totally greek (i.e, ethnic, as well as baffling) to the outside observer. Trying to moderate the expectations of society, many do try to strike a balance between the ostentatious and the unpretentious.

In preparation for her impending departure (to her new home), the Chinese bride-to-be secludes herself in a separate part of the house with her closest friends. During this period, the young women sang laments, mourning the bride's impending separation from her family.

Meanwhile, "at a propitious hour, a 'good luck woman' or 'good luck man', (someone with many children) would install a newly purchased bed. Children are invited onto the bed as an omen of fertility – the more, the merrier. The bed is scattered with red dates, oranges, lotus seeds, peanuts, pomegranates and other fruits. Part of the fun is watching the children scramble for the goodies.

On the day of the Wedding, the bridal "Hair Dressing" ritual and the groom's "Capping" (cap decorated with cypress leaves) ritual signal their initiation into adulthood. The colour red symbolizing joy, is reflected in the dress and other paraphernalia.

To the accompaniment of firecrackers, loud gongs and drums the procession makes its way from the groom's home to the bride's. The groom leads the procession accompanied by a child as an omen of his future sons. The reverse procession, bringing the bride-to-be, happens in the same manner, with the bride riding the bridal chair or palanquin.

After all the pep of the pre-nuptial preambles, the actual wedding ceremony seems rather anti-climactic. The bride and groom are stood before the family alter and make obeisance to the ancestors and to the kitchen god. The Tea Ceremony follows. And then in the evening, it perks up again – The banquet! Very likely, it would be in a grand ballroom somewhere, or a posh restaurant.

Like the Chinese, the Indian wedding preludes include an insane number of rituals. So, cutting to the actual ceremony, the pair are seated in lotus pose under a floral *pandhal* (covered dais). She is on his right. They would have exchanged garlands already. The priest, chanting away while feeding the fire with ghee, blesses and hands the groom the *thaali* (sacred thread with pendant) that rests on a coconut. Earlier, the thaali would have gone around the assemblage of guests for a blessing. As the Nadhaswaram – Thavil ensemble uptempos in a crescendo, the groom ties two knots of the thaali behind the bride's neck. The third knot is tied by the groom's sister. This is equivalent to the western ring exchange. Only, the bride doesn't return the favour. Or maybe she does. Henceforth, the Tamil groom is to wear a ring (*metti*) on his right second toe, so women (who shouldn't look directly at men) can know if he is married. As the thaali tying is done, the whole congregation rises to throw their handfuls of turmeric stained rice at the couple, in an overhand arch. Rice is a metaphor of prosperity, progeny, and protection.The music continues.

The *saptapadi* (seven steps) is when the corner of the bride's saree is knotted to the groom's little finger. He leads her seven times around the sacred fire, which is supposed to denote the seven sacred vows of marriage. And thence the reception dinner, which used to be veritable vegetarian victuals, but no more.

The dinner is either in a public hall or ballroom. The Indians still tie a pair of banana trees with the *thaar* (fruit bunch and flower) forming an arch at the entrance of the wedding hall or tent (*Pandhal*). Its significance is that of fertility. The banana tree, sprouts new shoots all around it, like a family. In yesteryears, a simple tarp tent was set up for the reception area, with young coconut frond *thoranam* (festoons) hanging all round. Each thoranam resembles five birds in flight (3 for funerals). Me remembers we boys going into the forest reserve of the Kenny Hills (now, Bukit Tunku) area in KL to search for vines and wild palm leaves, to wrap the pillars. The entire lower area of the tent is tied with coconut frond mats to form a half-wall. The night is spent making a "ceiling" of colourful crepe paper ribbons under the tent, blowing and tying coloured balloon bunches at the central junction. Its all history now. The whole setup reflected a *kaavanam/kaavu* ("grove"), perhaps harking back to the days when they lived in the forest. Its all history now. What else can be expected in a concrete forest?

As part of the post wedding programs, I witnessed a newlywed couple engaged in a public tussle. A ring was tossed into a narrow necked, wide bodied bronze pot (*kudam*) filled with water. The neck was enough for an arm to go in. So, imagine if the couple had to fight to get to the ring! It made for a few tries before one of them could get the ring, which was theirs to keep. Most times the gent would lose, so as not to be rough with his wife. Or, the bride's slender hand slid in easier! The idea was kind of an ice-breaker for the two, since it would have been their first "physical" meeting. The elders of long ago, in their wisdom, would have created this game as warm-up for the intense activity that would follow! I also remember joining in a water fight with the wedding entourage, splashing turmeric water on each other. That too, seems to be history

At Tamil weddings, not withstanding religion, elders bless the newlyweds who would kneel and touch their feet. The elders would bless, *"Pathinaarum petru peruvaazhvu vaazhga."* Literally means, "May you attain all sixteen and live the great life." As a child, I always took that to mean a blessing to literally produce 16 children (not uncommon in those days). As a matter fact, *Petru/Peru* means to "receive" or "give birth to", anyway. It is identical to the confusion in English where, "Have" can mean either, "get" or "give birth to." Only later did I learn that it meant acquiring 16 blessings or virtues that make for a successful marriage.

The 16 are: –

1. Fame   *(Pugazh)*
2. Education   *(Kalvi)*
3. Firmness of mind   *(Mana Uruthi)*
4. Victory   *(Vetri)*
5. Progeny   *(Puthra Santhadhi)*
6. Bravery   *(Thunivu)*
7. Wealth   *(Dana Sampath)*
8. Granary   *(Dhaanya Sampath)*
9. Prosperity   *(Soubaaghyam)*
10. Comforts   *(Sukham)*
11. Intelligence   *(Arivu)*
12. Greatness   *(Perumai)*
13. Good family life   *(Narkudi)*
14. Health   *(Aaroghyam)*
15. Longevity   *(Neenda aayul)* and,
16. Discernment   *(Buddhi koormai)*

Like the Chinese and Indian weddings, the Malay kampung wedding too, has its days of frenetic preliminaries. The main venue is the bride's house.

With the relatives and neighbours on hand, it's a hive of activity in *gotong-royong* (community team work) style. There'll be the kitchen team, usually comprised of men – aren't they always the best at big banquets? The cow and goat slaughter team is responsible for the meat prep with government licence, so no worries about food safety. Another team will set up the wedding tent and decoration.

Meanwhile, inside the house the women are busy being *sous chefs*, prepping the ingredients. Some will engage in house cleaning, interior decoration and making the *bunga telor* ("egg flower"), a party gift given to the guests. Its like a colourful flower stalk (the egg forms the flower). The egg is supposed to denote fertility. Note that the fertility theme is echoed in the Chinese children clambering onto the bridal bed, while the Tamil fertility is symbolized by the twin banana trees.

The day prior to the wedding day, there is the *Khatam Al – Quran* ceremony, where the bride recites the Holy Book. In the afternoon is the *berinai* (henna dyeing) activity. This is followed in the eveing by the make-up done by the *mak andam,* or professional beautician.

On the day itself, in the AM, is the *Akad Nikah* or marrriage contract. The Imam holds the groom's right hand in a handshake and says, "Ahmad, I thee with Aminah wed with *mas kahwin* (dowry) of RM22.50 cash ". The groom repeats it in the first person and full name, just like in a western wedding. Then it's the *"membatal air sembahyang"* session whereby the groom will be allowed to touch the bride's hands to insert the wedding ring. It is now proper and legal for the man to touch the woman who is now his wife. The bride may now kiss the hands of the man who is now her husband – Not, the other way! A thousand apologies, no English-style liplock here.

The main event of the day is the reception, or *Bersanding* ("sitting side by side"). The couple sits on a *pelamin* (wedding dais) and receives the well wishers, who bless them by sprinkling the *tepong tawar* on their upturned palms. It consists of white rice (for fertility), yellow rice (for nobility), kernel (for wealth), and rose water (for family harmony). As the guests take their leave a strangle thing happens, a kind of sleight of hand, known to insiders as the *salam changkuk,* aka secret money transfer. You would have already placed a multiple times folded over money envelop in the hollow of your palm, see? Under the pretext of shaking hands with the bride/groom, the note exchanges hands. Abracadabra!

All this while, dinner is going on. It is all come and go. You come and go between about 11 am to say, 5 o'clock pm. There are no toasts, boasts or roasts (of the couple) as in Chinese weddings. Just eat, greet and beat the retreat. Or, hang around and mingle with the other guests, of course.

Conception and Cofinement: Pantang, Paththiyam, Zouyuzei

So, the two became one. And the one becomes three. Individuals become a couple and the couple becomes a family, the smallest unit of society.

The word for the birthing process, as in other aspects of life, varies with the cultures. The English phrase for the arrival of the VIP is, "was born." That the mother "gave birth" or "delivered" gives the nod to her as the active, creative person in the process. She, afterall, "conceives", "bears", and "births" the tot. The Tamil language begs to differ. The phrase *pillai peru*, means "to receive" or "to accept child". "She received the baby at 7.00 this morning". From whom did she receive it? We assume she received it from the higher authority, naturally. The Malay counterpart is equivalently poignant. *Dikurniakan*, that is, "to be awarded" or "blessed" with child. The common phrase *beranak*, can mean "to have child". The more literary *bersalin* is queer because besides birthing it also means, "to change" into a new set of clothing. To change from being pregnant to being non-pregnant? The root, *salin*, also means "copy". Does that imply we now have a zerox of the parent? The Chinese, *shēng hái zi*, "to give birth to a child", is straightforward enough. The child is "shanghai"-ed from one space to another?

If you ask me, opposite to the mother, the foetus is the passive player in the process. Why then, is it referred to in the passive voice as in, "was born", "was delivered", etc. ? In Malay, it is *dilahir*, or, "was born". *Melahir*, ascribes some autonomy to the mother. It means, "to beget". However, the Tamil baby, unlike its mother's passivity, has its own mind. *Pirappu* (appearance, or dawn of something). "The baby appeared (*piranthathu*) late last night". Well, in the Tamil context, it only makes sense that the baby "appear/arrive", so that its mother can "receive" it with joy. The mother may have carried the baby for ¾ of a year, but who grew from zygote to neonate, and survived the journey? A recent Tamil motivational song goes:

Didn't you exit your mother's womb unscathed?
Weren't you O human, at that instant a winner?

Most of the pre-natal activities, or non-activities have to with avoidance (passive) and protection (active).

During conception, the Indian woman is not allowed to sleep alone or go out after dusk or eat spicy foods. At eclipses she has to lie down without moving her legs. She is not supposed to cross a river or climb a hill during pregnancy. The expectant Chinese mothers are, strongly discouraged from moving furniture or renovating the house during their pregnancy. In addition, they are urged to avoid activities such as digging, slaughtering, hammering and looking at unsightly images as these would lead to undesirable consequences. Expectant mothers should also refrain from uttering words that are considered taboo or offensive to deities and spirits.

"Chinese mothers also abstain from certain types of food during their pregnancy that are believed to be harmful to the baby. Cantonese women are warned against consuming mutton as the Cantonese word for the meat has the same pronunciation as the word for epilepsy. On the other hand, Hokkien mothers are advised to avoid crabs as it is believed that doing so will result in the birth of a naughty child – literally born with as many "hands" as a crab. "Cooling" foods, which are associated with the reduction of heat or vitality, are also avoided as they may weaken the womb. At the same time, it is believed that certain foods should be taken to help strengthen the womb and ensure a smooth delivery. To give the child a smooth and fair complexion, expected mothers are recommended to take gingko fruits and strips of dried soya paste."

Malays tend to avoid the use of drugs and anesthetics to relieve pain during delivery fearing it could lead to potential side effects to the mum and baby. Coconut oil is widely used as prenatal treatment to ease delivery. It is believed that taking a few tablespoonfuls of coconut oil daily a few weeks before delivery can facilitate labor and delivery. Daily application of a little coconut oil in and around the vagina opening, from the 6th month onwards, will reduce the need for episiotomy (making slit around the vagina opening to avoid tears).

A Tamil ceremony called *Valaikappu* is held in the fifth or seventh month of pregnancy, when the expectant mother is presented with new sets of bangles. Her mother-in-law or sister-in-law leads her to the temple and to a bangle shop where she selects the bangles of her choice. Some families arrange to get the bangle-seller to their houses and the purchase of the bangles is a part of the ritual. She seeks blessing of elderly men and women after putting on the bangles.

During the sixth or eighth month of pregnancy, a ceremony called *Seemantham*, a sacrificial fire is lit and the husband and his wife pray jointly for the gift of child and for safe delivery by circumambulating the fire. The woman prays that she may beget a son in her first pregnancy, possibly to prevent the husband or his mother nursing a grievance if a girl is born. This is not the general case anymore.

After the prenatal, now the post-partum. In some parts of south India, the confinement period lasts for sixty days. Although, a Malay colleague overseeing irrigation works in the Indian parcel of the Tanjung Karang paddy area was surprised at finding an Indian farmer working the fields the day after giving birth. An elderly member of the house will take charge of preparing *Paththiya Samayal* (stringent diet) a well-balanced nutritional food for the new mother. Food to avoid during the period are pickles, chilies, spices, oily food, sour curd, and fruits like grapes. In place of *thuvaram paruppu* (pigeon pea), which is the main ingredient of saambaar, *paasi paruppu* (mung bean) is used as toor dal causes gas problems. Fenugreek leaves, gourds both bitter and bottle, drumsticks are all suitable.

Half teaspoon of turmeric is mixed with lukewarm water or milk and is given to new mom once daily to increase the healing of internal wounds. Dry ginger powder with jaggery or dry ginger powder in lukewarm water is also given. Steamed food items like idly and idiyappam are preferred for breakfast.

Body massage: Gingelly oil is widely used in south India for body massage during the confinement period. Head, hip, and stomach are applied with lukewarm gingelly oil

Bath: Water for the bathing is boiled with turmeric pieces, tamarind leaves, and neem leaves too. Shikakai powder used to wash the hair. Turmeric powder can be applied to the whole body. After the bath, Sambrani (incense) smoke is made, and hair has to be dried over it. It is to prevent the mother from catching a cold

Belly binding is done for the first thirty days with a tightly wrapped large piece of thick felt cloth. It is done to compress the abdominal region

In Chinese, *Zouyuzei* literally means "sitting out the month." During the first 30 days, mothers are expected to remain indoors and follow a complex set of rules to care for themselves. One of the most extreme rules is not touching cold water.

"For one full month after giving birth, the mother is confined to the house with her baby so she can properly rest and heal during the most crucial period of recovery. In addition, the mother must also follow a very strict diet. "Confinement meals" are prepared during the month, and postpartum mothers must only eat what is given and nothing else. This age-old tradition dates back to year 960 and is still very commonly practiced in Asia.

my confinement nanny, *pui yuet* took the baby and handled everything. I can't stress enough how crucial this was for my mental health.

As for that ginger bath, all I can say is, after each bath, my skin felt incredibly smooth, my body felt energized and my face was glowing. The hot ginger water left a tingly sensation on my skin that made me feel great from head to toe, as if someone just gave me a great scrubdown. It felt like I walked out of a spa."

In the Malay community, the confinement period is 44-days and even 100-days for some people! It's a test of patience for most of the women in the Malay community as it restricted most of the things that women usually do. Its purpose is to maintain the Malay women's femininity and beauty from the within, which is the womb.

Here is a direct lift from one of the confinement packages promoted for the Malay confinement. Looks like a 5-star vacation!

Confinement Lady Malaysia/Mothercare

Daily Visit: 14 days, 9am – 5pm

Body Massage	– (*Urut*) (1x/day)
Hot Stone Therapy	– (*Tungku*) (2x/day)
Tummy Binding	– (*Ikat Kain Bengkung*) (2x/day)
	– *Param, Pilis, Tapel* (2x/day)
Herbal Bath	– (*Mandi Herba*) (2x/day)
Body Scrub	– (*Lulur*) (1x/week)
Vaginal Steam	– (*Tangas*) (1x/week)
Breast Engorgement Massage	– (*Urut Bengkak Susu*) (3x/week)
Head and Scalp Massage	– (*Urut Kepala Buang Angin*) (3x/week)

Babycare

– Baby Bath	– (*Mandi*) (2x/day)
– Baby Massage	– (*Urut*) (2x/day)
– Poultice	– (*Tuam*) (2x/day)
– Babysitting	

Food

– Pantang food
– Pantang beverages
– Herbal tea

Midwifery is alive and well even if births are happening in sterile hospital suites.

Post-Birth: Cukur Jambul, Mottai Aditthal, Taimaobi

Every nation has a name, and every house an address. Every newborn child is given an address in the form of a personal name. The naming is the first formal event in its life. Hindus call the child's name aloud three times, and it is official. Usually someone of senior status, is invited to do the favours. Often, that person also chooses the name. At other times, the name is calibrated horoscopically and suggested by the priest.

The Muslim father, having chosen the name in advance, whispers it three times, into the ears of his child.

Christians – Catholics do the naming in a ritual. It is christened, or "christianized" by being baptized with the sprinkling of water on its forehead.

Taoist – After three months, a naming ceremony would be held, attended by all the senior female members of the family, such as grandmothers and aunts. The mother would have a bath and change of clothes, and the baby's hair would be shaved leaving only a section of hair that would be tied in a pair of little horns.

A common observance among the world's communities, is baby's first tonsure. *Cukur jambul* (shaving forelock), is the Malay name. The cukur jambul ceremony generally coincides with the end of the confinement period (*pantang*) observed by the new mother, which lasts between 40 and 44 days. It is festive, with a kenduri for the extended family. The venue is usually either one of the grandparents' homes.

Indian households observe the *mottai adiththal* (shaving bald). This is usually done during the first or the third year (odd years) of the child. The hair is consecrated and offered to the respective family deities. The child receives new dresses from its parents, maternal uncles and grand-parents. In Tamil society (not much anymore) the maternal uncle, *thaai maaman*, is the VIP, possibly because he is expected to foot the bill, or provide the goat for the feast.

At the family temple, the child sits on the maternal uncle's lap, as the barber does his thing. A paste of sandal and turmeric is slathered on the bald pate for cooling and antiseptic purposes. The belief behind the shaving ceremony is a detachment from the past. The Hindus, as is common knowledge, would rather not have the ghosts of the past life follow the child into it's current avatar. At around the same time, or concurrently is the *kaathu kutthhu* (ear piercing) administered by a goldsmith, who makes the earrings. The Hindu rationale for this is the ear hole completes the ear-like shape of the Tamil alphabetic representation of AUM or OM (ॐ), the cosmic sound of heaven.

Chinese trim the birth hair at one month, or baby's first "full moon". The month also coincides with the mother's period of "confinement" or recuperation. There is an old custom, of collecting strands of the hair in a red pouche and stiching them to the baby's pillow, for soothing. There is another ancient custom, now reviving, of using the downy hair to make a calligraphy brush called *Taimaobi* (Baby Hair Brush), and engraved with best wishes for the baby's future.

Full moon celebrations are extended family focused and event-managed by specialist caterers. Though much sweet stuff is present the two must haves are red *Ang Koo Kueh* and red painted eggs. The red represents good luck, of course. The guests get goody boxes with eatables, while giving *Ang Pao* for the child.

In all cases, confinement periods are excuses to be pampered with special baths, be it warm water, herbal etc. All races used to have special *midwives*: *Bidans, Aayamah* or *Zhù chǎn shì* and administer baths, concoctions, and massages. All races, used to wrap their mid-sections with a length of thick airtight material known in Malay as *bengkung*. It was a kind of woollen tweed, almost canvassy in thickness and air-tightness. These practices have probably gone the same route as squatting outhouses went the toilet seats way.

Coming of Age: Manjal Neeraattu, Khitan/Khatam, Guan and Fu

In Christendom, Roman Catholics have their "First Holy Communion" at about age 7 to 13. It follows later, with the "Confirmation" (completing basic religious knowledge); Jews have a Bar/Bat Mitzvah at ages 13 and 12 respectively for boys and girls. Latino girls celebrate Quinceanera (age 15). These days across the board, coming of age is the 21ˢᵗ birthday, where someone become truly adult. Age 12 seems to be common everywhere as that is about when girls begin to menstruate, boys sprout facial hair, loose all their birth teeth, etc.

The Tamil community reserves greater importance to girls, to the extent that boy's feel left out in a kind of gender envy. Most Hindu ceremonies are done by men, but this one is primarily done by women. At the first "monthly", the womenfolk gather for a special meal followed by a *Nalangu* ceremony in which her feet are painted with a paste of red ochre, turmeric and lime. Finally the young lady is banished to a purpose-built *kudisai* or hut, made of bamboo, coconut fronds and mango and neem leaves. Inside, she will have all her necessities, including clothing and toiletries. Food will be brought in daily, and she is bathed by the women alternating between head and body baths. The seclusion lasts for 9,11 or 13 days – note the odd number again.

The grand finale is the *Manjal Neerattu Vizha*, or "turmeric water bath ceremony". It's a grand public event with the men included. Here again, the maternal uncle, or *Thaai Maaman* figures prominently. The girl gets her first saree. She is dressed almost like a bride, with a silk saree, and much gold jewelry. Some say that this function is the announcement of a marriageable woman, and serves as notice to prospective husbands and their families, of a bridal possibility.

Age 11 marks the start of Muslim boys being able to celebrate *Khatam Al – Koran*. This ritual marks a coming of age ceremony showing growth and maturity presented in their local mosque. Years are spent rehearsing and reciting the Koran to recite the final chapter to their families and friends. Khatan is attributed to a Hadith from An Nas, who recalled Prophet Muhammad saying it was good practice to open and recite the Quran. The khatam is done with selected verses from surah Wadhuha till surah An Nas, interspersed between surahs with calls of "Allahu Akbar". The exercise is finished with reciting the Al-Fatihah, the first chapter of the Quran.

Another aspect of coming of age is the *Khitan*, which is circumcision. The circumcision ceremony for a boy is an elaborate event and happens between the age of 7-12, while female circumcision is mostly discreet and or not practiced at all.

Female circumcision, said to be on the increase in Malaysia, is the removal of all or part of a child's clitoris. This an area of great controversy as it has some religious basis (Hadith), while the rest of the world considers it female genital mutilation (FGM). Malaysian clinics who do it don't have a clear SOP. Some say it is only a pin prick on the organ, while traditional practioners use a special blade. Malay parents decide on it only after much soul searching, as it is banned in Muslim countries like Egypt. Dato' Dr. Mohd. Asri Zainul Abidin, Perlis Mufti, proposes a solution to the fix – let the girl grow up and decide for herself.

Chinese coming of age falls between ages 12-20. The culmination is the wearing of a ceremonial hat (*guan*) and dress (*fu*) – to signify the new status. Women get a special hairdo (hairpinning) and ornaments. A series of steps take place before the final 'full dress" presentation. The "man" first get his inner cap, then a cap and finally a scarf. After these three steps, the man's hair is combed into a bun. Symbolically this means that he has become an adult.

The guest of honour then gives a speech congratulating the new adult man. After the speech the new adult man would take a bow to his mother. Then the guest of honour would give him a new name." The new name is actually an honorific or "literary" name. Henceforth only elders could refer to him by his given name. Everyone else had to address him by the new name. He then kowtows to parents and guests at end of ceremony.

Age of Accountability: Baptism, Bersunat, Bar Mitzvah.

When is a child a believer? Muslim, Hindu, Buddhist, Christians all have their own times when a child becomes an adult, or able to make life decisions.

Every newborn child is named according to the religion of the parents. It is assumed by the community, that they are followers of the "family faith". The Muslims believe that a child is a Muslim by virtue of its birth, so much so, that some believe that if one partner of a non-muslim couple converts to Islam, the convert parent has an automatic right to "convert" his or her children. It was official policy until recently, when the (then) young administration of Prime Minister Najib Tun Abdul Razak stepped in to stop the practice, following a public outcry. That was the case of one Mogarajah converting to Islam and forcibly converting his two children. Years on, the case is still dragging in the high court. The mother, S.Shamala, has meanwhile moved to Australia with the two children in question. (Note: Mirroring Shamala's situation, are the recent cases of M. Indira Gandhi and Loh Siew Hong, whose *muallaf* (new convert) husbands also forcibly "converted" their children.

Prophet Muhammad is reported to have said, "All are born Muslims. It is the parents who make them Christians, or Jew, or Magi." If children are born Muslims, as per the prophet's alleged words, why did Mogarajah feel compelled to "convert" his children? The Christian view is similar (to Muhammad's). Only, it does not consider underaged children "Christians". Such children don't know to confess faith, and don't need to, having a free pass to heaven should they die. When they attain the age of accountability (around age 10 or so), they must choose their religious identity and determine their destiny. No excuses like, "I didn't know that I had to!"

The Hindus are no different from the Muslims, and believe that a child born into a Hindu household is to be considered Hindu. They would go kilometers further, by asserting that their child is born into one of their caste groups, with all the attendant priviledges or privations of that group. The medieval implication of this is, if you are born to parents who are fishermen, you become and remain one yourself. In modern context, that makes you scratch your head. Hindus do not have specific conversion rituals like the Muslims or Christians. They consider anyone Hindu as long as they display the slightest hint of a hinduistic outlook, like perhaps, being spotted in a temple. Neither to do they have the concept of proselytization.

The Mormons, considered a sect, stretch this idea even further. They vicariously "baptize" people in their family trees or contact lists, who have long since died. There is this recent absurd case of President Barack Obama's late mother being baptized into their church. Doesn't the dead person have a say in it? In a similar vein, we have recurring stories of state Islamic departments in Malaysia digging up graves of Non-Muslims suspected, or supposed to have converted to Islam. The bodies are appropriated and reburied according to Muslim rights. This is by no means, a phenomenon peculiar to the Malaysian State Islamic Departments. Over a decade ago, a Christian friend had married a Hindu girl and died shortly thereafter. She had become estranged from the boy's family and decided that she was going to give her husband a Hindu burial. The deceased's father finally gave up the tussle over the corpse, saying, "She can have his body, but his soul already belongs to my God."

The Catholics baptize their newborn infant to their faith by "christening" (Chrisianize them?). They used to boast, "Give me a child, and I will make him a Catholic for life". The "evangelical" Christians get the Bible message that baptism is only for the believing adult – called "Believer's Baptism". They ask how can an 8 days old infant know right from wrong and make decisions? They point to the Bible's teaching that children are innocent, and therefore all of them have an automatic ticket to heaven. The minimum age at which one becomes a "believer" and gets baptized, is at the age of accountability, usually around the age of 10 and above, depending on level of maturation. Interestingly, this is about the age when Catholics "confirm" their pre-adolescents and the Muslims circumcise their pre-pubescent boys. Those are basically rights of passage into the fellowship or community of faith. It is commonly known as coming of age.

There is no mention of circumcision in the Koran, but the prophet Muhammad is reported to have stated that "Circumcision is a *sunnah* (customary) for the men and a *makrumah* (meritorious) for the women".

It is not one of the Five Pillars of the Faith (*Arkan Al-Islam*), which consists of: daily prayer (*salaat*), the profession of faith (*shahada*), the giving of alms (*zakat*), fasting at Ramadan (*sawm*), and the pilgrimage to Mecca (*hajj*). Muhammd laid down five further rules (*fitrah*), for Muslim men; shaving pubic hair; circumcision; trimming moustache; plucking hair from the armpits; and clipping nails" – *(Bukhari, Book 72, Hadith 779)*. Note that it excludes children and women. Sami Aldeeb says, "They are not compulsory, but simply advisable". Good advice, at that. Circumcision carries the same weightage as trimming moustache and shaving pubic hair.

What's in a Name?: Yuva*(raj)* s/o A. Gun*(segaran)*, Yu*(nus)* Sandokan, Sun Ah Gan.

In as much as humans want to possess belongings and to exercise ownership, they also want to belong to an address and to be possessed, of a family, group or nation. Similarly, in as much as we want to possess the earth, the earth is awaiting the day it will possess us, six feet under it. It has always been waiting a game between earth and earthling.

Perhaps, nowhere is this sense of belonging more obvious and surreptitious at the same time, as in our surnames, which function as our social identifier and familial address. Surnames may identify us by city as in the Arab (Al-Bukhari = of Bokhara), and the German Frankfurter (of Frankfurt). They can identify country of origin as in Al-Hindi ("the

Indian"), Schweitzer (Swiss) etc. They advertise clans, as in the Chinese *Chong* or *Cheah*, or the Scottish, *McMillan* or *McCarthy*. They can also proclaim families like the Irish *O'Hara* or *O'Connor*, and royal houses such as the *Hanovers* and *Windsors* of Britain or the *Sauds* of Arabia, and the *Bolkiahs* of Brunei.

Malays follow the Semitic, Arabic style of a given name followed by the name of the father (patronym). Like the Hebrew *Ben*, Bin (Ibn) or Binti meaning "son of" or "daughter of" connects the person to his/her family. Since it only tells who the father is, it is strictly a family identifier not a social group identifier. Even in the father's family, his brothers' children will carry their own first names as surnames while his sisters' children will carry their husbands respective first names. If you want to mention both father's name and the clan name, it would be long. For instance the Bedouin Arab camel trader by the name Ali Hassan, with a father named Ahmad Hussaini, will be rendered as, Ali Hassan bin Ahmad Hussaini Al-Badawi. That would be, Ali Hassan son of Ahmad Hussaini, of the Bedouin tribe. Malay names are simpler than that because, they don't have the tribal appendage to carry around. In daily conversation, it often shrinks to Ali Ahmad, or A.Ahmad, or plain Ahmad. The famous Malaysian cultural icon, P.Ramlee supposedly shortened his name in the style of the Indian directors (of old Malay movies). His full name? Teuku Zakaria bin Teuku Nyak Puteh would hardly ring a bell today, would it?

Across the board, it seems that Malay personal names have been entirely arabized. There are a few holdovers from local names. Tompel, P.Ramlee's contemporary and co-comedian, sounds very Malay. So does his son and comedian, Badul bin Tompel. Even so, the local sounding Badul could be a variation of Abdul. So there. Badul's name reminds me of Badam Malek. Back in my DID (Drainage and Irrigation Department) days in Tanjung Karang, payday was by calling the roll of workers and handing out cash. I helped to count and arrange the pay packets. On my first month there, an Indian guy responded to Badam bin Malek, so I assumed he was an Indian Muslim. It turned out that he was actually Vadamalai ("Northern Hill", in Tamil). Such comical situations as a result of clerical mistakes at the Registration Office, abound. But let's leave that for a different forum. Check out the, 'Name Mashup." Section that follows.

Like the Malay naming system, the Indians use s/o or d/o ("son of" or "daughter of" respectively), to denote patrilineage. Munusamy s/o Muthusamy, is usually said, Munusamy Muthusamy. Or, it might be further constricted to M.Munusamy, the father's name initialized and placed in front. Like the Malay system, this is not conducive to tracing lineage beyond the first (or father's) generation, unless a good system of record keeping is practiced by succeeding generations and passed on down the family tree. In the epic book *Roots* by Arthur Haley, the author traces his African ancestry, with the help of the oral history of his older relatives. He later hits the mother lode in the person of a *griot*, or professional oral historian, in the West African branch of his family, in the ancestral homeland in Gambia. Otherwise, it would have been mission implausible.

The Chinese name begins with the clan, or surname and followed by a descriptive two part given name. When Sun Ah Gan introduces himself, he is basically saying, "I am Ah Gan, of the clan Sun." A kin of Dr.Sun Yat Sen, the founder of Taiwan? But how does one determine if Ah Gan is a boy or a girl, since there is no *Bin* or *Son of* ? Perhaps the secret is in the sound. Ah Chong, Ah Kow, and Ah Gan sound "loud" and must be masculine, whereas Ah Moi or Siew Lien, have decidedly soft, feminine sound.

The Chinese will tell you that it used to be forbidden to marry within the clan, or someone with the same surname. These days, with millions of people with the same clan name, it should not be a problem. Besides, in addition to Chinese Lees, there are Korean Lees and Scottish Lees (Leighs). The original prohibition against same clan name marriages, however, is brilliant. No danger of in-breeding, see? The clan system grew out of a strong sense of family, whereby the descendants of the historic procreator of the clan are able to help each other out like a self-help cooperative. Indeed, the Chinese clan associations in Malaysia were founded out of such need and still do such services. Young men who immigrated to Malaya in the 19th century, had their needs taken care of, and work or businesses set up for them by the clan associations.

The grouping by clan names like the Scottish clan system, or the European trade based groups like Baylor, Saylor, Taylor, or Schumacher (cobbler),

Schroeder (Tailor) and Bauer (builder), is useful in determining genealogies, though not necessarily foolproof in the absence of written church records. A Chinese acquaintance claims to have managed to trace his family back 500 hundred years back to China, using his clan name. I didn't ask how he did it.

A similar thing happens in Malay families with names beginning in *Syed* (female, *Sharifah*) or *Sheikh*. The Syeds are those who claim direct descent from the Prophet Muhammad. Sheikh is chieftain in Arabic, and Malays who use these titles may be claiming an Arab leader in their genealogy. It is doubtful if the genealogical branches can be positively delineated, though. There are other prefixes like *Wan* and *Nik* prevalent in Kelantan and Trengganu, and *Datu* in Sabah, or *Abang* in Sarawak. *Megat, Daeng* (Bugis). The above are just titles, but can serve as surnames, when tracing trees. Family trees, that is. Some Arab-Malay surnames, like *Al-Attas, Alsagoff*, can be a constant that will help in tracing the tree roots.

Tamil Muslims, and some Malays with Tamil Muslim forebears have surnames such as *Marican* attached to their given (first) names. The *Marakaiyar* or *Maricars* of Tamil Nadu, are actually a very progressive Tamil Muslim caste-like group. They get their name from *marakalam* (Tamil: *maram* = wood, and *kalam* = vessel). They were great shipbuilders who built and traveled the seas around South Asia and South East-Asia. They may have even have travelled as far as New New Zealand 500 years ago. The New Zealand national museum in Wellington, the Te Papa Tongarewa has a bell on display referred to simply as, "The Tamil bell". It is a bronze bell that has the Tamil inscription, "Muhaiyatheen Buks's ship's bell." It was bought by William Colenso, British missionary and witness to the famous New Zealand Treaty of Waitangi between the British and Maoris. When Colenso bartered for the bell in 1836, some Maoris had been cooking sweet potatoes in it for decades! The British first landing there had just occurred about 60 years earlier. Research has found the founding (construction) date of the bell to about 1450 AD, from Nagapattinam in Tamil Nadu. And so? So, Muhaiyatheen Buks, the Maricar possibly (plausibly, probably, presumably, potentially, perchance, peradventure) sailed down to northern North Island of NZ earlier than Abel Tasman, the first European! Of course, the Maori Malay cousins were there way earlier.

Some Malays have *Keling* (e.g. Zainal Keling) which refers to a South Indian, and has attained a somewhat derogatary connotation. The Minangkabau version is *kaliang.* The original root of that is likely *Kalinga*, an ancient kingdom in present day Orissa state, India. To the Malay Keling clan, it is badge of honour, an ancestral address, and a peg in which to hang their genealogical hat. Malays with North Indian or Pakistni, Iranian forebears are Khan, Shah etc.

Similarly, the Hindus use caste names as a peg to hang their identities on. This is prevalent in India, but in Malaysia caste sentiments are repressed and generally expressed only within the confines of the home and caste group. To use caste in their names is considered to be a rascist, or casteist, behavior. This is thanks to the Dravidian movement in Tamil Nadu, which discouraged caste distinctions. Originally, caste functioned similar to the trade guilds of Europe with names like Butcher, Taylor, Barber, and Saylor. However with the Hindu concept of *varna*, it became confused and convoluted into a thousand caste divisions. While the guilds were trade associations one freely chose and joined, castes became such rigid hereditary situations that, if one were born into a certain caste, you were pigeon-holed into that job and status for your lifetime. Modernity has made such practices obsolete. Today, the untouchable stitcher of leather shoes (*Shakkilyar* caste) can be a stitcher (a surgeon) of broken Brahmins. Conversely, the top of the totem Brahmin can be a glorified purveyor of leather shoes, albeit, Armanis and Guccis etc.

About Portuguese surnames, they continue to be a living testament of Portuguese presence in Asia. Each ethnicity has its own exclusive, trademark Portuguese name that is not used by the others. Like the food fusions they have left behind in their various Asian outposts, Portuguese surnames tend to be place specific. The Malacca Portuguese names of D'Costa, Oliveiro, Lazaroo, Santa Maria, and Texeira et cetera, are rarely found in the following groups and vice versa. Malayali Catholics generally use Gomez, Lopez, Pereira (for Ferreira), and Verghese (for Vargas). Tamil Catholics of a fisher community in southern Tamil Nadu use D' Cruz. Other Tamils commonly use Santiago, but mostly as first name, rather than surname. Goan Catholics are called Paes, Fernandez, Cunha. East

Timorese have names like Horta, Soares, Lobato. Among the Sinhalese, you find Fonseka, Perera (always without the "i" as in the Malayali "Pereira"). Macanese Catholics maintain Portuguese forenames but retain Chinese surnames.

Separated, as they are, by such distance, it is puzzling how these disparate communities can have settled on their own limited choice of Portuguese surnames. Did they somehow communicate with each other and come to an agreement? Perhaps someone should study this curious case of localized adaptation of foreign names. I didn't mention the Filipinos, with surnames such as Marcos, Aquino, Ramos, etc, as their tradition is Spanish, rather than Portuguese. These two crazy Iberian nations somehow had the notion that the world was a pie they could slice in two. With the mediation of the Pope (*Treaty of Tordesillas*), they drew a line on South America, which effectively divided it into Portuguese Brazil and the Spanish rest. The line that cut through the globe, brought Africa, India, Malacca, East Timor into the Portuguese sphere, and the Philippines, Japan and smaller pacific islands into the Spanish zone. That still doesn't account for the Portuguese possession of Macao and Taiwan (Formosa) in the Spanish area. That episode didn't last of course, as the Dutch, British, French and Americans soon came and helped themselves to the sweet pie. The lesson of history? Don't grab what doesn't belong to you. Somebody else is always hanging around to grab it from you. It's a monkey grab from monkey world. Or is it, "dog eat dog" world?

You are reminded of a nursery rhyme that describes this cycle of history. You don't remember the words, but it is similar to Ambrose Bierce's, "Edible, adj.: Good to eat, and wholesome to digest, as a worm to a toad, a toad to a snake, a snake to a pig, a pig to a man, and a man to a worm." I might add, "and a worm to a germ, and germ to a worm, and a worm to a toad..........", and so on, Ad Infinitem. William Shakespeare had a similar thought, "A man may fish with the worm that hath eat of a king, and eat of the fish that hath fed of that worm."

Indonesians have single names, such as Suharto, Sukarno etc. Indonesian Chinese wearing very Indian names – Haryanto, Darmawan, Setiawan. All these have been star badminton players, over the years. Filipino Chinese use Chinese names spelled Spanish stye.

As we saw at the beginning of this article, that names are a kind of address for identfying us. They are also descriptive. All of them. As we have seen, Malay, or Arab based names are meaningful. *Muhammad*, means "praiseworthy". Eventhough it is a personal name, it can function as a titular name, as in Muhammad Fasly bin Muhammad Ali. Muhammad is commonly used as a mark of respect. Abdul is another such 'prefix', conveying "servant, or slave of ...". Abdul Malik can mean, "Servant of the King." Abdul Rahim is, "Servant of Mercy"

While Muslims adverstise the greatness of Muhammad in their names, Christians shun Jesus as too holy for mere mortals. They would happily go for Joshua (the Jewish equivalent of Jesus) or Christian, Christopher, Chris etc. Jesus is used in context as in, Yesudasan/Yesadian (Servant of Jesus).There was a time, two generations ago, when every Tamil Catholic girl was a Mary — Mary Elizabeth, Mary Fatima, Santhanamary, Amalorpavamary, Jeyamary, Visuvasamary, Salathmary, Soosaimary, Annamary etc.

Tamil name — male names often end in '..an" such as Ilangovan, Mathialagan. The "an" is a shortening of *avan,* meaning, "he" or "the one who is..". For example, Parameswaran, is a composite of *Param* (universe); *Easwara* (Lord); and *Avan* (He). So, Parameswaran equals, "He who is Lord of the universe." It is a title for Shiva. Ilangovan is Ilam (young), Ko (king), and avan (He), meaning, "The young king". *Mathialagan* is "He who is of a beautiful (*alagu*) mind (*mathi*). Tamil muslims also have interesting ways of coining names. Allapitchay, is *Allah* and *pitchai* (*alms*). "The alms (grace) of God." Christians have Jesudasan — Jesu (Jesus) Das (servant/slave), an (He) — "The slave of Jesus."

While on the subject, modern parents, especially, are fond of sound synchronizing their names. You may have Malay siblings named Mohd. Anil and Mohd. Azil, or a constellation of Mohd. Fadhi, Fikri, Fitri. There are Chinese brothers named Lee Yi Rou and Lee E Ray, or Liew Shu Yi, Zhen Yi, and Zhen Yang. There are Indian sisters named Shalini, Sharini, and Shantini (my nieces, actually). You suppose, parents are able to keep track of them, and others too, after a time. But what is the principle at work here, for such monotonous monikers? You would think that children would appreciate a dose of individual Identity.

Another thing about names, is conformity to astrological demands, and get crazy instances where a perfect name such as Gayatri is changed to Khayatry and such. Well, It could be worse – Khadafi, for a girl. While Indians alter names to fit astrological requirements, Malays do so for style or gaya as they say it. Rossalennah Natassyiah Asshaferah, is an actual celebrity wife.

Young Malay couples love to name their babies in an explosion of sound – Hanisyafiqah Syazwany Yaakub named her daughter Nur Raisha Delisha Mohamad Amirul Affis. The Sy sound is Sh in common use. It is borrowed from the Bahasa Indonesia model of spelling. How's this for the longest name in Malaysia? Princess Aura Nurr Emily Amara Auliya Bidadari Nawal El Zendra Mohd Sufian. How will she fill up her name on an embarkation card with only 15 spaces?

Named!

Clerical slip-ups at the NRD (National Registration Department) result in many awkward situations. For the poor child, not the parents. The hilarity is a result of three types of commission or omission. One is in a straight reading in the context of a different culture or language. For instance real-life, clean freak, Malaysian Chinese sisters, Wai Ping and Swee Ping are normal enough in the original language. It only assumes humour when read in English. The second "trigger"is when a name is misspelled, like the Badam bin Malek (Vadamalai) in the preceding article. The third source of funny and lame, depending on perspective, is when some parents deliberately name their children just to draw (unwanted) attention. Tomato bin Potato, is my coinage, but similar pathetic namings have occurred before, which has made the NRD come up with strict rules about namings as well lengths of names – no more than 80 alphabets.

Though it may look like it belongs to the last class of namings, Suparman bin Batman, belonging to a Singapore ID, is veritably legitimate. Suparman is a common Javanese name, and Batman is also Javanese, if less common.

Situation 3 – Tomato bin Potato, is deliberate and unfunny. Situation 2 – Mispelled Badam bin Malek can be occasionally and situationally funny. Situation 1 – Wai Ping and Swee Ping are most funny if you are an outside ignoramus peeking in. To the native, it is seriously most meaningful. Chinese names, being monosyllabic, easily lends to puns in English. You can easily make up your own Chinese name. "You are fat" can easily transform to Yeoh Ah Fatt. Similarly, we play sardar puns like, Balan Singh – tightrope artist.

As beauty lies in the eyes of the beholder, so too funny is in the ears of the hearer. A body's name is no laughing matter, except for the ignorant outsider. Though not as serious as calling names, laughing at one can also bring a knuckle to one's chuckle.

Having said thus, shall we – funny business (names)

Death and Dying: Bank of Heaven notes, Forehead coin, Coins wrapped in paper

Everyone has an anxiety about the unknown, of which death is the big one. Even though others may be just as freaked out about death, the Chinese appear to be more so, because of certain archaic attitudes. The mere proximity to death is considered bad luck. The taxi driver won't take a dead body in his vehicle. The neighbor will raise hell if you start an elder-care facility next door to him. The possibility of death occurring next door has them running scared, as if it is a vicious virulent vapour that spreads in the air. Or, could it do with ideas of negative energies and vibes (Chi), in keeping with Feng Shui foolosophy?

How then, do they handle death in their own homes? I don't know. I don't want to generalize this to the whole community, but two decades ago a Chinese colleague died young, of cancer and his family refused to have his body inside the house. They laid him in his coffin, in his hospital clothes, in the driveway, under a makeshift tent. The same mindset used to prevail in unnatural deaths like accidents and suicides.

There must be some extenuating explanations for such phobic behavior, since their funeral rituals are elaborate and well attended. The body is often kept for days to allow for maximum mourning. No expense is spared, to ensure the grandest send-off. As a child in the Sentul of the sixties, I witnessed a Chinese funeral procession that could have rivalled the Macy's Thanksgiving Day parade of that time. Being a wealthy businessman, his hearse was followed by his whole fleet of lorries and mourners' cars stretching three blocks. Added to these were people carrying life-sized paper cars, money safes and boats and anything the man needed in his new home in heaven. Gold paper money was burned to deposit in his other-world bank account. A lot of drum banging and cymbal clanging added to the clamourous cacophony raised by the choir of professional criers doing their sing-song wailing.

Mrs. Reginald Sanderson again (British Malaya),*: "The uneducated Chinese have a superstitious dread of deaths taking place in their private houses, and therefore, when any one is ill beyond the hope of recovery, he or she is removed to a 'death-house,' or if there be no such place available, to the nearest piece of waste-ground.*

The funeral of a rich Chinaman is well worth seeing. From 3,000 to 5,000 dollars is not considered too lavish a sum to spend on the arrangements. Preceding the sandalwood coffin are preappointed "guides" and a Buddhist high priest, all in carriages, in advance of whom, again, is a seemingly endless procession of flags, bannerets, and musicians of all ages playing all sorts of Chinese instruments. Alongside the coffin itself, walk the male relatives of the deceased all clothed in sackcloth; they are followed by many hundreds of funeral guests; and last of all come the female relatives of the deceased, attired as mourners. On arrival at the cemetery the coffin is placed temporarily in a mortuary, there to await interment at some future date to be arranged by astrologers. The proceedings are characterised by great reverence."

Modern Chinese funerals are less ostentatious and Chinese are discarding the antiquated attitudes about death and dying. As an economically progressed community, they have not escaped progressive thinking in other areas. Toaists still have week-long ceremonies for their deceased, especially senior relatives. Food is catered on all the days of the wake and funeral. Visitors sign a ledger and drop monies into a money box. During the wake there is usually a group of people gambling in the front courtyard of the deceased's house because the corpse must be "guarded," and gambling helps the guards stay "awake."

A recent funeral, two doors away went on for five days. Every once in a while, in the evenings the beating of small gongs, flute, and tortoise shells would start, accompanied by some prayer and chanting. The flute music was very like the music at a Wayang Kulit performance. The vocals didn't seem to carry any particular sentiment, but *"hey yaa hey hai yai yaa"* similar to a Native American (Red Indian) war whoop.

On the day of the funeral there was a band ensemble, that played short, catchy tunes that included Western pieces like *Auld Lang Syne*. Another funeral procession that passed by had groups of dancers leading, followed by a marching western band, a Chinese traditional orchestra on a lorry. This was followed by some uniformed youth on unicycles, and the eye catching horde of bearded Chinese mythological characters on stilts. Then came florally decorated lorries, with a group of mourners in white gowns. A larger crowd of younger people in blue pyjama – like dresses came next, just ahead of the hearse car. The other cars brought up the long tail of the procession.

Malays practice the Muslim custom of same day burial or burial in the shortest possible time frame. If death occurs on a Friday morning, burial is expected before noon, before the Friday congregational prayers. In a sense this urgency derives from a kind of fear, the fear of quick decomposition of the body. In the Middle East, where Islam originated, the hot dry climate may cause such concerns. Both the Jewish and Muslim teachings require such haste in burials.

Significantly, there is, or was, another Middle-Eastern culture that practiced elaborate burial rituals that extended for days. The ancient Egyptians solved the problem of decomposition, by perfecting the science of embalming. Just as the Egyptians buried their dead in elaborate tombs, old Jewish and Arab cultures buried their dead in tombs cut out of rocks. To get the maximum burial space for families inside the tomb chambers, they would carve crevices or shelves in which to lay the shrouded bodies. Perhaps that is why Muslims as well as Jews today, wash and wrap the bodies in white linen, *kafan*. As they dig the grave (*liang lahad*), a side chamber is dug at the bottom, like an "L", *"Al-Lahad"*. The horizontal leg of the L functions like a ledge or shelf that becomes the final resting place. Another version is the *"Al-Shaq"*, with a trench at the bottom of the pit. The other two types are regular holes where the *janaza,* or body is covered by a leaning, or overhead board. In other words, no soil hits the body. In all the 4 cases, the body is laid at an angle on its right, against one corner. It is propped uped up by a bed of soil underneath. This is to faciltate facing Mecca (*qiblat*). Similarly, Chinese cemetaries are located on hill slopes, so as to face the sea – good feng shui.

Unlike the Chinese, some Indians think that handling dead bodies brings them good luck. One guy helped to bathe and dress the body of a friend's deceased relative. He claimed hitting prizes in multiple consecutive draws of the 4-D lottery. The winning streak only ended after the dead man's relative jinxed the bull run by wondering why the dearly departed only blessed strangers and not his survivors!

This is not to say that Indians do not have fears and anxieties about death situations. Like the Chinese, Indians too have an aversion about dead bodies. It goes directly to the infamous caste system, whereby handling of dead animals and their by-products is considered unclean. Hence, a whole caste (hereditary) business is created for those who handle dead bodies, grave-digging, and cremation – the *Vettiyars* or *Vettiyaans*. *Vettiyaan* actually means, "digger." The *Chakkiliyar* are shoemakers and those who work with leather – a dead animal product. The *Paraiyar* (Pariah), are drummers and heralds who made announcements (auspicious and inauspicious). *Parai* refers to a *kompang*-like drum and a verb "to proclaim".They were probably relegated to this position because their drums were made of cow leather. All these caste groups are considered unclean enough to be "untouchables", thrown outside the caste hierarchy. Outcastes.

So, the Hindu/Indian aversion to dead bodies is of a more "advanced" and pronounced level then that of the Chinese. The Chinese only fears or avoids a negative situation, whereas the Hindu has taken the phobia to a level of social engineering and restructuring, passing the buck, leaving the cleaning of unclean things to the weakest members of society.

The question that comes to your mind is, how come the so-called higher castes, including the Brahmins, who are practically the salt of the earth according to that system (*varnashramam*), can wear leather items like shoes, belts and sandals and still be considered "clean"? The foremost mrdangam drummers and tavil (another drum) vidwans come from the

Brahmin and Pillai groups. Perhaps there are other criteria that determine a person's caste stature.

The Hindus, and Sikhs and Buddhists have perhaps the most economical (in terms of land use) and clean way of dispatching – cremation. Planting or Burning – (Burial or Cremation) – either way the result is dust. The Parsees of Bombay, practice the Zoroastrian faith and allow their dead to be eaten by vultures. They build special towers for that.

The Hindus do sometimes bury their departed. The reasons may range from death in infancy, death of a Sadhu, death by snakebite to death of someone with skin disease. South Indians place a coin on the forehead of the deceased. It is explained as transportation fare to heaven. The ancients Greeks had a similar custom to pay the ferry man to heaven. Another explanation is that it shows one cannot carry possesions to the hereafter. The Greek great, Alexander is said to have asked to have his right hand hanging out of the his casket, during the funeral procession. It would show that he went empty handed. A not too disimilar thing happens in a Malay funeral. At the end of the burial, the son gives each man at the gravesite, coins wrapped in paper. This indicates that he has let his father go to *alam barzakh* (netherworld), without emotional tug, just as he gives away money without regrets. Interestingly, at Taoist funerals, you are given a "good morning" face towel with coins knotted in one corner.

The Funeral: Pengebumian, Karuma Kiriyai, shou ling

Kinship connections are very pronounced at funerals and other occasions of social gathering. In all these ceremonies, there are fixed rights and duties for the maternal relations. For example, a hindu widow's white dress has to be presented by the head of her mother's family. They have to bear a small part of the funeral expense either in cash or kind as a token of sympathy.

It is considered a boon to die on *Margazhi Thiruvadharai* day in December-January or on an *Ekadasi* day (eleventh day of either the waxing or waning phases of the moon). Death during a temple festival period in the village is considered unlucky for the dying person since no music can be played before funeral houses. At such times, the person has to die 'unsung'.

Death on a Saturday is believed to lead to another death in the same household. The saying is *'Sani-ponaa Thaniye pokathu'* i.e. "the dead do not go alone on Saturdays". To circumvent the effects of a death on Saturday, a portion of the house where death has occurred is dismantled or a new exit gate created to remove corpse. Sometimes; a fowl; is tied to the bier and buried or cremated along with the corpse.

When a person dies, the chief mourner is his wife. She breaks her bangles, loosens her hair and laments his death. The period of mourning; is about 12 to16 days among the well-to-do castes and lesser duration in castes which earn their bread through daily labour. The traditional periods are observed only in the rural areas and more rigidly by the leisured classes. Attendance at the house of the dead is a compulsory social duty.

Every person visiting the house of the dead person during the mourning period is believed to suffer from pollution. The first thing; he is expected to do on leaving the house of the dead person is to have purificatory bath. Only after this bath, he is entitled by custom and usage to have a drink of even a glass of water or to eat and enter the main parts of his own house.

After the kith and kin have assembled and had a last look at the departed, the corpse is bathed, perfumed and attired in new clothes. The widow is brought near the dead body of her husband; and given white garments to wear ever-after. The women do not; go the cremation ground.

A popular Tamil movie song of the 60's goes,

> *Relationships extend within the home*
> *The wife accompanies up to the street*
> *The child accompanies up to the grave*
> *But who will go with you till the end?*

All along the funeral procession, film music is played in a raucous rhythm. At cross-roads, the bearers of the dead body circle the place thrice. This is done to misguide the spirits; and prevent further calamities to the village.

When the departed was at peace with himself and with the world at the moment of truth, it is known as *Kalyana Saavu*, or, "wedding funeral". Consequently, the funeral assumes a poignant and auspicious feel. It is a celebratory occasion. A "good death", is another way they say it.

At the cremation bier, the oldest son, wearing white Vaeshti, is required to walk around it three times while carrying an earthen pot of water on his left shoulder. As he starts the cycle, someone follows behind and punches a hole on the side of the pot so the it drips behind him. Each time he comes around, a hole is added for a total of three leaky holes. After that, he lets it drop behind him and the smashed pot denotes the breaking of ties between the dead and the living. The son then lights the fire to the pyre.

After the funeral service, neigbours usually, take turns to cook vegetarian food for the bereaving family. No cooking is done in the house of mourning. The Tamil phrase *"There is no fire in the stove"*, is a euphemism that the household was in mourning. Matter of fact, when someone curses, *"Your stove won't burn tomorrow"*, it is usually a threat to kill you or someone of yours."

Before taking leave from the death house you wash your feet from the pail of water set at the front gate. You don't say goodbye – The Tamil good bye translates as, "I'll go and come" similar to the English, "see you again.' The implication being, that you want to meet under similar circumstances. Therefore, you simply walk away. Afterall, you'd already expressed your condolences earlier and paid your respects.

There is common choice of the colour white. The white cloth tied to the Malay grave posts, the white funeral shroud, white cloth tied to a Chinese hearse, and Indian widows wear white thereafter. Western mourning is the exception, where black prevails.

At the Muslim gravesite, the last *Azan* is called into the ear of the deceased. The son hands a clump of earth to men in the pit, who let the deceased "sniff" it before depositing by the side.The others hand down their handfuls. After the grave is filled, two *batu nisan* (headstone or stela) are planted at the head and waist respectively. The stones are either cylindrical (male) or flat (female) poles jutting out about two feet above ground. The name and dates of birth and death are engraved. The material ranges from granite to marble to concrete to hardwood.

The imam prays and sprinkles fragrant *attar* or rose water from head to toe, of the backfilled grave. The others follow suit and scatter *bunga rampai*, assorted flower petals. White strips of cloth are tied to the two grave markers. The attendees at the grave are invited to a *kenduri arwah* or feast in memory of the deceased.

Everyone joins in a *kenduri arwah* (memorial feast) which includes a reading from the Koran. The prayers (*tahlil*) will be held again on the third, fourteenth, fortieth and hundredth day.

When a Taoist takes leave, all the deities and mirrors in the house of the deceased which is also where the wake is usually held are covered with white paper. This is because the deities would never allow the deceased (who is now a spirit) in the house and the non-reflection of his/her image in the mirror would scare him/her.

A new suit of clothes is bought. The coat and tie ensemble is favoured. All the pockets of that suit must be cut so that it "leaks". It is believed that if the deceased tries to take anything away with him in his pockets, it will just leak back into the family. Doesn't it recall the leaking Hindu water pot? All is not lost, for the family will incinerate virtual property and bank notes for use in paradise.

The mourners are asked to turn away while the coffin is carried to the hearse. This is to show that the family no longer takes an interest, thus allowing the deceased to go in peace. On the way to the cemetery, the older son will ride on the hearse and will need to call out to the spirit when they cross bridges or bodies of water as the spirits are 'simple' and will not know how to cross.

With that journey (funeral) completed. and all the paper stuff which includes a big house for the deceased, car, bicycle, servants are all burnt in a bonfire with the mourners surrounding it in a final goodbye. The paper dolls that are burnt as servants are first given names and 'activated' by the Taoist priest. The family is required to remember those names and not to give anyone in the family the same names.

With that the rites are complete and the mourners return home with the eldest son carrying the picture that was on the front of the hearse which will be used for the temporary altar to be set up. As the spirit is still 'new' it will not be left at the cemetery but allowed to return home for 49 days.

Back at the house the cooks have been busy and the house has been cleaned, the deities have their coverings removed and a piece of red cloth is hung across the main door to celebrate. The mourners return but before being allowed back into the house, the spirit is received and set up at a separate temporary altar. The mourners wash their hands, face and feet in water containing petals of 7 kinds of flowers and pomelo leaves to rid themselves of bad luck. The mourners then shower and change before feasting.

In Memoriam: Tahlil, Thivasam, jìchén

Solomon, author of the *Book of Proverbs* in the Bible, says that there is a season for everything, giving a list, including death. A time for everything. Everything in its time.

Malays believe it is a good idea to die on the Haj – the pilgrimage to Mecca. It is somewhat similar to the common idea that dying on the battlefield is more honourable than while retreating from it. Die with the arrow in your heart rather than on your hind.

Among Hindus, it is considered a boon to die on Margazhi Thiruvadharai day in December-January or on an Ekadasi day. Death during a festival period in the village is considered unlucky for the dying person since no music can be played before funeral houses on such days and so the person has to die 'unsung'.

Tradional Chinese culture doesn't appear to have such a thing as auspicious days to die. Rather, death as whole, is taboo. Merely talking about it, is said to bring bad fortune and aging parents avoid discussing it with their children. They would go to lengths to avoid the number 4 (sei, si), which is homophonic to "die". Organ donations and will writing are also given wide berth for fear of speeding up death. Naturally, attutudes are changing with the younger and more enlightened.

Generally there are two important ceremonies after death of a person in Hindu Culture. First is the third day ceremony (collecting bones after cremation) and second is the fortieth day ceremony *Karumathi*, which marks the end of the mourning period. On the 16th day, *Athmasanthi* (peace of the soul) prayers are held. The Hindus observe a death anniversary, *Thivasam*, which is attended by invitees. Sikh's observe what is called *Path da Bhog* (Completion of the reading of the Guru Granth Sahib). Among other situations, it also done at deaths.

In the Christian, depending on family tradition and denomination etc, post-funeral rituals vary. In my own memory as about a 10 year-old, our Catholic family had the *urumaa* tying ceremony. At my grandfather's memorial (he had passed away while on visit to India). All his male offspring including me, had an oil massage administered by grandpa's in-laws side – the *maamans* and *machaans* (uncles and cousins) – followed by a shower and veshti – shirt dress up. Then, we were made to sit in a row before each one of then came up with new veshti and tied a turban on us. The turban kept growing taller and taller as relatives kept coming up with their "gift". It made for quite some fun and gaiety. A homecooked dinner followed, provided by the deceased's family. The significance of the ritual has been lost to me – except, that it was probably a ancestral village "import" and a comfort giving mechanism. Apparently, up to the sixties our extended family had a "20 (India) village" sangam (society) in those days, so relatives were plenty. Sadly, their current generations have dissipated, along with the queer custom.

If the Chinese run scared of death, they embrace the funeral itself with elaborate and lengthy sendoffs. Similar to condemning the sin but loving the sinner, fear the idea of death, but respect the dead. The mourning period is 49 days. Buddhists consider that the rebirth happens within 49 days of death. Traditional prayers are conducted in 7-day installments of 7 reps. (There is also a 100 day memorial service called *Gong Teck*, to pray for a ideal rebirth for the deceased.

In Islamic tradition, "When a person passes away, the family and the community get together seven days after for the *spoua*. And 40 days after what is called the *arbyin*, and one year after the one year anniversary. When we gather in these gatherings, we recite the Quran, we give to charity, we do good deeds on the behalf of the deceased," Imam Saleh Qazwini,

Concepts of Life and Death: lái shì, Kiamat, Karma,

Being a microcosm of world cultures, Malaysians hold different concepts of death. Those who profess the monotheistic faiths of Judaism, Christianity, and Islam look at death as the beginning rather than the end. That is to say, a new everlasting life of peace awaits the faithful who live righteously on earth. They anticipate a judgment day, or *hari kiamat/khayamat*, in which rulings as where a soul would go – heaven or hell – will be written.

The Jewish and Islamic religions believe a Messiah, or Masihi respectively, will judge the world. For the Christians their Messiah, Jesus Christ, has already come and will come again as judge on the day of judgment.

For Hindus death, rather than a beginning, is a continuation in the cycle. While in the monotheistic religions time is linear, the Hindu-Buddhist time is cyclical. The Hindu too believes in a soul, spirit and body, just as everybody else. The soul actually has a chance to upgrade itself. Hence, it can be reborn in lower/higher form in different persons depending on conduct in the past life. So, is there any end to the cycle? Hindus believe that it ends when the soul attains *Mukthi* (aka *Moksha*) or oneness with God. Hence, instead of a fixed cycle, it is more a spiral that can end in the soul (atma) finally blending with god. Which leaves a puzzle as to the attitude of some towards their fellow man. The supposed high caste Brahmin sage (upgraded from a cockroach in the former life), now suppresses his fellow human of low birth (downgraded from her previous life of a cruel royal) – is he on the downward spiral again? Which begs the question – does the atman easily forget its past, once reborn?

While the Hindu cycle of death goes through many lifetimes, some Western literati have an interesting take on the single lifetime cycle of death. A few follow:

> "Life is hard. Then you die. Then they throw dirt in your face. Then the worms eat you. Be grateful it happens in that order."
>
> – David Gerrold

> "Edible, adj.: Good to eat, and wholesome to digest, as a worm to a toad, a toad to a snake, a snake to a pig, a pig to a man, and a man to a worm."
>
> – Ambrose Bierce

> "A man may fish with the worm that hath eat of a king, and eat of the fish that hath fed of that worm."
>
> – William Shakespeare

The message in all the above, is unmistakable: Nothing is permanent. You will be eaten !

There is no concept of the afterlife or life after death in Chinese thought. Death is the end. Hence, they are more focused on preserving and prolonging the current life. Confucius taught to avoid focussing on the afterlife as nothing much was known about it, but rather, to focus to on everyday issues such as duty, honour, and moral living. If living the moral life for its own sake (without expectation of reward in the hereafter), it surely must be the purest morality. Unless Confucius is advocating a quid pro quo equation in the here and now and the hereafter transaction, without spelling it out. Other signs pointing to afterlife concerns in Chinese culture, are Confucius' emphasis on filial piety and the Chinese concept of a 18 level hell (Diyu).

All Saints Day: Ziarah Kubur, Qingming, Thivasam

With the exception of the Hindus, Sikhs and some Buddhists, most everyone else gets buried at death. The sprawling old Loke Yew Road cemetery has sections for Hindus, Sikhs (crematorium), Buddhists, Christians, Europeans and Japanese (wartime dead), and separate sections for the different Chinese dialect groups, Cantonese, Hakka, Hokkien, Teochew etc. It witnessed its last burial in the 60s. Situated in the middle of town, it is one of the the prime real estates in the city. The interred are PR (permanent residents), and RIP (resting in perpetuity). So thanks to them, the area will likely continue to be a green lung indefinitely. With VIP (very intellectual property) neighbours like *Dewan Bahasa dan Pustaka* (Language and Literature Council), and also *Wisma Putra* (*Foreign Office*), you can grant that the graveyard gets gross ghastly glances from gawdawfully greedy landgrubbers.

All Malaysians visit the graves of their dearly departed. The Catholic and Chinese have special days called All Saints Day. Muslims visit the graves every chance they get, to clean it. Festive days like Hari Raya Puasa are an excuse to visit.

Normally, families and friends would gather around gravesites of their fallen relatives and friends, clad in their festive baju raya attires, to pray and even taking time to clean and spruce up their loved ones' final resting places in the spirit of Hari Raya.

Two months before the dawn of Ramadhan, the Muslim cemetery on Langat road in Klang gets a spruce up. Overnight, one notices that the gentle sloped garden of rest had been cleared of weeds and snow white clothes wrapped around the headstones and footstones. Now, at Ramadhan, the place still looks like an explosion of white mushrooms in a green meadow. About a few weeks before the Muslim memorial park makeover, the Chinese burial ground received the same treatment. The only difference was, there had been no sign of human activity on the Muslim plot. It seemed like a contract job, as all the graves were uniformly dressed. Whereas, the Chinese section was overrun by relatives clambering up the steeply sloping hillside, cleaning their respective family momuments. You couldn't be taken by surprise, as cars were lined up by the roadside for a distance, slowing down traffic.

Meanwhile, the sleeping residents of the adjacent, ancient Christian Calvary, continued their perpetual repose, undisturbed by visitors. The Catholic All Saints Day had not arrived. The Hindu crematorium and graveyard, also in the vicinity, continued undisturbed in its secluded location further up the hill. Now, doesn't that hill seem like a metaphor for the premise of this book? Everyone sleeps peacefully in his/her own piece of earth and in their own communal section. Yet, they are all together, on a common hill. But graveyards shouldn't be the only place for communal peace and harmony. Why should only the dead rest in peace. Why not the living too?

Those who opt for cremation too observe anniversaries of death, variously called, *Thivasam* (Hindu), *Barsi* (Sikh prayers)) etc.

One year after death, an annual funeral memorial will be observed, called *"Thithi"*. Thithi literally means "Date". The only date the ancient Hindus bothered about was this death ceremony. Even today the same custom survives without much change. Still, it is the most important ceremony to be done by a son for his dead parents and ancestors. Ancient Hindus believed that and present day Hindu also still believe, that if the annual ceremony is not held properly, the soul will not reach heaven and also will not get nourishment. Further the soul will be neglected in heaven or even worse scenario that the souls of ancestors will be sent to hell. Such is the burden on a living decendent that he had to conduct the annual death ceremony (Thivasam). Without that his *Pithrus* (Fathers and fore fathers) will be put into eternal punishments. It is said that the ancestor comes a calling on the death anniversary. The modus operandi of the preist is based on Brahmanical rites and rituals, involving the offering of *pindam* (balls of rice) to be eaten by crows, special food to cows etc. The crows are thought to be representatives of the pithru (deceased elders).

The Qingming or Ching Ming festival, also known as Tomb-Sweeping Day in English (sometimes also called Chinese Memorial Day or Ancestors' Day), is a traditional Chinese festival observed by the Han Chinese of Mainland China, Taiwan, Hong Kong, Macau, Malaysia, Singapore, Indonesia, Thailand and by the Peranakan of Malaysia and Singapore. It falls on the first day of the fifth solar term of the traditional Chinese lunisolar calendar. This makes it the 15th day after the Spring Equinox, either 4, 5 or 6 April in a given year. During Qingming, Chinese families visit the tombs of their ancestors to clean the gravesites, pray to their ancestors, and make ritual offerings. Offerings would typically include traditional food dishes, and the burning of joss sticks and joss paper. The holiday recognizes the traditional reverence of one's ancestors in Chinese culture.

The Qingming Festival has been observed by the Chinese for over 2500 years. It became a public holiday in mainland China in 2008.

The Qingming Festival commemorates the life of the departed in an elaborate set of rituals often mistranslated in the West as ancestral worship. Actually, it is a Confucian form of posthumous respect and filial piety offered to a Chinese person's ancestors.

Young and old kneel down to offer prayers before tombs of the ancestors, offer the burning of joss in both the forms of incense sticks (joss-sticks) and silver-leafed paper (joss paper), sweep the tombs and offer food, tea, wine, chopsticks, and/or libations in memory of the ancestors. Depending on the religion of the observers, some pray to a higher deity to honour their ancestors while others may pray directly to the ancestral spirits.

These rites have a long tradition in Asia, especially among the royalty who legislated these rituals into a national religion. They have been preserved especially by the peasantry and are most popular with farmers today, who believe that continued observances will ensure fruitful harvests ahead by appeasing the spirits in the other world.

Religious symbols of ritual purity, such as pomegranate and willow branches, are popular at this time. Some people carry willow branches with them on Qingming or stick willow branches on their gates and/or front doors. There are similarities to palm leaves used on Palm Sundays in Christianity; both are religious rituals. Furthermore, the belief is that the willow branches will help ward off the unappeased, troubled and troubling spirits, and/or evil spirits that may be wandering in the earthly realms on Qingming.

Midwives: Bidan, Maruthuvacchi, Zhùchǎnshì

Before the Ob-Gyn, there was the midwife. She was the one who made house calls on D-day (delivery day), and who monitored the incubational progress of foetus and mother prior to that.

Meaning of: Maruthuvachchi – "Medicine woman" (nurse)

One of the victims of modernization is the traditional (!). Traditional healing, traditional midwifery, traditional medicine and what have you. Midwives have become modern, with special degrees and coursework in universities.

Some of the duties of the traditional midwives/healers have been described in the previous section on confinement.

Grandmothers of old were natural traditional healers. My own grandmother had her own bag of tricks. Once, when I complained of sore throat, she took some lime (from limestone) spat out her betel leaf juice and mixed it so that a pastel pink paste was formed. She then smeared it on my throat. Voila! The pain disappeared shortly after. Similary, when we were working in the garden removing rocks, I got stung by a scorpion. My mother immediately halfed an onion and squeezed the juice on the throbbing toe. The pain subsided quite soon after. Now, we won't know if it was actual science, or virtual serendipity. But at that moment it worked, didn't it?

I remember witnessing both my parents stretching a length of saree (5 to 8 meters) at waist level, placing my screaming baby sister in the middle and rolling it back and forth like a skateboarder on the half-pipe. Baby's stiff neck problem solved! These are history now, overtaken by modernity. Every household will have a similar story of miraculous healing in their family memories. Every kitchen had a box of spices and dried herbs on standby, for medicinal use. All the above ailments are now referred to the nearest dispensary (clinic, rather) to be treated.

The other day a friend reported going to an 80-year old sinseh as he just been confirmed as having diabetes and some vision issues. The old uncle bent his patient's two ears, till he felt a click. The patient says that that at least his sight was immediately, and recognizably much better! What other tricks does the sinseh hide up his sleeves?

Well, the cycle seems to have turned. While we looked to science for answers, science is now turning to good old grandmother cures! Recent cases of the efficacy of turmeric, moringa (murungai), yoga, etc. abound. Scholarly research papers on the benefits of all kinds of herbs and fruits are legion, and our forebears used it without knowing it? Forget it, they have been recorded in the traditional medicine handbooks of the millennium old TCM (Chinese traditional medicine), the Siddha system of the Tamils, and orally preserved by Malay dukuns.

As far the practice of midwifery, it has been detailed in the preceding sections on *Conception and Birth* and *Confinement*.

Nannies: Aamah, Aaayah, (peng) Asuh

Aamah, and *Aayah/Aayamma*, are Chinese and Tamil personal pronouns respectively, for older women who do child care. Asuh, is a Malay verb root, "to mentor". The noun, *Pengasuh* refers to an older woman who does the same things as the aayah and aamah. In other words, all three are nannies. They may not be the young and attractive, "Nanny Fine" (of *The Nanny* TV comedy series) but they are fine nannies (fannies ?), nevertheless. These are some titles given to a caregiver of little children – Au Pair, Babysitter, Childminder, Chaperone, Duenna, Governess, Nanny, Nursemaid, Mrs. Doubtfire (?), Wet-nurse. The *Mrs.Doubtfire* movie is based on the 1987 novel by Anne Fine (any relation to Nanny Fine?!). What a fine coincidence.

Aamah is Chinese for an elderly household help. This excerpt from an article in the South China Morning Post (9th July 2020) gives some insight into their history. The article was titled *"Malaysia's last living amah seeks family, searches for her roots, hopes to reunite with family in China"*. Her Cantonese name is Ngan Dou Tai, aged 105, and living in residential care.

"Ngan's lineage as a *ma jie* dates back to 17th-century China when silk was considered the world's most luxurious fabric.

Few knew at the time, that silk threads came from silkworm cocoons because the production of silk floss was a closely guarded secret in an industry run only by women – the ma jie (literally, mother-sister).

Going against the grain of a male-dominated society then, the ma jie took a vow of celibacy and kept the economic power they enjoyed as silk floss producers to themselves.

But in the 1920s, the silk industry collapsed with the creation of synthetic fabrics.

This led the ma jie to change occupations, and they left China by the thousands and became domestic helpers in well-to-do families throughout Hong Kong and Southeast Asia.

They became multitasking governesses or female butlers, renowned for their loyalty and dedication to the master of the household.

Many people today still have fond memories of being raised under the care of the ma jie."

The Aayah, more commonly Aayamah. It is a combination of Aayah – granny, and Amma – Mother. Granny mother? I remember those carefree childhood days when my father was the Headmaster of an estate school. Before sunrise, the women rubber tappers would leave their babies and toddlers in the *aayah kottaai* (Litt: "nanny barn") – or nursery. The mothers left the requisite milk and baby food in wicker baskets.The infants slept in *thottils* or swinging cradles *(*Malay: *buaian)*, which were basically hammocks – sarees or sarongs, ends tied together and slung from overhead beams. The bigger children slept on mats on the floor. The aayah had no particular nanny training, being just another estate employee. The likely basic qualification was, an advanced age, a knowledge of children's maladies (cholic etc.) and a knack for pacifying children. I recall our estate aayamma had to handle about 10 to 15 children of various ages, from babes in arms (*kai kulanthai*) to the terrible twos and threes, to the fidgety fours and fives.

As old is always gold, grandmothers make the best nannies. Nowadays you hear horror stories of children being hurt, even killed at young nannys' homes. Many a CCTV clip has circulated where a maid is seen roughing up a child (Shaken Baby Syndrome) or an elder. Strangely, a boyfriend (of the nanny) is often involved in the deaths. Many a nanny wannabe who advertises her services are not registered and rigourously regulated, as in more advanced countries.

The Malay word for nanny is *Pengasuh*, or one who nurtures or instructs. The root word is *asuh* (to guide). This not to be confused with *Ah Soh*, a title for Chinese grandma. Pengasuh is used for registered, trained teachers at pre-kindergarten or day care centres, as opposed to the fly by night, or fly under the radar, home based operators.

TASKA (Taman Asuhan Kanak-Kanak) are government registered day care providers. Below is a list of their duties under TASKA Registration (Section I)

Registered childcare providers at the workplace, community, and institutions have the following responsibilities:

(a) Caring for children according duties assigned.

(b) Ensuring feeding methods follow ways recommended by the Health Department.

(c) Immediately report any suspicion of abuse or injustice, to the supervisor.

(d) Inform the supervisor of any early signs of disease on the child.

(e) Prepare daily reports to the supervisor, on the day to day activities of the children.

(f) Prepare trimonthly report on childrens' development and copy to parents and guardians.

Like the midwife, the nanny too, is becoming modernized, with training and certification. Looks like it is one of the few old time jobs that will not be extinct due to modernization.

Traditional Medicine: Siddhar, Sinseh, Dukun

Before there were MDs, there were traditional healers and herbalists. These herbalists are of the proactive mindset. That is, they focused on medicines to prevent disease, and treated diseases with what is regular food as medicine. Not medicine as food supplement.

Siddha is the Tamil counterpart of *Ayurveda* medicine and has been around for over two millennia. It has a slew of ancient medical texts. The Siddhar hagiography consists of 18 personages over varous time periods including the first, Agathiyar from the 7th century BCE.

Scores of leafy greens and seeds form the base of this school of native medicine. They have exotic sounding names like *musumusukai, karisalanganni, mudakkathaan, thottarsinungi etc. Musumusukai* (melothria maderasapatana) is a common ingredient. Note of interest: Madrasa Pattinam (Madras) was the old name of Chennai, Tamil Nadu. The English name for the plant is Madras Pea Pumpkin. It is a little creeper with yellow flowers and blood red cherry sized fruit. When green, it is a veritable thumb sized watermelon, stripes and all! The properties of this plant are "Astringent, Expectorant, vaatham (intestine related), pittham (stomach related), Adaptogenic, anti oxidant, pungent, sweet, anti inflammatory, hypoglycaemic, antispasmodic, anti pyritic, hepato protective components". Too technical? Well, it is medicine, ain't it?

The Siddhars use plant, mineral and animal products in the making of, *Leghiyam* (paste), *Sooranam* (powder), *Thailam* (liniment/ointment), *Kashayam* (decoction) and *Mezhugu (capsules)*, Kuligai (*tablet*) and Arishtam (*tonic*).

The operating principle is the homeostasis (*Thannilai*) of the three humours – *Vali, Azhal*, and *Iyam* corresponding to the *Vatham, Piththam,* and *Kapham*, of Ayurveda. Vali (air), Azhal (fire), Iyam (earth) are present in the body in a healthy ratio of 1: ½: ¼ respectively and distruptions in the equilibrium leads to disease.

According to the Siddha medicine, various psychological and physiological functions of the body are made up of the combination of seven elements namely:

1. *ooneer* (plasma) is responsible for growth, development, and nourishment;
2. *ischeneer* (blood) is responsible for nourishing muscles, imparting color, and improving intellect;
3. *oon* (muscle) is responsible for the shape of the body;
4. *koluppu/Kozhuppu* (fatty tissue) is responsible for lubricating joints as well as oil balance;
5. *elumbu* (bone) is responsible for body structure and posture and movement;

6. *elumbu majjai* (bone marrow) is responsible for the formation of blood corpuscles; and
7. *sukkilam* (semen) which is responsible for human reproduction.

The Siddha principle predicates that the universe is composed of two forces: 1) Matter and 2) Energy, hence its, "*man is nature, nature is man*" axiom. It refers to it as *Siva* and *Sakti*. Both are co-existent and inseparable. Siva the husband and sakti his wife, are often represented as *ardhanareeswara*, a male-female form. It is quite similar to the *Yin* (male, heat) – *Yang* (female, cold) principle in Chinese philosophy.

The Traditional Chinese Medicine (TCM) shop and its Sinseh, are a familiar sight in any sizable town in Malaysia.

The philosophy is based on the balance of *Yin* (heat) and *Yang* (cold), *Chi* (energy). With its dependence on exotic animal parts, the use of traditional medicine in China has been a major generator of illegal wildlife smuggling, linked to the endangerment and potential extinction of exotic animals. Being a primary part of the illegal ivory trade, it is a major factor for the endangerment of the wild African elephant and rhinocerous population.

There are roughly 13,000 compounds used in China and over 100,000 TCM recipes recorded in the ancient literature. Plant elements and extracts are by far the most common elements used. In the classic *Handbook of Traditional Drugs* from 1941, 517 drugs were listed – out of these, 45 were animal parts, and 30 were minerals.

Qi shows itself inside the body in five different ways, which are collectively known as the <u>five vital substances</u>

- *Jing*/essence — jing is associated with growth, core organs, and reproduction. Deficiencies in jing can manifest in a weak constitution or a weak mind
- *Qi*/life force — qi flows around the body, and imbalances manifest as fatigue and poor digestion (qi deficiency), or stress and insomnia (qi excess)
- *Shen*/spirit — associated with emotions and mental condition, shen imbalances manifest as psychological illnesses
- *Xue*/blood — blood nourishes the organs and the mind. Imbalances in xue manifest as fatigue and poor memory.

- *Jinye*/body fluids — body fluids provide moisture and lubrication around the body, like the thin/light tears, sweat, saliva (Jin) and the viscuous mucus, semen, milk (Ye). Imbalances interfere with the production of other vital substances.

Modern acupuncture actually emerged in 1930's and gained popularity in the 60's. It is the insertion of needles into superficial structures of the body (skin, subcutaneous tissue, muscles) – usually at acupuncture points (acupoints) – and their subsequent manipulation; this aims at influencing the flow of qi.

The dukun's (aka tabib, bomoh, pawang) primary role is that of a healer. They may use herbalism, incantations (*jampi*), chants (*mantra*), animal parts, inanimate objects, spiritual communication or guidance, prayers, offerings, the keris or any combination to effect their curatives.

Malay traditional medicine is based on the 4 elements, fire, water, earth and wind, one less than the Siddha or TCM. Siddha (earth, water, fire, air, and ether); TCM (water, fire, metal, wood, earth). While it is certainly not short of documented cures and treatment, Malay traditional medicine lacks a defined principle or philosophy of it such as classification, causation, and confirmation of disease. The *semangat* (soul substance) of a person is said to determine an individual's susceptibility to various illnesses. But, how does it work?

"The practices of Traditional Malay Medicine involve a combination of animist, Hindu and Islamic traditions. Healing may involve rituals, physiological aspects such as massage and bone-setting, as well as the use of medicine that are derived from plants, animals and minerals." – ROOTS, a Singapore government website.

The Malay medicine man uses a variety of herbs such as aloe vera, amaranth (spinach), cassia alata, coriander, nutmeg etc which are used in combinations, to make Jamu. Jamu is a traditional colloidal concoction originating from Indonesia. It is predominantly a herbal medicine made from natural materials, such as roots, bark, flowers, seeds, leaves and fruits. Materials acquired from animals, such as honey, royal jelly, milk and country chicken eggs are often used as well.

In 2019, jamu was officially recognized as one of Indonesia's intangible cultural heritage by the Indonesian government. Malaysia has its own Jamu and medicinal entrepreuners, and a LOT of celebrity beauty care producers.

Massage: Urut, Uruvuthal, Tui Na

Chiropracty and physiotherapy are modern avatars of the old grandmother massage therapy.

Traditional Malay massage, known locally as "Urut Melayu", involves soft-tissue manipulation of the whole body applied using the hands and fingers.

The main focus of massage is the elimination of *angin* (air/wind) which said to block the *urat* (blood vessesl, lymphatic sytem, and nerves). Forms of message include, *bekam* (cupping), *lumur* (soaking) etc.

The few types of massage include post-natal, post stroke, blind massage (performed by blind masseurs), urut batin, or sexual enhancement/ enlargement massage. The latter appears most common of the Urut Melayu. It is a kind of chiropractic of the male implement, aimed at vamping up waning venereal vigour, in combo with pill form Viagra wannabes – or prototypes, as the case may be. With the market for such treatment so in demand, impersonators abound. One guy, opting for a masseuse (female), ended up getting a handjob, leaving job in hand unaccomplished.

Massage of Chinese Medicine is known as An Mo (pressing and rubbing) or Qigong Massage, and is the foundation of Japan's Anma. Categories include Pu Tong An Mo (general massage), Tui Na An Mo (pushing and grasping massage), Dian Xue An Mo (cavity pressing massage), and Qi An Mo (energy massage). Tui na focuses on pushing, stretching, and kneading muscles, and Zhi Ya focuses on pinching and pressing at acupressure points. Technique such as friction and vibration are used as well.

Tui na is a form of massage akin to acupressure (from which shiatsu evolved). Asian massage is typically administered with the person fully clothed, without the application of grease or oils. Techniques employed may include thumb presses, rubbing, percussion, and assisted stretching. Tui na aims to improve the flow of chi through the meridians.

Reflexology, also known as "zone therapy", is an alternative medicine involving application of pressure to the feet and hands with specific thumb, finger, and hand techniques without the use of oil or lotion. It is based on a pseudoscientific system of zones and reflex areas that purportedly reflect an image of body parts on the feet and hands, with the premise that such work effects a physical change to the body.

Massage in Tamil is *Uruvuthal*, from the verb root *Uruvu* (to massage, draw, shape or stretch). Indian massage is popularly known as Ayurvedic massage or Abhyangam ("oil application") in Sanskrit. According to the Ayurvedic Classics, Abhayngam is an important *dincharya* (Daily Regimen) that is needed for maintaining a healthy lifestyle. The massage technique used during Ayurvedic Massage aims to stimulate the lymphatic system. Practitioners claim that the benefits of regular Ayurvedic massage include pain relief, reduction of fatigue, improved immune system, and improved longevity.

Indian massages inevitably involve herbal oils. During Deepavalis of yore, family members got up early in the morning to take the "oil bath" – actually an oil rub. It was accompanied by simple massages by the parents. After an hour's soak in the sun, the gingelly oil was washed off with a mungbean paste scrubdown, an excellent degreaser. Friday's also saw such activity. The result was complete body cooling and a luxurious nap after an invigorating vegetarian meal. This a now an extinct item in our customs. Even the oldos don't do it anymore.

The message of massage is a transaction of therapist pain for client pleasure. One curious aspect of east and south east Asian massage is the concept of the masseur absorbing the toxicity of his patient. I have witnessed many a foot reflexologist acting tired and burpy, saying that they actually absorb the client's bad vibes.

"So, when a therapist makes skin contact with an electron-deficient client, electrons will be drawn away from the therapist to the person receiving the treatment. This is an energy transfer, a major component of feeling drained by the end of a busy day.

The physical laws of electrostatics require that this charge transfer begins immediately and continues as tense, painful, and inflamed tissues are relaxed. As the walls of inflammatory pockets dissolve under the therapist's skillful hands, more free radicals are released, leading to more charge transfer from therapist to client. The process obviously helps clients feel better, but who is paying the price?"

(excerpted from: Massage and Bodywork Magazine for the Visually Impaired – Earthing. March/April 2016 Issue.

Earthing, or grounding is a technique for therapists to regain their electron balance.

Shamans: Wu, Bomoh, Samiyadi

A shaman is someone who purportedly heals with the help of benevolent spirits. They are traditional native medicine men. The word itself comes from Siberian Tungusic, *saman* ("one who knows".

Chinese shamanism has the longest recorded history in the world. The word *wu* "shaman; spirit medium; healer", first appeared on oracle bones from the late Shang Dynasty (ca. 1600-1046 BCE). Chinese classics from the Zhou Dynasty (1045-256 BCE) provide details about male and female shamans serving as exorcists, healers, rainmakers, oneiromancers, soothsayers, and officials. Ever since Emperor Wu of Han (r. 141-87 BCE) established Confucianism as the "state religion", the male-dominated Confucian ruling class had marginalized shamanism, especially female shamans. Shamanic practices continue in present day Chinese culture.

Various ritual traditions are rooted in original Chinese shamanism: contemporary Chinese ritual masters are sometimes identified as wu by outsiders, though most orders don't self-identify as such. Also Taoism has some of its origins from Chinese shamanism: it developed around the pursuit of long life (shou 壽/寿), or the status of a xian (仙, "mountain man", "holy man").

In the Malaysian context: "Ah Yuk Je is a successful Hakka Chinese spirit medium practicing in a small Chinese community in Malaysia. Her clientele consists largely of young children suffering from a culturally specific condition called haak geng or 'soul loss' and women concerned about infertility, prenatal problems and errant spouses. While in a trance state, assisted by her tutelary spirits, she diagnoses, prescribes and treats illnesses. Her treatment includes naturalistic and magico-religious elements such as 'cooling' herbal teas, tonics to strengthen the body, rituals and amulets. Because Ah Yuk Je is a wife and mother, women find her sympathetic and astute at solving family problems. When faced with an illness herself, which she suspects to be the result of kong tao (black magic) instigated by someone in her own village, she seeks assistance from a healer outside her own ethnic group as well as outside her community. "(Excerpted – Social Science & Medicine, Volume 18, Issue 2, 1984, Pages 147-157)

The Shaman King (*Raja Bomoh*) is a self certification by a certain Ibrahim Mat Zin, originally of Bagan Datoh, Perak. He was a mahaguru (grand master) of the Seni Silat Gayung Ghaib (Silat Martial Arts) association of Malaysia. He is more notorious (nutty odious) internationally, for his unsolicited exploits trying to located the whereabouts of flight MH370 in 2014. Remember that? Lest we forget. His scientific methods included waving fresh coconuts and peering through two bamboo tubes for binoculars. When he asserts that, *"The plane is in a parallel realm. It will be missing for 25 years before it returns, but the people may still be alive because the air is different, a month is like a day to them"*, we shall reach our own conclusions.

In 2017, he reappeared on the international stage when he used the same methods to try and stop a North Korean bomb entering Malaysia space. *"We don't have modern weapons like (North) Korea. If we go to war with weapons, we will lose. But we use ancient methods to fence the air, the earth and the water, so that missiles will go missing and not reach Malaysia."* That was during the diplomatic crisis following Malaysia's detention of some North Koreans under suspicion in the (VX nerve agent) murder of Kim Jong Nam, Kim Jong Un's elder brother. The assassination, by VX nerve agent was carried out at the KL International Airport.

The most well-known bomoh outfit in Malaysia is Darussyifa' (House of Healing), run by followers of the late Datuk Haron Din, spiritual leader of PAS until his death last September. (From a Star report.}

Main puteri literally means "playing princess," believed to refer to Puteri Saadong, a legendary 17th-century Kelantan princess driven insane by her husband's marital infidelities. Her spirit is now said to watch over Kelantan and she is regularly invoked as the ultimate emotionally troubled main puteri patient. But conservative Islam has steadily gained sway in the historically moderate country, and religious bodies monitor magian warlocks' Islamic incongruities and contradictory practices.

More acceptable to Malaysian authorities, are the Islamic bomohs. Mazlan Hakim is one of a new breed of bomohs who are well-educated, plugged-in to the modern world (a computer programmer), and base their ghostbusting and healing on Islamic precepts instead of animist or otherworldly techniques.

The 56-year-old has been a bomoh for 30 plus years and unlike his un-Islamic counterparts who say they use demons known as "jinn" to do their bidding, he unleashes verses of the Koran to heal the sick and drive out evil spirits.

"There are two types of jinn, the Muslim and the non-Muslim jinn," he says.

"The worst is the Muslim jinn as the other jinns come out of the body when I read passages from the Koran, but the Muslim jinn are immune to the Koran so I have to use my telekinetic abilities to pull the demon out."

Catholic exorcists are legion. Recall the priests in the movies *The Exorcist* (1973) and *The Omen* (1976). I still remember a monk of the Capuchine order from Rawang's church of St.Jude, who came and blessed our house in Bukit Badong Estate, Batang Berjuntai. I remember his brown robed and hooded image, as he went around the house muttering a prayer and sprinkling 'holy water'.

The Pentecostal brand of Christianity is rife with so-called pastors who prance and flail with boisterous commands to the demon, to exit the possessed. They make fantastic claims of healing sicknesses, driving out devils, and making prophecies. It is always a spectacle.

The "in-betweens" between the Catholic and the Pentecostal, are the Churches of Christ.They believe that while Jesus did drive out evil spirits and performed miracles, the Bible does not empower humans to do exorcisms, miraculous healings, and prophecies, which are the exclusive domain of the Divine. Man ought not to ascribe such powers to himself, or he is in danger of trying to become God.

"Eight people have been arrested for allegedly exhuming and consuming human flesh during a temple festival at Sakthi Pothi Sudalai Madasamy

Temple in Tenkasi tehsil of Tamil Nadu.The men reportedly belong to the 'Samiyadi' community." That was the intro to a report on the July 28, 2021 article of the India Today magazine.

Saamiyadi ("spirit dancer") and *Peyoti* (exorcist) refer to Tamil shamans. The story was, a Saamiyadi was seen entering a trance, dancing and holding a human skull on a sword. "When the police asked them about allegedly having exhumed and consumed human remains, they said they were not aware of the human remains and did not know what they were doing since they were in a trance," added the report.

"Samiyaadis" are people who claim to get possessed by local gods and make prophecies in a trance-like state, providing solutions and judgments to people's problems. They are bestowed with respect in their respective communities.

Saamiyadis were common in Malaysia in the rubber estate era. With most estates gone and the populace relocating to urban housing estates, there might be a few holdovers. The dancer (trancer, prancer) probably made more money from this side business, than from his full time rubber tapping job. With his paraphernalia of limes, coconut, *vibhuthi* (holy ash), *kunkumam* (turmeric + slaked lime), *mai* (ink), betel leaves etc, he gets into trance to describe *dosham* (defects), prescribe *pariharam* (remedies), and predict results. As a boy, I was privy to such an act in our estate, my legs in the stance of a sprinter – just in case.

Sorcery: Sihir, Wugu, Maanthrikam

While shamanism can be seen as benign white magic, sorcery can be labelled as black magic.: *Silap Mata* (litt: "mistaken eyes"), *Kann Katti Vitthai* (Litt: "eyes tied trick", *Gu* ("poison")

Shamans, sham or not, actually do try to help people. In those days, they functioned much like today's psychotherapist. The practicioner of black magic, or sorcerer, has no such qualms. His end, is to inflict emotional and psychological damage. His weapon is fear, which paralyses the mind of his gullible victims. Ignorant people who are so brainwashed, go to any extent to achieve powers. Many a time it involves the macabre and the murder, of innocent and unsuspecting victims, very often, their own children.

Modern science and rational thought may have reduced his numbers, but he still continues to thrive in the rural areas and among the poor in Malaysia. He engages the help of sinister beings such as spirits and demons in their activities. The Tamil *Kuttisaathaan;* Malay *Jinn, Toyol etc*; Chinese *Yaogui.* In other words, these practitioners have sold their souls to the devil.

In the Malay world, sorcery is/was quite widespread, carried out by bomohs and dukuns. The usual paraphernalia include, the kris, blood, eggs, needles, and dolls. Among his "assistants" are Jinns and devils such as the *hantu bungkus* ("packet devil") having powers to infiltrate the human body. *Langsuir* are spirits of females who died in childbirth and are used for purposes of disturbance. *Polong* suck victims' blood. They are a type of female looking spirit, the size of a distal phalange of the finger, i.e 1/3 the size of a finger. Bomohs use *Jembalang* ("goblin") as security patrol at sites that are encroached upon by outsiders. These are acquired as family heirloom, or through training in the art.

The types of sorcery include the usage of *patung* (dolls – voodoo?) that are attached with the victim's body parts like hair or nails. They are then pinned with needles to the accompaniment of invocations and incantatations – torturous and death causing. *Santau* is murder, either by ingesting poisoned items into a victims body or by blowing spellcast dust (*santau angin*) at the person. *Telur layang* ("flying eggs") – spell cast egg wrapped in yellow cloth and stuck with needle. Agonizing death. *Tangkal/Azimat* (amulets). *Sihir kasih sayang/pembenci* (love/ hate sorcery) – intended to join together or separate couples. Spells are written on paper and burnt, and the ash mixed into drinks and served to the intended target.

Wugu – "sorcery" or:"art of casting spells" is the Chinese sorceror's art and like shamanism, has a long history in the culture, especially in Taoism.

The following is an old prescription for a sorcerous act – Chinese style.

"To start with, take hold of a vessel made of some earthen elements, preferably clay, best be dark black in color. Next, you need to get hold as of something directly related to the thing you long for. If it is a person or living being, you need to get some things of them like for example, if it is a girl you love, then get hold of her hair strand, a handkerchief which she has used, etc.

Next, choose any full moon night and start with the rituals by getting hold of a white mouse. Keep this mouse directly under the rays of the full moon for three such full moon nights. Fill the earthen vessel with water such that when you throw the mouse in, it should not be able to escape from it. Once you have the said quantity of water in the vessel, you need to hold the mouse by the tail and drop it in the earthen vessel. Hold a lighted candle and let the light of the candle fall on the mouse when it fights for its life in desperation. Then start chanting these below said lines looking directly in the eyes of the mouse (you need to do this without blinking your eyes).

"Oh, powers of the universe here I beseech, listen to this wounded heart weep, take the life which struggles within and in return get me (mention what you want in life for which you are performing this ritual). Say these lines with utter concentration for seven nights, and you would see the powers of magic bringing impossible things happen."

Historian Philip Kuhn, records the "Chinese Sorcery Scare of 1768," referring to a series of sorcery practices in central and eastern China in the lower Yangtze river delta region. These involved the idea of "soul stealing" giving the sorcerer power and causing the victim to fall ill or die. That episode mostly involved the act of cutting off a man's queue (hair knot). The act of cutting off a man's queue possessed political significance. Emperor Qianlong of that time initiated a large scale hunt for the perpetrators.

Tamil culture has its share of the dark arts,. The list of various "treatments", is a follows: –

Pilli (Demon) – bringing someone's thoughts and actions under one's complete control

Sooniyam ("zero") – Making someone's life utterly meaningless, a total waste – done using his personal effects like clothing, hair, foot print, etc. *pilli-sooniyam*, is a combition of the above two.

Seivinai ("to do someone") – Making an enemy miserable in every which way.

Vasiyam ("enchantment") – making someone to fall for, or obey you

Eval ("incitement") – Impel someone do things against their wish

Vaippu ("placement") – similar to *seivinai*, by placing a magic charged object near the victim.

All these nefarious, malfeasant deeds are effected with the help of odious spirits and gory artifacts.

Street Medicine: Minyak Biawak, Tang shui she, Karna Puraa Thailam

Like the black magic artist, the street vendor of snake oil plays on the fears and gullibility of his clents. Snake oil or snake oil salesman, generally refers to quackery. Nowadays, the WWW and Youtube etc. function as digital streets for unscrupulous purveyors of questionable medicine.

There was a time in the sixties and earlier, where you could see street salesmen selling snake oil – actually it was crocodile, or monitor lizard (iguana/biawak/udumbu) oil. The Chow Kit Road market area in KL, was their popular playround. Whether he sold any or not, he attracted a constant, jostling audience. Such was his persuasive prowess, thespian talent and showbiz swag, as he incorporated sorcery and sleight of hand into the bargain.

"Oil from Chinese water snakes has for centuries been used in Chinese traditional medicine to treat joint pain such as arthritis and bursitis. It has been suggested that the use of snake oil in the United States may have originated with Chinese railway labourers in the mid-19th century, who worked long days of physical toil in the US trnscontinental railroad. Chinese snake oil may have had real benefits due to its high concentration of the omega–3 fatty acid eicosapentaenoic acid (EPA)—more than that of salmon." – Wikipedia. Wild West charlatans who got wind of this started their own bottled oils. Clark Stanley's Snake Oil Liniment – produced by Clark Stanley, the "Rattlesnake King" – was tested by the United States government›s Bureau of Chemistry, the precursor to the Food and Drug Administration (FDA) in 1916. It was found to contain: mineral oil, 1% fatty oil (assumed to be tallow), capsaicin from chili peppers, turpentine, and camphor.

Minyak Biawak ("Monitor Lizard Oil") is the Malay oil for treating multiple malaise. It touts its efficacies as:

1. Skin treatment
2. Smoothing the skin
3. Treating acne
4. Healing burns on the skin
5. Enhance male performance – "This oil is believed to increase the size of the male apparatus. This drug can be applied like a smear drug in general."

Karna Puraa Thailam ("Wild Pigeon Oil") is not a "snake oil". Nor is it made from pigeons. As a matter of fact, it is even sold on Shopee and Lazada. It occurs here only because it is an oil and represents the Tamil culture. I remember using it in the 1960's. It states its uses as: –

1. Bleeding from cuts and wounds stopped immediately on application.
2. When applied to burns and scalds, it stops burning sensation instantly and prevents deterioration of skin.
3. Toothache – Apply a cotton dipped in oil on the spot where it pains, Pigeon Oil is also an effective cure for puss oozing from the ears
4. Skin-itch – Apply lightly on the spot
5. Bodily pain – Apply where affected.

Those are old stuff. These days, in a single day, you come across a range of oils and liniments on internet street. The modern avatar of the snake oil saleman is here! Here is a list of such street pushers offering cures from scalp to "performane enhancing" oil on Youtube advertisements.

Minyak Arnab Cernuai (Rabbit oil) for the enlargement and durability of the you know what. Minyak Ustaz – is another rabbit oil for marital bliss, treatment of magic spells etc. Wait a minute. Rabbit oil, did you say? You mean the non-stop energizer bunny?

This is purportedly from Islamic medicine, the hadith etc. On the seemingly plausible side, one guy promotes musk oil perfume favoured by Prophet Muhammad. Surimass oil, Franch oil also make their presence in the videos. Ashwagandha KSM 66 (BP, cholesterol, Diabetes) by Astraherbs Ashwagandha out of Puchong, is a herbal product that also makes an entry. Many more such purveyors proliferate the cyber space. Don't expect to see any research data or institutional endorsement, only word of mouth and big talk by the bottler.

Faith Healers: Pozhi Saamiyar, Xìnyǎng zhìliáo shī, Penyembuh iman

The way I sees it, methinks faith is a personal thing between the person and his God. So wherein in do these "healers" come in? Most often, they have zero input in their client's faiths, and usurp God's role as healer and redeemer.The gullible disciple's faith in the fallible "apostle", seems the only faith here. Indeed, scenes of bodies swaying in ecstacy and "hallelujah"s heavenward soaring, are requisite at Pentecostal "healing services". It might even put a Woodstock rock concert to shame.

Modern Malay faith healers claim to use koranic verses in their "treatment", and Islamic officials are very wary of the healers' applications and seek to regulate them closely, when they blow into water containers to turn the H2O into *Air Jampi* (blessed water).

The Catholic priest uses holy oil and incantations to treat his flock. The Pentecostal pastor cavorts on stage, clamours, and claims to heal anything in the name of the Holy Spirt. Chinese "mediums" – yes, they all claim to be mediums and intermediaries between God and man. The Chinese medium mediates between the patient and certain spirits. Is this what makes them "faith" healers? Interestingly, the Tamil term for a faith healer is, *Pozhi Saamiyaar,* or "fake priest/healer." The line between faith healer and fake dealer is thin indeed, like that between a qualified and a quack. While well meaning, faith healers are generally viewed as askewed and affected. Except for their diehard disciples and fervent followers, of course. Their very public shows somehow attract press attention for the wrong reasons.

Since most of these faith healing sessions, notwithstanding the religion they represent, are run by in*SPIRIT*ional characters and involve mass frenzy and hysteria, they are ripe for monetary milking, charging for "holy oils", "phone consultations, "Prayer Towers", "memberships", "Fast Tracks" etc. Indeed the Pentecostal pulpiteers honestly and openly (shamelessly?) do flaunt their enormous wealth, mansions, personal jets etc. Shouldn't the Holy Spirit get the accolades? As the Malay proverb says it, *"Lembu punya* *susu, Sapi dapat nama"* – The cow gives the milk, but the buffalo gets the name. The words of Jesus Christ: – *"One sows and another reaps"* [John 4: 37], could also apply.

Since medicine, while science based also subscribes to placebo or "sugar pill", perhaps it is also faith based. As everyone knows, placebo is all in the patients head. When patients place their health in the hands of doctors, the healers become like gods, wielding powers of life and death. So much more, the faith healers, when they promise the sky.

Hindu faith healers refuse to be outdone. Many have been caught exploiting the gullibilities of their clients, milking them of monies and mortifying their modesties. Many stories have come out, about these *pozhi saamiyars* ("fake healers") being beaten and run out of town. While suckers may be born every minute as per P.T. Barnum, a bugger may also be born every day. As the Tamil saying goes, *ellu metula eli puzhukaiyum sernthu kaaiyithu* – "Rat poop also sun dries on that pile of black sesame."

Herbal Medicine: Ginseng, Vallaarai, Misai Kuching

Reality is a child of the times. Priorities and fashions change with its ebb and flow, and traditional medicine has been relegated to the backrooms in the backlanes of the outback of our medical consciousness.The so-called alternative medicine of today used to be the almighty cures of yesteryear. Alternative, though conveying runner-up status, is not entirely old school or outdated. Medical research is realizing the effectiveness of the medicinal herbs and roots of our old ways. Westerners have patented the turmeric (*manjal*), which Tamils have long held as an anti-bacterial, and anti-septic. Desert bound Israel is cultivating the lemongrass (*serai*) and exporting it overseas! *Ginseng* is now a worldwide phenomenon and common item in our medical vocabulary.

The list of Mal*Asian* herbs that are being appropriated and usurped by western pharma grows by the day. *Tongkat Ali* (Ali's rod), *Misai Kucing* (Cat's whiskers), *Kacip Fatimah* (Fatimah's Betel Scissors) are Malay traditional herbs. While Ali's Rod is supposed to boost testosterone, Fatima's Scissors are touted to increase estrogen. *Murungai* (Moringa), *manjal* (turmeric) and *Veppilai*/Neem (*Azadirachta indica)* are common Tamil herbs. TCM's traditional herbs include cordyceps (a fungus), *rén shēn* (ginseng) and *gǒu qǐ* (goji berry).

The wall-to-wall, floor-to-ceiling glass show case displaying laboratory type specimen jars containing dried plant and animal parts, or the same secreted away in a hardwood wall-to-wall chest of drawers, is both awe inspiring and confidence building. The Sinseh/Dukun Cina, diagnoses your situation, extracts the herbs, processes and compounds, hands it to you in a neat paper pack, with instructions on usage. That is comforting – what you see is what you get. Otherwise, you might opt for his pre-prepared stuff in a little bottle.

One endearingly enduring embrocation is the world famous Tiger Balm out of Singapore. It all began when Aw Chu Kin, a Chinese herbalist working in the Emperor's court, left China and set up a small medicine shop called Eng Aun Tong in Rangoon in the late 1870s, where he would make and sell his special ointment that was effective in relieving all kinds of aches and pains.

When Aw Chu Kin died in 1908, he left his business to his two sons Aw Boon Haw (meaning 'gentle tiger') and Aw Boon Par (meaning 'gentle leopard'). They took the business to Singapore and successfully sold their ointment to surrounding countries like Malaya, Hong Kong, Batavia, Siam and various cities in China. Aw Boon Haw was the marketing genius who named the product Tiger Balm.

The Tamil Siddha medical system relies heavily on herbs, besides, animal and metal/chemical items. Some of the plant products commonly used are, *nellikai* (Indian gooseberry), *inji* (ginger), *manjal* (turmeric), *thulasi* (holy basil), and *amukkuraan kizhangu* (ashwaghanda), or Indian ginseng. Unlike the *buah cermai*, which is thick thumb shaped, the nellikai (*buah melaka*) is its bigger cousin, about golf ball sized.

Siddhar are the ancient formulators of the siddha system, and there are only 18 of them in the hagiography. *Vaidyars*, like the Sinsehs and Dukuns, are the current practioners, who undergo 5½ years of courses in government approved institutions in Tamil Nadu. They are trained to diagnose (through pulse reading), and prescribe the herbal remedies. They too, will compound the cures on the spot. Whereas in the past, the powders (sooranam) and pastes (leghiyams) had to be shipped in from India, there a number of practioners in Malaysia.

Some of the many Malay medicinal herbs (*ulam*) are *petai* (butter bean), *jering* (dog fruit), *pegaga* (vallarai in Tamil), *temulawak* (java ginger), and *terung pipit* (pea eggplant).

Not to be outdone by the supplements industry and the other traditional systems, Malay herbalists are producing herbal pills and capsules in impressive packaging. While the three main ethnicities source their raw materials from gardens and wild expanses, our original people have had their own healing systems for aeons, in the jungles where they live. Just like western interlopers have pilfered much knowledge from the tribes of the Amazon, and other jungles and forests, perhaps Malaysia can learn much from our own orang asli/asal.

Psychology: Koro, Suo Yang, Suudu

There are certain psychological disorders that are culture specific and occur only in that particular environment. As such, Malaysia has given the psychology handbook, the *DSM-5: Diagnostic and Statistical Manual of Mental Disorders,* a few words such as *koro, amok,* and *latah.* The Chineses and Indians have their own disturbances. *Koro, Suo Yang*, and *Suudu*, are Malay, Chinese, and Tamil respectively, and refer to a paranoia about the loss of one's private parts, specifically the penis. Koro apparently derives from the Malay *kura-kura* (tortoise), a reference to the tortoise's retracting head.

An excerpt from a psychology journal, *"Koro is probably one of the better known of the culture-bound disorders. The primary symptoms is that the penis (in males) or the vulva and breasts (in women) are receding into the body, possibly causing death. It is more common in males, who will go to great lengths to stop this from happening. Similar to dhat, or semen-loss syndrome, Koro is sometimes believed to be caused by inappropriate sex, such as masturbation or sex outside of marriage, which result in an imbalance of the male/female principle (yin and yang). It may also be caused by outside causes – a recent rise in cases was caused by reports that eating pork from pigs innoculated against swine flu caused two cases of koro.*

In other parts of the world, the belief may be that, rather than the genitals shrinking into the body, they are being stolen by supernatural methods. In the Guangdong region in China, it is believed that a fox spirit can steal penises, while it is more likely to be ascribed to sorcerers or black magic in regions of Africa. Often, those believed to be responsible are publicly accused. The theft is carried out when the sorcerer touches the affected person. The person may believe that, although his penis has been returned, it is smaller, malformed or the property of another person entirely." Koro: A Natural History of Penis Panic

Amok: The origin of the English phrase "running amuck". This is a dissociative episode featuring a period of brooding followed by an outburst of aggressive, violent or homicidal behavior aimed at people and objects. It seems to occur only among males, and is often precipitated by a perceived slight or insult. It is often accompanied by persecutory ideas, automatism, amnesia or exhaustion, following which the individual returns to their premorbid state. The victim, who is almost always a male between 20-45, has often experienced a loss of social status or a major life change. It is now rare, and occurs primarily in rural regions.

Frank Swettenham ("The Real Malay"),: *"A Malay is intolerant of insult, or slight; it is something that to him should be wiped out in blood.He will brood over a real or fancied stain on his honour until he is possessed by the desire for revenge. If he cannot wreak it on the offender, he will strike out at the first human being that comes in his way, male or female, old or young. It is this state of blind fury, this vision of blood, that produces the amok."*

That was over a century ago. Thankfully, there is such a thing as change and progress. Everyone is safe in the streets of Malaysia. If anything, cases of amok are more prevalent in the West today. It parades in the form of "serial killers" and "psychopaths" as seen in the Columbine High School, USA (April 20, 1999); and in Swettenham's home country, Britain.

This is an excerpt from a British op-ed piece (June 2, 2010): "It's beginning to look like Derrick Bird shot some victims on purpose, while others were shot randomly. When in a trance-like state, he drove around a Cumbrian countryside shooting anyone he saw, who just happened to be in the wrong spot." Police suspect a family feud as the cause.

"*Latah* is an exaggerated startle response, typically found among past middle age Malay women. Being surprised may result in screaming, cursing, dancing and hysterical laughter that might last a half hour or more. They may imitate the people around them or things they see or hear in the media. Relatives and friends may provoke episodes for the entertainment value, and are not considered to be worthy of referral to the psychologist.

Latah often occurs following a traumatic episode. There are many cultures which have similar syndromes, but it is unclear how or if they relate to each other."

I witnessed a somewhat similar event in Abilene, Texas, my university hometown in the late 90s. I had walked up to a gentleman bending iron, his back to me. Stupid me should have called out from further down at the roadside. Before I could finish asking him for direction, he shot up a clear two feet off the ground. That was a normal response.

Somewhat similar to latah (individual action), is mass hysteria or collective delusions, defined as "the spontaneous and rapid spread of false or exaggerated beliefs within a population". Outbreaks usually occur in small, tight-knit groups in enclosed surrounding such as school hostels, orphanages and factories. Robert Bartholomew, a sociologist has researched mass hysteria in Malaysia. Though it has happened in New York, USA, and the UK, as far as Malaysia is concerned, it has so far been a solely Malay female phenomenon, and that too, in rural areas.

Methinks mass hysteria should not be classified as a psychological problem at all. It happens quite naturally in society, especially when sense take a leave of absence and the body goes into auto overdrive. It happens in rock concerts, political rallies, and Pentecostal healing rallies, where bodies twitch and convulse onto the ground. It happens when a political fake news spreads through society at Covid-19 speed, and every other person forwards the virus through Whatsapp. People may also autonomically gather on streets to protest something or other. Oh, how psychologically messed up we are!

"Qi-gong (exercise of vital energy) is a Chinese method of meditation, based on traditional Chinese medicine. The best known in the West is Tai Chi, although there are around 2,200 methods in total. The DSM-IV and the Chinese Classification of Mental Disorders define it as an acute, time-limited episode characterized by dissociative, paranoid and other psychotic and non-psychotic symptoms that occur after participation in Qigong. An alternate name for the syndrome is Qigong Deviation Syndrome. According to a recent study by Dr. Huaihai Shan, folk-beliefs attribute the condition to "adverse flow in the body," "uncontrollable behavior," "over-meditation" and "spirit possession". Over a third of 129 respondents described sensory problems (32%), mood symptoms (90%) and behavioral problems (37%). Other symptoms listed were memory problems (24%), attention difficulties (26%), thought disorders (18%) and disordered consciousness (2%). Nearly all patients report "the Qi moving within the body, and dashing or rushing into the head." Somatic symptoms may include headaches, dizziness or disorientation, and strange sensations in the lower abdomen (the Dan-Tian point). They may demonstrate hypochondriasis, anxiety, sadness and feelings of being out of control. In addition, they may experience visual and auditory hallucinations. The symptoms occur after Qigong practice and may last two weeks to a month

Tamils are an over emotional group and relationship slights have led to many suicides in the past. It was common in the days of the rubber estates, where the chief method of self murder was weed killer from the estate stores, or hanging. They have a long history of invented self immolation at the death of a political leader, or in political protest. Its earlier precedent must have been *saati*, the ancient Hindu practice of widows jumping into their husband's funeral pyre. Therefore doesn't surprise anyone, that Tamils of the Liberation Tigers of Taml Ealam (LTTE) were the pioneer suicide bombers. They had given it up for formal warfare, when the Al-Qaeda co-opted and adopted it for their own.

Unlike the Malay *mengamuk,* when an individual goes beserk over a perceived slight and attacks others, the Tamil tends to react inwardly by suicide. Perhaps, they see it as a way to get even at the family member, or as an escape from whatever situation. Although all of the above have been tagged with ethnic identification, they are actually universal.

Extreme sports: Basikal Lajak/Mat Rempit, Gambling, Gang involvement

Let's place this matter here, instead of the sports and games section. This where the thin line between healthy sports and deathly mania intersect. Parkour? Base Jumping? No thanks! Bungy Jumping or Wall Climbing? Fine, if they have harnesses attached to a secure place.

As in the preceding piece, there seems to be some culture specific psychology at play here. The recent rash of accidents and scare stories concerning the *basikal lajak* (speedster bikes) comes to mind. This is a game where teens ages thirteen to sixteen, race down sloping streets at night. The rules (law breaking rather) of the game, are to modify children's bikes, adjust the handlebar and seat so as to be same level. Remove the brakes and lights. As you pick up speed on the down slope, you get into the "superman" position by laying head at the bar and pelvis on the seat, legs stretched out back. Sounds like a dare devil act, which is what youth at that age seek. There is a senior version of it where older teens and young adults, the *Mat Rempit*, let loose on 2-stroke motorbikes at night on the highways. Rempit is said to derive from the English, "ramp-it" i.e to ramp up the throttle. They assume the same superman postures. The specific culture here, generally, is suburban Malay. Many reasons are given as to why this is – boredom, thrill seeking, peer pressure.

Youth of all races indulge in playstation video games and the earlier Nintendo, although Chinese youth may be overwhelmingly into it. That is another form of daredevilry, of a more passive kind. It is virtual more than actual action. It only becomes problematic and psychological if you engage for hours. Then it becomes an obsession, mania and and addiction. While Chinese are not averse to extreme sports, they generally seem to stick to the generic, rules based games like badminton or basketball. Or, to rules based extreme sports, for that matter.

I am hard pressed to think of a wantonly daredevil sport that Malaysian Chinese indulge in. Therefore let's change the definitions a bit, to include gambling as a sport, which it can, considering the factors of persistence, luck, rules etc. This sport is carried to extremes, when players (older people) get addicted, lose their inhibitions and push their luck. A peek into the casinos at Genting Highlands, will reveal how they revel in their risky ventures.

Indian youth specific psychopathy is not in leisure terms, but rather in a need to get rich quick. Their psychosis manifests in the disproportionate distribution of their gang involvement and drug mule convictions compared to the larger communities. Many reasons have been given – low education, depressed social environment, lack of social support etc., even going back to British colonial times. However it ultimately falls to the individual to avoid the traps set by drug czars and gang lords. The British colonial and early independence period witnessed the opposite of today's situation. There was an inordinate number of Indians who excelled in individual and team sports, like Manikavasagam Jegathesan and Mailvaganam Rajamani, sportsman and sportswoman of the the year 1966. Researchers, who are into correlations and connections, would have a field day (pun incidental) on how the social situation of the day determines the attitude of Indian youth.

Massage: Foot, Body, Herbal

Tamil grandmothers of old, were expert bone setters and cramp and twist (*sulukku*) removers. Beside being village midwives, they were also consulted for all kinds of ailments. *Paati Vaidhyam* (Granny therapy) is fondly recalled by baby boomers, themselves grandparents now. I remember vividly, my own grandmother's soothing back scratch, her skillful loosening of your neck knot. Or, her cure for sore throat – a pink potion made by compounding white lime and her betel leaf spittle and smeared on the front of the throat. I can vouch for its quick effect, as the paste dries and tightens the skin.

Foot massage, or foot reflexology is associated with Chinese culture as they were the ones who have formulated a philosophy or science of it, with body charts, pressure point diagrams etc. Similar practices have existed in the Indian, Egyptian regions. Well off Indians had their household *ladka* (lads) employed to massage their feet before bed.

Imagine a central control panel with switches and buttons that activate and motivate different parts of a system. That is what the Chinese foot reflexology resembles. *"One of the core principles in Traditional Chinese Medicine is qi, which can be described as life force or vital energy. Similar to how we have a circulatory system for blood, our bodies have energy pathways for the flow of qi. When qi is flowing properly, our bodies are in harmony and we experience wellness.*

The major energy pathways in the body connect with your feet. Thus, your foot is considered the headquarters for the energy pathways in your body. It's a microcosm of your entire body as reflex points on your feet connect energetically to different organs and areas of the body.

If a reflex point is sensitive to the touch, this indicates that the corresponding area of the body is experiencing a disruption in the flow of qi. Massaging these reflex points helps to clear toxins and improve the flow of energy."

Maalish is Indian hair and scalp massage using oil. Kerala ayurvedic massage is basically plain massage with ayurvedic herbal oils rubbed into the skin. No pinching, kneading, stretching, pushing or pulling is involved – just a rough, deep rub. A steam bath, afterwards, is supposed to sweat out the suffused oil and clear the pores.

Kansa Vatki is a foot massage using a metal bowl of copper, zinc and tin alloy. Six *marma* (secret) points on each feet out of a total, 107 points in the body, are worked, releasing and realizing the flow of *prana* (life force) throughout the body.

Urut Melayu, is Malay deep tissue massage with the hands and fingers. *"Key concept in Urut Melayu is the elimination of Angin (wind) which is said to cause physical blockages in blood vessels, the lymphatic system and nerves (together called Urat). If left untreated it's thought that these blockages lead to a variety of diseases or discomforts.*

Malay Traditional Massage uses a variety of massage techniques, such as jabbing (poking), stretches, cupping (called *Bekam in Malay),* daubing or smearing *(called Lumur)* and acupressure, all depending on the needs of the receiver. Herbal compresses and herbal or palm oils maybe used also during a session if deemed necessary. Typically the masseuse applies a lot of kneading while using long strokes to expel *Angin* (wind). Strokes directed towards the heart are aimed to invigorate, while strokes going away from the heart are aimed at calming." This is similar to the rubbing action of Kerala massage."

Blind massage is done by masseuse specially trained by MAB – Malaysia Association for the Blind, which neighbourhood in Brickfields, KL is also a popular as a blind massage hub. Blind massage in Malaysia is said to have started when a Taiwanese vision impaired man began training masseuse in 1986. It is today, a place where clients can get the twin benefits of getting a cheap and quality (not, cheap quality) massage as well as helping out a not physically endowed human. The disability is only physical, as the service is top notch. Their absence of sight, apparently compensates with enhanced sense of touch. "Seeing hands", can find the muscle knots and tangles better than seeing eyes, you suppose.

Personal Hygiene: Wash vs Wipe, Bidet vs Toilet Roll

One could safely consider daily ablutions as good medical practice. While the inhabitants of the Tundra can get away without showering for days, even weeks, we of the tropics often shower twice or more a day. We frequently flush face, teeth, hands and feet. More so, after the covid contagon. But curiously, the west steers clear of their derrieres (rear). Wonder what they used before the toilet r   oll? The exception may be the French – as inferable from their words *bidet* ("throne"), *derriere* (buttocks), *douche* (ablution), *serviette* (napkin), *toilet* (WC – water closet). All common English words, now.

Back to Malaysia, and Asia – Africa, we tend to go for the full wash, meaning running water. Most homes nowadays have taps in the toilet or flexible fixings that function as water jets. Unlike the temperate climes, with their sometimes frozen water sources, we have year round supply of it. Long before our modern amenities, our ancestors squatted or stood waist deep in the river facing upstream. The rear exiting excreta naturally escaped downstream. The guy washing up downstream of you had better duck!

Malays and Indians, being of a more traditional mindset, are almost entirely in the washer camp. Chinese, perhaps due to their easier adaptability to western norms, are mostly wipers.

Washing up Malaysian style was quite a challenge in the US. In public toilets, after the initial dry wiping, I wet a piece of folded tissue paper in the toilet tank (cistern) and finished the business. Often, wet wipes came in handy. In the house, a dipper of water is used, from the adjacent bathtub tap. The bathroom room includes toilet seat, see? That, and soap (for hind wash and handwash) concluded the process.

Aikk! How does one handle one's filth? That is why 1 has 2 hands. One for dirty work and one for clean work. Generally, the left hand is the cleaner – not the comparative adjective, but the actor. What would this world be, without the cleaners. It is referred to as *tangan najis* in Malay, *peecha kai* in Tamil and *goushi shou* in Mandarin. All mean "shit hand.

Washing versus Wiping: pros and cons. In the west, considering their toilet set up, wiping may be the most convenient. Otherwise, washing comes up tops. Healthwise, regular washing is expected. Leaving out a part of the body most exposed to bacterial contamination seems like mopping the entire house and leaving out the latrine. Environment wise, it comes down to the cost of paper production versus water douching. There are figures available, but suffice to consider that besides murdering trees, the amount of water needed to process and bleach to create the white sheets. Finally, the environmental impact of flushing paper down the drain, compared to plain water. Which one degrades faster in the sewerage pond – paper, or excrement?

Speaking of toilets, why do Malaysian businesses – malls, stalls, halls, hotels and office blocks have more squatting toilets than sitting? Some restaurants have exclusively squatters. Do the architects even consider the elderly and aged with their knee issues? For that matter, after long time sitting, even the young are not able to squat anymore.

Dirty Minds:

What is the psychological term for a pathological fear of a harmless word that has lately assumed an unflattering connotation, Verbophobia? Perhaps, but fasten your seatbelt. Gripe session, incoming.

In the West, especially in the US, it is no longer polite to address or refer to a woman of high social status as 'lady". Try saying, "she's a nice lady" before a female executive in business suit, and you are most likely to receive a frighteningly furrow foreheaded frozen frown from that direction. This is PC (political correctness) gone berserk. Just how can a term of dignity (the spouse of a Lord, the mistress of the manor etc.) become so unsavoury? It is probably an attempt by the socialite female to get away from the negative connotations, the word assumed much later. *Lady of the Night* is a euphemism for the prostitute. The unpolished, lowly New York taxi driver might address you politely as lady, and that apparently drops the value of the word by a 100 Dow points. Words that have been perfectly acceptable and aristocratic, have overnight become dirty and objectionable. Gay, is not so gay?

It is not as if Lady has changed over the milleniums. Just a generation earlier, Tom Jones was effusing (not, abusing) his lady in "She's a Lady." "She's got style, she's got grace. She's a winner. She's a lady. Wo oo, wo oo wo oo wo oo, she's a lady."

Psst! Talking about lady, didn't we recently experience a gripe session by some, over the name "Timah" for a local whisky? While the logo and the word pointed to Malaya's tin (timah) industry, some were upset that Timah (diminutive of Fatimah, the prophet's daughter), degraded a muslim female.

Many of us Malaysians, as well as other internationals cringe when the American immigration authorities and media categorize us as aliens. Why do we have such an averse reaction to a harmless word? *Alien*, alias "different", has never been any different from *foreigner*. It only acquired the negative connotation from the recent rash of *Alien* movies out of Hollywood. You see, in our dirty thinking, we associate the word with the ugly creatures in the film. It was never the dictionary definition.

Back in our neck of the woods, we will never more hear of Bukit Cherakah (now Bukit Chahaya), Batang Berjuntai (Bestari Jaya). Jalan Alor, off Jalan Bukit Bintang, almost got wiped off the map by City Hall staffers, who thought it reflected too much of its red light area image. It is still on the road sign thanks to the objections of the locals and foreigners alike. Ejecting those historical, unique, and descriptive place names, to me, is equal to cultural cleansing. It smacks very much, of a dirty, jaundiced mind. And to think these cultural policemen are no more than low level staff of local governments, not the powers that be in the state or federal governments, is no surprise. What do these know of the finer points of language? Shouldn't they be doing something more in their area of expertise, and let Dewan Bahasa dan Pustaka, custodian of the national language, deal with its linguistic correctness and etymology? Or, is DBP in it too?

There is a sort of psychological disease, a Paranoia, that seems to beset these local government low rankers. The Agriculture Park in Shah Alam started off on a good footing, as the Bukit Cherakah Agriculture Park. Somewhere along the way, somebody had a philosophic moment about the word "Cherakah". We won't know what it means exactly, but we know for a fact, that it is a historic name that existed in British times and beyond. All this time, the *rakyat* (citizens) were perfectly comfortable with it. The word *Cherakah* does sound similar to *celaka* (rascal). So, Cherakah went the way of *lady*. So, what's wrong with *Rascal Hill* ? Living in the States at the time, I imagine this debate would have centred on how the latter word would corrupt young minds. So now, who had the "dirty mind" in the first place? There are a couple of hills nearby, that sound similar to a local two syllable word describing a body part, or its function. Bukit Lanjan, and Bukit Lanchong. The offensive word is colloqial Chinese, but is used by men and boys of all races, as an explosive expletive to convey something like, "penis!", or, "dick". They also resemble a Malay word for "masturbate". Shouldn't we urgently rename those hills too?

So, you traded Cherakah for *Cahaya*. How imaginative can you get? Cahaya ("light") is a bland, tired word that does not add character to the place name. But it sure is very sterile and stereotyped, just like you want it. You hear of Taman Cahaya, Bangunan Cahaya Suria, Seri Cahaya, Cahaya this, Cahaya that. Batang Berjuntai, my onetime hometown, probably went the same way. The name Batang Berjuntai, which means, "swaying branch" fell off the locals' tongues so smoothly. The local authority that changed it thought like a numerologist or geomantist – change a number here, shift an object there and all will be right. You see, in their minds the perfectly poetic and meaningful "swaying branch" did not register. What did, was the baser connotation of branch/batang, namely a phallus. So, you have Batang Berjuntai equals swinging penis. So, you might have an occasional laugh about it. So, did the world come to an end? So, did it kill anybody? So, who has the dirty mind? It so happens that those who bicker about bikinied beachgoers, wouldn't have anything to babble about, if only they didn't so ogle in the first place. So, what were you doing on a bikini beach, in the first place?

Going on, on this theme of changing names in the interest of public decency, local officials with dirty minds also seem to have poor imaginations. What brilliant mind came up with "Bestari Jaya" as a replacement for Batang Berjuntai? A survey of place names in the Klang Valley alone that have "Jaya" in them, makes you *muak* (nauseous) with giddiness. Ampang Jaya, Pandan Jaya, Damansara Jaya, Kelana Jaya, Kelang Jaya, Subang Jaya, Petaling Jaya, Puchong Jaya, Putra Jaya, this Jaya, that Jaya and on and on ad nauseum.

The last one, Putra Jaya, brings up another one of those irritating repeaters. Bukit Putra, Saujana Putra, Putra Nilai, Bandar Putera, Bandar Puteri (adjacent housing estates in Klang), this Putra, that Putra. Bukit Jelutong, Bukit Beruntung, Bukit Cahaya, Bukit Tinggi, Bukit Rajah, Bukit Rimau, this bukit, that bukit. Kota Kemuning, Kota Raja, ... Shah Alam is fine, but, Setia Alam, Alam Setia, Alam Impian.... ? Pulau Indah, Pandan Indah, Kampung Indah, Taman Indah, ...Kampung Jawa, Padang Jawa, Bukit Jawa, ..., all kinds of Jawa. Puchong Perdana, Bayu Perdana, Sentul Perdana (?), Putra Perdana (?) With such an array of rhyming place names it isn't hard to arrange a song to the tune made famous by Johnny Cash, "I've been everywhere man."

I've seen every s'burb man, I've seen every s'burb man
Experienced foggy confusion man
I've tasted tedious heartburn man
Of puzzlement I've had my share man
I've seen every s'burb

I've been to Pulau indah, Pandan Indah, Kampung Indah, Sungai Indah,
Petaling Jaya, Subang Jaya, Klang Jaya, Putra Jaya, Kajang Jaya
Bukit Jelutong, Bukit Beruntung, Bukit Buntong, Bukit Bentong, Bukit
Banting, Buki Beruang, Bukit Rawang …….
I've seen every s'burb man, I've seen every s'burb man

Well, you get the drift. Not only are these toponymic (place name) clones mind numbing, they are utterly confusing to the outsider who wants to locate your address. With Bandar Damansara, Damansara Utama, Bukit Damansara, Damansara Jaya, Kota Damansara, Seri Damansara, Damansara Setia, Damansara Aman, Mutiara Damansara, Damansara Perdana, Damansara Putra etc, strung together along the NKVE (North Klang Valley Expressway), you would feel like looking for the needle in the you know what. I made up one of the places in the above list, but going by experience, such a place may actually be on the map. Just trust our local authorities.

Remember, these place names are of very recent origin – from 5 to 20 years old. Our simple-minded forebears have done so much better in this area. Place names like, Pahang, Selangor, Kelantan, Trengganu, Sarawak, glitter with uniqueness and character, as do district names like Janda Baik (The Good Widow), Gua Musang (Mongoose Cave), Cherok Tok Kun (Tok Kun's Corner).

The recent place names above have local council/developer input. The individual resident has no say in the matter. It is another matter, when it comes to christening your business. Here too, imagination is found wanting. Especially of restaurants, it appears that herd mentality gallops wild when it comes to name branding (mixed metaphor intended). Let someone's enterprise prove successful, and every **Tom**, **Dick** and **Harry** wants to join the bandwagon, trying to keep up with the **Joneses**. "I want what he has", rather than, "I have what he wants."

Some progressive Indian Muslim restaurateur names his shop a "Restoran (something something) Maju". He does a galloping business. Then, every other Mamak establishment begins adding "Maju" to its name. Every *Mastaan*, *Siddique*, and *Bukharry* jumps on the maju express. There is even a roadside cendol stall in Klang that calls itself, "Gerai Cendol ……. Maju." Folks, we are *maju* (progressive) in everything but creativity. Any wonder why we get very sparse international awards, especially those that count, like the Nobel, Man Booker etc? 60 years of *Merdeka* (Independence), and every year new marches are written. However, the tunes seem to be the same year after year. And, aren't we famous for imitating things already existing elsewhere? Like a little 3-year old, we want what the other one has – twin towers, giant ferris wheels, other peoples' cars. Perhaps, the local authorities and businesses should engage the LimKokWing University of creativity as their place name consultants.

Kopitiam was not an uncommon usage in those days, donkey years ago. It was used in general conversation, but not on shopfront signboards. We always had the *Kedai Kopi Ah Fatt,* or "Ah Fatt Coffee Shop" or other. Then along comes someone who names it a kopitiam, and it made a big impact on the populace's consciousness. The kopitiam war explodes. Every **Ah Tong, Ah Dick**, and **Ah Harry** clambers aboard the kopitiam convoy. Here a tiam, there a tiam, ever where a kopitiam. Perhaps the original fellow should have trademarked his establishment, just to prevent the mindless copycatting.

The Indian Muslim *Restoran Maju* and the Chinese *Kopitiam* phenomena were a surprise to me when I returned to Malaysia. They had occurred during my 14 year hiatus in the US. The story doesn't end there, of course. Imagine my reverse culture shock when I discovered the near complete disappearance of the *Restoran Daun Pisang, or* banana leaf restaurant. Instead, it was "*Curry House*" on almost every Indian restaurant. Now, I have not been to Britain, where I hear that the natives are quite curry crazy. I have a mild suspicion that Indian restaurants there are called curry houses, so perhaps somebody tried it here, just to currify and spice up the storefront sign. It did, and the next thing you know, every **Thamb**iraj, **Deek**shithan, and **Hari**haran hops on the curry house carousel. Surprisingly, no Indian curry place has jumped on the *Curry 'n a Hurry* (Indian fast food?) craze. That one is a popular eatery name in Britain, I believe.

The Malay restaurateur sticks by the *kedai* or *gerai makanan,* which simply means food shop or stall, respectively. But there was a time though, when they went through a phase, and food stalls were calling themselves *warong* this, *warong* that, and what not. Every *Thamrin, Sidek*, and *Khairi* wanted to be on the warong wagon. It was apparently a passing fad, of indo(nesia) philia. Warongs are not so fashionable these days, as stall names. What we have these days are, a proliferation of *Tom Yam Gerai* (stalls). So, this Tom Yam, that Tom Yam, and some other Tom Yam. Looks like Tom's got the Yum! Draw level Dick! Hurry up Harry!

By the way, it appears that we have distinct and different models of doing the restaurant trade. The corner Chinese shop tends to be a food court where about 10 to 15 hawkers park their pushcarts on the outer edge and each sells a special dish. The owner of the shop reserves the right to sell the *nasi campur* or *economy rice,* and the drinks. This makes for a wide variety to choose from. The Malay seems to prefer the warong style, a little stall under a shady tree with a few tables, or stalls built by the local municipality. The Indian likes to have a corner shoplot, in which to serve a variety of snacks, tiffins as well as entree items. He might even have an upstairs, for parties or group functions.

Mom and Pop markets are known as *Mini Market.* However, the modern Indian ones, have gained an affinity to calling themselves the trendy trade name, *Cash 'N Carry.* Again, is this another case of galloping herd mindset? Knowingly, or unknowingly, these small businesses evoke ethnic identities. *Tom Yam* means Malay, *Kopitiam* conjures Chinese, *Curry House* indicates Indian, and *Maju* is a Mamak matter. May the day soon come, when Malaysians will say, "follow me", rather than play "follow the leader".

Concepts of Beauty: Of Fair skin, Facial Features, and Foot Binding

Times are changing, but old concepts and expectations of beauty still persist. For one, all races, Chinese, Malay, and Indian equate beauty with "fair" aka "pale" skin colour. We probably became entrenched in this when we wanted to become like our white-skinned colonial masters, the British. The hang-up is in no small part abetted by the media, especially the womens' magazines, women's pages in newspapers, female models (for anything under the sun!) etc. The curious factor in all this, is the fact that in the West, skin colour is of zero consideration in assessing beauty. Form (body shape, facial symmetry, etc), are the main considerations. The Somali maiden, Iman Abdul Majid is the world's top model; Halle Berry, Miss America, are all African or African American women. That fact speaks for itself.

Tamils, while generally blessed with good features and dusky dermis, value lighter complexion. Women of the old days tried to lighten their skin by applying turmeric paste.The fact that turmeric is a terrific antibiotic and cleansing agent, is a secondary matter. These days they might be seen shopping for products in the *Fair & Lovely* brand, out of India, of all places. Indian men who propose marriage want the "complete package" in a prospective bride – i.e., fair skin, on top of good financial, educational, and career status. Many indeed, hunt further afield for these qualities, marrying outside their race. The cultural instititutions seem to be abetting this attitude of mind. The Tamil movie industry (Kollywood) now has a fixation on featuring the lighter skinned north Indian actresses out of Bollywood, eventhough many "naturalistic" or "village" movies do very well, with dusky heroes and heroines. The dictionary definition of fairness, has nothing to do with colour, but rather facial symmetry and beauty. In fact, paleness is equivalent to sickness and zombies, and western women tan themselves to a ruddy look. "Fairer sex" may refer either to the attractiveness of women, or, to their impartial nature.

Going back about 1000 years till about the mid 1900s, the Chinese concept of female beauty was centred on the practice of foot binding. The Nationalist Chinese, and later, Communist, regimes abolished it. It was a kind of *bonsai* culture (Japanese tree dwarfing) on human feet. Tightly tying up a young girl's feet results in petite feet, which was pretty feet indeed, depending on the beholder. Modern medicine would define it otherwise, as club feet, and bad health practice. The fashionability of the dwarf foot has many origins, but it seems that it was predominantly prestigious in the upper classes and the nobility. The working classes were not bound (!) as strictly, by this social requirement. You don't expect women to be caught flat-footed trying to work their fields! In the aristocracy and taiko-dom, bound feet feet were a symbol of affluence, speaking volumes about husbands who could afford women who didn't need to work! Except conjugal service, of course. Perhaps this foot fetish or fixation can be compared to Cinderalla's golden slippers.

The Malay qualifier of beauty is also based on the so-called "Fairness", but also Caucasian features are fantasized. There used to be a craze in these parts, over Mat Salleh looking Bollywood heroes and heroines. Women swooned over the hunky ("Kacak") Kumars, Kapoors, and Khans of the day. The men secretly or overtly gushed over the Kumaris and Begums. As a society, the media induced "Pan Asian" look is something that is held up to. This has not escaped the Chinese too, as they go for blepharoplasty (eyelid folding) and rhinoplasty (nose lifts). Not too far away, from foot binding.

"To thine own self be true" – Act 1 Scene 3, *Hamlet* (Shakespeare). Looks like Shakespeare's bidding has no takers today, as then. Everyone is seeking someone else's approval.

Attitudes and Aspirations: Civil service, entrepreunership, patronage, Kleptocracy

Tamils have a well documented past, of maritime trade and global commerce on both the Indian and Chinese oceans. But their offshore excursions dwindled, with the demise of their kingdoms and consequently, their international trade dried up. The Chinese, after Cheng He's exploits, had their own self-isolation during the Ming dynasty. With the coming of the British, a half millennium later, Indians specifically Tamils, have had a subservient, menial mentality. A saying still in their cultural consciousness but less used nowadays, is *"Koli meichaalum, kumbiniyil meikkanum"* – "even if you tend chicken, its better to do it in the kumbini". Kumbini is the tamilized form of "company", the British

East India Company, EIC, that is. As they were the virtual government in those days, company meant ruling establishment/government. Hence, the import of the saying is, it is always ideal to be a civil servant.

These days, with government jobs in Malaysia less available or appealing to Indians, they have started out into business, trading, professions etc. The kumbini attitude seems to have shifted to the Malays, who love the security and stress-freeness of it. So much so, that some have even opted out of plum private sector jobs to join the government.

The British EIC destroyed most forms of local enterprise in India. Stories are told of looms being smashed in the Tanjavur and other centres of textile industry. Worker's fingers were smashed, to prevent them from resuming their trade – all to protect their monopoly on the cotton industry out of Liverpool. Indian martial arts took a beating when they outlawed those. They criminalized the so-called martial tribes like the Nairs and Kallars as "denotified tribes", as well as powerful "stealth" weapons such as the boomerang – like *Valari*. The Dutch are said to have restricted the trade of the Chitty's in Malacca.This drop in Tamils' seafaring and commercial skills, thus made it easier for the British to recruit them for indentured labour around the world.

The Chinese, even if they had had it bad from the European trade incursions into Shanghai, Hong Kong etc (opium wars), have largely kept away from the employ of the powers that be, of the day. Consequently, they have managed their own lives by engaging in entrepreunerships, as petty traders, tin miners, and smallholders. Perhaps there is a Confucian mind-set that drove this attitude of mind. The Punjabi Sikhs of Malaysia at one time seemed have their minds set on the military or police forces. At retirement, they were seen guarding banks and goldsmith shops. These days, they are prominent in the legal profession.

The Malays were minding their own business and tending their fields and flock when the British came to open up the jungles. While they brought Tamils from India and Ceylon for junior clerical positions and the larger labour groups for plantation work, Malays were more inclined to the less "muscular" work of local policemen and guards. This is not to say that that the different races didn't intermingle during british rule. Only, they were much more intertwined during the Malacca Sultanate, the likes of Malay and Tamil Bendahara and Temenggong as Chiefs of police and the Chinese (Han) Hang Tuah and henchman as royal security detail.

Malay aspirational attitudes have generally improved with many venturing into entrepreunerships and small businesses. This is seen in the young, who have move out of the village and into urban centres. There is yet a bit of the population that subscribes to the old easy life of the past. This is most visible in the kleptocratic nature of doing business, and in the giving and receiving of political patronages. Also, the governments' offers of freebies, benevolences, racial quotas, write-offs and recue of failed GLCs.

Who is Who?: Malay, Chinese, Indian

Following up with the foregoing theme and coming into the present, i.e. from Genesis to Gen-now, here is a conversation among modern Malays about their identity. Also, some insights from Sir Frank Swettenham, first Resident-General of the Federated Malay States, Mrs.Reginald Sanderson and Isabella Bird.

keroncong_asli   15-09-2004 02: 25 PM

Sorry for not being attentive on earlier posting.

Spent 20 mins surfing but cannot get defination whether Parameswara is a Malay.
Perhaps you may want to read about the power of Hinduism in Malacca those days:-

Malacca was founded in the 1400's by a Hindu prince named Parameswara. Although Parameswara embraced Islam during his rule, he gave many Hindus influential positions in his court. At that time South Indian, Tamil-speaking Hindus were coming to Malacca as prosperous traders from India. They were marrying local Malay and Chinese women, giving them Hindu names and teaching them their customs. However, the wives retained the Malay language, and the children – who spent more time with their mothers than their fathers – learned Malay rather than Tamil. The Malaccan Hindu community grew wealthy due to the lucrative trade business but suffered the loss of their Tamil language and culture from simple lack of practice. When Malacca came under the tough Dutch rule, many new trading restrictions forced the Chetties into farming and a far less exotic lifestyle.

http://www.hinduismtoday.com/archiv...989-06-08.shtml

isarahim   15-09-2004 03: 05 PM

Thank you very much for a very good link!

But there are other sources which claim that many Muslim Tamils came to Melaka as well.

So in a wonky sort of way, the tables where turned (!!!!) during the founding years of the Melaka empire:

– The Indians were mostly Muslims
– The Malays were mostly Hindus

Those were the days.....

In fact this odd circumstance (odd from a current day Malay's standpoint) is still in existence in Bali. The Indian traders there are principally Muslim, while the Malays are Hindu.

Coming to Bali and mixing with the local Malays there is in a way like travelling with a time machine 600-1000 years back in time. You frequently get these **magic eye openers** like WOW! this is how classic Malays used to be like during those years...it's just fantastic.

And you can relate to many customs and traditions which the Muslim Malaysian Malays have kept surviving through the ages...and you wondered where they came from...until you realise that similar phenomenas are still in practice in a more original form by the Hindu Balinese Malays.

keroncong_asli

15-09-2004 07: 42 PM

In Bali the Malys are Hindu, while the Indian traders are Muslim? Talk of role-reversal.

Rather amusing, there are ppl who're fascinated about 15th Century history. During our school days, we're least interested in Sejarah. Evolution indeed create a different community. One cannot imagine that the Malays were mostly Hindus at one time. If that happen today, one might be charged for being an apostate, ha-ha-ha.... The time machine experience will definately be an interesting one indeed. Isarahim, thanks for sharing about Hindu Balinese Malays altho I've not much info to exchange. Regards

Uchangeng   12-07-2004 02: 08 PM

Isaibrahim, my friend. You seems to know something about the Malays heritage and history that I do not. Do you know any books I can read up on the Malay people? I am a bit 'malu' calling myself a Malaysian but know absolutely nothing about my Malay history. I think we should include the Malay history in our school like we study about the Chinese and Indian.

I though the word "Malay" stands for "peopel who run away" in Jawa. Is this true?

I travel to Riau, Pulau Batam and Bintan once in a while and I do know, there, you could find Malay locals who speak our brand of the Malay language.

Ed's note: This from a Wikipedia entry under Parameswara:

Hindu-Malay and Tamil-Muslim conflict

During the time of Raja Ibrahim, tension occurred in Melaka between the growing Tamil Muslim community and the traditional Hindu Malay because Raja Ibrahim only has islamic name but did not embraced the new religion but instead adopted the traditional Hindu title Sri Parameswara Dewa Shah. As a result, Raja Ibrahim ruled for less than seventeen months and he was stabbed to death.

Raja Ibrahim's elder half-brother, Raja Kasim, by a Tamil Muslim mother, assumed the throne and taking on the Islamic title Sultan Mudzafar Shah. This signalled a new golden era for the Melaka Sultanate.

Cultural Identity: Religion, Language, Confucianism

Generally, the cultural badge or identity of a group focuses on one major aspect apart from minor ones like dress or food. That major aspect is the one that the group promotes and cultivates as unique to itself. Food and clothing may change, especially in these digital times.

The Malay has very recently increasingly inclined toward a more Islamic identity. His/her dressing is more arabized and outlook shifted to a more conservative islamic one. This is obvious from the so-called "green wave" shift of his support for PAS, the Islamist party in the general elections. A 2015 survey by Merdeka Centre found that the Malay of today considers himself as Muslim first (60%), as Malaysian first (27%) and as Malay first (6%). This goes with the old saying that to be a Malay, one has to be a Muslim, as per the constitution. In fact the oldtimers way of converting to Islam was "Masuk Melayu" – convert to Malay. Does this recent surge in a midle-eastern identity point to a drastic drop in his traditional culture? An iconoclasm of unique Malay customs in favour of the Arab/Muslim image?

There may be many reasons for this situation. It is not that the Malay has "lost it" or surrendered his native culture. The 6% who claim to be Malay first represents the historic fact that they have always been a receiving population. As mentioned elsewhere in this book, the Malay, like the English have always been astute students of other cultures. First they received Indianization, followed by Islamization, and finally European influences. Their vocabulary is but 90% foreign words (Chinese, Tamil, Sanskrit, Portuguese, Arabic, English etc), with currently English words being added on a daily basis. Given this level of mix, the dichotomous attitude of some Malay politicians, using malay culture and language as a tool of racial superiority is interesting. The very fact of Malay culture's multicultural composition could rather be sold as a unifying factor.

Secondly, this move towards a more Islamic/arabic outlook can be reactions to global Islamic situations such as political upheavels (Afghanistan, Palestine), islamophobia etc. The process of standing with your fellow muslim can take many forms and with the Malay, it is almost going whole hog.

The Tamil identity largely hangs on pride in language, eventhough many today hardly speak it, much leass read or write it. This language pride is mostly thanks to the British linguists in 19th century India, who assiduously began accessing and assessing previousy lost Tamil manuscripts and determining their 1000 to 2000 year antiquities. This gave the Tamils who had lost their kingdoms and national honour for about seven centuries, renewed pride and self-respect. The fact that Tamil comes up on top in any discussion of the oldest existing language, is an added booster of pride.

Religion comes second as cultural identifier although not to the entire race. There are Tamil Hindus, Tamil Muslims and Tamil Christians, with the Tamil language or race as the prime descriptor.

The Chinese identity can perhaps be stated as Han, as a way of separating them from the other groups such as the Tibetans, Uighurs and aboriginal people.Though of many dialects, they are all classified as Han. Another way of classifying them is by Confusionism, which is not a religion but a philosophy that underlies their worlview and attitudes. Owing to that, their most identifying mark is their attitude towards education and upgrading themselves in knowledge which reflects in their industriousness and business acumen. Religion comes third, with Taoist, Buddhist, Christian and Muslim Chinese common in Malaysia. Here, differences (in religions) are not deterrents to a common culture.

As a nation, Malaysians don't seem to have a broad or deep national identity. Each group exists as its own. The racial-religious politics practiced by some quarters, has only served to further dilute whatever nationalism there was.

Ancestral Village: Nanyang, Coromandel, Nusantara

Though Malaysians originate from India, China and Malay areas, it appears more specific that that. There is a distinct pattern of Indians generally issuing from South India (the Coromandel coast), and the Chinese coming from South China (Nanyang) and the Malays materializing from the Malayur area of Sumatra. Naturally, the Originals of the peninsula and Sabah/Sarawak have always been with us.

Nanyang refers to the coastal area of Southern China and the warm places in the "South Seas" that they migrated to, namely Malaysia/Singapore, Phillippines, Indonesia and Thailand, aka South-East Asia. As we saw in the section on food, the 8 styles of Chinese cuisine include Hokkien, Cantonese, Hailam which thrive in South East Asia. They are the original inhabitants of the areas in South China – Guangdong (Cantonese), Fujian (Hokkiens) and the Hailam (Hainan Island)

Besides the above, we also have Teochews, Hakkas who also have their own deep mark here in population and cuisine. The Teochews and Hakka, though southern Chinese, consider themselves immigrants – Teochew from Henan in Central China and Hakka also from the Central plains of China. Both are said to have left their homes to escape disturbances in the northern kingdoms, as well as famines and bad weather. Both settled in the hilly areas of Southern China. Both groups have maintained their own dialects and culture. Both had come south through Fujian before moving to their present areas, and the Hakka/Khek had majorly settled in Guangdong further south. Both are major groups in South-East-Asia, along with the larger Hokkien and Cantonese. Former Singapore PM Lee Kuan Yew is of Hakka extraction.

The Indians, with their Indic looks and culture are like the Chinese, with their Sinitic looks and culture. Just as the Chinese are many clans and dialects, so are the Indians, many castes and languages.. The Malays, on their part are no longer a single race (biology), but are now an ethnicity (culture) encompassing many islands and suku kaum (tribes). However, this is only in the Malay Peninsula, the land of coming together. In Indonesia, the same tribes are as discrete as their scattered islands and the Malay is a tiny minority. Perhaps the occasional times the Malaysian Malays, i.e. Islamized South-East Asians, think about their ancestral villages is when they gather in their tribal groups, the Minangkabaus of Negeri Sembilan or the Javanese of Johore and Selangor, or the Bawean and the Bugis.

The Coromandel coast refers to the area of South India historically known as *Cholamandalam* (Chola Domain). Being the west coast (on the Bay of Bengal), Tamils and Telugus call it their homeland. The Malayalis who were part of ancient Tamilakam, come from the west coast (Malabar) of south India. However, like the Tamils and Telugus, they invariably embarked from the ports of Madras and Nagapatnam on the Coromandel. The odd ones here, are the Punjabis from north-west India who embarked from the north-east india port of Calcutta, 1000 miles away from home. Curiously, very few Bengalis (Calcutta natives) got on the boat here. Go figure! The neighbouring Biharis did go to Fiji and and Caribbean, because they had famine, unlike the Bengalis.

The wave of indentured South Indians to Malaysia, Mauritius and South Africa also corresponds to the Great Famine of 1876-1878, which struck South India, China, South America and parts of Africa. The Bengal Famine of 1943, which took 3 million lives, was caused by Winston Churchill, who instead of feeding the people, diverted the provisons to his troops who were fighting the Japanese in Burma.

Quite unlike the Chinese who are Hans all over, South Indians are distinct from the Northerns, in linguistics, genetics, phenotype, origin myths and beliefs. Even if all Indians are mixed in various levels, they are divisible into three distict groups, Tibeto-Burman and Aryan, and Dravidian. Malaysian Indians largely fall into the latter category. While they still have connections to the Indian and Chinese landmasses, History speaks of both these groups living and working in South-East Asia for 2000 years.

Most Malays have so settled into the land that there is no touch with their original villages in Malayur. This is in contrast to the Chinese and Indians, who still maintain contact with distant relatives and their ancestral villages. What? You tend to forget the nearby old country but remember the far away? Anything to do with the saying, "Distance maketh the heart grow fonder?" Perhaps there is room for sociology to shine some light here.

Nusantara, is an Old Javanese term for "outer islands", basically archipelago, which it is. The modern Malay is a composite of people who come these islands, such as Sumatra, Java, Riau, Bawean, Borneo, Sulawesi (Bugis) etc. Thus it would stand to reason (logical), that the Malay has a homeland everywhere, but nowhere in particular. Alternatively, the only Malay homeland today is *Tanah Melayu*, "Malay Land" or Peninsula Malaya, away from the ancestral home. This is exactly it for all Malaysians, Australians, Americans etc.

Europhobia: Mat Salleh, Gweilo, Vellaiyan

The white man has quite a presence in the consciousness of all Malaysians. The British, Dutch, and Portuguese have all had their fingers on India, China and Malaya. Hence, the relationship was not always amicable. But these days he is welcomed anywhere, anytime, by anyone. He has a sure ticket into the Malaysian heart and hearth. Hard as Tun Mahathir might push his

Look East policy, young Malaysians seem to *"Look The Other Way"* – West in everything from food, dress, music to what have you. The Malay term for the Caucasian is *Mat Salleh.*

That, in itself, is a strange appellation. *Salleh* means virtuous or pious. *Mat* is the diminutive of Muhammad, no less. Matt won't do because it is short for Mathew. So how did the white man get be called "Virtuous Mohammad"? The only virtuous Europeans of the days of yore were the Christian missionaries and educators, crème de la crème of humanity who give up everything and lived for and among the people. The others were colonists – land grubbers, profit mongers, superiorists and supremacists. In recent memory, Singapore's neatly kept house was were vandalized twice by young Mat Sallehs. They got to taste the rotan (cane) for all their troubles, spray painting public property.

Speaking of intrusions, there was a true native Mat Salleh (his actual name) in Sabah, who was killed by the *Mat Salleh* forces as he led a rebellion there! So, that certainly cannot be the source of this term.

The most plausible story as to the origin of this term, goes back to the Portuguese period in Malacca. Or, it could be Dutch or British colonial eras. As the story goes, some European sailors had disembarked and gotten into a rowdy drunken state. The locals were wondering who these foreigners were. A passerby muttered, "Mad Sailors!" To the Malay ear, it sounded like 'Mat Salleh'. That apparently, is how the European came to be called "virtuous Mohammad". It must have been some British, as a Portuguese would have said, "Marinaro Loco!" These things are known to happen. *Gostan!* is a local command to "reverse" the vehicle. It is a rendering of "Go Astern!", another sailing term. Going the other direction, *Godown,* is a perfectly English sounding word by way of Portuguese (Gudao), by way of perhaps the Malay (*Gudang*) but ultimately from the Tamil *Kidangu* (storehouse).

While the Malay nickname for the Caucasian is harmless and even flattering in a sense, the Chinese term is scary and terrifying! *Gweilo,* meaning "ghost man" or, "foreign devil" was used in southern China specifically in Cantonese speaking areas to refer to westerners. We must remember that the people of the Middle Kingdom (Chinese name for China), had had a 4,000 year paranoia about outsiders and barbarians.

Consider the Great Wall of China. The lengths they went, to keep the devils out. Even we in Malaysia have born the brunt of it. I remember, as primary school students in the early 60's being called Keeling *kuei,* or Maalaai *kuei* (Indian or Malay devils). We in turn called them Cheena *kuei* (Chinese devils). It was more friendly banter, than anything else, not knowing what it meant.

Somewhat in a self-fulfilling prophecy, the Europeans did behave badly in China, especially in Shanghai where they were allowed to establish trading bases. If my primary school history memory serves me right, the Opium Wars were a Chinese reaction to European drug pushing in Shanghai. *Gweilo,* thus had negative or even derogatory connotations then. Nowadays, it is almost a term of endearment. Even *Gweilos* use it on themselves. *Gweilo* could almost be the same as *Gringo,* the Spanish term for Anglos, that derives from *Griego,* meaning "Greek".

Besides *Gringo,* the Japanese have *Gaiju.* The Thais use the term *Farang,* The Tamils use *Parangi,* and Malays use *Ferringhi.* There's even a popular beach in Penang called Batu Ferringhi, or "Europeans Rock". The widespread use of this word, doesn't give a clue to its origin or meaning. The Persians use *Farang to refer* to the *Franks, a Germanic tribe,* and hence, Europeans.

The Tamils, as part of their freedom fight againt the British in India, used *Vellaiyan* againt their colonial rulers. "*Vellaiyane Veliyeru",* was the war cry, meaning "Whitie get out". There was no rancour but strong sentiments of independence.

Overall, Malaysian attitude towards the Caucasian has been one of deference and admiration. Malay, Chinese, Indian. We all like to wear his clothing style, speak his language, do business with him, and generally jump at the opportunity to be of any assisstance. We do not often extend the same welcome to our own differently tinted fellow Malaysians. The Mat Salleh, is a priviledged person in Malaysia, and need not be apprehensive, like in some other places you know. There is no phobia, as such, of the European. Rather, a partiality. The phobia was in the earlier time when he ruled us. Now that he has let go, we kinda miss him. Absence makes the heart grow fonder, you wonder?

Anglophilia: Banana, Mangosteen, Ketupat

The big draw for fair skin is not entirely to be laid on the Europeans. It on us, actually. The black man gazed upon his first white man as a god. The Hindu caste system is graded on skin shade – *Varnasrama Dharma*. Varna, of course means colour. Skin whitening creams are billion dollar considerations for Asian women and perhaps other non-whites. It is still on us, for looking up to the western and white image as the gold standard of beauty. How many of our Malaysian, Phillipine, Thai, Indonesian "eurolook" women, have been chosen as Miss universe representative for their countries? The so-called pan-asian look.

Not only physical appearance, the world has entirely bought into its daily dress, customs, idioms etc. When the west sniffs, we get a cold, as the saying goes. When one of our own becomes irritating in the imitating, we'll intimate a scornful scoffing sneering sarcasm. Humans are so creative in coming up with nicknames and appellations, be it for an individual or for a whole group. I recently came across an incidence of Chinese on Chinese name-calling. In a Chinese cultural website, a young man wanted to know what a "banana" meant. He had heard some friends refer to others of his race as "banana".

Apparently, it is a common reference to a Chinese (or any oriental) person who has essentially lost his cultural identifiers (language, culture etc.) and has become anglicized or europhilic. The only remaining ethnic marker is his skin color and facial contours. Hence the banana – yellow on the outside, all white in the inside. Now, this should not be construed as derogatory, as it is used by and within the community. It can only be derogatory in the true sense if an outside group uses this against the Chinese.

This is similar to the situation in America, where some African Americans freely and unabashedly call each other "nigga" without denigration, to refer to fellow blacks. It can be used in friendly banter to mean, "bugger", "buddy", "loser", etc. But let an outsider use that word, and all hell breaks loose, as happended in the case of Eminem in one of his raps. With the increasing popularity of rap band and hip-hop, the term has become more widely used among some black youth. Chris Rock, the black comedian used *nigga* to describe African Americans who brought shame to the community by their behavior. He stopped using it when he sensed that non-blacks were using it in the same way. "N****" is the current PC form. By the way, our common usage of the word "bugger" to mean "fellow" or "chap", is far from its original denotation for a sodomite/homosexual. Think of that! Bugger off that usage!

While we are on the subject, how would the other races refer to someone they perceive to have abandoned their mother culture? Surprisingly, it is difficult to find a fruity appellation for the Indian Anglophile, given the well established fact that a large number of Indian middle class families do not speak their mother tongue at home. English is their default language. An old term that family members used, to describe a relative who acted "more English than the English", was *Karuppu Vellaikaran*, or, "Black White man." A snarkier version was, *Vellaikaran, karuppu sooththu* or "White guy, black ass'" Even more disparagingly, they were the butt of, "He thinks he's the big Dorai!" – "He thinks he's the big white Boss/Tuan/Buana/Massa."

Now, an Oreo is an American term that used to describe a black American who is succeesful. It is named after the black cookies sandwiching the white cream sugar. In other words, a black white wannabe. Perhaps along the same lines, there is the Malaysian refreshment that is called the Michael Jackon. "Waiter! A cool Michael Jackson for me and my friend here." Some people like to mix the milky white soya drink with the black grass jelly (*Cincau*) and what you get is a somewhat pastel drink with bits of black jelly floating in it. There is also the Tiawanese milk tea with black tapioca pearls called bubble tea. That is a frontal attack on Jackon's seeming obsession with attaining a certain cosmetic look, namely a Caucasian one. Some say it was actually a skin condition. Poor guy.

Both the above names won't describe the Indian Anglophile, for obvious reasons. Perhaps indignant Indians should stick to the fruit theme. Perhaps they might want to pick the Mangosteen as the ideal candidate. It is a local fruit, just like the banana. The dark purple rind belies the gleaming white interior. Split the tennis ball-sized fruit between the heels of your palms, and it instantly flashes a pearly white Darlie grin, rimmed by reddish pink lips. Perfetto. Now you have a mental image for the ages! While that is my contribution to this conversation, South Asians already have another fruit (nut) in mind. The coconut, as everyone knows, is brown on the outside, and snow white on the inside. Need we stretch the metaphor?

The Malay equivalent to the banana and mangosteen is elusive. Duku/ Langsat won't do, as the flesh is translucent, not white. Perhaps we have potential in the rice, with its golden husk encasing the white grain. Or, what about the *ketupat,* the little basket woven out of coconut frond, filled with rice and boiled. The cooked ketupt has the right outside coloration, and the caked rice inside is white as white is. It is settled then. In the absence of a fruit metaphor, the Malay Europhiliac might be called a ketupat. It is quite in context too, for the Minangkabau (Malay sub-group) description of their skin tone, is *sawo matang.* It literally means a golden, harvest-ready paddy field.

The latest fruity epithet, or even slur, if it comes to that, is the tembikai (watermelon). Thanks to the PAS – UMNO nexus circa 2017, It describes a PAS member (green) who is ideologically UMNO (red). Does that make Pas in 2015, when they backed BERSIH, another type of watermelon. The kind with green (PAS) skin and yellow (BERSIH) heart?

In this globalized and enlightened age, what makes people make such pronouncements and judgements on their own kind? Perhaps they feel threatened. Perhaps they feel inadequate about their own parochial mentality. Perhaps they are envious of your progressive outlook. That would make them a kiwi fruit. Brown on the outside, and envious green on the inside.

Dwelling on fruits makes one want look at some peculiar positive qualities about them This a children's prayer from Liz Curtis Higgs called "Pumpkin Prayer" The American tradition of *Halloween,* is a time when families carve holes on the vegetable and place a candle inside it. Placed on the front porche, it looks a like a lantern with a "Smiley" face.

"Pumpkin Prayer"

{cut off top of pumpkin}
Lord, open my mind so I can learn new things about you.

{remove innards}
Remove the things in my life that don't please you.
Forgive the wrong things I do and help me to forgive others.

{cut open eyes}
Open my eyes to see the beauty you've made in the world around me.

{cut out nose}
I'm sorry for the times I've turned my nose at the good food you provide.

{cut out mouth}
Let everything I say please You.

{light the candle}
Lord, help me show your light to others through the things I do. Amen

Now, the starfruit is an interesting local fruit that I never found in the supermarkets in the US. No matter how many slices you cut cross-wise, it always yields a star. Starfruit – star on the outside as you cut it crosswise. In the Phillippine island of Tawi-Tawi just off Sabah, the balimbing fruit (our belimbing) has accrued the derogatory connotation for a turncoat or traitor, due to its multiple sides. American teens call their unfaithful friends "two-faced". The Starfruit is actually 10-faced. A diamond has even more facets. So, is the belimbing a metaphor for a diamond, or a diabolism? No matter how many times you cut it cross-wise, it always yields a star. Couldn't that be taken as a token of consistency, of truthful person?

Coming to think of, it the apple does it too, revealing a star inside it as you cut it cross-wise. No human characterization here, except a metaphor for biological life cycle and regeneration.

Star inside the apple

from Ellis Paul – The Dragonfly Races

There's a star inside my apple
I know it's hard to grapple
but if you cut it side to side
there's a star alone, no lie.
And in my star inside my apple
are sleepy little seeds

and in those seeds found in my star
are could-be apple trees.

Out in the ground, I'll put my seeds
and an apple tree will grow
And in that tree soon will be apples,
red or gold with stars and seeds and apple trees
for people, birds, bears and bees,
For months, for years, for centuries
And on and on it goes you see
And on and on it goes.

Carrying on in this fruity theme, I recall a certain Dato Menteri, when he was Minister of Agriculture in the 80s or 90's, giving a parable on fruits. The details escape me, but he said something about a coconut tree with its thick erect trunk and relativeely small nuts hidden under spread-eagled fronds. The watermelon, on the other hand, has a long thin droopy stem that crawls on the ground unable to support its comparatively huge fruits. I don't mean to read the YAB's (Rt.Hon) mind, but he may have gone on to describe an intermediate state like a pineapple perched atop a short upright stem rising out of a rough thorny bush. I didn't stay to listen to the rest of the story as I was busy in the hotel kitchen lining up with the next course to serve the banquet guests. You could hear the hoots of laughter all the way back there.

The banana, mangosteen, and ketupat may seem to describe someone who is untruthful and disingenuous, displaying a certain outward identity but their heart beating to a different cultural ethos. But it is not like they are closet westerners, yet to "come out" to their community. They do flaunt their anglophilia and occidental outlook. However, the mangosteen is not the epitome of a lie. Rather, the opposite. It is the truest and most honest fruit you will ever find. At its base, every mangosteen has a 4 to 8 pointed, raised star that resembles an asterisk *. They are the remnants of the stigma, when it was a flower. The number of points the asterisk has, is the exact number of the wedge-like edible flesh, or arils, you'll find inside. You see, what you see, is what you get. Get it? This fact is guaranteed, or your money back.

The white aril is the tasty part of the fruit that is eaten, the outer exocarp is discarded. However, the current mangosteen juice craze is all about the skin! Chemical analysis has shown that the shell has the most nutrient content, including the anti-disease zanthones. The aril has no such, while the deep purple skin is nonesuch! (N*onesuch:* – 1590: a person or thing without an equal, *adjective,* Merriam-Webster). Does this say something about the worth of our indigenous culture? Whatever you are outwardly, whatever culture you are born into, treasure it. Be a philiac (lover) of another culture, but not after discarding your own. In that case you would be no more than one of those plastic imitations.

The mangosteen is called the queen of fruits due to its cooling properties. It is a common accompaniment to the heaty durian, the unanimously crowned king of fruits. What does the durian represent? With its outer rough shell and prickly thorns, and aromatic flavourful flesh, it is definitely a sweetheart. Many Westerners have been put off by the roughness of the fruit and its off-putting odour, only to fall in love with its custardy pulpy nectar. What is this? Is it a metaphor for a gentleman, who is misunderstood because of his appearance. A diamond in the rough. A book that was judged too soon, by its cover. In other words, this does not describe your anglophile. It describes that which is presumably despised by the anglophile. That, of course, is the unassuming simpleton nurtured on the milk of his mother culture, who exhibits the highest traits.

Now, what about the coconut? It may be descriptive of a seemingly tough-minded, hard-headed, nut-case who is inwardly capable of weeping buckets of tears. A real softy. A gentle giant? Folk heroes (in movies, novels, comics etc.) often present such crude outward facade and are bleeding hearts for social justice. Somewhat along these lines (or not), a popular Tamil song of the 60's goes thus:

When you beget a coconut tree (Thennai), you get coconut water (Ilanir)
When you begat a prodigal child (Pillai), you will cry "eye-water" (Kannir)

The antithesis of all the above fruits is the orange. Same on the inside as well as outside. To be fair, our anglophiliacs are not all that bad. We all speaka de Inglis, si?, and we all dress western, we all enjoy Hollywood (be honest!), we all root for English soccer teams and wear their colours on our torsos. May be some of us get too carried away and lose our mother tongues – but the loss is the losers, not yours. Bilingual is better than unilingual, just like a bicycle gets you places faster than a unicycle. Culture is a choice we must make: trim the bad in your culture and take the good from other cultures. Did you notice that religion has not been made a criterion to decide on the type of fruit you are. You can be an active Christian, Muslim, Hindu or Buddhist, and still be a true Chinese. Perhaps, we should just do away with mouthing fruity metaphors and just enjoy the fruits!

Colonial Perspectives: What they said about us

Oftentimes, we tend to be poor assessors of ourselves – looking at concave and convex mirrors that show us as greater or lesser than our true selves. Like someone having himself for a lawyer, our judgment becomes clouded by sentimental bias. Outside observers with more objective eyes, are like a well polished straight mirror. A candid camera. European observers, commenting about us in the 19th century, have given us writeups that rings true, even today. Their journals feel like today's news, rather than those in the National Archives. Here's a brief sampling: –

The images of Malaysians living in trees, is also from the West, but that is the from the runaway imagination of those who did not visit these shores.

European descriptions of Malaysians. This is from, ***"Travellers' Singapore: An Anthology"***, compiled by John Bastin.

Isabella Bird, writing in 1897, writes of the Tamil woman thus, *"The Kling women are, I think, beautiful – not so much in face as in form and carriage. I am never weary of watching and admiring them for their inimitable grace of movement. Their clothing – or rather drapery, is a mystery, for it covers and drapes perfectly, yet has no 'make', far less 'fit', and leaves every movement unimpeded. These women are tall, and straight as arrows: their limbs are long and rounded; their appearance is timid – one might almost say modest – and their walk is poetry of movement. A tall, graceful Kling woman, draped as I have described, gliding along the pavement, her statuesque figure the perfection of graceful ease, a dark pitcher on her head, just touched by the hand, showing the finely-moulded arm, is a beautiful object, classic in form, exquisite in movement, and artistic in colouring, a child of the tropic sun. What thinks she, I wonder – if she thinks at all, of the pale European, paler for want of exercise and engrosssing occupation, who steps out of her carriage in front of her, an ungraceful heap of poufs and frills, tottering painfully on high heels, in tight boots, every movement a struggle or a jerk, the clothing utterly unsuited to this climate, or any climate, impeding motion, and affecting health, comfort, and beauty alike?"*

What would Bird say today, about that womans's (lumpy?) modern descendents? Housebound and lacking an active lifestyle, all the kitchen prep of pounding, pulverizing, grinding, blending, even slaughtering taken over by machines and maids, why sure.

What is a Malay, Chinese, Indian in colonial British eyes, for an unbiased third person perspective. Will the real Malay stand up?

Winstedt, Swettenham etc: ***"The Real Malay"*** (1895) – 2nd paragraph

"The real Malay is short, thick set, well built man with straight black hair, a dark brown complexion, thick nose and lips, and bright intelligent eyes. His disposition is generally kindly, his manners are polite and easy. Never cringing, he is reserved with strangers, and suspicious, though he does not show it. He is courageous and trustworthy in the discharge of an undertaking; but is extravagant, fond of borrowing money, and very slow in repaying it. He is a good talker, speaking in parables, quotes proverbs and wise saws, has a strong sense of humour, and is very fond of a good joke. He takes an interest in the affairs of his neighbor and is consequently a gossip. He is a Muhammadan and a fatalist but he is also very superstitious. He never drinks intoxicants, he is rarely an opium smoker. But he is fond of gambling, cock fighting and kindred sports. He is by nature a sportsman; catches and tames elephants; is a skilled fisherman, and thoroughly at home in a boat.

Above all things, he is conservative to a degree, is proud and fond of country and his people, venerates his ancient customs and traditions, fears his Rajas, and has a proper respect for constituted authority – while he looks askance on all innovation and will resist their sudden introduction. But if he has time to examine them acrefully, and they are not thrust upon him, he is willing to be convinced of their advantage. At the same time, he is a good imitative learner, and, when has energy and ambition enough for the task, makes a good mechanic. He is however lazy to a degree, is without method or order of any kind, knows know regularity even in the hours of his meal, and considers time as of no importance. His house is untidy, even dirty but he bathes twice a day, and is very fond of personal adornment in the shape of smrt clothes.

About the Tamil, Mrs.Reginald Sanderson, wrote an article in the, **Twentieth century impressions of British Malaya: its history, people, commerce, industries, and resources (1908). She writes,**

"Singapore being in close proximity to India, black races are conspicuous for their numbers, their peculiarities of dress. Both Singapore and Malacca were at one time ruled by Hindu kings who were disposed by the portuguese and henceforth relegated to the position of traders only.

Klings is a name given to the lowest classes of the immigrants, who clear the jungles, do the rough part of road-making, and drive bullock carts, while the most degraded become herdsmen to the natives and wander round with the water buffaloes, half starved, and barely clothed in strange fragments of rags. The designation Klings was originally by no means a derogatory term; it signified only the tribe of black traders from the ancient kingdom of Kalinga. This poor class of Tamils are patient and enduring. They have developed some a mount of muscle with hard work, and walk with an upright carriage. Even the women and children might have been drilled in the best gymnasiums. Once a year, they rejoice in the Pongul Feast, when they troop down to the sea to wash away all sin in the flowing waters and then feast for three days."

Here is Isabella Bird, describing the Chinese. "They can bear with impunity the fiercest tropical heat, and can thrive and save where Englishmen would starve". However, she also adds, "along with their industrious habits and their character for fair trading, they have brought negative habits like gambling and opium-smoking". This was on her trip to Malacca. Her trip to Sungai Ujong with British Superintendent of Police, Mr. Hayward, got this reaction: "poor, half-naked creatures...staking every cent they earn on the turn of the dice", making them "a truly sad spectacle", while the "opium inebriates" are "lean like skeletons, and very vacant in expression"

(Letter XIII January 1879, 179-80). ***The Golden Chersonese and the Way Thither*** (1883).

In the article in the *Travellers's Handbook,* Bird describes Malay servants as *"charming but work-shy"*, and the *"unreliability" of the Indians, "who can be very good indeed, but often are not."* And while the Chinese provide *"value for money"* service, they still require close supervision as *"one cannot expect them to conform to European standards"* – ***The Colonizer: Travellers Handbook for British Malaya*** (1937)

The two British women and a male colonial administrator, provide a balanced pro and con report. To us, it may be half-truths. Bird's single sentence, positive – negative, da-da-da – but – dada da tone ending in a letdown, is a little biting.

Race relations: Sino – Indo – Malay ….

The old Chinese merchant class had a reputation for being inscrutable and unscrupulous.They have been called the Jews of the East. And stingy with information. Malaysians of earlier generations have memories of Chinese disdain for others. Many will still tell you that the Chinese oldtimer would never give someone of another ethnicity, the time of day. Ask for directions, and the stock answer was, *"Ta tau"* or "Don't know." The Chinese of today are more enlightened, and would gladly guide you with good directions. Even go out of the way and lead you there.

Perhaps there is a reason for the erstwhile Chinaman's apparent inscrutability. It may not be that the old Chinese wanted to disassociate from the others or was being insolently insular. It may not be that he was applying his concept of financial parsimony or penury to the realm of information giving. It may simply be a communications issue, being unable to give information in the lingua franca, Malay. When replying, "ta tau", s/he probably meant that they "ta tau" how to say it in Malay. The sad part was, "ta tau", sounded like "bug off!". Remember, their centuries old paranoia about barbarians overrunning the Middle Kingdom, and the resultant Great Wall?

An Indian friend has a slightly different take on it. He says that the Chinese are practical people, who work with solid facts. They probably shied away from volunteering information because they didn't want to risk misleading people with wrong or incomplete information, like most of us well-meaning "guides" sometimes do. How many times have you had to ask two or three people just get from here to there? How many times have they forgotten to mention, to take the second left not the first?

Or, perhaps it is cultural. Did the Chinese petty trader carry the accepted concept of not giving away trade secrets, beyond its business application. The rest of us have learned from the Baba-Nonyas, the superstition of withholding some ingredient when giving out a recipe. Or, you replace an ingredient with another. To give away the whole recipe, supposedly means that your cooking of it henceforth won't "jadi" – won't "materialize" – perfectly.

What about the names each gives the other? Malays and those of Nusantara (Indonesia) call South Indians *Keling* – due to a historico-geographic misunderstanding. Tamils' domain consisted of the Pallava, Pandya, Chola (Raja Chulan) and Chera kingdoms.To Malay forebears, the *Benua Keling* of Sejarah Melayu (Malay Annals) referred to the Tamil area instead of Kalinga, which was more northerly and distant, somewhere near modern Orissa. So, *Keling*, or Kalinga came to refer to South Indians, generally. Tamils resent being called Keling, not because of any inherent derogation there. There is none, the Kalingas being a proud and majestic race. In fact a respected Tamil personal name is *Kaalingarayan*, or "King of the Kalingas", or *Kaalingan* – "He of Kalinga". The reason for their resentment is the same as, if a Malay is called a Sundanese, or a Chinese is referred to as a Mongol, even though all four are classified as belonging to the Mongoloid race of humankind.

The same historic mistake happens in the case of Punjabi Sikhs. All Malaysians, including fellow Indians, refer to them as Bengali. When the tall and bearded Portuguese first landed in Malacca, the locals started calling them "White Bengalis", because they looked like Punjabis! Duh! Another theory says that modern Punjabi soldiers of British India boarded the Malaya bound ship at Calcutta, in Bengal. So, there. It is to their credit that Punjabis have not complained about the labeling mix-up. First of all, there are very few Malaysian Bengalis. Bengalis are of shorter stature, darker skinned, and don't wear turbans, much less, beards! The true Bengalis that one sees every day, believe it or not, are our Bangladeshi guest workers. Malaysian Punjabis, who are mostly of the Sikh faith, are also called *Bayee*, a corruption of *Bhai* or brother. Pakistan also has a Punjab province, so there are millions of Muslim Punjabis in this world. No one calls them Bengali. You only hear, "Pakistani". Perhaps, Tamils should cease being so prickly with the kling word. People who who want to stir you up won't have anything to stir you with, if you are not easily stirred, in the first place. Understirred?

Chinese referred to Malays as *Mah Laai Kuie*. They call Indians *Kee ling Kuei*.

Indian descriptions of their fellow Malays and Chinese is often more descriptive. Up to the mid sixties, Tamils referred to Malays as *Valayaangkatti*. Officially, they were and are, *Malaaikaarar* (Malay person). The currently popular colloquial designation is *Nattukkaaran* (He of the land/native) after they were officially designated as *Bumiputras* (sons of the soil) in the 70's. It became a kind of code word among Indians.

Back to *Valayaangatti*, its meaning is literally, "a fastener of rings". The secret of its origin only recently came to me. An Indian friend of mine was told this by his Malay friend. According to this Malay, the nickname was given by Indian rubber tappers to their Malay co-workers. Apparently, the British plantation owner, in a bit of his divide and rule tendency, assigned the lightweight duties of tying the rings (*valayam*) that held the latex cup, around the trees. Needless to say, the British considered the Tamils as workhorses and used them as dumb mules for the hard labour of tapping, collecting, and manually transporting the latex. This title was merely descriptive rather than derogatory, likely used in jestful camaraderie. "Dey Valayaangatti!" "Hey, Ring-tier!"

Tamil designation for the Chinese was *Sadaiyan* (wearer of braids) possibly due to the old Chinese coolie habit of wearing a long single braid. Sadai, means braid.

From the names we give each other, to our conceptions of each other, it is undeniable that Malaysian ethnic groups have always held certain preconceived ideas about other groups. Other Malaysians have generally had this notion of Indians as drunks or as easily inebriated and loud. Indeed, some of the poorer class of Indians, who went for cheaper intoxicants like *samsu*, tended to make a scene after imbibing the stuff. The Chinese were known as the pushers of samsu.

Malays were thought to be indolent and loving the easy life. They were labeled as easy going and carefree in their ways. The rest of us, considered Chinese as unscrupulous and willing to do anything to make a buck. Someone noted, a long time ago, that a Chinaman will even pimp his daughter in order to make a sweetheart business deal. All the above are generalizations, of course. It is something we humans do only too well. Not all Indians drink, and if they drink, not all make a scene. Not all Malays *curi tulang* ("steal bones"), the Malay term for a lazy bones. And, not all Chinese worship at the altar of fithy lucre. The majority are decent people, with high moral (Confucian) values.

Things seem to have changed in our perceptions of each other, but only in the content, not the attitudes. These days, the Indian youth is associated with banditry, burglary and drug mulery. Chinese youths used to have that distinction in the 60's, when the likes of Botak Chin and gang gave police a run for their money. Malay youth are synonymous with *Mat Rempit* (highway hogs on motorbikes) and their young girls are implicated in out of wedlock pregnancies and baby dumping cases. Chinese are blamed for bribe giving, to grease dealings with the civil authorities. Most loan sharks tend to be Chinese, and so are criminal cases pertaining to their collection activities. Again, these are generalizations. Taking the mindsets and mouthings of a miniscule minority and imputing it to the whole community, is what we seem to do best. We seem to prefer spray-paint sweeps, to dainty Chinese brush strokes. Not all of us are prone to making sweeping statements. Indeed, we have gotten along very well all these centuries, with *sopan santun*. Sopan santun – not "soap and sun tan", as the Western tongue is wont to say, but "Soft and sound tone". In other words, "courtesy and good manners."

No matter how we look at it, each has its own flaws. The sad part is, such polarized thinking appears stronger now than ever before, amongst the youth. It is such a total change from the colonial days, when everyone attended the "English school", and got along famously. These days, children attend vernacular schools, shielded from the other races. Heaven knows, what such places can breed – racial labeling, racial myopia, and racial stereotyping. National schools (Sekolah Kebangsaan) don't fare that much better, either. The recent rash of racial slurs uttered by some teachers and school principals, is worrying. Even so, we shouldn't generalize it to the whole of the teaching profession. Politicians do that too. No less than a special representative of Prime Minister Najib for ethnic unity, had to resign, after questioning the inalienable citizenship rights of Chinese and Indians! At least, that guy blurted his mind. But, you have to beware the one who appears to say the right things, but is a racist at heart. Like a scorpion hiding under the rock, he is difficult to spot.

And now, a brief look at another subset of name calling or labelling – religious. Sikhs in the US have often fallen victim to the smear, "Raghead". It was originally directed at the likes of Osama bin Laden and the thick turbaned Talibans. The Americans, flopping spectacularly as usual in general knowledge, mistook the innocent Sardars for the Suicide Squads. Hindus are called Dot-heads, for obvious reasons. Likewise in India's Tamilnadu, Christians are called *Paavaadai* ("skirts"), due perhaps to the gown-like robes of Catholic Priests and Nuns. Come to think of it, even Muftis and Taoist priests wear skirts of some sort, don't they? There was a time when "tent" had currency among Malaysian Indians, to describe the rare *Burqa* – clad muslimah

Religion

Whether aware or unawares, religion is central to the daily grind of your typical Malaysian. Every day in the week you find you will find the Muslim Ummah, the Hindu Mahajanam, The Catholic Parishoners, The Christian Koinonia, The Buddhist Bhaktas, and the Taoist Throngs, doing their thing for and towards God. The closest thing to an atheist you will find in Malaysia, is the inactive theist. That's the one who prays once a year, on a special occassion. This section, though on religion, is not about Theology (Sunnah, Shénxué, Siddhantham) but about the practice of it (Ibadah, Zōngjiào Shíjiàn, Vazhipaadu).

The Catch: Wow, Niat, Nerthikadan

I am the last person to pretend to understand an atheist. I understand atheists to be those who have no proven rationale for their ravings, but an irrational hatred of the Almighty rooted in some early life deprivation. I believe that no child who had a happy life, becomes an atheist. The atheist's agenda rests in the fact that at some critical point in his early life, God seems to have absconded and become irrelevant. From then on, he grasps at any and every reason to support his view that God is nought (not). It is much the same with religious terrorists, who have an irreligiously irrational hatred of people or things, not of their religious outlook. The advanced scientist may be another class of atheist. Perhaps, having discovered the "answers" to all questions of science, he might feel equal to the Almighty. But looks like he has only scratched the surface. The fabled Tamil grandmother, *Avvaiyaar* (1ˢᵗ Century BCE) had already said thus:

> *Katrathu kai mann alavu* – What has been learned is as a handful of soil
> *Kallaathathu Ulagalavu*   – Yet to be learned is as the whole earthful

Note: Interestingly, the scientific community generally has the "Beginner's Mind" of Zen. Afterall, Avvaiyar has been included in NASA's Cosmic Questions Exhibit. In 1991, a 20.6 km-wide crater in Venus was named the Avviyar crater by the International Astronomical Union

That is not to say that theists are bona fide believers. I find there generally is a catch, or trade off, to the God – believer relationship. It's a quid pro quo (*this, for that)* barter trade. Not every believer is bona fide (*in good faith*!). Belief in God becomes conditional on what the "believer" can get out of the relationship. It is a one-sided marriage of convenience, If you please.

The Hindu hums, "if you grant my wish I will break a hundred coconuts in your name next Thaipusam." The Taoist thinks, "If business booms, I will burn incense incessantly and intensively. The Buddhist blurts that he will dutifully do the dhamma. The Muslim murmurs, "I will play a more active role in the religious affairs of the local mosque." The Christian cries, "I will do mission, or charity work." IF!

Yet, there are Hindus who renounce worldly ways, and assume lives of simple sadhus. They give their lives to acts of piety, poverty, and praise of the Almighty. There are Taoists who are true monks in every sense, and model human beings. There are Buddhist bhikkhus who renounce worldy ways and live off the charity of others. There are Muslim fakirs who live sainted lives and are models for others to emulate. There are Christians who live only to serve others and not self. Unlike the self servers, who live miserable lives pestering God for earthly comforts, these servers of others have found true happiness without resorting to the ABBA style "gimme, gimme, gimme" mantra.

Those are the ones who have tapped into the motherlode of true religion. It is never the failure of the religion. It is the failure of the particular practioner to understand its deeper truths. The The charismatist pastor, I observe, is a good man, committed to his work. But he seems to know no other prayer but the, "gimme, gimme, "prayer. "Lord, show him the good life. Take away her pain. Bless them with child." Crowds flock to his church because, they too, want the miracles and goodies that he claims God has given him.

There is a "gimme" prayer that is almost never asked. "Lord, gimme the strength to bear this pain. Gimme the faith to weather this trying phase of my life. Thank you, God, for allowing this tribulation, for it is shaping me into a better person. "Indeed, the pastor's Bible says that the Holy Spirit is a comforter of the soul, not a provider of his every material lust. Doesn't the gimme culture in religion smack a wee bit like a manipulation of God. It is like a little 3 year old in a toy store, throwing a tantrum at his father. "I want that, and I want it now!"

This happens when the concept of man serving God, becomes the notion of God at your beck and call, heeding your every whim and whine. Most believers fall into the cavalier category of Alladins expecting Allah to be their gentle genuflecting genie. It is a shallow, surface level faith. The surface of the sea is where the waves, whirlpools, and violent weather are. Diving deeper, you find still waters. The believer who transcends the material mind, spirals up to a higher/or deeper, spiritual plane. No longer is his focus on getting the most from God, but in giving his utmost to the High one. Personal pain, suffering, and setback in divine service, is considered a blessing. An honour. A calling. These true believers are your saints and savants, sadhus and sanyasis, Xian and shèng, sufi and orang suci. They are a minority in all the faiths, but a blessing to all.

This materialistic state of affairs in personal religion, is probably a by product of progress. We want what the Jones' have. It has infected and infested the Christian Mega churches. Joel Osteen, the youngish and handsome pastor of the largest congregation in the US, supposedly subscribes to the "gospel of health and wealth." It is an anti-biblical concept that says God will bless all true believers with great personal wealth and comfort. The implication being, that if you are poor, you are not doing your religion right.The other implication is, if you are not rich, you don't belong in his church. Of course, the more Osteen can convince you of the the gospel of wealth, the fatter his wallet gets. It is like the fortune teller, who builds his fortune on your unfortunate greed and gullibility.

Thousands, from various religions, made pilgrimages to Sathya Sai Baba (now deceased) in India. He supposedly made things appear out of thin air. Now, that is not a bad thing, in and of itself. Very good entertainment value. But you question the motives of these devotees. Would they flock there if he only gave them moral teachings and injunctions? Don't their scriptures offer that already?

The occasional Taoist is not averse to burn incense to Buddha or Shiva. His shrine may include an idol of one or both of these. His idea of religion is to get material blessing, no matter the source. In a sense, for all these people of religion, the supreme and ultimate god seems to be the holy Moolah – money! The fastest way to fill up your religious building is, to start a rumour that all your problems will be solved if you go there.

Atheists – In what ways are they also similarly agenda-ed? The atheist communist has said that religion is the opium of the poor. The religion of communism that grew in the lifetime of my grandfather has become a flop in my lifetime. Atheists too, have an "instant coffee" mentality. Because they didn't get something from God that very instant, they decided that he didn't exist.

The Catch: When you ask the average person why he prays to a particular god, or attends a particular church, or embraced a particular religion, you are likely to get answers like these: "That idol is 'powerful' because he/she answers all my prayers." "I attend that church because it is big and exciting." "I chose this religion because it suits my personal philosophy." Can it not be all about the self ("Ego", "I"}? If only people would practice what their religion says, and not what they want it to say, the world would be a far better place. Wouldn't it?

Symbolism: Thopukaranam, Ruku, Sign of the Cross, Josstick waving

Hinduism as most of us know, is chock full of symbolism and sagas. It is the most ritualistic and "physical" of all religions. Other than animism, of course. Every aspect of the faith is wrapped around a physical object. Example: The white ash on the forehead, the *thiruniru,* represents the Hindu's proclamation of his humility. He is telling himself (or others) that he is nothing before his Almighty. You would think that they could show their humility in other ways, not so graphic. Afterall, all agree that God is a spirit and an unseeble force.

If you thought that the Hindu is too preoccupied with the physical. If you thought that they might express their religiosity in ways not so graphic and tangible. If you thought that they might be simpler in their worship – not having to spend small fortunes on flowerss and garlands, you might want to rethink. If you think the Hindu is symbolism heavy in his worship act, then he is most simple in dispatching his dearly departed. While the rest of us tend to build elaborate tombs and mausoleums for the dead, the

Hindu cremates his relative. Tell me if that is not the most environmental friendly – No land wastage, instant bio-degrade, literally dust to dust and ashes to ashes. What a simple, uncluttered concept!

The Taoist, while not as full of *Ithikasa* (traditions), is also ceremonious, waving jossticks and banging tortoise shells. The Muslim too, goes through the elaborate ritual of washing before prayers and ritual postures during prayers, the *ruku*, which represents a stance of humility. During the Sunday service, Christians stand, kneel or bow for prayers.

The Catholic dips his fingers in a font of "holy water" and makes the sign of cross on his forehead, chest and across the shoulders. He then makes a half kneel (dip) before entering the sanctum. The Muslim makes a detailed wash (wuduk) before entering the mosque. During worship, he turns his head left and right, addressing two Jinns sitting there.

Well, that was symbolic action. Now, about symbols.

All Malaysians of different religions, have forms that are a kind of ritual language.

While islam itself, being a monotheistic faith, eschews association with cultural symbolism as *shirik* (associating islam with an alien object), there is a movement to ban symbols such as the crescent moon and star from mosques and other Islamic worship centers.

The crescent moon and star symbol actually pre-dates Islam by several thousand years. These symbols were used by the peoples of Central Asia and Siberia in their worship of sun, moon, and sky gods. It was associated with the Carthaginian goddess Tanit and the Greek goddess Diana. In pre-islamic Arabia itself, al – Lat was worshipped as moon goddess.

It wasn't until the Ottoman Empire that the crescent moon and star became affiliated with the Muslim world. When the Turks conquered Constantinople (Istanbul) in 1453, they adopted the city's existing flag and symbol. For hundreds of years, the Ottoman Empire ruled over the Muslim world. After centuries of battles with Christian Europe, it is understandable how the symbols of this empire became linked in people's minds with the faith of Islam as a whole.

Based on this history, many Muslims reject using the crescent moon as a symbol of Islam. The faith of Islam has historically had no symbol, and many refuse to accept what is essentially an ancient pagan icon. It is certainly not in uniform use among Muslims.

The Star of David is the symbol of Judaism. The star is has six points created by two equilateral triangles overlayed in opposite directions. Anthropologic researchers believed that the triangles were used to symbolize male (pointing up) and female (pointing down), thereby noting unity, balance or harmony.

In Judaism, the Star is referred to as *Magen David,* which means, literally, Shield of David. Interestingly, in ancient times, the Menorah (candelabra) was symbolic of Judaism, not the Star, which was believed to be a symbol used by Kabbalists. It was also known as the Seal of Solomon. Modern Jewish scholars write that the six-pointed star is the reminder of God's rule over all. The six points represent the four cardinal directions (north, south, east, west) as well as up and down.

While there is no reference to the Star in the Talmud, some scholars believe the use of the Star came about in the first century when warriors made shields using two inverted triangles.

The Cross is the symbol of the Christian faith. Jesus Christ was accused of raising the population against the Jewish priestly hierarchy with his radical teachings of love and brotherhood. The common form of execution at that time was for criminals to be nailed to a cross until dead. So Christians have a taken a symbol of shame and converted it into a thing of pride and sacrifice. Other symbols of Christianity are the Fish (Jesus was a "fisher of men"), the Butterfly (Resurrection and new life). The cross is a later addition, and was preceded by the fish sign. Fish (*IKTHYS* in Greek), is an acronym for "*Iēsoûs Khrīstós, Theoû Huiós, Sōtér*" or, "Jesus Christ, Son of God, Savior".

Hinduism is symbolized by the AUM (OM, OHM) symbol, indicating three states of mind. These states are waking (A), dreaming (U), deep sleep (M) and silence. It is also said to represent the three aspects of the Hindu godhead – Brahma (A), Vishnu (U), and Shiva (M). It is supposed to be the first sound heard, at creation. The Dharma Wheel of the Buddhism is believed to originate in from the 7-9th centuries. This symbol represents birth and rebirth, the eternal cycle of life.

Taoism is typified by the Yin-Yang symbol. The origin of this ancient sign is unclear. It represents the harmonious equilibrium between the polarities of nature (light/dark, male/female, peace/conflict). Clearly, religious symbols (so-called) are not enjoined by any scripture, but by human design, as a way of self identification. These symbols, appearing on flags, is no different from individuals wearing them on their necks or tattoed on body parts.

The colour green has been appropriated by Islam, and is symbolic of life and vegetation, harking back to the notion that those in Paradise will be clothed in the fine green silk. If you live in a desert, surely a green shoot is a sight for sore eyes! The Hindu desires the colour of saffron, which signifies agni, or fire, which in turn portrays purity, and the search for knowledge. When ascetics and sadhus move from place to place, a saffron cloured flag acts as a satisfactory alternative to the burden of lugging around a hot fire bowl. Yellow or orange is the major colour of Buddhism. It harks back to the days when the Buddha himself instructed his bhikkus (monks) to dress in soiled or discarded clothing materials, which they sanitised by boiling in turmeric water. While many colours are used, blue/white is predominant in Christianity. It represents heaven, sky, water, cleansing, baptism etc.

Has it come to this? That religion, instead of reflecting wisdom from the scriptures, is now reflected by man made signs? There was even a case in Kuala Lumpur, where a mob mobilized, offended by the cross on a church in their neighbourhood. Whatever happened to the scriptures' strictures against outward forms but to reflect holiness through inherent qualities?

The Call: Azaan, Temple Bell, Tortoise Shell

Everyboy announces the call to prayer. The Muslim answers the *Azaan* – which is a recitation by the *Muezzin* (professional caller). The content of the azaan, is the *Kalimah Shahaadah* (profession of faith) along with an invitation.

The Catholics also announce weddings and deaths with the tolling of bells. In earlier times, it was for announcing news from battlefields. Bells are rung at certain points during the mass (worship) to highlight what was happening at the altar, for those at the back. This is archaic, as in modern times better lighting, sound systems, and video live streaming bring the action close the the worshipper.

Unlike the Jewish, Christian, Muslim and Sikh worship which are congregational, the others are individual or family worship. Hindu priests ring hand held bells to create a serene environment in the sanctuary. Rather than getting the attention of the *bhakta*s (believers), it is more for the deity. So, the ringing of bell with the left hand while the right hand does the *Aaaraathi* or, *Theeba Aaraathanai* (circular waving of flames before the lord or lady of the house) is an ambidextrous action. This, accompanied by mouthing of mantras, completes the picture. The tinkling silvery sound of ringing bells announces to the passerby, of *puja* (worship) in progress. They also tap tiny bells that hang from the ceiling, to sign in to face the deity.

Taoist prayers are accompanied by the knocking of wooden tortoises. The torroise/turtle has been used as a medium to ask favours from heaven. The turtle, as in the rabbit and turtle tale, are said to be slow and steady and had reserves of energy for last minute dashes. Sages and hermits are said to mirror the turtle in character. Buddhist temples call with the banging of a big bronze drum that booms out the welcoming bellow.

Generally, since the loud calls to prayer are remnants of archaic technology, perhaps it should be upgraded to modern times. Some countries, like adjacent Singapore have banned such public town crying in the interest of communal peace and noise reduction. Well, if we have foregone camel carts and horse carriages in favour of motor vehicles, why not? There already exists technology such as prayertime reminders on phone and radio as well as whatsapp-like features, to gently remind us of our appointments with the Almighty. Indeed, the practiced adherent already has the schedule indelibly imprinted in his consciousness. That would make one's worship and prayer an automatic self-driven act, rather than forced and externally induced wouldn't it?

The distant sound of the azaan, or a church bell, is rather soothing to one's ear since it is not an incessant din, and breaks the overall quietness. Right on your street, it can be noise pollution.

Chants: Suprabaatham, Zikir, Gregorian, dàojiào shèngge

A chant is often a choppy, peppy tune, more like the beat of a military march. The idea is to rouse the spirit and mind of the believer. The Murugan baktha who carries a kavadi at Thaipusam is encouraged by his entourage with shouts of "Vel, Vel, Vetrivel." Vel being his spear. A school chant or cheer is similarly, to stir the team spirit.

Here's sample of a cheer for a MU (not University of Malaya) player. There are scores of such written team and individual tunes.

He's big, he's bad, he's Wesley Brown,
He's the hardest man in all the town.
With orange hair beware.
Come and have a go if you dare...

Every Hindu deity in the temples or at home, is woken up in the morning and laid to sleep in the evening. The morning begins by the chanting of the *Suprabatham*. Each deity has its own "anthem", if you please. Suprabhatham is Sanskrit for "auspicious dawn". The most famous is the Lord Venkateshwara Suprabhatham recited at Tirupati to waken a form of Vishnu. During Ekanta/Panupu Seva, a lullaby is sung, to put the Lord to sleep.

Tamil Nadu temples also have special singers known as *Othuvaars* who chant the *Thevaaram* ("Garland of the Lord") and *Thiruvasagam* ("Sacred utterance"), in Shaivite temples.

In Buddhism, chanting is the traditional means of preparing the mind for meditation; especially as part of formal practice (in either a lay or monastic context). Some forms of Buddhism also use chanting for rituals.

Here is a sample of a very popular chant, the triratna ("{three jewels") from the Theravada branch of Buddhism.

- Buddham saranam gacchāmi – I go for refuge in the Buddha.
- Dhammam saranam gacchāmi – I go for refuge in the Dharma.
- Sangham saranam gacchāmi – I go for refuge in the Sangha

The Taoist Chant/Incantation has 6 healing sounds.

- SSSSS metal – white – fall season. SHHHHH wood – green – spring. WOOOO water – deep blue – winter.

- HOOOOO earth – yellow gold – Indian Summer. HEEEEE fire (endocrine glands) – violet.
- HAAAAA fire (cardiovascular) – red – summer.
  Of course, Taoist chants are sing song and just sound bites, like above.

Sikh chants (Jap) are slow, soft reading in undertones, of the *Gurbani*, the text of the Sikh Bible, *Guru Granth Sahib*. Those are meditations on the relationship of the Sikh to his Waheguru (God).

The Christian, Gregorian chant originated in Monastic life, in which singing the 'Divine Service' nine times a day at the proper hours was upheld according to the Rule of St. Benedict. Singing psalms made up a large part of the life in a monastic community, while a smaller group and soloists sang the chants. In its long history the Gregorian Chant has been subjected to many gradual changes and some reforms. The tones are haunting and echoing, probably because they were sung in the cavermous vaults of the monasteries.

Muslim chant, the Azan cannot be considered a strict chant but more a song, since it is melodious, smooth, drawn out and almost Operatic or Carnatic. But if the Gregorian hymn, with its mellifluous rhythm can be called a chant, the same could said of the azan. If the early early morning *suprabatham* is meant to wake up the god, the muslim *azan* is to "wake" or remind the faithful to attend the five prescribed daily prayers. But there is a certain prayer that one hears at the local surau during Ramadhan. It has a predictable cadence as the phrase, "La Ilaha illalla", is recited non-stop in the evenings, just before *buka puasa* or, breaking of fast.

Chants are superlatively soothing no matter the decibel level. On a scale from the undertonal Jap, Gregorian, Buddhist, Azan, Suprabatham and Taoist, all are calming to the spirit, far away from hard rock.

Worship Posture: Ruku, Toppukaranam, Kneeling, Kow Tow

They say they worship the same almighty but in different forms of theology and practice. The difference in form also applies to the physical stance and worshipful attitude of the dvotee.

The Hindu temple has a main sanctum sanctorum in which resides the chief diety. Somewhat reminiscent of the high priest in the now extinct

Jewish Levitical priesthood, the Hindu priest or *Ayyar* stands inside the sanctuary. All others must stand in rows on either side of the entrance. You are not allowed a close encounter of the full frontal, face-to face kind with the deity. You line up on both sides of the aisle as if welcoming a visiting VVIP. Most temples have iron railings to facilitate this formation, in the off chance that a delirious devotee might go face-to-face and then inadvertantly do the unthinkable – turn his back to the holy one.

While thus positioned, the devotee might do one of several things, as the priest chants and does the pooja. One might mock knock her temples three or five times with her knuckles – the *Pillaiyar Kuttu.* Just to be sure, temples in this case are the sides of the head between eye and ear, not the religious building you do the knocking in.

Another devotee may be seen crossing his arms, pinching the opposite ear lobe, and bobbing by doing a slight squat. The significance of this action is unclear, but you do remember from your primary school days, the schoolteacher would punish misbehavior by having the student do this motion. It is called the *Thoppu-karanam.* Perhaps, the devotee in this case, is repenting of some indiscretion? You wonder which came first? Did the teacher appropriate a temple ritual to his disciplinary repetoir, or vice a versa? Thoppukaranam is also known as "super brain yoga", supposedly a concentration activator.

As the priest comes out of the sanctum bearing a tray of *Prasadam* – basically ash powder, and Kum-kum – the devotees cross their palms and tap the opposite sides of their jaws. They them help themselves to the prasadam and smear their foreheads with the ash and apply the kum-kum pottu.

The Catholics do their one-on-one worship before icons of Mary, Jesus and a host of saintly figures. They are allowed to come up close and personal with these images. They do the "sign of the cross", first touching the forehead with their forefingers saying *"in the name of the Father"*, and then the heart *"and of the Son"*, followed by the left and right shoulders *"and of the Holy Spirit"*. That, basically traces the shape of the cross. Pentecostals sway and swoon, lifting up arms heavenward. Church of Christ worship is the most intellectual, and cerebral. No icons, music, or (e) motion – just mind, soul, and body.

As the Catholics do the sign of the cross, they do a slow motion drop on one knee (genuflection), or kneel on both knees. Alternatively, they might do a half dip, kind of a little curtsy. The significance of the sign of the cross and curtsy is a little fuzzy. Lighting of candles is something that the Catholics share in common with the Taoists, Buddhists and Hindus, who light oil lamps and incense sticks.

The Chinese Taoist worshipper is not to be outdone in the matter of worship "form". He or she will purchase a handful of fragrant joss sticks and light them up. They will hold the handles with both hands at about chest height and wave them back and forth before the deity with wrist motion. Then they'll pinch a few sticks and stick it in the brass urn in front of the idol. The process continues until they have appeased all of the idols in the temple.

The Muslims not only observe the congregational Friday worship, they also pray five times a day either individually or in groups. The worship includes a sermon or *khutbah*. It is preceded or followed by a series of standing, bowing, kneeling, touching forehead to ground, etc. This constitutes the *ruku* (bowing) and *sujud* (obeisance/bow low kow-tow). Occasionally, one might espy a someone in a skullcap with a pronounced dark mark on his forehead, and decide it is from systematic sujud. There is a group of bare bodied Saivites in Jaffna, who have prominent humps on their necks. They will explain that as due to carrying the Lord's palanquin (litter) across their shoulders.

In summary, the Christian bows his head while standing upright.The Taoist slightly tilts from the hips, and waves josssticks. The Catholic goes on his knees. The Muslim drops to his knees and bows low (sujud) so that his forehead touches the floor. The Hindu sometimes outdoes them all, as he prostrates himself on his stomach, stretching his arms towards the altar. It is all in the worship of the Almighty.

The Hindu, sometimes outdoes everybody, when s/he circumambulates the temple. Circumambulation (*Angapradakshinam*) is rolling your soaked body like a log, around the temple's periphery, arms stretched forward. In the process, the devotee hits all the cardinal directions and degrees of the compass, and heaven too, as she faces the sky on the upturn. What happens when she is on the downturn? Is she facing hell, then? It is a silly thought, but whatever the direction one faces, anyone would agree that what is paramount, is the state of mind of the believer. Whether it is sham or sincere.

Circumambulation is circular motion, and everone does it. The Hindu walks around the shrine of the deity, imagining himself a planet circling the sun. The Muslims circumambulate en mass during the *Tawaf* or circling the Kaaba seven times. The Catholic priest circles the altar while waving an incense emitting censer. On Good Friday, they go in procession around the cathedral waving palm leaves, recollecting Jesus's entry into Jerusalem. Jews perform the *Hakafah* ("to circle" in Hebrew) at the end of the Sukkot festival. Zen Buddhism has the *Jundo*. In Sikhism, the *Lavan Pheras,* where a wedding couple circle the Guru Granth Sahib four times to readings from the scripture. The Hindu couple circles the fire seven times (*Saptapadi*) on their wedding.

As to where they face when praying, The Muslim faces Mecca, where the Kaabah is. It is said that before Mecca became the direction of prayer (*qiblat*), the prophet faced Jerusalem, as the Jews did. When you are in Mecca, you could could possibly face any direction, standing in the square as long as facing the Kaabah. The Hindu and Taoist face the idol of the deity wherever it is placed. Although, Hindu temples, by design, are built in the direction of the rising sun, the devotee in the temple will face west towards the deity. In those days of no electricity, the rising sun lit up the temple and provided some positive energy. The Christian, when s/he prays, does so vertically, that is, heavenwards. Eventhough he may face in any direction, his mind is directed vertically.

Ritual Washing: Wuduk, Snaanam, Baptism, Ching Jing

Wudu(k) is the Islamic act of bodily cleansing as a sign of purity, before prayers. Though the Koran mentions (2: 222) that God loves one who is *"clean and pure"*, Muhammad said that, *"cleanliness is half of faith."* The actual details of the act (of ablution) are from the Hadiths. The finer details vary with each Madhhab (denomination). As a Muslim mentally prepares for prayer and does the wudu, s/he follows these steps:

1. Washing the face
2. Washing both arms from the tips of the fingers up to and including the elbows

3. Wiping the head. However, there is a difference of opinion on the sufficient portion.
4. Washing both the feet up to and including the ankles.

While Hindus practice ritual cleansing before weddings, after deaths, bathing of deities, they also bathe before going to the temple. However brahmins, especially the priests among them, undergo more rigourous and ritualistic cleansings. It would be ideal if there is a flowing river nearby and inimitable if it happens to be the ganges itself. Occasional pilgrims (*thirtha yatra* – sacred river pilgrimage) and once-in-12 years (*kumbha melas)* witness masses dipping and dunking in the Ganges etc.

The Christian way of cleansing is baptism, which happens only once in a person'e life. It is not for cleaning physical dirt, but as a sign of being inducted into the *koinonia* – faith community. The Catholics do baptism by sprinkling on the forehead of the newborn, whence it is given a name. True baptism, according to the Greek meaning (*baptizo*), is dunking the entire body under water (signifyng burial to the old life) and emerging from it (signifying entering the new new life/rebirth).

It doesn't have to be water that purifies. Apparentlty the Koran exempts desert dwellers from water wudu and allows clean sand as cleanser. Other religions make no mention of other media.

The hangup on ritual cleanliness is based on the fear that the divine cannot endure uncleanness – which can include anything from soiled clothing, to menstruating women, to being of an outcast group, etc. these are all physical aspects but strangely, the divine looks not at the outward flesh but the inward spirit of the believer. The New Testament (Matthew. 5: 8) says, *"Blessed are the pure in heart: for they shall see God.*

This is one of the conundrums in the practice of religion. While the Bible, in another of the *beatitudes* (Matthew 5: 5) says, *"Blessed are the meek, for they shall inherit the earth"*, Popes and Cardinals, dress like Lords and live in gilded palaces. Similarly, while the Hindu sincerely believes that life in his hereafter depends on his conduct in the here and now, yet feels compelled to stomp on his fellow man as unclean and below his dignity. Does anyone notice the glaring dissonance between belief and being? Between talk and walk? Between hallowed and hollow, between dinkum and bunkum, between pukka and put-on and so on and so on?

The Taoist cleansing *Ching* ("clearing") *Jing* (purifying") is mental rather than physical. *"To clear, you must REMOVE what is there that is unwanted".* To purify is to be, "Aligned with the Tao, it is then positive and good for you. When energy is aligned, evils are gone, impurities are gone, you will change to become more positive" – Tin Jee, Tin Yat Dragon Blog.

Mirroring the Taoist Ching/Jing, is the secular Tamil tome, Thirukkural (1ˢᵗ Century AD). Kural 341 i.e, *Yaadhanin Yaadhanin Neengiyaan, Nodhal Adhanin Adhanin Ilan.* Translation: "Whatsoever it is you detach yourself from, that will never distress you." Even closer to Ching Jing's "Remove the unwanted", is the common Tamil saying, "The sculptor must chisel away the unwanted bits before the (shiny) statue can reveal itself."

Wow. Talk about internal cleansing rather the outward. In Matthew 23: 26, Jesus scolds, "You blind Pharisee, first clean the inside of the cup and of the dish, so that the outside of it may become clean also". Allah says: "He has succeeded who purifies the soul, and he has failed who corrupts the soul." (Quran, 91: 9-10). The Yoga-Sutra of Patanjali (2: 41) describes Shaucha (cleanliness) thus: *"Shaucha gives rise to* <u>purity</u> *of mind, contentment, one-pointedness, conquest of the senses and competency to attain Atma-Darshana (Self-Realization)". Note the nexus between the Sanskrit shaucha and the Malay suci (*<u>purity</u>*).*

It must be realized that it is never the fault of religion, but of the human. While religion teaches all the right things, man tends to interpret them as he fancies. Romans 3: 4: "God forbid: yea, let God be true, but every man a liar; ...."

The Fast: Nonbu, Puasa, Bigu, Lent

Fasting was never a religious thing with our hunter-gatherer forebears. They ate when they had a kill or pick. They fasted when it was a lean day. Fasting probably gained significance after they had mastered farming and had stocks. So now they could recall their days of the "fast" or hunger.

Fasting is not obligatory for Hindus, but for health and spiritual purposes. It usually involves abstention from basic urges like food, sex, meat, entertainment, shopping etc. Fasts are done on *Ekadashi*, i.e, the waxing (moonlit) and *Amavasai* (moonless) days of the month. In the months of July and august, they undertake a fast and vegetarian diet until evening.

Women of the Vaishavite denomination also do the *eka paththini viratham* ("fast of the faithful wife") for their husbands. This is in reference to, when Rama refused an offer by Agni Deva to have a second wife, besides Sita. Hindus who prepare for penance on Thaipusam are required to fast (single daily meal) during the entire 10th month of Thai.

During the Muslm holy month of Ramadan, which occurs on the ninth month of the lunar-based Islamic calendar, all able Muslims are required to abstain from food and drink from dawn till dusk for 30 days. Because Ramadan shifts approximately 11 days forwards each year on the solar-based Gregorian calendar, Muslims experience Ramadan in different times of the year. Note: Gregorian calender – 365 days. Islamic calender – 354 days. There is also the confusion on start dates, when some countries start earlier or later than others. Even the in same country, they have many viewing lookouts, so as to get "choice" of options to spot the new moon.

"Some of you may be thinking, 'Wow, that sounds like a great way to lose weight! I'm going to try it!' But in fact, Ramadan is actually notorious for often causing weight *gain*. That's because eating large meals super early in the morning and late at night with a long period of low activity bordering on lethargy in between, can wreak havoc on your metabolism." – google quote

"One meta-analysis of scientific studies on the effects of Ramadan fasting on body weight found that "[w]eight changes during Ramadan were relatively small and mostly reversed after Ramadan, gradually returning to pre-Ramadan status. Ramadan provides an opportunity to lose weight, but structured and consistent lifestyle modifications are necessary to achieve lasting weight loss." – *Islamic fasting and weight loss: a systematic review and meta-analysis* (Public Health Nutr. 2014 Feb).

Iftar and suhur look like epicurean bookends to the long lean time. Even if Ramadan itself does not contribute much to weight gain/loss, there is the 3 three day orgy of open houses and holiday feasts post Aidil-fitri, to account for weight gain. This not a judgement on the fast itself, but on the practice of it. Afterall, the main purpose of fasting is moderation.

"Even though the Taoist fasting method of Bigu claims to have roots more than 2,000 years old, most people in China today are only just now hearing about it. It is suddenly everywhere!"

"In Chinese, "bi" means "stop," and "gu" means "grain." So, literally, bigu means to stop eating grain. Ge Hong wrote the book on Bigu in 320 a.d., *Baopuzi*, which means *Book of the* Master *Who Embraces Simplicity*. In it he wrote:

"I have personally observed for two or three years, men who were foregoing starches, and in general their bodies were slight and their complexions good. They could withstand wind, cold, heat, or dampness, but there was not a fat one among them."

"Bigu students often ingest tea and supplements to help provide them with some nutrients and to bring their qi into balance".

The biblical practice of fasting dates back to the Old Testament, as a spiritual discipline to deepen our communion with God. Today, fasting is still practiced by many Christian denominations and annually observed during the time of Lent in preparation for Easter Sunday.

"Lent is a 40 day period of reflection and prayer to remember the 40 days of Jesus Christ's life in the wilderness. Christians have observed Lent for roughly 2,000 years as a way to praise and memorialize Jesus's death and burial before glorifying His resurrection. One of the central traditions of Lent is fasting, the discipline of abstaining from specific foods or something you enjoy for a set amount of time".

While there are many quotes in the Old and New Testaments of the Bible regarding fasting, there is nothing in there that mentions the so called lent. The Christians in the Bible celebrated the Lord's Supper/Communion during Sunday worship, to celebrate Christs's resurrection. So the fourty day lent is an entirely fabricated tradition of man. So it is, with the celebration of Christmas, which is neither mentioned nor obligated. Human's may be forgiven their over-zealousness in wanting to honor the almighty through the creation of extra-biblical holidays and acts of piety. But, to call a spade a spade, the world should know that these are, but traditions of man.

Sleepless in Spiritual: Midnight Mass, Malam qiamullail, Vaikunda Ekadasi

Midnight mass is celebrated on the eve of Christmas, by the so-called High Churches, of Catholicism, Methodism, Anglicanism, Lutheranism and any other ism out there. They mirror the shepherds who gathered to await the birth of Jesus Christ. Whereas, watchnight services are prevalently celebrated by African American Christians on New Year's eve. *"It symbolizes the historical fact, that on the night of Dec. 31, 1862 during the Civil War, free and freed blacks living in the Union States gathered at churches and/or other safe spaces, while thousands of their enslaved black sisters and brothers stood, knelt and prayed on plantations and other slave holding sites in America – waiting for President Abraham Lincoln to sign the Emancipation Proclamation into law"*. While the former awaited the birth of Christ, the latter anticipated the birth of a new dawn for the race.

Certainly, when you excitedly look forward to a great event, losing sleep is of no consequence. Remember your wedding day, award, flight, vacation, meeting a loved one etc?

Waking up nights and standing in prayer is known as *qiammullail* in Islam. Most direct references to it are in the Hadith. Qiammullail is usually observed during Ramadhan, after the usual prayers and tarawih (long readings of the Quran, after Isyak prayers). The time of it is not specified – it could continue after midnight.

A special qiamullail is *Lailatul Qadar*, honouring the day the Quran descended from heaven during Ramadhaan. It is recommended to observe the Lailatul Qadar in the mosque, and starting from 12 pm do the *tajahud* (8 rakaat – sets), and *witir* (3 rakaat).

If it seems like a lot of work, look at the payback. The prophet is said have said,*"Allah likes one second spent on Qadar night, more than a year of fasting." "He likes one verse of the Quran read on Qadar night, better than an entire reading on other nights." "Whosoever does qiamullail on Ramadhaan with faith and anticipating reward will be forgiven all his previous sins."*(Hadith Bukhari dan Muslim).

In Taoist culture, the hungry ghost season (Zhongyuan Festival) begins at midnight on the fifteenth day of the seventh month in the lunar calendar, whence the denizens of the underworld return to the upper world for their annual visit. The day is called the Ghost Day and the seventh month in general is regarded as the Ghost Month. People leave out food for them to feed on, especially the orphaned or lost ones. Having no living relatives to remember them, naturally they are hungry. We presume the whole affair would be a kind of midnight thing, followed by the days.

Ekadasis are overnight wakes observed during the waxing (full moon) and waning (new moon) periods of the month. It is associated with Vishnu, who loves those days. The days are observed with fasts, especially fruits, and carbohydrates are avoided. Observers are blessed with better health, peace of mind, happiness and redemption from malefic planetary influences.

Vaikunda ekadasi is a special ekadasi on the the 11th lunar day of the fortnight of the waxing moon in the month of *margazhi* (late December till early January). Vaikundam is the abode of Vishnu and on this day *Vaikuntha Vaasal*, 'The Gates of Vaikuntam' are believed to open. You may enter therein and access the Lord's feet, *Parama Patham*. Naturally, you can only do this in spirit, as access to parama patham is only at death.

My only childhood recollection of vaikunda ekadasi is, of the double matinee at the Mido Theater in Sentul, across from the Methodist Boys' School. Theaters ran two consecutive Tamil movies (for the price of one), beginning with a late night show. I couldn't endure the vigil and would fall asleep sitting, to be be roused at dawn by my Hindu companions.

This midnight madness is not limited to a certain type of religious act. There is an even widespread religious fervour – that of sports. Soccer World Cup livecasts especially, will have diehard fans staying up late to root for their teams. Naturally, you don't want to hear of the exciting moments from your friends the next day. You want to get in your own two cents worth of play by play of the game. So, you might force yourself to stay up. A game starting at 6.00 PM in London would be 2.00 AM in KL.

Generally, most Malaysians sit up and wait for the birth of a new year, driven by an eagerness for welcoming something new. Something to forget and say goodbye to. A change of some sort. Media writeups and commentaries on the events of the past year summarize its positives and negatives. The same media also brings out Nostradamus and Baba Vanga out of year old dust, to highlight their predictions for the new year. Astrologers gaze into their glass globes and gush their gassy gossipy guessings at their gullible goons grasping at scraps of glad tidings. But the common man just wants that closure at midnight.

Futures Trading: Bank of Hell currency, Indulgence, 72 Virgins, Pindam

The spiritual focus of religion, be that as it may, some practices or understandings of it seem to have a physical skew.

The inter – galactic forex trading is worth bezillions daily. Taoists burn currency notes valued from 10,000 to 10 billion $ (!) as a form of direct deposit into the other worldly bank accounts of the deceased. The notes *"usually bear an image of the Jade Emperor, the presiding monarch of heaven in Taoism (Yu Wong, or Yuk Wong) and the signature of Yanluo, King of Hell (Yen Loo)".*

The Taoist idea of hell (Diyu) is not like the western one, but a place of purgatory where the naughty one gets judged and atones his sins. Indeed, there is a belief that burning real money brings good luck in the present.

The bank notes are a modern iteration of the joss paper. Heaven imitates earth.

"Despite the disclaimer by some Muslims, the truth is very clear. The *72 Virgins* notion has its origins in the Qurʾan. Although the holy book does not specify the number as 72, it does say that those who fight in the way of Allah and are killed will be given a great reward. It goes on to stipulate that Muslims will be awarded with women in Islamic heaven. It even describes their physical attributes—large eyes (Q 56: 22) and big, firm, round "swelling breasts" that are not inclined to sagging (Q 78: 33). The Qurʾan refers to these virgins as houri, companions of equal age, but the highly-flavored emphasis of their bodily characteristics, including their virginity, gave rise to many hadiths and other Islamic writings".

"Hadith 2687 is where the number 72 is mentioned. *"The smallest reward for the people of Heaven is an abode where there are eighty thousand servants and 72 houri, over which stands a dome decorated with pearls, aquamarine and ruby, as wide as the distance from al-Jabiyyah to San'a."*
– Avi Perry, 06/26/2010

These are in the context of *shaheed* (martyrdom) during *Jihad* (Holy war). Groups like Hamas, Al-Qaeda, and ISIS are known to use these promises as draws in the recruiting of new members. So, heaven in an earthly fashion.

The Catholic world went through a spell in the Middle Ages, when the clergy offered *indulgences,* temporary/partial forgiveness from the effects of sin while alive. To get complete forgiveness in the hereafter, one had to turn over a new leaf. To get the indulgence, the believer could pay a sum (sounds like a bail?) to the priest.

These days, the pope (not God), still enforces the indulgence. Only, no money is exchanged, but you secure indulgence by doing things like prayers, charity, penance, spiritual retreats, etc. etc. *"On 20 March 2020, the Apostolic Penitentiary issued three plenary indulgences. The first indulgence was for victims of COVID-19 and those helping them. The actions that the indulgence was attached to included praying the rosary, the Stations of the Cross, or at least praying the Creed, Lord's Prayer, and a Marian prayer"*. In short, it's a quid pro quo, a barter trade.

The hindu system, without saying, is chock full of such human made transactions, called *parihaaram* (remedies). These are usually in the context of astrology, when you do certain physical acts (breaking coconuts, fasting etc) to remove *doshams* (afflictions due to negative planetary alignments). Hindus also prepare *pindam* (balls) of rice, ghee and black sesame seeds, which they feed to (only) crows which are said to represent their deceased ancestors (*pithru*). The pithrus bless them accordingly. Of course, the Hindu and Buddhist system of rebirth promises an upgrade to higher life-form, for the life lived in the present.

Mormonism, which Christians consider a cultic moronism, has this thing called proxy baptism for the dead. It is an indefensible concept that a dead person's soul can be saved merely by someone else standing in for the baptism. It is a souped up version of the Catholic prayer for a departed soul. You would assume that when a soul "crosses over", there is no "reset" button.

Heaven: Tian Tang, Jannah, Paralokam

The Chinese concept of heaven is that of being, rather than of a place or idea. It is depicted in modern Chinese writing as well as in the oracle bone script (1000+ BCE) as a stick figure. All teachers from Confucius, Lao Tzu, to Mencius talk of heaven in those terms. Hence, a clear picture of heaven as a place is not forthcoming, unlike the detailed aspects of hell (Diyu).

"Confucius honored Heaven as the supreme source of goodness:

The Master said, "Great indeed was Yao as a sovereign! How majestic was he! It is only Heaven that is grand, and only Yao corresponded to it. How vast was his virtue! The people could find no name for it. How majestic was he in the works which he accomplished! How glorious in the elegant regulations which he instituted!" (VIII, xix, tr. Legge 1893: 214)

While the Chinese concept of heaven is as a creative personality, the Hindu heaven is depicted in terrestrial terms.

"Attaining heaven is not the final pursuit in Hinduism as heaven itself is ephemeral and related to physical body. Only being tied by the bhoot-tatvas, heaven cannot be perfect either and is just another name for pleasurable and mundane material life. According to Hindu cosmology, above the earthly plane, are other planes: (1) Bhuva Loka, (2) Swarga Loka, meaning Good Kingdom, is the general name for heaven in Hinduism, a heavenly paradise of pleasure, where most of the Hindu Devatas (Deva) reside along with the king of Devas, Indra, and beatified mortals. Some other planes are Mahar Loka, Jana Loka, Tapa Loka and Satya Loka. Since heavenly abodes are also tied to the cycle of birth and death, any dweller of heaven or hell will again be recycled to a different plane and in a different form per the karma and "maya" i.e. the illusion of Samsara. This cycle is broken only by self-realization by the Jivatma. This self-realization is Moksha (Turiya, Kaivalya).

The concept of moksha is unique to Hinduism. Moksha stands for liberation from the cycle of birth and death and final communion with Brahman. With moksha, a liberated soul attains the stature and oneness with Brahman or Paramatma. Different schools such as Vedanta, Mimansa, Sankhya, Nyaya, Vaisheshika, and Yoga offer subtle differences in the concept of Brahman, obvious Universe, its genesis and regular destruction, Jivatma, Nature (Prakriti) and also the right way in attaining perfect bliss or moksha.

In the Vaishnava traditions the highest heaven is Vaikuntha, which exists above the six heavenly lokas and outside of the mahat-tattva or mundane world. It›s where eternally liberated souls who have attained moksha reside in eternal sublime beauty with Lakshmi and Narayana (a manifestation of Vishnu).

In the Nasadiya Sukta, the heavens/sky Vyoman is mentioned as a place from which an overseeing entity surveys what has been created. However, the Nasadiya Sukta questions the omniscience of this overseer." – Wikipedia.

The Christian construct of heaven is a non-physical space (kingdom of God) where the throne of God is. It is a place every Christian desires to go after the judgment. Since God is a spirit and everyone there, including angels and the arrivals from earth will be spirits, there won't be any shade of the earthly. As Jesus Christ says, in the resurrected state people, *"neither marry nor are given in marriage ….. for they are like angels"* (Luke 20: 34-36). Even if heaven sounds boring, with no earthly pleasures, the Bible promises a beautiful experience, that the human mind can't yet imagine. Phillippians 4: 7, speaks of a *".. peace that passeth* [surpasses/transcends] *understanding"*. The streets are paved with gold (figurative), and the only activity mentioned, is non stop praise of the almighty. There are no hierarchies of heavenly experience, as the saved are all on the super deluxe ticket.

In contrast, the Islamic heaven *Jannah*, is described thus: *"The afterlife experiences are described as physical, psychic and spiritual. Jannah is described with physical pleasures such as gardens, houris, wine that does not make drunk, and "divine pleasure". Their reward of pleasure will vary according to the righteousness of the person. The characteristics of Jannah often have direct parallels with those of Jahannam (hell). The pleasure and delights of Jannah described in the Quran, are matched by the excruciating pain and horror of Jahannam. Both Jannah and Jahannam are believed to have several levels, in both cases, the higher the level, the more desirable in Jannah the higher the prestige and pleasure, in Jahannam, the less the suffering."* – Wikipedia.

Hell: Paathaalam, Hell, Jahannam, Diyu

The hindu hell is called Paathaalam. i.e, seven levels or realms of it underground. These realms are each ruled by demons and nagas. These have no specific stated purposes, except as communities of the individual demons and nagas. *"The lowest realm is called Patalam or Nagalokam, the region of the Nagas, ruled by Vasuki. Here live several Nagas with many hoods. Each of their hood is decorated by a jewel, whose light illuminates this realm"*. Sheshan, the serpentine *vahanam* (vehicle) of Vishnu is also said to live here.

Below the regions of Patalam, lies *narakam/yamalokam*, the Hindu Hell – the realm of death where sinners are punished. This is the abode of *Yama Dharmaraja*, judge and enforcer of punishments. The *Manu Smriti* mentions 21 hells, or cell blocks, each for sins like bestialty, taking another's property/wife, cooking animals alive (will be cooked in boiling oil), pride, alcoholism, incest, corruption etc. Unlike the monotheistic religions, narakam is a temporary state (recyling unit), before the rebirth.

The hell of the Bible, while described in physical terms ("lake of fire") is more likely to be symbolic, spiritual, or a state of mind, just like the biblical heaven. As 2 Thessalonians 2: 9 says, *"eternal destruction = separation from the presence God and His glory."* Those who have been separated from their loved ones, can relate to it as the most painful of sufferings. So what is more excruciating than a living, emotional hell? Psychological hell? There is no processing unit, holding cell, appellate court, or degrees of conviction. Once consigned, might as well be resigned to it.

In the Taoist tradition, 10 courts are mentioned, and 18 hells. All will go to Diyu ("earth prison") after death but the period of time one spends in Diyu is not forever – it depends on the severity of the sins one committed. After receiving due punishment, one will eventually be sent for reincarnation.

"The 18 hells vary from narrative to narrative but some commonly mentioned tortures include: being steamed; being fried in oil cauldrons; being sawed into half; being run over by vehicles; being pounded in a mortar and pestle; being ground in a mill; being crushed by boulders; being made to shed blood by climbing trees or mountains of knives; having sharp objects driven into their bodies; having hooks pierced into their bodies and being hung upside down; drowning in a pool of filthy blood; being left naked in the freezing cold; being set aflame or cast into infernos; being tied naked to a bronze cylinder with a fire lit at its base; being forced to consume boiling liquids; tongue ripping; eye gouging; teeth extraction; heart digging; disembowelment; skinning; being trampled, gored, mauled, eaten, stung, bitten, pecked, etc., by animals". Whew! anything left out? Seems right out of a horror film script.

"Punishment and suffering in hell in mainstream Islam, is physical, psychological and spiritual, and varies according to the sins of the condemned person. Its excruciating pain and horror described in the Quran often parallels the pleasure and delights of heaven (*Jannah*). It is commonly believed by Muslims that confinement to hell is temporary for Muslims but not for others, and Muslim scholars disagree over whether hell itself will last for eternity (the mainstream view), or whether God's mercy will lead to it eventually being eliminated".

The common belief among Muslims holds that *Jahannam* (corresponding to the Hebrew, *ge-hinnom*) coexists with the temporal world, just as Jannah (the Islamic heaven) does, rather than being created after Judgement Day. Hell is described physically in different ways by different sources of Islamic literature. It is enormous in size, and located below heaven. It has seven levels (each one more severe than the one above it), (the Quran specifically refers to "seven gates"); but it is also said to be a huge pit over which the bridge of As-Sirāt crosses and the resurrected walk; to have mountains, rivers, valleys and "even oceans" filled with disgusting fluids; and also to be able to walk (controlled by reins), and ask questions, much like a sentient being".

Hell is described as being located below heaven, having seven gates and "for every gate there shall be a specific party" of sinners (Q.15: 43-44).

1. *Jahannam* was reserved for Muslims who had committed grave sins.
2. *al-Laza* (the blaze) for the Jews
3. *al-Hutama* (the consuming fire) for the Christians
4. *al-Sa'ir* for the Sabaeans
5. *al-Saqar* (the scorching fire) for the Zoroastrians
6. *al-jahim* (the hot place) for the idolaters
7. *al-Hawiya* (the abyss) for the hypocrites.

"The common belief among Muslims (as indicated above) is that duration in hell is temporary for Muslims but not for others. And also the issue of whether People of the Book, are a variety of believer or unbelievers destined for hell. In two places in the Quran, almost identical verses seem to indicate they are saved:

'Surely those who believe, and those who are Jews, and the Christians, and the Sabians, whoever believes in Allah and the Last day and does good, they shall have their reward from their Lord, and there is no fear for them, nor shall they grieve" (Q.2: 62; cf. 5: 69)'

Warrior gods: Madurai Veeran, General Wu, Datuk Keramat

The Hindu pantheon of gods and goddesses is similar to that of the Greeks, Romans, and Vikings. They all have voluminous convoluted tales and mythologies about the exploits of their gods. This unity is perhaps related to the Indo-Aryan speaking Aryans originating closer to Europe. The Tamil folk religion finds a parallel in Chinese religion. Taoism does not have complex hierarchies of gods, leaders of gods, gods begetting gods, and gods warring with each other. However, there is much commonality and similarity between Chinese mythology and the Tamil folk belief system, which is non-brahminical and entirely Dravidian or South Indian.

For one, Chinese and Tamil folk beliefs subscribe to the concept of hero worship, literally. That is to say, humans who attained the status of folk diety through bravery, chivalry and glory.

Tamil folk (village) gods such as Madurai Veeran ("hero of Madurai city"), Ayyanar, Karuppasamy, and Muneeswarar (Muniandy), began their incarnations as war heroes. After a hero fell in battle, people set up memorial rocks (nadukkal) and commemorated them on their death annivesaries. In time, they evolved into religious icons. They are often depicted as fierce looking warriors with bulging eyes on horseback or standing upright, and carrying executioner'sswords (*aruvaal*).

All the above deities are considered boundary gods who do their midnight rounds (*Oor Kaaval = Village Protection*) at the village borders. Their shrines are also located at the edges of villages. Their statues are in open space. Not in buildings. Praying and offering puja to them brings protection and peace to the village. Unlike the Vedic Hindu gods who receive flowers, the folk gods are offered animal sacrifice or meat and blood, and toddy, a natural alcoholic beverage tapped from the coconut flower. Muniandy is often depicted with cheroot (Tamil: *Suruttu = "to roll", or "rolled")* in hand.

Now, the ending, Eeswaran as in Muneeswaran, Parameswaran etc is common to names of male gods. Eeswaran means "lord" or "god". Eeswari denotes the lady. Parameswaran means Parama (almighty) plus Easwaran (lord) "almighty lord".

The Chinese god, General Wu, is comparatively similar to Madurai Veeran and company. In fact in Malaysian Chinese shrines, Toaist and Tamil dieties often share space, as "Datuks" who dole out lottery numbers. General Wu's mythology tells that he was an unremorseful butcher of animals, and later had an epiphany that turned him into a benefactor. He is portrayed as a fierce looking, red faced, black bearded, bulging eyed warrior with a sword-like spear, or an executioner's sword attached to a pole.

He is sometimes shown with two of his aides, General Wan Gong and General Ma, who handle local issues like childbirth, medication, family matters, as well as feng shui consultation. General Wu is known by other names, such as Luan Wu aka dark Lord of the North or the Lord of True Martiality, or True Warrior, or The Kong in Hokkien. The Malay culture does not have a warrior god per se, as Islam is a monotheistic faith. If they had such a god in the old days, it has long since disappeared from consciousness. If there is any surviving concept similar to the warrior gods of the Chinese and Indians, it may be the Datuk Keramat.

The religious belief of the *Datuk Keramat* worship can be found in Malaysia, Singapore and along the Straits of Malacca. It is a fusion of pre-Islamic spirit belief, Sufi saint worship and Chinese folk religion.

According to local Malay legend, all Datuks were once human and were considered the "Forefathers of The Land" and may sometimes be also known as the "Spirit of The Land" as the locals would call them. They may sometimes be referred to as semangat (spirit).

Around the Malaysian countryside some small, red painted shrines by the roadside or under a tree can be found, and these shrines are usually worshipped by the residents living around the neighbourhood. The shrines are normally of a fusion Chinese-Malay design, with Islamic elements such as the crescent moon decorations. Inside the simple room, a small, decorated statue is venerated, depicting the datuk. Around the statue offerings are brought, sometimes on a small altar in front of the datuk statue.

It is believed that there are a total of nine types of Datuks, and that each of them were once great warriors and expert in Malay local martial arts, the *Silat,* except for the last Datuk. They were also known to possess great magical powers. Worshippers usually pray to Datuks for protection, good health, and good luck, and sometimes seek divine help to overcome their problems.

Worshippers, almost always Chinese, usually offer fresh flowers, *sireh* (betel leaves), *rokok daun* (local hand rolled cigarettes), sliced *pinang* (areca nuts) and local fruits. An important part of the praying ritual is also to burn some *kemenyan* (benzoin – made of a local gum tree, when burnt will emit a smoky fragrance).

If their prayers are answered, the worshippers usually return to the shrine and make offerings or hold a *Kenduri* (feast).

The kenduri items usually consist of yellow saffron rice, lamb or chicken curries, vegetables, *pisang rastali* (Manazana bananas), young coconuts, rose syrup, *cheroots* (local cigars) and local fruits. Below are the nine Datuks named according to their seniority from the eldest to the youngest:

1. *Datuk Panglima Ali* (Ali)
2. *Datuk Panglima Hitam* (Black)
3. *Datuk Panglima Harimau* (Tiger)
4. *Datuk Panglima Hijau* (Green)
5. *Datuk Panglima Kuning* (Yellow)
6. *Datuk Panglima Putih* (White)
7. *Datuk Panglima Bisu* (Mute)
8. *Datuk Panglima Merah* (Red)
9. *Datuk Panglima Bongsu* (Youngest)

Pork items are considered impure and are therefore totally forbidden in a shrine; visitors are also asked to not show disrespect when inside or around a shrine.

In Taman Sentosa's Jalan Raja Nong, in Klang, one notices a red Chinese shrinette in front of a tree that is draped in yellow cloth. The resident datuk is obviously Chinese, wearing a flowing snowy beard (with centre parting) and white brows. He wears a typical Chinese nobleman's robe and headgear. Crowding the limited space are containers with constantly fuming joss sticks, water with a kalamansi lime in it. There is also a banana bunch. The datuk wears a jasmine garland (the Indian flavour). On the roof of the shrine, a plastic nameplate is attached, that reads: Dato Haji Hassan Musa Hitam. That is the Malay aspect.

Mother Goddess: Kuan Yin, Amman, Ibu Pertiwi

Another similarity between Chinese and Tamil folk deities is the concept of the mother goddess. Kuan Yin is a goddess venerated by the Buddhists as Bodhisatva (Buddha form). In the Taoist tradition she is known as an "Immortal", one of eight in Chinese mythology. Her full name is Guan Shi Yin meaning, "observing the sounds (or cries) of the world." Hence her title, "Goddess of Mercy". She is also known as the "Queen Mother of the West".

The Tamil form of the mother goddess is the "Amman" from Amma (Mother), a manifestation of Parvathi, w/o Sivaa. Many of the Hindu temples in Malaysia are devoted to the different manifestations of the Amman. Mariamman (Mari = rain, symbolizing small pox) is the commonest. Spite her, and she'll rain the pox on you! She supposedly cures smallpox and other heat caused diseases like rashes, and her cure is the Veppilai or Neem leaf. You wont miss a neem tree in an Indian home. If you come across an anthill that looks like it has had some ceremony done to it, chances are some mariamman devotee considers it sacred ground. The anthill is believed to be the abode of the sacred snake, messenger of Mariamman.

Kaliamman (black Amman, or Bhadra Kali, or Durga) is a vengeful goddess indeed. You don't want to upset her with stupid actions. The forms of Amman also include the Draupadi, Isakki, Pidari, Kateri and Karumari Ammans.

"These Amman manisfestations are protectors of the downtrodden, and human rights abusers beware. The Tamil classics of the Sangam age refer to her as Kotravai, a war goddess worshipped by soldiers before going into war. The Telugus, a South Indian sub-group, have their equivalent in Jakkamma. She is Yellamma in Karnataka state. The Malayalees have their Bhagavati Amma. In the vedic religion the equivalent are the three Devis, spouses of the Hindu trinity (Devas/Murthis) who are Brahma, Shiva and Vishnu. Brahma's wife Sarasvati, Shiva's wife Parvati, and Vishnus's wife Lakshmi, make up the female trinity known in Tamil as *Moondru Deviyar* (three Devis) or *Mupperum Deviyar* (Three Great Devis). Don't confuse these Moondru Devis for Moodevi. It is a reference to a shrewish, unruly female.

The Roman Catholics have a form of Mother Goddess, though not strictly in the sense we are discussing. Mary, whom they worship as the "Mother of God", supposedly acts as a conduit to approach Jesus Christ. This concept is considered to be blasphemous by other Christians. Before jumping to any conclusion that they are assigning a higher status to her than to God himself, I shall try to parse it as a literal understanding of the Bible. You see, the book portrays Jesus Christ as an aspect/facet of the Almighty. Mary is the birth mother of Jesus. Hence Mary, the mother of God. Mary was actually the mother of the human Jesus, not of Christ the divine aspect.Therefore, there is no mother Goddess or mother of God, in the real sense.

The Malay community, having long shed Hinduism and put on Islam, have nothing whatsoever to do with gods and goddesses. Some vestiges of mother goddess honoring may yet be seen in the usage of the term *Ibu Pertiwi* (Mother Earth). It is the personification of Indonesia, and the East Malaysian state of Sarawak, whose state anthem is Ibu Pertiwi. The early inhabitants of Indonesia/Malaysia hallowed the earth as mother. With the coming of Hindu influences at the beginning of the Christian Era, mother earth took the name Ibu Pertiwi from Sanskrit *Prithvi*, (mother goddess of the earth). Countries, except for Nazi Germany, have always been considered as motherlands, and languages as mother tongues.

(Sathia) − "Since prehistoric times, worship of the Mother Goddess in many forms was the standard practice in many cultures. It still continues in some cultures especially in Asia.

For example there are similarities between the Goddess *Ma Tsu* (Chinese) and Goddess *Mariamman* (Tamil), both of whom are Goddesses of the Sea. In Indian traditional culture, *Mariamman* is one of the numerous forms of *Amman*, the Supreme Mother of all beings in the universe".

Saints: Wali, Xian, Siddhar

Malaysian Hindus are increasingly tending to worship human beings who have exhibited great holiness, spirituality, and poverty. It is a natural progression from the worship of handmade objects and animals (snake, rat and cows). You hear of people increasingly making pilgrimages to these "holy men", both living and dead. Satya Sri Sai Baba (deceased), Shreedi Sai Baba (deceased), and Raaghavendra Swamy (deceased), are some of these. Then there are those who go to the Himalayan foothills to seek blessings from the sadhus, yogis, and hermits residing there.

It seems that Hindus are not the only ones adhering to this practice. The Taoist have always worshipped their ancestors. But, that is more a reverence than actual worship.

The Roman Catholics have an ever expanding list of saints whom they pray to, or, at least use as intermediaries. The most important of their saints is Mary, whom they consider the "mother of God." And then there is Joseph, her husband, the 12 apostles and early church leaders. Every year, the Pope unveils the latest inductees into the hall of sainthood. Each saint is assigned some special area of need. For instance, you will find Catholics wearing a coin with the figure of St. Christopher, the patron saint of travellers. No, it does not refer to Christopher Columbus, the great maritime traveller. You pray to St. Jude, if you want to overcome desperate cases and lost causes. Mother Theresa is now Saint Theresa.

Among the Muslims, there is a group who subscribe to praying at the graves of holy men (the alim) known as Wali. Especially among Indian Muslims, is the practice of building shrines to the deceased and regular praying there. In india, these are called *dargah*. The Malay equivalent is *keramat*. There is a famous one on Pulau Besar ("Big Island") off Malacca. Growing up in Sentul, in what used to be Kampung Puah, there was one such popular dargah just behind my grandparents' house. The place still exists. It was known as the *Thanggacchi-amma (little sister/mother)* kovil. Apparently, the two mounds there were of a mother and daughter. We just assumed. I was witness to the annual feast that the Indian Muslims held there. The highlights were prayers and chants, a *qawwali* (Persian influenced vocal music) concert, and the best part, ghee rice cooked in large aluminum *andaas* (cauldrons). The heavenly aroma of the rice, as it was prepared, is not a thing to be forgotten. While the celebrants feasted, the neighbourhood scrambled for the packed rice. Ours was delivered directly to the house.

On the theme of human shrines, the mother of them all is the Taj Mahal. Of course, it was built and still stands for, worship of a different kind: human L-O-V-E. When you are emotionally and intellectually drawn to another person, I suppose worship is unavoidable – hero/heroine worship, that is. From there, it is a short step to worshipping the person as deity. My question is not aimed at the devotee, but at the so called holy man. Why does he accept that kind of devotion, instead of forbidding the practice. Wouldn't that make them equal to the Hitlers of history, who basked in the glow of hero worship?

However, holy men, ascetics, saints who have lived in the past, and whose influence still lives in the present have earned their adoration. Many of them would have refused to receive that adulation, but who could stop humans from doing what they want to or are wont to do?

The Chinese, needless to say, have a devotion to ancestors. They also have a hagiography of old sainted people, the *Xian*. Chief among them are the Eight Immortals, the *Baxian*.

Xian semantically developed from meaning spiritual "immortality; enlightenment", to physical "immortality; longevity" involving methods such as alchemy, breath meditation, and tai chi chuan, and eventually to legendary and figurative "immortality".

Victor H. Mair describes the xian archetype as:

"They are immune to heat and cold, untouched by the elements, and can fly, mounting upward with a fluttering motion. They dwell apart from the chaotic world of man, subsist on air and dew, are not anxious like ordinary people, and have the smooth skin and innocent faces of children. The transcendents live an effortless existence that is best described as spontaneous. They recall the ancient Indian ascetics and holy men known as rishi who possessed similar traits." (1994: 376) Śūraṅgama Sūtra

The Śūraṅgama Sūtra, in an approach to Taoist teachings, discusses the characteristics of ten types of xian who exist between the world of devas ("gods") and that of human beings. This position, in Buddhist literature, is usually occupied by asuras ("Titans", "antigods"), but these beings are of another type. These xian are not considered true cultivators of samadhi ("unification of mind"), as their methods differ from the practice of dhyāna ("meditation").

Dìxiān (地(行) 仙; Dìxíng xiān, "earth-travelling immortals") – Xian who constantly ingest special food called fuer (服餌).

Fēixiān (飛(行) 仙; Fēixíng xiān, "flying immortals") – Xian who constantly ingest certain herbs and plants.

Yóuxiān (遊(行) 仙; Yóuxíng xiān, "roaming immortals") – Xian who "transform" by constantly ingesting metals and minerals.

Kōngxiān (空(行) 仙; Kōngxíng xiān, "void-travelling immortals") – Xian who perfect their qi and essence through unceasing movement and stillness (dongzhi 動止).

Tiānxiān (天(行) 仙; Tiānxíng xiān, "heaven-travelling immortals") – Xian who constantly practice control of their fluids and saliva.

Tōngxiān (通(行) 仙; Tōngxíng xiān, "all-penetrating immortals") – Xian who constantly practice the inhalation of unadulterated essences.

Dàoxiān (道(行) 仙; Dàoxíng xiān, "immortals of the Way") – Xian who achieve transcendence through unceasing recitation of spells and prohibitions.

Zhàoxiān (照(行) 仙; Zhàoxíng xiān, "illuminated immortals") – Xian who achieve transcendence through constant periods of thought and recollection.

Jīngxiān (精(行) 仙; Jīngxíng xiān, "seminal immortals") – Xian who have mastered the stimuli and responses of intercourse.

Juéxiān (絕(行) 仙; Juéxíng xiān, "absolute immortals") – Xian who "have attained the end" and perfected their awakening through constant transformation.

"In Tamil Nadu, South India, a siddhar refers to a being who has achieved a high degree of physical as well as spiritual perfection or enlightenment. The ultimate demonstration of this is that siddhars allegedly attained physical immortality. Thus siddhar, refers to a person who has realised the goal of a type of sadhana (detachment) and become a perfected being. The siddha tradition is still practiced there, special individuals are recognized as and called siddhas (or siddhars or cittars) who are on the path to that assumed perfection after they have taken special secret rasayanas (chemicals) to perfect their bodies, in order to be able to sustain prolonged meditation along with a form of pranayama which considerably reduces the number of breaths they take. Siddhars were said to have special powers including flight. These eight powers are collectively known as attamasiddhigal (ashtasiddhi). In Hindu cosmology, Siddhaloka is a subtle world (loka) where perfected beings (siddhas) take birth. They are endowed with the eight primary siddhis at birth". – Wikipedia

The 18 personages in the siddhar hagiography are listed as follows: Agasthiyar, Kamalamuni, Thirumoolar, Kuthambai, Korakkar, Thanvandri, Konganar, Sattamuni, Vanmeegar, Ramadevar, Nandeeswarar (Nandidevar), Edaikkadar, Machamuni, Karuvoorar, Bogar, Pambatti Siddhar, Sundarandandar, Patanjali.

Wali (Arabic: وَلِيّ, walīy; plural أَوْلِيَاء, 'awliyā') is an Arabic word whose literal meanings include "master", "authority", "custodian", "protector" and "friend". In the vernacular, it is most commonly used by Muslims to indicate an Islamic saint, otherwise referred to by the more literal "friend of God". In the traditional Islamic understanding of saints, the saint is portrayed as someone *"marked by [special] divine favor... [and] holiness"*, and who is specifically *"chosen by God and endowed with exceptional gifts, such as the ability to work miracles"*. The doctrine of saints was articulated by Islamic scholars very early on in Muslim history, and particular verses of the Quran and certain hadith were interpreted by early Muslim thinkers as "documentary evidence" of the existence of saints. Graves of saints around the Muslim world became centers of pilgrimage — especially after 1200 CE — for masses of Muslims seeking their barakah (blessing).

Since the first Muslim hagiographies were written during the period when the Islamic mystical trend of Sufism began its rapid expansion, many of the figures who later came to be regarded as the major saints in orthodox Sunni Islam were the early Sufi mystics, like Hasan of Basra (d. 728), Farqad Sabakhi (d. 729), Dawud Tai (d. 777-781), Rabia of Basra (d. 801), Maruf Karkhi (d. 815), and Junayd of Baghdad (d. 910). From the twelfth to the fourteenth century, *"the general veneration of saints, among both people and sovereigns, reached its definitive form with the organization of Sufism into orders or brotherhoods"*. In the common expressions of Islamic piety of this period, the saint was understood to be *"a contemplative whose state of spiritual perfection [found] permanent expression in the teaching bequeathed to his disciples"*. In many prominent Sunni Islamic creeds of the time, such as the famous Creed of Tahawi (c. 900) and the Creed of Nasafi (c. 1000), a belief in the existence and miracles of saints was presented as "a requirement" for being an orthodox Muslim believer.

In the modern world, the traditional Sunni and Shia idea of saints has been challenged by movements such as the Salafi movement, Wahhabism, and Islamic Modernism, all three of which have, to a greater or lesser degree, *"formed a front against the veneration and theory of saints."* As has been noted by scholars, the development of these movements has indirectly led to a trend amongst some mainstream Muslims to resist *"acknowledging the existence of Muslim saints altogether or... [to view] their presence and veneration as unacceptable deviations"*. However, despite the presence of these opposing streams of thought, the classical doctrine of saint-veneration continues to thrive in many parts of the Islamic world today, playing a vital role in daily expressions of piety among vast segments of Muslim populations in Muslim countries." – Wikipedia

In the Turkic Islamic lands, saints have been referred to by many terms, including the Arabic *Walī,* the Persian *S̲h̲āh* and *Pīr*, and Turkish alternatives like *Baba* in Anatolia, *Ata* in Central Asia, *Hazrat* (Urdu).

Schisms: Sunni/Shia, Catholic/Protestant, Shaivite/ Vaishnavite, Theravada/Mahayana

The human embryo grows by the continual division of the initial cell. Do you suppose it also applies to human communities? Adam is now split into multiple races and polities. His religion undergoes binary fission into sects, schisms, splits, splinters, separations and severances

Islam is divided into Sunni (90%), subdivided into Shafie, Wahhabi, and Salafi streams. And then there are Syiah, Ahmaddiyya, Ibadi, Sufi and other minor branches that appear and disappear. As with all religions, they agree in the main points, like the holiness of the Quran, the oneness of Allah, the prophet and his hadith etc. They differ only in the interpretation of the finer points. That is only too human, as we noted in the cell division analogy. It is never about the Almighty or the Scripture, which are infallible. As Romans 3: 4 of the Bible says, "Let God be true and every human being a liar."

Christendom, likewise, is divided into a ton of denominations. The Catholics form the largest block (50%), followed by Protestants (37 %) and the rest made up of Orthodoxies and others. Here again, they all stand united in the concept of one God with three aspects, salvation only through Jesus Christ as the son of God etc. The divisions are based on particular interpretations of certain doctrines. Say, you all love steak, but prefer certains cuts and doneness (medium, rare, medium-rare etc).

The Hindu pantheon is made up of *muppaththu mukkodi devarkal,* or 330,000,000 (330 million) gods, if one takes a literal understanding of the term. Hindus are likely say that *mukkkodi* (30 million) refers to a Sanskrit word meaning "33%". It refers to the ⅓ of human nature that is divine. However, by that token if all humans are ⅓ gods, we have 6 billion partial gods? Anyway, there are many sects in modern Hinduism, beginning from Shaivism (Shiva worship), Vaishnavism (Vishnu worship), Kaumaaram (Murugan), Shaktism (Amman), Ganapathiyam (Ganesha), Smarthism (twice born Brahmins). Shaivism has its own divisions (Veerasaivam, Lingayat, Aghoram, etc). Vaishnavism is, divided too (Vadakalai (northern), Tenkalai (southern), Gaudiya, Rudra etc). Then there are 3 types of gods they have: Ishta deivam (Personal god), Kula deivam (family god), Oor deivam – (Village deity).

Buddhism has broken up into Theravada (Way of the Elders), Mahayana (The Great Vehicle), Vajrayana (Diamond Vehicle), and more. Theravada thrives in Sri Lanka, Thailand, Burma etc. Mahayana is mainstream in China and the Far East. Tibetan buddhism is another class.

The bisections as usual, were due to differences in understanding. After Budhha's time, his disciples gathered a council to formulate the teachings, the *Tripitaka.* A certain group didn't fully buy the teachings. This went on for another four councils under different kings including Asoka. Finally, a king by the name Kanishka, formed two sects. The more numerous group became the Mahayana (great vehicle) and the other the Hinayana (lesser vehicle). Only based on the numerical strength of each. Hinayana were truer to the original and the Mahayana were more liberal. Theravada Buddhism is an offshoot of the Hinayana branch.

"Taoism was formally established at the end of Eastern Han Dynasty (202 BC – 220 AD), with the emergence of *Taiping* Tao and *Wudoumi* Tao as its indication. Apart from the above two sects, other sects such as *Shangqing* (upper clear) and *Lingbao* (quick and precious) also appeared in the Jin Dynasty (265-420) and the Southern and Northern Dynasties (420-581). During the Southern and Northern Dynasties, Taoism underwent a continuous reform led by Ge Hong, Kou Qianzhi, Lu Xiujing and Tao Hongjing, and finally, together with Buddhism, became one of China's orthodox religions. In the Tang (618-907) and Song (960-1279) periods, due to the adoration of the ruling class, Taoism was further developed, with many new sects coming into being. Since the Yuan Dynasty (1271-1368), *Quanzhen* (totally true) Sect and *Zhengyi* (exact one) Sect have gradually become the two main sects of Taoism.

Be that as it may, the Islamic, Christian, Hindu, Buddhist and Taoist sectarians still consider everyone in the group as the Ummah, Koinonia, Mahajanam, Sangha, and dào jiào tuán qì respectively. You may argue among yourselves, but still uphold the main identity. It is like people within a country divided into rival ethnicities, but sign up for conscription against an outside enemy, in the name of unity.

This can be an OK situation. The bad situation is when groups quibble over minor matters and forget the majors. As the Bible admonishes in Mathew 23: 23, "…. but you have neglected the more important matters of the law—justice, mercy and faithfulness". A modern way of saying it would be, "Majoring in the minors, and minoring in the Majors". Or, "Throwing out the baby along with the bathwater."? Or, "Complaining about getting wet while drowning."?

The Patriarchs: Megat Iskandar Shah, Mani Purindan, Hang Li-Po

This topic gets its own chapter. It often appears that the Malaysian royal houses are only relevant to Malays and that the others have little personal investment in, or identification with them. This is far from the truth as there are many reasons to identify with them, apart from the fact that they are the symbol of our national identity to the world.

Everyone knows that the nine Malay royal houses take turns to send their Sultan/Raja to become the Paramount Ruler of Malaysia who goes by the title, *Duli Yang Maha Mulia Yang Di Pertuan Agung*. The United Arab Emirates does something similar with its seven Emirs. Everyone also knows that the first Sultan on peninsula Malaysia was a Hindu Raja named Parameswara who converted to Islam, and became Sultan Megat Iskandar Shah. His son, Muhammad Shah married a Tamil woman and her son Raja Kassim also briefly ruled Malacca. The fifth Sultan, Mansur Shah married a Chinese princess Hang Li-Poh. So we know that Malaysian royalty have mixed blood right from the outset. A genealogy of the respective royal *Dar-ul* (s) (Arabic: "House of") will be very revealing indeed.

Palace language itself has many words of Tamil and Sanskrit origin, harking back to the pre-islamic hindu/buddhist kingdoms of the region. The long title of the paramount ruler is *Kebawah Duli Yang Maha Mulia, Yang DiPertuan Agong,* followed by the equally lengthy personal *name*. Parsing the phrase word by word will perhaps shed light on the confusing string of words. *Kebawah* (Malay – "below"); *Duli* (Skt – Dhool "Dust"); *Yang* (Malay, "That is"); *Maha* (Skt. "Great" referring to the Almighty); *Mulia* (Skt. "worthy"); *Seri* (Skt. "The Radiant/Graceful "); *Paduka* (Skt. "Sandal" or "Footpint"); *Baginda* (Skt. (fortunate – a references to Prophet Mohammad); *Yang diPertuan* (Malay, "Who is made lord"); *Agong* (Tamil – *Kohn*, "King"/"Paramount"/"Mountain"). The last word, Agung, sums up the gist of the long title. The ancient Tamil word for Mount Everest, is *Ven Ko,* or, "White Mountain". Some common Tamil boy names include: Ilan ko or Ilango – "Young king", Komahan – "Son of the king", Ventharkon (Vendargon) – "King of kings".

A direct English rendition of the title might yield thus: *"Underfeet of the most honored (Allah) and the radiant footprint of his excellency (The Prophet), he who is made lord, the paramount ruler Sultan ...... "*In pre-islamic times, in place of Allah and his Prophet, it would have been Shiva and the Rajaguru (King's royal mentor).

Kebawah Duli literally means "below the dust". In the epic Ramayana, Rama's half-brother Baratha, was left behind to hold the fort while the other one went off to the forest on self imposed exile. Baratha asked for and placed his older brother's sandals (paduka) on the throne, to signify the continuation of his rule.

Looking even earlier in Malaysia's timeline in the north of Malaysia, The rulers of Kedah were Tamil mixed? Archeological evidences of Hindu settlements attest to it. Someone has even observed that it is small wonder that Kedah Malays, generally, are of a darker hue than in the rest of the country. In fact it is said that Langkasuka was one of the names proposed for the new nation. At the southern tip of the Malay pensinsula (Singapore), Parameswara's forebears, from Sang Nila Utama are said to be descended from a Tamil merchant called Mani Purindan, originally from "Benua Keling", a reference to present day Tamilnadu. This is according to *The Malay Annals,* recorded by Tun Seri Lanang. The Tamil element in the royal households of Malacca and Pasai, are recorded to have been at the centre of many a court intrigue (politics) of that time. Lineages of Bendahara and other court officials had been Tamil. Mani Purindan is as Tamil as (Tan Sri) Mani Jegathesan, the Malaysian sports icon. Manipravalam is the type of Tamil with strong Sanskrit admixture, used by Tamil Brahmins of yore to write their religious commentaries. Mani in Tamil means gem or jewel. It is also a diminutive of Subramaniam, subramani, selvamani, navamani, maniratnam, manimaran etc, all Tamil names.

"Acheh was the first court in Southeast Asia to convert to Islam in 1204 A.D. Hence it took nearly 500 years for the new religion to reach here. The

Malays of Malacca did not embrace Islam until 1276 A.D. According to some scholars Malacca waited for the Indians to be converted. Both Gujerat and South India have strong claims for the conversion. It was not to Persia or Arabia but to India that Southeast Asia had always looked to for cultural inspiration combined with commercial prestige. The acceptance of Islam had therefore to wait its acceptance by Indians who were prominently engaged in the overseas trade between India and Southeast Asia. This condition was fulfilled in 13th century.

With the establishment of Malacca, trade again picked up between India and SEA. The Indian traders especially the Gujeratis and the Tamils were great favorites with the Sultans and other aristocrats. The Tamil Muslims, in particular, enjoyed extraordinary privileges and also married into the noble families. As the Portuguese historian Tome Pires observed, the Tamil Muslims were a mighty force in the royal court and they acted as real kingmakers. As Muslims the Tamils naturally had an edge over others.

Their offsprings wielded considerable influence and acquired chief positions.

A Tamil prince Raja Kassim born to a Tamil muslim mother in the royal court ascended to the throne of Malacca under the name of Sultan Muzaffar Shah, the first Muslim ruler in Malaccan history. He reigned till 1456 A.D. His uncle Tun Ali, a Tamil noble became his Bendahara or Prime Minister. Tun Ali, after a while, relinquished his post in favour of Tun Perak, a dignitary of pure Malay blood. For that favour Tun Perak rewarded him with the hand of his sister Tun Kudu. Tun Ali's son by Tun Kudu by the name of Tun Mutahir (∞) assumed the offices of Temenggong and Bendahara. And his son Hassan too rose to the post of Temenggong later. Tun Mutahir became a very influential person and with his position he was bound to make grave mistakes. In 1510, one year before Malacca fell to the Portuguese Tun Mutahir was put to death by Sultan Mahmud on the charge that he aspired to become a Sultan by himself." – Bala Baskaran

The Malay royalty, post Malacca have other mixtures. The house of Selangor and Johore claim Bugis blood. The house of Negeri Sembilan has Minangkabau markers, genetically speaking.

The nine Dar-ul of Malaysia, by the way, are:

Perlis, Darul Jamallullail	(House of Beauty of the Night)
Kedah, Darul Aman	(House of Peace)
Perak, Darul Ridzuan	(House of Contentment)
Selangor, Darul Ehsan	(House of Sincerity)
Negeri Sembilan, Darul Khusus	(House of Specialness)
Johore, Darul Takzim	(House of Dignity)
Pahang, Darul Makmur	(House of Prosperity)
Trengganu, Darul Iman	(House of Faith) and,
Kelantan, Darul Naim	(House of Bliss)

The state of Negeri Sembilan literally means, "Nine States", referring to its nine districts actually. If we were to count Negeri Sembilan as such, Malaysia should actually have 23 states, including the non royal states of Penang, Malacca, Sabah and Sarawak!

And, this has nothing to do with the nine royal houses of Malaysia, but is only incidental. The Hindu horoscope has nine "abodes/houses" in which reside the nine astral "rulers" (planets) who supposedly influence the events of your life, depending on your proximimity to them!

Malay court ceremonies contain many Indian practices such as the clasped palms of the subject in saluting the king.

Arab influence occurs in the use of the Koran and prayers. The first part of the hail, "Daulat Tuanku!" meaning, "Long Live", is Arabic. Hence *Daulat Tuanku,* renders as "Long live, my Leige!".

Of course, the Malay royalty also seek to claim lineage to Alexander the Great (Iskandar Zulkarnain). This is by way of Persian influences. Although why Persians will claim Alexander as a forefather is beyond comprehension, since he is the one who routed their king, Cyrus the great. Todays Iranians would rather be called Darius or Cyrus. Not Iskandar. To them, Alexander was a Macedonian usurper with a lust for world dominance. The only lasting conquest the Greeks did was in the realms of culture, language, and philosophy.

Malay royalty also embrace Solomon (Sulaiman) as a link to their past. This is fair enough, even if not supported by historical or genetic evidence. Every society has its own story of its hoary origins.

Alexander never entered India. He was stopped at the border by the Indian Maurya king Porus (Purushothaman), on his Elephant cavalry. Thereafter, history says that Alex retreated back to Macedonia, installing his generals as Satraps (governors) of the conquered territories. Punjabis and Rajasthanis too claim descent from Alexander the Great, whom they call Sikander. The Rajasthani elevated castes today call themselves raiputs (sons of kings). Are these Indians claiming ties to a loser in Indian history? Herein, is the great anomaly of alexandrine ancestry. History is conclusive that Alexander never married, nor had children, was even homosexual. Did he father whole races of people? Malay royalty's claim to Alexander is that some prince from Rajasthan may have contributed to the royal gene pool of the Malacca court at some point. The Sejarah Melayu has a take on Mani Purindan, the Tamil progenitor of Malaccan royalty. Alexander was stopped at the western fringe of India, near Eastern Afghanistan. So would this be a case of double fault? First the Rajasthani myth. Then, carried over into a Malay myth?

There are some royal houses that claim descent from the Prophet Muhammad himself. The ruler of Perlis state has an Indian title (*Raja*) and a lineage from Muhammad (*Syed*), in a double dose of non-native identity. Raja is a common title for members of the extended royal family both male and female. The immediate children are addressed as *Tengku*, probably abbreviated from *Tuan Ku* (M'lord). Tuanku as it is, is reserved for His Highness.

Chinese influence in court ceremonies. The colour yellow is (was) the royal colour of the Chinese emperor. If you are lucky enough to catch a Chinese opera in a Taoist temple, look out for the emperor in his loose yellow house coat (er, robe). Tumeric (*manjal*), with its bright sunny hue is an age old favourite of the Tamils, as an anti-bacterial and beauty treatment stuff. The name *manjal* has evolved into *mangalam*, to denote auspiciousness. If you happen to receive an invitation to a Tamil wedding, be sure to observe a smear of turmeric at the top right corner of the envelop (where the stamp is supposed to be).

As we have noted in the section on male dresses, the *Baju Melayu*, the malay royalty's official attire, is a tapestry of Chinese, Indian, and Arab influences. The collars of the baju (shirt) and the jacket are clearly chinese ispired. So are the loose pants. Watch a Kung Fu movie (Bruce Lee or anyone else), and judge for yourself. The *samping* (waist wrap) is Indian. Old Indian kings, priests, and even the Hindu gods, are depicted with a *Karchchai* (waist wrap). The *tengkolok* (headdress) made out of a single length of silk, could hark back to Indian or Arab influences, where the turban is still a common wear.

Hence, is it actually baju melayu or baju Malaysia? Now, who is to say the Malay ruler is relevant to Malays only and not to all Malaysians? And why are they called Malay Rulers (Raja-Raja Melayu), instead of Malaysian Rulers?

Catalogued!: Kaum, Clans, Castes

Indians in Malaysia are divided by languages, Chinese by dialects, and Malays by islands of origin. Indians are Tamils, Telugus, Malayalis, and Punjabis etc; Chinese are Cantonese, Hokkiens, Hakkas, Hainanese, and Teochew etc; and Malays are Melayu, Minangkabau, Javanese, Boyanese and Bugis etc.

Indians are further split into castes, Chinese into clans, and Malays into suku kaum (sub-groups). The Indian caste system is perhaps the most divisive and invidious/insidious apartheid system ever devised by man. The Hindu would deny that Sanatana Dharma (another name for Hinduism) engenders casteism. That the four original castes are only social categories, as in any social hierarchy. But no other system has descended this low. Call a spade by any another name, it is still a spade. A rose is a rose is a rose by any name. The Tamil poet Ottakoothar, when confronting Shiva in a literary debate had said, "Even if your middle eye opens, your error is still an error."

Malay royalty, with their sequestered lives, and affluent lifestyles are the pinnacle of their community pyramid. The next layer, are mostly to do with admistrative and political connection. UMNO, PAS, Bersatu connections has granted ordinary Malays access to upper middle class comforts and priviledges. They are the equivalent to Bangsawan (Aristocracy) of old. Then, there are the clerks and secretaries. As in all human societies the B40 group who make up the basement, homeless and subsistence livelihoods. Many have been on welfare and now they are given direct handouts like BRIM, engineered, naturally, by the political elites to keep themselves politically relevant through patronage.

Another layer of influence are those in positions of social control, like the Police; enforcement directorates, and the Military. These, being overwhelmingly Malay led, are subservient to the government of the day. There has never been, and probabably never will be, any coup or takeovers from these quarters as happened in neighbours like Burma, Thailand, or Indonesia. Malaysia, being multiracial, you won't see one Malay dominant entity knock out another. It would reflect badly on Malay unity and the need to protect the upper hand of the race. Unless of course, they coalesce with a minority "king maker" party.

Chinese clans are kinship groups. Never has there been a more stable human social structure than the family. Chinese clans evolved on the basis of a common surname, usually consisting of a common descent from a real or fictitious ancient person of that name.

"Clans provided a way in which Chinese who travelled away from home regions could locate putative kinsmen and procure assistance if necessary." State, and district level clan associations proliferate in Malaysia. Sometimes, you see dialect based associations and they are large and well organized, like the Hokkien Asociation of Klang and the Teochew Association of Klang and Coast. This raises a question. Are clans like "Lee" spread all over China or are they confined to the dialect areas? Certainly the Hokkien Asociation in Klang, big as it is, has many clans represented in their membership rolls. Aren't there "Lee"s in Korea too. But it would be a different Lee altogether.

Since clans were a people unit to serve their self-interests, conflict often arose among different clans. *Kongsi Gelap* (Secret Societies) were common in early British Malaya, providing social and financial networks for new immigrants from China. A curious case of such inter-clan rivalry still exists in the Larut district of Perak. You are hardpresed to find *Hakka* food in Kamunting and cannot find *Hokkien mee* in Taiping, just next door. And vice versa. This harks back to the 1800s when there was a running war between the *Ghee Hins* (Kamunting − Cantonese/Hokkien) and the *Hai Sans* (Taiping − Hakka) over the tin prospects of the area. The Larut Wars (1867-1873) include 4 wars. Peace (Pax Brittanica?) was mediated between the two by Andrew Clarke, Governor of the Straits Settlements. Incidentally, Taiping, the town, means *Eternal Peace* in Chinese. It was renamed from Klian Pauh, by the Hakka, who had escaped the Taiping Rebellion in China. Kamunting (formerly Klian Bahru) also sounds quite like Kuomintang, Dr. Sun Yat Sen's Chinese Nationalist Party.

Confucianism is credited with making Chinese society fiercely patriarchal and defining its social stratification with: 1) scholar-bureaucrats at the top, because they had the knowledge and wisdom to maintain social order; followed by 2) farmers, because they produced the necessary goods; and 3) the artisans, because they possessed necessary skills. At the bottom 4) were merchants. All they did was buy and sell things. Sounds quite similar to the Hindu division of castes into 1. Priests (Brahmins), 2. Nobility (Kshatriya), 3. Vaisya (Merchants), 4. Sudra (Artisans). As if on hindsight, another group was created 5) the untouchables or outcasts. The Confucian placement of scholars at the top corresponds to the Brahmins at number one on the Hindu list. Both are scholars! It is somewhat universal in that scholars and the intelligentia have always been respected and feared. Or, did they get there through brain rather than brawn? Education – the way forward.

Casteisim while not overtly visible among Malaysian Indians, lives on in their homes. The political fallout of former MIC president Samy Velu and M.G.Pandithan is parallel to the Mahathir – Anwar Ibrahim split, and occurred concurrently. While the latter was over plain politics, the former is said to be due to caste politics. While Anwar, after the fallout went on to start a new movement, PKR (People's Justice Party), Pandithan started the IPF (All Malaysian Indian Progressive Front). While Chinese found clan associations, Indians have their caste associations, though they are not as visible as the clan houses.

Caste is kind of the built-in DNA of Indians that explains their "crab mentality". It is an Indian metaphor to describe their national trait. A crab, it seems, would grab and pull down another crab that is climbing out of their cage. The attitude of sabotaging another, who is making his upward mobility in life. The caste system, it seems is like the food chain of humans treating other humans badly. The tiger eats the fox that eats the monitor lizard that eats the frog that eats the fly that eats the food waste. Even the *Paraiyar* (low caste drum beaters) look down on the *Pallar* (field labourers.), *Chakkilyar* (toilet cleaners), and *Vannaar* (washermen). It goes all the way up the totem pole.

The recent hue and cry by the Indian community, over the use of the word *pariah* in a school literature text, is an interesting study in sociology. Since most Indians, still subscribe (privately) to casteism, it is not surprising that they would go up in arms over the application of the offensive word to them (the so-called higher castes). Wouldn't it have been most noble of them to stand with their brother of the downtrodden pariah class, thereby removing the taint? Instead, by treating the word as offensive, they are actually reinforcing the pariah as a low person and that they are liable to get offended when a Malay writer uses it broadly, to include themselves. How does that make their fellow Indian of the said caste feel? Like being kicked by his own brother, when down? Ask the Australian. He would proudly boast his lowly pedigree, descended from British criminals exiled to Botany Bay, Sydney.

A great example of standing with your brother is the case of Charlie Hebdo, the French cartoon Publication. 12 cartoonists were gunned down in 2015 in retaliation for a caricature of prophet Muhammad. People around the world came up with *Je suis Charlie*, French for "I am Charlie", Similarly, in the case of George Floyd's murder by a white cop in Minneapolis in 2020, people came out with "I am George Floyd" and "Black lives Matter."

Tamil Muslims, while not as caste conscious as their Hindu cousins, do seem to exhibit some caste-like behavior. For instance, the Maricars and Rawthers, among them, even use those names as part of their surnames. Indian Christians, still observe caste tendencies, though not using caste names. While outwardly egalitarian, caste in Malaysia rears its head when it comes to matters of marriage. Of course, that is dying out with the passing of the old guard. Younger people don't subscribe to such cultural dinosaurs from a dark age.

Chinese tend segregate among themselves, not on the basis of birth, but on wealth and individual attitudes. Confucian dictates look down on laziness and lack of drive to make money. Indians, are of the opposite mold. They segregate based on "purity" as established by their religion. So, a person of the "impure" caste can be a rich tycoon and yet be considered "unsuitable" for a son or daughter-in-law. As in every nationality, this is an old man's disease. The current generation has largely eschewed this kind of thinking. Even before the field-levelling factor of Islam, Malays have always been welcoming of outsiders. In the past, their own society segregated on social class. "Darjat", or aristocracy, used to determine human interactions.

Even the tiny Portuguese community of Malacca has had its own schisms, according to one of its own. At the lower rung are the poor fisher folk at the "settlement" at Ujong Pasir with Portuguese surnames like, Santa Maria, Texeira, De Costa and Monteiro. They are the simple, darker skinned, Malay looking person. The upper crust were the fairer skinned, Eurasian looking persons with Dutch names like Danker, Kraal, Marbeck etc. Those with Dutch or English names, had dispersed to the other parts of the country, as professionals. They were the ones who spoke for the community. At least, that was the situation at *Merdeka* (Independence). Things seem to have reversed, after an official visit to Malacca, by a government leader of Portugal. Since then, the residents of Ujong Pasir ("Edge of the Sand"), Malacca, took over charge of Portuguese affairs. The upper crust, tended to fall in, assuming a Portuguese identity, rather than Dutch ethos. Ujong Pasir, is the showcase fishing village of the Portuguese community. The Indian version, (the Anglo-Indian) can be a Sanderson, Atkinson or a Darlington.

The Chinese of antiquity, while phobic about foreign devils, the modern Chinese are very open to marrying and mixing outside the race. Even their old requirement, that forbade or restricted marriage within the clan, is very scientific and modern. Everyone is game. The old Chinese boast, that they will eat anything that moves, is metaphorical of their attitudes to life. The old (Circa 6th century BCE) Tamil saying, *"Yaathum Oorey, Yaavarum Keylir"*, or "Every city is mine, everyone my relative" does not have a resonance in the caste system that has engulfed it. Like the old Chinese fear of foreigners, the Tamil caste rigidity engenders social distance, but is not as pronounced in Malaysia, at least outwardly. They may eat and fellowship together freely, but the last holdout of the curse of caste is marriage. The best of friends (of different castes) might balk at their children marrying for love, perhaps due to considerations of their relatives' sentiments. The Malay is basically not a race, but a mix of many races. They are not socially stratified, like those days of the bangsawan and bangsa biasa. They would, however draw a firm line and insist on marrying within the religion. This segues into the next section.

Honorifics: Thiru, Encik, Xiānsheng

Tamil gentleman are referred to as Thiru or Thiruvalar. Thiru (sacred) is affixed to hallowed books (Thirukkural), pilgrimage towns (Thirupathi) etc. In this case it refers more to "esteemed." The Sanskrt "Shri" also assigns holiness or greatness – Shrimad Bhagavad Gita. In South-East Asia we have the ancient Sriwijaya kingdom, Nakhon Si Thammarat (Nagara Sri Dharmarajah) in Thailand, and Dato Seri, Tan Sri etc. No Tun Sri, eventhough there is an occurrence of Tun Sri Lanang the author of the Sejarah Melayu (Malay Annals). Tun probably derives from Tuan, as does the Tan in Tan Sri. Tuan is used to refer to any gentleman who does not have a ruler given title. Dato or Datuk derives from Datu, common in Autronesian languages, referring to a person of influence and respect. Datu is prevalent the Phillipines, Sarawak and Sabah states, and is cognate with Ratu of Fiji, as titles of chiefs. The Sikh title is Sardar (leader).

Menteri refers to minister derived from Sanskrit Mantri. From whence it went to China by way of the Europeans, as Mandarin, basically a prime minister in old China. In fact, Prime Minister (PM) is Pratama Mantri (PM) in India and Perdana Menteri (PM) in Malaysia. Pertama/Pratama (first), and Perdana/Pradana (chief) and Prime (chief) are cognates, as are Minister, Mantri, Menteri, and Mandarin.

Uniquely, Tamil speakers worldwide and the government of Tamil Nadu state don't say Mantri in any form. They use Amaicchar (minister). That is because that particular language, of all the languages in india, has enough vocabulary of its own, not to depend on Sanskrit hand-me-downs. In fact, the modern guardians of Tamil have not spared any effort to eject Sanskrit from the vocabulary.

Hang, was a popular title applied to warriors and heroes of yore. It is equivalent to "knight" and indeed Sultan Mansur Shah the 6th Sultan of Malacca had an inner circle of 5 knights that was fiercely loyal to him – Hang Tuah (Sir Lancelot ?), Hang Kasturi, Hang Jebat, Hang Lekiu and Hang Lekir. Hang may be Chinese in origin. Hang Li Poh was the Chinese Princess whom Sultan Mansur Shah married, as part of a treaty he made with the Ming emperor Yongle. Han is a collective term to describe the Chinese race, as opposed to Tibetan, Uighur or Manchurian Chinese.

Then, there is the *Sang* used in Malay folk tales – Sang Kancil, Sang Harimau, Sang Buaya, Sang Suria etc. It is the equivalent of the American *B'rer* (B'rer Rabbit, B'rer Fox etc). The origin of Sang, is not clear, although we may have a clear connection to the Chinese (Cantonese) *Saang,* meaning

"Mister". Lee Saang is Mr. Lee. Of course, if Mr. Lee went to Japan, he would be addressed as Lee San.

Often, you hear people referred to as *Si,* or the article "the"as in, *Si Arab*, "the Arab". And it is not always flattering. *Si bodoh*, is, "the fool". Si bedebah, "the rascal". *Si gemuk,* "the fatso". *Si Lokek*/Kedekut, "the miser".

On another note, there is the recurring, hereditary title in Malay society. Following, is lengthy list. Mostly, it travels patrilineally.

Syed/Sharifah, is the male and female title attached to the forename of a person claiming descent from the Prophet Muhammad himself. *Meor* (Perak), is one title that is matrilineal and also of Arab origin, that is given to children of a Sharifah who is not married to a Syed. Indian muslims use *Mir* (Emir, prince) and *Pir* (elder) before their names, but not as a title. *Wan* are descendants of Cik Siti Wan Kembang of Kelantan lore. The Wans of Kedah are possibly a dimunitive of Pahlawan. *Che*, is another kedah designation possibly a dimunitive of Enche. The former Prime Minister Dr.Mahathir Mohammad, gives himself the pen name Che Det. *Nik,* is predominant in Kelantan, Trengganu and Pattani. *Megat*, another Perakian pedigree, derives from the Minangkabau *"Maha Gaek"*, or "Great One". Apparently, an early heir apparent to the Pagaruyung (Minangkabau) throne, Megat Terawis, decided to give it up for the Bendahara-ship of Perak, and his descendants are the Megat. The female of the Megat have *Puteri*, as their prefix.

Perak also has *Ngah* and *Long* (remember Ngah Ibrahim and Long Jaafar from our history books? They look suspiciously like constrictions of Tengah and Sulong ("Middle, and Younger"). Hence, it could indicate hierarchy in age or seniority. *Raja*, is a common prefix, also originating from Perak royalty. Tengku, Tunku, Engku, Ungku, Ku, U (?), is common in the northern states. *Khir*, is another title that is common among Javanese, and could be related to the Arabic, *Khair,* "good". The continuing usage of hereditary titles points to the very aristocratic nature of Malay society in the past, and present.

Government issued titles seem to be collectible items and can lead to funny situations. Tun Tan Sri Tan Tian Tong – made up of course. Or, how's this for an Indian guru who has the Indian government title of Padmashri, for contribution to society ? Shri Shri Tan Sri Dato Sri Padmashri ShivaSri Swamy Sai Sriram.

Across the South China Sea in the Bornean states of Sabah and Sarawak, we find a preponderance of hereditary titles like *Awang* (Sabah and Brunei) and *Abang* (Sarawak). The female equivalents of these would be *Dayang*. The daughters of the Brooke Dynasty, White Rajahs were designated as Dayang. Datu is used among the Sabah natives of the Moro/Sulu group.

If Abang is elder brother in Malay, Thambi is younger brother in Tamil. Dato Rahim Thambi Chik. *Chik* is a dimunitive of the Malay Kechik or Kechil, meaning, "little". Hence, Thambi Chik is "Little little brother". Jalan Thamby Abdullah (Brickfields), Changkat Thambi Dollah (off Pudu Road). Who is this Thamby Abdullah, anyway?

The Chinese in Malaysia, deriving from the common business and labour classes, don't have the tradition of hereditary titles, like the Malays. That is unless we count the term *Baba*. Which is a applied to a whole community. Mister in Mandarin is Xiansheng.

The Indians have a whole of lot suffixes like Khan (*chief*), Singh (*lion*), Lal (*red*) plus caste names, that don't qualify as titles. Whatever titles they used to have now exist in their given names. Thambiran, was used for a chief. Tham – own self, piraan (Lord). Maran – knight. Varman – he who binds. Mallan – wrestler. These used be titles of kings and princes. The current formal titles for king are Mannan, Ko, Vendhan, Arasan (rajah), now part of common names.

Nick's Names: Ahmad, Ah Long, Arumugam

So you don't know the name of the waiter whose attention you want to get. You call out thus, "Captain!", or "Boss!", or just plain "Waiter!" In Germany, he is called *Herr Ober*!, or "Mr. Supervisor". In an Indian restaurant, you shout out, *Annengh* !, simply meaning "Elder Brother!" just as you would hail the Malay waiter, *Abang*!, meaning the same thing. Note that you call everyone *Annei* or *Abang*, notwithstanding age differences. They are less patronising and presumptuous. Taking a junior stance with a waiter ensures prompt service and smile. To hail a Chinese waiter, it used to be, "Towkay!" meaning, "Boss!". The former, is close to "taiko" from whence English got, "Tycoon"

If you are in England, you would address your driver as "James", even though he is not.

The Malaysian driver is "Ahmad". A Malaysian Indian driver might be called "Muthu?" Indeed our First Prime Minister, Tunku Abdul Rahman's official driver was R.Kalimuthu, deceased 24.11.2012.

The Chinese Hokkien dialect has lots of such designations. "Ah Long" is now the all Malaysian term for a loan shark.

Tamils seem to have an affinity for the use of numbers as coded adjectives and nouns. I remember on my visits home in BB (Batang Berjuntai), my younger siblings devised a mathematical code for Chinese pork noodles. They lived next door to an Indian Muslim family, separated by a cardboard wall. So as not to offend their sensibilities, they would speak in terms of ordering take-outs of 1.20 or 2.50 which referred to the type or quantity of noodle.

Please don't try this at home. Don't say to anyone in particular about anyone in particular, that, he's a 9 (Onbathu). Don't ask me why, but that is colloquial Tamil, for a transgender person. Some say it originates from the English adjective, femi**NINE** to describe them.

Indians say "tubelight", when they mean a fluorescent light. When you refer to someone as a tubelight, you are commenting on his slowness in "getting it". Get it? If you didn't, here it is: regular bulbs light up instantly. Fluorescent tubes take time (to get the point, the joke, the meaning etc). Got it? Good!

The male Sikh has "Singh" (lion) as his surname. His distintictive turban sets him apart in any crowd. Look at a picture of a crowd, and you are likely to spot a Sikh first even if he is in the background. Your eyes are simply drawn to it (the turban, that is). It is part of his religion's 5 Ks.

However, these days young Singhs (Singhlets, as my form one history teacher, Mr. Scully, called them.) Pig – Piglet, Eagle – Eaglet, Singh – Singhlet. Wait! I didn't finish the sentence. Young Singhs these days, often, or mostly, do away with the turban altogether. They are known as *turbanators*. Terminate the turban, get it?

Like the prevalent Irish jokes and Jewish jokes, Malaysians have a lot of Sikh jokes, and some of them can be really sick and unflattering. One class of jokes, similar to the *knock, knock* jokes, is the *What is a …. Singh* type. What is a unique Singh – *Jaswant* (Just one) *Singh*. What is a beer guzzling Singh – *Jasbir* (Just Beer) *Singh*. What is a lazy Singh – *Relaxing*. As you can see, this one has many possibilities. For instance, "what do you call a Singh who stamps letters at the post office?" – Embossing. What is a Singh that doesn't appreciate these kinds of jokes? – *Menacing*.

Nair, and Menon are common surnames in the Malayalee community. What is a good looking Nair? – *Debonair.* What is an amazing Menon? – *Phenomenon.*

In the earlier section on names we Malaysians give each other (Mat Salleh, Kuei, Keling, Valayaggatti) we proved very subtle. Subtlety is a mark of creativity and control, rather than in-your-face directness and offensiveness. Sometimes subtlety, like a good satire, can be more hard hitting than full frontal offence.

Some even give themselves nicknames to heighten their political currency and relevance. Dato Najib Razak, gave himself the nickname "Bossku" – my boss – after he had lost his election and his reputation. He probably did not attempt to give himself "Tuanku" – my liege – because that was already taken. Still, he had his lackeys who treated him like royalty wherever he went.

Come to think about it, some of "The Greats" (Alexander, Czar Peter, Cyrus, Catherine, Akbar, Ashoka etc.etc) were likely self-designations crafted by their public relations departments.

Etiquette: Right hand, Rubber time, Gift wrap colour

Some aspects of etiquette have already been discussed especially in the section on food (Table Manners) and in funeral houses. An etiquette is not the same level as an edict of any kind. Since it is community or culture specific, outsiders are easily forgiven any faux pas. However, it is proper and civil to know and observe the other's idiosyncracies when entering his/her space.

After so much time together, Malaysians generally have a set of social rules that are similar among the races. The following are some of those.

Giving and receiving of gifts and serving and passing of food around the dinner table are always with the right hand. This goes back to the practice of "washing up" after "doing the business", with the left hand. Hence it becomes the "pee hand". You should give gifts with both hands. The good hand and the bad hand cancel each other out. Another thing we don't do with either hand is, point with the forefinger, in the off chance that someone comes into the line of fire. But, isn't that what the forefinger is for? Observe any babe in arms. Nevertheless, you use either the thumb or the entire upturned palm, to point. And we don't point to things on the ground with our feet, either. We don't cross our legs in front of elders, or smoke, or any hanky panky. When passing the elder, we spontaneously stoop slightly. Address the most senior member first and go down the line whenever it is feasible.

When it comes to gifting, for the Chinese, timepieces and things associated with the number 4 remind them of the grim reaper (death). Scissors and sharp objects elicit the thought, "Is he trying to snip off our relationship?" But the outsider is generally forgiven most gaffes. Of course these days, these cultural cues have gone the way of the morse code and mind reading.

Indians, even the one who hasn't been within a mile of a school building, will instictively react when he accidently steps on a book — or anything printed. He will touch it and bring his fingers towards his eyes. Eyes are a metaphor for something very precious. Somehow, it is in the ethos of the Indian, perhaps equating the alphabet, word etc to scripture. When you accidentally step on someone's toes, you bend slightly to pretend touch the offended part and make a namaste gesture.

When visiting, we do what mystifies westerners — the absence of the concept of punctuality. We are almost proud of stretching time, calling it "rubber time", "Malaysia time", etc. That is one sick "etiquette". What a shittiquette! Perhaps the "come and go" way of organizing a dinner, is one way of getting around this Mal-aysian malaise. Surely, turning up late for the party must be deemed the height of rudeness. The sad part of it is, we have become so benumbed and conditioned to accept tardiness as a national trait. The only medicine for this ailment is, hosts sticking to their schedule and not waiting for quorum.

We remove shoes when entering a house, including our own. Even if it is a public building (mosque, temple, or community hall) the pile of shoes strewn around should alert us to shed our own. It is nice to visit a friend or family, with a *buah tangan* ("fruit of the hands"), usually a fruit basket, biscuits, candy, or a craft item.

Wrapped gifts are not opened immediately. Only after you get home. This is to avoid potential embarrassments when the said gift is not revolting to the receiver. In the western style, where you are expected to open gifts in front of the giver, don't you pretend to love it and play the drama? Now, scissors and knives are innocent enough as gifts, but you never know how the other will take it. "Is he trying to snip off our friendship. When in Rome, do as they do. When at home, do as you please.

And then, there are race specific boo-boos, such as wrapping gifts in white for Malays; blue, white and black for Chinese and black or white for Indians. These are colours of mourning. Red, yellow and pink are auspicious for the Chinese and red, yellow and green for Indians. I humbly submit that culture and customs should stand on elevated moral teachings, civility, humanity, literature, arts, sports etc instead of meaningless notions, suppositions and superstitions that don't show up (!) under the laboratory microscope.

Order of Service: Kuththu-vilakku, Doa Selamat, Gong,

Important events are variously preceded by the national anthem, a prayer, by a bang of gong etc. The cultures of Malaysia, similarly have their own unique ways of beginning their cultural events.

For starters – beginning the event – starts with the audience seated. After what seems like an eternity past the publicized start time – generally i.e – the chief guest is marched in, by the organizing committee. It may be preceded by a thumping *kompang* combo and bunga manggar bearers. The guest in the Tamil event is marched in to the spirited flourish of the Thavil, Nathaswaram duet. In some instances, a colourful parasol may be carried in as well. In some cases, Chinese programs may be preceded by the parading of prancing lions and the booming of daluo drum and clanging cymbals and gongs.

As a sign of formal start to the program, a *Kuththuvilakku* ("standing oil lamp"), is lit by the chief guest. The fire connoting the dispelling of ignorance and gaining of knowledge. Whereas In the Malay situation, the chief guest strikes a brass gong to signiy the official opening of a program/project/enterprise. This would usually happen towards the end of the official program, after the speeches.

The MC, after the formal and lengthy welcome, invites the Imam to say the *Doa Selamat*, for the success of the meet. The Tamil MC calls for the audience to stand for the *Thamizh Thaai Vaazththu* ("Praise of Mother Tamil"). This anthem is either a playback or sung on stage by a designated singer. That takes care of giving the higher power its requisite due. However, something that often happens only in Malaysia occurred. During a school Tamil language carnival in Penang (December 2023), the *Tamil Thaai Vazhththu* and *Kadavul Vazhththu* ("Praise of God") was banned by a junior education officer, which caused a stir. The non-Tamil officer concerned was later transferred to another department.

The prelude, or interlude may include some performances, such as choir, solo, vocal or instrumental and group or solo dance.

When the VIP guest is invited on stage and before his his speech, the organizing chairman might present him with a memento of the event, say, a document pertaining to the event. In the Tamil version, he is draped with a silk shawl ("Saalvai"), and garlanded with a Jasmine "Maalai" as a way of honouring.

The ending usually does not follow rules of deference to the VIPs, as the audience rushes out to the cafeteria for the requisite catered tea. The VIPs will hang back and wait to make their way to the VIP table, or quietly leave for the next appointment. Needless to say, Chinese functions are apt to include a sumptuous post-meeting meal, either in situ or at a high end restaurant.

Across communities and cultures, Malaysians are notoriously late, lackadaisical and lacking in punctuality, thus seriously lagging in character, morally languid, ethically lax, and plain lazy. In fact, we proudly dismiss it as "Malaysian Time" or "Rubber Time", as if we indeed possess the UN charter to this malaise. Functions, events and dos don't. Happen on time, that is. Organizers and event managers are at the mercy of the tardy and push the clock back for "quorum". Nothing short of a law can change this mindset. I have a law of my own. Dinner starts on the dot. First come, first served. Latecomers are free to avail of the scraps.

Latecoming VVIPs will have to contend with cold food in the "domes" at their reserved table.

Business as usual: The way we do it

Malaysian meetings from the JKKK (village committee) to cabinet huddles have catered meals. Even a breakfast meeting will have a comprehensive array of kuehs. Food figures prominently in meetings perhaps to ensure a quorum. Introductions by the MC begin with lengthy preambles, giving a nod to every YAB (Rt.Hon), YB (Hon), Yg Mulia (Esteemed), Yg Ariff (Learned), Tun, Tan Sri, Dato Sri, Dato right down to Tuan – Tuan dan Puan-Puan (Ladies and Gentlemen). Ten minutes could be taken up if everyone is mentioned by name. More time will be taken by every speaker who comes to the podium in a repeat of the long list. When will they come to the point?

You see, you don't want to upset anyone by rushing through – they will likely *merajuk* (be miffed, piqued). Whereas, the leader of the so-called most powerful country in the world gets by with, "Mr.President" and "Ladies and gentlemen". Our condition is either a holdover from British aristocracy or local tribal hierarchy.

In Malay circles, mirroring the family, no one rocks the boat. Face, or *air muka*, is saved. A look at the politics will reveal smooth transitions from President to his deputy in UMNO and from Prime Minister to his deputy in the cabinet. The rare times there has been a direct challenge for the UMNO presidency, the challenger lost, or was forced out of the party. Mahathir's prime – ministership is notable for his inability to keep 5 out of his 6 consecutive deputies! All 5 of those, he either sacked, or he sacked himself when he resigned on his second innings. The only time he passed the baton was to Tun Abdullah Ahmad Badawi, considered to be a weak and "safe" deputy. Then again, Mahathir played a major role in bringing down Abdullah, and his successor Najib. Now, he seems bent on trying to trip his ex deputy and current PM, Anwar. Looks like a lifelong career doesn't it?

The Chinese too, value face and meetings are conducted over catered meals. This is not to say politics is smooth, as happened a few time in MCA. It didn't reach the heights of the chair throwing of the Taiwanese parliament. Generally business gets done without hitch, as proven by the success of their business houses.

Indians are liable to speak their minds. While they are largely of servile stock and lower castes brought over from famine starved areas of South India by the British estate holders, they seem to have found their voice. A look at the early and current trade and labour union movements, the NGOs agitating for human rights (Hindraf, etc), and criminial defence lawyers, seem to be preponderantly Indian. You'd suppose you would need big talkers for this kind of work.

Being vociferous and garrulous, their political meetings can be rowdy. For a miniscule minority, Indians boast more registered political parties and splinters than anyone.

It seems that some things never change in government, eventhough the incoming administration came in by vociferously sniping at the previous one's record. Quite apparently, or very glaringly, sloganeering is part of everyone's political DNA. They don't waste much time announcing it, as soon as they form the cabinet. A survey of the slogans of past governments bears out this rebrand/makeover/paint over foolishness.

Personage	**Term**	**Slogan**
Tunku Abdul Rahman	(31 August 1957-22 September 1970)	– Happy Malaysia
Tun Abdul Razak	(22 September 1970-14 January 1976)	– Onward Malaysia
Tun Hussein Onn	(14 January 1976-16 July 1981)	–
Tun Mahathir Mohamed	(16 July 1981-31 October 2003)	– Vision 2020
Tun Abdullah Badawi	(31 October 2003-3 April 2009)	– Islam Hadhari
Dato Sri Najib Razak	(3 April 2009-9 May 2009)	– 1 Malaysia
Tan Sri Muhyiddin Yassin	(1 March 2020-16 August 2021)	– Abah ("Daddy M")
Dato Sri Ismaii Sabri	(21 August 2021-24 November 2022)	– Malaysian Family
Dato Sri Anwar Ibrahim	(24 November 2022-)	– Malaysia Madani

It doesn't matter the lifespan of the administration, you will still have your slogan. Muhyiddin and Ismail had a slightly over a year's life each, one after the other. Mahathir effectively used his 20 + years in antipathy towards the West, with his Look East policy. Most of the youth still looked west! Najibs's 1 Malaysia was anything but. It was just after his entry that Malaysia experienced a spurt in already worrisome levels of racism. The most surprising is the new guy on the block, Anwar. His supporters expected a sea change from the past 60 years of independent Malaysia, with his awowed *Reformasi* platform. Status appears Quo.

Besides slogans, Malaysian PMs were also fond of prefixing their names with, besides royal titles like Tun, Tan Sri, and Datuk Sri, self-aggrandizements like *Bapa* ("Father of..."). Looking at the above list, it would look like this: – Tunku (Father of Independence), Tun Razak (Father of Development), Tun Hussein (Father of Unity), Tun Mahathir (Father of Modernization), Tun Abdullah (Father of Human Capital Development), Dato Sri Najib (Father of Transformation). Tan Sri Muhyiddin and Dato Sri Ismail Sabri are "fatherless", possibly because they didn't have time enough in their 1 year terms to prove anything. Although, Muhyiddin did call himself *"Abah"* (daddy) of the *rakyat* (people). The current one, Dato Sri Anwar might yet get his accreditation. Methinks that this trend of 'Fathering" this or that or other is merely an ego trip, much like Alexander's or Akbar's, "The Great", suffixation.

Malaysians all these years, have become benumbed to sloganeering. They had seen that nothing actually changed. The status quo was the same old same old. Being perceived and felt as a whole lot of blustery hot wind and no action, the citizenry had innoculated to it. New ministers often come up with frivolous plans just to be seen as being relevant. One guy, immediately after appointment as education minister, proclaimed that shoes henceforth would be black! He was of course, shot down by the public. Speaking of the education ministry, it is still finding its feet (!) after all these years. Every so often old SOPs are taken out and new schemes introduced by the – yeah. Maths and Science to be taught in English and then revert to Malay and back again etc. etc. The pupils are the ones to suffer. If at all, education policy should be the most stable and entrenched, of the government's concerns. The education system of the US has not changed in aeons, for a reason. They got it right outright.

What about ABC — Accountability, Bribery, Corruption at all levels? Well, that would need to wait for tommorow's tome — too widespread and way deep a topic! What with our infamous mother of all kleptocracies (1MDB). *Klepto* (thief) — *Cracy* (Power).The endemic, top down corruption leading to corrosions of confidence as well as corresponding citizen's discontent Is very disconcerting. By the by, keeping the peace, stabilizing the boat, saving the face, *jaga air muka*, is what led to the IMDB fiasco in the first place. None of PM6 Najib's yes men, dared to point out irregularities. His deputy, who did voice out, was kicket out of the cabinet. In a strange twist in the script, he (the deputy) who became PM8, and his minions are also embroiled in a similar situation as his bossku. This kind of attitude is well reflected by the *Abilene Paradox*, a management parable that highlights the pitfalls of "going along".

Texas Line Dance: Now, everyone move to the middle!

Now together to the left, y'all

This time it is a horizontal coach. That is to say, the seats are placed along the walls, in two rows facing each other. The overflow crowd has plenty of standing room in the corridor, betwixt.

Everyone seems deep-frozen in their individual, invisible shrink wraps, indifferent to the presence of their fellow riders. Half of them are engrossed text-messaging, mostly girls. Agile thumbs agitatedly tap-dance on the phone keys, raising quite a clickophony. Still others are shut-eyed in pretend sleep, ostrich-like. This, afterall, is the morning rush hour after your requisite night-time sleep. Perhaps the sleep is real, induced by the rhythmic swaying of the coach and the incessant white noise of the engine as well as by the grind of wheels on the sleepers. Horrors, not that! Iron wheels on iron tracks, that is! Soon, the cabin will fill up with upright passengers.

The daily morning KTM commute affords a unique opportunity for the amateur social anthropologist, to observe human behavior under lab-like conditions.

It is lab-like because the subjects are in such close range. The subjects are enclosed in a hermetically sealed observation chamber – albeit, a fast moving one. The subjects don't know that they are….well, subjects.

The immersion into text-messaging, is part of the withdrawing into personal cocoons, that we do when in crowded situations. The non-texters withdraw into their own soundless world, staring blankly into nothing, staring right through you.

Did you notice that conversation is non-existent on public transport, unless friends are travelling together or someone is on the phone? Somehow, when you are with someone familiar, either in person or disembodied, as on a phone, you lose the inhibitions. Otherwise, the silence is palpable.

Something similar happens in crowded lifts. Have you noticed? This is strange, because humans normally fear silence and want to fill in the void. Remember the occasional pregnant pause or the awkward silence at a dinner table? Everyone's brain works overtime to come up with a smart comment that would jumpstart the stalled soiree. Boy, isn't that band of Bangla *bhayyas* boisterous, as they come aboard?

The text-messaging *tabiat* (habit), while it may have its saving grace, seems to affect communication skills. For one, it garbles and garbages grammar, shrinks spelling (LOL!), and contaminates content etc. Most importantly, it appears to diminish verbal facility.

Recent research out of India reveals that people who text-messaged or used the cell-phone solely for socializing, underperformed in job interviews compared to those who did not. They could not express ideas, elucidate aims or explain concepts.

Back to the subject(s) [pun indeed intended], you notice an anomaly or discrepancy in the coach. While crowded trains are conversation killers, as we have already observed, personal boundaries are significantly relaxed. What a surprising discovery! EUREKA – A – A – A !

No homophobia! No opposite-sex stranger stress!, Look Ma, no claustrophobia! Agoraphobics (scared of public places) probably won't be on the passenger list, in the first place.

The human mind is a beautiful thing, indeed. Whereas in ordinary circumstances you would put up defense walls when another intrudes your physical space, the mind allows it in crowded situations.

People push and press, or are pushed and pressed, against each other, and their train etiquette deems it A OK. A whole lot bumping, pumping and thumping happens.Flesh squeezes flesh when the Komuter suddenly makes a large lurch forward, a backward whiplash, or does a sideways shimmy. A jell-o-like jiggle, is what it is. Bodies bounce off each other like numbered balls in a lottery draw machine. But it is all sanitary and sensuality free. Sterile, as in a doctor's examination room.

Perhaps, the same principle that allows a person to detach and dissociate by text-messaging, also works in the matter of en masse close proximity. It is as if the invisible bubble wrap that encapsulates commuters, also immunizes them from erotic shocks as bodies make contact. Insulated wires don't cause sparks when they cross, do they? By the by, check this out. 'Close proximity' is the Malaysian media euphemism for adultery or fornication. Does it apply in this case?

Is there also some principle of herd behavior involved here? Since everybody is in the same boat, er… coach, it is not so bad. Now, if it is only I who am the recipient of unwanted body contact, I should be so embarrassed, ashamed, angry and outraged. When everybody is being bumped and humped, it is somehow acceptable.

Have you noticed people as they board trains at the initial stations? Be sure to diligently observe as they take their seats. Be assured that they will zoom in to a seat that is at least one removed from the next person. Be very assured that they will sit right beside you only if there are no more seats with a corner lot.

The usual comfort zone with strangers is one arm's length radius. At the Teluk Pulai (Klang) station, my embarkation/disembarkation point, there are 10 shiny, silver-plated, three-seater benches along the sides of the carriage. Guess what? There is one human sitting on each bench. Others are standing.

I think I see a parable in this. We Malaysians are akin to molecules of varying valences (lab lingo) bubbling and bouncing buoyantly off each other in a boiling beaker. Even though race relations currently appears to be at a low boiling point (per the sociologists), when the heat is up (economic crisis, foreign aggression etc.), we generally react and combine well, thank you. There is less political volatility, compared to our relatively homogenuous northern neighbours, Thailand, Myanmar, Cambodia who are prone to military coups.

Pardon me, we didn't do a comparative study of the on-train attitudes of the different races in Malaysia. Only the Malaysian race as a whole. We are all, including the world at large, adamantly adamic after all. That is to say, despite the varying socio-religio-cultural norms, we are homogenously human, behavior wise. On the Komuter, everyone has unspoken contact, camaraderie, and communication with another. This is just Malaysia, only Malaysia, one Malaysia. For one brief moment, there is no multiplicity of races. Rather, one amazing race.

The KTM Komuter experience is the Malaysian experience. In a brief daylight time, we move and mingle together as one, until night when the trains stop running. Everybody returns to their roost and rests their legs on their own private Lazy Boy. Are we merely going through the motions? (pun unintended). Or, have we found a miracle formula for chemical stability under all kinds of conditions? In any case, we Malaysians are more miscible than say the ethnic groups of the US, who often live on opposite sides of the tracks and seldom cross paths.

National Culture — can there be such a thing? In the context of the unique entity, quality, quantity, and personality of the cultures, it will need to take a long time. The government has tried but abandoned the idea of forcing or hastening such an evolution. With individual cultures so rich in their own right, who needs rojak (tossed salad)? Need we reinvent the wheel? The closest thing we have, to a national culture is the Malay culture, if only because it already has chunks and layers of the Chinese, Indian, Arab, Persian and Western cultures in it. True blue cultural coalescence will probably look more like the Peranakan culture — Baba Nonya, Malacca Chitty, Portuguese Kristang, Peranakan Jawi. However, as you can guess, they are miniscule cultures gasping for air in the throes of survival. The lesson from this? In a live and let live way, let everybody be as they are. Let the individual cultures be what they are, like singly sassy, saucy, spicy, savoury, sweet items on a *Friday Special*, banana leaf vegetarian spread in Indian street. It is much more palatable than hurriedly rushed mush from a multi-ethnic mish mash of what was originally decent grub.

Societies that have not experienced the kind of respectful distance and relative closeness that we have had, are not so lucky. With so many mutual commonalities, we cannot point a finger at the other(s). Four others point right back at us. The mark of an intolerant person is the haughty, holier than thou spirit that one's race, culture or religion is the crème de la creme in terms of values, rightness, wholeness etc. Others are deemed inferior, fit to be condemned and ridiculed.

One Malaysia is real. It already is. It was and it shall continue to be as it is. Doesn't it exist in the lives and values of your average Malaysian Joe (Johari, Jong Fatt, and Jothilingam or Joginder? Or, Jonaidah, Jo Yee (Lim), or Jothika). However the media, instead of being 1 Malaysia savvy, are a rather sorry story, notoriously lacking and lagging in the mindset. Surveying the advertisements and news media, you would think that Indians, Ibans and indigenes don't exist in this country. A survey of young peoples' preferences, published by *The Star* newspaper carried photos and views of 14 youth, 7 Malay and 7 Chinese! And it claims to be the *Peoples Paper!* Hooh!

Happy Komuting!